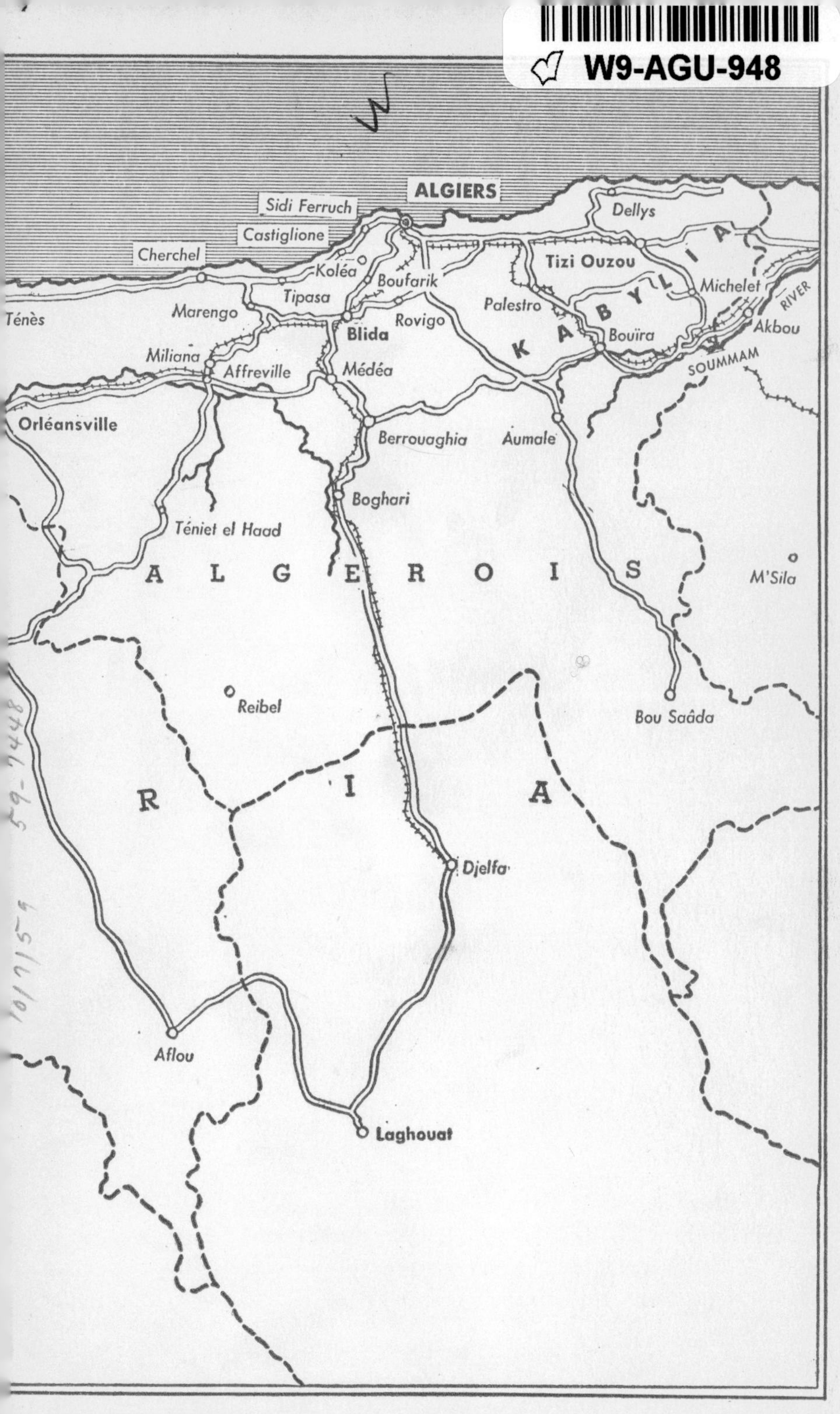
ALGIERS
Sidi Ferruch
Castiglione
Cherchel
Koléa
Boufarik
Tipasa
Ténès
Marengo
Blida
Rovigo
Dellys
Tizi Ouzou
Palestro
Michelet
KABYLIA
Bouïra
Akbou
RIVER
SOUMMAM
Miliana
Affreville
Médéa
Orléansville
Berrouaghia
Aumale
Boghari
Téniet el Haad
ALGEROIS
M'Sila
Reibel
Bou Saâda
R I A
Djelfa
Aflou
Laghouat

ALGERIA IN TURMOIL

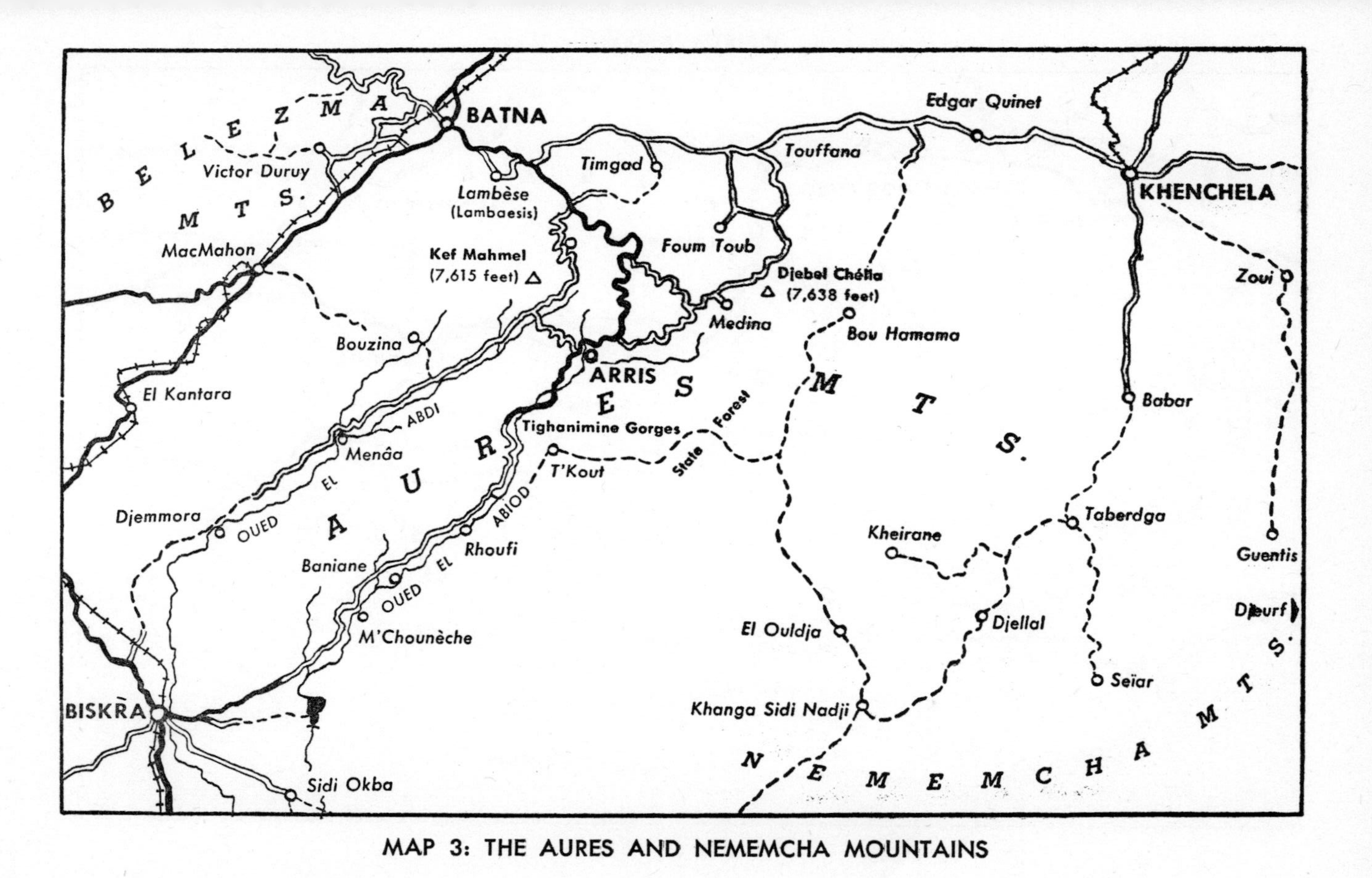

MAP 3: THE AURES AND NEMEMCHA MOUNTAINS

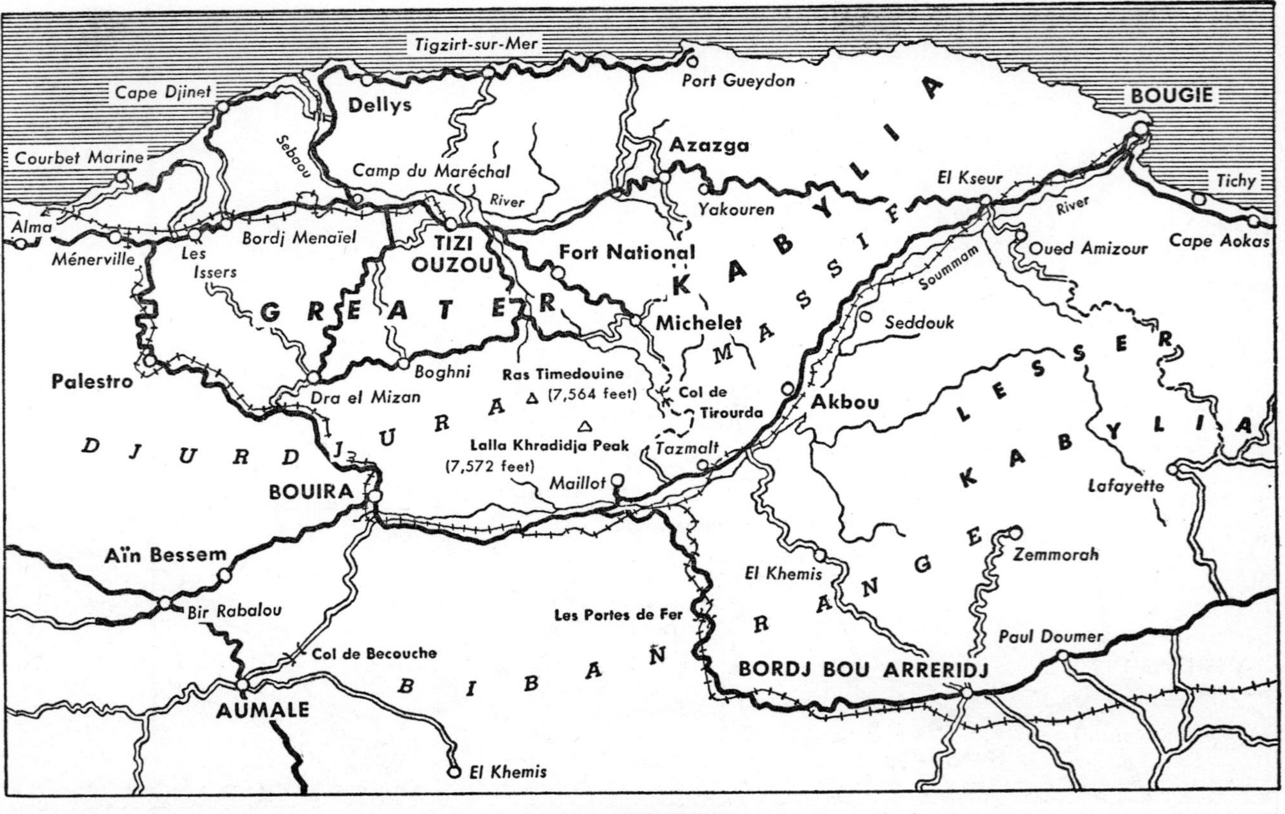

MAP 4: KABYLIA

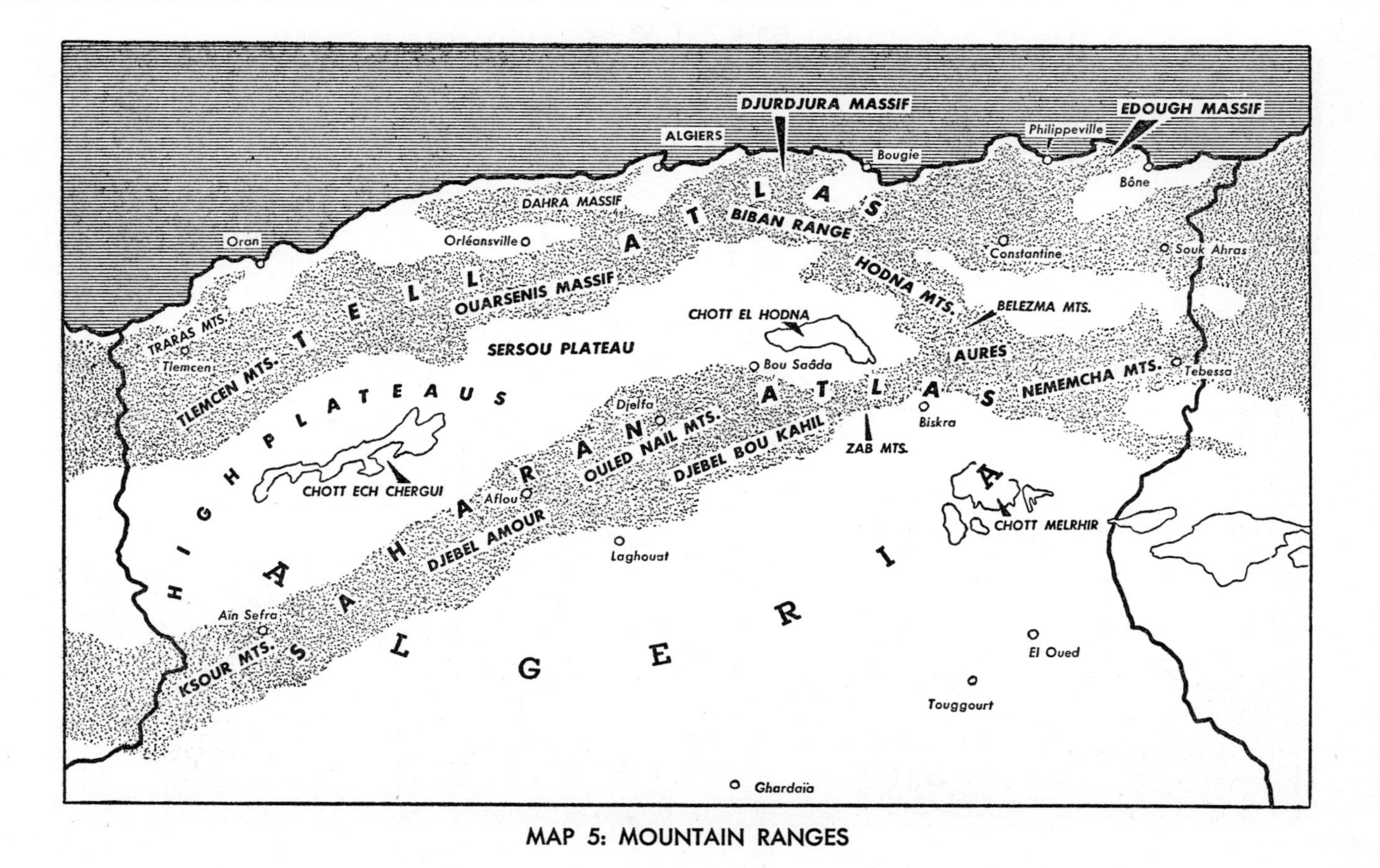

MAP 5: MOUNTAIN RANGES

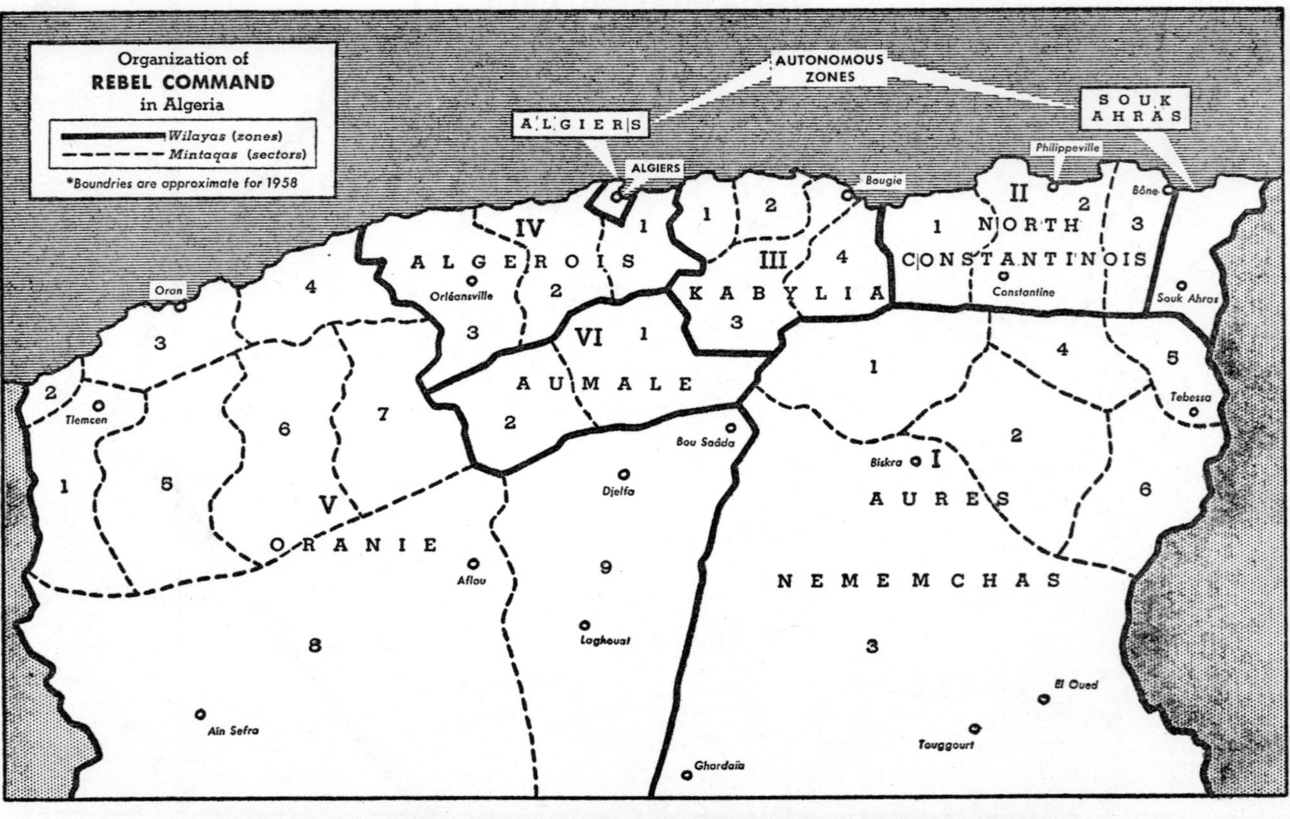

MAP 6: THE ORGANIZATION OF THE REBEL COMMAND IN ALGERIA

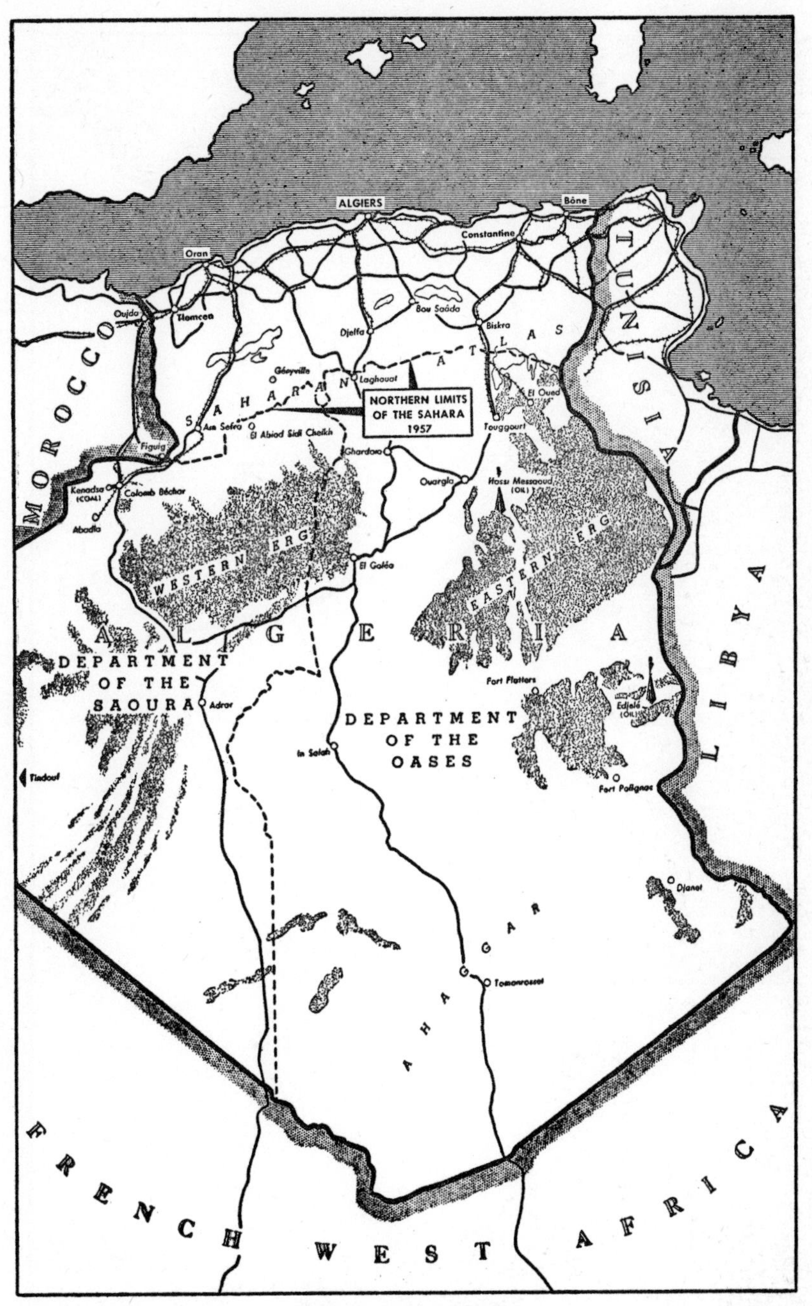

MAP 7: THE SAHARA

ALGERIA IN TURMOIL

A HISTORY OF THE REBELLION

by Michael K. Clark

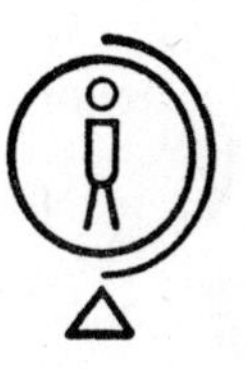

FREDERICK A. PRAEGER, *Publishers*
New York

BOOKS THAT MATTER

First published in the United States of America in 1959
by Frederick A. Praeger, Inc., Publishers
15 West 47th Street, New York 36, N. Y.

Library of Congress catalog card number 59-7448

Printed in the United States of America

PREFACE

"Autre est de savoir en gros l'existence d'une chose, autre d'en connaître les particularités."
CHATEAUBRIAND

This book, like a newspaper, contains both fact and comment. My purpose, first of all, has been to make a contribution to the record. But in chronicling the Algerian story from 1943 to 1958 (with brief flashbacks to the French conquest and to the first stirrings of Algerian nationalism prior to World War II), I have pursued the goal of analytical, rather than merely descriptive, objectivity. This has involved an attempt to seize the meaning of events and to anticipate their consequences. It was essential, therefore, to present the nationalist rebellion as far as possible in its rather intricate historical setting. The rebellion itself has so profoundly altered the outlook in Algeria that I felt compelled to follow the first year or so of its development with some attention to detail. If the outbreak of the rebellion on November 1, 1954, was an important landmark, the demonstrations of February, 1956, were another, for they revealed the depth and intensity of the European reaction. By March, 1956, the issues had largely crystallized; the matter stands now virtually as it did then. I have, as a result, been able to carry the story forward into 1957 and 1958 in broader sweeps.

I am aware that, even in the light of fuller knowledge, many Americans will reject my opinions. For, despite the ruthless colonization of our forebears, the United States is a country where anticolonialism remains a national dogma. It is a country, too, where precedent and convention too often hold individual judgment in a vise of conformity. Paul Valéry once wrote: "Obedient to a sort of law of the least effort, reluctant to create, to respond with imagination to the originality of a situation, hesitant thinking tends toward automatism; it looks for precedents and surrenders to the historical spirit that induces it to remember first, even when an entirely new case has to be provided for." My appeal to the reader is not to adopt all the views expressed in this book, but to look upon the Algerian problem as something wholly without precedent, something for which a fresh approach is needed.

The singularity of Algeria will, I think, be quickly apparent to the reader of these pages. Essentially, it derives from the presence of two distinct communities, the one Moslem and the other European, rooted in the soil of the same country. These are not political communities to which a basic ideal and basic assumptions are common; they are ethnic and religious communities living, to a large extent, under separate systems of law. Until race becomes irrelevant, and until a single system of law receives the consent of all, any attempt to impose majority rule on one of the communities, or minority rule on the other, will be felt by thousands of Algerians to be an intolerable injustice and will prevent the civil concord without which a country cannot live. The contemporary world offers no example of a true racial partnership. Yet such a partnership, guaranteeing the freedom of each individual both as a member of his community and as a citizen, is what Algeria must have if it is to survive in its present form.

American correspondents often refer indiscriminately to the European inhabitants of Algeria as "die-hard colonials." I reckon that anyone worth his salt dies hard. But in the interests of accuracy, correspondents and editorial writers should perhaps bear in mind the fact that European settlement is, after all, older in Algeria than in many parts of the United States, and that when Algeria was annexed to France, only twenty-four states had been admitted to the Union. Colonel J. M. Chivington issued his famous order to kill all Indians, "big and little," in 1864. By then, Frenchmen and Moslems had been living side by side in Algeria for years, not in equality to be sure, but at least in relative peace.

It has repeatedly been asserted in the American press that the European Algerians are trying to preserve a system of colonial privilege. This may be true of some, but not of the many. European Algerians want first of all to defend their homes, their freedoms, and their self-governing institutions. Under the Republic, this could be possible for them and for the Moslems as well. But the Europeans have no confidence in Moslem rule and will, no doubt, go to extreme lengths to block it. They react to it as a threat to their freedom and way of life, on a par with Communism. In a sense, then, Algeria is a vital testing ground. If it cannot be shown there that a workable alternative to European domination can be found in racial partnership, many honest men and women will conclude that the South African theory of *apartheid* stands vindicated.

These are the thoughts I submit to the reader who is about to take a closer look at recent developments in Algeria. They will, I hope, help him understand and judge fairly the attitudes and reactions of people whose moral standards and sense of social responsibility are at least equal to his own.

MICHAEL K. CLARK

New York City,
April, 1959.

CONTENTS

LIST OF MAPS

ALGERIA IN TURMOIL

PART I: 1830-1954

The Seeds of Trouble

1. FROM THE PARTICULAR TO THE GENERAL

"The Arabs are determined to be lord and master of their homeland from the Atlantic Ocean to the Arabian Gulf."

AHMED SHUKAIRY

On November 1, 1954—All Saints' Day—at 2:52 A.M., Jean Deleplanque, youthful subprefect of Batna, was called to the phone. Biskra was on the wire. That oasis town on the edge of the Sahara, seventy-three miles farther south, had just been shaken by the explosion of several bombs. The exact number was not yet known. Shots, too, had been fired. A French policeman had been picked up with two bullets in his thigh.

Eleven minutes later, Batna itself, administrative center and garrison town at the foot of the lofty Aurès range in eastern Algeria, was invested by groups of armed Arabs who appeared as from nowhere. These "commandos," it was learned later, had come down from the hills in trucks.

Colonel Lucien Blanche, commanding the Batna garrison, alerted by M. Deleplanque, was shot at as he drove to his headquarters in a staff car. For an instant, a group of rebels came within range of the car's headlights. This brief glimpse told a long story. There could be no doubt in the colonel's mind as to what was afoot. But the rebels were already on the move. They made off in the direction of Lambèse to the east, shooting to cover their retreat. Two French sentinels were killed in front of the army barracks.

Instantly, the alarm went out. Arris, administrative center in the heart of the Aurès mountains, was warned of the danger a few minutes before the telephone lines were cut. But for this timely call, the lonely village perched high above the upper El Abiod Valley might have fallen into rebel hands. Arris, beset on all sides, was delivered that afternoon by two relief columns, one of which had had to blast its way through four rebel roadblocks.

Khenchela, sixty-four miles east of Batna, was caught by surprise. The administrative building, the barracks, and the power station were attacked simultaneously. The French lieutenant commanding the garrison and a soldier were killed before the rebels withdrew.

A particularly tragic incident occurred that Monday morning. A bus on its way up from M'Chounèche to Arris was ambushed in the wild Tighanimine gorges by a group of fifteen rebels armed with automatic weapons. Most of them were dressed in military-type uniforms; all were masked. The leader of the group stuck his head into the bus and, addressing himself to the driver, twenty-two-year-old Brahim Halimi, said: "I know you have Caïd Saddok in this bus. Make him get out."

The *caïd* (native chief) was in the road in an instant. "I am Caïd Saddok, captain of the French Army," he said, "and I order you to allow this bus to proceed." The answer was a burst of machine-gun fire. Ben Hadj Saddok, *caïd* of M'Chounèche, former captain in the crack Spahi cavalry regiment, fell, mortally wounded.

The bandits then spotted among the passengers a European couple, Guy Monnerot, rural schoolteacher, and his bride of two months. Both were escorted out of the bus at the point of a gun and robbed of their money. "Now you may go," said the rebel chief. The two were shot as they turned to get back into the bus. The rebels, having sent the bus on its way with the wounded *caïd*, left M. and Mme. Monnerot to die by the roadside. Guy Monnerot did die before help could be sent out from Arris; Mme. Monnerot, though grievously wounded, survived.*

Meanwhile, reports from other parts of Algeria indicated that a widespread campaign of terrorist agitation was under way. No less than seventy attacks occurred in the early hours of All Saints' Day. Public

* This version of the incident in the Tighanimine gorges, based on the testimony of Brahim Halimi, the bus driver, as reported in the *Journal d'Alger* for November 5, 1954, is offered without guarantee of accuracy. Jean Servier, the young ethnologist who rescued Mme. Monnerat, gives a slightly different version in his book, *Dans l'Aurès sur les Pas des Rebelles* (Paris: Editions France Empire, 1955). According to M. Servier, Caïd Saddok was murdered when he intervened in an attempt to save M. and Mme. Monnerot from death at the hands of the rebels.

buildings and conveyances were shot at, bombs exploded (two of them in Algiers), and fires were started. Seven persons were killed and four wounded. Property damage was substantial.

These events burst upon the country like a clap of thunder in a summer sky. Nothing could have been more unexpected. The protectorates—Tunisia and Morocco—were, it was true, seething with trouble, but French Algeria was assumed to be proof against nationalist violence. The "unequivocal loyalty" for which Premier Pierre Mendès-France was to commend the Moslem population of Algeria a few days later had been taken for granted. Despite the Premier's optimistic pronouncement, this was no longer possible after November 1, 1954. In the space of a single night, Algerian nationalism had pushed itself into a conspicuous place among the revolutionary movements of Africa and Asia. The reaction in France was one of surprise, indignation, and dismay. The French had not bargained for an Arab revolt in making Algeria what it is today: a highly developed, plural state administered as an extension of Metropolitan France, but drawing its personality in part from the desert, in part from the four corners of the Mediterranean.

The rebellion was at the start, and has remained, the work of a small minority. It has never taken the form of a general uprising. The apathy of the Moslem population as a whole has resisted the pressures of incessant propaganda, intimidation, and outright terror. By the end of April, 1957, the rebels had killed 5,576 Moslems and wounded or abducted 5,480 more. It is unlikely that such a hecatomb would have been necessary if the rebellion had had the spontaneous and unanimous support claimed for it by its instigators. On January 31, 1957, the rector of El Azhar University in Cairo, a renowned seat of Islamic learning, appealed to the Arab and Moslem peoples of the world to "demonstrate their hostility toward the French colonialists, who are exterminating a people aspiring to national independence." Who, one was tempted to ask, was exterminating whom?

But the passiveness of the Algerian Moslems as the rebellion broke over their heads provided little solace for the French and certainly no excuse for complacency. A decisive page was turned when the first shots were fired. The French were safe in Algeria as long as a successful challenge to their authority remained unthinkable. Their superior force had placed the Moslems in a "state of necessity" justifying resignation, acceptance, and even cooperation. "Those who believe shall not take misbelievers for their patrons, rather than believers, and he who does this has no part with God at all, unless, indeed, ye fear some danger from them." (Koran, III:26)

There was thus a certain scandal, dimly perceived even by the ignorant, implicit in the fact that this part of Islam lingered on under an infidel flag. The rebels, though their literature was full of such modern concepts as "national state" and "self-determination," appealed to the people on a more primitive level. They stopped at nothing in their effort to prove that the time for a change was, by providential decree, at hand. The failure of the French to crush the rebellion when it had been weak was later presented as a sign of divine intervention and gave added credence to rebel prophecies of impending glory. A further aim was to convince every Moslem that, since the French were doomed, revolt was an inescapable duty. Again and again the Koran enjoins the faithful to "strive in the Way of God"; this is the obligation of the *jihad*, or holy war. The time to do God's will, the rebels said, was now, for the star and crescent had at last been raised over Moslem encampments in Algeria, and the battle was joined.

The French, on the other hand, soon showed, by their weakness and vacillation and by their internal differences that there was little security in their camp. It was not hard to put oneself in the shoes of an Algerian Moslem. His first question was: "Are the French really here to stay?" Doubt on this score, if widely shared, could be disastrous for the French. Jacques Soustelle, who became Governor General of Algeria the next year, was close to the truth when he said: "If the conviction that France will remain in Algeria is not inculcated in everyone, no Moslem, no matter how closely he may be bound to us by heart or by interest, will remain at our side. He will tremble to pay for his loyalty with his life, or with that of his family, after our departure, which our hesitations necessarily suggest as a possibility. Any political move, any statement, any article in the press giving the impression that we will come to terms with terrorism—in other words, that the terrorists will some day be in a position to settle outstanding scores—drives the Algerian Moslems further from us." M. Soustelle's remark was made in the winter of 1956. The rebels soon demonstrated their ability to settle outstanding scores without waiting for the French to leave. No wonder defections to the rebels were frequent.

Some were sudden and dramatic. The crime of Maadi Lakhdar comes to mind as an example of this. Roger Ancel, subprefect of Djidjelli, a coastal town 205 miles east of Algiers, was wounded in the bathroom of his home one day in May, 1956, when his cook, Lakhdar, entered suddenly and fired two shots at point-blank range. Mme. Ancel, rushing in to see what had happened, also was shot and seriously wounded. Lakhdar had been in the Ancels' service for twelve years. It is worth noting, too, that M. Ancel, a native of Djidjelli and an accomplished Arabist, had won a reputation for liberalism in twenty-nine years as a servant of the Algerian Administration.

A similar incident occurred at Bouzaréa in the suburbs of Algiers, where an Arab employed as bottle-washer in the modest Hôtel de France walked up to a French soldier taking breakfast, shot him dead from behind, and fled. In this case, as in many others, the culprit could reasonably expect to be rewarded by the rebels for meritorious service. He might even be accepted as a *moujahid* (or combatant; cf. *jihad*). Had not Cairo radio said: "If each Arab were to kill one Frenchman, it would be possible to exterminate all the French. Kill them without pity. Destroy them all!"?

The French were impressed by the synchronism of the first terrorist attacks. The means at the disposal of the rebels were rudimentary: their artificers had not yet progressed beyond the Molotov cocktail and the castaway tin filled with powder and gasoline. Nevertheless, seventy attacks had occurred on the same night at widely separated points. Three questions demanded urgent answers: Who had planned the outbreak? Who had executed the plans? How could a plot of such magnitude have been hatched without the French getting wind of it?

The last of these questions caused no little embarrassment precisely because it could hardly be said that the French had had no warning. In Tunisia, on Algeria's eastern flank, bands of armed rebels known as *fellaga* (highwaymen in Arabic) had been fighting the French since March 19, 1954, and ominous rumblings had been heard for some time in the Aurès mountains and elsewhere in eastern Algeria. On the night of September 23, 1954, a group of ten *fellaga*, in search of arms, had forced their way into the house of an Arab notable at Hadada, a frontier village near Souk Ahras. The incident had attracted little notice, but by mid-October rebel action along the border was conceded to be a threat to law and order on the Algerian side, particularly in the Souk Ahras district, where raids had become an almost daily occurrence despite the "security curtain" said to be in place to protect Algerian soil.

On October 15, Lieutenant General Pierre Boyer de Latour du Moulin, French Resident General in Tunisia, and Roger Léonard, Governor General of Algeria, met at Constantine with their principal advisors to examine the security problem on the Algerian-Tunisian confines. M. Léonard said afterwards: "So far, the *fellaga* have limited their activity to isolated raids launched in the hope of obtaining money, arms, and food. It would be wrong to attach importance to these acts, which are more in the nature of banditry than of organized political action."

This sanguine view was not shared by General Boyer de Latour, who had gathered from *goumiers* (native soldiers) recruited in the Aurès mountains that the political atmosphere on the Algerian side was anything but wholesome. The general's misgivings, supported by more corroborating evidence each day, were so great that he made serious representations in Paris, apparently to no effect. He reports in his book, *Vérités sur l'Afrique du Nord,** that André Pélabon, chief of Premier Pierre Mendès-France's personal staff, had laughed at the thought of an uprising in Algeria.

The Algerian Administration itself had tragic shortcomings. It was top-heavy, half-atrophied, improvident, and without roots deep in the country. M. Soustelle, in his book, *Aimée et Souffrante Algérie,*† compares it to a raft floating on an unsounded sea. This had not always been the case. The shifting shoals of Arab life had, in the past, been charted, and the various currents prevalent in the country had been accurately measured by an agency known in its earliest form as the *Direction des Affaires Arabes.* This remarkable institution, put on a permanent basis by Marshal Bugeaud in 1841, spawned the famous *Bureaux Arabes* in 1844.

The Arab Bureaus were the instrument of government in all areas under military administration; gradually, as the civil administration took over in the north, they moved south with the army.‡ However, the *Direction Générale des Affaires Indigènes et des Territoires du Sud,* set up in 1934, brought the management of native affairs once again under a single wing. The word *indigène* (native) having become objectionable, the central agency became the *Direction des Affaires Musulmanes* in 1941. The Ordinance of March 7, 1944, which abolished, in principle, all distinction between Frenchmen of different faiths, was foolishly interpreted to mean that the *Direction des Affaires Musulmanes* would have to disappear. Its existence was ended in August, 1945, by decision of Yves Chataigneau, Socialist Governor General of Algeria, who, as a result, has much to answer for.§

The whole structure has since had to be resurrected in the heat of action. The first "Specialized Administrative Sections" (Arab Bureaus in a new guise) were organized in the summer of 1955 with Algerian (meaning native) Affairs Officers in charge; and the *Direction Générale des Affaires Politiques et de la Fonction Publique,* invested with virtually all the prerogatives of the old *Direction des Affaires Musulmanes,* was set up in June, 1956.

* Paris: Plon, 1956.

† Paris: Plon, 1956.

‡ The Southern Territories under military administration were: Aïn Sefra, Ghardaïa, Touggourt, and Oasis.

§ The *Direction des Territoires du Sud* survived.

A high French official, asked on November 7, 1954, how French intelligence could have failed to alert the authorities in good time to the possibility of a terrorist outbreak, replied with a saying that had gained currency during World War II: "Information is difficult to get, more difficult still to transmit, and almost impossible to use." The official listed six different and often competing information-gathering agencies. Nevertheless, alarming reports are known to have reached the top. The Revolutionary Committee for Unity and Action (C.R.U.A.), the group responsible for the terrorist outbreak, is believed to have been mentioned for the first time in an official report on April 15, 1954. By May 5, the activities of the C.R.U.A. and its links with Cairo were known in some detail. Its leaders had been identified. A report dated August 12 called attention to the presence of an embryo army of fifty-odd armed rebels in the Aurès mountains. The C.R.U.A. was described on August 28 as being "in ferment"; the danger of acts of terrorism in response to possible orders from Cairo was stressed. An equally pressing report was sent up on September 22. To no avail. M. Léonard, apparently, had decided that the danger was not to be taken seriously.

At all events, the rebels, few in number, kept their secrets well enough to make the element of surprise work fully to their advantage. The French were caught off guard. Quite naturally, the rebel organization, which had previously been the object of professional curiosity only, aroused the lively interest of the public at large after the first shots were fired. Numerous articles purporting to explain the origin of the rebellion appeared in the press in those early days. But the picture could not be brought fully into view unless recent developments were seen in their relation to the remoter background.

It is essential to remember that the outbreak of the Algerian rebellion on November 1, 1954, was closely connected with the rise of Lieutenant Colonel Gamal Abdel Nasser to power in Egypt. Out of the 1952 revolution in Cairo came a new fusion of forces, and this in turn provided the vital spark, without which nationalist undertakings could not be carried successfully and impetuously forward in Algeria. The new Egyptian regime was found to possess what the Arab League had so woefully lacked—a will to move mountains in pursuit of the ideal of Arab folk nationalism.

The chronology of events itself helps to bring the origins of the Algerian rebellion into focus. The old regime in Egypt, with its administrative and financial corruption and with its tradition of rivalry between the Palace and the nationalist Wafd party, was destroyed by the military *coup d'état* of July 23, 1952. King Farouk's abdication in favor of his infant son, Ahmed Fouad, gave the monarchy a temporary reprieve, but by degrees the Revolutionary Council, composed of young officers and headed by Nasser, took into its hands all the reins of power. Major General Mohammed Naguib, the council's figurehead, succeeded Aly Maher as Premier in September, 1952. In June, 1953, General Naguib proclaimed Egypt to be a republic with himself as President and Premier. However, in April, 1954, the Revolutionary Council forced President Naguib to abandon the office of Premier; this office was taken over by Nasser.

Two months later, a correspondent of the London *Times* reported that "outside the armed forces it is difficult to find any positive support for the military regime." The indifference noted by this and other observers soon turned to enthusiasm, however; for in July, 1954, the agreement by which Britain undertook to evacuate the Suez Canal Zone was initialed in Cairo. Cairo radio announced ecstatically that Egypt had "cast away the last fetter on glorious independence."

The following autumn the Nasser regime dared to challenge the deeply pervasive influence of the fanatical Moslem Brotherhood, long protected by a mystique of sanctity. Sheikh Hassan el-Hodeiby, the Brothers' "Supreme Guide," was thrown into prison; six of his associates were executed, and the organization itself was dissolved. Once this contest with the chief advocates of Islamic reaction and theocratic government was decisively settled in Nasser's favor, it was clear that the new regime had the strength, as well as the determination, to maintain a type of secular polity comparable to contemporary Western models. President Naguib himself was ousted in November, 1954, despite his apparent popularity, and Nasser became the head of the state.

In the midst of the momentous events of 1952 and 1953, Colonel Nasser was struggling to get his thoughts on paper. These were ultimately published by the Cairo weekly *Akher Sa'a* in three installments toward the end of 1953 under the title, "The Philosophy of the Egyptian Revolution." Being more of a profession of faith and manifesto for the future than a philosophical treatise, this work provides an excellent glimpse of what Nasser had in mind when he began to turn his attention to the problems of North Africa. He speaks of the Arab world as a single, though artificially divided, community faced with a common enemy—imperialism. He also makes a strong plea for united action, adding: "I do not doubt for a moment that our common struggle will achieve for us and our peoples everything we desire and long for. For I shall always maintain that we are strong. The only trouble is, we do not realize just how strong we are."

When these words appeared, there was, in Cairo, a group of waiting men—Algerians, Tunisians, and Moroccans who had come to the capital of the most powerful Arab state in quest of the very message they now heard. Making their headquarters at the Maghrib Office, rendezvous of North African nationalists, they had plotted, intrigued, bickered among themselves, and hounded the Arab League collectively and individually, but they had got nowhere. Two men—Mohammed Ben Bella, a former warrant officer in the French Army, and Mohammed Khider, a former nationalist deputy in the French National Assembly—dominated the Algerian contingent. They were soon to find in Colonel Nasser and in the Revolutionary Council the kind of support needed to make significant action possible.

It is ironical that the point of combustion should have been reached in a distant city between men only beginning to emerge from obscurity. For the Algerian national movement had produced a leader of commanding stature, Messali Hadj, founder in 1933 of the *Glorieuse Etoile Nord-Africaine* and in 1946 of the Movement for the Triumph of Democratic Liberties (M.T.L.D.). But the M.T.L.D. was racked with dissension in 1954, and Messali himself had been under house arrest in France for two years.

Messali had organized the M.T.L.D. as a vehicle for legal political activities and also as a cover for illegal agitation and subversion. Its latter function was the most important, for Messali believed in violence. Thus, while some of Messali's followers ran for office and sat in the councils of government, others, chosen for their courage and contempt for the law, were incorporated into a select group called the Special Organization (O.S.). The purpose of the O.S. was to prepare and execute plans for widespread terrorist agitation leading to an insurrection against the French. The organization was discovered by the French in 1950, however, and many of its leaders were tried and convicted for plotting against the security of the state.

Ben Bella, "national chief" of the O.S., was one of them. But he escaped from prison in 1952 and made his way to Cairo. There he joined Mohammed Khider, the former deputy, who had fled to Cairo the previous year to escape arrest. Both were in Egypt when the old regime came tumbling down.

Later in this book the signal services rendered by the Egyptian Army to the Algerian and other North African nationalists, beginning in 1952, will become apparent. The creation in Algeria of a Revolutionary Committee for Unity and Action (C.R.U.A.) in 1954 was one of the fruits of Algerian and Egyptian plotting in Cairo. This new committee, though its membership was drawn from the ranks of the old O.S., stood resolutely apart from the quarrels that had pitted Messali Hadj against his central committee in Algiers. When it became apparent that the rival M.T.L.D. factions could not be brought together behind a bold plan for revolutionary action, the C.R.U.A. and the Algerian *émigrés* in Cairo resolved to go it alone with Egyptian support. The result was the formation of the National Liberation Front (F.L.N.) and the outbreak of the rebellion.

Although Premier Pierre Mendès-France vowed at the outset that reinforcements exceeding the need would be sent to Algeria and that his government would yield nothing to "sedition," the rebellion was to go from strength to strength in the months and years that lay ahead until virtually the whole country was enmeshed in it. As we shall see, the F.L.N. has consistently kept its ultimate goal—undivided power—clearly before its eyes. Recognizing its most precious allies to be naked fear among the Moslems and confusion among the French, the F.L.N. has cultivated both in a multitude of ways. The French, on the other hand, have misunderstood the issue at almost every point. Again and again they have interpreted fear reactions as the expression of political aspirations; and, although personal security has from the start been a desperate need, they have usually responded only with offers of more bread and more social justice. The accession of General de Gaulle to power has modified but not abolished this concept. Some nations seem wedded to a single solution to all problems. In every recent crisis, the United States has proposed economic aid as the essential remedy. Similarly, the French have tended to place almost mystic faith in the virtues of *liberté, égalité, fraternité.* The tragedy in Algeria is that reliance on this formula and the promise of a more abundant life to come have shielded nobody from the terrorist's bullet.

The rebellion was greatly strengthened in March, 1956, by the grant of independence to the former French protectorates of Tunisia and Morocco. The sanctuary behind friendly frontiers that then became available to the Algerian rebels was in itself an invaluable asset. But the Tunisian regime of Habib Bourguiba was to provide direct assistance as well. Without this, the rebellion might well have been crushed by the French before the end of 1957.

Nevertheless, through all vicissitudes and every internal convulsion, the essential, sustaining link has been with Cairo. This was true even when a Berber group inside Algeria wrested control of the rebel apparatus from the Arab *émigrés* in 1956. It was true even after the rebel high command had established its headquarters at Tunis early in 1957. The link transcends mere shipments of arms and ammunition. It is more than ideological. It might almost be described as historical in the sense that the Algerian rebellion is in part a product of Nasserism.

Mr. Bourguiba has had many difficulties with the F.L.N. It is not easy to play host to 5,000 or more armed men from a next-door country in the throes of civil war. But the basic differences stem from the fact the F.L.N. is, and Tunisia is not, in political communion with Cairo.

It was inevitable, of course, that resurgent Arab nationalism should infect Algeria in its sweep across North Africa. But it is not necessarily written that this force shall carry all before it there or elsewhere. Where a vital Western interest is at stake, it must obviously be protected, for the alternative is an acceleration of Western retreat.

Recent events in the Middle East—notably the bloody destruction of the Iraqi monarchy in July, 1958—have led to some rather hysterical thinking in this country on the subject of Arab nationalism. The dramatic successes of Arab nationalism (under the banner of Nasserism) are presented as evidence of its invincible power. Eric Johnston, chairman of the Committee for International Economic Growth, has described it as a "surging revolutionary tide." And he warned: "Those who deal with the Middle East must go with this tide or be overwhelmed by it."* Clearly, if Arab nationalism is assumed to be irresistible, it will be just that, but not necessarily as a result of its own intrinsic strength. Communism, too, is regarded in some parts of the world as an irresistible force, but I doubt that Mr. Johnston would accept this contention. And who does not remember the deluded people who, before World War II, claimed fascism to be the wave of the future?

The fact that the force of Arab nationalism has been magnified by the weakness of the forces that have been brought to bear against it sometimes seems to be wholly lost from sight. The historian of the future will undoubtedly associate the advance of Arab nationalism very closely with the decline of the West. He may, indeed, compare it to the early conquests of Islam. When the followers of the Prophet burst out of the desert and flung themselves against the civilized world, they found their principal adversaries—the Byzantines and the Persians—exhausted by war and divided against themselves. At the death of the Prophet in 632, the conquest of Arabia had yet to be completed. When Omar, the second caliph, died twelve years later, the whole of Persia, Syria, Egypt, and Cyrenaica were conquered and regularly administered. But the caliphate was to be no match for the Tartars.

It is not to deny the legitimate aspirations of Arab nationalism to point out that its advance since the end of World War II—encouraged first by Britain against France, later by the United States in contempt of British and French interests, and finally by the Soviet Union against the

---

* See *The New York Times Magazine*, August 10, 1958.

West as a whole—has, too often, held up a cruel mirror to Western folly and weakness. London committed a tragic mistake in 1945 when, with Washington's blessing, it compelled the French to relinquish their League of Nations mandate in the Levant States and to pull out entirely without concluding treaties similar to the 1931 treaty giving Britain a privileged position in Iraq. This was the first decisive blow at the underpinnings of Western influence in the Middle East, for, by analogy, there could be no further justification for the Anglo-Iraqi and Anglo-Egyptian treaties. The subsequent loss of the Suez Canal base and of the canal itself followed logically from the precedent set in Beirut and Damascus.

Nevertheless, at some point the Western powers with vital interests in the Arab world—and the United States is one of them—must decide to prevent further nationalist expansion at their expense. All past and present appeasement and propitiation, all betrayals of Western solidarity, will not indefinitely stave off the day when, if Arab nationalism is not challenged, the last Western position in the Arab world will fall—no doubt to others. Where is the final stand to be made? For the United States, the answer may be, along the frontiers of Israel. For France, the vital position is Algeria.

2. THE CONQUEST

In a sense, Algerian nationalism can be said to go back to the French conquest in the 1830's and 1840's. The Emir Abd-el-Kader symbolized, more nobly perhaps than any of his successors, Algerian resistance to French domination. Although the great emir, vanquished in 1847, later became a loyal friend of France, and even saved a number of Christians from death during the Damascus massacre of 1860, his countrymen showed little love at first for their new, infidel masters. Gérard de Nerval, who visited Cairo in 1843, was urged by his friend, M. Jean, a "glorious remnant" of Napoleon's Army of Egypt, to attend the festivities marking the feast of the Prophet Mohammed. "Only I advise you," said M. Jean, "to disguise yourself as an Arab, because the feast coincides this year with the return of the pilgrims from Mecca, among them many Maghribi, who dislike Frankish dress, particularly since the conquest of Algiers."

The poet, disguised as a Syrian, was at the El Futûh gate when the pilgrims entered the city. "It would be impossible," he wrote, "to find anything more hirsute, more bristly, and more fierce than the immense throng of Maghribi, men from Tunis, Tripoli and Morocco, and our compatriots from Algiers. The Cossacks entering Paris in 1814 give only a faint idea of what these men were like."*

But Algeria as the French found it in 1830 was not a nation; it was a conglomerate of warring tribes. The decline of Turkish power had led to a resurgence of anarchy, North Africa's traditional alternative to empire. Hussein Ben Hussein, the last Dey of Algiers, and the lesser Deys of Constantine, Oran, and Médéa held about one-sixth of what is now Algeria in their grip, but neither they nor their predecessors had ever been able to subjugate the intractable Berber tribes in the mountains or the nomads of the desert. Even in the cities, crawling with turbulent Janizaries, the exercise of power was a perilous game. Fourteen of Hussein's twenty-nine predecessors had met with violent death. In the interior, the tribes fought among themselves for the best pasture land each spring and for the best barley land each autumn. Their *razzias* kept the blood flowing in the off-season. It is not to be wondered at that the native population of Algeria should have remained constant at about 1,500,000 for fourteen centuries; it now stands at about 9,000,000.

The Arab nationalists are fond of depicting the pre-French period as a golden age when Algeria was free, prosperous, and respected by the nations of the world. Treaties concluded with the Powers are cited as evidence of the Dey's former sovereign status. The treaties, made necessary by the Dey's predatory habits, are real; the rest is twaddle. Every schoolchild knows how Stephen Decatur successfully sailed in 1815 against the Barbary pirates of Algiers that had preyed on Mediterranean shipping for so long and how, a year later, Lord Exmouth, in command of an Anglo-Dutch fleet, bombarded Algiers, forcing the Dey to free his Christian slaves. The conventions to which the Dey was a party had to do with piracy, slavery, and tribute. They should not be cited without reference to their contents.

But it remained for France to give the Barbary pirates their quietus. The famous incident which was to lead to the French expedition of 1830 and to the fall of Algiers has long since become part of the Algerian legend. On April 30, 1827, the French consul in Algiers, a M. Deval, hied himself to the *Kasbah* (citadel) to present his compliments to the Dey on the occasion of Lesser Bairam, the feast that marks the end of the Moslem lenten month of Ramadan. Hussein, it is said, made testy by long fasting, responded to the consul's compliment with an ill grace that

* Gérard de Nerval, *Voyage en Orient* (Paris: 1856).

led to words. In a fit of passion, he struck the consul with his fly whisk and threatened to throw him into irons. Hussein explained in a recently discovered letter to his suzerain, Mahmoud II, Sultan of Turkey, that he had been moved by the consul's offensive words to strike "light blows" two or three times with the fly whisk he had held in his "humble hand."

King Charles X of France may also have had an eye on the Dey's treasury. This had been spoken of as a fabulous hoard of ill-gotten gold stored up in the inner recesses of the *Kasbah;* it turned out to be a starved reserve amounting to some 48 million francs. In any case, the expedition mounted against the Dey was in no sense a war of conquest. It took King Louis Philippe's Government four years to make up its mind after interminable wavering that Algiers should be kept.

The Government of the "French possessions in the north of Africa" was established by decree in July, 1834. Until 1840 it was hoped that Algiers could be held without deeper penetration, but the tribes were not so easily reduced to vassalage. The rise of Abd-el-Kader compelled the French Army to dispute possession of the ground pace by pace until Algeria was entirely won.

It was the independent Berber spirit combined with allegiance to Islam and a taste for war that Marshal Bugeaud had to contend with in Algeria. His difficulties did not stem from the resistance of a defiled nation or the revolt of outraged nationalism. The Algerian state had no existence in fact, none even in the minds of men. The Dey could not have transferred his sovereignty to the French if he had wanted to; it was less than a fiction. The word Algeria itself gained currency only in 1835. It was given official sanction in 1839, when the French Minister of War first used it to designate what had previously been known as the "French possessions in the north of Africa." The entity Algeria must therefore be regarded as a French invention.

3. FIRST STIRRINGS OF NATIONALISM

Ferhat Abbas, now a prominent member of the rebel command in Cairo, was hurt to the quick twenty-two years ago when he heard the word "nationalist" used to describe the coterie he had gathered about him. He claimed to be falsely accused. To prove his point, he published an article still remembered and, no doubt to his sorrow, widely quoted. "If I had encountered the Algerian nation," he wrote, "I would be a nationalist and, as such, would have nothing to be ashamed of. Men who have died for a patriotic ideal are honored and respected every day. My life is worth no more than theirs. And yet I will not die for the Algerian fatherland, for this fatherland does not exist. I have not encountered it. I have questioned history. I have questioned the quick and the dead. I have visited cemeteries. No one has spoken to me of such a thing. . . . You cannot build on wind. We have eliminated all fogginess and vain imaginings to link our future once and for all to that of French endeavor in this country." It would be interesting to know what recollection Mr. Abbas has today of his former dialogues with the ghosts of his forebears.

One of the first to contest the validity of Mr. Abbas's stand was the late fiery Sheikh Abd-el-Hamid Ben Badis, a Moslem Savonarola driven by an immense desire to rid Algeria of the French and to restore Islam to its primitive purity. After reading Mr. Abbas's article, he published a countercredo, which said: "We have examined the past and the present and have found that the Algerian nation has taken shape and exists. This nation has its history, marked by deeds of the highest order. It possesses its culture, its traditions, and its characteristics, good and bad, as do all the nations of the earth. We maintain further that this Algerian nation is not France, cannot be France, and does not wish to be France." Mr. Ben Badis also held that "independence is the natural right of all peoples." There you have it: the issue was as clearly stated on both sides in the spring of 1936 as it has been since.

Mr. Ben Badis was an early master in the art of fighting the West with arms stolen from the arsenal of Western thought. The hirsute pilgrims mentioned by Gérard de Nerval had only the Koran to go on: "Fight in God's Way with those who fight with you, but transgress not; verily, God loves not those who do transgress. Kill them wherever you find them, and drive them out from whence they drive you out; for sedition is worse than slaughter." (II: 186–187) Or again: "And when ye meet those who misbelieve—then strike off heads until ye have massacred them, and bind fast the bonds!" (XLVII: 4)

Mr. Ben Badis recognized that prescripts such as these, their divine origin notwithstanding, would no longer do outside the mosques; but he also realized that the enemy might be confounded with a vigorous Western idea like national self-determination. This he wielded with telling effect. But he may have committed a grave imprudence, for an alien idea is a sword that cuts both ways, and Mr. Ben Badis was not prepared to let down Moslem defenses against the onslaught of modernism. On the contrary, his primary object and that of his Algerian Association of Ulema (doctors of Islamic law) was to save Algeria for a hermetic and puritanical form of Islam derived from the teachings of the Wahabite school in Arabia.

Mr. Ben Badis, like the Wahabis, proscribed smoking, drinking, and dancing. He denounced as polytheistic the cult of saints and of *marabouts* (holy men) and other heterodox practices prevalent in North Africa. He deemed modern science to be a source, not of truth, but of evil. In 1938, he issued a *fatwa* (authorized opinion) according to which the acquisition by a Moslem of French nationality was tantamount to apostasy. It would be wrong to think that his message failed to sink in.

The Association of Ulema, with its slogan, "Islam is my religion, Arabic is my language, Algeria is my fatherland," was in the forefront of the nationalist movement from the start, fanning the fires of Moslem fanaticism and combatting all Sufistic tendencies destructive of Islamic unity. Its secretary-general, Ahmed Tewfik el-Madani, became titular head of the Algerian Liberation Committee in Cairo in October, 1956. He had previously achieved a reputation of sorts as editor of the Ulema's weekly organ *El Bassaïr*, now banned.

I vividly recall the day I went around to see the Ulema with Piero Mignanego of the *Corriere della Sera*. We were received on the morning of November 25, 1954, by Mr. Tewfik el-Madani and other officers of the Association in an elegant Moorish palace in the Kasbah, the teeming Arab quarter that derives its name from the citadel above it.

The conversation, conducted in an atmosphere of stiff oriental politeness, was not frank enough to be rewarding. Why, we asked, did the Ulema, which clamored for the emancipation of Algeria, do nothing to emancipate the female half of its Moslem population? It was a fair question, we felt, because in this respect at least the Ulema had power to act, and because the Moslem women were still veiled and half-sequestered. They have not yet been rescued from the evils of child marriage and divorce by repudiation. The answer given by the Ulema was that the existing barriers had to be maintained to protect Moslem womanhood from European immorality.

The Ulema might have cited, but did not, the pure word of God: "Men stand superior to women in that God hath preferred some of them over others, and in that they expend of their wealth: and the virtuous women, devoted, careful (in their husbands') absence, as God has cared for them. But those whose perverseness ye fear, admonish them and remove them into bedchambers and beat them; but if they submit to you, then do not seek a way against them; verily, God is high and great." (Koran, IV: 38)

Hadj Ben Ahmed Messali, as crafty a demagogue as ever raised the banner of revolt, occupies the undisputed place of honor in the hall of fame of Algerian nationalism. Born of humble parentage in 1898, Messali is a native of Tlemcen, one of the few authentic Arab cities in Algeria. He became an obscure Communist agitator in Paris after serving in the French Army during World War I. His early occupations as peddler, laborer, and student at the Sorbonne left little scope for his rabble-rousing talents, which came fully into play only when he blossomed forth in 1927 as leader of the *Etoile Nord-Africaine*, an outgrowth of a Communist-front organization called the *Secours Rouge International.** The *Etoile* was banned by the French in 1929, but it rose from its ashes in 1933 to become the *Glorieuse Etoile Nord-Africaine*. Messali and two of his associates were thrown into prison for reactivating an illegal association, for subverting soldiers, and for "inciting to murder in the interests of anarchist propaganda."

The National Union of North African Moslems was then formed to keep the torch of nationalism aloft in adversity. However, a mistrial soon restored Messali to freedom, and the Glorious Star resumed its ascension. As it rose, it moved out of the Communist firmament and into that of pan-Arabism. In 1935, to escape arrest, Messali fled to Geneva, where he came under the influence of the Emir Chekib Arslan, the Lebanese apostle of the pan-Islamic ideal. As a result, Messali soon ditched his Communist friends completely and made peace with the Ulema. His conversion was later to be reflected in his outward appearance, for he grew a beard and began to play the part of a seer.

The advent of Premier Léon Blum's Popular Front in 1936 aroused great hopes in the ranks of the Glorious Star. Messali, amnestied and allowed to return to France, campaigned vigorously in public places and in the columns of his journal *El Oumma* (The Nation) for the independence of North Africa. "Brothers," he cried, addressing a huge rally in the Algiers municipal stadium on August 2, 1936, "we must not be lulled to sleep; our action has barely begun." But the balmy days were soon over. Outlawed again in January, 1937, the Glorious Star disappeared forever. Its place was taken by the Algerian People's party (P.P.A.).

Messali, finding it expedient to lower his sights, made Algerian independence his goal and dismissed the dream of becoming a North African Bolívar. But his tongue had lost none of its vitriol, and his paper, *El*

* The French Communist party had resolved at its Fifth Congress at Lille in March, 1926, to "establish closer contact with the native masses and give more effective support to the revolutionary movements directed against French imperialism."

Oumma, none of its violence. In July, 1939, *El Oumma* stated: "No sentiment links North Africa to France except the hatred that a hundred years of colonialism have bred in our hearts." In August, Messali was arrested for "inciting to disorderly acts inimical to the sovereignty of the state" and incarcerated in Algiers. In 1941, a military court sentenced him to sixteen years at hard labor for sedition. He was pardoned in 1943 as a consequence of the Allied landings in North Africa, but only to be banished soon afterwards, first to Reibel, 230 miles south of Algiers, then to French Equatorial Africa. The P.P.A., although officially banned in September, 1939, lived on as an underground organization.

4. THE ALLIED LANDINGS AND NATIONALIST RESURGENCE

When the French had thus whisked Messali into the wings, Ferhat Abbas stepped to the front of the stage. The newcomer was a well-to-do druggist from Sétif, the forty-four-year-old son of a highly decorated former *caïd*. He had, as we have seen, made something of a name for himself as a publicist and an ardent advocate of assimilation. Mr. Abbas is often represented as a romantic modernist deeply hurt by the failure of the French to accept him as an equal. In a petition to Marshal Pétain, "revered chief of the French state," he had, in 1941, professed to speak in the name of men "pledged to strive and act in all circumstances, at all times, and under every regime until the law in Algeria is the same for all." He could not yet be regarded as a dangerous revolutionary.

But the Atlantic Charter, with its promise of universal self-determination, and, to an even greater extent, the dramatic Allied landings on the North African coast, opened new horizons toward which Mr. Abbas was irresistibly drawn. It could hardly have been otherwise, for the persuasive Mr. Robert D. Murphy, President Roosevelt's personal envoy, was there, explaining that the end of colonialism was an American war aim. All this had Mr. Abbas so dazzled that at one point he addressed a petition, not to the French, but to the Allied "authorities." He quickly recovered himself, however, and, in February, 1943, produced his famous *Manifesto*. This incondite and laborious document was essentially a long diatribe against French colonialism, combined with an assertion of Algeria's right to home rule. The following excerpts are samples of Mr. Abbas's style and line of argument:

> It is enough to examine the process of colonization in Algeria to realize how the policy of "assimilation," automatically applied to some and denied to others, has reduced Moslem society to utter servitude. . . .
>
> The salient and continuing characteristic of French colonization is the subjection of the entire country, its humanity, its wealth, its equipment, and its administration, to the European and French element. It is here that the policy of linking Algeria to Metropolitan France, the so-called "policy of assimilation," finds its source, its justification, and its truest expression.
>
> Politically and morally, this colonization can have but one concept, that of two mutually alien societies. Its systematic or disguised refusal to allow the Moslem Algerians into the French community has discouraged all those who have favored a policy of assimilation extended to the aborigines. This policy appears today, in the eyes of all, as an inaccessible dream, as a dangerous device in the hands of colonization.

The document, long on criticism but short on constructive proposals, ended with a demand for the grant of an Algerian constitution that would:

1. Abolish colonialism;
2. Guarantee the freedom and equality of all Algerians without regard to race or religion;
3. Destroy the power of the French land barons by dividing their estates among the Arab peasants;
4. Make Arabic as well as French an official language;
5. Insure freedom of speech and association;
6. Provide free, compulsory education for children of both sexes;
7. Establish the principle of religious freedom and the separation of church and state;
8. Bring the Moslems into the new Algerian Government;
9. Free all political prisoners.

It cannot be said that the *Manifesto* contained a fully developed nationalist creed. Mr. Abbas was still groping. The idea of nationhood underlay his proposals but was not made explicit. The contemplated constitution was not even presented as an expression of popular sovereignty. However, a glowing reference to Mustapha Kemal, father of modern Turkey, suggests that Mr. Abbas had a secular rather than a Moslem state in mind. The pan-Arab ideal was not mentioned. Nothing was said about Algeria's relations with France. The idea seemed to be that once colonialism was laid low, Algeria's political future would take care of itself.

One surprising thing about the *Manifesto* is that it apparently had official French blessing from conception to birth. The exact extent of the French undertaking cannot easily be ascertained fifteen years after the event, but this much is certain: Mr. Abbas was in touch with Marcel Peyrouton, the Governor General, and with the late Augustin Berque, the Director of Moslem Affairs, and was led to believe that the authorities took a favorable view of his efforts.

The fifty-five Moslem politicians who added their signatures to the manifesto were under the same impression. Some of them would have given the document wide berth at the slightest hint of official hostility; defiance of the Administration on such basic issues was not common in those days. It is known, too, that M. Berque had seen the *Manifesto* in draft form. He is said actually to have gone out of his way to round up signatures.

However, there must have been some wavering among the politicians despite M. Berque's encouragements, for the nationalists felt called upon to throw a few threats into the balance, a time-honored trick in Algeria for making a minority opinion prevail. A letter bearing the imprint of something called the "Union of Algerian Moslems" was sent out to remind the recalcitrant that those "who refuse to join the reform movement of the Algerian *Manifesto* will be sentenced by public hatred to certain punishment."

The *Manifesto* was handed to M. Peyrouton and to the representatives of the Allied Powers in Algeria on March 31, 1943. Mr. Abbas claimed later that M. Peyrouton had accepted the *Manifesto* as the basis for discussions leading to a new statute for Algeria. This may or may not be entirely true. In any case, a Commission for Moslem Economic and Social Studies was appointed to prepare a plan of reforms that could be implemented at once without damage to the war effort. On May 26, Mr. Abbas and twenty-one other Moslem delegates to Algeria's consultative financial assembly came forward with an *Addition to the Manifesto* prepared in response to a request from the Governor General for "concrete proposals." The new document went further than the first in terms of nationalist ideology.

> It is an established fact, proclaimed by French statesmen and jurists [the delegates wrote], that France, a Christian and Latin nation, cannot, without compromising her national unity, accept within her community and family an Algerian who does not abjure

his faith. In these circumstances, it is only fair and human that an Algerian should at least be a citizen of his own country. This is the clearest and simplest justification for the recognition of the Algerian nation.

The word "nation" was to become the theme of Mr. Abbas's subsequent pronouncements. Mr. Abbas was getting closer to his cherished "Algerian Republic" of later years. Specifically, the *Addition to the Manifesto* demanded a guarantee of Algeria's territorial integrity and a recognition of her "political autonomy as a sovereign nation." France was to be conceded only a *droit de regard,* whatever that may mean. On the other hand, a federation of the three North African countries—Tunisia, Algeria, and Morocco—was held out as the ultimate goal. For some obscure reason, Mr. Abbas and his friends were moved to take a strong stand against economic planning and especially against measures to coordinate rail and road transport.

5. GENERAL CATROUX STEPS IN

The nationalists had spoken, but, much to their surprise, nothing happened. It is stated in a pamphlet published by Mr. Abbas's party in 1948 that the *Addition* was "adopted" by the Commission for Moslem Economic and Social Studies on June 26, 1943, with the approval of M. Berque. The pamphlet goes on to accuse the Governor General of "disloyalty," his sole aim being, in the words of the pamphlet, to "save the colonial regime in its entirety and to safeguard colonial privileges on Algerian soil." The record does not confirm these statements.

The facts are these: M. Peyrouton resigned on June 1, 1943, two days after General de Gaulle's arrival in Algiers. General Georges Catroux, appointed Governor General of Algeria on June 3, made his position clear from the start: Algeria was part of France and secession was unthinkable. In September, to put an end to the continuing political agitation, General Catroux had Mr. Abbas and Abdelkader Saïah, president of the Arab section of the financial assembly, interned; whereupon twelve financial delegates, including Dr. Abdennour Tamzali, president of the Kabyle section, quit the nationalist group with professions of undying affection for France. Messrs. Abbas and Saïah were released in December.

There was nothing equivocal in General Catroux's approach to the Algerian problem. Independence, in his view, could not be entertained for an instant, nor was nationalist agitation to be countenanced. But the new Governor General, who also served the French Committee of National Liberation as Commissioner of State for Moslem Affairs, was aware of the need for a new deal in Algeria. The prestige of France was at a low ebb among the Arabs. The French, humbled by the Germans, then rescued by the Americans, could no longer count on the respect and loyalty that impregnable might commands. Moreover, as General Catroux himself has noted, "French North Africa was caught in a wind of emancipation coming at once from the East and from across the Atlantic, coming also from the depths of naturally intractable Berber souls and from the religious intolerance of Islam."* There had already been squalls. General Catroux's object was to "prevent the storm." This was, indeed, an imperative because General de Gaulle and his French Committee of National Liberation had undertaken to build on African soil a powerful new army as the primary instrument of their policy and as the promise of France's return to greatness. Colonial troops were needed in vast numbers. It was no time to complicate matters with political turmoil at the rear.

In seeking a way out, General Catroux felt that he had to combat a "blind spirit of social conservatism" among the Europeans and to promote a "symbiosis" of the European and Moslem communities. This, to his mind, meant lifting up the Moslems socially and economically; it meant bringing their leaders into the French community on an equal basis. Unfortunately, his solution was too easy to be sound, and France is still paying the price of his blunder. He persuaded the Committee of National Liberation to extend full French citizenship to a native elite without prejudice to their personal status as Moslems and to increase Moslem representation in the councils of local government. General de Gaulle, who accepted this plan as a genuine advance, asserts in his *Mémoires*† that many Arabs and Kabyles reacted with an upsurge of hope and gratitude. The reform was announced by General de Gaulle in a dramatic speech before a huge crowd packed into the Place de la Brèche in Constantine on December 12, 1943. He reports in his *Mémoires* that,

* G. Catroux, *Dans la bataille de la Méditerranée* (Paris: René Julliard, 1949).

† *Mémoires de Guerre*, Vol. II: *L'Unité 1942-1943* (Paris: Plon, 1956).

as he was speaking, he saw Mohammed Salah Bendjelloul (a former stalwart of the *Manifesto*) and other Moslems with tears of emotion running down their faces.

However, the reform proposed by General Catroux and adopted by the Committee of National Liberation also had noxious effects. By setting the few apart for special privilege, it made the many more painfully conscious than before of their inferior status and increased their resentment. Was the reform, in fact, a decoy designed to entice the Moslem elite into the ruling circle and thus to pervert their natural loyalties? Or was it rather a step toward assimilation? If it was in good faith, the least that can be said is that General Catroux took little account of the lessons of the past. For assimilation had been tried and found wanting. A quick but critical retrospective glance would surely have made this clear.

The Algerian Moslems became French by virtue of the annexation of their country. A *senatus consultum* of 1865 gave solemn recognition to their status as French nationals but made a distinction between French citizens and French subjects. An Algerian Moslem was stated to be a French subject unless, repudiating the Sharia, or canonical law of Islam, he accepted the French civil code, in which case he could become a French citizen. For seventy-nine years—until General de Gaulle decreed otherwise—religious personal status was, under the law, incompatible with French citizenship (just as it is incompatible with United States citizenship). No French citizen, for instance, could legally keep four wives, or divorce them by simple repudiation, as authorized in Moslem sacred writ.

In 1919, the French Parliament adopted a measure simplifying the formalities involved in the acquisition of French citizenship. The great hope was that the Algerian Moslems would ask for citizenship in droves and that a large measure of assimilation would result. No such thing happened. The vast majority obdurately resisted any change in their personal status as repugnant to custom and the revealed way of Islam.

General Catroux was not the first to hold the idea that resistance to assimilation could be overcome if citizenship were conferred by decree on a restricted number of Moslems without prejudice to their personal status. A bill embodying this principle had been introduced in the French Parliament by Premier Léon Blum's Popular Front Government in 1936. The author of the bill, Maurice Viollette, a former Governor General of Algeria, was convinced that his plan to extend the political benefits of French citizenship to some 20,000 selected Moslems would suffice to keep Algeria within the gravitational pull of France.

The French *colons*, quite naturally, opposed the bill; they were afraid it would lead to trouble. Messali had no use for it either; he denounced the contemplated measure as a disguised attempt to apply the principle of divide and rule. The Blum-Viollette bill was tabled and ultimately dropped. Who can be sure what the effect would have been if the bill had been enacted into law? The immediate aspirations of the beneficiaries would doubtless have been satisfied, but not, I venture to believe, for long. The chances are that the communal structure of Moslem society would have weathered the storm and that the violation of its integrity would have been repaired in time.

But General Catroux did not hesitate to take up where M. Viollette had left off, even though the circumstances were by then far less auspicious. Fewer Moslem leaders still looked to France for a share in the spoils of power. The prospects of national self-determination seemed so much brighter! There were many signs, past and present, that General Catroux would have done well to ponder before trotting out the old Blum-Violette scheme, renovated and refurbished for the occasion. He might have realized that the Moslem community, so long impervious to persuasion, would also be proof against rupture by fiat and would indeed remain intact were the privileges of citizenship to be conferred upon every Moslem in the country.

The problem went far deeper than General Catroux appears to have suspected. For Algeria was, in fact if not in law, as authentic a binational, or biracial, state as Palestine before partition. The bulk of the Moslems had yet to be integrated into the modern world. By European standards, their economy was primitive and unproductive. The system of law and ways of life to which they clung belonged to another century. These barriers could not be legislated away. Nothing was to be gained by treating a few Moslems as semidetached entities. Until Moslems in large numbers were equipped by schooling and training to take their places in a developing Algeria, the "symbiosis" sought by General Catroux was bound to remain a fiction. His reforms served only to throw a deceptive cloak over the Algerian reality and its cleavages.

The results obtained by General Catroux were, inevitably, meager. The "upsurge of hope and gratitude" spoken of by General de Gaulle was imperceptible. Disaffection had gone too far among the educated Moslems. And the lower orders, when not wholly unconscious of what was going on in spheres far distant from their own, were stung by a new sense of their inferiority.

As often as not in those days, the attitude of the little Moslem toward the European was uncolored by sympathy or aversion; it was one of acceptance born of long habit. In the countryside, the French *colon* was to the Moslem peasant or farm hand as much a part of the natural order as the cold of winter and the heat of summer. On the other hand, the Moslem usually respected the Army, for under its standards public peace had been made to prevail over anarchy. In addition, the uniform had come to symbolize a code of disinterested service and uncomplicated equity particularly suited to Algeria. But the Army had not yet identified itself with a political option that could be understood by the multitude. This was to be one of the most important fruits of the nationalist rebellion.

Subsequent events were to show, however, that religious fanaticism, accompanied by cruel atavisms, including a taste for ritualistic murder, could sometimes be brought to the surface in the more backward parts of the country. It is curious to notice, too, that opinion at the top of the social scale was singularly devoid of critical or moral reference. The Melouza massacre, in which 302 defenseless Arab peasants were butchered on May 28, 1957, for failing to support the rebels, caused no twinge of conscience among the nationalist leaders, who were always so quick to denounce French "atrocities," real or imagined. There was one, but only one, Moslem protest—that of Mohammed el-Aziz Kessous, a former senator for Constantine.

A committee of six Frenchmen, six Moslems, and four government officials (including M. Berque) was appointed on December 14, 1943, to work out the details of General Catroux's new policy. The committee conducted a series of hearings before adopting a final report on January 31, 1944. The report, prepared by Senator Paul Giacobbi, contained a draft Ordinance under which all Algerian-born Moslems would be declared French citizens. However, the committee did not recommend a common electoral roll for Moslems and Europeans, the only provision that could have given real substance to an ostensibly revolutionary reform.

In promulgating the Ordinance on March 7, 1944, the Committee of National Liberation hedged even more.

Article One of the Ordinance stated that French Moslems had the same rights and duties as non-Moslems.

Article Two stipulated that the law was to apply without any discrimination to Frenchmen of all faiths and automatically revoked all measures applicable to Moslems only. However, the Moslems, who remained free to choose religious or civil personal status, were thereby guaranteed a privilege denied to other Frenchmen.

Article Three extended French citizenship on a personal rather than hereditary basis to selected Moslems, including former army officers, graduates of certain schools, public officials, members of recognized elected and appointed bodies, and the recipients of various decorations.

Article Four held out the promise of eventual French citizenship to all other Moslems but kept them, in the meantime, on a separate electoral roll. This so-called second college was allowed to elect two-fifths of the members of city and regional councils and of the Financial Delegations. To all outward appearance, Article Four was a negation of Articles One and Two and a damaging measure of French sincerity.

The right of a provisional government to make permanent constitutional changes was seriously questioned at the time. But apart from its dubious legality, the Ordinance bore the mark of hasty thinking. Equal rights implied an equal share in the benefits distributed by the welfare state. But how, for example, could the authors of the Ordinance have expected a system of family allowances devised for a rich country with a low birth rate to make sense in a poor country with a runaway birth rate? How did they think the nomad tribes of the desert could be brought within the framework of French social security? If the Government, in the name of equal treatment, had to provide free, compulsory schooling for all Arab children, the financial burden would be out of all proportion with Algeria's ability to produce.*

Apparently, it did not occur to anyone in 1944 that the principle of equality might one day bring to the bench Moslem magistrates bound by duty to enforce upon others the observance of a civil code they rejected for themselves. Yet this is exactly what has happened. In 1957, there were in Algeria four Moslem magistrates—a judge in Guelma and three deputy justices of the peace—whose personal status is that of the Koran, not of the French law they administered. Clearly, in 1944, logic had taken a holiday.

The first effect of the Ordinance was to put some 40,000 Moslems on the first-college electoral roll, where they remained until the roll was abolished in 1958, constituting a strong minority (about 13 per cent of

---

* Even the present effort is too great to be economically sound. In 1955, with 300,000 Moslem pupils—13 per cent of the Moslem children of school age—and 125,000 European pupils in Algeria's free public primary schools, the cost was about $45 million, or 15 per cent, of the ordinary budget, plus $21,545,000 for new schools. Only 20,000 applicants were turned away for want of space. By 1957, the carrying charge had risen to $63 million and the appropriation for new schools to $22 million. Sixty-five per cent of the Algerian budget was covered by Metropolitan France. The rest of the burden fell largely on the European taxpayer in Algeria.

the whole). The rest of the Moslem electorate—about 1,500,000 voters—constituted the second college. Events were soon to prove that the Moslems, even the selected few, had still to acquire a sense of "belonging."

6. THE 1945 UPRISING

In 1944, Algeria was, in fact, heading for one of the worst convulsions in its turbulent history. Opposition to the Ordinance crystallized around the feverish figure of Ferhat Abbas, whose new party, the Friends of the Manifesto and of Liberty, was launched in Sétif on March 14, 1944, with the followers of Messali Hadj aboard as well as the Ulema. A militant periodical, *Egalité,* started the following September, beat the drums for the party's three-point platform: the fight against colonialism, the establishment of a self-governing Algerian republic in federation with France, and the elimination of special privilege. But Mr. Abbas and his friends, mere dabblers in the art of troublemaking, were soon outflanked by activists trained in the school of the Glorious Star. A motion hailing Messali Hadj as "undisputed leader of the Algerian people" and demanding his release was voted by a congress of the Friends of the Manifesto in March, 1945. The congress went further. It repudiated the idea of a federation with France and came out instead for an independent Algerian Government free to choose its own alliances.

The psychological "build-up" in progress at the time was anything but reassuring. Nationalist handbills and wall inscriptions kindled the spirit of revolt with such slogans as: "Kill the French and the Jews!" (at Djelfa), "Moslems unite!" (at Aïn Bessem), "Frenchmen, by God you will be massacred by the Moslems!" (at Sétif), "It is the Moslem flag that will fly over North African soil" (also at Sétif) and "Moslems, awake!" (at Tlemcen).

Mr. Abbas, understandably alarmed by the trend of events, was soon heard appealing for a little moderation; but it was too late: the fat was already in the fire.

Simultaneous developments in the Middle East undoubtedly helped bring extremist agitation to a paroxysm in Algeria. Mr. Abbas lost control of his party just as the Arab League was being born in Cairo, the wave of pan-Arab enthusiasm having swept over Sirte, where the desert comes down to the sea, to engulf the distant Maghrib. Nationalist leaders from North Africa—including Habib Bourguiba, future premier of Tunisia—all of them convinced a new day was about to dawn, flocked eagerly to Cairo. But there they found the Arab League so absorbed in problems closer at hand that perfunctory support was the best it could offer. Abdel Rahman Azzam, secretary-general of the League, talked vaguely about the virtues of North African independence but avoided any positive commitment. Nevertheless, the great hope that had sprung from the founding of the League continued to fire the zeal of the North African nationalist leaders.

The atmosphere of incipient rebellion prevailing that spring in eastern Algeria is reflected in a letter of urgent warning sent on April 24, 1945, to André Lestrade-Carbonnel, Prefect of Constantine, by seven General (Departmental) Councilors, among them Eugène Vallet, who reproduces the letter in his book, *Un Drame Algérien.**

> "Everywhere," the Councilors wrote, "insecurity is increasing. There have been reports of attacks on property, of willful damage to water mains, of undisguised threats on the lives of isolated French inhabitants. In the cities, despite the official ban on processions, the streets are full of demonstrators openly proclaiming that Algeria belongs to the Arabs.
>
> "Local organizations—combat groups and, as in El Milia and Châteaudun, groups formed to replace the French Administration—have burgeoned in front of our eyes.
>
> "These facts, taken together, are as many alarming signs of possible serious disturbances ahead, disturbances that could break out tomorrow, exposing French farmers to mortal peril, especially in the outlying districts, where illicit but virtually open traffic in the weapons of war has flourished for three years. When it is considered that Algeria is about to experience a famine without precedent in recent years,† and that this circumstance could produce a sudden and widespread upheaval, the disastrous consequences of which could be contained only with the greatest difficulty, the least prejudiced mind is bound to conclude that words of prudence and appeals to reason are not enough to conjure away the impending evil and that measures conveying stern warnings will alone be adequate to spare public order and the dignity of France any untoward surprise."

---

* Paris: Les Grandes Editions Françaises, 1948.

† A reference to the 1945 drought.

No such measures were taken, despite an avalanche of similar warnings. The explosion came a fortnight later, at Sétif, Ferhat Abbas's home stamping-ground. The city, gaily decorated and festooned for V-E-Day, the Tricolor fluttering above the public buildings and every balcony bedecked with flags, was in a holiday mood on the morning of May 8.

A grand parade was in prospect. But before it got under way, a Moslem mob invaded the street, frenzied demonstrators waving a strange flag—red, white, and green, with a star and crescent in the middle—and banners inscribed with such slogans as: "Long live Messali," "Long live Algeria, free and independent" and "Down with colonialism." Permission had, in fact, been given for a separate Moslem parade, but only with the express understanding that it would be strictly non-political and that no banners would be carried. A French police inspector, when he saw that the agreement had been flouted, ordered the marchers to lay down their banners. In the face of their defiant refusal, he tried to seize the banners himself. A shot was fired and the riot was on.

A French writer, Charles-André Julien,* who seeks to saddle the police with the onus of shooting first, does not, however, deny that the Moslem demonstrators, having protested their peaceful intent, were nevertheless in the street armed with pistols, knives, and clubs, which they promptly used with murderous effect on all Europeans they encountered, killing twenty-two and wounding forty-eight (official figures).

The riot was broken up as soon as the available police and army forces could be brought into action, but a native taxi had already left to carry the word of the revolt to expectant Arabs in the surrounding towns, villages, and hamlets. That evening and in the days that followed, a shiver of fury and fear ran through the whole of eastern Algeria. The pattern set at Sétif repeated itself, with variants, again and again.

Guelma, once the Roman *municipium* and colony of Calama, forty miles south of St. Augustine's Hippo, had a narrow brush with disaster when a horde of nationalist demonstrators, colliding with the official procession, engaged the police in a pitched battle before being thrown back. French aircraft flew several strafing missions on May 9 and 10 in an attempt to free Guelma from the pressure of armed insurgents investing it on all sides.

A near riot occurred in Bône on May 8; and hostile crowds of Moslems roamed the streets in El Arrouch, Jemmapes, Condé Smendou, Oued Amizour, El Milia, and Oued Zenati. In the countryside, murder,

---

* Sorbonne professor and Socialist politician, author of a pronationalist but informative book entitled *L'Afrique du Nord en Marche* (Paris: René Julliard, 1952).

rape, and arson were the order of the day. The casualty figures give some indication of the extent of the uprising but convey nothing of its horror, for the massacres were accompanied, as always in Algeria, by unspeakable mutilations.

One after another, little French farming communities, most of them settled in the last century by hardy pioneers, reported their death toll: Sillègue, two men and a woman butchered; El Ouricia, a priest cut to pieces; La Fayette, three Jews killed, including a woman and a fifteen-year-old boy; Périgotville, fourteen killed; Chevreul, four killed; Kerrata, seven killed; Cape Aokas, three killed; Tamentout, seven killed, including two women and a three-year-old boy; Petit, seven killed. Altogether, according to an official figure, 103 men, women, and children perished in that brief but bloody reign of terror.

The fate of Basile Grousset and of his wife and daughter, peaceful citizens of Chevreul, is a fair example of what the demented Moslems had in store for all they could lay their hands on. At the approach of a hostile mob, M. Grousset, taking his wife and daughter with him, sought refuge first in the home of an Arab neighbor, then, finding no welcome there, in a thicket on the edge of the village, where the unfortunate farmer was quickly overtaken, bludgeoned to the point of death, and finished off with a bullet in his head before the eyes of his wife and daughter, who were promptly delivered up to the appetites of the assailants. André Halbedel, manager of a farm near Villars, was axed to death in the presence of his wife and daughter Josée. And so it went.

The testimony given later by a Moslem youth brought to book for the murder of Mme. Devèze, a French forester's wife, casts a lurid light on the psychological background of such crimes. Ayache Ben Hanachi Boudria, twenty years old, of Menar village in the Fedj M'Zala district, was, acording to his own deposition (reproduced by M. Vallet), on his way to market when he met another Moslem, who said: "The Holy War has been proclaimed. The French are beaten everywhere. The time has come to exterminate them."

Without a moment's hesitation, apparently, Boudria, his head throbbing with strange exaltation, marched with the mob to attack the nearby Aïn Settah forestry station. Mme. Devèze, whose husband had already been slain, was found hiding in a native hut. Boudria, being the youngest, was the last of forty-odd Moslems to assault the hapless woman; by the same token, his was the privilege of killing her. He attempted this with a blast of buckshot in the back, but it fell to others to complete the job. Mme. Devèze's unclad and disfigured body was recovered by French troops six days later. The civil administrator at Fedj M'Zala reported later that he had heard the mob attack his village to cries of "*El jihad fsabil Allah!*" (Holy War in God's cause).

Europeans caught in the midst of the uprising were appalled by the behavior of the Moslem women, who filled the air with their strident you-yous, an unearthly, modulated clamor that had the effect of driving the men to ever greater heights of frenzy. I can never hear these cries of Moslem women without going back in my mind to the massacre that took seventy-seven European and Jewish lives at Oued Zem and Aït Amar in Morocco on August 20, 1955. Crimes hideous beyond words, notably the ritual murder of seven hospital and maternity patients and the cremation of their dismembered bodies, were committed at Oued Zem to the accompaniment of piercing you-yous. On September 22, when General Pierre Boyer de Latour du Moulin, newly appointed Resident General, visited the town, steps had to be taken to silence a group of women who had begun to utter their you-yous in token of welcome. The sound had become unbearable to European ears.

The 1945 uprising has gone down in nationalist literature as a French plot against the legitimate aspirations of the Algerian people. The version issued by Ferhat Abbas and his associates in 1948 is worth keeping on the record as a sample of nationalist history-writing:

> But as the movement [The Friends of the Manifesto and of Liberty] was getting organized openly and legally, and just as its local branches were beginning to function, the Administration, which could not tolerate such a success, plotted our undoing and posted troublemakers in strategic positions.
>
> At Sétif, on May 8, these police accomplices, masquerading as ultra-nationalists, undertook, without the knowledge of the Friends of the Manifesto but in agreement with the prefectural administration of the sinister Lestrade-Carbonnel, to organize a disorderly demonstration on market day. The police, in pursuance of prior orders to prepare a trap, opened fire on the procession. Two demonstrators fell. The riot ensued, with its train of crimes, affliction, and terror.
>
> The colonialists had attained their object. The armed repression was reminiscent of the conquest. It was barbarous and inhuman. The leaders and members of the Friends of the Manifesto were arrested, many were assassinated, others sent to prison, and a great number were interned in concentration camps. The organization was outlawed.
>
> Once again the colonial regime had triumphed easily, by

trickery and crime, over the inexperience of our masses athirst for freedom and justice. But this ephemeral victory, it must be said, would not have been so easy if the colonialists had not, as always, used the native to betray the native.*

The Communists were still following the wartime party line when the uprising occurred on May 8, 1945. That is why, in their first pronouncements, they laid the initial violence at the door of the nationalists. It was not until a week later, revised orders having been issued in the meantime, that they denounced the uprising as a "colonialist plot."

General Raymond Duval, commanding in eastern Algeria, moved quickly to crush the rebellion. The military action that followed the uprising was, by all reliable accounts, brutal. An official estimate put the number of native dead at 1,500. M. Julien thinks 6,000 to 8,000 were killed. The nationalists, claiming that 15,000 or 20,000 had perished,† accused the French of "genocide" and of "collective extermination." "We refuse," said one‡ in a moment of grandiloquence, "to discuss terms with men who, reviving an act of two thousand years ago—the barbarous act of Rome ploughing up the accursed soil of Carthage—ran the plough, in 1945, over the burned villages of the region of Sétif."

M. Julien dwells on the retribution meted out to the natives, on the wholesale executions imputed to European vigilantes hastily recruited into a civil militia at Guelma. A similar account, heightened in color for the American reader, appears in *North African Powder Keg*,§ a book by Edmund Stevens, an American journalist who visited Algeria in December, 1954, as correspondent of the *Christian Science Monitor*. Mr. Stevens devotes twelve embarrassed words to the uprising, but 301 words to the ensuing "open season on natives." "The Senegalese troops and the Foreign Legion," he writes, "were turned loose on the countryside with unlimited license to kill, rape, and plunder¶ . . . As is ever

---

* *Du Manifeste à la République Algérienne* (Algiers: Editions "Libération," 1948).

† *El Bassaïr,* organ of the Association of Ulema, once advanced the figure of 80,000 victims.

‡ Senator Abdelkader Mahdad, before the Council of the Republic on August 29, 1947.

§ New York: Coward-McCann, Inc., 1955.

¶ This sentence, in Julien, reads as follows: "Dans la campagne, les Sénégalais et les Légionnaires pillèrent, incendièrent, violèrent et tuèrent en toute liberté." But the statement did not originate with M. Julien, whose source, unacknowledged, was none other than Mohammed Salah Bendjelloul, signer of the *Algerian Manifesto*. On February 28, 1946, in an impassioned speech to the First Constituent Assembly in Paris, Mr. Bendjelloul said: "Tabors mathe case in North Africa, estimates of the number of victims differ widely. French sources place the figure at between 8,000 and 10,000, but other observers' estimates range as high as 45,000."

This, I have found, is the kind of reporting the American reader generally gets from North Africa. The anti-French slant has become so much the rule that editors are now apt to question the reliability of an honest dispatch. There is an abundance of detail, usually presented in panting style, when the news gets "hot," but little or nothing the rest of the time, the silence being broken only by the peremptory judgments of itinerant commentators like Mr. Stevens.*

I often wondered how such a grave disservice could be done until I found the explanation in a remark by that unquestioned master of the trade, Henry Wales, Paris correspondent of the *Chicago Tribune*, who advised a stringer in Rabat to leave the constructive stories alone: "What the United States wants to read first is scandal about our air bases; second, scandal about French oppression of the poor natives."† In Algeria, where there are no American air bases, the visiting correspondent can always, and usually does, fall back on the "French oppression of the poor natives."

This is not to say that the truth is invariably pretty; sometimes it is grim. But for a more balanced and more truthful account of what happened in the wake of the May 8 uprising, I prefer to turn to Edouard Sablier of *Le Monde*, who took part in the action as a section leader. Here is his account:

> In all haste, the officers were recalled to quarters. The available troops were organized as mobile groups, each composed of a company of Foreign Legion and a section of Algerian Rifles. Already, in the coastal area, the Marines were on the spot. For

---

rocains, Sénégalais, Légion étrangère eurent quartier libre pour dévaster les *mechtas*, piller les demeures, violer les femmes et les enfants, voire même les adultes, et de brûler le tout après s'être acquittés de cette odieuse mission."

* The first reflex of an American correspondent in a foreign city is to make for the friendly haven of the local United States embassy or consulate. There he gets a courteous briefing in line with American policy, which, in Algeria, is to ease the French out as painlessly as possible. The vestigial positions of colonialism are described in these consular talks as untenable in the world of Bandung. The French are blamed for their reluctance to recognize that an Arab country must be won for the West by more enlightened methods. The listening correspondent, I have observed, is usually convinced that the official views are sound.

† Quoted by Marvine Howe in her book *The Prince and I* (New York: John Day, 1955).

our part, we were ordered with our Foreign Legion section to proceed to Constantine. A squadron of South African R.A.F. Dakotas carried us to the airport of that city.

For a month and a half, across the whole department, the mobile groups were to be occupied restoring order. At Sétif, at Périgotville, at Kerrata, at Chevreul, the scene was that of houses destroyed, schools burned, victims still unburied. The victims had been killed under horrible conditions, subjected in most cases to hideous cruelty and mutilations: at Kerrata, the judge and his young wife; at Chevreul, an octogenarian and a little girl; almost everywhere, the murderous madness had struck without discrimination.

The repression was at no point carried out with greater discernment. Summary executions struck more often than not at random. The *mechtas* [hamlets] were destroyed; wretched huts, emptied as well of their occupants as of their poor furnishings. Everywhere, troop detachments undertook searches after harassing marches. Woe to the village where a weapon was found! Often, newly dug caches revealed the intention of putting some compromising object out of sight, but rarely was a truly deadly arm found. Here and there, in the path of the mobile groups, a *caïd* in full dress—scarlet lined with blue—would perform a ceremonious surrender of arms; on such days, mules carried off old flintlocks, scimitars, and pistols that had once belonged to the Barbary pirates.

Day after day, the exasperation grew worse. The residents, whom we were supposed to protect against a new outbreak, were not able to hide their anxiety or their desire to terrify the presumed adversary. How many times, setting off to inspect an isolated mountain village, I heard them say: "To punish them, take their crops away."

On all sides, in the cities, barbed-wire camps held hundreds of suspects. On the roads, most of the Moslems one met put their arms in the air. The *colons* went about heavily armed; civil militias, whose intervention had, no doubt, prevented the spread of the troubles at the outset, complicated the task of the authorities by carrying out operations that went further than the initial objective. On all sides, "interrogations" were conducted in public, too often, alas, enlivened by third degree. All that left a frightful memory everywhere.

Soon, the re-establishment of order was pursued methodically. The investigations became tedious. The mobile groups were now known as "sovereignty units." Fanning out across the whole Constantine region, the detachments traveled the roads from Djidjelli and Batna, from Lambèse to Bougie. The death toll cannot accurately be computed. The victims of the uprising reached 120 in number. The victims of the repression were more difficult to count: 80,000, 12,000, it has been said. For my part, I should more readily accept the figure of 1,200.*

It is only fair to add that troops sent to rescue French civilians bottled up in their homes and villages had frequently to fight their way through rebel barrages of rifle or machine-gun fire. Such was the case, according to M. Vallet, at Périgotville, at Chevreul, at Taher, and in the Fedj M'Zala district. At Kerrata and Chevreul, relief reached the besieged in the nick of time. Such resistance was put down with no quarter given. The French Army lost twelve dead and twenty wounded in these operations.

The events of May, 1945, have given rise to interminable controversy. Wild accusations have been hurled about. Unfortunately, the truth may never be known in full. A commission of inquiry headed by General of Gendarmerie Paul Tubert, pro-Communist deputy for Algiers in the First Constituent Assembly,† was recalled to Algiers before it had accomplished much. The commission did, however, submit a report on its curtailed mission. The report drew attention to the "fear psychosis" sweeping the European community and also to the discontent and suspicion prevalent among the Moslems. It stressed the necessity of reassuring both communities, since they were doomed to live together in the same country, and proposed the formation of permanent, mobile security units as a means of restoring confidence and of preventing further recourse to vigilante action.

To keep the 1945 tragedy in perspective, reference should also be made to the fear of a general insurrection. Was there such a real and present danger in May, 1945? Yes, says M. Vallet. If he is right, the loss of life may possibly be considered a lesser evil. The 1954 outbreak, not nearly as murderous as that of 1945, was nevertheless allowed to get out of hand. The appalling result, in terms of human life, is plain for all to see: 21,179 known dead and 1,833 missing in the space of two years, and the killing has continued since. The story might have been very different if a man of General Duval's decision had been in command in eastern Algeria on November 1, 1954.

The record contains evidence to show that plans for a widespread revolt were, in fact, brewing in the spring of 1945, and that the insurgents in eastern Algeria, deceived by the flare-up at Sétif, had merely

* See *Le Monde* for November 3, 1954.

† General Tubert was also mayor of Algiers from October, 1945, to May, 1947.

jumped the gun. Another false start could as easily have been made at Blida, thirty miles inland from Algiers, where Moslem demonstrators, carrying banners and shouting slogans, clashed with police on May 8, or at Sidi Bel Abbès, fifty-one miles south of Oran, where a similar demonstration took place. On the night of May 18, the town hall at Saïda, 108 miles southeast of Oran, was attacked by Moslems who, when caught, asserted that they had been ordered to assassinate the local authorities. The same day, before dawn, an Algerian Communist named Mohammed Saïd Ladjali was killed by police in a running gun battle in an Algiers street. Counterfeit rubber stamps, copies of clandestine nationalist newspapers, and other underground paraphernalia were found on his person. A secret arms depot was discovered at Djidjelli, a coastal town ninety-four miles northwest of Constantine, on May 12.

An anti-French plot came to light at Cherchel, sixty miles west of Algiers, on May 15, and another at Tigzirt-sur-Mer, seventy-eight miles east of Algiers, on May 23. That night twenty-eight telephone lines were cut at Haussonvillers, fifty miles east of Algiers, and a length of railway track was unbolted. A spate of terrorist agitation in the area took twelve lives between June and September. The conspirators of Cherchel, brought to trial in September, complained that their plans had been wrecked by the "premature" action at Sétif. Mere straws in the wind, perhaps, but highly suggestive.

General Duval, who left Constantine soon after the uprising to become French commander in Tunisia, was appointed commander of the French forces in Morocco in 1949. He died in the crash of his personal aircraft twelve miles from Kasbah Tadla in central Morocco two days after the Oued Zem massacre. He had devoted the last day of his life to a tour of operational command posts in an area infested with rebel Berber tribesmen.

7. THE AMNESTY

The man at the helm in Algiers during the squall of 1945 was Yves Chataigneau, who had succeeded General Catroux in September, 1944. A Socialist diplomat, M. Chataigneau had been very close to Premier

Léon Blum in the days of the Popular Front. His subsequent experience as French Minister to Kabul and as secretary general of the French mandate administration in the Levant states (where he had weathered the crisis resulting from British efforts to oust the French in 1943) should have stood him in good stead in Algiers. Yet, by temperament and by political inclination he was, perhaps, inadequately equipped to deal with riot and violent attempts on the security of the state.

On the other hand, M. Chataigneau, ably assisted by Lucien Paye, his planning director, did much for the well-being of the natives. The impetus he gave to rural improvement and soil conservation had a profound effect, changing the whole outlook for countless Moslem peasants. He is remembered, too, for his efforts to free Algeria from the shackles of a purely agrarian economy. His search for new sources of energy and wealth led to the construction of one of the world's great solar furnaces, that of Bouzaréa, 1,000 feet above the city of Algiers. M. Chataigneau left Algiers in 1948 to become French ambassador to Moscow.

"All is now calm." Such was the reassuring word that went out from M. Chataigneau's office toward the end of May, 1945. Several thousand arrests had been made, and the expectation in European circles was that the guilty would be punished. The European community was particularly relieved to hear that the Friends of the Manifesto had been declared illegal and that two of its leaders, Messrs. Abbas and Saadane, had been packed off to prison.

Had all danger of a recurrence of trouble been removed? There could be reasonable doubt on that score. Nevertheless, M. Chataigneau and the Provisional Government in Paris soon felt the time had come to sweeten the atmosphere with kindness. All would be well, they reasoned, if only the Moslems could be made to feel the loving solicitude of France. And so, to wash away the last vestige of bad blood, they drew up plans for a general amnesty. But they do not seem to have asked themselves whether the desire for reconciliation was mutual.

Their amnesty bill came up for discussion in the First Constituent Assembly in February, 1946, and was quickly adopted. Only Antoine Colonna, deputy representing the French community in Tunisia, raised his voice in protest and solemn warning. "Twenty thousand French citizens accused of collaboration with the enemy are still awaiting judicial examination," he said. "Many of them, presumably, are innocent; yet they have been in prison for eighteen months. The men of Sétif and Guelma, meanwhile, officially indicted for horrible crimes of assassination, pillage, and rape in connection with a plot against France, have been in prison for barely eight months; and yet they are already demanding their release." André Le Troquer, Minister of the Interior, concluded his defense of the measure with a ringing peroration: "But, ladies and gentlemen, we must go to the heart of the matter, start by eliminating force and restraint as a way of government, and have confidence in understanding, solidarity, and union. I say what I think, with all my heart and the strength of my reason: France is great and powerful enough to be benevolent, generous, and human." Poor man!

A glance at the amnesty bill should have been enough to give pause even to the dreamiest of deputies. Article One granted "full and plenary amnesty" to those guilty of such "crimes, misdemeanors, and offenses" as:

1. Rebellion by one or two persons, armed or unarmed;
2. Contempt of, and violence to, persons in authority;
3. Theft of official documents;
4. Vandalism;
5. Threats of death or of violence;
6. Assault and battery not resulting in death or permanent injury;
7. Participation in illegal meetings and gatherings;
8. Revival of outlawed organizations;
9. Plots against the internal or external security of the state.

Article Two specified that certain crimes, though subject to pardon, would not automatically be covered by the amnesty. These were murder and assassination, acts of savagery, mutilation of human bodies, rape, abduction, assault and battery resulting in death or permanent injury, pillage, arson, destruction of crops or of public works, and theft. Article Three revoked all administrative sanctions taken against persons implicated in the disorders. Article Four stipulated that those guilty of crimes listed in Article Two could be pardoned by a special commission provided for in Article Five.

It was stated at the time that, of 4,500 Moslems arrested in connection with the uprising, 1,500 had been released pending trial, ninety-nine had been sentenced to death, twenty-two had been executed, sixty-four had been sentenced to hard labor for life, and 329 to lesser prison terms. The rest were in prison awaiting trial. The record does not say how many criminals and confirmed agitators went scot-free as a result of the amnesty, but the number must have been great. I cannot help wondering what the promoters of this measure really expected to come of it. Were they artless enough to think the culprits would, out of gratitude, behave like changed men? If so, disillusion was soon to follow. The following April, handbills came out with the warning: "Frenchmen, prepare your valises or your coffins!"

The 1946 amnesty set a precedent that the French have since had reason to regret. It put the nation on record as favoring lenience as the way to deal with armed rebellion. How then can the French, without damage to their reputation as a logical people, criticize others for following their example? The Moroccans, for instance. On October 23, 1956, an anti-French demonstration in Meknès degenerated into a bloody riot in the course of which the mob stormed a Moroccan (but French-manned) police station. Several native constables in uniform, joining the rioters, massacred five French police officials. One of the victims was cut to pieces. Another was thrown on an improvised pyre and burned. In February, 1957, four native constables were tried for this crime by a Moroccan military court in Meknès. The public prosecutor, Ali Benjelloun, had the courage to demand their heads. Counsel for the defense declared that the accused had merely acted "as they ought to have done" in the circumstances. He begged the court not to reopen old wounds by giving publicity to forgotten events.

The verdict—a four-year prison term and three acquittals—was hailed with a thunderous ovation in the courtroom. But the French inhabitants of Meknès were shocked. Some, who until then had clung to the hope that the Moroccan authorities would yet be able to maintain law and order, prepared to leave the country for good. The verdict caused a storm of protest in the French press. The Paris newspaper *Le Figaro*, under a three-column head, "Scandalous Verdict at Meknès," accused the Moroccan court of "inconceivable concessions to political passion." The paper denounced the verdict as an "odious parody of justice." But what about 1946? Who first preached the doctrine of forgive and forget?

The Algerian voters were called to the polls in October, 1945, to elect deputies to the First Constituent Assembly in Paris.* The Moslem "citizens" as defined in the Ordinance of March 7, 1944, voted with the Europeans, this "first college" having thirteen seats to fill. The non-citizen voters were put on a separate electoral roll with an equal number of seats to fill. The election, conducted in the absence of the nationalist leaders, was relatively free of acrimony. The ever versatile Dr. Bendjelloul, no longer a "Friend of the Manifesto," led a group of second-college deputies in demanding the complete integration of Algeria with Metropolitan France and the immediate grant of full citizenship to the entire Moslem population. His plan, if accepted, would have given Algeria at least a fifth of the seats in the French Parliament. The plan was not accepted, however; it was, in fact, barely noticed.

The peaceful interlude was over when the time came, in June, 1946,

---

* Convened to draw up the Constitution of the Fourth Republic.

to elect the Second Constituent Assembly. The amnesty had restored any number of agitators to their usual activities, and the political pot was again bubbling and sputtering. Ferhat Abbas, at the head of a new party called the Democratic Union of the Algerian Manifesto (U.D.M.A.), lashed out against the "crime" of colonialism and against official "prevarication." He did not try to revive the old cohort of nationalist "Friends"–Ulema, Messalists and Moslem zealots. Instead, he went to the people on a platform calling for the establishment of an Algerian republic untainted by either colonialism or Moslem theocracy. The result was a resounding victory at the polls. Mr. Abbas and his party won eleven of the thirteen second-college seats.

But this victory was deceptive. If Mr. Abbas looked like the true standard-bearer of Algerian nationalists, it was because he was alone in a field of pygmies. He did not have to try conclusions with Messali Hadj, the still-banished leader of the clandestine Algerian People's party (P.P.A.). Mr. Bendjelloul had withdrawn from the race, throwing his support to Mr. Abbas. The Communists, defeated at the polls, also fell in behind the U.D.M.A.

Mr. Abbas had propitious circumstances to thank for his aggrandizement. Actually, he had already lost much of his punch and was beginning to lapse into intellectualism, the bane of his party ever after. He was still posturing as a popular leader when I first saw him in the corridors of the Algerian Assembly in 1953. But by then, although the U.D.M.A. retained a little middle-class following, its rank and file had long since deserted to Messali. In January, 1956, Mr. Abbas declared that the rebels alone could speak for Algeria, and he put the U.D.M.A. on ice. In April, he joined the rebel committee in Cairo.

Paris, still pursuing the mirage of reconciliation in the summer of 1946, decided, not without persistent prompting from the ingenuous Mr. Abbas, to release Messali Hadj. The old enemy of the law, back from darkest Africa, set up shop at Bouzaréa in the suburbs of Algiers, where he launched a new party, the Movement for the Triumph of Democratic Liberties (M.T.L.D.), in time for the November general election. The French hoped to put a crimp in Messali's style by keeping him out of Algiers. Idle precaution! His friends beat a path to his door, and Bouzaréa became the focus of nationalist agitation.

While Mr. Abbas, in Paris, was vainly trying to interest the Second Constituent Assembly in his scheme for an autonomous Algerian republic, the Messalists were operating in depth among Algeria's anonymous millions. Their watchword was as simple as it was effective: "You are the have-nots. The French have grabbed everything. We must throw them out!" Mr. Messali geared his organization to the immediate task of wiping the floor with Mr. Abbas. According to a report in the Paris newspaper *Le Monde*, voices were heard in native villages at night intoning such warnings as: "If you do not vote for us, the malediction of Allah will be upon you and upon your flocks."

Ferhat Abbas, empty-handed despite his best endeavor in Paris, chose to stand down in favor of the Communists. In November, the second college sent five M.T.L.D. deputies to the National Assembly in Paris, along with two Communists and eight moderates ("collaborators" in nationalist parlance). However, an indirect election, in which the M.T.L.D. took no part, gave the U.D.M.A. four of seven second-college seats in the Council of the Republic, upper house of the French Parliament.

But Mr. Messali, who had no faith in orderly processes, kept his eye on the longer-term objective of revolution by force and violence. To this end he retained the outlawed Algerian People's party (P.P.A.) as the clandestine nucleus of a future underground resistance movement. "Shock groups" recruited from the ranks of the P.P.A. were later to be banded together to form the terrorist Special Organization (O.S.), the bush league in which many a future guerrilla fighter got his basic training.

The French journalist, Pierre Frédérix, who visited Mr. Messali in his den at Bouzaréa, gives us this portrait of the man: "I found myself in the presence of a singular character, as oriental in appearance as Ferhat Abbas is western. He was dressed in a black *djellabah* [native robe] with the open collar of a white shirt showing at the neck. Long ringlets fell from under his red fez. His wide face was set off by the curly wisps of a greying beard. I listened to him speak—his French is impeccable—and the surprising softness of his voice, his unctuous manner, brought to mind . . ., curiously enough, a pope of the Greek church, Rasputin of 1916, Gapon of 1905. As I was leaving, I suddenly realized what he resembled. Messali is a magus, a prophet, a thaumaturge. When you call on Abbas you meet other bourgeois like your host: doctors, lawyers, professional people. Those who haunt Messali's home are the lean Algerians who, in France, served Doriot, the [Vichy] militia, the Communist party without discrimination: Jacks-of-all-trades, the products of pauperism."

Turning to the religious context of the nationalist movement, M. Frédérix wisely observed: "In Abbas's party, no doubt about it, religious passion plays a very subsidiary part. With Messali, on the other hand, religion and politics are inseparable, although Islam seems to be more the means than the goal." *

* See *Le Monde* for April 4, 1952.

In terms of social change, Mr. Abbas represented the rising third estate, while Mr. Messali relied on the rabble. It would be stretching a point to compare the two men with, say, Mirabeau and Marat or with Kerenski and Lenin, for the class struggle is always blurred in Islam; but social forces do come into play and must be taken into account. Mohammed Mossadegh and Gamal Abdel Nasser cannot otherwise be fully understood.*

8. THE ALGERIAN STATUTE

The new Constitution, which came into effect in December, 1946, left the Algerian problem in the air. Indeed, the contradictions resulting from previous efforts to assimilate the Moslems were written into the charter of the Fourth Republic as though they were meant to last forever. Article Eighty-one stated that all natives of oversea departments and territories were "citizens of the French Union" and, as such, enjoyed the human rights set forth in the preamble, among them the equality of men and women "in all respects." Article Eighty-Two stipulated that the "rights inherent in French citizenship" could not be denied on grounds of personal status. No attempt was made to reconcile this provision with the servitude of Moslem women. John Gunther says in his book *Inside Africa*† that the right of personal status gives the Moslem citizens the "best of both worlds." Certainly it gives them the best of a man's world. Mr. Gunther himself speaks of a French journalist who had *never* seen the wives of several Arab friends encountered every day for twenty years.

It remained for the new Parliament to get down to cases. The legislators had before them seven bills providing for various degrees of Algerian home rule. The Communists and Socialists were on deck with separate proposals for Algerian statehood within the French Union. Ferhat Abbas's scheme for an Algerian republic, a hardy perennial, was introduced as a bill in the Council of the Republic, upper house of the French Parliament. The coalition Government headed by Socialist

* As is often the case among nationalist leaders, both Abbas and Messali have French wives.

† New York: Harper & Brothers, 1953.

Premier Paul Ramadier submitted a draft Algerian statute, which ultimately prevailed in the teeth of bitter opposition from the Moslem deputies and senators. The Government's bill was carried with minor amendments in the National Assembly in August, 1947, by a vote of 320 to eighty-eight. It was enacted into law on September 20.

A more hybrid document could not be imagined. It was a potpourri of half a dozen abstract concepts such as "integration," "association," "assimilation" and "autonomy"—in short, a hopeless hodgepodge, largely inapplicable and conducive only to endless confusion.

It is, I must say, hard to go along with Léon Blum, who is quoted by M. Julien as having passed this judgment on the statute at the time: "It breaks once and for all with the century-old illusion summed up in the expression, 'policy of assimilation.' It comes to grips with the reality of the Algerian problem. It seeks to regulate, within the framework of the French Union, the relations of two peoples living on the same soil, but different, distinct, not to be amalgamated. . . . The *colons* abhor it, but this reaction should cause neither surprise nor concern. The Algerian *colons* still seem to be beguiled by the chimera of assimilation. They cannot bring themselves to give up what they call the maintenance of French sovereignty and what is, in fact, their own domination. They are invariably revolted every time the relations of the two peoples that coexist in the land of Algeria are considered in the light of relative equality."

This is an example of the fuddled thinking prevalent in Paris in 1947. Alas, the statute could hardly justify such glowing tribute. It defined Algeria as a "group of [French] departments" distinguished by their separate civil status, by their financial autonomy, and by a common administrative structure. The Governor General, who remained the chief executive official in the country, was, under the statute, to be assisted in the management of Algerian affairs by a Council of Government and by an elected Algerian Assembly* with special responsibility for voting the budget.

---

* From 1898 to 1945, Algeria possessed a non-political assembly called the Financial Delegations. These Delegations were based on the principle of "representation of interests," a concept long held to be particularly well-suited to a country where material interests were of paramount importance and where the inhabitants, belonging to separate communities, could not easily be welded together into a single electorate. Each of the three delegations comprising the assembly—farmers, non-farmers, and natives—was composed of twenty-four members elected for six years. The members of the native delegation—seventeen Arabs and seven Kabyles—were nominated by the Governor General and elected by a small electoral college. The assembly's essential task was to vote the budget.

In other words, Algeria, though still an integral part of the Republic "one and indivisible," was endowed with embryonic institutions of home rule. There was to be no taxation without representation. Arabic, formerly relegated to the position of a privileged foreign language, was henceforth to be honored as a native tongue and taught in the schools at all levels. But French alone would continue to be the official language. Algeria was also denied national colors. The French Parliament relinquished none of its sovereign powers, and the Government clung to its exclusive privilege of executing the laws of the Republic. Thus were reconciled, on paper at least, the apparently conflicting principles of integration and autonomy.

The doctrine of assimilation was emasculated but by no means discarded, M. Blum's assertion to the contrary notwithstanding. The double-college system of voting was retained for the Algerian Assembly on the basis of equality and parity, each college being allotted sixty seats. The statute did not give effect to Article Four of the Ordinance of March 7, 1944, which held out the promise of full French citizenship to all Moslems without prejudice to their personal status. It merely carried the principle of automatic assimilation a step further.

The number of voters registered on the two rolls in 1947 were:

First college: 469,023 Europeans (88.1 per cent); 63,194 Moslems (11.9 per cent)
Second college: 1,301,072 Moslems

It was estimated that some 159,000 Moslems were entitled to vote as citizens under the electoral law of October 5, 1946, an essentially transitory measure which, for the purposes of the November general election, had added veterans of World War I and elementary-school graduates to the list contained in the 1944 Ordinance. The great question was: should an elementary education continue to qualify Moslems for admission to the first college? To say yes would be to put Algeria on the road to a common electoral roll and Arab domination, for the Moslem citizen-voters could soon be expected to outnumber the Europeans. (There were 306,737 Moslem pupils in Algeria's elementary schools in 1955.) The debate on this vital point brought out the absence

---

The Financial Delegations, incompatible with the Ordinance of March 7, 1944, which gave the second college two-fifths representation in all elected bodies, were abolished in September, 1945. They were superseded by a Financial Assembly of thirty-seven members—twenty-two for the first college and fifteen for the second. The new assembly differed from its predecessor in that all its members were elected by the people, and deliberated together as a single whole and not as the representatives of "interests." The Financial Assembly was superseded by the Algerian Assembly in 1948.

of any guiding doctrine. "We must have confidence in the loyalty and affection of the Moslems," said the advocates of a common roll. "You cannot turn an Arab into a Frenchman simply by sticking a label on him," said the advocates of separate rolls.

Premier Ramadier summed up in these terms: "The double-college system is based on the principle of homogeneity. But we are not treading on virgin soil. We cannot overlook the solemn promises that have been made." He left the matter of the aging war veterans to the Assembly, but added: "It seems to us that the registration of elementary-school graduates, whose number is increasing with the development of public education, would deal the principle of homogeneity such a blow that the regulations would have to be entirely reviewed in a very few years' time." What he was saying, in effect, was: "We are on the wrong track, ladies and gentlemen, but it is too late to do anything about it now except to throttle down as hard as we can." The Assembly, accepting the Government's view, voted 316 to 286 to prevent any further registration of elementary-school graduates as citizen voters.

The myth of assimilation, repudiated by M. Ramadier with such disarming candor, lived on in the statute to vex Algerian politics for years to come. Thousands of Moslems, who should have been available to serve the interests of their own community, were drained off and frozen into the first college, where they became political eunuchs, unable to elect a single Moslem candidate, capable only of upsetting the cohesion of the European electorate. The statute betrayed the principle of equality by setting the first college above the second in point of prestige and quality. The result was easy to foresee: the second college, humiliated, deprived of many of its natural leaders, was delivered up to the rabble-rousers, those who had no use for co-operation with the French and nothing but scorn for the privileged caste represented in the first college.

An even more inherent vice of the statute was to saddle Algeria with an electoral system based on the false assumption that the ordinary Moslem was yet able to make up his own mind on broad public issues and to vote accordingly. Nothing could be more alien to his tradition and to his nature; wherever you find Moslems banded together, you also find a *caïd* (chief). The ordinary Moslem, unchanged by the right to vote, faithful to himself, continued to move with the herd. He was easy prey for Messali and his henchmen. The statute, therefore, left the French administration in Algeria in an awesome predicament: democratic institutions, manifestly unsuited to the country, had to be made to work; yet free elections were out of the question. The Moslem electorate could not be isolated from almost irresistible pressures hostile to the regime itself. Nationalist extremists of every stripe, at large since the amnesty, could, and certainly would, use the Koran and the threat of retribution, now and hereafter, to regiment the second college against the French and so checkmate the racial partnership without which Algeria was lost.

The administration had no choice. The elections, since they were mandatory, had to be rigged. A shameful chapter in Algerian history was about to begin. The Parliament, in the exercise of its sovereignty, had reduced the representatives of the Republic in Algeria to the stuffing of ballot boxes and other such forms of deceit and trickery, all of which gave France a bad name, offended the Moslem's native sense of justice, and obscured the future. The French Governors General had a difficult course to steer. Those who conducted "good" elections were congratulated in Paris. But woe to those whose elections were too "good" or not "good" enough!

Article Fifty-Three of the statute was intended by its authors to be the death warrant of the *communes mixtes*, or administrative townships, a time-honored institution of colonial rule. These entities, of which there were seventy-eight in 1947, covered vast areas where the European population was sparse. Each was headed by a civil or, in the south, by a military administrator who acted as mayor. The administrator was at once the representative of the central government and of the township. He was also registrar, judicial police officer, and public prosecutor. Until 1927, he had power to punish certain infractions committed by the natives. This type of township, though not nearly as bad in practice as one might expect, was nevertheless no better than the man in charge, and was, naturally enough, bitterly opposed by the nationalists. Most Europeans lived within 332 self-governing townships on the French model. Many of these were, so to speak, enclaved in administrative townships, the two systems existing side by side.

The idea in 1947 was to carve the administrative townships up into a multitude of self-governing townships in which the Moslems, assimilating the rudiments of democracy, would learn to manage their own local affairs. It was recognized, however, that this reform could not be carried into effect overnight, particularly in the distant reaches of the Sahara. Article Fifty-Three, drafted with this thought in mind, said: "Local government units in Algeria are: townships and departments. Consequently, administrative townships are abolished. The progressive application of this stipulation will result from decisions taken by the Algerian Assembly." However, as the European delegates to the Algerian Assembly were hostile to the reform, the necessary decisions were never taken, and the administrative townships were still functioning when the Algerian Assembly was dissolved by a decree of the French Government on April 11, 1956.

The Parliament, in voting the statute, dumped another thorny problem into the lap of the Algerian Assembly, that of freeing the mosques from government control. It was assumed, on the strength of vehement nationalist protests, that the Administration in Algeria had been meddling with the right of the Moslems to run their own religious affairs. "Flagrant inequality," cried independent Deputy Emmanuel Temple, a former prefect of the Algiers Department. It will perhaps be well to see what the dither was all about.

The French, in the early days of the conquest, took over Algeria's *habbous* properties or *wakfs*. These, as elsewhere in Islam, were charitable legacies and foundations. The *habbous* revenues served a multitude of purposes, among them the maintenance of mosques and religious institutions, the remuneration of religious personnel, teachers, and magistrates, and the endowment of hospices, fountains, and other public facilities. Having seized the revenue-producing properties, the French undertook in return to maintain the existing services and institutions at public expense. This policy wrecked much that had remained of the Middle Ages in Algeria. It cleared the way for a modern form of government. But the Moslems, who take comfort in permanence—it tends to compensate for their chronic anarchy and the fickleness of fate—were deeply offended. In those days, however, they had no recourse.

The 1905 Separation of Church and State Act was exended to Algeria by decree in 1907. Nevertheless, the state retained title to churches, mosques, and synagogues in Algeria, and also to the *habbous* properties. By then, however, most of the original *habbous* properties were either alienated or inextricably intermingled with other public holdings. Religious ministrants of all faiths were knocked off the public payroll and put on allowance. The hitch, as regards the mosques, was that although the Moslem religious associations, newly created, were free to appoint whom they pleased as *mufti* (expounder of the law), *imam* (officiant), *muezzin* (crier of the hour of prayer), *khatib* (preacher), *mouderrès* (teacher), *hazzab* (reader of the Koran), and beadle, the allowance was available only to those approved by the Administration.

French control never covered matters of faith or ritual. There was nothing to prevent the Moslems from building as many new mosques or from appointing as many unapproved religious officials as they were willing to pay for (although it must be remembered that collections are not normally taken up in mosques). The agitation, largely stimulated by the Ulema, who wanted control of the religious apparatus to further their political ends, had nothing to do with freedom of worship. It centered around demands for the restitution of *habbous* properties and for the removal of all government control as distinct from government subsidies.

Article Fifty-Six of the statute left the Algerian Assembly with the task of making the "independence of the Moslem faith" work in practice. The Assembly, slow in bestirring itself, turned the matter over to a special committee in November, 1951. The committee, headed by Abdelkader Chergui, delegate for Aïn Témouchent in the Oran Department, began by asking the Governor General to consider no further applications for allowances until the Assembly had come forward with new proposals. This request was granted. The Government went further: it expressed its willingness to pay a reasonable perpetuity in lieu of the lost *habbous* revenues. This annuity plus the annual appropriations voted by the Algerian Assembly could be expected to produce upwards of 700 million francs ($2 million) a year, a goodly sum.

Despite their differences, the Moslem leaders consulted by the committee agreed that the funds should be administered by a central religious authority in which the orthodox Ulema and the heterodox *zaouïas* (religious confraternities) would be equitably represented. However, the French Council of State ruled in October, 1953, that a central religious body of the kind contemplated by the committee was incompatible with the Separation of Church and State Act. The committee was still struggling with the problem when the Algerian Assembly vanished in April, 1956. The Ulema have long since dropped their demand for religious "independence" on the grounds that this question will automatically sort itself out when Algeria becomes a sovereign nation.

9. FIRST ELECTIONS UNDER THE STATUTE

The municipal elections of October, 1947, swept the nationalists into city councils all over the country. The M.T.L.D., in particular, had waged a bitter and often brutal campaign. But M. Julien exaggerates when he says the Messalists won "almost all the second-college seats." The figures show that the M.T.L.D., very successful in the larger cities, played second fiddle to the U.D.M.A. in many smaller centers, the over-all breakdown being:

M.T.L.D.	31 per cent
U.D.M.A.	27 per cent
Algerian Communist party (P.C.A.)	4 per cent
Others	38 per cent

Fifty-six per cent of the registered second-college voters cast their ballots. The nationalist landslide was a lesson to those who still had faith in M. Chataigneau's "liberal" policies as an instrument of reconciliation. The Europeans, however, remained in full control of the city councils, since the first college had not been deprived of its statutory right to three-fifths of the seats. The Governor General got another douse of cold water when the natives in the countryside were called to the polls in November and December to elect new *djemaas* (rural councils). Despite the vigilance of the Administration, 28 per cent of the votes cast went to the "secessionists" (M.T.L.D., U.D.M.A., and P.C.A.). The elections were accompanied by a wave of terrorist agitation in the coastal area east of Algiers. Secret courts set up by the M.T.L.D. tried "traitors" to the party, fining some, ostracizing others, and sentencing a few to death. Four assassinations were reported.

M. Chataigneau, whose elections were criticized in Algiers and Paris as not "good" enough, was succeeded in February, 1948, by another Socialist, Marcel-Edmond Naegelen, deputy for the Bas-Rhin department (Alsace). For several months, a group of first-college deputies for Algiers led by Jacques Chevallier had been agitating for M. Chataigneau's removal. Their efforts had encountered the stiff opposition of the Socialist party. The coalition cabinet headed by Premier Robert Schuman, a Popular Republican, was almost torn asunder when the ministers fell to quarreling over this issue. René Mayer, Finance Minister and Radical deputy for Constantine, vowed he would resign if M. Chataigneau stayed in Algiers. Jules Moch, Socialist Minister of the Interior, countered with a threat to resign if M. Chataigneau were ousted. In the end, however, the ministers agreed to split the difference by appointing a Socialist to succeed a Socialist. The compromise was eminently satisfactory to the Algerian deputies, who, disregarding M. Naegelen's political affiliation, interpreted his appointment as a repudiation of M. Chataigneau's "soft" policies. "At last!" exclaimed the *Echo d'Alger* in an exultant editorial.

The event was soon to show that the Algerian deputies were not mistaken. M. Naegelen announced at the start that in Algiers he would represent the whole nation, not just the Socialist party. He ruled out any concessions to what he called the "backhanded racism that consists in denying the French the right to live."

The new Governor General arrived in Algiers on February 25. He made it his job, in the first weeks of his incumbency, to state his position clearly. Freedom, he said in one of his early speeches, belongs to "those who deserve it," that is, to those who "respect the freedom of others." He warned that any attempt on the part of the few to impose their will by terror would be nipped in the bud. "We will crush terror in all its forms," he declared. "We will stamp out violence wherever it occurs. We will see that order and justice prevail in this land."

In an address to a gathering of mayors, he said his hands were outstretched in brotherhood to all who strove to make Algeria a harmonious member of the French family. "We shall," he promised, "attempt to reason with those who might be tempted to pursue other goals or who, carried away by I know not what paroxysm of pride and vanity, claim to be able to get along without France. And if they refuse to see the bright light of truth, it will be no fault of ours, and we shall not be responsible."

These were strong words. Algeria had heard nothing like them in a coon's age. "The voice of colonialism," cried the nationalists. "The threshold of a new era," said the *Echo d'Alger*.

M. Naegelen did not have long to wait for a chance to put his theories into practice: elections for the new Algerian Assembly were coming up, and the nationalists were quite prepared to play havoc with the polls. On April 2, an M.T.L.D. agitator, arrested in Kabylia, was found to possess an instruction sheet prepared by his superiors. It said: "If our defeat becomes certain, the ballot boxes must be broken at all costs, by force if necessary. It is imperative, in these circumstances, to keep cool and not to go beyond the destruction of the ballot box. A ballot box must never be broken in a district where we are certain to win, but only in places where the outlook is hopeless."

This was a big order, far beyond the party's ability to deliver. Nevertheless, a few isolated attempts were made on election day (April 4). A detachment of mobile guards sent to relieve a besieged polling station at Deschmya near Aumale seventy-five miles southeast of Algiers got caught in a barrage of stones hurled from the side of the road and shot its way through, killing seven demonstrators. At Champlain, further to the west on the road to Médéa, a mob stormed a café in which a police superintendent, two inspectors, and a driver had taken refuge. Shots were fired, and the assailants dispersed. The polling station at Tiara in the Tablat district (forty-two miles south of Algiers) was set on fire. In western Algeria, polling stations were attacked at Ammi Moussa, Trézel, and Hammam Bou Hadjar. And that was all.

Messali Hadj, meanwhile, writing in his paper, *El Maghreb El Arabi*, had put the issue, as he saw it, to the voters in his usual forthright way: "It must be said that once again two utterly irreconcilable forces are to meet head-on: on the one hand, backsliding colonialism, determined to retain its hideous privileges; on the other, the national liberating movement, struggling to restore the sovereignty of the Algerian people."

The first results of the election left people wondering whether the Administration had matters fully in hand. The M.T.L.D. got off to a flying start. Its candidates—thirty-two of whom were under arrest for plotting against the security of the state*—ran up 30 per cent of the second-college votes cast on the first day of balloting. The U.D.M.A. got 18 per cent and the P.C.A. 2 per cent. In other words, 50 per cent of the Moslem electorate had voted for secessionist candidates (nationalists and Communists).

It may be surmised that M. Naegelen experienced an anxious moment or two when the returns were in. But a runoff election on April 11 put an end to all earlier alarms. The secessionist vote fell to 24 per cent, and the M.T.L.D. ended with only nine seats. The U.D.M.A. won eight seats and the Communists none. The French could breathe easy in the knowledge that forty-three second-college seats in the new Assembly would be occupied by dependable Moslems. The first college gave most of its votes to the *Union Algérienne*, a coalition of all French parties except the Socialists and Communists. The breakdown in the first college was: Union, forty seats; Socialists, four; Communists, one; others, fifteen.

The election results were a source of jubilation in European circles. Jacques Chevallier summed up the feelings of his constituents with the comment, "A great hope has been born!" The *Echo d'Alger* waxed even more lyric: "On this day of peace and glory, in this newspaper where we have striven unceasingly to bring forth this radiant and assuaging dawn, we may say with pride: in Algeria, henceforth, France marches on." M. Naegelen himself noted that the "populations have demonstrated their attachment to the union of France and Algeria."

The satisfaction of the Europeans would have been more than

---

* One of the arrested candidates was Mohammed Yazid, who, after serving a two-year prison term, became secretary-general of the M.T.L.D. organization in France. With Hocine Aït Ahmed, he represented the Algerian rebels at the Bandung conference in April, 1955; he later acted as rebel spokesman at the United Nations.

legitimate if it could truly have been said that the Moslem electorate had spoken. Alas, the second college was voiceless in the sense that if the right to vote implied the right to think, it was not exercised. With few exceptions, the Moslems at the polls obviously responded to the balance of power rather than the dictates of their individual consciences, casting a "communal" vote in places where the threat of nationalist reprisals seemed real, supporting Administration candidates elsewhere. Undoubtedly, there was manipulation of votes as well. I dare say M. Frédérix of *Le Monde* was close to the mark when he estimated that of the forty-odd "administrative" delegates, a mere half-dozen could claim to be the authentic representatives of a group or of a religious force. A few others commanded some personal following. But, according to M. Frédérix, more than half the second-college delegates, and perhaps two-thirds, represented only themselves. They were at the beck and call of the Administration or of their European colleagues. The era of the "beni-oui-ouis" (yes men) had begun.

The "beni-oui-ouis," often handsomely beturbaned gentlemen full of years and dignity, have been held in much derision. Such disparagement is ridiculous and unjust. Men who try conscientiously to do the bidding of their rulers are not necessarily clowns or rascals, especially in Moslem countries, used to government by command. Any number of "beni-oui-ouis" have latterly paid for their fidelity with their lives. And yet they were fish out of water in a democratic body supposed to reflect the will of the people. Their presence facilitated the work of the Assembly from day to day without enhancing its prestige. The basic evil lay, not in the men, but in the institution itself, virtually meaningless as far as the Moslems were concerned, for their country was without the slightest trace of a democratic tradition.* A lasting racial partnership, Algeria's greatest need, could hardly be built upon the equivocal foundations provided for it.

The inaugural session of the Algerian Assembly on April 22 was marred by the belligerence of Ferhat Abbas, delegate for Sétif. Governor General Naegelen had just opened the session with a solemn charge to the delegates. The dean of the assembly, acting as speaker *pro tempore*, invited the two youngest members of each college to assist him pending the election of officers. Mostefa Ferroukhi, M.T.L.D. delegate for Miliana, rose when his name was called and launched into a venomous

* The *djemaas* or village councils in the mountains of Kabylia are frequently cited as evidence of an indigenous democratic tradition. From what I know of the *djemaas*, they are akin to the councils of elders to be found in the African bush—synods, the primary function of which is to protect the clan and respect the immemorial customs of the race.

diatribe, the burden of which was that the honor conferred upon him rightfully belonged to an M.T.L.D. colleague arrested only a few minutes before and that the Assembly as a whole was the product of "terror and repression." Mr. Ferroukhi and the three other M.T.L.D. delegates present then filed out of the Palais Carnot, whereupon Mr. Abbas leaped to his feet to make an "interlocutory statement." Ruled out of order and denied the floor, Mr. Abbas nevertheless raised his voice above shouts of protest and the din of banging desk tops (a traditional sign of displeasure in French legislative bodies). "If I am not allowed to speak, no one will speak," he thundered, purple with rage. The phrase lives on in the memory of his contemporaries.

On November 11, 1948, the "grand electors"* were convened to choose new members of the Council of the Republic. The results of this indirect election reflected the trend of the times. Secessionist votes fell from 55 per cent in the December, 1946, senatorial election to 43 per cent. The breakdown in the second college was:

M.T.L.D.	16 per cent
U.D.M.A.	26 per cent
P.C.A.	1 per cent
Others	57 per cent

Elections to the General (departmental) Councils in March, 1949, carried the decline of the secessionist parties a step further. The M.T.L.D., accepting defeat by default, put up no candidates and recommended abstention—discreetly, so as not to vex the U.D.M.A. and P.C.A., with which unity talks were then in progress. The results, highly satisfactory from the Administration's point of view, were:

U.D.M.A.	10 per cent
P.C.A.	3 per cent
Others	87 per cent

The participation of the registered second-college voters was put at 64 per cent.

However, polling was reported to have been marked by irregularities in a number of localities, and the official figures must always, in such cases, be treated skeptically. On April 14, Jacques Fonlupt-Esperaber, Popular Republican (M.R.P.) deputy for the Haut-Rhin (Alsace), who

* The "grand electors" of each college were its deputies to the National Assembly, its delegates to the Algerian Assembly, and delegates elected by its city councilors on the basis of one delegate for 500 registered voters. Algeria was represented in the Council of the Republic (319 members) by fourteen senators, seven for each college.

had traveled to Vialar, 155 miles southwest of Algiers, to watch over his party's second-college candidate there, a certain Ouazane, sent a blistering letter to Jules Moch, Socialist deputy, then Interior Minister.

"It is beyond argument," M. Fonlupt-Esperaber wrote, "that, in the district I visited, the election was neither free nor sincere. It is not the voters who chose the successful candidate. The Administration chose him by using the tested methods which, in Algeria, are the fruit of disgraceful experience. This fact is not only indisputable; it is admitted. It occurred to none of the officials I saw to deny for an instant that, in Algeria, elections are the business of the Administration. . . . One of them declared outright, in the presence of our colleague, M. Pierre-Henri Teitgen [another M.R.P. deputy], that he 'made the elections,' because such were the orders he had received from above. . . . Allow me to say with all frankness that the methods I witnessed, and which I have good reason to believe are generally employed for second-college elections to the General Councils, are properly intolerable."

The testimony of M. Fonlupt-Esperaber is cited with satisfaction by M. Julien as irremediably damaging to the Administration. Yet the deputy could not be called an impartial witness. His party's candidate was soundly beaten in a district where no secessionist–nationalist or Communist–candidate was running. Why? It is convenient for M. Fonlupt-Esperaber to accuse the Administration, and the Administration may be guilty. But M. Fonlupt-Esperaber and his admirers fail to mention one or two pertinent facts, to wit: Mr. Ouazane, a former *oukil* (native lawyer) convicted for malfeasance, could hardly have hoped to defeat his rival, Belkacem Ferhat, *bachagha* (the highest rank of *caïd*) and a member of the most influential family in the area.

10. THE TERROR BEGINS

On April 5, 1949, before dawn, a daring robbery was committed in Oran. Raphael Fabre and Gustave Barraut, cashiers at the Oran central post office, were counting the previous day's receipts when three armed men burst in upon them. "Hands up!" said one, pointing a Sten gun at the cashiers. No danger, however, that the man would use the gun: silence was essential to the success of the venture. Realizing this, the two cashiers flung themselves at the robbers, but only to encounter the swinging butt of the Sten gun, which knocked them out. Frantically, the robbers stuffed wads of bills into a pouch. Then they fled, leaving a trail of bank notes behind them. They escaped in a car they had stolen the night before from Dr. Pierre Moutier, a well-known Oran practitioner who, abducted in the process, had spent the night in a cave. The take was 3,170,000 francs ($9,057). About 33 million francs were found strewn on the post office floor when the robbers had gone.

The press next day was full of details, but it was not thought that the culprits were any different from the criminals who, only a short time before, had mugged a taxi driver and robbed the Loubet garage. Nobody could have guessed that the crime had been masterminded by a member of the French National Assembly, M.T.L.D. deputy Mohammed Khider, to help finance a contemplated insurrection against the French in Algeria. It was not until the following year that the facts became known, almost fortuitously.

On March 18, 1950, a nationalist "commando" was sent out from Bône, port city in eastern Algeria, with orders to kidnap Abdelkader Khiari of Tebessa, repentant M.T.L.D. member who knew too much. However, Mr. Khiari, fearing that he might be the object of punitive measures, was ready. He repulsed the attack. The assailants, two of whom had tried to get away in a car, fell into the hands of the police. They were questioned by officials extremely curious to know exactly what was going on.

The three put the police on the track of a secret paramilitary branch of the old Algerian People's party (P.P.A.) with ramifications throughout eastern Algeria. By the end of March, more than 100 members of this so-called Special Organization (O.S.) had been rounded up. Cached stores uncovered by the police yielded three light machine guns, thirteen rifles, fourteen pistols, and assorted explosives, together with binoculars, compasses, and pharmaceutical supplies. An "instruction book" figuring among a collection of seized documents summoned each member to be ready at all times to suffer, if caught, "the inexorable fate that awaits him: death." There were also summary courses in topography, military drill, police technique, secret codes, disguise, and espionage. The members of the O.S. were bidden to avoid contact with members of the political wing of the Messali movement. A "guerrilla manual" was found to contain ten lessons covering such subjects as sabotage, ambushes, surprise attacks, attrition tactics, and close combat.

It was discovered soon afterwards that the O.S. had organized active cells in central and western Algeria as well as in the eastern part of the country and that the "secret army" as a whole came under a nine-man "general staff." A statement issued by the Governor General's office on

April 21—the investigation was then in its earlier phases—reviewed the evidence that had been gathered and said: "A total of 154 persons have been arrested and held for trial. The search continues under rogatory commission issued by the investigating magistrates involved, the aim being to hunt down the responsible leaders and all the elements of this organization recently set up by the M.T.L.D.–P.P.A. and now comprising, as far as is known, only a few hundred individuals." It was later learned that the O.S., conceived in 1947, began to take shape in 1948 and that its effectives had reached about 1,800 in 1950.

On May 10, 1950, Mohammed Ben Bella, a former warrant officer in the 141st Algerian Rifles (four citations; Military Medal) and deputy mayor of Marnia, a town 120 miles southwest of Oran, was arrested in Algiers. A pistol of German manufacture and a roll of banknotes amounting to 223,000 francs ($637) were found on his person. Ben Bella, then thirty-four years old, was quickly identified as "national chief" of the O.S. and as one of the instigators of the Oran post office robbery. He had previously been "departmental chief" in western Algeria. His promotion had come in September, 1949, following the dismissal of Hocine Aït Ahmed, twenty-four-year-old Kabyle who had sided with the "Berberists," a group formed in opposition to Messali Hadj's "dictatorial" leadership and to the concept of Algeria as an essentially Arab nation.*

As "national chief" of the O.S., Ben Bella took his orders directly from M.T.L.D. deputy Mohammed Khider. One of Ben Bella's three "departmental chiefs" in 1950 was Mohammed Boudiaf, who, like Ben Bella himself, was later to play a key part in the rebellion.† Khider, Ben Bella, Aït Ahmed, Boudiaf, and a fifth rebel leader named Mustapha Lacheraf were caught by the French on October 22, 1956, when the plane on which they were traveling from Rabat to Tunis was intercepted and brought down at Maison Blanche, near Algiers.

The O.S., responsive to the law of natural affinities, was in touch early in the game with notorious brigand chiefs in the Kabylia mountains, notably with Belkacem Krim, Amar Ouamrane, Ali Rabia, and Amar

---

* This was not the first time dissension had broken out in the ranks of the M.T.L.D. From the start, relations had been strained between the veterans of the old P.P.A. underground and the newly elected party politicians. In 1948, the veterans formed an ephemeral "Opposition Committee" in Algiers for the avowed purpose of purging the "traitors" and the "spineless." The "Berberists," whose opposition developed the following year, were encouraged in their stand by the Communists, always eager to confuse any issue to their own advantage.

† Boudiaf was responsible for the Constantine Department. It may be surmised that the rebels, when they struck in that same area five years later, were indebted to Boudiaf for much of the preparatory work that had gone before.

Haddad, and had sought their help in organizing gangs of saboteurs. Krim and Ouamrane, Kabyles both, were not only to emerge as patriots with the outbreak of the nationalist rebellion, but actually to assume a commanding position in the rebel camp at the expense of their Arab brethren. Belkacem Grine, another Berber bandit whose normal activities were to be transfigured by the rebellion, was beginning to rise to fame in the Aurès mountains in 1950. The following year, he and four accomplices gave a good account of themselves by holding up the Arris-Khenchela bus and relieving its passengers of 40,000 francs.

The nationalists raised the cry of "repression" when the French set up three new security posts in the Aurès mountains in 1951. It will be seen later on that the word "repression," no matter how indiscriminately used, usually brings deep-seated guilt feelings to the surface of the French mind. This conditioned reflex, destructive of self-confidence and determination, has probably stood the rebels in better stead than their powder. The average Frenchman would accept almost any indignity rather than appear to contest the legitimacy of a fight for freedom, even when a portion of his nation's sovereignty and the security of his fellow citizens are at stake. Consequently, Paris has never quite dared equate the rebellion with ordinary lawlessness.* This is reflected in official efforts to taboo the old-fashioned word "repression" and to substitute the euphemistic "pacification."

11. THE ROLE OF JACQUES CHEVALLIER

Jacques Chevallier, weathercock deputy for Algiers, set tongues wagging early in 1951 by resigning his seat in the National Assembly to stand for election to the Algerian Assembly. His decision, he said, sprang from a

* Ben Bella and the four rebel leaders incarcerated with him at the Santé prison in Paris were given the status of political prisoners. Thus, despite the fact that, with the exception of Mustapha Lacheraf, each had a criminal record as long as his arm, the five were allowed visitors and other privileges. The French police were surprised to learn in March, 1957, that, eluding the affable vigilance of their guards, the rebel leaders had continued, from their cells, to take a hand in the management of the rebellion. Handwritten notes sent out by Ben Bella and his companions were found in the home of Ahmed Taleb, arrested deputy head of the rebel organization in Metropolitan France.

conviction that Algeria's future could best be forged not in Paris, but in Algiers. This view had M. Chevallier's peers bristling with indignation. General Adolphe Aumeran, Fernand Chevalier, Auguste Rencurel, and Paul-Emile Viard, deputies for Algiers, and Senators Henri Borgeaud and Marcel Rogier, stated in a letter to Count Alain de Sérigny, publisher of the *Echo d'Alger*, that they were unalterably opposed to any move to turn the Algerian Assembly into a parliament. For good measure, they also denounced the "mad idea" of an Algerian republic and repudiated federalism in all its forms—the implication being that M. Chevallier's position was dangerously close to that of Ferhat Abbas.

But M. Chevallier had already sallied forth as knight-errant of Algerian politics. In December, 1950, in a series of articles published in the *Echo d'Alger* under the general head "*Faisons le Point*" ("Let Us Take Our Bearings"), he came out for what he called a "genuine Franco-Moslem union," which alone, he wrote, could create the necessary atmosphere of mutual confidence and foster the emergence of latent Moslem elites. He refused to limit the spectrum of Algerian public life to two tendencies, the one "colonialist" and the other "secessionist." He insisted that the "no man's land" between the two should be explored, that it was safer to deal with "semirebels than with menials."

Unfortunately, his arguments, based on a fond belief in the possibility of nonconformism as a force in Islam, won him few disciples; but they gave rise to many doubts as to the consistency of his thinking. Was he not the man who in 1947 had told the National Assembly that the only valid objective in Algeria was the "Frenchification" of the natives? Had he not raised his voice against the teaching of Arabic in the schools and against the pernicious influence of Islam? Was he not the villain of innumerable nationalist tracts for defending the "exorbitant interests of the agrarian caste"?

The terms of one-half of the members of the Algerian Assembly having expired, an election to fill their seats was held in February, 1951. An analysis of the revised electoral rolls showed that, in the first college, the number of Moslem voters had reached 63,762, or 12 per cent of the whole. Moslems accounted for 40 per cent of the first-college rolls at Tebessa and at Bougie.

The M.T.L.D., pursuing the course adopted at the time of the 1949 election to the General Councils, stayed out of the race. This maneuver automatically cost the party four of its eight seats.* The U.D.M.A., with

* The M.T.L.D. delegates who lost their seats were: Mohammed Cherchalli (Koléa), Chouki Mostefai (Constantine), Mohammed Lamine Belhadi (Le Kroubs) and Boualem Baki (Aïn Sefra). Mohammed Boulkeroua (Philippeville) had already lost his seat as the result of a conviction in court.

four seats falling vacant, put up candidates in sixteen constituencies and let the other fourteen go. The results proved that the secessionists, whether for natural or contrived reasons, were still on the skids. Second-college participation was put at 67 per cent, the breakdown of the votes cast being:

M.T.L.D.	0.7 per cent
U.D.M.A.	11.0 per cent
P.C.A.	4.3 per cent
Others	84.0 per cent

The election left the secessionists with nine seats instead of seventeen. Of the successful second-college candidates, two had been sponsored by the Popular Republic party and one by the Socialist party. The others were without French party affiliation. The Communist daily, *Alger Républicain*, as was its custom on such occasions, ran a "fraudulent election" column. The paper intimated on February 6, for example, that the Administration had engineered the election of Tahar Imalhayène in the Blida constituency. It pointed out that Ahmed Saoudi, up for re-election, had defeated Mr. Imalhayène by 16,559 votes to 2,791 in 1948 but had polled only 2,691 votes in 1951. (Neither Mr. Saoudi nor Mr. Imalhayène was then a nationalist.) In the Dupleix district of the same constituency, according to *Alger Républicain*, Mr. Imalhayène got 400 of 419 votes cast, whereas two nationalist candidates got none.*

The new faces in the Algerian Assembly included that of Jacques Chevallier, who made his presence felt in the spring by sponsoring a "liberal" movement among the delegates of both colleges. M. Chevallier's "liberalism" was welcomed with delight by the members of the U.D.M.A. group, who conceived immoderate hopes—soon to be dashed, for the "liberalism" involved no concessions to the demand for Algerian statehood.† However, the new tack was a prosperous one for M. Chevallier; it marked the beginning of a political alliance that was ultimately to carry him to ministerial rank in the Government of Premier Pierre Mendès-France.‡

* One of the two was a young lawyer named Ali Boumendjel, a U.D.M.A. candidate. Mr. Boumendjel was later to become political boss for the rebels in the south section of Algiers. Caught by French paratroopers in Algiers on February 9, 1957, he committed suicide or was killed on March 23, 1957. His brother, Ahmed Boumendjel, a member of the Paris bar and of the Assembly of the French Union, was to become Ben Bella's lawyer; he subsequently took charge of the rebel weekly, *El Moudjahid*, in Tunis.

† However, in February, 1956, and again in September of that year, M. Chevallier recommended a negotiated settlement of the Algerian conflict.

‡ He was appointed Secretary of State for War in June, 1954, and Minister of Defense in January, 1955.

The extent of the "liberalism" invented by M. Chevallier could be measured when his friends in the National Assembly, led by Georges Blachette, multimillionaire esparto king and deputy for Algiers, joined the conservatives in voting down the Benchennouf bill to give the second college parity of representation in the Algerian city councils. The new liberalism could be seen at work again in October, 1951, when Abderrahmane Farès, in those days a staunch "integrationist,"* was elected president of the Algiers General Council with the united support of the liberals and conservatives.

M. Chevallier, his talents apparently finding insufficient scope in the Algerian Assembly, won a by-election in January, 1952, and went back to the National Assembly in Paris. "No one," the *Echo d'Alger* commented, "can be unaware of the mandate Jacques Chevallier has received from his constituents: it is to defend French Algeria in company with Georges Blachette, Marcel Ribère, and Marcel Paternot" (deputies elected in June, 1951).

When he became mayor of Algiers in May, 1953, M. Chevallier succeeded in securing the cooperation of the nationalist members of the city council. His incumbency, which ended in June, 1958, was distinguished by a notable effort in public housing, which, he has said, proved that "men of good will, however divergent or conflicting their opinions and however different their racial origins may be, can in all loyalty achieve a common denominator uniting them in the bonds of a shared enthusiasm." He claimed to have done away with the "racial complexes and the spirit of segregation." Unfortunately, the common enthusiasm of which he was so proud vanished into thin air when political issues came to the fore. M. Chevallier's social-minded and reformist approach has, indeed, been called "neocolonialism" and denounced by the nationalists as one of the worst forms of perfidy.

The February, 1951, election put an abrupt end to M. Naegelen's career as Governor General. Though his mission had just been extended for an additional period of six months, M. Naegelen tendered his resignations in March after a squabble with Interior Minister Henri Queuille.†

---

* He declared for the rebels in September, 1956.

† The incident, a futile one, involved the election of Hachémi Benchennouf, a Popular Republican deputy in the outgoing legislature, as delegate to the Algerian Assembly for Khenchela. Mr. Benchennouf, fearing that the Administration's curse might be upon him, got three Popular Republican deputies down from Paris to watch the electoral proceedings. His success at the polls does not seem to have pleased M. Naegelen, who, accusing the civil administrator at Khenchela, a M. Laussel, of "partiality," assigned the guilty official

Roger Léonard, the Paris Prefect of Police, appointed Governor General of Algeria on April 11, 1951, arrived on May 16. The Socialist politician was succeeded by a distinguished and cultivated servant of the state, the epitome of prudent rectitude. It was clear, when M. Léonard addressed the Algerian Assembly on May 22, that the florid oratory to which M. Naegelen had accustomed the delegates would no longer be heard, though the tenor of the Governor General's pronouncements was to be much the same. M. Léonard likened France to a mother, but added: "I shall oppose the undertakings of those who seek to destroy our national unity and who do not hesitate to preach disorder and hatred."

The general election in June, 1951, was a disaster for the secessionists; it wiped out their entire representation in the National Assembly. The M.T.L.D. lost its five seats, and the P.C.A., its two seats. The U.D.M.A., it will be recalled, had none to start with. The breakdown of the second-college vote (67 per cent participation) was:

M.T.L.D.	8 per cent
U.D.M.A.	9 per cent
P.C.A.	3 per cent
Others	80 per cent

Instances of violence on election day were few. However, the polling station at El Oustia, in the Aurès mountains, was occupied by two self-styled "electoral agents" who had appeared on the scene with several hundred Chaouïa tribesmen spoiling for trouble. The local *caïd* was knocked to the ground with a bludgeon, and balloting had to be called off.

Mohammed Khider, implicated in the Oran post office robbery and other dark doings, had not been a candidate for re-election. Even if he had been able to retain his seat—a highly unlikely contingency—he would have had to fight action, then pending, to deprive him of his parliamentary immunity. He fled to Cairo at the end of his term and joined the Maghrib Office, rendezvous of exiled North African nationalists. He

---

to a lesser charge at Châteaudun-du-Rhumel between Constantine and Sétif. A hue and cry went up from Mr. Benchennouf's political friends in Paris; and M. Queuille, impressed, ordered the immediate reinstatement of M. Laussel. M. Naegelen felt he had every right, in the circumstances, to put his resignation on M. Queuille's desk in protest, but he was surprised and hurt when it was accepted without a demur from his Socialist colleagues. He at least had the satisfaction of making M. Benchennouf feel the bite of irony; he published a letter in which the Moslem deputy for Constantine had, in 1948, railed against M. Laussel, who, the letter said, "in his desire to harm me at any cost, has been led to bully the whole population."

had put himself beyond the reach of the French police in the nick of time: two warrants for his arrest were issued in July, 1951. Khider replaced Chadly Mekki as head of the Algerian Section of the Maghrib Office in October, 1952.

12. THE NATIONALIST SEARCH FOR UNITY

There had been talk of a united nationalist front in Algeria for years, and intermittent negotiations to this end had been conducted since Messali's return from banishment in 1946. However, the dangers of an unduly chummy attitude had been made manifest to Mr. Abbas when his party was virtually commandeered by the Messalists in 1945. Messali himself was too much of a megalomaniac to take kindly to the overweening Mr. Abbas. Messali's primary ambition in 1946 had been to thrust all rivals aside and to become Algeria's uncontested man of destiny. Nevertheless, unity remained a hope and a recurrent theme in Algerian nationalism.

A step in the direction of unity was made when the U.D.M.A., already in close communion with the Association of Ulema, succumbed to Communist blandishments. Ferhat Abbas, proclaiming that there could be no peace with colonialism, was the toast of the Communist-managed Partisans of Peace Congress in Paris in April, 1949. Later, at a U.D.M.A. party meeting in Tlemcen, he declared: "The French Communist party has adopted, apart from a few matters of mere detail, the very position that we ourselves are defending. We are assured of its support. This is something that, in all fairness, must be said. The French working class is the best of our allies and, for this, deserves our thanks."

But it was not until August, 1951, with the birth of the *Front Algérien pour la Défense et le Respect de la Liberté* that all four secessionist groups–M.T.L.D., U.D.M.A., P.C.A., and Ulema–succeeded in getting together for joint action. The Front agitated for the invalidation of previous second-college elections, for the release of political prisoners, and for religious "independence." But its action was never very effective. Messali, seasoned by long exposure to Communist theory and practice, was warier than Mr. Abbas of treacherous entanglements on the left.

Ahmed Mezerna, one of Messali's chief lieutenants and editor of the party paper, *L'Algérie Libre*, felt obliged to explain that the understanding with the P.C.A. was, in his party's view, merely "transitory," its purpose being to retain the good graces of the French Communist party and to scare the United States. The Front gradually crumbled away. It should be remembered, however, if only because three Frenchmen sat on its executive committee. They were General Paul Tubert, pro-Communist former deputy and former Mayor of Algiers; André Mandouze, professor of classical languages and literature at the University of Algiers, and an obscure secondary-school teacher named Marcel Domerc.

One of the three, M. Mandouze, a fervent Peace Partisan, later rose to fame for his tireless efforts in behalf of the rebel cause. An examining magistrate at Blida, in the process of getting up a case against members of a local terrorist cell in May, 1956, stumbled upon evidence implicating M. Mandouze. It was discovered that *Conscience Moghrébine*, a semi-confidential sheet put out by M. Mandouze, had, in December, 1955, carried nationalist material, including rebel "victory bulletins" along with lists of "traitors executed" and of "patriots who have given their lives for the Algerian cause." This material was later reproduced in a clandestine rebel publication printed in Belgium. The examining magistrate concluded that the evidence was incriminating enough to indict M. Mandouze for plotting against the security of the state. A second information was lodged against M. Mandouze in November, 1956, this time in Paris by the military magistrate who had been examining Mohammed Ben Bella and the four other rebel leaders caught on October 22, 1956. The new charge, based on evidence got from the captive rebels, was for "activities tending to undermine the morale of the Army and of the nation." On November 10, M. Mandouze was committed to the Santé prison to await trial. He remained there until paroled on December 19.

News of M. Mandouze's arrest and imprisonment was met with a great outcry of indignation in Paris, particularly in leftist and intellectual circles. A committee headed by François Mauriac, the distinguished novelist and Nobel prize winner, was formed for his defense. The authorities were soon deluged with petitions. One was signed by 161 university professors, another by 118 professors at the University of Strasbourg (to which M. Mandouze had just been appointed), still another by some 800 secondary-school teachers. "We consider it inadmissible," M. Mauriac's committee said in a handout to the press, "that indictment and imprisonment should await those who, in accordance with the policy approved at the polls, seek to establish the basis for an understanding with the representatives of the Algerian people" (meaning, of course, the rebels). M. Mandouze himself explained in a statement that the Government had been privy to his commerce with the rebel leaders and had encouraged him to persevere in the course he had chosen. He dismissed *Conscience Moghrébine* as an essentially "pedagogical" venture.

Nothing to my mind better symbolizes the confusion into which the French had fallen than the case of André Mandouze. Here was a man who, without danger to himself, sided with those who had taken up arms against his country. He served a cause that had claimed thousands of innocent lives. Yet he was magnified by many as the witness and martyr of some higher spiritual order. It did not seem to have occurred to the indignant petitioners that M. Mandouze was a spurious victim. Prison was grist for his mill, for it could only lead him to a position of greater eminence.

The real tragedy was not his; it was, and is, that of the maimed and bereaved in Algeria, that also of those whose farmsteads are sacked, whose crops are burned, whose cattle are slaughtered. The humble victims of Arab terror—Arabs for the most part—have no learned doctors to defend them; they must suffer in obscurity and silence. In a better-ordered world, they would surely be held to deserve the concern and solicitude of the righteous; and Messrs. Mauriac, Mandouze, and company, who defend the rebels in the name of lofty political and ethical convictions, would justly incur the opprobrium of their countrymen. The symptoms strike me as extremely serious: "Every kingdom divided against itself is brought to desolation," says the Gospel.

Messali Hadj, who had been elected vice-president of the World Moslem Conference in Pakistan, made a pilgrimage to Mecca in 1951. Meanwhile, his henchmen in Algeria were being haled into court in droves for their activities as members of the O.S. Sixty Messalists were tried at Blida, eleven at Tizi Ouzou, 135 at Bône. Mohammed Khider, tried *in absentia* at Tizi Ouzou, was sentenced to five years in prison. Belkacem Krim, the Kabyle bandit-turned-patriot, was found to have served the O.S. as second in command of the northern Kabylia zone under Hanefi Fernane. Krim, still at large, was sentenced to five years in prison while Fernane, who had fallen into French hands, got four years.

The trial at Blida in March, 1952, was an all-star show with many famous terrorists, including the redoubtable Mohammed Ben Bella, present in person. Fifty-six accused were in the dock; four had got away. Forty in all were sent to prison for plotting against the state (and some also for the "illegal possession of arms and ammuntion of war"); twelve were given suspended sentences, and four were acquitted. Mohammed Khider, among the absent, was sentenced to eight years in prison and fined

120,000 francs ($342). The accused came into court singing the nationalist battle hymn: "In the way of salvation, we consecrate our efforts to the service of glory and of the *jihad*" (fifth couplet). Demonstrators outside, taking up the militant refrains and shouting slogans, had to be dispersed by the police.

Ben Bella, who had been sentenced to seven years, and Ahmed Mahsas, who had been sentenced to five years, escaped from prison on March 16 and were soon on their way to Cairo. They had sawed through the bars of their cell with a blade sent to them by the party in an enormous dish of *couscous* (steamed groats with meat).

The terrorists implicated in the Oran post office robbery* were tried by the Oran criminal court in June. Seven accused, among them Ben Bella and Khider, were sentenced *in absentia* to hard labor for life. Four others—Hamou Boutlelis, Rabah Lourgouioui, Benzerga Benaoun, and Fellouh Mesquine—were given long prison terms (up to twenty years at hard labor). It came out at the trial that the proceeds of the robbery had been handed over to Khider by Boutlelis.

The elections held in that period were as good from the Administration's point of view as any that had gone before. In October, 1951, the voters were called to the polls to fill the seats that had fallen vacant in the General Councils—thirty-six for the second college and fifty for the first (roughly half the total). The 66,000 Moslems registered as first-college voters that year accounted for 13 per cent of the roll; in several constituencies, the Moslems outnumbered the Europeans in the first college. The Communists alone among the secessionist parties contested the election. But though the M.T.L.D. and the U.D.M.A., with the approval of the Ulema, had preached abstention, the turnout of second-college voters was fairly heavy (55 per cent). In Algiers, many Messalists, disregarding the boycott decreed by their party, voted for the Communist candidate, Rachid Dalibey, who was re-elected. The results were:

P.C.A.	2.6 per cent (one seat)
Others	97.4 per cent (thirty-five seats)

The election left the U.D.M.A. with only two General Councilors, both in the Constantine Department, instead of seven as before. The M.T.L.D. had never even tried to get a candidate into the General Councils. The Communist representation remained unchanged: one councilor (in Algiers).

In May, 1952, the "grand electors" were convened in the Oran and Constantine Departments to fill five vacated seats in the Council of the

* See pp. 56–57.

Republic (three for Constantine and two for Oran). Four of the outgoing senators, one of them a U.D.M.A. candidate, were re-elected. In Constantine, an "independent" incumbent was beaten by a "Republican Union" candidate; in other words, the balance of power remained unchanged. The U.D.M.A. lost ground in the Oran Department (207 votes as against 255 in 1948) but picked up eighty-five votes in the Constantine Department. The M.T.L.D., which had made a fair showing in 1948 (16 per cent of the votes cast), was not in the race but could probably claim the seventy blank ballots cast in the Oran Department (ninety votes in 1948) and the 125 blank ballots cast in the Constantine Department (222 votes in 1948).

13. MESSALI SPURS DIRECT ACTION

The year of Messali's apotheosis was 1952; it also marked the beginning of his decline. Back from Mecca, the veteran leader tarried for a time in France. He was afraid perhaps that if the situation got worse in Tunisia —that country was already caught in the vicious circle of agitation and counteragitation*—the French might be tempted to harry the nationalist movements elsewhere in North Africa. In any case, when Habib Bour-

* A nationalist Tunisian Government headed by Premier M'Hamed Chenik had, on October 30, 1951, demanded immediate negotiations with France leading to Tunisian home rule. The demand was rejected by the French Government on December 15. M. Jean de Hauteclocque, the new Resident General, arrived at Tunis aboard a warship on January 13 and two days later handed the Bey a letter in which French Foreign Minister Robert Schuman ordered the dismissal of the Chenik Government. The Bey demurred. Rioting broke out in Bizerte and Béja. The leading nationalists were rounded up by the French on January 18. The next day, a general strike was proclaimed, and more rioting occurred. For five days beginning January 28, the French Army scoured the Cape Bon region for suspects. M. de Hauteclocque tried in vain to obtain the resignation of the Government on March 25. The Bey immediately sent a letter of protest to the President of France. On March 26, the Tunisian ministers were apprehended by order of General Pierre Garbay, commanding the French Forces in Tunisia, and the friendly Salaheddine Baccouche became Premier of Tunisia.

guiba and a host of other Tunisian nationalists were arrested in January and interned, Messali found that his presence in France was essential. What better excuse could he have than a nationalist conclave? And so, on January 28, a group of North African nationalist leaders including Sheikh Bachir Brahimi, president of the Association of Ulema, Ferhat Abbas, the Tunisian Mohammed Masmoudi, and the Moroccan Mohammed Hassan Ouezzani gathered at Chantilly for a meeting at which Messali presided.

A "common declaration" was issued afterwards. It called for an end to "repression" in Tunisia, for the release of Bourguiba and "all the political prisoners," for the recognition of Tunisian independence, and for an appeal to the United Nations. Plans for a "North African National Front" also were discussed, the idea being to unite the anti-French forces in North Africa under the symbolic leadership of the old Riff warlord, Abd-el-Krim, then in Cairo. It was later announced that a "North African Unity and Action Front" had been formed under the lesser auspices of Sheikh Brahimi. However, nothing seems ever to have come of this "Front" even though its charter was signed by such luminaries as Abbas, Masmoudi, and Ouezzani.

The themes developed at Chantilly were taken up by the Congress of Peoples against Imperialism* at its meeting in Paris on February 1. The speakers on that occasion included men who later became outspoken friends of the Algerian rebels: Emile Kahn, president of the League for the Rights of Man;† Claude Bourdet, editor of the leftist weekly *France-Observateur,* and our old friend, Charles-André Julien.

In February, Messali, seeing that the lid had been clamped down in Tunisia without noticeable effect in the form of increased agitation in Algeria, resolved to correct this anomaly himself. The great homecoming could not, therefore, be longer delayed. By February 16, Messali was doing business again at the old stand. His first move was to summon the faithful to banquet in his own honor at Bouzaréa. Reporting on his trip to the Orient, Messali paid warm tribute to the "tireless activity" of his man in Cairo, Chadly Mekki. All, it was reported, was buoyancy and enthusiasm in that hour of Messali's triumph. The leader, it was decided, would set out as soon as possible on a barnstorming tour across the country; he would fire the zeal of the people, rally the wavering, rouse the indifferent, and lead the whole nation on to glory.

---

* Chairman: Fenner Brockway, Labor M.P. for Eton and Slough. Secretary: Jean Rous, French socialist and publicist.

† M. Kahn died in 1958.

But there was nothing haphazard about the venture. Messali had an articulate and well-managed organization behind him at the center and in the provinces. He was assisted at the top by a "sacred trio"—Ahmed Mezerna, a former deputy for Algiers; Hocine Lahouel,* secretary-general of the M.T.L.D., and Ahmed Ben Amar Boudaa, a delegate to the Algerian Assembly. Other members of the Messalist executive board ("*Comité Directeur*") were: Sid Ali Abdelhamid and Abdelli Aïssa, members of the Algiers city council, and M'Barek Ben Salah Djilani and Mostefa Ben Mohammed Ferroukhi, delegates to the Algerian Assembly. Responsibilities within the party leadership were divided as follows:

Planning: Hocine Lahouel, assisted by Taher Zerargui.

Press and Propaganda: M'Barek Djilani, assisted by Larbi Ben Sahli Demaghlatrous (a delegate to the Algerian Assembly).

Controller: Abderrahmane Kiouane (a member of the Algiers city council).

"*Complicity Network*": Saïd Amrani, assisted by Moulay Merbah.

Relations with Morocco: Mostefa Ferroukhi.

Relations with Tunisia: Ahmed Boudaa, assisted by Sid Ali Abdelhamid.

"*Prefect*" *for the Department of Algiers* (the city of Algiers excepted): Moulay Merbah.

"*Prefect*" *for the Department of Oran:* Zitouni Messaoudi (a member of the Algiers city council).

"*Prefect*" *for the Department of Constantine:* Ahmed Boudaa.

Head of the Clandestine Organization in the Algiers Region: Sid Ali Abdelhamid.

The party's pyramidal structure, patterned after that of the Communist party, provided the summit with a disciplined hierarchy capable of carrying the chain of command without interruption from level to level down to the innumerable cells at the bottom. A system of reporting enabled the high command to keep tabs on the execution of policy and on the results obtained. The party executive committee, organically conceived as a steering group within the larger Central Committee (about forty members), met in Algiers at the end of each month to map policy and to draft directives for use in the *wilayas*, or provinces.† The pro-

* Lahouel was elected to the Algiers city council in October, 1947, but was declared ineligible and deprived of his seat in December of that year. He was born at Philippeville in 1917.

† Compare "vilayet," an Anglicized Turkish word derived from the Arabic *wali*, meaning "governor." A vilayet, in Turkey, is a province.

vincial leaders, all of them salaried party officials, converged on Algiers at the beginning of each month for a meeting with the executive committee. This so-called National Council gave the provincial leaders a chance to turn in their reports and get their marching orders for the month ahead before returning to their various posts. Periodical meetings were a part of the nationalist apparatus at all levels.

As far as is known, the country was divided into five *wilayas*, thirty-three *dairas* (districts), and a hundred-odd *kasmas* (sectors). In each province, the *daira* leaders convened at regular intervals to form the *wilaya* council. So, further down the scale, each *daira* had a council made up of its *kasma* leaders. The salaried official in charge of each *kasma* was assisted by a committee on which sat: 1) a financial officer (known as "R.F.," meaning "*Responsable aux finances*"); 2) an "R.A.L." ("*Responsable aux assemblées locales*") to direct the M.T.L.D. representatives in local government councils; 3) an "R.A.S." ("*Responsable aux affaires syndicales*") to control the party's organized workers in the area; 4) an "R.P.I." ("*Responsable à la propagande-information*") to dispense party literature; 5) an "R.O.L." ("*Responsable à l'organisation locale*") to supervise the local party apparatus in the town; 6) an "R.O.R." ("*Responsable à l'organisation régionale*"), in charge of rural activities. The ramifications of the party in each city and large town were called "quarters," "sections," "groups," and "cells"; these entities, taken together, constituted the "center." Their leaders met as a "Local Organization Committee." The ramifications in the countryside were: "Sectors," "*douars*" (groups of hamlets), "fractions," "*dechras*" (villages), "groups," and "cells." The "*dechras,*" "groups," and "cells" in outlying districts frequently came directly under a *kasma*. The active membership of the party was estimated at upwards of twelve thousand. It was reported in January, 1952, that "Action Groups" had been recruited in Algiers by Sid Ali Abdelhamid, Djillali Reguimi, and Saïd Amrani. Other such groups were said to have come into existence at Boghari, Tlemcen, and Marnia. Persistent rumors spoke of traffic in arms and ammunition along the frontier of Spanish Morocco.

When Messali took to the road on April 15, he headed east. At every stop his people had a huge and excited crowd on hand to cheer the leader, to vibrate with his words, to wax hot with indignation, to vow vengeance, and to enroll under the banner of the star and crescent: 2,000 at Oued Zenati, 2,500 at Souk Ahras, 6,000 at El Arrouch, 2,000 at Philippeville. The effervescence gained in intensity with each passing day until the French authorities got alarmed. They feared the result might easily be a serious breach of the peace. It was decided on April

24 that enough mischief had been done: Messali was apprehended at Philippeville by order of the Governor General and whisked back to Bouzaréa, where it was assumed he would stay put.

Not at all! Too good a start had been made. Messali, surer than ever before of the sanctity of his mission, of its infallible success, set out again, this time south and west. In an atmosphere charged with fervor and emotion, Messali traveled to Boghari, Reibel, Affreville, Blida, Miliana, and Orléansville—party strongholds all. He preached to the convinced; he carried them to a degree of frenzy and hysteria rarely reached. The street was invaded again and again; processions were formed; slogans were shouted. At Blida, 300 demonstrators clashed with police. At Orléansville, a mob of P.P.A. demonstrators, many of them armed with blunt objects, attacked a police cordon and stoned passing cars. The police, hard pressed, opened fire, killing two demonstrators and seriously wounding a third. Six policemen were injured. "This," said the French in effect, "has gone far enough."

Messali's next stop was to have been Mostaganem, where, party organizers boasted, 6,000 followers were ready to pour into the street to welcome the "National Chief." But Messali never got there, for his tour came to an abrupt end on May 14. In a matter of hours, he was declared undesirable in Algeria, put on a plane at Orléansville and sent to Niort in the Deux-Sèvres department of France (near La Rochelle), where he was assigned to live.*

This move caused a tempest in nationalist circles. Messali protested vigorously against the "arbitrary" action taken against him. His followers, as soon as they recovered from their surprise, made a frightful fuss: handbills were issued, motions voted, articles written, and telegrams sent to the United Nations. The Communists joined in and trumpeted their protests. The U.D.M.A. and the Ulema were indignant, too, but perhaps a little more perfunctorily so.

The Messalists, stepping up their campaign, decreed May 23 to be a "day of protest" and summoned the Moslem shopkeepers to close their shops on pain of reprisal, not excluding death. The people were urged in Messalist and Communist handbills to demonstrate in the

---

*Messali's two trips were not all propaganda; collections were taken up at every stop. The party, fully aware that money is the sinews of war, engaged in a relentless drive for funds. Some of the contributions were voluntary; most were exacted. The P.P.A. excise system was based on the protection racket, highly organized and ruthlessly imposed, but other tricks were often resorted to. One was a tax on everything ordered in a café catering, by fiat, to party members.

street "for the release of Messali and against the repression." The "day of protest" was, in most places, a fizzle. Sure enough, the Arab shops were closed in the native sections of Algiers. The stevedores went on strike. A nationalist demonstration had to be broken up in Philippeville. But elsewhere, disturbances were few and activity was normal.

Mr. Abbas, meanwhile, was stumping the country with a message of sweet reasonableness that could interest none but the thinking few. At U.D.M.A. meetings held to commemorate the ninth anniversary of the *Manifesto*, Mr. Abbas recommended non-violence and patience in the pursuit of the nationalist ideal. "Sticks," he said, "are of no avail against guns." Or again: "Force is no solution." He even went so far as to reject complete separation from France, uttering words that, today, would brand him as a traitor: "I still prefer the yoke of French imperialism to that of Algerian imperialism." Only an Algerian republic closely associated with the "great French democracy" could, in his view, open the avenues to a brighter future.

In July, Mr. Abbas rashly decided to contest the seat in the National Assembly left vacant by the death of Dr. Youssef Kessous, independent deputy for Constantine. The hapless Abbas was beaten by the conformist candidate, Amar Naroun, by 115,326 votes to 14,079. He did not yet realize that there could be no "third force" between the centripetal pull of the French Administration and the centrifugal pull of extreme Arab nationalism.

The multiracial state, the working partnership of the Algerian communities, was the undeniable fruit of French rule. Mr. Abbas hoped, no doubt, by infusing his nationalism with social enlightenment, to save the existing partnership and so preserve the country from the dangers that a rupture would entail. His attitude in this respect was commendable but unrealistic, as he has since discovered. Of course, when the crisis came, he opted for Arab, and not for French, imperialism. If taxed with inconsistency, Mr. Abbas would probably reply that the French are to blame for not making concessions in good time to his earlier point of view.

In this he would, I think, be only partly right, for the Abbas card was never strong. If the French had played it, they would at best have delayed the day of reckoning, at worst have secured nothing but the rancor of the Europeans.

It was not to be hoped that Mr. Abbas, in the role of a moderate nationalist leader, could ever rally a force substantial enough to offer the French a lasting settlement in return for concessions. He lacked the essential quality of a national leader—he was not representative. He spoke neither for the inarticulate masses nor for the politically-minded intelligentsia.

The true Arab nationalist, whatever his slogans may be, has no use for equality within a biracial or multiracial system. What he wants is the total benefit of majority status, that is, domination. The Prophet himself set the example. After an early attempt to establish a mixed community at Medina, Mohammed broke with the Jews and ultimately expelled them. He and his Arab followers quickly established themselves as sole masters.

By drawing on the legacy of the emancipation movements of Europe for their slogans and doctrinal pronouncements, the Arab nationalists have created an illusion useful to their cause. They have made their action look like a drive to redress social as well as political wrongs. Many Europeans have been led to conclude that a measure of appeasement could result from social reforms and the granting of equal civil rights. A segregated racial minority—the Negroes in the American South, for instance—will naturally strive for social and political equality. But the Arab nationalists are in a totally different position. Claiming to express the aspirations of the indigenous racial majority, they feel they need no further argument—except force—to establish their right to rule.

It follows that any proposal embodying a concept of shared power —and this is what Mr. Abbas seems to have been talking about—must be rejected by the true nationalist as a form of treason. This also explains the fury with which the nationalists denounced the "neocolonialists"— European advocates of equalitarian reforms.

The ordinary Moslem in Algeria, particularly the older man, does not need to examine conditions in the newly independent Arab states to realize that independence may not be an unmixed blessing. I can testify to his intuitive perspicacity from many friendly talks with Arab neighbors at Bouzaréa, where I lived for two years. Centuries of domination have given the unsophisticated Moslems a kind of wisdom in such matters. Experience tells them that independence is likely to mean only a change of masters unaccompanied by any improvement in the lot of the poor. Their presentiment of what lies ahead goes far, I think, to explain the mass apathy that the rebels never succeeded in vanquishing.

Non-violence has never recommended itself to Algerian Moslems as the right or virile way of settling a dispute. Clans and vendettas in the hills, tribes and raids in the plains—the pattern is as old as the race.

It was, therefore, quite naturally an article of faith in the councils of the P.P.A. that, in the conflict with France, nothing would be final until powder had spoken.

In preparation for the ultimate contest, the P.P.A. had, as we have seen, started to recruit and train a secret army known as the O.S. (*Organisation Spéciale*). It must not be thought that the arrests in 1950 and the subsequent trials had removed the danger. The underground continued to organize and to enlist the support of the professional bandits. A guerrilla band armed with weapons obtained in Spanish Morocco was reported in July, 1952, to have been formed in the Marnia-Nedroma-Nemours-Port Say quadrilateral in the mountainous northwestern corner of the country. In the Aurès mountains to the east, lawlessness was increasing. A shooting that cost two inhabitants of Ghassira village their lives on May 13 was found to be the work of three bandits armed with army rifles. The French authorities were convinced that at least twenty armed outlaws in the mountains–bandits, deserters, and fugitives from justice–were in league with the P.P.A., among them Hocine Berail, Lakhdar Zelmat, Mekki Aïssi, Saddok Chebchoub, Belkacem Grine, and Messaoud Maache.* Their raids were, as the occasion warranted, personal or political ventures. They served the P.P.A. by collecting "imposts" and inflicting "fines." On June 7, a village headman named Tahar Beloukil was killed in the Khenchela district by Messaoud Maache–in execution, it was said, of a death sentence passed by a bandit conclave. Beloukil had testified in a French court against one of the perpetrators of the bus holdup between Arris and Khenchela on February 12, 1951.† In September, 1952, Berail, Chebchoub, and Maache were, it was learned, in the coastal area near Djidjelli organizing a guerrilla unit there. But those who stayed behind –Grine, Aïssi, and Lakhdar Zelmat–consolidated zones of influence in the Ichmoul, Ouled Labiod, and Zellatou districts. Aïssi, however, was killed by a French security force in November.

In 1953, a batch of secret P.P.A. documents fell into French hands. The haul was an unusually good one, for it included the "General Directives" sent each month to the chiefs of *wilaya* from November, 1951, to December, 1952, and, in addition, three reports from the Constantine *wilaya*–documents so secret that their recpients were supposed to burn them as quickly as possible.

---

*Not to be confused with Messaoud Zelmat and other "bandits of honor" who refused to corrupt their profession with politics–but whose position was none too secure. Messaoud Zelmat himself was "liquidated" by rivals in May, 1954.

† See. p. 59.

The P.P.A. documents reveal nothing but scorn for the U.D.M.A., the Ulema,* and the "reformists" in general. "Reformism" was described in one of the "Directives" as a Hydra-headed evil that could never be completely eliminated. It was pointed out that the U.D.M.A. and the Ulema, if destroyed, would soon reappear, different in name, perhaps, but the same in essence, for the corrupt spirit of "reformism" never died. The P.P.A. executive, therefore, concluded that past efforts to combat the U.D.M.A. and the Ulema had been a mistake and that accommodation was the better policy. The orders issued in consequence of this declaration were: "Involve the reformist parties with us in every way for as long a time as possible." It was anticipated that the new tactic would increase the "fighting potential of the Algerian people." The P.P.A. hoped also to better its chances of proselytizing among the "reformists" and, in any case, to avoid the danger of rapprochement between the "reformists" and the Administration. The principal instrument of the P.P.A.'s smiling campaign was, of course, the *Front Algérien pour la Défense et le Respect de la Liberté* formed in August, 1951.†

But the P.P.A.'s position as a member of the "Front" was complicated by the fact that one of its partners there, the Algerian Communist party (P.C.A.), was also a revolutionary party using lamb's clothing for a similar purpose. Obviously, great care would have to be exercised at every turn. The P.C.A., with powerful organs of propaganda at its disposal (notably the daily, *Alger Républicain*), could not be treated with disdain. The problem, made clear by the P.P.A. high command in various warnings and recommendations, was to take what help could safely be accepted and to reject the rest. The P.C.A., presented as "the party's only dangerous rival," was to be "isolated" within the "Front," and lesser party officials were advised to be watchful against Communist efforts to outflank the P.P.A. by mass action at the bottom of the social scale.

Indeed, the "Directives" showed to what extreme lengths the P.P.A. was prepared to go to retain the initiative, to establish a monopoly of agitation, at the lowest level. They were perfectly explicit: the street was to belong to the P.P.A. Consequently, the forward echelons, in preparing the masses for the struggle against "repression," would be expected to organize demonstrations against the legal authority when-

---

* It was recognized, however, that the Ulema had set an example to be followed by establishing *medersas* (Koranic schools) all over the country and that the P.P.A. had a long way to go before its educational effort could be called competitive. The P.P.A. is thought to have had about fifteen Koranic schools of its own at the time.

† See pp. 64–65.

ever possible and at all other times to keep the party's objectives before the people by disseminating slogans and by exploiting instances of injustice. "Interventions," "reactions," and "demonstrations," each adapted to the circumstances of the moment, were to be controlled with "vigilance and *sang-froid*"; "excesses" were to be avoided.

This, judging from a candid report sent up by the Constantine *wilaya* in September, 1952, was easier said than done. "The masses follow when our militants set the example," the report said, "but tend to lose their heads, especially in the presence of rural elements. Our people are not yet able to control a demonstration, particularly in the cities. At Bône, for instance, the demonstrators got out of hand and began throwing diverse projectiles (chairs, stones). Our people, too, rather forgot themselves in the course of the demonstration."

The main conclusions to be drawn from an analysis of the "Directives" are:

1. The party's determination to achieve full independence for Algeria led it systematically to take advantage of every possible chance to stir up trouble for the French.
2. The P.P.A., though its primary effort was directed toward the Moslem masses, sought in a multitude of ways to win certain specific groups—civil servants, students, women, and even children—to its revolutionary doctrine. Much of its propaganda was therefore slanted to have special rather than universal appeal.
3. The internal organization of the party was improving all the time in obedience to Messali's dictum: "If I were a teacher and the Algerian people my pupil, I would have him conjugate the verb 'to organize' every day." Iron discipline was the goal sought by the party executive, whose directives became more precise as the months went by. Inspections and sanctions were frequent.
4. A parallel effort was made to improve party leadership. The educational circulars prepared for this purpose were often well thought-out and well presented.
5. The formulation of policy was the exclusive prerogative of the *Comité Directeur*, whose deliberations were secret and whose decisions were cynically made in the light of immediate contingencies. The subordinate leaders and the rank and file had only to listen and obey. The system, taken from the Communist party, permitted sudden switches in policy without danger of disconcerting the membership.
6. The Messalists, imitating the Communists in another respect, allowed many of their activities to be conducted by front organiza-

tions. The most important of these were the *Scouts Musulmans Algériens* (boy scouts), the *Association des Femmes Musulmanes d'Algérie* (women), the *Union Générale des Etudiants Musulmans Algériens* (students), and the *Comité de Soutien aux Victimes de la Répression*, but the full list included religious societies, social clubs, school committees, sporting associations, and groups of organized unemployed.

7. The P.P.A. underground was merely secret. But there was also a supersecret network of activists whose names never appeared on any document. Some were intellectuals consulted on matters of doctrine and policy; others were party couriers and inspectors; still others were spies assigned to rival parties and to the French Administration.
8. Though the effort was impressive, the results were meager. The rank and file* was, on the whole, poorly led by petty agitators often wanting in experience, ability, and even in zeal. The rural Moslem population—76 per cent of the whole—remained largely impervious to nationalist indoctrination; the *fellahin* could be stirred to sudden outbursts of fanaticism but could not be organized for political action.

In October, 1952, Ahmed Mezerna and Ahmed Boudaa, on a party mission to Egypt, dismissed Chadly Mekki, the man Messali had praised so highly only eight months before, and appointed Mohammed Khider to be P.P.A. representative in Cairo.† It was alleged that Mekki had pocketed Arab League funds made available to the party and that he had served the cause of King Farouk, lately deposed (in July, 1952). Mekki, denying all charges with high indignation, refused to take his dismissal lying down. He set up an office of his own called the "Middle East Algerian Bureau" and conducted business there as though he were

* The membership was divided into three classes: "Militants" (dues: 100 francs a month), "Members" (dues: 50 to 100 francs a month), and "Sympathizers." A distinction was later made between "organized" and "contributing" sympathizers. Party members of eighteen years or more were admitted as "Militants" only after a period of probation by which could be tested their ability to submit to party discipline. By 1953, the estimated membership (all classes) had reached 24,000 in Algeria and 6,800 in France.

† The "Algerian delegation" in Cairo also included Hocine Aït Ahmed and Mohammed Ben Bella. Khider and Ben Bella were soon heard making violently anti-French speeches on Cairo radio's "Voice of the Arabs" program. They were rivaled in the use of intemperate language by Aït Ahmed, who, under the name of Saïd Ferhi, carried the party's message to such distant lands as Burma and Indonesia before coming back to roost in Cairo.

still the uncontested representative of the Algerian nationalist movement, although it was not quite clear where his operating revenues came from.

The municipal elections in April, 1953, were a full-scale political grab bag—3,012 second-college seats to be had—the last before the outbreak of the rebellion. In the first college, the Communists maintained their voting strength but lost the two city councils they had still controlled (Sidi Bel Abbès and Ténès). In the second college, the secessionist candidates (nationalists and Communists) were for the most part badly trampled upon, although they scored heavily in Algiers. Their popular vote was 35 per cent of the total as against 62 per cent in 1947. In Algiers, however, the secessionist candidates won 93.8 per cent of the votes cast (turnout: 52 per cent), the local results there being:

M.T.L.D.	63.5 per cent (4,852 votes)
U.D.M.A.–P.C.A. (joint ticket)	30.3 per cent (2,313 votes)
Others	6.2 per cent (476 votes)

The picture in the country as a whole was quite different, as will be seen from the following table:

Turnout: 70.48 per cent (58.96 per cent in 1947)

Parties	*Percentage of Popular Vote*		*Seats Won (1953)*	*Percentage of Total*	*Losses and Gains*
	1947	*1953*			
M.T.L.D.	31	19	408	13.5	Loss of: 14,272 votes 502 seats
U.D.M.A.	27	12	289	9.5	Loss of: 20,832 votes 275 seats
P.C.A.	4	4	49	1.6	Gain of: 545 votes Loss of: 57 seats
Total Secessionist	62	35	746	24.6	Loss of: 34,559 votes 834 seats
Others	38	65	2,266	75.4	

The elections were orderly everywhere but in Oran, where M.T.L.D. and P.C.A. troublemakers had to be ejected from a polling station. The incident, frantically played up by the Messalists, led to intense agitation that irrupted into open rioting on May 3. It was the usual thing—police attacked, cars stoned, buildings damaged—but for once the police, heavily reinforced, managed to contain the mob without the use of firearms. However, the box score at the end of the day was: forty demonstrators and 100 other civilians injured; seventy policemen, forty-three Republican Guards, and thirty-eight gendarmes wounded; ninety-seven demonstrators arrested and fifty-three held for trial (forty-three were later convicted and given short prison terms).

The nationalist agitation spread to France in July, the M.T.L.D. having instructed its French "Federation" to bring out the Algerian laborers on Bastille Day. The Algerians, pitifully gullible, appeared with their banners, marched defiantly in the Communist parade, and ran headlong into a police cordon as the demonstration was breaking up.* Six Arabs were killed and many more were injured. The Communists and the Messalists were, of course, quick to make what political capital they could of the day's tragic events, but the P.C.A. was the first to organize a "Committee for the Defense of the Victims of the July 14 Fusillade." The Communist committee and nationalist delegations were waiting on the dock when the bodies of four of the victims were disembarked at Algiers on July 25. Diligent hands draped the coffins in green and white with the red star and crescent showing on top so that the martyred four could be borne by Moslem boy scouts in uniform to a mortuary chapel, where, in response to their parties' call, some 2,500 Moslems filed silently past.

New statutes adopted by the M.T.L.D. at its second congress in April, 1953, reconciled theory with practice by giving written sanction to the total merger of the M.T.L.D. and the P.P.A. (*Parti du Peuple Algérien*). If there has been any confusion in the reader's mind as to the exact relationship between the two, it is suggested he compare the whole Messalist structure to an iceberg. A small part of its bulk emerged; this was the M.T.L.D., an entity seen and recognized. The rest, below the surface

---

* It would, however, be a mistake to exaggerate the strength of the M.T.L.D. organization in France. It was by no means able to muster the bulk of the Algerian labor force in the Paris area, estimated at the time to number 132,000 men. Three thousand of these clashed with the police in the Place de la Nation on the evening of July 14, 1953; the rest stayed home.

and mostly out of sight, was the P.P.A., the clandestine party machine. The M.T.L.D. was, therefore, not at all the "movement" it purported to be but rather the legal façade of a revolutionary party conceived in the best bolshevik tradition. Messali took over as president of both branches of the organization in 1953. Previously, he had been president of the P.P.A. and honorary president of the M.T.L.D., the titular president of the latter having been Ahmed Mezerna. Hocine Lahouel stayed on as secretary-general. It will be seen, however, that the family circle was by no means united.

The year 1953 also saw the beginning of a long but star-crossed love affair between the M.T.L.D. and the International Confederation of Free Trade Unions (I.C.F.T.U.). The object of their overtures was to start a Moslem labor movement in Algeria on a mutually advantageous basis: the M.T.L.D. would use the new organization for purely political purposes but would, in return for I.C.F.T.U. approval and support, take an anti-Communist line and swing the Algerian workers into the I.C.F.T.U. orbit. The scheme, propounded, apparently, by Abderrahmane Kiouane of the party executive committee, recommended itself at once as eminently desirable. The M.T.L.D. was, despite a measure of success, tired of trying to compete with the Communists for control of the Algerian branch of the French General Confederation of Labor (C.G.T.). The party was fully aware that the positions held by the Communist labor leaders could be undermined but never completely destroyed by boring from within; too many strings were pulled from above by French Communists whose influence was felt among the numerous European members of the local unions in Algeria. It was realized, too, that if the Algerian C.G.T. could be stripped of its Moslem membership, the Communist labor leaders would be left with a millstone round their necks, for they would then no longer be able to pose as a nationalist force. To put the Communists in this predicament, the M.T.L.D. was quite prepared to forget its policy of friendly cooperation and to take out a mortgage with "American imperialism" (as the Communists said).

The leaders of the I.C.F.T.U., particularly Irving Brown, European representative of the American Federation of Labor, rejoiced at the thought of such a triumph. It mattered little to them that the maneuver was strictly political and had nothing whatever to do with the advancement of trade unionism. All previous objections to racial separation were forgotten. The tentative beginnings of a multiracial trade union movement in Algeria under French Socialist auspices weighed no more in the balance than doubts as to the wisdom of pitting Moslem workers against their European employers in the context of a nationalist struggle that could end in economic ruin for both. Only one consideration counted: the discomfiture of the Communists, of the hated rival, the World Trade Union Federation (to which the C.G.T. belonged). And what a prize: the Algerian workers for the free world! The nationalist trade-union movement in Tunisia had long since been brought under the wing of the I.C.F.T.U., and the trick was about to be turned in Morocco. But Algeria, the biggest of the three, would have to be brought in, too, if victory was to be complete. However, the negotiations begun in 1953 never came to successful issue. The I.C.F.T.U., as we shall see, later ditched the Messalists as "non-representative" and did business with another lot.

I remember calling on Mr. Brown one day in July, 1954, at his Paris office. He was just back from Tunisia, where he had lavished encouragement on the local nationalists in the name of the American workers and of the I.C.F.T.U. "I have come here," he had told a meeting of the *Union Générale Tunisienne du Travail* on July 2, "fully conscious of the struggle in progress in the world today, not only to bring you the greetings of my organization, but also to assure you of the total solidarity of the American labor movement in your struggle to raise the living standard of the masses of your country and finally to achieve your objectives—national freedom and independence."

I asked Mr. Brown who would employ the Tunisian workers when his friends down there had thrown the French employers out of the country. He turned the question by stating that if the free world (meaning essentially the I.C.F.T.U.) failed to support the resurgent nationalisms in Africa, the Soviets would soon win over the still uncommitted peoples on that continent. When I asked how he expected economic collapse to constitute an effective rampart against the spread of Communism, he challenged the premise, stating that I was too pessimistic. He pooh-poohed the idea that the Tunisian *Syndicat des Chômeurs* (Union of Unemployed) would ultimately, as I suggested, become the largest in the country. Yet more than four years have passed, Tunisia is now independent, and the army of unemployed there has increased from some 350,000 to almost 500,000, or about one-third of the active male population.

In July, 1957, Mr. Brown was back in Tunis for the I.C.F.T.U. Fifth World Congress. The people were hungry; one man in three was out of work. Mr. Brown was bursting with satisfaction because his side was in and the Communists were out. But at what price? And for how long?

The first anniversary of the Egyptian *coup d'état* found Ferhat Abbas in Cairo at the head of a U.D.M.A. delegation officially invited by the Egyptian Government. The Egyptians were, naturally enough, eager to hear about the situation in Algeria as Mr. Abbas saw it, but only confused and embarrassed explanations were forthcoming. In his first statement, Mr. Abbas said that, although he would welcome United Nations action to hasten the emancipation of his country, the future Algerian republic, a nation of Moslems and Europeans living in fraternal union, could not join the Arab League; the country's special nature would necessarily keep it somewhat apart.

These remarks, hardly pleasing to Egyptian ears, quickly required amplification, if not correction. "The Algerians live like aliens in their own land," Mr. Abbas was soon telling the Cairo newspaper *El Balagh*. "France prevents them from sending their sons to be educated in the Arab countries and refuses to admit missions of El Azhar to North Africa. Our primary object is the liberation of our country."

Other voices were raised in the East that summer to anathematize the French for their conduct in Morocco. The Arab world reacted as though its vitals had suffered injury when, on August 20, 1953, General Augustin Guillaume, French Resident General in Morocco, banished the nationalist-minded Sultan, Sidi Mohammed Ben Youssef, and allowed a coalition of *caïds* led by Si Thami el-Glaoui, Pasha of Marrakech, to hoist the gentle, doddering Sidi Mohammed Ben Moulay Arafa upon the Sherifian throne. "France is the enemy of Islam," cried Khader Hussein, Tunisian rector of El Azhar. General Mohammed Naguib, President of Egypt, draped in unsewn sheets (for he was a pilgrim), stood on the sacred hill of Arafat near Mecca and implored God to avenge Morocco.

The U.D.M.A.–Ulema representatives in Cairo, meanwhile, had joined with the representatives of minority nationalist groups in Tunisia and Morocco to form a "North African Liberation Committee" in competition with the Maghrib Office.* Abd-el-Krim, the truculent old *rogui* (insurgent pretender) of the Riff war, having broken with the "upstarts" of the Maghrib Office, gave his blessing to the new committee. But that was not enough to save it from early oblivion, for it was only one in a series of shifting alliances and realignments among the

---

* The minority group in Morocco was the Democratic Independence party (P.D.I.) headed by Mohammed Hassan Ouezzani. In Tunisia, it was the Old Destour headed by Salah Ferhat. The Moroccan Istiqlal party headed by Allal el-Fassi (then in Cairo) and the Tunisian Neo-Destour party headed by Habib Bourguiba (then in detention on the Ile de la Galite off the northern coast of Tunis) were partners of the M.T.L.D. in the Maghrib Office.

North African exiles in Cairo. The titular members of the committee were:

For Morocco: Mohammed Hassan Ouezzani, Ahmed Bensouda, Mohammed Cherkaoui;
For Algeria: Ahmed Ahmed-Bioud, Mohammed Larbi Boudjemline;
For Tunisia: Mahieddine Klibi.

In October, a bitter incident at Nedroma* near the Moroccan frontier, 122 miles southwest of Oran, showed how effective P.P.A. tactics could sometimes be. It began with a vendor selling copies of the M.T.L.D. organ, *L'Algérie Libre,* in the Nedroma market place. A policeman sent to arrest the interloper found himself caught in the midst of a hostile gathering. Reinforcements were instantly dispatched, but the small French force was thrown back by a crowd of about 300 natives armed with knives and clubs. The civil administrator leapt into the fray, only to be struck on the head with a bludgeon. A customs inspector and a policeman, clubbed and stabbed, were picked up in a seriously wounded condition. One of the demonstrators suffered a bullet wound of which he died the following day. After an hour or two of tumult and confusion in front of the civil administrator's office —the windows of which were smashed—the crowd dispersed. Thirty-six ringleaders were later arrested, tried, and sent to prison for terms of from one to four years, a circumstance that enabled the M.T.L.D. to denounce a "new colonialist crime."

The P.C.A., meanwhile, having hit on the idea of a "National Democratic Front" in Algeria, kept harping away on it indefatigably. The party's Central Committee ended a session on November 1, 1953, with a "solemn appeal" for united action by all "anticolonialist" Algerians to achieve such "minimum" objectives as: a general amnesty, the defense of civil liberties, social and economic betterment, more schools, the recognition of Arabic as an official language, withdrawal from the Atlantic Pact, and the maintenance of peace. The appeal, penned, no doubt, by Larbi Bouhali, secretary of the P.C.A., also called for agreement on "higher aims," notably on the "prospect of a democratic Algerian republic . . . and of an assembly truly representative of the Algerian people."

Nobody fell into Mr. Bouhali's trap, although the M.T.L.D. paid

* Nedroma, once a fortified native city, lies in the heart of the mountainous district from which sprang the Almohade dynasty. Abd el-Moumin, the Almohade conqueror of Morocco and Spain in the twelfth century, was born into a Berber tribe known as the Koumia, then in control of the area.

tribute to it in a way by proposing a similar scheme. The party executive issued an "appeal" of its own on December 11, not for a "National Democratic Front," but for a "National Algerian Congress," conceived as a sort of embryo constituent assembly to which the nationalist parties, social and cultural groups, and trade guilds would send their delegates. It was thought that "independent personalities" should also take part in the deliberations of the forthcoming "Congress." The plan was not followed up, however, and I suspect it was not even meant to be. The P.P.A. was preparing for other work ahead, for the kind of "direct action" that brings results.

An election was held on January 31, 1954—with a runoff ballot on February 7—to fill fifty-nine vacated seats in the Algerian Assembly, those assigned to the even-numbered constituencies. The M.T.L.D. announced early in the game that, as in 1951, it would put up no candidates. Orders sent down the line from party headquarters were: "Stay away from the polls." The party, it was officially explained, was guided by a desire to do nothing that might sully the aims or prejudice the success of the contemplated "National Algerian Congress." Actually, the Algerian Assembly no longer had much bearing on the tasks in store for the party and was considered a waste of time. The U.D.M.A., on the other hand, hoping perhaps to take up some of the slack left by the M.T.L.D., had candidates running in seven second-college constituencies, and the P.C.A. had candidates in all thirty.*

The M.T.L.D., by its abstention, forfeited its four seats† and disappeared from the Assembly. The U.D.M.A., to the surprise of all, made no headway. Two outgoing U.D.M.A. candidates—Ferhat Abbas and Ahmed Francis—were re-elected; the third, Dr. Abdesselam Benkhelil, was beaten at Batna; but the success of another U.D.M.A. candidate, Chérif Bouyoussef, at Mila, compensated for the loss. Thus, although the U.D.M.A. got 43,443 fewer votes than in 1951, it still held five seats. In the previous session, the U.D.M.A. delegates, abandoning their attitude of systematic opposition, had cooperated loyally with the majority whenever their basic principles were not at stake. Their courtesy, greatly appreciated in the Assembly, was poorly requited at the polls. In truth, Mr. Abbas, flanked as he was by the moderates on one

* For all the good it did them: every Communist candidate in the second college was defeated. In the first college, however, René Justrabo, former Communist mayor of Sidi Bel Abbès, was re-elected.

† The outgoing M.T.L.D. delegates were Ahmed Boudaa (Maison Carrée), Larbi Demaghlatrous (El Milia), M'Barek Djilani (Mila), and Mostefa Ferroukhi (Miliana).

side and the M.T.L.D. on the other, had little room in which to maneuver.

The M.T.L.D. boycott was very telling in some constituencies, less so in others. The total turnout—61 per cent—although substantially below the 1948 mark (70 per cent), compared well enough with that of more recent years. At Mila, however, only 28 per cent of the registered second-college voters cast ballots. The figure was 37 per cent at Tizi Ouzou and 39 per cent at El Milia and Maison Carrée. The consolation, for the Europeans, was an Assembly that could best be described as eminently manageable: its make-up, as regards the second college at least, had changed for the better:

	1948		*1951*		*1954*	
	%	*Seats*	%	*Seats*	%	*Seats*
M.T.L.D.	30	9*	0.7	4	0	0
U.D.M.A.	18	8	11.0	5	5	5
P.C.A.	2	0	4.3	0	1.3	0
Others	50	43	84.0	51†	93.7	55‡

* Including one lost later by the arrest of the incumbent.

† Including one seat held by a Socialist and two seats held by Popular Republicans.

‡ Including one seat held by a Socialist and three seats held by Popular Republicans.

14. DIVISION IN THE RANKS

In February, 1954, a fissure appeared in the monolithic façade of the M.T.L.D.–P.P.A. The party had been torn by dissension before, but this time the cleavage was deep enough to rip it asunder.

Messali Hadj, brooding at Niort on his own and on his country's plight, seethed with rage to hear how the party executive under Hocine

Lahouel still countenanced truckling to the French in Algeria. The thought of Kiouane, Abdelhamid, and others on the Algiers city council voting at M. Chevallier's call rankled and festered until he could bear it no more. He knew, too, that the Lahouel group was scheming against him and would, at the first opportunity, stamp him a "dictator" and divest him of all power.

But cooped up as he was in a remote corner of the French provinces, he could not easily reassert his authority. He was unable to reach out and fetch back the sheep that had strayed into the green but poisoned pastures of French colonialism, unable to crack down on the derelict shepherds. In his impotence, he could only gather his disciples about him—Ahmed Mezerna, Moulay Merbah, Abdelli Aïssa—appoint *missi dominici,* and commit his fate to their devotion. This he did. The *missi* went forth, their first task being to alert the faithful in France and Algeria to the dangers to which the Lahouel group had exposed the party. If necessary, they were to set up "public safety committees" ready and willing to seize power by force in Messali's name.

The outlook for Messali did not seem hopeless. He could count on the almost unanimous support of the M.T.L.D. Federation in France. And even in Algeria, the men in control of the party machine were powerless to destroy, and therefore bound to consider, the veneration in which Messali was held by a multitude of followers everywhere.

In preparation for the impending showdown, Mr. Lahouel and his friends on the Central Committee—Abderrahmane Kiouane, Benyoussef Benkhedda, Ahmed Boudaa (treasurer), Mostefa Ferroukhi, M'Barek Djilani, Ali Abdelhamid, Larbi Demaghlatrous, and Mohammed Yazid—took the precaution of putting the party funds under lock and key, along with the assets of the *Comité de Soutien aux Victimes de la Répression* (C.S.V.R.) and of the party print shop. The deeds to the premises occupied by the party were also duly sequestered. The party organs, *L'Algérie Libre* and *Saout el Djezaïr* ("Voice of Algeria"), remained at Mr. Lahouel's disposal, and although Messali was not attacked outright in the party press, the attentive reader could easily detect an undertone of hostility and disparagement.

In March, Messali dipped his pen in vitriol and issued a "Message from the National Chief to the Militants of the Algerian National Movement" in France. "Warning!" the message said. "In my capacity as chief of the party, answerable to God, to you, and to my conscience, . . . I must tell you that our movement is going through a crisis." In the long diatribe that followed, Messali spoke of his past efforts to keep the revolutionary ideal alive, of the "sloth and dishonesty" that nevertheless had permeated the party, and of the "policy of ease and compromise" that had been followed. He said the rank and file could not understand why the party had failed to denounce French crimes in Tunisia and Morocco. Referring to the death of six Algerian demonstrators on July 14, 1953, he deplored the negligence that had made it possible for another party to "exploit the blood of patriots." He railed at the party "bureaucracy" for "haggling over seats and flap-seats" in the councils of government and reviled it for proposing a "National Algerian Congress" after the dismal failure of the *Front Algérien pour la Défense et le Respect de la Liberté.*

He denounced attempts to "lead the movement into the path of compromise and concessions to reformism." "I have been compelled to deprive the party executive committee of my confidence," he declared. "In spite of that, the executive committee . . . clings to its privileges." In these circumstances, he said, the Federation in France would be put under a "Committee of Public Safety" pending the election of a new executive committee by a "congress that we shall convene." "The colonialist budget of the city of Algiers has been voted by our representatives," he wrote, almost beside himself with indignation. "Lawyer Kiouane made a speech . . ., declaring that a new era of understanding had dawned at the Algiers City Hall. This seems unbelievable . . . I have taken a stand against this policy of surrender and disavowal . . . I appeal to the people . . . Your absent chief bids you, FORWARD!"

For a moment, at the end of March, it looked as though a settlement might be in sight—to Messali's advantage. On March 27, the Central Committee convened in emergency session to examine all outstanding differences. The meeting, at which Ahmed Mezerna spoke for Messali, ended in compromise the following day. It was agreed that an extraordinary congress would be held in July. But where? This question—an important one because Messali, invincible in France, could more easily be countered in Algeria—was left undecided. However, Lahouel and his committee consented to withdraw pending action by the congress. In the meantime, Messali would be allotted five million francs (about $14,000) plus current income to cover operating expenses. The agreement stipulated that the rest of the party's reserves (thought to exceed thirty million francs or about $85,000) would be placed in the custody of a treasurer appointed by the committee.

On the face of it, Messali had little ground for complaint. The terms of the agreement were, on the whole, favorable to him. Yet he appears to have suspected his former companions of evil designs. At all events, on April 3 he issued a "Message from the National Chief, Messali Hadj, to the Algerian People." In it, he denounced the party "bureaucracy" for its "plotting" and summoned those among the subordinate leaders who until then had refrained from taking sides to make available to him the funds in their possession.

It must be recorded that, despite their ostensible withdrawal, Lahouel and his friends were far from admitting defeat. They put a spoke in Messali's wheel whenever they could, and the opportunities were many. Their first move was to sabotage the new arrangements by bringing the party machine to a virtual standstill. Salaried party officials were given three months' pay in advance and told to suspend all further activity. The campaign of disparagement, given new impetus, did much to accredit the notion that Messali was a "played-out old man," a "pleasure-seeker," and a "blunderer." A mimeographed bulletin called "The Voice of the Militant" described Mezerna as a "blind and unscrupulous climber."

The protagonists were thus wholly engaged in their squabble when, without any warning, a voice out of nowhere cried, "Halt!" The voice, that of a mysterious group calling itself the "Revolutionary Committee for Unity and Action" (C.R.U.A.), took the form of a mimeographed "proclamation," which said in essence:

> Faced with the present crisis, a group of party leaders, men of integrity in no way responsible for the present conflict, has decided to act with a view to saving the party from destruction. This stand means that you must join with us to preserve the unity of the party, to call a sovereign congress into being, and to make our party a truly effective revolutionary instrument, one that will, in association with the brother parties of Morocco and Tunisia, hasten the destruction of French colonialism. We call on all leaders and militants to rally round our committee, which must compel the two factions to come before it and to explain their conduct. Meanwhile, the Committee will undertake to enlighten our brethren by means of a party bulletin, *The Patriot*. It will take measures to see that all traitors are exposed and punished. Help us save our party from anarchy and inaction. Down with those who seek to divide and to sow the seeds of hatred!

Soon afterwards the first issue of *The Algerian Patriot* appeared, an unsigned, mimeographed sheet. It was learned that the C.R.U.A. had been formed at the instance of Mohammed Boudiaf, Mohammed Ben Bella, Ahmed Mahsas, Mohammed Khider, and others who, after having organized the old O.S., had fled to Cairo to avoid arrest. These men, it was said, had followed political developments in Algeria from afar with dismay and disgust and had, in addition, suffered the bitter remonstrances of the Cairo regime. Little else was known of the C.R.U.A. except that it was directed by a "committee of four" (Mohammed Boudiaf, Mohammed Larbi Ben M'Hidi,* Mourad Didouche,† and Rabah Bitat‡). Who could have foreseen then that, before the year was out, this obscure committee, apparently bent only on healing the party's wounds, would have succeeded in thrusting both factions aside and in plunging Algeria into civil war?

Not the intriguing Lahouel, surely, nor his friends. But Lahouel, who felt painfully insecure as the fateful day of the "extraordinary congress" approached, was quick to guess what use might be made of the C.R.U.A. to improve his own prospects. For one thing, he could no longer be called supine with the manly C.R.U.A. behind him. It was conceivable, too, that the alliance, if effective, could help him muster a majority at the forthcoming congress. To this end, Lahouel secretly sought to ingratiate himself with the C.R.U.A., helping out with a mimeograph machine, lists of party members and possibly even with funds. Lahouel was pleased to observe that, at the behest of the C.R.U.A., a number of *kasma* leaders had decided not to make their funds available to Messali and his aides.

The second and third issues of *The Patriot* appeared in May, and although its demand was still for action to convene a "truly representative and democratic congress," it was evident that the C.R.U.A., discouraged by the persistence of the conflict, was beginning to think in terms of simply taking over from the P.P.A.

But the factions paid no heed and went on quarreling. Messrs. Lahouel, Kiouane, and Yazid, in a statement, demanded a congress "giving adequate protection to the Central Committee." The statement was followed by a "declaration" in which the committee announced that it had met on May 22 and 23 and still claimed to be the "sole sovereign body" within the party until relieved of its mandate by the congress. It accused the temporary executive under Messali of "misuse of authority."

Messali reacted by impeaching the committee. He charged that it had held an illegal meeting and had "paralyzed the activities of the party." He ranted against its "acts of insubordination, discord, and factiousness" and summoned its members to appear before the coming

---

* Arrested by the French on February 23, 1957; committed suicide on March 3, 1957.

† Killed in combat in January, 1955.

‡ Arrested by the French on March 22, 1955.

congress to answer for their "deviation." In the meantime, the committee was directed to turn all the party's assets over to the temporary executive headed by Moulay Merbah so that the congress could be called into session without delay.

But Messali did not make the congress subject to the committee's will and pleasure in any way. Instead, he convened it himself and on his own terms. Time, place, and order of business were laid down from Niort. The procedure was a little highhanded even for Messali; it did not bring him luck. His congress, held from July 14 to 16 in the Star Cinema at Hornu, Belgium, across the border from Valenciennes, and attended by 150 delegates who had traveled there in greatest secrecy, was, by all accounts, a strange affair. For three days the delegates were kept in their seats; nobody was allowed to leave the hall while the ponderously regulated wheels of excommunication were in motion. For the congress had but one purpose: to put Lahouel and his confederates beyond the pale. The accused were absent; their case was not heard. The views of the C.R.U.A. and of the Cairo group were, likewise, neither sought nor given. The meeting in the Star Cinema was, indeed, a sort of Star Chamber.

A long report prepared by Messali in his usual style was read at the outset. In it, Messali inveighed against the Lahouel group, which, he said, had "led the party to M. Jacques Chevallier's feet." Messrs. Boudaa, Yazid, Benkhedda, Abdelhamid, and Kiouane were singled out as particularly unworthy types. These, according to Messali, were men who acted as though some good were possible under colonial rule, a belief contrary to the true doctrine of the party, one that could only lead to repeated disillusion and ultimately to prison. Genuine institutional reform, Messali insisted, could be undertaken only by a national Algerian government. He condemned "corruption" as the first step in the path of "deviation"; he denounced the "neutralists" of the C.R.U.A. and their works; he called for measures to "internationalize" the Algerian problem; he denounced the "bankrupt" policy pursued by the party "bureaucracy" and at the end asked the "whole Algerian National Movement" for a vote of confidence in himself.

Satisfaction on all scores was instantly forthcoming. The congress adopted (with four dissenting votes) a motion of confidence and a resolution providing for:

1. The plenary rehabilitation of all expelled "militants";
2. The dissolution of the Central Committee;
3. The recovery, by force if necessary, of party assets held by the opposition;

4. Action to support the nationalist struggle in Tunisia and Morocco, including an immediate public protest and a message to the United Nations;
5. The adoption of an active and revolutionary policy based on the principles of the P.P.A. underground (but without immediate recourse to force and violence).

Before ending its session, the congress heard a final message from Messali and charged four emissaries with the task of conveying to Niort the results of its labors.

Messali's success was more apparent than real. The congress had been that of a mere faction; it did not restore the party's lost unity, but rather aggravated its divisions. The Messalists went home firmly convinced, no doubt, that they were the custodians of the party's true tradition and the architects of its triumph to come. However, their congress had not disarmed the opposition, which still held, in addition to the party's physical assets, a flattering opinion of itself. Indeed, the Algiers committee heaped as much contempt on Messali after the congress as before, taxing him with muddleheadedness, incompetence, conceit, primitive thinking, and factionalism. Certainly, if the roll could have been called, the force of numbers would have favored Messali's cause, for his name was a symbol and a magnet. But a roll call was out of the question.* Messali himself had fashioned the party on hierarchical and totalitarian lines and could not, therefore, with others in control of the party machine, obtain a democratically expressed mandate from the membership at large.

Nevertheless, wielding the power now theoretically vested in him as "life president" of the M.T.L.D., Messali fulminated a bull of exclusion against Lahouel, Benkhedda, Ferroukhi, Yazid, Boudaa, and Mohammed Salah Louanchi† and pronounced the Central Committee dissolved. Kiouane and the other M.T.L.D. members of the Algiers city council were summoned to swear allegiance to the new party leadership or follow Lahouel into disgrace. Mezerna, accompanied by Saïd Boudjeroudi (a "good" member of the Algiers city council), managed to wrest from Lahouel's grip the premises occupied by the party in Algiers, including the print shop, and to recover two party motorcars, but that was all: the funds remained in Lahouel's possession. The good work

* Except in France, where Kaoua Moussa, one of Messali's chief lieutenants, had the M.T.L.D. Federation well in hand.

† Formerly an official of the *Scouts Musulmans Algériens*, Louanchi was later to become head of the rebel organization in France. He was arrested by the French on February 28, 1957.

prompted Moulay Merbah, whose new title was secretary-general of the M.T.L.D., to state that the crisis was "virtually over."

Later, in a statement to *Le Monde,* Merbah hazarded a look into the future. "It is evident," he said, "that the settlement of the crisis must put an end to the immobility that was one of the causes of the breach. This means that the party will henceforth return to the principles of struggle that have guided it from the start. . . . As in the past, it will struggle with dignity to win its demands without forgetting for a single instant or prejudicing its primary objective: the independence of Algeria." Messali, it was recalled in this connection, had, in his report to the Hornu congress, admired the methods used by the Tunisian and Moroccan nationalist leaders to "internationalize" the problem in their countries. "Let us say," he had added, "that the situation in Morocco and Tunisia verges on insurrection."

The implication was clear: an "end to immobility" and methods leading to near insurrection connoted mobs in the street again and new attempts to let violence bring the Algerian problem to the attention of the world. Disorderly demonstrations that could probably be considered trial heats occurred on October 2 at Roubaix and Tourcoing, Messalist strongholds in France. On October 10, Algerians demanding Messali's release demonstrated at Lille, Douai, and Maubeuge. At Lille, 400 demonstrators, many of them armed with bludgeons, would have marched on the prefecture if the police had not barred the way.

Lahouel and consorts, in the meantime, had not been idle. Braving the thunderbolts hurled at them from Niort and Hornu, they met on July 17 and 18 to repudiate Messali's "prefabricated congress" and lay plans for a congress of their own, to be held "on national soil." Their deliberations bore fruit on August 13 when the representatives of the dissident faction assembled in solemn session at the Nadi Ar-Rachid Club in Algiers. The schism was consummated before the opposition congress ended three days later. The expulsion of Messali, Mezerna, and Merbah, pronounced in short order, was followed by the election of a new Central Committee of thirty members, among them Lahouel, Benkhedda, Kiouane, Demaghlatrous, Boudaa, Djilani, Ferroukhi, and Louanchi. *L'Algérie Libre* having reverted to Messali, the dissidents resolved to found a new organ to be known as *La Nation Algérienne.* The search for guiding principles, however, did not lead them out of the dialectical morass in which they had long been caught. Their doctrine remained "Messalism" watered down. Joint action with the P.C.A. was rejected; instead, an understanding was to be sought with the "left wing" of the U.D.M.A.

Although it was agreed that opposition thrusts would have to be parried, and even countered, the delegates shied away from a frontal attack on Messali; they preferred, if possible, to sap his strength by attrition from without and boring from within. Sid Ali Abdelhamid was put in command of the street gangs recruited for the protection of the new committee's holdings and freedom of action. But apart from that, the inclination of the congress was to concentrate on the "elite" and to leave the "masses" more or less to their own devices.

The debate was, however, soon taken into the street. The vendors of *La Nation Algérienne* and their bodyguards, provided by Mr. Abdelhamid, were, as might be expected, set upon by Messali's thugs; and although the resulting free-for-alls merely gave a little zest to life in the native quarters of Algiers, the police took a more serious view of the matter when a group of Messalists, appearing in force at the Koechlin printing plant, attempted to prevent *La Nation Algérienne* from coming off the press. The mob was dispersed.

The first issue of *La Nation Algérienne* (September 3, 1954) carried a manifesto in which the Lahouel group stated its position in these terms:

> The M.T.L.D. is for the establishment of a democratic and social Algerian republic. All Algerians, regardless of race, have the right, and are in duty bound, to take part in this endeavor. . . . In addition, the M.T.L.D. believes that the struggle for immediate demands is not incompatible with the struggle for freedom. That is why it has encouraged and guided the action of the workers, young people, women, unemployed, etc. That is why it has joined in the struggle for the development of the Arabic language, for the separation of state and religion; that is why it has organized campaigns for the release of political prisoners and against repression. . . .*

Halfhearted language, this, in sharp contrast with the sulphurous invective of *L'Algérie Libre*, which continued to excoriate all "opportunists" who would seek to gain by ruse some advantage of imperialism. In later issues, the editors of *La Nation Algérienne* cast Messali in as unfavorable a light as possible and exhumed the old proposal for a "National Algerian Congress," presented as a "valid platform for discussion." Meanwhile, emissaries fanned out in all directions with orders to rally the *kasmas* to Lahouel's standard.

It would be wrong to think, however, that the leaders of the P.P.A. underground viewed these efforts with ready acquiescence. They, who had forged an instrument of violent revolution, sometimes at the peril of their lives, were little inclined to stand by and wait while the La-

* See *Le Monde* for October 13, 1954.

houelists pondered the question, "Is the time ripe yet for action?" The logic of their position inevitably brought some P.P.A. activists into alliance with the C.R.U.A. for the better hope it offered. From this alliance the rebellion was later to spring.

For the C.R.U.A., too, its remonstrances ignored, its mediation rejected, was undergoing a change. The obduracy of the contending factions within the P.P.A. soon convinced the leaders of the C.R.U.A. that, to bring about the desired result, there was no effective catalyst but violence. Consequently, they scuttled *The Patriot* and began pulling together the body of partisans whose action, they hoped, would attract, revivify, and impel forward all the energies of Algerian nationalism until freedom was won. The C.R.U.A., it is safe to assume, was strengthened in this resolve by pressing encouragement from Cairo.

Early in July, 1954, the *émigré* leaders, including Ben Bella and Khider, visited Switzerland for the double purpose of inducing Messali and Lahouel to bury the hatchet and of plotting alternative action with the C.R.U.A. Meeting separately with Lahouel and with Messali's representative, M'Barek Filali, the travelers had reportedly urged not only reconciliation but joint street demonstrations to give substance to Arab complaints at the United Nations. Messali seems to have taken the second of the two admonitions to heart but not the first; in the Lahouel camp, both fell on deaf ears. Khider and Ben Bella, it was said, had gone back to Cairo with but one thought in mind: to get an insurrectionary movement going in Algeria by hook or crook, and a plague on Lahouel and Messali.

This was Cairo's view as well; so it remained only to find the ways and means. The Arab League's "Fund to Aid the Liberation Movements in the Arab Maghrib" was in a position to finance the operation.* And had not the C.R.U.A. already claimed that its effectives were ready to go into action in sixteen Algerian localities, including Batna, Khenchela, Arris, and Foum Toub? On their return from Switzerland, the principal leaders of the C.R.U.A., meeting in Algiers on July 10, 1954, adopted a master plan by virtue of which Algeria was divided into six *wilayas* in preparation for the impending showdown:

Wilaya 1: The Aurès. Chief: Mostefa Ben Boulaïd.

Wilaya 2: The northern part of the Constantine Department. Chief: Rabah Bitat.

Wilaya 3: Kabylia. Chiefs: Belkacem Krim and Amar Ouamrane.

Wilaya 4: The central and western parts of the Algiers Department. Chief: Mourad Didouche.

---

* One report spoke of an initial subsidy of £15,000.

Wilaya 5: The Oran Department. Chief: Larbi M'Hidi.
Wilaya 6: The Sahara. No chief designated.

Bitat and Didouche later switched "commands." Boudiaf fled to Cairo before the outbreak of the rebellion.

M. Soustelle rightly concludes in his book, *Aimée et Souffrante Algérie*, that the rebellion resulted from the conjunction of two forces: Algerian activism and Egyptian expansionism. "Just as two inert chemical substances produce, when combined, a violent explosion," he writes, "so Cairo's dreams of power and the rancor of the veterans of the old O.S. derived a redoubtable charge from their encounter." Early in September, Mostefa Ben Boulaïd, a trucker from Arris and chief of the underground in the Aurès mountains, met Ben Bella at Tripoli, in Libya; the "Army of National Liberation" came into being when Ben Boulaïd returned to Algeria on September 5. A final "summit conference" between the Cairo *émigrés* and the C.R.U.A. was held in Switzerland in September.

Ferhat Abbas, still chasing rainbows in the summer of 1954, was heard from occasionally, although his utterances had no bearing on the inexorable trend of events. In June, he sent a telegram to Pierre Mendès-France hailing the new premier's investiture as the "dawn of a new policy capable of reconciling the grandeur of France with the freedom of the oversea peoples." He got into trouble on his return from a visit to Cairo in July by making a statement to *Le Monde* in which he said: "As far as I am concerned, my position is simple. I explained it again only yesterday to a very highly placed Egyptian: 'I am an Arab and a Moslem, but only to the extent that this is compatible with the relations of affection that I intend to retain with France.'"* Accused of being a "collaborationist," Mr. Abbas hastened to exculpate himself, explaining that by "France" he had only meant the Mendès-France Government. "The truth is," he added, "that the Algerian people in its overwhelming majority is Arab and Moslem. But this does not prevent us from remaining attached to French culture, which we do not intend to disavow. That is why we believe that an Algerian state, our party's object, will be achieved, in cooperation with democratic France, by the formation of a fraternal community incorporating the Algerians of European origin."† Nobody paid much attention to Mr. Abbas. His party had lapsed into lethargy of thought and action and was not destined to be aroused again before the outbreak of the rebellion.

The P.C.A., no more alive to the winning forces at work than was the U.D.M.A., rather stupidly sidled close to the Lahouel faction. The

* See *Le Monde* for August 1, 1954.
† See *Le Monde* for August 15, 1954.

party's *politburo*, in a statement issued in September, claimed not to have taken sides in the quarrel between Messali and Lahouel but went on to criticize Messali's "narrow and outdated" views. Lahouel, on the other hand, got a pat on the back for reviving the idea of an "Algerian National Congress." The P.C.A. found Lahouel's plan to be not far different from its own proposal for a "National Democratic Front" and therefore well worth serious consideration. "The 'National Congress,'" the P.C.A. statement said, "could give birth to a true National Charter and, by the same token, to a concrete and lasting framework for the union of the Algerian people, a framework that could take the form of a National Democratic Front as proposed by the Communists."

Messali, whose withers were unwrung, answered the Communist criticism with a tongue-lashing. An editorial in *L'Algérie Libre* compared the union advocated by the P.C.A. to that of the "rat and the cheese." "Our fight," the paper said, "is one we wish to wage for ourselves, not for others. You have your struggle and we have ours. Let us pursue them honestly, with the mask off, each side on its own. If our efforts are sometimes joined, so much the better. But, just as we refrain from propagating our message among you, do not try to come and palm off on us your message with its sugar-coating of independence."

If Messali was a trial to the French, he was one also to the manager of his hotel. The manager, tired of having his establishment constantly cluttered with policemen, resolved at length to ask his guest kindly to look for other lodgings. It was for this reason that, on September 30, 1954, after canvassing the possibilities at La Roche-sur-Yon and at Saint-Jean-de-Monts, Messali, followed by his cumbersome retinue, moved to the Hôtel de la Comète at Les Sables-d'Olonne, a resort and fishing town on the Vendée coast.

15. THE CRUMBLING OF FRENCH AUTHORITY

If I have focused attention on the activities of the separatists, it was not with any intention of forgetting the other inhabitants of the country, the vast majority; it was merely to keep an eye on the gathering storm.

The Europeans, unaware of the imminent threat to the very fabric of their lives, carried on as before. They never dreamed that the world might soon contest their right to call themselves Algerians. Human realities were still assumed to be a more potent force than nationalist ideology. And European Algeria was undeniably a human reality.

So was Moslem Algeria, of course. But the mingling of the two communities on the land and in the economy had become so complete that the Moslems, too, had a vital stake in the existing racial partnership. To repudiate it, as did the nationalists, was to court disaster. To establish it on a basis of greater justice was the ambition of many Moslems. The multitude merely accepted the imperfect association as a fatality and as the source of their livelihood.

That the conduct of some European Algerians had reflected little glory on France was a demonstrable fact. But evil is mixed with good in most human enterprises. Notable instances of both had been numerous in the recent history of Algeria. Nothing, therefore, could have been more natural than the impatience the Europeans felt when told by their countrymen across the Mediterranean that ultimately their crimes would destroy them.* Their answer often was that, though wrongs would certainly have to be redressed, those who looked for redress in vengeance merely damned themselves and Algeria as well.

For all their confidence, the Europeans could not help casting frequent anxious glances at the deterioration of French authority in the neighboring protectorates, particularly in Tunisia. On July 31, Premier Mendès-France flew to Tunis and, in a dramatic move, called the nationalists to power, undertaking to negotiate with them the conventions of home rule. It was understood, of course, that French interests, and those of the European minority, would be jealously protected. In his proclamation, the Premier said: "The French, in return for their services past and present and for the part they can and must play in the future, have acquired the right to live and work in Tunisia, a right that no one would think of denying them. It is not a matter only of defending positions they have already attained. In truth, they must continue, they, their sons and their sons' sons, a task that serves the interest of the country and of all its inhabitants." But M. Mendès-France's persuasive words could not hide the fact that an irrevocable step had been taken. Tunisia was clearly on the road to independence.†

---

* This thesis has been developed by two French writers, Colette and Francis Jeanson, in a book celebrating the rebel cause (*L'Algérie Hors la Loi*, Paris: Editions du Seuil, 1955). Must France yield to violence in Algeria? Yes, say the Jeansons, because the violence in the first instance is French—a reference to the accumulated wrongs of a century of colonial rule.

† Premier Mendès-France must have been intelligent enough to know—even if he did not care—what disestablishment would inevitably mean to the Euro-

Juridically speaking, the Premier's decision was unassailable. Protectorates are temporary by definition; the alienation of sovereignty is neither complete nor permanent. But Tunisia had developed *organically* as though French protection were to last forever. Its large European establishment, its cosmopolitan economy, its very personality were the fruits of French rule. It was, in short, a synthesis, a binational state, repugnant perhaps to the aspirations of some, but real, existing in fact. The folly was to believe that this vital synthesis could survive with the Moslem Tunisians in sole command of the state, that a withering of the nation could be avoided after the disestablishment of the European community. I do not have to labor the point; Tunisia's sad plight is there to bear me out. It is now painfully apparent that, in a poor country like Tunisia, the decline of the productive potential, the result of the disaffection of its most active inhabitants, spells misery to the many.

M. Mendès-France, who is a lawyer, may have thought that the precedent set in Tunisia could be shown to be inapplicable in Algeria, juridically an integral part of the French Republic. If so, he was on thin ice. Tunisia, though smaller, was the same kind of a country as Algeria. Legal subtleties could not change that. The French Government, having once granted the Moslem majority the right to rule in Tunisia, set a dangerous precedent for Algeria.*

Unfortunately, France, weary and deeply divided, failed to seize what may have been one of the great opportunities of history. The challenge was to fashion, while she still held Tunisia's fate in her hands, the bold new contours of a multiracial state. If France had risen to the occasion, the peoples of two contrasting civilizations and ways of life, might, perhaps, for the first time since Rome, have found the institutional basis for harmonious cohabitation rooted in justice and equality. Tunisia

---

pean community. The year 1956 saw the departure of the French civil servants. The French garrison was evacuated in 1958. In a speech at Metouya on November 29, 1958, President Bourguiba announced his intention to recover all land held by "foreigners"—this, of course, to include the 2,000-odd French holdings. There were about 180,000 French residents in Tunisia when that country's independence was proclaimed in March, 1956. By 1958, the number had shrunk to about 80,000. It cannot be long before the French colony in Tunisia will be merely a vestigial thing.

* François Quilici, a former deputy for Oran, once remarked, in answer to those who claimed that Algeria and Tunisia could be treated separately, that it was idle to believe that a provision of public law, "this rampart of paper," as he called it, could "contain the contagion of the passions of an Orient in full ebullience." He was right, although, of course, when a "rampart of paper" is all one has, it must be maintained.

would then have given the world an example of tremendous import instead of sinking, as she has done, into poverty-stricken mediocrity. The task, however, would have required imagination and tenacity to an unusual degree, and in these, France was then lacking. She was unable even to protect those who had placed their trust in her. The policy defined by M. Mendès-France, presented as courageous and enlightened, was in essence an abject surrender to the agitation of men with nothing to offer but sterile nationalism.*

In Algeria, the Moslems and the Europeans interpreted M. Mendès-France's policy as a sign of weakness and impending capitulation, and wondered with concern what the future held in store for them.

François Mitterrand, Interior Minister in the Mendès-France Government, was, however, as cheerful as a lark when he visited Algeria in October. "We must study," he said in a speech at Oran, "the way to bring more Algerians into the management of public affairs. We must have a clear vision of what democratic Algeria will be like at the end of the century." To the apprehensive, he declared enthusiastically that Algerian affairs were as close to the Government's heart as those of France itself.

Poor solace! Tension, as we have seen, was already building up along the Tunisian frontier. The first *fellaga* foray on Algerian soil† had occurred on August 15, when a 50,000-franc ransom was exacted from a Moslem merchant at El Miridj in the Morsott district north of Tebessa. The next day, a group of ten *fellaga* descended on the nearby village of Dyr. Such incursions became more frequent in September and October.

---

* When the Tunisian Republic was proclaimed on July 25, 1957, and Habib Bourguiba became President, *The New York Times,* in an enthusiastic editorial, hailed the "establishment of democratic self-government" in Tunisia. The facts hardly warranted such generous praise. Tunisia, for all its many charms, is politically no more than a dictatorship based on a one-party system. The fact that the Tunisian monarchy, venerable if not resplendent, was overthrown by the unanimous vote of the Constituent Assembly, that not a single voice in the whole country was raised in its defense, should have awakened the suspicions of the editorial writer of *The New York Times.* In a country without any real checks and balances, the monarchy was the only possible counterpoise to the misuse of executive power; it represented, in symbol at least, a last recourse for the wronged.

† But not their first appearance. Three French gendarmes guarding the Bir el Ater security post at the Tenoukla pass had been attacked, and one of them wounded, by a group of *fellaga* on June 26. Six inhabitants of Ouled Sidi Abid village in the Tebessa district were later arrested for having harbored *fellaga* several times between June 20 and 30.

I have mentioned the Hadada raid on September 23.* On October 14, Caïd Abderrahmane Beddiar of Hammama in the Souk Ahras district, who had been abducted with his *khodja* (secretary), turned up in Souk Ahras with a letter for the French administrator. The writer of the letter signed himself "Generalissimo Hadj Ali" and purported to speak for the "Algerian revolutionaries." Athmane Benouarab, *ouakaf* (headman) of Bourouba village in the Lamy district north of Souk Ahras, and his brother were carried off on October 25 and butchered. Blood had been spilled only ten days after M. Léonard's security meeting with General Boyer de Latour at Constantine. Meanwhile, on October 24, the P.P.A. had held an improvised street meeting in Government Square at the foot of the Kasbah in Algiers to announce that it was ready for action. Something, beyond a doubt, was in the wind. Secret marching orders from Cairo had, indeed, already reached the C.R.U.A.; it is said that the date set for the outbreak was known by perhaps sixty people in Algeria.

The Lahouelists, in frequent touch with the C.R.U.A. leaders—Boudiaf, Mourad Didouche, Ben M'Hidi, Ben Boulaïd, and Rabah Bitat—were quite aware of what was brewing but viewed the contemplated insurrection with the gravest misgivings. They considered it wholly premature. The P.P.A.'s fighting potential was well known to them, for they had been instrumental, before the schism, in organizing the party's principal instruments of action—"Surveillance Groups" in Souk Ahras, "Shock Units" with hidden arms in Bône, "Support Groups" in Tlemcen, "Action Groups" in Philippeville. Bandits friendly to the P.P.A. had been subsidized with funds controlled by the Central Committee. Lahouel and his friends maintained that more was needed. The organization, they said, would have to be further consolidated before it was ready to take the field with some hope of success. Their idea was to "top up" the party's membership, to strengthen its fighting wing, and to rally to its cause as many U.D.M.A. and P.C.A. members as possible. All that would take time. The Lahouelists suggested scheduling "direct action" to begin in September, 1955, and thus to coincide with that year's session of the United Nations General Assembly.

When it became clear that matters were about to be precipitated without regard to these prudent urgings, concern in the Lahouelist camp gave way to alarm. Lahouel himself, accompanied by Yazid, flew to Cairo on October 10 to press in the most insistent terms for delay. But their reasons were spurned. This left Lahouel, who did not want to be called a shirker, with no choice but to declare that his purpose in visiting Cairo had been to request more aid from the Arab League.

Mezerna also traveled to Cairo in October, his object being not to

---

* See p. 7.

forestall an insurrection of which he had no knowledge, but to plead Messali's case, to claim for his faction the right to be considered the true expression of Algerian nationalism. Mezerna won no hearing at all; his failure was even more dismal than Lahouel's. For Lahouel was later allowed to serve the rebels in a modest capacity, whereas poor Mezerna was rejected; he was destined to be thrown into an Egyptian prison with Chadly Mekki.

PART II: 1954-1958

The Rebellion

16. INSURRECTION

On October 31, the order went out to the waiting "action groups," terrorist cells, and teams of saboteurs: the moment had come! The course to be followed had been irrevocably set; there was no turning back now.

The events of the first hours of the rebellion have already been briefly described: seventy simultaneous attacks at scattered points across the country; seven people killed, four wounded; total surprise. But when the dust had settled, it was observed that, despite the remarkable synchronism of their action, the rebels were few in number and, for the most part, poorly equipped. The bombs used were of the homemade variety and caused no great damage; 500 such primitive engines of destruction, ready for use or only partly completed, were seized by the police in the days immediately following the outbreak.

The Aurès mountains and the cities at their foot—Batna, Biskra, and Khenchela—bore the main brunt of the rebel onset. In the mountains, the rebel bands, swollen with local recruits and Tunisian *fellaga*, invested Arris, attacked T'Kout and murdered Caïd Saddok and Guy Monnerot, the young French schoolteacher, in the Tighanimine gorges. At Biskra, six bombs were thrown, an attempt was made to set fire to the railway station, and the gas works were shot at. It was learned afterwards that these attacks had been directed by Taieb Kherraz, a former Moslem scoutmaster, in pursuance of orders given him orally by Ben Boulaïd himself. At Batna, as already reported, two French soldiers were killed. At Khenchela, a sublieutenant at the head of a small force repulsed a rebel attack but was killed in the action; a French private was mortally wounded.

Further north, at Le Kroubs, near Constantine, and at Condé Smendou, shots were fired. Night watchmen were stripped of their weapons at Saint-Charles. At Dra el Mizan, in the Kabyle mountains seventy-two miles east of Algiers, a native constable was shot at point-blank range and killed by a terrorist who escaped. A second policeman was murdered in that town later in the day. In Algiers, bombs exploded near the government radio station and in an oil depot; damage was slight. Fires were set in an agricultural cooperative at Boufarik and in a paper factory at Baba Ali near Algiers. An attempt was made to destroy a power transmitter at Ouillis in the coastal area northeast of Oran. Two French farms were attacked near Cassaigne a little further inland. Laurent François, on his way to give the alarm, was killed at the wheel of his car by a sniper hiding beside the road. A rural constable on his round near Turgot, forty-two miles southwest of Oran, was brought down with a bullet in his head.

Like many another tourist attracted by the austere but vivid beauty of the Aurès and by the call of the desert just beyond, Pierre Weiss, a retired Air Force general, had traveled to Batna that autumn. He reported having seen vultures in the sky as he motored north toward Constantine on November 1. "You at least," he said to the vultures, "when you sweep down upon your prey, respond to a natural need. You are truer to the universal order than these assassins."

The first care of the French authorities was to relieve rebel pressures in the Aurès. The means at their disposal were meager. Apart from the years of improvidence, French military commitments in Europe and the Indochinese war had greatly reduced the strength of the Algerian garrisons. The effectives available in Algeria at the time did not exceed 50,000 men—little enough for a country four times the size of France. The security forces stationed in Algeria were officially stated to be only a third of those of Metropolitan France in proportion to population. However, reinforcements began coming into the country by air and sea on November 2. A parachute battalion was the first to arrive. Batna, Khenchela, and Biskra were designated as mustering points.

Jacques Chevallier, Secretary of State for War, who had toured the troubled area with René Mayer, deputy for Constantine, and Pierre Dupuch, prefect of Constantine, exclaimed excitedly when he returned to Algiers on November 3 that the Aurès was "practically in a state of insurrection." Four hundred rebels or more, he said, equipped with automatic weapons and two-way radio sets, controlled the Aurès high country; Belkacem Grine, the well-known bandit, was their chief.* Newspaper reporters on the spot found that, though French armor had

* M. Chevallier had recovered his equanimity by the time he got back to Paris on November 9. "The situation is developing quickly and favorably in Algeria," he told reporters. "I am very optimistic."

got through to Arris, helicopters were still being used to fly food and other supplies to the beleaguered town. The village of Foum Toub near ancient Timgad on the northern edge of the Aurès was cut off for three days and all but fell into rebel hands. The progress of French troops was frequently impeded by rebel roadblocks and by bridges hewn down or blown up. The rebel objective, in the words of a French official at Batna, was to "turn the whole region into a sort of impregnable citadel that two extremely mobile divisions could not reduce."

Batna breathed a sigh of relief to hear, on November 5, that the 1,500 pounds of dynamite stocked at the Ichmoul zinc mine had been recovered intact. The mine had been one of the first objects of rebel attention, although the affair seems to have been more sound than fury. Instead of taking the installations by storm, fifty-odd rebel besiegers had, apparently, indulged in a spectacular nocturnal fantasia, burning up 600 rounds of ammunition. The night watchman, a native, had returned fire with an old cavalry magazine rifle; then, thinking better of it, had crawled under his bed, as surprised as could be to realize, a few moments later, that the rebels had made off. November 5 brought a second blessing: a troop of French boy scouts on a hiking trip in the Aurès returned safe and sound to Batna. However, some forty rural schools had to be closed and the teachers withdrawn to safety; isolated foresters also were removed.

By the time I visited the Aurès on November 11, strong points had been established at Foum Toub, Arris, Bou Hamama, and M'Chounèche; columns of paratroopers, Spahi cavalrymen, and Algerian riflemen assisted by local levies were attempting to "comb out" contaminated areas within an enveloping *cordon sanitaire*. It was estimated that about 30,000 inhabitants of the Aurès—possibly one-sixth of the total—were in these areas and, therefore, subject to rebel exactions. A senior officer at operational headquarters in Batna described the rebel bands as "extremely fluid"; he stressed the difficulty of tracking them across 4,600 square miles of desperately rugged country. The job, he thought, might take three months.

So it did—and more! The officer was right about the difficulties of the terrain. For the Aurès, fascinating but little known to the world at large before November, 1954, bristled with very special problems. It was the natural matrix of the rebellion. The Aurès range is lofty and almost impenetrable; it includes Algeria's highest peaks—Chélia (7,638 feet) and Kef Mahmel (7,615 feet)—and deepest valleys. Its inhabitants are a Berber people called Chaouïas, whose religion is Islam and whose language is a variety of Kabyle.

From time immemorial, turbulent tribes, secure in the fastness of the Aurès, have constituted a threat to the established order. The Romans, the Byzantines, and the Arab conquerors learned this long before the French appeared on the scene. The Roman Third *Legio Augusta* held the tribes in check from the fortress town of Lambaesis, seven miles from modern Batna. The Byzantines, determined to stamp out the ever-glowing embers of Berber rebellion, drove to the heart of the Aurès; but, taking no chances, they also girdled Theveste (modern Tebessa) with mighty walls, which yet remain.

The Arab conquerors, advancing from their caravansary-stronghold at Kairouan, also ran afoul of the Berbers of the Aurès. Sidi Okba, emir of the Arab army, perished at the hands of the Berber chief Kosayla at Tehouda near Biskra in 682; a *kubba*, or small shrine, now marks the spot. In 688, the famous Kahena, queen of the Djeraoua, a Judaized Berber tribe then dominant in the eastern Aurès, defeated Hassan Ibn en-Noman el-Ghassani, governor of Cairo, on the Meskiana river and pursued him all the way to Gabès and beyond. Hassan returned, however, at the head of a stronger army, and crushed the Berber tribesmen. Queen Kahena herself was killed in the Aurès at a place long known thereafter as Bir el Kahena, meaning Kahena's well.

For centuries, the policy of the Arabs and then of the Turks was to circumvent rather than subdue the Aurès. Taxes were rarely collected there because it took a costly military expedition to make the inhabitants pay. The French occupied the Aurès in 1845, but the area was not completely pacified until five years later. And even then, the peace was precarious; the Aurès was swept by revolt three times under French rule –in 1859, 1879, and 1916.

It is, therefore, no exaggeration to say that the people of the Aurès have always displayed a mutinous spirit. The Circumcellions of the fourth century found refuge and welcome in their midst. So did the nationalist rebels in the autumn of 1954.

But the warlike Chaouïas are also a credulous and fanatical people. They had been told by the tellers of tales, and firmly believed, that the day appointed by God for the end of French rule had come. Their heads swam with the prophecies they had heard, about a great Egyptian army –70,000 horsemen dressed in green– even then on its way to the Aurès, galloping across the Sahara behind "General Grine" mounted on a pure white steed, or, according to some soothsayers, riding in a glittering airplane.

Unfortunately, the first plane seen over the Aurès was a yellow Piper Cub, a French observation plane trying to spot rebel concentrations for the guidance of artillery units below. The Chaouïas rushed out of their hiding places to acclaim "General Grine." They were amazed to see that, although badly battered themselves by the shelling that followed,

"General Grine" in his plane swooped and glided with perfect impunity, miraculously unscathed however low he flew.

The wild fancies of the Aurès were recorded by Jean Servier, a young ethnologist who, after rescuing Mme. Monnerot, had taken command of a native unit; he heard them from the mouths of glum, bewildered prisoners.* M. Servier also learned that the rebels had offered a premium of 30,000 francs ($85) to each Chaouïa peasant who joined the rebellion, recruits having, however, to provide their own firearms.

It was not at all clear at first, as I have said, whose brain had concocted the plot consummated on November 1. The M.T.L.D., of course, immediately suggested itself as a probable moving force behind the rebellion. The presumptions were strong enough at any rate to bring down upon the M.T.L.D. the full force of French retaliation. The M.T.L.D. and its "subsidiary organizations and associations"† were "dissolved" on November 5 by decree of the Council of Ministers. The two factions, assumed to be equally guilty, got equal treatment: their publications were banned, their offices in Algeria and in Metropolitan France searched, and many of their leaders apprehended. In Algeria, 196 arrests were made in the course of a police operation dubbed "Bitter Orange." Moulay Merbah, the first of the ranking Messalists to land in prison, was charged with illegal possession of "arms of war." Messali himself was put under closer guard and compelled to take his meals in his room. In Paris, the Government initiated a legal action against "persons unknown" for plotting against the security of the state.

17. WORD FROM REBEL HEADQUARTERS

That the Government might be barking up the wrong tree was a thought that had occurred to many, even in official circles. But no matter: the show of energy was in itself commendable; besides, there was always the

* See *France Soir* for December 21 and December 22, 1954. I am indebted to M. Servier also for the account of the attack on the Ichmoul zinc mine.

† The "subsidiary organizations and associations" were, it seems, only two in number: the *Société Algérienne de Presse et d'Edition* and the *Comité de Soutien aux Victimes de la Répression.*

fear that the M.T.L.D., though perhaps not directly implicated, might take advantage of the troubles to advance its own revolutionary designs. However, the Government, with greater discernment, also pointed an accusing finger at Cairo.

For months, the "Voice of the Arabs," broadcast over Cairo radio, had been calling on the Algerians to revolt. "Brethren," it exulted on All Saints' Day, "Algeria has returned to the heroic and glorious struggle for the cause of freedom, Arabism, and Islam! After a retreat contrived by imperialism, and which lasted nine years, Algeria today proudly lifted her head everywhere. Today, fifth day of the month of Rabia I, corresponding to November 1, 1954, at one o'clock in the morning, Algeria began to live a worthy and honorable life. Today a powerful elite of the free children of Algeria started the insurrection of Algerian freedom against French imperialism in North Africa. . . . This is the impetuous, crushing insurrection by which Algeria joins the struggle of the Maghrib and which must lead the whole Arab Maghrib to liberty and dignity." Subsequent broadcasts were also full of references to the "glorious and heroic struggle" of the "forces of the Algerian Liberation Army"—sometimes called the "redeemers"—against French imperialism, described as being exceeded in perfidy only by that of the Zionists in Palestine. French efforts to put down the rebellion were, to the "Voice," an unspeakable outrage: "Genocide!" it screamed; "extermination of the Arabs!" News items embroidered out of all recognition, or simply invented, were a "Voice" staple; these often concerned Algerian villages allegedly bombed off the face of the map. Ahmed Saïd, a "Voice" commentator, announced one day in a moment of passionate indignation that Egypt was prepared to "offer her sons in holocaust for the Arabs of the whole world." This struck some in Algeria as not such a bad idea. The Mendès-France Government made representations in Cairo, but to almost no effect. The "Voice" continued—with valuable assistance from Damascus and Budapest*—to keep a hysterical, high-pitched sound track running in the background.

The Arab League, in the person of Ahmed Shukairy, its deputy secretary-general, gave the French a clue as to what they were up against by announcing on November 3 that the Algerian rebels had its full backing, although "others are with us in this struggle." Mohammed Khider said in Cairo on November 9 that guerrilla warfare would spread in North Africa and that the French could do nothing to prevent it. Word had thus been received from headquarters. It was even more interesting to hear what the local command had to say.

---

* Tetuán, Rabat, and Tunis later chimed in.

The C.R.U.A., however, or the "Autonomous Group," as it had come to be called, was no more. Having once brought within its fold the "neutralist" *kasmas,* those that were neither Messalist nor Lahouelist,* the C.R.U.A. had resolved itself into two distinct but interlocking entities—the "Army of National Liberation" (A.L.N.) and the "National Liberation Front" (F.L.N.), the one military, the other political. The rebellion was the work of the A.L.N., which, on November 1, proclaimed its existence with a "Call" in the form of a handbill. The "Call" of the A.L.N. said:

> Algerian people:
>
> Reflect on your humiliating, colonized condition. Under colonialism, justice, democracy, and equality are but bait and dupery. To these misfortunes must be added the bankruptcy of the parties claiming to defend you. Side by side with our brothers to the east and to the west who are dying that their fatherlands may live, we call upon you to reconquer your freedom at the price of your blood.
>
> Organize your action beside the Forces of Liberation, to which you must give aid, comfort, and protection. To take no interest in the struggle is a crime; to oppose this action is treason.
>
> God is with the fighters of just causes, and no force can stop them now save glorious death or National Liberation.
>
> Long live the Army of Liberation!
>
> Long live independent Algeria! †

Terms of service in the rebel "army" were set out in the seven articles of an A.L.N. "standing order" seized at Saint-Lucien, southeast of Oran. Enlistment was stated to be open to men between the ages of eighteen and forty years; tour of duty, unlimited. Men accepted or drafted for service would be required to remain at their places of residence until called, any infraction of this regulation to be considered desertion in time of war. A *moujahid* (combatant) could be transferred from one region to another by written order. Minor offenders would be disciplined by the regional command, whereas serious offenders would be court-martialed, the possible sanctions being reduction to the ranks, "national indignity," and death. All sentences would be final and subject to immediate execution. The rewards for meritorious conduct would be promotion and citation.

---

* The "neutralist" *kasmas* (sectors) included Boufarik, Souma, Lourmel, El Arrouch, Condé Smendou, Jemmapes, Batna, Arris, and Foum Toub.

† The text is here somewhat condensed in translation from the French original.

"Directives" and "practical advice" issued to the guerrilla units contained rules to be followed when engaged in such activities as laying ambushes (mountain roads to be preferred), attacking isolated French soldiers, gendarmes, or policemen (the "trigger man" to be protected by two or three "cover men" and shot in case of failure to act), pitching camp or bivouacking in the hills, patrolling at night, organizing night and day marches (scouts to be employed in the front and in the rear), and spying on the Administration. The "practical advice" ruled out rape, the massacre of women, children, and old people, and the profanation of sacred precincts, but, as events have proved, this good counsel was frequently to be ignored in practice.

The F.L.N. also emerged into view on the first day of the rebellion, giving notice of its pretensions in a handbill. The F.L.N. "Proclamation," pruned to its essentials, read as follows:

> To the Algerian People!
>
> To the militants of the National Cause!
>
> After decades of struggle, the National Movement has reached its final phase of fulfillment. At home, the people are united behind the watchwords of independence and action. Abroad, the atmosphere is favorable, especially with the diplomatic support of our Arab and Moslem brothers.
>
> Our National Movement, prostrated by years of immobility and routine, badly directed, was disintegrating little by little. Faced with this situation, a youthful group, gathering about it the majority of wholesome and resolute elements, judged that the moment had come to take the National Movement out of the impasse into which it had been forced by the conflicts of persons and of influence and to launch it into the true revolutionary struggle at the side of the Moroccan and Tunisian brothers.
>
> We are independent of the two factions that are vying for power. Our movement gives to compatriots of every social position, to all the purely Algerian parties and movements, the possibility of joining in the liberation struggle.
>
> *GOAL:* National independence through: 1) the restoration of the Algerian state, sovereign, democratic, and social, within the framework of the principles of Islam; 2) the preservation of all fundamental freedoms, without distinction of race or religion.
>
> *INTERNAL OBJECTIVE:* Political house-cleaning through the destruction of the last vestiges of corruption and reformism.
>
> *EXTERNAL OBJECTIVES:* 1) The internationalization of the Algerian problem; 2) The pursuit of North African unity in its national Arabo-Islamic context; 3) The assertion, through

United Nations channels, of our active sympathy toward all nations that may support our liberating action.

MEANS OF STRUGGLE: Struggle by every means until our goal is attained. Exertion at home and abroad through political and direct action, with a view to making the Algerian problem a reality for the entire world. The struggle will be long, but the outcome is certain.

To limit the bloodshed, we propose an honorable platform for discussions with the French authorities:

1. The opening of negotiations with the authorized spokesmen of the Algerian people, on the basis of a recognition of Algerian sovereignty, one and indivisible.
2. The inception of an atmosphere of confidence brought about by freeing all those who are detained, by annulling all measures of exception, and by ending all legal action against the combatant forces.
3. The recognition of Algerian nationhood by an official declaration abrogating all edicts, decrees, and laws by virtue of which Algeria was "French soil."

In return for which:

1. French cultural and economic interests will be respected, as well as persons and families.
2. All French citizens desiring to remain in Algeria will be allowed to opt for their original nationality, in which case they will be considered as foreigners, or for Algerian nationality, in which case they will be considered as Algerians, equal both as to rights and as to duties.
3. The ties between France and Algeria will be the object of agreement between the two Powers on the basis of equality and mutual respect.

Algerians: The F.L.N. is your front; its victory is your victory. For our part, strong in your support, we shall give the best of ourselves to the Fatherland.

The two M.T.L.D. factions, totally disoriented by the outbreak of the rebellion, floundered between acceptance and rejection. To accept the F.L.N. and its works was to take a back seat for the rest of the ride; to reject them was to challenge a redoubtable adversary. After much anguish, the Lahouelists were to choose the former, and the Messalists the latter course.

At the beginning, the leaders of the Messalist faction—Moulay Merbah, secretary general; Arezki Ladjali, chairman of the organization committee; Mohammed Abdelaziz, chief of information and propaganda;

Abdelli Aïssa, financial officer and chairman of the *Comité de Soutien aux Victimes de la Répression;* and Saïd Boudjeroudi, overseer of the party's municipal councilors–preferred merely to stand by for instructions. Their quandary must have been great, for despite their insistence on revolution now, the party apparatus was, in Algeria at least, badly disorganized. Besides, Messali's release was one of their primary objectives, and a revolt could, in this respect, only queer the pitch.

Nevertheless, the orders, when they came, were to integrate or control the C.R.U.A. and the rebels, to hire the jobless for terrorist agitation, and to "liquidate" pro-French Moslems. Isolated efforts in this direction had already been made by the more impatient members of the faction; Abdelaziz and Ladjali undertook to make the policy general. Indeed, Abdelaziz went so far as to turn 1,800,000 francs ($5,000) over to Mourad Didouche of the C.R.U.A. A dozen terrorist cells were organized in Algiers. However, the areas of Messali's greatest strength–the southern and western parts of the Algiers Department–remained relatively undisturbed.

Meanwhile, the French had begun to cut a swath in the Messalist high command. Merbah was arrested on November 7; Boudjeroudi was caught on November 22; Abdelaziz, on December 23; Ladjali and six others, on December 28. A warrant for the arrest of the absent Mezerna was issued on November 24. The only public pronouncement made by the Messalists was that of the leader himself, who, at Les Sables-d'Olonne, declared on November 8 that the explosion of the Algerian people was the consequence of the colonial regime to which they were subjected.

The Lahouelists, in no less of a predicament, tried to get off the ground on November 4 with a lame statement protesting against the "repression" and demanding a "political solution." The next thing they knew, as though in answer to their complaint, the party had been "dissolved" by the French authorities and its Algiers headquarters ransacked by the police. Although the party funds had once again been removed in good time to a safe place, Mohammed Laichaoui, the office manager, was nabbed. It was he who had run off *The Patriot* and the F.L.N. "Proclamation" on Lahouel's mimeograph machine. On November 23, Kiouane, Boudaa, and Benkhedda explained in the columns of *Alger Républicain* that those who had clung to the *status quo* were to be blamed for the troubles. Two days later, Benkhedda, Boudaa, and Ferroukhi produced a "letter to the Minister of the Interior," which reached the public through the courtesy of *Alger Républicain.* The three protested in their letter against the "repression" but longed for a "future of peace and harmony between the two communities that must necessarily live together." With that, they relapsed into silence. Benkhedda was arrested on November 25; Kiouane, on November 26. On December 22, Ali Abdelhamid, Boudaa, and Larbi Demaghlatrous headed for prison, to be followed on the 28th by Ferroukhi.*

Ferhat Abbas, who could not be suspected of trying to overthrow the Government with anything but the force of words, naturally felt called on to make his position known. He did so on November 4 in these terms:

> The action of the Army, the repression, and the *ratissages*† provide no solution for the Algerian problem. The political bureau of the U.D.M.A. recalls that for years it has incessantly directed the attention of the authorities to the necessity of putting an end to the colonial regime and of satisfying the legitimate aspirations of our populations. Similarly, it has denounced the poverty, the unemployment, the systematic violations of the law, the contempt in which the people are held. Our appeals to reason and wisdom have unfortunately found no echo in governmental spheres. The U.D.M.A. reasserts its doctrinal position, which is to seek, in an atmosphere of understanding, a solution acceptable to all. In view of the present situation, the political bureau calls upon the European and Moslem populations to keep their heads, to analyze the facts with lucidity so as not to yield to panic and passion.

In a telegram to Premier Mendès-France, Mr. Abbas charged that the "omnipotent" *colons* were "cynically" pitting the populations against one another by their "criminal propaganda," causing "repression and hatred." To those who had taken up arms, however, all honor and deferential respect!

On November 26, Abbas, in the Algerian Assembly, demanded but was denied the floor.‡ The speech he had prepared for the occasion showed him to be in top form. "Beware!" he had planned to say. "Is it not to be feared that these are the premonitory signs of the great upheaval that could be upon us in a few years' time—the general revolt of the proletariat?" After stating that colonialism, compounded of injustice and want, was doomed, he continued: "The alternative is, in fact, federa-

---

* Most of the nationalists rounded up in November and December, 1954, were released during 1955.

† Literally, "rakings." The word, in French, is applied to systematic searches of the countryside or villages.

‡ By Raymond Laquière, mayor of Saint-Eugène (a suburb of Algiers), who had been elected to succeed Abderrahmane Farès as speaker of the Algerian Assembly on May 14, 1954.

tion or dismemberment. The extension of the unitary Republic is contrary to the nature of things, and the only course remaining to us lies in a union of peoples, a great human community gathered around France. . . . Let us sanction the existence of this Algerian state, which we will direct together. With democratic France remaining in our midst, peace and security will be secured, and the conditions of prosperity as well. . . ."

But, in Cairo, the U.D.M.A. spoke with a different voice. The party's bureau there, in a statement issued on December 12 and broadcast over Cairo radio, pinned entire blame for the uprising on the French authorities, who persisted in perpetuating a "regime of annexation." It called upon the "free men of the whole world to support the Algerian people in its gigantic combat for the right to live as a free nation."

The Algerian Communist Party (P.C.A.), quite as dazed by events as the other parties, puffed and wheezed in a pathetic effort to catch up with the already distant van. Never before had "common action" been, for the P.C.A., so vital and so hard to get. The party's only first-class asset was *Alger Républicain,* whose columns were sure to attract bidders deprived of their own means of expression. But the P.C.A. could not expect substantial rewards for little services rendered. A measure of initiative would have to be regained. But how? The answer was not to be found until much later, when the P.C.A. went in for blasting women and children to bits with superior bombs of its own manufacture. The party was reduced in the earlier days to the unsatisfactory exercise of making noises in the background. It followed the lead of the other parties in explaining the troubles as the fruit of the French policy of "colonial oppression." The Communists, too, fumed against the "repression" and "police brutality"; they, too, clamored for the release of the political prisoners. They expended energy organizing "vigilance committees" and demanding "commissions of inquiry."

The Communist line at the beginning of the rebellion, as defined by *L'Humanité* on November 9, was to avoid individual acts of terrorism and to support the "Algerian people in their mass struggle against repression and for the defense of their rights." The disaffection of many European members of the P.C.A. was to be the inevitable consequence of this policy, for the party could not always be the friend of the working man and of the nationalist at the same time. On November 17, the rebels, by removing a length of track, sent a phosphate train hurtling off the rails between Bône and Souk Ahras. Two *cheminots* were killed and six wounded in the wreck. A good many of their fellows, unlike the P.C.A., vowed they would have no truck with those who killed, or with those who condoned the killing of, innocent workers. What could be more damaging at such a time than the silence of the Communist trade union organization?* But it must be said, to their credit, that the Communists never flinched; once the order to support the rebels had been received, they sacrificed their European clientèle without a murmur. When it is considered that the bulk of their Moslem following was also soon to be snatched away from them, their devotion to the party line and their unflagging efforts to make headway in the face of adversity are seen as something akin to heroism.

18. THE FRENCH RESPONSE

To the European Algerians, the rebel outbreak came as a profound shock. The Europeans were heartened, certainly, by the Government's good show of resolution. But they remained nervous and uneasy. However distant the rebel-infested hills might seem to be, the Europeans sensed a threat to their security; not the "oligarchy" of *colons* only, but ordinary people everywhere, especially those whose horizons had never extended beyond their native Algeria. Security is a primary human need; there is an intuition that tells us, at every age in life, how it goes with our own security. The Europeans demanded energetic measures in defense of their lives and homes; their purpose was not, as has been charged by many, to pit European against Moslem in an atmosphere of implacable hatred.

L'Echo d'Alger, on November 2, recommended strong, quick action in response to what it called "this bloody provocation." Senator Henri Borgeaud wrote in the Algiers *Dépêche Quotidienne:* "The evil must be sought where it is to be found and the ringleaders routed out where they are. They are known. It is enough to reinforce the security measures. . . . A blow must be struck at this handful of agitators and struck high; the organization must be decapitated." Georges Blachette, deputy

* The Algerian branch of the French C.G.T. had, at its Fifth Conference in June, 1954, draped itself in a semblance of autonomy by adopting a new name, *Union Générale des Syndicats Algériens*. The tactical advantage resulting from this move appears to have been slight.

for Algiers, published an editorial entitled, "First the *Fellaga,* Now the Terrorists," in his paper, *Le Journal d'Alger.* "We have reached the point logically foreseen by clear-sighted minds and forecast by all those who, living in contact with daily realities, possess the feel of events: Algeria was shaken yesterday. Terrorism has now made its appearance in Algeria. . . . Henceforth, errors will be faults." Only *Alger Républicain* among the dailies commented on the outbreak without the shadow of a rebuke for the rebels. It called for a "democratic solution" but did not really warm to the subject until a few days later, with a ringing denunciation of the "bestial repression."

The thoughts of many were well expressed by François Quilici, deputy for Oran, who, in an interview, said:

> Years of ease, of weakness, and especially of ideological dreaming have brought us to this pass. But when M. Mendès-France proclaimed Tunisia's internal sovereignty and turned the government and Tunisia itself over to the Neo-Destour, he showed that terrorism paid off. Our protectorate half thrown down, the French inhabitants legally declared to be foreigners and, as such, excluded from public affairs—that is more than enough to fire the dreams of all the troublemakers in North Africa, Algeria inevitably included. The Government did not even get peace in the streets and in the countryside as a consequence of this unmistakable political revolution. The evil is spreading. The admirable Algerian peace, French peace in Algeria, is ruined, for . . . weakness always encourages new ventures.*

François Mitterrand explained the Government's position to the Interior Committee of the National Assembly on November 5, saying that although it was quite prepared to listen to demands put forward by the Tunisian and Moroccan nationalists, since the protectorates were legally separate states, it could not contemplate any such talks with the Algerian nationalists. Algeria, he asserted, was, and would remain, an integral part of the Republic; consequently, all Algerians taking a stand in contradiction with the unity and integrity of the nation would have the law to contend with. On the other hand, M. Mitterrand continued, the Government would lend a very sympathetic ear to demands made within the context of the nation, particularly if such demands came from Algerians who had repudiated the rebellion. Meanwhile, he said, the Government's determination to bring the rebels and terrorists to book was "total."

---

* See *Le Monde* for November 3, 1954.

On November 12, Premier Pierre Mendès-France rose in the National Assembly to make a policy statement on Algeria.

> A few weeks ago [he said] at the time of the Orléansville catastrophe,* I stressed the solidarity of the entire nation with the Algerian populations. Faced with a new test, the result this time of the criminal purpose of a few men, a pointless and blindly stupid test, the nation must assert its unity and its solidarity. A blow struck at the French of Algeria, be they Moslem or European, is a blow struck at the whole nation. With them, France grieves to count so many innocent victims, but she also shares with them, in her sorrow, the satisfaction of seeing that the overwhelming majority of our Moslem fellow countrymen has not ceased to display, during these tragic days, a faultless civic sense and unequivocal loyalty. Like them, we know that the repression must be kept within bounds, that it must fall only on those that are truly guilty and avoid even the appearance of a reprisal that might hurt innocent people. But, thus circumscribed, the repression must be without weakness, for it is without injustice.

After referring to the reinforcements already sent to Algeria, the Premier went on to say:

> Other reinforcements will follow, just as massive as hitherto—indeed, more massive than necessary, for to maintain order I prefer to have more than ample means. Let there be no mistake about it: the Government will act without hesitation, delay, or half-measures.
>
> Let no one expect us to have the slightest consideration for sedition or to make any concession to it. The defense of the internal peace of the nation and the integrity of the Republic admit of no compromise. The Algerian departments form part of the Republic; they have long been French; their population, which

* Orléansville—5,000 Europeans and 31,000 Moslem inhabitants—and the surrounding region were hit by a severe earthquake on September 9. A second tremor occurred a week later. The stricken area covered 1,740 square miles with a population of 250,000. The number of dead and missing was put at 1,400; 5,000 persons were injured. The number of homeless exceeded 60,000. Then, toward the end of October, torrential rains struck the region. Ruins collapsed, tents were washed out, streets were flooded. An emergency relief agency supervised the distribution of 6,000 tents, 2,300 tarpaulins, 20,000 blankets, and 500 tons of food. Voluntary contributions flowed in from all over France and Algeria; more than $5,700,000 was raised in this way, $1,700,000 of it in Algeria. The reconstruction of Orléansville, though well advanced, is still proceeding.

enjoys French citizenship and is represented in Parliament, has given proof enough of its loyalty to France for France to thwart any attempt on its unity. It is inconceivable that Algeria should secede from Metropolitan France. This should be clear forever and to all, in Algeria, in Metropolitan France, and abroad. [Applause.] France will never, no Parliament, no Government will ever, yield on this basic principle.

The Premier deplored also attempts to liken Algeria to Tunisia. "Algeria," he declared, "is France, and not a foreign country under our protection."

Alas, what was to become of these fine words? Did M. Mendès-France keep his solemn promises? Was the situation in Algeria less critical when M. Mendès-France spoke, not for the Government, but for the leftist opposition? Anyone listening to the former Premier in 1957 would be tempted to think so. For then he was piping a different tune. "It is fascism," he cried, "that holds sway in Algeria at present. By degrees it grinds more and more Frenchmen. The liberal press is seized; that of the ultras has never been touched."* The rebel designs? The tragedy of those who had not been protected? There was neither a word nor a thought for them. All M. Mendès-France's solicitude went to the poor "liberals" in hot—not very hot—water because they had chosen the rebel cause.

* See *Le Monde* for May 5, 1957.

19. WAR IN THE MOUNTAINS

"Men are so constituted that they are prone to support a cause which they believe to be assured of victory."
H. A. L. Fisher

It was apparent from the start that a modern striking force was ill-suited to conditions in the Aurès. Heavily equipped units dependent on motor transport lost much of their mobility in the hills and were easily outmaneuvered. The military authorities on the spot did the best they could to remedy the deficiencies with requisitioned mules and hastily recruited *goums* (groups of native irregulars), but these were not enough. M. Mitterrand announced that the old *Armée d'Afrique*, a specialized force experienced in the ways of the country, would be reconstituted largely with troops withdrawn from Indochina.

But meanwhile, for the units engaged in the Aurès, the contest was a harassing and inconclusive one. The rebels, slithering through the thousand gullies and defiles of a region the size of Connecticut and as wild as the Mountains of the Moon, had every advantage; they could have eluded an army corps. When I was in Foum Toub, I heard a company commander who had spent two fruitless and sleepless nights with his men in the rain-soaked hills say: "This is not Indochina. This is not Korea. But it is a nasty piece of work." Caïd Abderrahmane Maaoui of M'Chounèche told me the next day how for four hours he and his forty *goumiers* had, by moonlight, beaten off waves of attacking rebels. The village below us was, as he spoke, silent, frightened, vulnerable, and, it seemed to me, noncommittal. The stark mountains above formed an ominous screen behind which armed men roamed almost at will. At night, fires were lit on distant slopes, an unnerving sight even for those in protected villages.

Who had the initiative? If the French could not, in short order, give a convincing answer to that question—the only one that really mattered—there was every reason to fear that the guerrilla, the "little," war would grow in cruelty and intensity. I remember thinking at the time that, despite the undeniable valor of the troops in action against the rebels, the French retaliation was wanting in vigor and sinew. It would be presumptuous to offer military advice, even in retrospect, but I do believe the situation would have developed differently if strong points had quickly been established all through the mountains, fortlets linked together by troops always on the move; if new roads and tracks had furrowed the face of the Aurès; if each post had been given its administrative complement so as to serve as a pole of attraction. Then there would have been no mistaking French intentions. The French, I am told, threw 100,000 men against the insurgent Kabyles in 1871. Was a comparable effort impossible in 1954?

The presidents of the local *djemaas,* meeting at Batna on November 6, estimated rebel strength at more than 2,000 armed men. Of this number, half at least, the presidents thought, had been pressed into service and could, therefore, be induced to desert if ironclad protection could be provided. The troubles, they insisted, were to be attributed not to any tribe as such, but to subversion by "strangers" whose exactions were widely and painfully felt. The fate of "Generalissimo" Hadj Ali Mohammed Ben Saïd, already mentioned, whose body was found in an abandoned mine shaft near Souk Ahras, suggests that the rough methods employed by the rebels did not always meet with docile acceptance; the "Generalissimo" had, apparently, been killed by his own men. One of the documents found on Hadj Ali's body bore the stamp of the "Committee for the Liberation of the Arab Maghrib" and the signature of Mohammed Khider.

It was announced on November 20 that the peaceful population of the Aurès would be concentrated in "security zones" prior to the drive that was to carry French troops to the heart of rebel-held territory in an all-out attempt to force a decision before the first snows. To this end, more than 50,000 handbills were dropped from the air carrying this message in French and Arabic:

> Agitators, among them strangers, have brought bloody strife to our country and have, in particular, established themselves in your area. They are living off your own resources. They inflict their exactions upon you and attempt to lead the men of your

homes into a criminal adventure. They have been followed by the misguided few whose notion is to start a civil war.

Moslems: You will not follow them but will assemble immediately, and not later than November 21 at 6 P.M., in the security zones with your families and your goods. The location of these security zones will be explained to you by the French troops stationed in your area and by the village administrative authorities.

Men: Those of you who have enlisted without thinking, if you have no crime on your conscience, proceed immediately to the security zones with your arms, and no harm will come to you.

Soon a terrifying calamity will overtake the rebels, after which French peace will reign again.

The response to this ill-considered injunction could have been anticipated. The rebels had freely predicted the total eviction of the French; at best, the issue, in the eyes of the Chaouïas, was still in doubt. And so, guided by an instinct as old as the race, the Chaouïas preferred to wait and see. In the end, only one security zone was announced, that of Touffana, near Foum Toub. After protracted negotiations, the representatives of two native villages—Ichmoul and Yabous—agreed to the evacuation demanded by the French. The people began coming down from the hills on November 26; they came in groups of a dozen or so at a time until about 1,600 men, women, and children—239 families—had gathered at Touffana.* But among the men, few were young enough to carry a gun. As for arms, none, to my knowledge, were surrendered. With that, a venture that could be called "Operation Bombast" came to an end. The damage to the French cause, in terms of loss of face, had been incalculable: the Chaouïas had learned to measure the weight of French threats.

Luckily, the French could point to more positive results in the field. The rebels, though not wiped out, were severely mauled. On November 29, two companies of paratroopers on reconnaissance patrol in the Oued Taga district northeast of Arris fell upon a strong rebel band at Aïn Tinn. Twenty-three rebels were killed in the encounter and eighteen were captured. The French lost two killed and nine wounded. One of the rebel dead, distinguished by his uniform, which was of stylish American cut, turned out to be Belkacem Grine himself, killed at the age of twenty-seven. This success prompted the president of the Oued Taga *djemaa* to place his village under French protection—an instance of what might have been if the French had managed to show their force everywhere. But Grine's spirit was kept alive. A few days later, R. G. Soulé

* Total estimated population of the Aurès: 200,000.

of the *Echo d'Alger* met an ancient Chaouïa who said: "Grine is not dead. The French can never catch him. He is stronger than their guns, their tanks, and their planes." And where had the man heard all this? Why, in the village. "They" had told him that Grine would return to "punish traitors." The rebel psychological warfare branch at work!

That the rebels were able to bring modern weapons of war into play, soon amply demonstrated, raised the intriguing question of their sources of supply. It was known, of course, that the armies of World War II had left firearms in large quantities strewn about the battlefields of North Africa and that the Arabs, with their passion for powder, had kept up brisk trading in salvaged weapons ever since. It was known, too, that the P.P.A. had arms stashed away. But the rebels had obviously been able to lay their hands on guns of more recent vintage. The late André Leveuf, a conscientious reporter whose memory I should like to pay tribute to here,* got the answer from a hardbitten lieutenant of *méharistes* at Khanga Sidi Nadji on the southern confines of the Aurès somewhere east of Biskra. Here is what the lieutenant said:

> In the *djebel* [hills], they [the rebels] are banded together in groups of forty or fifty men, highly mobile and perfectly trained in the methods of combat currently used. Most of them possess uniforms on which the star and crescent are emblazoned, uniforms cut for them by tailors in neighboring villages. Contrary to the commonly accredited belief, their weapons are modern: American Garands, German Mausers, Thompson submachine guns. All this equipment is new and came directly from Libya. From the Libyan frontier, the arms reach the Ghadamès oasis; then, heading north in packsaddles carried by camels, they pass to the east of the Melrir chott, cross the Khanga-Ferkane track and end up at Guentis, seat of the most flourishing arms mart in North Africa. For a few thousand francs, anyone can acquire there the rifle or submachine gun of his dreams. From Guentis, the arms enter the Aurès by way of the track leading in from Babar to the east.†

Such were the modest beginnings of what was later to become a highly organized operation involving regular shipments of contraband arms by camel caravan and by sea. The rebels were ultimately to receive up to 1,000 weapons a month, more than enough to make good their losses. By the end of 1955, arms depots had been set up in northern

* Leveuf, then of *France-Soir,* Roger Lavedèze, his photographer, and Roland Jourdan, "stringer" for the National Broadcasting Company's television network, were ambushed and murdered by insurgent tribesmen between Khenifra and Kasbah Tadla in central Morocco on August 20, 1955.

† See *Le Monde* for November 13, 1954.

Libya under the supervision of Mohammed Ben Bella; the caravans themselves set out from transshipment points in southern Tripolitania. A caravan would occasionally be intercepted by the French, but most of the shipments presumably got through.

The grant of independence to Tunisia on March 20, 1956, greatly facilitated rebel logistics, for it enabled the A.L.N. to move men and supplies across the Tunisian frontier and thence directly into the Aurès-Nememcha ranges. Similarly, the independence of Morocco, proclaimed in Paris on March 2, 1956, gave new impetus to contraband by sea. Soon small vessels loaded to the gunwales with arms and ammunition were plying between Alexandria and Nador in the former Spanish zone of Morocco.

One of these vessels, the 400-ton "Athos," seized by the French off Oran on October 17, 1956, was found to be carrying seventy tons of war material, including twelve mortars, six machine guns, fifty British-made automatic rifles of a type not yet delivered to the troops of the North Atlantic Treaty Organization, 600 Beretta and Sten light machine guns, 2,000 war rifles, 300,000 cartridges, and six two-way radio sets. The "Juan Illueca," seized by the Spanish authorities at Ceuta on June 16, 1957, made the "Athos" look "small time"; her bowels yielded 800 tons of war material—3,000 rifles, 3,600,000 cartridges, 550 machine rifles, 1,595 submachine guns with 2,280,00 rounds of ammunition, 750 mortars, 60,000 hand grenades, and miscellaneous ammunition—enough to equip a force of more than 10,000 men. The "Swanee," caught by the Spanish and taken to Almería on June 26, 1956, had 300 tons of war material and transmission equipment in her hold.

Elsewhere in Algeria, the French were generally able to break up the terrorist groups that had been formed prior to November 1, 1954. Their success was particularly notable in the Oran department, where the natives themselves spontaneously came forward to assist the police.

On the evening of November 4, a terrorist gang roaming the Moulay Ismail state forest twenty-five miles southeast of Oran broke into the government forestry station and murdered the forester, François Braun, after binding and gagging his wife and daughter. The crime did not long go unpunished. The gang, engaged on the night of November 7, lost two killed and five captured. At Cassaigne, twelve terrorists, including the assassin of Laurent François, were arrested with the help of the local population. Two terrorists were killed in an exchange of fire with a security unit near Turgot. The Oran department was quiet for many months thereafter.

On November 4, troops of the Blida garrison southwest of Algiers, combing the Mount Marmoucha district near Souma, bagged a group of ten rebels who had undertaken to organize a "second Aurès" from headquarters in the abandoned Tizi N'Taga copper mine.

In Kabylia, the outlook was rather less reassuring. A bus on its way from Camp du Maréchal, fifty-six miles east of Algiers, to Dellys on the coast, was caught in a burst of submachine-gun fire near Ben N'Choud. The driver, Roger Meyzer, was mortally wounded. In the days that followed, the French learned that nationalist guerrillas had established themselves in several of the remoter reaches of the Kabyle mountains and notably on the craggy slopes below the Makouda pass between Tizi Ouzou and the sea. An operation in this area brought French troops into contact with a rebel band on November 14. One of three rebel prisoners taken in the encounter still had a smoking submachine gun in his hands.

René Janon of *Le Figaro,* who toured higher Kabylia in December, found the atmosphere there tense and anxious, particularly as he approached the high Djurdjura massif. He reported a sore spot in the densely-populated Beni Ouacif tribal area on the slopes of Mount Kouriet, where forty or fifty rebels had subjected the inhabitants to a reign of terror. "The bandits have relatives, friends, in all the little eagle-nest villages," M. Janon wrote. "The people there live in the grip of fear, yet not daring to speak, much less to point the rebels out to the authorities. And yet with a single voice they implore the aid and protection of our troops and long for some sign of French presence. 'Insure our security!' is what one hears at every turn; 'then we will be able to help you rid us of the handful of rebels who now give the law to us all.'"* The problem was elemental, but its solution required something more than an occasional passing column of troops and periodical *ratissages,* however thorough; a permanent and massive military and civil occupation of the upcountry was wanted at the start; but that, unfortunately, was not the kind of effort the French were geared to provide. They still hoped "police action" would suffice. As a result, one after another, the Kabyle villages came under rebel control, making the task a thousand times more difficult for the French.

Nevertheless, the year ended on a note of moderate optimism. The bandit chiefs Belkacem Krim and Amar Ouamrane had, it is true, been able to maintain nine troublesome bands in the mountains of Kabylia; "traitors" had been assassinated; roads had been blocked; telephone and telegraph lines had been hacked down. But Major General Paul Pardes, commanding the Algiers garrison, had thrown 4,000 of his best troops—

* See *Le Figaro* for December 13, 1954.

the 9th regiment of Zouaves, the 13th Senegalese, the 16th Light Infantry, the 18th Parachute—into the area, and decisive results were expected.

Operations in the Aurès, directed by Colonel Paul Ducournau, were also being pushed with increased vigor. The rebels, though not often sighted by Colonel Ducournau's paratroopers, fought back furiously when forced to make a stand. The French reported the destruction of a rebel band in the Beni Imloul forest southeast of Arris on December 14, but conceded that their troops had suffered losses. An engagement near Duvivier, between Bône and Souk Ahras, on November 20 had revealed the presence of armed rebels in the low country north and northeast of the Aurès. Their numbers were not great; but, in the Duvivier affair at least, they had put up a spirited resistance, yielding only after the French had shelled their "fort," an abandoned forestry station.

The Governor General, Roger Léonard, conscious of the threat to Algeria's Libyan and Tunisian confines, traveled to El Oued, 440 miles southeast of Algiers, on December 17 with Lieutenant General Paul Cherrière, commanding the French troops in Algeria, and Brigadier General Robert Quénard, commanding the Southern Territories. The ostensible object of the trip was to attend a colorful annual ceremony during which the standard of the Saharan (native) troops passes from the custody of one company into that of another. But M. Léonard and the generals accompanying him also conferred at length with the local civil and military authorities, first at El Oued and then, on December 19, at Souk Ahras.

"We need your help in restoring the peace that will enable you to work," M. Léonard said at Souk Ahras addressing himself to the Moslem population. "But I give you here the assurance that you will always be protected against possible reprisals. Measures have been taken to insure that the friends of France will not be bothered by the outlaws." Rash words! If M. Léonard and his successors had been able to keep this promise, it is probable that the course of subsequent events would have been quite different. But on that very day, the body of Lakhdar Bentaieb, president of the *djemaa* of Aïn el Ksar near Batna, was found at the bottom of a well; that of his brother was discovered in a nearby thicket; the two notables had been abducted by the rebels. Meanwhile, in Kabylia, a native farmer who had incurred the displeasure of the rebels was shot dead in his field near Dra el Mizan.

"We are certainly not yet at the end of our difficulties," M. Léonard told a press conference on the last day of the year. "But we must be at once optimistic and vigilant. Our security services have proved their efficacy. We must apply ourselves to the further development of French endeavor in Algeria." He stated that 1,431 persons had been apprehended by the police, that ninety-five terrorists or rebels had been killed, and that fourteen terrorist cells had been broken up before they had gone into action.

The outbreak of the rebellion and the uncertainties that it implied put the Moslem politicians in an awkward position. Nothing, certainly, could have been further from their minds than to disavow the French or to declare for the rebels; the situation had not deteriorated far enough for that. But it was equally evident that the rebels, having dared to defy French authority, might conceivably get away with it. The sense of insecurity resulting from this realization had prompted the European politicians to demand stringent measures against all troublemongers. Among the Moslem politicians, it had an opposite effect: it impelled them to denounce as harsh and unjust the measures already taken. Thus they put an anchor out to windward, drawing what comfort they could from the thought that, if worst came to worst, they might be remembered for the stand they had taken against the oppressors of the Algerian people—an oblique stand, to be sure, and devoid of risk, but a stand just the same.

The Moslem and European members of the Algerian Assembly were bound, in these circumstances, to drift further and further apart. The divorce became apparent on January 21, 1955, when forty-six second-college delegates, meeting as a caucus, adopted a motion which said:

> The second-college delegates of the Algerian Assembly, fully aware of the responsibilities they assume at a time when the country is going through a painful ordeal,
>
> Protest energetically against the illegal searches, the arbitrary arrests, the inhuman brutalities to which the prisoners whom the law considers innocent are subjected, pending the declaration of guilt by the jurisdiction of judgment, and also against the extreme sentences passed by the courts;
>
> Demand that a policy of complete equality of rights and duties be quickly carried into effect in Algeria within the framework of the French democracy and the removal of any system of exception;
>
> Call on their colleagues of the first college, animated by the same ideal of concord and progress, to join with them for the fulfillment of our country's future in unity and complete brotherhood;
>
> Appeal in pressing terms to the Government to remedy the situation of which they complain and to remove the cause of their legitimate grievances;

Finally, appoint a delegation whose task will be to approach the authorities, both in Algiers and in Paris.

A stranger reading this document would not guess that a violent revolution was then in progress, claiming the lives of innocent people. The meaning of the motion was clear to anyone with eyes to see and ears to hear: the Moslem politicians, if they were not yet abandoning a sinking ship, were jolly well scrambling into their life belts. The comments that appeared in the French press, and particularly the subtle exegesis of *Le Monde*, missed the point entirely. Aïssa Bensalem, delegate for M'Sila, was chosen to head the contemplated eight-man delegation. The members were to include Mohammed Bensouna, delegate for Aïn Sefra, and Hachémi Benchennouf, delegate for Khenchela.

20. JACQUES SOUSTELLE TAKES OVER

Jacques Soustelle, distinguished ethnologist and Social Republican (Gaullist) deputy for Lyons—an "active and progressive disciple of General de Gaulle," the London *Times* called him—was appointed on January 26 to succeed Roger Léonard as Governor General of Algeria. For some reason, M. Soustelle's political views were generally thought to be "pinkish." The second-college delegates were delighted by the appointment; they thought that, if French policy was about to be inflected toward greater leniency, they could claim at least part of the credit. "The new Governor General will, we do not doubt, be the capable architect of reforms indispensable to Algeria," Mr. Bensalem exclaimed.

The Europeans, when not openly hostile, expected little good of the appointment. The fact that he had been picked by M. Mendès-France counted against him. It was also recalled that he had recently visited Warsaw. *Le Monde* quoted an unnamed mayor as having commented: "We will judge him [Soustelle] by his works, but if he supports the second college in the crazy dreams of their motion, he will find us ranged against him."* A vicious whispering campaign, playing on the

* See *Le Monde* for January 28, 1955.

anti-Semitism common to the Christian and Moslem communities in Algeria, had it that M. Soustelle was in reality a Jew named Ben Soussan. Poor man, it availed him little to be of rocky Protestant stock, long rooted in the south of France.

M. Soustelle's perplexities were great before he even set foot on Algerian soil, for the Mendès-France Government, blasted in the National Assembly by those opposed to its vacillating North African policies, and notably by René Mayer, Radical deputy for Constantine, fell on February 5. The new Governor General was kept in a state of suspended animation while the National Assembly thrashed about in search of a new Government. An important fact had emerged, however, from the tumultuous debates of February 2 and 3: it would be difficult, if not impossible, for any new Government to go back on M. Mendès-France's plan for making pacification in Algeria go hand in hand with political reform and economic betterment. When the former Premier had undertaken to increase appropriations for economic development in Algeria from 28 billion francs ($80 million) to 40 billion francs ($114 million), he had made a commitment of a kind not easily forgotten.

M. Soustelle took up his new post in Algeria on February 15 without waiting for a government to be formed; he did so to prevent a power vacuum in Algiers consequent to the departure of M. Léonard, who had been called to Paris on February 12 to become president of the Court of Accounts. Luckily, M. Soustelle found himself in agreement with the government formed by Edgar Faure on February 23. He stresses, in his book, *Aimée et Souffrante Algérie*, the high value he attached to the friendship of the new Interior Minister, Maurice Bourgès-Maunoury, whom he had known as a resistance leader in France during World War II.

On February 20, five days after his arrival in Algiers, M. Soustelle set out for a tour that was to take him to Biskra, M'Chounèche, Baniane, Rhoufi, Arris, Batna, Tebessa, and Khenchela. What was the situation in the Aurès as he found it? He gives this answer in his book:

> The rebellion was then tending to become an endemic evil, that of permanent and diffuse guerrilla warfare with ambushes, isolated attacks, and individual assaults. Now a forestry station burned, now a patrol, at a turn in some rugged defile, ran into the fire of well-hidden snipers, now a native dignitary or a simple peasant was found by the roadside in the morning with his throat slit. Isolated at first, these attacks on Moslems soon became more and more frequent and atrocious, accompanied, the better to

strike the imagination, by gruesome effects: revolting mutilations, threatening messages pinned to the clothes of victims.

When I made my first trip to the Aurès, the first of many, terror had taken hold. No one spoke. The Administration and the Army had seen information dry up as soon as any informer, any native suspected of friendly relations with the authorities, ran the risk of mutilation or assassination. Fear closed mouths and hardened faces. A few brave men, certainly, stood out from the rest, like the *caïd* of M'Chounèche, who had already escaped, as though by a miracle, several attempts on his life. But the population as a whole, without throwing in their lot with the rebels—there has never been a general uprising—remained frightened and noncommittal.

Several aspects of the Algerian reality impressed themselves strongly on M. Soustelle's mind and greatly influenced his approach to the problem. He was struck in the first place by the appalling poverty of the Aurès, epitome of all the ills that beset the Algerian countryside—a difficult and capricious climate, deep erosion of the soil, ancestral methods of agriculture, a fantastic birth rate, and the goat, relentless destroyer of vegetation and sole measure of each native's personal estate. Unfortunately, the remedial measures—the introduction of improved methods of agriculture, reforestation, the substitution of the sheep for the goat, the construction of roads, and the digging of wells—could hardly be seen through to completion in the midst of a civil war.

M. Soustelle was also struck by the defects of a skeleton administration. He found huge rural townships like Arris and Khenchela, comparable in size to departments of France but stretching, as he puts it, "from the high plateau to the Sahara across Cyclopean deposits of lunar mountains," committed to the responsibility of a single administrator. Some, but not all, of the administrators were men of high caliber; beneath them, there was a sort of administrative void, peopled only by a few *caïds*, frequently absent, and *ouakafs* (headmen). It was clear that the Administration would have to get closer to the inhabitants if its purpose was to improve their lot—and to know what was going on.

The new Governor General had grave doubts, too, about the efficacy of the action undertaken by the military. Two huge operations, dubbed "Violette" and "Véronique," had been launched in the Aurès without success. "It goes without saying," M. Soustelle writes, "that several battalions noisily brought together to encircle, then to search, a *djebel* found nobody there save only, perhaps, a few cunning *fellaga* who, their rifles hidden in a safe place, had taken their goats to graze among the rocks." Worse still, the Army had been unable, for want of troops, to bring the whole area within a close-knit security system, and many a native village, finding its requests for protection ignored, had of necessity come to terms with the rebels. Other villages and clans might have been, but were not, armed for their own protection.

Another anomaly was the absence of any legal provisions for dealing with the emergency. As a result, a rebel caught with a smoking gun in his hands was duly brought before the civil courts, where he would, as M. Soustelle says, "take refuge in the *maquis* of procedure, safer for him than that of the hills." The death of a rebel naturally gave rise to a judicial inquiry. M. Soustelle was astonished to discover that officers and men, cited by an examining magistrate, were compelled to answer for their conduct in the field as though, in returning fire, they might have been guilty of a criminal act. Much has since been done to eliminate such absurdities, but the ponderous ritual of French justice still serves the rebels well on innumerable occasions. It has also had the unfortunate effect of inciting French soldiers to deal with captured rebels ruthlessly and on the spot, in accordance, not with the laws of the Republic, but with those of revolutionary strife.

The civil and military authorities were powerless under existing regulations to control internal communications or the movements of people, to conduct night searches or to ban seditious meetings. The Government, in short, three and a half months after the outbreak of the rebellion, had not yet recognized the true nature of the Algerian situation.

It was General de Gaulle, I think, who said on one occasion that the health of a nation could best be measured by its reflex in matters pertaining to national defense. Judged by this criterion, France was truly a "sick man." The politicians, engaged in their sterile games, the intellectuals, absorbed in polemics and casuistry, seemed, with few exceptions, not to have realized that the French state was dissolving before their eyes. Algeria was the vital test: everything here was at stake—the integrity of the nation, the right of citizens to life and property, the defense of the frontiers. The loss of the Levant States, of Indochina, of the Indian establishments, of Tunisia, of Morocco—all this, however serious for what it revealed of the nation's will to resist, was not to be compared to the loss of Algeria. France, if brought to her knees in Algeria, would have been vanquished, not by the rebels, but by her own inner rot, just as Rome was when the Rhine and Danube frontiers buckled.

Marshal Juin, in his book, *Le Maghreb en Feu,** quotes a Moroccan

* Paris: Plon, 1958.

nationalist as having told a countryman serving in the French Army, in an attempt to shake his loyalty, that he had no idea of the degree of degeneracy and folly to which the French had fallen, that with France anything might now be ventured. These words, apocryphal or real—the man to whom they are attributed, former Premier Si Bekkai of Morocco, denied having uttered them—nevertheless reflected an opinion widely held among North African nationalists, and among many others as well. The F.L.N., in any case, based its whole action on the belief that the French would weary and cave in, even though there was no decision in the field; that no interest, however vital, could now distract the French from their divisions, their quarrels, and their pleasures. The F.L.N. had dared strike at the heart; events suggested that its boldness might be vindicated by success.

But who could be sure the French would not show in the end that they had the stamina and the will to save the threatened part of their national patrimony? It was to be hoped that in this contest the French would not fail, for if they did, they could be counted out for the defense of the wider, and therefore less intimately perceived, interests of the Western Alliance; and they would, by the same token, abdicate in advance any claim to leadership in the federated Europe of tomorrow.

The Governor General's address to the Algerian Assembly was awaited with intense curiosity on all sides. What, exactly, were his views, his intentions? Everyone wondered; much depended on the answer. The Palais Carnot was, therefore, buzzing with excitement when M. Soustelle appeared on February 23, to present, with his comments, the 1955-56 budget for the Assembly's consideration. He did not announce specific policy decisions—it was too soon for that—but he did define the principles by which he intended to be guided and the spirit in which he approached the tasks ahead. He promised to make "pacification" his first duty; he said that by this he meant "peace and security, justice and equality for all." In other words, the military and police action would be accompanied and, he hoped, reinforced by political, social, and economic measures. And he went on to say:

> No uncertainty must be allowed to remain as to our inflexible determination to preserve Algeria from the terrible destiny that some are seeking to prepare for it. France is at home here, or rather, Algeria and all its inhabitants form an integral part of France, one and indivisible. All must know, here and elsewhere, that France will not leave Algeria any more than she will leave Provence or Brittany. Whatever happens, the destiny of Algeria is French. This means that a choice has been made. The choice is

> called integration; it is to make Algeria each day more completely a province, different from the others certainly, but fully French. . . .
>
> At the present time, we have a charter voted by the Parliament, and which is our law; I refer to the Algerian Statute. Its progressive and loyal application is a duty incumbent upon us all.

The Governor General called for a "crusade against hunger." The pressures of a rapidly expanding population, he said, demanded a much more productive economy. The Government was, therefore, submitting a record works budget of 52 billion francs ($148 million), four-fifths of which was to be provided by France. M. Soustelle also announced that in the coming fiscal year, France would contribute for the first time to Algeria's ordinary budget.

"The aid provided by Metropolitan France," he said, "enables us to present a balanced budget that the Algerian Assembly will be able to vote without imposing any further burden on the population. It is not material aid only that we receive from Metropolitan France, but the precious comfort of her solicitude, the concrete and tangible demonstration of her solidarity.

"What better reply could we give to those who might be tempted to assert that France is turning away from her African province? And what a lie given to the voices abroad that denounce the so-called colonialism of France, when our country, far from exploiting Algeria selfishly, draws on her own resources to help Algeria live through a period of crisis!"

The rebellion, meanwhile, was spreading. By February, it had reached the Nememcha mountains to the south and to the east of the Aurès. Intelligence reports spoke of two strong bands in the area, well equipped with automatic weapons and presumably intent on opening a supply route to southern Tunisia. On February 16, a sergeant and six men of the 1st Regiment of Airborne Hussars stationed at Seiar in the Nememchas, fifty-two miles south of Khenchela, set out to patrol the Djebel Chechar and vanished.*

In the Aurès fastness, the bands, some 300 or 400 strong altogether, but with up to 1,000 active auxiliaries, gave repeated evidence of their fighting spirit. In January 4, a French lieutenant and four paratroopers perished in a rebel ambush between Foum Toub and Medina. On January 8, two paratroopers and eight rebels were killed in a sharp

* The sergeant never returned; the six hussars, caught by the rebels, escaped on May 23.

engagement near Ichmoul. On January 18, a patrol of the 18th Parachute Regiment, falling into a rebel ambush near Oued Taga, lost two lieutenants, a sergeant, and four men killed. Two supply convoys were attacked on February 23 and one on February 26. The French military position seems to have improved slightly in February with the arrival of Moroccan *tabors,* native troops noted for their mobility and toughness.

A small rebel band showed its teeth near Condé Smendou north of Constantine on January 18, killing a French gendarme and wounding another before being cut to pieces in a French counterattack.* Other bands were detected in the Jemmapes and El Milia districts between Constantine and the sea, and in the Edough massif west of Bône, while, in the Souk Ahras district, the rebel chief Amor Djebar was reportedly active. In Kabylia, a Senegalese unit holding an isolated position near Michelet at an altitude of 3,600 feet was stormed in the early hours of January 9 by a force of about thirty rebels. The assailants, thought to have been led by Ouamrane himself, were driven off; but by their action, the rebels had shown, for the first time in Kabylia, that they dared throw themselves against troops in quarters. A rash of terrorist agitation was also breaking out in the Dra el Mizan district, seventy-two miles east of Algiers, in the high Sidi Ali Bou Nab hills further to the north and in the area between Azazga, east of Tizi Ouzou, and Port Gueydon on the coast.

21. GOOD AND BAD LUCK FOR THE FRENCH

The rebels, wherever they had managed to get a foothold, were showing signs of better organization and coordination in the fourth month of the rebellion. Little by little, the Army of National Liberation (A.L.N.) was becoming a reality, tangible, effective, dangerous; little by little, as reinforcements filtered in from Libya, it was able to con-

* One of the six rebels killed on that occasion was identified as Mourad Didouche, a founding member of the old C.R.U.A.

solidate and extend its control. With its supreme council in Cairo, its training camps in Egypt and Libya, its headquarters at Tripoli, its military regulations, its underground network, and its fifth column, the A.L.N. was in a position to adjust its strategy to the long pull and, in the meantime, to absorb many a hard knock. It had taken prisoners, executed "traitors," put out "victory bulletins" over Cairo radio. This was enough to give it the prestige that, in the eyes of the Moslem populace, rightfully belongs to all "heroes of Islam"; a patriotic ideal was beginning to crystallize around it.

The challenge, clearly, was not one to be taken lightly. But instead of tightening up right down the line, the French dallied. Dangerous agitators slipped through their fingers. The Government and the Parliament quibbled about the terms of the contemplated emergency powers act as though they had all the time in the world. The French forces in Algeria were, it is true, brought up to 84,000 men; a far greater number was urgently needed. Algerians living in France were allowed to return to Algeria in droves without any check on their reasons and intentions. No effort was made to counter the flood of rebel propaganda.

François Mauriac in *L'Express* and Claude Bourdet in *France-Observateur*, both of them fast friends of the rebels, raised the cry of police brutalities in January. Buckets of tears were shed in Paris for the misfortunes of Moulay Merbah and Mohammed Laichaoui, none for the victims of the rebels. Police officials in Algeria got so jittery about possible sanctions that some preferred to take no initiative whatsoever. The rebellion was, in short, prospering like bacteria in a culture medium.

But the French could claim one notable success: the capture of Mostefa Ben Boulaïd. The rebel leader, on his way to Tripoli for a meeting with Mohammed Ben Bella, was caught near the Libyan frontier on February 11. The circumstances of his capture prove that if, as the French say, "there is a god for drunkards," there is sometimes one also for the French. On February 10, at Ben Gardane in southern Tunisia, a native constable spotted two suspicious-looking characters among the passengers of the bus from Gabès. Ordering the two to follow him for an identity check, the constable started off toward the native affairs office; a few moments later, one of his charges whipped out a gun and shot him dead. A general alarm went out, and the two fugitives, pursued across the desert, were picked up the next morning at a point thirty-four miles southeast of Ben Gardane just as they were about to enter Libyan territory. Their identity was quickly established, one of the two being none other than Mostefa Ben Ahmed Ben Boulaïd, thirty-eight years old, of the Aurès. The other, previously unknown, was a certain Amar Ben Mohammed Ferchichi, thirty-nine.

Alas, good luck cannot last forever! Ben Boulaïd, sentenced to death in June, 1955, given the benefit of a mistrial, sentenced to death a second time in October, escaped with ten others from the Constantine prison on November 10 and lived to command his men in the Aurès against the French again.

"And of those who say, 'Verily, we are Christians,' we have taken a compact; but they have forgotten a portion of what they were reminded of; wherefore have we excited amongst them enmity and hatred till the resurrection day" (Koran, V: 17). Allah's malediction has, certainly, been upon Christendom ever since these words were revealed. A Christian may, however, console himself with the thought that Islam has apparently been in the same boat: God seems to have thrown discord among the Moslems for all time. Dissension was rife in the Arab world and also in the ranks of the Algerian rebels; it was to do Ben Boulaïd in at last. After he had ordered the execution of several of his subordinates for failing to toe the mark in various ways, Ben Boulaïd perished with his lieutenant, Lakhdar Chelili, and two other rebels in the explosion of a booby-trapped radio set on March 27, 1956.

On February 26, a group of gendarmes from Boghni and Dra el Mizan, on patrol near Maatkas, north of Boghni, were shot at by three Arabs. An exchange of fire ensued, and when it was over, the gendarmes had two prisoners, one of them wounded. The wounded man, who claimed to be Mahmoud Fetah of MacMahon, a town south of Batna, was found to have, in fact, a different and far more interesting identity: Mohammed Ben Hamadi el-Aziz by name, alias El Riffi; he hailed from Tetuán in the Spanish zone of Morocco, where he had been born in 1929. According to his own account,* Hamadi traveled in 1948 first to Cairo, then to Baghdad, to enter the cadet college there. Emerging in 1951 with a diploma equivalent to a second lieutenant's commission, he returned to Cairo to assist the old Riffian leader, Abd-el-Krim, and his brother, M'Hamed el-Khattabi, both of whom were then busy recruiting "commandos" for action against the French in North Africa. Hamadi's first mission for Abd-el-Krim took him to Benghazi to look into the possibilities of purchasing some arms there; but the mission was an abortive one, and Hamadi moved on to Morocco, where he seems to have been at loose ends for a time in 1952 before reporting back to Cairo.

Thirty-odd Moroccan students, recruited by Hamadi's countryman and Baghdad classmate, Hachémi Taouad, were accepted by the Egyp-

---

* As given to André Blanchet of *Le Monde*. See *Le Monde* for April 22, 1955.

tian Army for military training. This success excited the envy of Salah Ben Youssef, extremist secretary-general of the Tunisian Neo-Destour party, who, hoping to do as much for his own country, turned the task of recruiting Tunisian trainees over to Abdallah Abaad, a deserter from the Ben Gardane constabulary and a graduate of the Baghdad cadet college. Mohammed Ben Bella, anxious to get some Algerians into training as well, approached Taouad and Abaad on the subject, and the scheme was agreed to; it even got the blessing of Majors Mohammed Fathi el-Dib and Soleiman Ezzat, Egyptian intelligence officers in charge of Arab and North African affairs. Abaad managed to bring about sixty Tunisians into the country as a starter and to "matriculate" them for a four-month course under the auspices of the Egyptian National Guard at Cairo's Koubri el-Koubba camp in the summer of 1954. A few Moroccans and Algerians rounded up by Hamadi also joined the course.

In Tripoli, meanwhile, Azzeddine Azzouz, leader of a Tunisian faction hostile to a settlement with France, had undertaken to rally his countrymen to the idea of total resistance. In this he was opposed by Ali Zlitni, head of the official Neo-Destour "military" organization. When the quarrel landed Azzouz in a Libyan prison, Hamadi was sent from Cairo to extricate him. The Libyan authorities agreed at Hamadi's instance to treat Zlitni and Azzouz with equal respect. A free man again, Azzouz sold Hamadi and Ben Bella on the idea of a unified command for the North African "Liberation Army" with himself as supreme chief of staff. He suggested politely that Hamadi and Taouad should represent Morocco and that Ben Bella should represent Algeria. All this was accepted by Azzouz's confederates; but when word of the compact got back to Cairo, Abd-el-Krim flew into a rage and dispatched an indignant letter asking the Arab League to cut the scalawags off without a piaster.

At this juncture, who should appear on the scene in Tripoli but Mostefa Ben Boulaïd with the latest news from the *Comité Révolutionnaire d'Unité et d'Action* (C.R.U.A.). The impression gained from his report was that the "Algerian brothers" would soon be ready for business. On the strength of this, after having drawn £3,500 from the Egyptian consulate in Benghazi for the purchase of arms, Ben Bella and Azzouz took off for a top-level conference with Boudiaf in Bern, where the final details of the coming "offensive" in Algeria were settled. It was also decided that Hamadi would serve as military adviser to Boudiaf. In consequence of this decision, Hamadi set out from Cairo on October 15 with an Algerian identity card in the name of Mahmoud Fetah, the good wishes of Majors Fathi and Ezzat, and a letter of introduction to the paymaster at the Egyptian consulate in Benghazi. After stopping briefly in Tripoli to confer again with Azzouz and Ben Bella, Hamadi continued his journey; he was only in Gabès when the rebellion broke out, but, as calmly as you please, he took a train to Algiers and a bus from there to Tizi Ouzou. On December 9, somewhere in Kabylia, the young officer appeared before the bandit chief, Belkacem Krim, who, it seems, was rather less than glad to see him. For forty-seven days, Hamadi shared the life of Krim's guerrillas without being given any particular command.

Hamadi's testimony gave the French a glimpse of what was going on behind their backs in Egypt, Iraq, and Libya. The real Mahmoud Fetah, incidentally, a well-established citizen of MacMahon, was amazed to hear the story of Second Lieutenant Hamadi. Three months before, Mr. Fetah had reported the theft of his identity card.

In February and March, 1955, the Algerian Communist party (P.C.A.) made a serious effort to get its grappling irons on the rebellion. A by-election to fill the vacancy caused by the death of Abdelkader Cadi, moderate deputy for Constantine, was due to be held in the middle of March. This circumstance, it was perceived, provided an excellent opportunity for prospecting the rebel-infested parts of the eastern department. A Communist candidate was put up in the person of Saïd Lamrani, a Batna lawyer, who campaigned vigorously, though more for his party than himself. His platform, pledge, and slogan involved the immediate establishment of "popular committees for the struggle against the repression and for a general amnesty." He denounced the authorities for their "brutality," called for the cessation of all military operations in the Aurès and in Kabylia, and demanded that full and prompt compensation be paid to the "victims of the repression." A P.C.A. "delegation" comprising Mme. Alice Sportisse, Communist deputy for Oran, René Justrabo, Communist delegate to the Algerian Assembly for Sidi Bel Abbès, and Mohammed Guerrouf of the P.C.A. central committee, turned up to help Mr. Lamrani keep his campaign lively—and to have a look around. Candidate and delegation traveled through the Aurès without let or hindrance, taking roads reputedly controlled by the rebels and long since forsaken by all other civilians. That there was collusion of sorts between the Communists and the rebels could hardly be doubted, but real cooperation was another matter. The P.C.A. had not achieved that.

Guerrouf, instead of returning to Algiers with Mme. Sportisse and M. Justrabo, stayed on in the Aurès; he had business there. A native of the area, he was already well introduced among the rebels. In the first days of the rebellion, he had taken a rebel chief known as Si Slimane to Algiers for conferences with the Communist leaders. Later he had been in touch with a lesser rebel named Messaoud Ifrih, who, unluckily, fell into French hands and spilled all he knew. It was learned, for instance, that a token monetary contribution from the *Secours Populaire Algérien*, a Communist front organization, had been channeled through Guerrouf to Ifrih. The man's testimony was said to be damaging in other respects. In any case, it put the police on Guerrouf's trail; the Communist was arrested on March 7 at Oulach in the Aurès, taken to Batna, and charged with being in league with the rebels.*

The results of the by-election, held on March 13, were a surprise to no one. Dr. Ali Cadi, independent nationalist and brother of the deceased deputy, led the field with 48,787 votes, or 53 per cent of the votes cast. Hachémi Benchennouf, Popular Republican, was second with 35 per cent; Boulakras Ben Gana, independent, third with 8 per cent, and Lamrani last with 4 per cent. The turnout, as might be expected at such a time, was not heavy: 42.6 per cent. A runoff ballot on March 27 brought Dr. Cadi's vote up to 36 per cent—he won—and Lamrani's down to 3 per cent. Pierre Gabelle, Popular Republican deputy for Orléans, declared on his return from a visit to the Constantine department that the election had been entirely "free."

The Communists—need it be said?—were in no way disturbed by their candidate's poor showing at the polls. The object of the exercise had been to spread a little propaganda and to get the lay of the land, not to win a hopeless election. What rankled was Guerrouf's arrest; he had made such a promising start!

22. STATE OF EMERGENCY

On March 19, nearly five months after the outbreak of the rebellion, it was announced in Paris that the Government was now almost ready with special legislation to help cope with the Algerian problem. A bill

---

* Guerrouf was convicted in September, 1955, and sentenced to two years in prison.

to authorize the declaration of a "state of emergency" in parts of Algeria (or even of France), it was said, would be submitted to the National Assembly with a request for urgent consideration. The announcement, couched in almost apologetic terms, is worth quoting as a reflection of the Government's understanding of what was needed in Algeria. It said:

> The administrative and judicial arrangements currently in force are not adapted to the conditions in which outlaw bands have been developing their criminal actions since November, 1954—bands which, though still small in numbers, infest certain difficult regions of Algeria—and hence it is practically impossible for the Government to insure the security of the bulk of the population against the exactions of the rebels.
>
> Consequently, this population runs great risks in failing to comply with the requirements of the outlaws and would inevitably become their victim or accomplice, and in the end turn away from us for fear of reprisals. To remedy this deficiency, our present store of judicial means offers only one solution: the declaration of martial law, which transfers wide powers to the military authorities.
>
> But this solution also raises serious objections at once because of its exceptional gravity and because of the disorganization of the traditional administrative structure that it implies.
>
> Therefore, so as to avoid having recourse to this extreme solution, which the present situation in no way justifies, it seemed necessary to bring into existence judicial arrangements which, while leaving the exercise of the traditional powers to the civil authorities, reinforces and concentrates these powers in such a way as to make them better adapted to events having the nature of a public calamity likely to endanger public order or to violate national sovereignty. These arrangements are called a "state of emergency." Every care will be taken to see that their duration and extent of application are made subject to the prior agreement of the Parliament.*

Let us stand back for a moment and judge this announcement in the light of subsequent events. The Government recognized that the deficiencies of which it spoke could be remedied by a declaration of

---

* *Le Monde*, in reporting this announcement in its issue of March 20, 1955, did well to recall that the military authorities are not allowed, in times of peace, to make an arrest without the assistance of the civil authorities except in cases of *flagrante delicto*.

martial law, a step held, however, to be in no way justified by the situation. But could it reasonably be hoped that a "state of emergency" was adequate? The rebellion was to go from strength to strength in the months that followed. It was not difficult to anticipate that such would be the case. Why, then, did the Government, after much costly delay, come forward with a pipsqueak proposal? The answer, I fear, lies in the fact that the Government did not want to ask for more than it could expect to get from that divided and umbrageous body, the National Assembly.

The bill, submitted on March 22, was prefaced with a long preamble which added little to the announcement already made except to say that the object of the contemplated measures was to "put an end" to the insecurity and fear "psychosis" existing in Algeria. The main provisions of the bill, essentially an enabling act, were:

> A "state of emergency" may be declared by act of Parliament in all or part of French territory in case of imminent peril. Within the area covered by such an act, the Government is authorized to determine by decree the specific zones to which the special powers resulting from the "state of emergency" are to be applied. The duration of the "state of emergency" is set by Parliament and can be extended only by another act of Parliament. When the Parliament is not sitting, the "state of emergency" may be declared by governmental decree, but if this happens, the Parliament must be convened within forty-eight hours to consider the matter. The "state of emergency" cannot be declared if the National Assembly is dissolved. The "state of emergency" gives the prefects concerned power to:
>
> 1. Ban the movements of vehicles and of persons within certain areas and at certain times as determined by prefectural decree;
> 2. Establish protection and security zones by decree and make persons residing in such zones subject to special controls;
> 3. Expel from the department any person seeking to impede the action of the authorities in any way.
>
> The Interior Minister and, in Algeria, the Governor General are empowered to assign a place of residence to anyone whose activity endangers public security and order, but persons to whom a place of residence is assigned may appeal for redress to a committee appointed for this purpose. The authorities may order the temporary closing of public establishments of all kinds and impound certain types of arms and ammunition. Searches may be

conducted at night (under Article Eleven) only if permission is specifically given by the Parliament when the "state of emergency" is declared. The same proviso applies to measures to control the press, radio, cinema, and theatre. Article Twelve gives the military courts wider jurisdiction. Infractions of measures taken in consequence of a "state of emergency" are made liable to prison terms of not more than two months and to fines of not more than 200,000 francs. Such cases, if *sub judice* when the "state of emergency" ends, will still be heard, but all other provisions of the bill will automatically lapse.

A bill to declare a "state of emergency" in Algeria for six months with application of Article Eleven (night searches and press controls) was submitted at the same time.

Immediately, the members of the Interior and Justice Committees began haggling and quibbling over the terms of the Government's bill, chipping off a provision here, tacking on an amendment there; in short, enjoying to the full their parliamentary prerogatives. They acted as though, by going through all the traditional motions, they could prove to themselves that the old world was the old world yet.

M. Bourgès-Maunoury felt he had to sugar-coat his plea for approval with assurances to the effect that the Government considered economic assistance to be just as important as the contemplated security measures. He promised up and down that the Government would never go beyond house arrest in pursuance of the "state of emergency" act; internment camps, he insisted, were out of the question. Robert Schuman, the Minister of Justice, begged the committees to believe that civil justice was not being thrust aside. Judicial inquiries, he said, would still be conducted by civil magistrates; the rights of the defense would suffer no prejudice. Certain criminal cases would, to be sure, be referred to the military courts to expedite the administration of justice, but the sentences of these courts would remain subject to appeal.

Mohammed Salah Bendjelloul, deputy for Constantine, and Robert Ballanger, a Communist deputy, tried unsuccessfully to have the bill thrown out in committee as unconstitutional. But before the bill was reported on March 31, the Interior Committee had removed the provision permitting the Government to declare a "state of emergency" by decree during a parliamentary recess and had added a provision to make the "state of emergency" end automatically in the event of a dissolution of the National Assembly. Another amendment barred the establishment of internment camps, which were, however, soon to become an evident necessity. The Government was made responsible for the subsistence of persons to whom a place of residence was assigned. It was further stipulated that the civil courts remained competent in cases not specifically asked for by the military courts. The whole effect of the committee's action had been to water down the bill.

Its adoption by the Assembly on April 1 at 4:20 A.M. illustrated one of the more dubious aspects of parliamentary procedure under the Fourth Republic. There was no debate, but a laborious pantomime interspersed with ritual phrases and the introduction of crippling amendments. The opposition naturally demanded, as was its right, a vote on each article of the bill, but with only a handful of deputies present—twenty-five in the final phases of the operation—and with the others voting by proxy, nothing could be carried by a show of hands. Time after time, all afternoon and all night, the proxies, frequently mere ushers, came down the aisles and stuffed their ballots in the box, and the counting had to begin all over again. The Communists, an occasional Socialist, and the indefatigable Mr. Bendjelloul kept the Assembly in session through long hours with their amendments, every one of which was voted down by a solid but incorporeal phalanx of some 360 deputies. The bill was carried in the end by a vote of 379 to 219.*

The adoption of the "state of emergency" act moved the nationalists and Communists to great outcries of protest. But Pierre Vignau, delegate to the Algerian Assembly for Médéa, summed up the feelings of the first college with the statement, "These measures, though they come late, are bound to have beneficial effects." It is, at any rate, no exaggeration to say that some remedial action was urgently needed, particularly in the Aurès, where the situation had deteriorated to a dangerous degree. René Janon gave the readers of *Le Figaro* an idea of what was happening there when he wrote:

> Although we motored by night from Arris to Batna in late December without fear of unpleasant encounters, the traveler going from one of these towns to the other must now take his place in one of the three escorted convoys that make the trip each week. Acts of terrorism are perpetrated almost on the outskirts of Batna. . . . On the Batna-Arris road, even military vehicles are frequently machine-gunned, and the staff car of a colonel of the Foreign Legion almost struck a mine a few days ago. . . . It is now certain that the chiefs of the organized bands, men like

* The declaration of a "state of emergency" in Algeria for six months with application of Article Eleven had been incorporated into the enabling act.

> Hocine Berail in the M'Chounèche district, Messaoud Maache between Bou Hamama and Arris, and Saddok Chebchoub between Foum Toub and Timgad, are in touch with Algiers on the one hand and with Tripoli and Cairo on the other. The rebels have divided the Aurès into eight or nine zones of operation, each under a separate command complete with ranks and uniforms. The various combat groups, generally three for each command, possess their own lookouts, shock troops, and auxiliaries. Contributions are levied throughout the area. . . . All the rebels look upon themselves as soldiers of the Army of National Liberation, and their crimes are aimed especially at dignitaries friendly to France or at Moslems who keep the French authorities informed. Thus, latterly, they have captured several of our auxiliaries and have freed them after mutilating their lips and tongues, cutting off their ears, or putting out their eyes. . . .*

By the end of April, 1955, eighty-eight Moslems, among them tribal chiefs, municipal councilors, and rural constables, had been murdered by the rebels; eighty-one had been mutilated or wounded; attempts had been made on 124 others. Each spectacular death, each humiliating disfigurement, marked an advance for the rebels; it put the local inhabitants in awe of them and secured for them the cloak of silence behind which their network of collaboration could begin to sap the foundations of French authority.

Wielding the imperfect sword put in his hand by the Parliament, Jacques Soustelle went resolutely into battle. The "state of emergency" was decreed to exist in the Tizi Ouzou, Batna, and Tebessa *arrondissements,* that is, in a large segment of Kabylia, in the greater part of the Aurès, and in the region of the Tunisian frontier, areas inhabited by about 1,200,000 people altogether. To appease the Moslem politicians, M. Soustelle let it be known that the provisions of the "state of emergency" act would not be felt outside the troubled areas and, even there, would be applied in the most considerate way possible.

On April 17, as the voters were going to the polls all over Algeria to elect new general councilors, a convoy of the 5th Battalion of Algerian Rifles fell into a rebel ambush between El Ouldja and Kheirane; the major commanding the battalion, a military chaplain, and two riflemen were killed. The same day the rebels attacked another convoy near Arris, wounding the mother of François Rey, civil administrator at Arris, her

* See *Le Figaro* for March 25, 1955.

driver, and three *goumiers*. The rebels had thus, symbolically, told the French what they thought of the "state of emergency." But the last word had perhaps not yet been spoken.

23. PACIFICATION TAKES ON A NEW MEANING

A bold, new policy based on the pacification techniques that had proved their worth in Morocco was about to be initiated in the Aurès. The appointment, on April 29, of Brigadier General Gaston Parlange, a seasoned native affairs officer from Morocco, to exercise, under the superior authority of the Prefect of Constantine, full military and civil powers in the eastern emergency zone could only prelude a radical and long-overdue change in method and approach. It was announced that General Parlange, himself an expert in the training and handling of native levies, and a select team of twenty-one native affairs officers—twelve from Morocco and nine from the Sahara—would undertake a total administrative reorganization of the area and, concomitantly, its reconquest in depth. The mailed fist was to be coupled with persuasion; the clash of arms was to be followed by peaceful penetration; the word "pacification" was to take on new meaning.

The three existing administrative centers—Batna, Arris, and Khenchela —would, according to the announced plan, be supplemented by twelve pacification zones corresponding roughly to tribal divisions. Each of the new zones would have at its center a *bordj*, at once a fort and an administrative building, to serve as a haven of security, as a pole of attraction, and as a token of France's determination to remain in the country forever. A school, a dispensary, a playing field, and a granary would be provided to infuse the seat of the *bordj* with communal life, and, perhaps, foster the growth of a future village. Each officer-in-charge would be given a *goum* of 180 *tabors* in addition to his personal guard of five mounted *mokhaznis* (auxiliaries). He would be expected to improve the lot of the people and to relieve unemployment by digging wells and irrigation ditches, by building roads and market places. He would be encouraged to arm the inhabitants for their own defense. It was hoped that in this way the rebel bands, having lost the cooperation of the inhabitants, could be isolated and destroyed.

But, of course, in the immediate situation, persuasion alone could not be expected to do the trick. The Army would continue to track the bands. To make its action more effective, severe measures of constraint were imposed: no travel was allowed between sunset and sunrise; native caravans were compelled to follow prescribed routes; the cities were put under curfew. A "zone of protection" covering the vast rural townships of Biskra and El Oued extended the emergency regulations far to the south. Later, the whole Constantine department was declared to be in a "state of emergency."

General Parlange established his headquarters at Batna early in May. He was assisted there by Lieutenant Colonel Guido Verlet, formerly chief of the Tahala district in the Middle Atlas between Taza and Fez. Major Jean-Baptiste Nivaggioni took over at Arris. We shall see that, as time went by, General Parlange and the native affairs officers under him gradually put the rebel bands in the Aurès on the defensive and reduced many to impotence.

In Kabylia, too, the "emergency zone" was organized in April and buttressed with "zones of protection" in the Palestro, Aïn Bessem, Bouïra, and Maillot districts. On April 23, the Minister of Justice decreed that the military courts could try persons accused of crimes committed after October 30, 1954, in the judicial districts of Batna, Guelma, and Tizi Ouzou. Another important step was taken when M. Soustelle ordered the formation throughout the country of Mobile Rural Police Groups (G.M.P.R.) composed essentially of French-officered Moslem war veterans. Some 1,800 French reservists, many of them officers with knowledge of Arabic or Berber, were called to active duty in May and assigned to native units. The total effectives in Algeria were brought up to 100,000 men.

The special powers granted under the "state of emergency" act enabled the authorities to round up and expel or put under surveillance persons held to be dangerous. Among these were a number of French Communist schoolteachers whose activities were irksome, to say the least. Jacques Galland, teacher at Tizi Rachid near Fort National in Kabylia, had, for instance, attracted notice by going from one village market place to another distributing handbills of protest against the "repression" and running errands for the *Secours Populaire Algérien,* that general purveyor to the rebels. He was expelled from the Algiers department. Guy Drouillard, teacher at Khenchela, was expelled from the Constantine department for "repeatedly getting in the way of the authorities." In

May, despite its rash promises, the Government set up five internment camps in Algeria and filled them with undesirables.

On the other hand, the Government enriched the rebellion by letting the cream of the old Messalist leadership out of prison. Abderrahmane Kiouane, who has since done yeoman's service in the cause of the F.L.N., was freed on April 2 at the behest of Jacques Chevallier. In May, fourteen other former leaders of the Movement for the Triumph of Democratic Liberties (M.T.L.D.), including Moulay Merbah, Benyoussef Benkhedda, Sid Ali Abdelhamid, and Ahmed Boudaa were released by court order. Merbah is, today, Messali's alter ego, chief amanuensis, and agent-at-large. Benkhedda became a member of the F.L.N. governing body.

Le Monde noted candidly at the time that the decision to release the fourteen, although made by a judicial authority, was in line with M. Soustelle's expressed desires, the idea being to give the Moslems "renewed hope."* Hope in what? one is tempted to ask. Seen in retrospect, the measure must be stamped as imprudent; it proves that even M. Soustelle, in the spring of 1955, labored under certain misconceptions.

The moment has come, perhaps, to cast a glance at the remnants of the defunct M.T.L.D. Quiescence is what we see among the followers of Hocine Lahouel. Mohammed Cherchalli, who had kept the organization together in the absence of Lahouel, turned his responsibilities over in May to a committee comprising Sid Ali Abdelhamid, Zitouni Messaoudi, Ahmed Boudaa, and Abdelhakim Bencheikh-Hocine. The faction was to be disbanded in November in response to an F.L.N. command; its members were allowed to join the F.L.N. on an individual basis, or not, as they chose.

The followers of Messali were, however, showing some signs of vitality. Their faction had survived the government dissolution order, but under a new name; it now called itself the Algerian National Movement (M.N.A.). Messali, who had by no means knuckled under to F.L.N. pretensions to supremacy, was nevertheless forced to recognize the existence of the rival organization; his thought was to dominate it, just as he had once dominated the Friends of the Manifesto. He was reported in April to have approached the F.L.N. indirectly with a plan whereby he would himself assume the presidency of a combined M.N.A.–F.L.N., control relations with the Arab states, and direct guerrilla operations in the Oran and Algiers departments, leaving only the Constantine department to the F.L.N. This plan, it seems, was haughtily rejected by the

* See *Le Monde* for May 15, 1955.

leaders of the F.L.N., who vowed they would wipe the floor with Messali—"Rasputin" as they called him—before they were through. In May, the F.L.N. issued a circular containing a bitter attack on the "revolutionaries in slippers and dressing gowns" who still shuffled along after that "old dodderer" Messali.

The General Council of the Vendée department had, in November, 1954, unanimously adopted a motion requesting the Government to assign some other place of residence to Messali, described as "undesirable in the department and more particularly in Les Sables-d'Olonne." Satisfaction was somewhat tardily given on April 16, 1955: Messali moved on that day with his cumbersome suite to the modest Hôtel-Restaurant de la Grande Cave at Angoulême, 280 miles southwest of Paris.

The 1955 cantonal elections, held on April 17 with runoff balloting on April 24, gave the second college parity of representation in the General Councils for the first time. Of the sixty-eight seats to be filled, thirty-three were new. The U.D.M.A. put up fifty-six candidates; the P.C.A., sixty-four. The M.T.L.D., of course, no longer existed; the Messalists and Lahouelists, however, recommended abstention. The U.D.M.A., actively supported by the Ulema, forged ahead in the Constantine department, picking up several of the new seats. The summary results are shown in the tabulation following.

	Percentage of the Popular Vote	*Number of Seats Gained*	*Total Number of Seats Held*
U.D.M.A.	11	10	11
P.C.A.	3	1	2
Others	86	24	88

(*Participation: 57 per cent*)

These elections marked the end of an era; no popular elections, free or otherwise, were held in Algeria for the next three years, except on a rudimentary village level. M. Soustelle says in his book that the electoral operations were, on the whole, honestly conducted. The most scandalous incident involved Abdelmadjid Mecheri, delegate to the Algerian Assembly for Tebessa, who was then standing for re-election to the Constantine General Council. At Morsott, where Abdelmadjid's brother, Tahar, was *caïd*, a gang of the candidate's supporters made off with the ballot boxes and stuffed them at their leisure. Abdelmadjid later declared for the rebels, went to Cairo, and posed as an enemy of France.* Another Mecheri brother, Chérif, is a French prefect who has served as Secretary-General of the French Union.

24. BANDUNG AND ITS CONSEQUENCES

An event that, morally at least, was to buoy up the rebellion as never before occurred in April some 6,000 miles away. The North Africans who traveled to Bandung in Indonesia to attend the great conference of African and Asian states from April 18 to 24 came back with thrilling reports: a third of humanity had, through its representatives, declared war on colonialism in all its forms; twenty-nine nations stood pledged to support the Algerians, the Tunisians, and the Moroccans in their struggle for independence.

Salah Ben Youssef, secretary-general of the Tunisian Neo-Destour party, headed a North African "delegation" which included Allal el-Fassi, leader of the Moroccan Istiqlal party, and Mohammed Yazid and Mohand Hocine Aït Ahmed for Algeria. Messali's man, Chadly Mekki, and Mohammed Hassan Ouezzani, leader of the Moroccan Democratic Independence party, chimed in with their counterpoint on the sidelines. The North Africans, although not officially recognized as delegates, did their utmost to damn the French and glorify the cause of North African independence; they were recompensed for their effort. An Egyptian motion, unanimously adopted by the conference, proclaimed the right of the populations of Algeria, Tunisia, and Morocco to self-determination and to national independence; it called on France to seek a peaceful settlement without delay.

The Arab delegates in private meetings pledged huge sums of money to help the North African insurgents; a Saudi delegate was heard to speak in terms of $20,000,000. Apart from its wider implications, the Bandung conference made the leaders of the Algerian rebellion fully conscious of the tremendous advantages to be derived from the grievance-ridden

* Mr. Mecheri did well to leave Algeria, where he had acquired a solid reputation as a profiteer. At the time of his departure, an information was pending against him for the embezzlement of more than 100 million francs from the native Provident Society at Tebessa.

solidarity of the Asian and African world. The Algerian problem was, to a dangerous degree, "internationalized" at Bandung. From this running start, the Algerians proposed to carry their offensive into the councils of the United Nations. There, too, a large measure of success was to attend their efforts.

On the home front, the F.L.N. intensified its psychological action by ordering all patriots to abstain from the use of tobacco. The tobacco industry is not a state monopoly in Algeria, as it is in France; indeed, several of the most affluent tobacco merchants in the country are Moslems. Moreover, some 15,000 Moslem peasants draw their livelihood from tobacco, pre-eminently a smallholder's crop. Nevertheless, the idea of a tobacco boycott, originally initiated by the Istiqlal in Morocco, had begun to catch on in western Algeria as far back as June, 1954.

The F.L.N., in search of a way to force the rebellion upon the consciousness of every Moslem, turned the tobacco boycott to its own account; every Moslem would henceforth have a sacrificial act to perform on pain of dire consequence. The F.L.N. handbill making the boycott compulsory stated that the "tobacco profits" were used to "manufacture shells and tanks," an instance of the dialectic truth so dear to the Communists. The French revolutionary Georges Sorel, if I am not mistaken, advocated the general strike as the quickest and most efficient device for winnowing the proletarian wheat from the bourgeois chaff. This notion lies at the heart of the F.L.N.'s revolutionary philosophy.

Pending a general strike, attempted at a later date, Sorel's principle was applied in the tobacco boycott, which soon led to dragonnades of a new type conducted by young bullies roaming through the Arab quarters and beating up all smokers they could find. There was talk of a "Liberation Tribunal" to punish offenders. Whether it actually existed I do not know; but revolutionary sentences, some of them primitive beyond belief, were repeatedly executed. The illicit smoker, when he could be caught and dealt with in defiance of the French, had his nose cut off. In the Constantine department, the interdiction was extended to cover spirits and games of chance, both contrary to Moslem law; European stores and cafés were also boycotted.

In the field, the rebellion continued to spread and to grow in virulence. Wide areas north of Constantine were caught in its sweep. On May 1, at 1 A.M., a band of about sixty rebels swooped down on a forestry station near Jemmapes where twenty-one men of the local *goum* were sleeping soundly. Before the slightest resistance could be offered, the rebels had made off with twenty-one rifles and 840 rounds of ammunition. In the days that followed, the rebels fanned out toward Philippeville, Collo, and Djidjelli, felling trees to block the roads, blasting bridges, cutting down telephone and telegraph lines, burning cork depots. On May 10, El Milia was isolated for several hours; two gendarmes on patrol near the town were killed on May 11.

There could no longer be any doubt: the whole of the northern Constantinois was contaminated. The rebel leader Youssef Zighout, with six bands and possibly 400 rifles at his disposal, had made a mockery of the French security arrangements. Colonel Ducournau and his paratroopers were hastily sent in, with orders to re-establish the situation. M. Soustelle himself traveled to El Milia and to El Arrouch seeking ways to restore confidence and to protect the crops. By the end of May, French effectives in the area were being increased from 2,000 to 8,000. But how revealing the whole performance! Once again the barn doors were flung shut after the horses had fled. Everything had to be improvised; nothing was solid.

The authorities could not claim, by way of excuse, that there had been no warning. The signs of rebel penetration had, on the contrary, been numerous and alarming. The engagement in which a French gendarme and six rebels perished near Condé Smendou on January 18 has already been mentioned. That was the beginning. André Leveuf of *Le Monde*, who toured the area in May, was told of a whole succession of later incidents, minor perhaps, but too ominous to be taken lightly.* A Moslem war veteran, for instance, was found on the morning of April 20 with his nose cut off at the root; a note was pulled from his pocket; it read:

> Committee of the Army of Liberation.
>
> War jurisdiction, April 20. The man Aïssani Ahmed, suspected of treason and of spying for the enemy, has been sentenced to the following punishment: national indignity and disfiguration by a mark for life. Sentenced, April 20; sentence executed, April 21.
>
> The Commander in Chief.

On May 2, French gendarmes getting out of a truck at Milia were spattered with lead by rebels ensconced behind a hedge; two gendarmes were wounded. On the same day, one rebel was killed and another wounded in an encounter with gendarmes seven miles south of Jemmapes. On May 8, a forester was killed near Collo after sustaining a bitter siege. Such little flashes of violence, too often repeated, had an unsettling effect on people's nerves.

---

* See *Le Monde* for May 24, 1955.

In April, a group of European farmers in the Redjas district near Mila, banding together for self-defense, attempted to form their own body of deputized crop-watchers. This move brought a hornet's nest about their ears. M. Soustelle himself let go with a blast: "Under no circumstances," he said on April 28, "will illegal or semilegal private groups, destined in the view of their sponsors to fight terrorism, be tolerated. Terrorism cannot be eliminated by methods tending to supplant the public powers." M. Soustelle's dilemma was real, but his words were those of a man who had the situation well in hand, who could justify his position by providing the protection to which every citizen has a right. Such was not, however, the case. The bucket was snatched from the householder's hands, but the house was allowed to burn.

In the Nememchas, the rebels struck a telling blow on May 24: they obliterated a French convoy on its way from Guentis to Tebessa. At dawn, a liaison patrol comprising a *goum* of thirty men under the command of a Lieutenant Guillemot set out from Tebessa and headed for Guentis. Nothing untoward marked the outward journey: the three vehicles—a staff car and two trucks—reached Guentis in good time and prepared to return. The administrator at Guentis, Maurice Dupuy, much in need of a respite after three months on the *qui vive* and several brushes with the rebels, resolved to go along with the convoy. Through the deep gorges of the Nememchas all was well; with the last mountain defile behind them and the safer plain ahead, the men of the convoy must have breathed easier. Yet it was there, on the edge of the desert, that the attack occurred.

The next day, word reached the gendarmerie at Chéria, southwest of Tebessa, that overturned trucks had been seen near Souk el Hadjaj, site of a weekly rural market. Two companies of Algerian Rifles and two groups of armored cars were instantly dispatched from Khenchela; a detachment of mobile gendarmes went out from Zoui, southeast of Khenchela. The burned carcasses of the staff car and of the two trucks were quickly found, and, beside them, on a bed of spent cartridges, six bodies, those of M. Dupuy, Lieutenant Guillemot, Corporals Brun, Cazeau, and Habibi, and municipal horseman Chérif Branki. M. Dupuy's head had been crushed with a rock; the throats of the two natives had been slit. Of the twenty-six other *goumiers*, not a trace: they and their weapons had vanished with their assailants. A poignant detail was reported in the press: Branki left eleven children; M. Dupuy, eight; and Lieutenant Guillemot, five.

André Leveuf, who was in the area at the time, found that a band operating from the fastness of Mount Tafrent northwest of Khenchela had by its repeated incursions terrorized the plain. Its members had exacted tribute from the Moslem peasants, cut off the noses or burned the faces of the recalcitrant, and murdered the hereditary enemies of their tribe. Even the European farmers, M. Leveuf wrote, had not been spared, sums of up to 200,000 francs ($570) having been exacted for "protection." Despite the havoc wrought by their raids, or perhaps because of it, many a village lad had gone off to Ouenza on the Tunisian frontier where a secret recruiting center had apparently been organized. And how, M. Leveuf asked the people at La Meskiana (between Tebessa and Aïn Beïda), had things come to such a pass? The answer was given that, prior to the outbreak of the rebellion, the entire township of La Meskiana —35,000 inhabitants; 853 square miles—had been administered by one administrator and his assistant and policed by five gendarmes.*

By the end of May, the rebellion had made tremendous strides. The rapid deterioration of law and order in the Constantinois had been the salient development of the month. Apart from that, the general impression was one of increased momentum. The number of acts of sabotage involving roads and telephone and telegraph lines had increased from sixty-four in April to 250 in May. The rebels, who previously had tended to wreak their vengeance only on Moslem "traitors to the Algerian fatherland," turned their attention in May to the Europeans as well, murdering three foresters, a mason, and a postal official. More European vineyards and orchards had been destroyed; reserves of cork and esparto grass had been burned; livestock had been poisoned.

In the Constantine department, rebel contingents had been levied by imperative summons; notices stipulating "in the name of the Algerian people" that non-compliance could result in death were sent out under the heading "Algerian Republic." An F.L.N. circular recommended that those who were able to do so should penetrate Government and "colonialist" circles and "sow confusion" there by pretending to betray the national cause.

The intense anxiety evident among the Europeans was, therefore, not to be wondered at. Their agitation, their verbal excesses, were the product of frustration, anger, and dismay. Faced with the vacillations of the French Government, staggered by the rebel onslaught, the Europeans could not decide what course to follow. Take up arms in their own defense? The idea, though it had occurred to all, could not be seriously entertained; Algeria was not Palestine. Shout from the rooftops their pent-up anguish and indignation? This outlet was frequently resorted to;

* See *Le Monde* for May 28, 1955.

the Algerians are, after all, a Mediterranean people. Resign themselves to their fate and salvage what they could from the wreck? The timid, perhaps, chose this last course; but on the whole, European Algeria gave evidence of an amazing will to survive.

M. Bourgès-Maunoury, visiting Algeria in May, was exposed to more than one outburst of European petulance. The mayors of the *arrondissement* of Tizi Ouzou and of the district of Koléa announced that they would refuse to welcome the minister officially in their townships. This stand was warmly endorsed by Gratien Faure, president of the Constantine chamber of agriculture, but opposed by Amédée Froger, president of the mayors' association in the Algiers department, who proposed instead to explain the European position to the minister in all serenity.

M. Bourgès-Maunoury did, in fact, receive a delegation of mayors, who, he said afterwards, were "fully reassured as to the Government's intentions." "Neither reassured nor satisfied," retorted several of the mayors.

Earlier in the same day—May 26—the Algerian Federation of Mayors, meeting in plenary session, had voted a resolution calling for stern measures commensurate with the gravity of the situation and for an unequivocal reassertion of French authority. Among the measures advocated were the "supreme penalty" for all persons convicted of terrorist acts, the dissolution of the Algerian Communist party, described as the refuge of extremists and secessionists, and the declaration of a state of emergency in the three departments of Algeria.

On May 28, returning to Algiers after a visit to Orléansville, M. Bourgès-Maunoury and his party stopped for lunch at Tipasa, an old Roman town on the coast of what was once Mauretania. The sylvan charm and quiet elegance of the outdoor meal, the music of native guitars and *darabukkas*, created an atmosphere of enchantment, unmarred until Henri Baretaud, mayor of Cherchel and delegate to the Algerian Assembly, rose to say: "There have been enough stupid and criminal subterfuges. You do not treat with hired killers, still less when they style themselves soldiers of the liberation. . . . We hope that the situation will be re-established and that the Government's reaction will be felt from Tunis to Rabat. Algeria must not be caught between two fires. Any political concession can only strengthen the position of the nationalists and swell their ranks. We look to the Government for action."

The next day, at Tizi Ouzou, M. Bourgès-Maunoury attended a reception, not at the city hall, but at the subprefecture. Courteously received by the mayor of Fort National, the minister was treated to a banquet and to words of protest at Michelet. "Serious events have occurred and are infinitely to be regretted," the minister said in reply, "but it behooves us not to lose our heads and not to yield to an impulse of panic, often played upon by those who serve their own interest in making the situation appear more serious than it is in fact." With that, he pirouetted away from the awkward subject.

M. Bourgès-Maunoury's visit may be remembered by some for the speech he made in the Algerian Assembly on May 27. "I should like to repeat once again," he said on that occasion, "that the Government, to solve the problems of these departments, will never look about for what are called 'valid interlocutors.' I go still further; I claim that no national Government after ours will be able to venture upon this path." Could it, I wonder, have occurred to him then that a little more than two years later a French Government headed by himself would dispatch an emissary to Tunis to sound out the intentions of the F.L.N.? Yet this was to happen.

At about the same time—on May 25—Jacques Chevallier, deputy, mayor, and late Minister of Defense, came up with a statement of at least passing interest. "When you play bridge with a sharper," he said, "you are sure to lose if you yourself persist in observing the rules of the game. You do not fight rebels with legal means; you fight rebels with means identical with theirs. It is the *lex talionis*—eye for eye, tooth for tooth; it is the law of self-defense on a country-wide scale." These words sound odd in the mouth of a man who was later to become an advocate of negotiations with the rebels.

25. THE MITTERRAND AND SOUSTELLE REFORMS

The question of the economic, social, and political reforms necessary to Algeria's salvation intruded itself from the start of the rebellion. Indeed, François Mitterrand, Interior Minister in the Government headed by Pierre Mendès-France, had, as we have seen, been talking about schemes for bringing more Moslems into the Administration even before the trouble began. The events of November, 1954, merely quickened his zeal, for he attributed the disorders in part to the inequalities that prevented the Moslems from identifying themselves and their hopes with France. In December, he warned the National Assembly that the unity of the nation would be but "lies and hypocrisy" as long as the equality of all its citizens had not been assured. This, he said, with a curious want of logic, meant that the provisions of the Algerian Statute would have to be carried into effect. By January he had elaborated a whole series of proposals known collectively as the "Mitterrand Plan."

Of the contemplated measures, two—the absorption of the Algerian police service into that of Metropolitan France and the reorganization of the Algerian section of the Interior Ministry—were implemented by the Mendès-France Government. A third, providing for the establishment of a special civil-service school at Algiers, was approved in principle. Still pending when the Government fell were plans to turn the huge administrative townships into self-governing entities, to bring the tiny municipal centers of Kabylia together into larger self-governing townships, to create three new departments with their administrative seats at Bône, Orléansville, and Colomb-Béchar, to extend the right to vote to literate Moslem women, and to put more Moslems on the first-college electoral roll.

Cries of indignation went up from many European politicians, who argued that law and order should come first and that political changes should, in any case, be preceded and conditioned by economic advance. The *Echo d'Alger* took a particularly hostile view of what it called "demagogic measures suddenly proposed." The influential *Echo d'Oran*, however, while reserving judgment on some aspects of the "Mitterrand Plan," was sharply critical of those who automatically said "no" at the slightest suggestion of change. The first-college deputies and delegates were all but unanimous in demanding that they be consulted before any action was taken. The second-college politicians expressed the opinion that the contemplated reforms did not go nearly far enough. Replying to his critics, M. Mitterrand insisted that he was merely trying to apply the 1947 Statute, which was, after all, he observed, the law of the land. Nevertheless, the "Mitterrand Plan" undoubtedly added force to the storm that was to overwhelm M. Mendès-France and his Government.

M. Soustelle took up where M. Mitterrand had left off. His first concern was to pump a little fresh money into the country for several hundred small improvement projects designed to have immediate tonic effect. To this end, he obtained on March 30, after a stiff battle with the Finance Ministry in Paris, a special allocation of 4,300 million francs ($12 million). He then resolved to tackle the problem of basic reforms. He began by sending out a circular making it incumbent on all persons in authority to pursue a "policy of consideration and confidence"; the European "superiority complex" was to go and with it all trace of discrimination and condescension, for, as he said, the Algerian native "legitimately values his dignity as a man." He then got down to cases with the help of his personal staff. The preparation of the "Soustelle Plan" required a close scrutiny of Algeria's needs and resources.

Agriculture, the country's primary source of revenue, was carefully surveyed. M. Soustelle saw at once that the land was not all in the hands of grasping *colons*. Some magnificent tracts, it was true, such as the Mitidja plain near Algiers, the plain of Bône, and the Chélif valley, had been created by hardy European settlers out of wastelands and swamps. Elsewhere, even European holdings were for the most part small and, by continental standards, unproductive.* Erosion claimed 100,000 acres a year, though an excellent and active soil conservation service almost succeeded in making good the loss. The 17 million acres of arable land, 98 per cent of them in the coastal belt, were divided into 652,769 holdings as shown in the following table (1951 figures):

	European	*Moslem*
Holdings of less than 25 acres	7,432	438,483
Holdings of more than 25 acres	14,605	192,249
	22,037	630,732

A little more than half the arable land was devoted to cereal crops, the rest to vineyards, orchards, orange groves, and market gardens.† It was estimated that, of Algeria's Moslem inhabitants, only about

* Thirty bushels of wheat per acre is a maximum yield in Algeria; in France, a good yield is between fifty-two and sixty bushels.

† It is frequently said that Algeria would be better off if the *colons* were made to go elsewhere, for then their vineyards could be converted to cereal and fruit crops for internal consumption, and luxury imports could be reduced. This is nonsense. Apart from the fact that the *colons* also produce wheat and fruit crops, it should be remembered that some land is good for wheat and some is good for the grape. Algeria has both. The hills of Mascara, for instance, are hardly more suitable for wheat than is the Nile Delta, and I doubt if anyone would suggest putting the Nile Delta under wheat. Algerian wine is, of course, like Egyptian cotton, primarily an export crop. But self-sufficiency is a medieval notion. Every country must both import and export, and the more the better. The Algerian population would, I am sure, hate to be deprived of its imported sugar, tea, and coffee. In addition, the vineyards provide a great deal of work. Acre for acre, a vineyard requires at least four times as many hands as a wheat field. Much of Algeria's fruit crop, especially its citrus fruits, also is exported to protected markets in France.

1,500,000 had been brought fully into a modern money economy; the others were still more or less confined to the archaic autarchy of their ancestors. Yet the Moslem population, essentially rural, was growing at the fantastic rate of 240,000 a year. The problem of making production keep pace with the birth rate was, therefore, a staggering one. Clearly, if the Moslem's lot was to be improved, the effort would have to be largely in the countryside, and there a herculean task awaited the reformers. The Moslem-held land, most of it poor and poorly worked, was further impoverished regularly by erosion and the goat, periodically by drought and the locust. Much was collectively owned or else morseled beyond belief. In Kabylia there were brothers and cousins each of whom held title to but a single branch of some ancestral olive tree. How, in these circumstances, could collateral be found for the grant of agricultural credit?

To meet the challenge of the countryside, M. Soustelle proposed the establishment of an agency with wide powers to acquire public and private land for redistribution to Moslem peasants and to secure for the beneficiaries the technical and financial assistance by means of which the new holdings could be improved. He also undertook to expand existing facilities, notably native Provident Societies and Rural Improvement Sectors, and to abolish the *khammessat,* a native system of sharecropping under which the tenant got one-fifth of the crop and the landowner four-fifths.

A survey of Algeria's industrial and commercial activity revealed the tremendous preponderance of European enterprise. In 1955, the 26,476 European concerns employed 305,000 people, whereas the 7,224 Moslem concerns employed only 23,314 people. It was estimated that the Moslem concerns accounted for 8 per cent of the year's gross earnings. The Moslem share of the country's total private investment of about $12,857,000,000 was also thought to be about 8 per cent. The Moslems, though nine times more numerous than the Europeans, carried only 50 per cent of the total tax burden. Their contribution to the total public and semipublic investment (including railways, gas and power, oil prospection, and coal mines) was put at about 20 per cent.* These findings pointed not only to the huge French stake in Algeria, but also to the part the French would have to play for many years to come if the country were to be saved from economic disaster. It is easier, as the French writer Thierry Maulnier has said,† to butcher innocent people than to

---

* Figures taken from an article by Senator Laurent Schiaffino in *Le Monde* for July 14, 1957.

† See *Le Figaro* for May 3, 1957.

push the desert back. The F.L.N. clamored for independence in the name of human dignity. But what dignity could there be in beggary and starvation?

M. Soustelle observed that although industry provided a livelihood for only 11 per cent of the Algerian population, the Algerian laborer was better off than his country cousin and was, in addition, a consumer. Hence the importance of industry and the necessity of expanding it. But if Algeria could not prosper as a purely agricultural country, it was equally evident that, without French aid on a massive scale, the industrial outlook was all but hopeless.

The great obstacle to industrial development had always been the dearth of natural resources and the absence of cheap power. The cost of power in Algeria was almost 60 per cent higher than in Metropolitan France. It is here that we see the full significance of the oil fields now being brought into production in the Sahara, where, according to present estimates, the reserves exceed 100 million tons. But in 1955 M. Soustelle looked for a temporary expedient in a plan to equate the power rates in Algeria with those prevailing in Metropolitan France, either through an amalgamation of the Algerian Gas and Power Company with the great nationalized *Electricité de France* or through a system of tax relief. He further proposed to set up an industrialization office in Paris to promote a decentralization of French industry toward Algeria.

Meanwhile, an economic study group headed by Roland Maspétiol of the Council of State had completed a detailed report containing a projected six-year "table of growth." M. Maspétiol and his associates were convinced that a policy of productive investment could, if rigorously pursued, raise the standard of living in Algeria by 6 per cent a year over a period of six years. This result could be achieved, however, only by an annual increase of 15 billion francs ($40 million) in French aid, plus the imposition of a progressively heavier tax burden within the country.

M. Soustelle, who attached great importance to M. Maspétiol's recommendations, was dismayed by the offhand manner with which they were treated in Paris. He noted in his book that the report, both in its descriptive chapters and its conclusions, brought clearly into view the fundamental fact that the economic and budgetary autonomy of Algeria was a myth if the Algerians were not to be reduced to "bestial misery."

But economic and land reform was, to M. Soustelle's mind, only part of a larger whole. He therefore struck out boldly upon the path of social and political reform as well. Like M. Mitterrand, he was haunted by the idea of bringing more Moslems into the Administration. Although, theoretically, Moslems could compete with Europeans for civil service jobs on equal terms, only 29 per cent of such jobs were actually held by Moslems. To correct this anomaly, M. Soustelle set up an Administrative Training Center in Algiers as a funnel through which to pour suitable Moslem candidates into jobs they were fitted to hold. He tried also, but without success, to institute a system whereby qualified Moslems could be exempted from competitive civil service examinations.

Schools were an obsession with M. Soustelle; there could never be enough to suit him. He fought like a tiger for appropriations to build 1,200 new classrooms in 1955-56 instead of 600 as originally planned. Faced with an avalanche of requests from teachers desiring to leave unsettled areas, M. Soustelle resolved to recruit auxiliary teachers and to keep the schools open. He planned also to cover the country with social centers equipped to combat illiteracy, promote hygiene, and encourage small crafts.

The inadequacies of the country's administrative structure were another of M. Soustelle's preoccupations. In pursuit of his goal, which was to break down the large, unwieldy territorial divisions into more manageable units and to bring the Administration closer to the people, he created a new department with its seat at Bône and twelve new *arrondissements;* other new departments were to follow, including that of the Sahara. Under the "Mitterrand Plan," the administrative townships, though endowed with the organs of self-government, would have kept their existing boundaries. M. Soustelle proposed instead to divide them into smaller "rural townships," these in turn to be composed of "rural centers," each corresponding to a *douar* or other natural community. The "rural townships" as envisaged by M. Soustelle would remain under the discreet tutelage of the administration until they were ready to become regular self-governing townships. Meanwhile, the Moslems were to be given parity of representation in the councils of all the old, established townships.

To fill the gap between the civil administrator and the widely dispersed inhabitants, M. Soustelle undertook to set up 400 Specialized Administrative Sections (S.A.S.) to be manned by a new corps of Algerian Affairs Officers. The pacification zones in the Aurès served as a model for the S.A.S., designed to catch up within their protective web populations that might otherwise be subjected by the rebels or trammeled by the Army or both.

The Government General itself had become such a maze that M. Soustelle, unable to unravel it, appointed M. Maspétiol to head a committee of experts, a sort of Hoover Commission, whose job it was to spot weaknesses and recommend remedial measures. He hoped that operations could, as a result, be simplified and improved.

Nothing fazed M. Soustelle; he dared tread even upon the prickly ground of religion. In a move to settle the bitter controversy stemming from government control of the mosques, he suggested that these be turned over to local religious associations and that the various Moslem groups receive compensation for the loss of the alienated *habbous* properties (pious endowments).* The plan called for the appointment of a Moslem commissioner for religious affairs who, assisted by a consultative body, would have authority to mediate disputes. M. Soustelle sought also to foster the emergence of a truly bilingual country by proposing that the study of Arabic be made compulsory, or at least optional, in all schools.

Such, in broad outline, were the elements of the "Soustelle Plan" as submitted to the Government in June. It was never fully carried out, although M. Soustelle's successor, Robert Lacoste, built his own plan of reforms on the foundations laid in 1955. The S.A.S. remain, however, a lasting tribute to M. Soustelle's initiative.

His great mistake, in my opinion, was to have believed that his reforms, except only for the S.A.S., could have the slightest effect on the rebellion. He looked upon them as crucial, as the vital part of his pacification effort. But there is a time for every task; even the most necessary have their season. No right, no benefit, is to be compared with the right to live. As M. Soustelle said himself in a speech to the Algerian Assembly on March 31: "The simple duty of any democratic authority is to put an end to murders, attacks, acts of pillage and of vandalism." This "simple duty" had first to be performed; as long as it was left undone, little else was possible. Precious time and energy were spent on matters that could wait.

How could it seriously be maintained that the prospect of land or a roof or a job or a better future could rouse any enthusiasm in the hearts and minds of men who lacked the essential—security? The Moslems, like the Europeans, asked first to be delivered from fear. Consequently, the "psychological shock" that was, thanks to the initiation of the reforms, to have won the Moslems over to the French did not, and could not, occur. The rebel cause suffered no perceptible damage; indeed, the rebels easily brought many of the reforms to nought, causing the French to lose face. The new schools were burned. The Administrative Training Center, utterly disrupted, ended in confusion. When M. Lacoste tried to distribute land to the Moslem peasants, the beneficiaries were slaughtered.

---

* See pp. 49–50.

26. THE CONFLICT SPREADS

> *"Que voulez-vous, les mesures prises ne sont pas suffisantes. C'est autrement qu'il faudrait agir. C'est le cri de toute l'Algérie."*
>
> A WOMAN OF VICTOR DURUY

Along about June 18, orders of mysterious origin went out over the grapevine telegraph: the rebellion demanded a boycott of the Mzabites. A curious Berber people from the M'Zab country in the northern Sahara, the Mzabites had for generations monopolized the grocery trade in the cities of the coastal belt. This in itself had been enough to arouse the jealousy and even the enmity of the more numerous Arabs and Kabyles. But there was more to it than that. The Mzabites, like the inhabitants of the island of Djerba in the gulf of Gabès, are Abadites, professing a puritanical form of Islam.* They were thus doubly damned, for in addi-

* When Ali, the fourth Caliph of Islam, was fighting Muawiya for control of the Moslem empire in 657, a group of Ali's followers deserted him rather than accept the mediation that had ended the battle of the Siffin plain in Syria to Muawiya's advantage. The Kharidjites, as these dissenters were called, became the first sect in Islam. Fierce and fanatical, the Kharidjites assassinated Ali and made war on the empire. The Abadites, a group of Kharidjite sectaries, rallying the Berbers to their standard, achieved supremacy for a time in North Africa, but ultimately went down to defeat before the Abbasside governors in the eighth century. Some Abadites, however, later took refuge in the distant and desolate M'Zab, where they watered the desert with deep-dug wells and founded thriving cities, including Ghardaïa. Few societies are as closely knit as that of the Mzabites. The men who trade in the north are tem-

tion to their minority status, they carried the stigma of heresy. It was surmised that the rebels, in decreeing the boycott, sought to punish the affluent Mzabites for their reluctance to contribute substantially to the rebel war chest.

At all events, the Mzabites lived through a period of great tribulation. Many, unable to honor their debts, had to throw themselves upon the mercy of their creditors. In some places the boycott was enforced by street boys whose badges were sticks of Spanish licorice held ostentatiously in their mouths in lieu of cigarettes. At Blida, hoodlums hurling potatoes larded with razor blades forced forty-five Mzabite grocers to close their shops entirely. In July, however, the boycott, condemned by the Ulema, by the Mufti of Algiers, and finally even by the F.L.N., began to peter out. It was rumored that the Mzabites had paid up.

The F.L.N. policy makers issued two documents in June to clarify their position—a "proclamation" very similar to that of November 1, 1954, and, far more revealing, a "directive" for the use of members only. Describing the F.L.N. as a combat organization rather than a political party, the authors of the "directive" insisted on the importance of unmasking the Messalists, who "sow confusion," and the Lahouelists, who "through cowardice take no part in the struggle." Talks of any kind with the French were strictly banned on the ground that anything suggestive of a possible agreement might weaken the Algerian case at the forthcoming session of the United Nations General Assembly. The A.L.N., it was stated, would not permit such people as Ferhat Abbas, Abderrahmane Kiouane, and Messali Hadj to speak in its name; they had only to "pitch in and lend a hand."

In July, the F.L.N. addressed itself in a handbill to the "intellectuals," whom it accused of merely looking on from the sidelines. "The people, though deprived of their natural guides, are performing their duty magnificently," the handbill said. "Arouse yourself from your lethargy. . . . You can give counsel, provide guidance, organize. . . . The day will come when the people will ask you this dread question: 'What did you do for the liberation of the fatherland?' "

In an attempt to make political capital out of the 125th anniversary of the capture of Algiers by the French, the F.L.N. ordered all native shopkeepers to close their shops on July 5 in token of their "active solidarity with the liberation fighters." Similarly, the Moslem feast of Greater Bairam was proclaimed to be a time of mourning; the tradi-

---

porary exiles, for their wives never leave the M'Zab. The Mzabites and the Djerbians are not without friends in the world: the Sultans of Muscat and of Zanzibar are Abadites.

tional immolation of sheep was forbidden.* European inhabitants of Algiers, opening their mailboxes in the morning, found there a cheery little handbill bearing the title, "French, do not forget: the valise or the coffin."

On the other side of the ledger, the French managed to bag two prominent F.L.N. leaders in June—Saadi Yacef, who had become rebel chief in the Algiers area after the arrest of Rabah Bitat on March 23, and Mohammed Terbouche, who, as member of the F.L.N. executive in charge of "external relations," had resolved to attend to the "physical liquidation" of Messali. Yacef, however, was soon released and resumed his former activities at the head of an accomplished gang of gunmen, arsonists, and bomb-throwers. By July, 1957, the elusive Yacef, still leading the French police a merry chase, had been sentenced in absentia twice to death and once to hard labor for life. He was caught again on September 24, 1957.

Dr. Mohammed Lamine-Debaghine, a former M.T.L.D. deputy who had been expelled from the party in 1949—he had, I believe, dabbled in "Berberism"—was arrested on June 24 and released the following September 9—one more instance of French imprudence; Lamine later became titular head of the F.L.N. and its chief spokesman.† Meanwhile, French officers interrogating a group of prisoners taken near Tebessa found they had caught another graduate of the Baghdad cadet college in the person of Abdelmadjid Adjebi, an Algerian student. Like the Moroccan Mohammed Ben Hamadi el-Aziz before him, Adjebi went on the air to say that he had been deceived by the F.L.N. leaders in Cairo and urged others to be warned by his example.

Seventy-two military engagements were reported in June as against seventy in May. On June 28, in the Aurès, the Foreign Legion put a rebel band to rout at a place called Ras-ou-Serhil. But the rebels were to get their revenge. Nine days later, a major and eight men of the 14th Battalion of Algerian Rifles, traveling in convoy from Guentis to Zoui, perished in a rebel ambush laid at the very spot where Maurice Dupuy, Lieutenant Guillemot, and four others had fallen on May 24. Worse was coming. On July 27 at dawn, a supply convoy of nine trucks

* It is customary in Algeria for each Moslem family of sufficient means to commemorate Greater Bairam by killing a sheep in memory of Abraham's sacrifice (Genesis, XXII: 9–13), symbol of total submission to the will of God. The meat is distributed to the poor.

† Dr. Lamine-Debaghine is reputed to have held the P.P.A. together during the period of Messali's banishment from 1943 to 1946.

protected by 140 men of the Foreign Legion left Taberdga in the Nememchas for Djellal twelve miles to the southwest, a point newly reoccupied by French troops. The vehicles were moving slowly through the difficult Taffassourt defile when they came under withering machine-gun and rifle fire. The first bursts, fired from positions among the rocks directly overhead, killed all the occupants of the last truck. The rebels then swarmed down into the road and burned three trucks before being driven off. The encounter cost the lives of twenty-one legionnaires, including an army surgeon, and thirteen rebels; eight legionnaires were wounded. Intelligence revealed that the assailants, attired in uniforms of khaki drill with a green crescent and skull embroidered on their patches, had attacked with new weapons—machine rifles, submachine guns, and army rifles. The scales tipped the other way on July 29, however, when men of the 1st Foreign Parachute Battalion flushed and decimated a rebel band near the Tunisian frontier north of Négrine.

At the end of July, the general picture presented new aspects of galloping deterioration. The Nememchas were entirely contaminated. Elsewhere in the Constantine department, whole *douars* had gone over to the rebellion. The rebel bands encountered by French troops tended to be bigger and better armed than in previous months. If General Parlange could point to some slight improvement in the Aurès, conditions in the Khenchela and Tebessa districts remained perilous to the highest degree. Alarming reports were received from La Meskiana and from Canrobert (between Aïn Beïda and Constantine); in the north, from El Milia, El Arrouch, and Philippeville. More ominous still, groups of rebels were known to be moving out of the Aurès and across the Hodna mountains south and southwest of Sétif toward Kabylia. The Kabyle rebels, too, could be expected to propagate new centers of infection; in fact, a band was sighted south of Blida, almost on the threshold of Algiers itself.

Acts of sabotage at Méchéria and Géryville, the first to be committed in the distant Aïn Sefra territory on the Algerian-Moroccan confines, gave a clue to the ultimate rebel goal of a continuous front from one end of the country to the other. Such, indeed, was thought to be the core of the four-year master plan worked out in Cairo by Lieutenant-Colonel Soleiman Ezzat and Major Mohammed Fathi el-Dib. Another rebel objective was to "free" some portion of Algerian soil, render it inaccessible to the French and there proclaim an independent Algerian state. The continuous front was later to be achieved, but not the "free" enclave. The F.L.N. leadership was so rent with internal quarrels that even the "free government in exile," many times heralded as imminent, did not come into existence until 1958.

As conditions became more and more insecure, the atmosphere among the European inhabitants became increasingly charged with emotion. The combustion point was just about reached when Jacques Fianna, mayor of Victor Duruy, a small agricultural community southwest of Batna, was murdered with his seventeen-year-old son, Claude Yvon, in June. The farmers in the area voted a motion expressing their feelings in such violent terms that the document, declared inadmissible at the Batna subprefecture, had to be toned down. "It is established," the farmers stated in the amended version of their motion, "that the situation is growing worse each day, that public authority is deteriorating, and that the very principle of French presence is becoming warped. The hour has come to put idle talk aside and to act as the present situation commands. They [the farmers] demand with insistence that the state of siege be proclaimed and that in consequence martial law be applied to the criminals." A delegation of farmers and tradespeople received by M. Soustelle at Batna on June 23 spoke their minds plainly: "The deliberate inertia of those who govern Algeria," they said, "has contributed to the spread of the contamination in this department and has allowed anti-French propaganda to work its mischief. . . . Only when law and order have been completely restored will it be possible to promote the necessary reforms without seeming to yield to banditry."

In Algiers itself the temperature was rising. The standing committee of the departmental association of mayors, meeting on June 21 with Amédée Froger, mayor of Boufarik,* in the chair, resolved to "withdraw its confidence from the Government and from the Governor General" on the ground that the promises made by the Interior Minister had not been kept and that, on the contrary, the situation had continued to worsen.

The anguish and intense misgivings of the European community inevitably led to a flowering of associations whose object was more effective protection or relief for the victims of terrorism. Although these associations were at one in opposing reforms while the troubles persisted, none of them succeeded in mobilizing European opinion or in becoming forces to be reckoned with. Peripheral at best, they were nonetheless to be kept in mind as symptomatic of the times. The most important of the associations formed in June and July were the *Rassemblement des Français d'Algérie*, headed by R. Peringuey, a prominent Algiers lawyer; the *Union Française Nord-Africaine*, headed by Louis Boyer-Banse, a retired government official, and René Reygasse, a dis-

---

* M. Froger was assassinated in the street near his Algiers apartment on December 29, 1956, by a terrorist who was later caught and executed.

missed civil administrator; and *Vigilances Africaines* (VIGILAF), headed by Henri Fayolle, mayor of Tizi Ouzou.

Politics came to the fore briefly in June when the "grand electors" in the Algiers department gathered to fill five vacated seats in the Council of the Republic. One outgoing senator, Léon Muscatelli, a former prefect of Algiers, stood down; his seat went to Laurent Schiaffino, a multimillionaire shipowner. The department's four other outgoing senators—Henri Borgeaud and Marcel Rogier in the first college, and Abdennour Tamzali and Marhoun Ferhat in the second college—were reelected.

Before adjourning for its summer recess, the National Assembly extended the "state of emergency" act on July 30 for a second six-month period, to end April 3, 1956. The Moslem deputies, needless to say, damned the authorities for indulging in "ruthless repression." Mohammed Salah Bendjelloul, in particular, was at his oratorical best: "The repression can never restore calm," he cried, "unless its object be total extermination, a solution which I myself am prepared to accept, for it is better to die than to continue to suffer the regime now imposed on Algeria." (Mr. Bendjelloul was, however, alive and bearing up remarkably well three years later, though the regime was the same.) Mostefa Benbahmed, Socialist deputy for Constantine, accused the European minority in Algeria of building its privileges on a philosophy of hatred imported from Nazi Germany and, imputing summary executions to the French police, claimed that a Moslem father had been compelled to carry away the dismembered remains of his son in a basket.

Jean Cayeux, Popular Republican deputy for Paris, also raked the *colons* over the coals. He demanded that the Algerian "latifundia" be broken up and that the wine, tobacco, cork, and esparto fortunes be stripped of their malignant power. Maurice Viollette, Radical deputy and former Governor General of Algeria, put the rebellion down, in part at least, to the "scandalous selfishness" of his countrymen. Quoting Jules Ferry to the effect that the violence of the *colons,* when not in their acts, was in their words and feelings, he declared that the Algerian French had never been moved by the sight of human suffering. The rebels, one gathered, were to be regarded as something in the nature of avenging angels.

"When a policy of repression is pursued in Algeria, it is not France that is defended but the colonial companies." So spoke Louis Vallon, independent deputy for Paris, who added: "It is false to say that the Algerian democracy would break its ties with France. Who made this accusation? Why, those who are ready to rely on the United States to safeguard their 'independence' and who proclaim their 'white dictatorship' as in Johannesburg." This was, I think—though I may be mistaken—a reference to the *colons;* if so, M. Vallon must have been unaware of the anti-American feeling prevalent among them.

Jacques Fonlupt-Esperaber, who had come to look upon himself as quite an expert on Algerian affairs, praised M. Soustelle but pilloried the directors of the Algerian Administration—"they represent a purely local point of view," he said—and complained of "tortures" allegedly inflicted by the police. The Socialist deputy Christian Pineau, who, as Foreign Minister in the Guy Mollet Government, was soon to be speaking with a different voice, rose to announce that his party, firm in its resolve never to condone a policy of "hatred," would vote against the "state of emergency."

M. Bourgès-Maunoury, appealing for support, said the "state of emergency" had already made it possible to "forestall the action of the rebels as well as to repress it and thus to reinforce the security of the populations." But the qualms affected by some deputies could not be so easily banished. Unable to present the "state of emergency" as a measure palatable to all, the Interior Minister tried to placate the querulous Assembly with a glowing description of the "Soustelle Plan." The policy defined by M. Bourgès-Maunoury was, in short, that of a little stick and of a big carrot. The "state of emergency" was extended by a hard-won vote of 382 to 233 at 4:30 A.M. The new department of Bône was approved at the same sitting by a vote of 493 to 100.

On July 5, the United States Air Force turned eight Sikorsky S-55 helicopters over to the French Air Force at Stuttgart. At the same time, it was learned from Washington that the French Government had been given a priority enabling it to purchase other military-type helicopters in the United States. The implication was clear: the United States Government would henceforth allow the French to use American military equipment against the Algerian rebels. It is safe to assume that this decision had brought perspiration to many brows in Washington, for the helicopter issue had involved all the conflicting concepts that held the United States and France so far apart on the question of colonialism. Helicopters were desperately needed by French troops operating against rebel bands in the *djebels* of Algeria, but none were then in production in France. The French turned, therefore, to their American allies. But Washington, fearful for what it considered its essential friendships in the Middle East, was loath to take any action that might offend Arab opinion.

The theory had been that no American military equipment was to be used in Algeria, although in fact the gap between theory and practice had been large enough to accommodate any number of half-tracks, G.M.C. trucks, jeeps, and other such items. The French Government, full of gratitude for the helicopters, obligingly put out a semiofficial statement in August to the effect that French units sent to Algeria left their American equipment behind and found French equipment waiting for them upon arrival. "It must also be stressed," the statement said, "that the kind of operations and the nature of the terrain do not lend themselves very much to the heavy equipment furnished by America." With that, the subject was dropped, and the half-tracks continued to rumble over the dusty roads of Algeria.

The French authorities in Morocco were acutely aware of the danger of wholesale violence on August 20. With the second anniversary of Sultan Mohammed Ben Youssef's banishment looming in fateful prospect, Gilbert Grandval, the Resident General, worked feverishly to find a solution to the problem of Morocco's disputed throne. The plan he had in mind called for the withdrawal of the reigning Sultan, Mohammed Ben Moulay Arafa, and for the establishment of a regency council; he hoped this drastic measure would clear the way for Moroccan home rule and, at the same time, obviate a humiliating restoration of the deposed Sultan. Unfortunately, as might be expected, the energetic Resident was hamstrung by hesitations and divergencies in Paris.

Morocco's dynastic troubles were, however, of little moment to Algeria, and M. Soustelle had no particular reason to apprehend an explosion of terror on August 20; indeed, he seems to have felt that the outlook was improving. Nevertheless, he hounded Paris for reinforcements. He admits in his book that he had been able to mass only 21,000 men in the Constantine department in May, whereas three times that number were needed. By July, he writes, the strength of the French forces in Algeria stood at only 114,000 men. Major General Henri Lorillot, who had succeeded Lieutenant General Paul Cherrière as supreme commander in Algeria, backed M. Soustelle's urgent request for thirty infantry battalions, eighteen squadrons of mechanized cavalry, ten transport companies, and more helicopters.

In a report to Paris in August, M. Soustelle dwelt on the extreme fragility of his security arrangements; he pointed out that these would collapse if the rebels succeeded in igniting a general revolt across the country. A concise inventory of the troops then available for action appears in his book: "Practically nothing in the Oran department; very little in the Algiers department outside of Kabylia; nothing or next to nothing west of El Milia and south of Khenchela and Tebessa; a very inadequate force along the Tunisian frontier. The bulk of our effectives were concentrated in the Aurès and at a few points in the north part of the Constantinois." Soon rumors of possible outbreaks on August 20 began reaching the authorities. On August 18, M. Soustelle put all units on the alert. However, he did not deem the danger serious enough to compel him to cancel a trip he had planned to eastern and southeastern Algeria. Accordingly, on August 16, he set out for Souk Ahras, Négrine, the Souf oases, Batna, and Arris.

The security curtain that had been drawn along both sides of the Tunisian frontier was, when M. Soustelle visited the area, in place, but, for want of troops, full of holes. M. Soustelle was very impressed, as well he might be, by the Ouenza iron mine, one of the largest in the world (10,000 tons of high-quality ore a day), and by the modern phosphate mines in the Kouif district northeast of Tebessa. Further to the south, the Governor General's helicopter put down at Djebel Foua where, in the midst of a most desolate landscape, a derrick, a cluster of prefabs, and a few watchtowers marked the site of a test oil well. The G.M.P.R. assigned to the protection of the camp had already beaten off several rebel attacks. Yet plans for mining the rich phosphate deposits in the nearby Djebel Onk area were under serious consideration. M. Soustelle was conscious at once of the hopes that could reasonably be founded on what had already been done and on what might yet be done in that part of Algeria for the good of all. "Nowhere," he writes, "had the criminal stupidity of the rebellion come home to me with greater force."

It was at Négrine that M. Soustelle first heard how the rebel chief, Lakhdar Hama, had come to the end of his trail in a fierce battle near El Oued a few days before. Hama's band, eighty strong and heavily armed, had slipped out of the Nememchas undetected and had moved southward toward the Souf oases. But there, betrayed by the Soufis, Hama had found himself caught on August 9 in a ring of French Saharan troops. It had been Hama's last stand, but he had made it a bloody and bitter one. Thirty-five rebels had perished, among them Hama himself, who had apparently committed suicide so as not to be taken alive; forty-six rebels had been captured. The French had lost twenty-two dead, including an officer.

M. Soustelle gives us this description of El Oued: "The next day I walked around El Oued, this astonishing city of brilliant cupolas that seem to be fragile bubbles under the sun ready to vanish like a mirage at the first breath of wind. The palm trees, which provide the delicious Deglet Noor date, grow at the bottom of immense, funnel-shaped hollows dug into the sand; and endless strings of *fellahin,* clinging to the steep and crumbling slopes, slave to carry up in baskets the sand that unceasingly flows toward the bottom—the exhausting struggle of these men who manage to survive only by the work of every hour. The tops of the palm trees barely rise above the level of the desert that would swallow them in a gulp if the dogged labor of human insects did not hold it in check."

Marked improvement was what M. Soustelle found in the Aurès. The native affairs officers had already begun to work their magic. At Ichmoul, the people were harvesting a bumper crop under the protection of their own *harka* (an irregular armed array). Faces that had recently been expressionless were now wreathed in smiles. Stone *bordjs* were rising from the ground in places that might otherwise have been rebel haunts. There was optimism in the air. But as evil a "hell-broth" as had ever been brewed in a witches' cauldron was boiling up in the north.

A general insurrection, a spontaneous rising of the people against the French, had been an essential rebel objective from the start. Nothing of the kind had been possible on November 1, 1954; but the lesson of May 8, 1945, seemed to be that if only the pump could be sufficiently primed, the latent fanaticism and atavistic bloodlust of the natives could be counted on to gush to the surface and carry all before it. The second anniversary of the Moroccan Sultan's banishment had been chosen by the Moroccan nationalists as the day for a bloody reckoning with the French; the F.L.N. resolved to do the same. Who could tell? Perhaps fires could be set that would sweep the whole of French North Africa. Such a prospect was surely worth the try. M. Soustelle reports in his book that the Algerians had made their decision at a meeting held in a neutral country and attended by a representative of the Egyptian dictator, Gamal Abdel Nasser.

While 2,000 Smala tribesmen in Morocco were turning Oued Zem and Aït Amar into an indescribable nightmare of death and destruction, the Algerian rebels, pushing hordes of maddened peasants before them, attacked everything French over wide areas within a quadrilateral extending inland from Collo and Bône to the points south of Constantine and Oued Zenati. This region, much of it mountainous, wooded, and loosely administered, was the domain of the rebel chief Youssef Zighout, whose judicious assassinations had in three months deprived the French of their antennae in the *douars*. The attacks, launched with the object of massacring Europeans and stealing arms, generally began at noon; the signal was given by the firing of shots, by the explosion of a bomb, or even—in two places, Sidi Mesrich and Robertville (between Constantine and Philippeville)—by the cry of the muezzin from the top of his minaret.

The city of Philippeville and its environs bore the brunt of the onslaught; but there the alert had been given, and the mobs, when they appeared to shouts of "The Egyptian Army is landing!" ran into French troops already at their posts. Some of the groups were led by flag-waving women. In one native district of the city, *fellaga*, resplendent in khaki uniforms, crossed cartridge belts, and sneakers, actually paraded six abreast, singing the P.P.A. battle hymn. Many were armed with automatic weapons. The auxiliaries came next with their hunting rifles, brush hooks, sickles, and mattocks. The nerve-rasping you-yous of the women filled the air. At Bizot, little children were used as bomb carriers. At Heliopolis, near Guelma, the cry was, "America is with us!"

In all, twenty-six localities came under attack on August 20 and ten on August 21. The mobs of assailants ranged in size from 100 to 700, including some women and children; they had for the most part been recruited only two or three days earlier. The technique used to unleash the primitive instinct of these wretched people had not changed: word excitedly carried from *douar* to *douar* spoke of the "holy war" now to begin. "The French will be crushed," rustic emissaries said. "You are the glorious army of the Prophet. Already Egyptian ships of war are landing troops at Collo. Airplanes from the east are raining bombs on Constantine."

These tidings were embellished with fabulous detail as they went from mouth to mouth. "The *fellaga* are invulnerable," it was said. "Yesterday in the Tahi pass, gendarmes stopped a truck carrying twenty *moujahidine*. When the French lifted the tarpaulin, they found twenty sheep. God had worked this miracle to save our *moujahidine*. As soon as the truck resumed its journey, the sheep became warriors again; our men are liberating angels jealously protected by God. The French can do nothing against them, but will be exterminated by the Algerian Army reinforced by Tahar Lassoued's* Tunisians. Tahar Lassoued has arrived. God turned him into a lion to enable him to cross the frontier."

When once these motley levies were under way, the "regulars" in uniform followed behind, ready to exploit any possible success. At several points, the "regulars" fled before they had taken part in the proceedings; but words cannot convey the horror of what occurred in places where the European settlements, undefended, fell prey to the mob.

"At Oued Zenati," M. Soustelle writes, "the slopes of the hill that rises above the town were suddenly covered with black dots as a crowd armed with clubs, knives, axes, and farming tools, descended upon the houses, but only to be mowed down by a machine gun brought into

---

* Tahar Lassoued was a well-known Tunisian *fellaga* chief.

action by the Senegalese. Faced with the failure of their venture, the *fellaga,* who had propelled the crowd from behind and who had been waiting in the safety of a river bed, took to their heels." However, news dispatches suggest that the matter was not quite so easily disposed of. The assailants, estimated to number 250, came in two groups, one of which reached the town hall before being driven off. A French officer and a Senegalese soldier were killed in the action; about thirty rebels lost their lives.

If the rebels had hoped to "free" a portion of Algerian soil, or even to overrun a French post and steal its arms, they were disappointed, but as a massacre, as I have said, the operation was a success. Peaceful citizens—men, women, children, and even babies—were butchered at Aïn Abid, Saint-Charles, El Arrouch, Condé Smendou, and Oued Zenati. But the ultimate in horror was reserved for the mining village of El Halia in the Fil-Fila hills east of Philippeville. All but a few of the 560 natives employed in the pyrite pits there threw themselves against the little European community attached to the mine. An appalling massacre followed. Brandishing sticks of dynamite, bottles of gasoline, guns, and axes, the assailants proceeded to butcher all the men they could find. They then turned their attention to the women and children; many of the victims were literally hacked to pieces. Thirty-seven Europeans, including ten children under fifteen years of age, perished. Altogether about 110 Europeans fell to the homicidal frenzy of Moslem assailants on August 20.

The sight that met M. Soustelle's eyes when he visited Aïn Abid and Oued Zenati on August 21 was not one that could easily be forgotten. I speak from experience, for on that same day, in Oued Zem, I saw the charred and mutilated remains of fifty European dead, many of them children, being laid in coffins; even Bishop Amédée Lefèvre of Morocco, I noticed, who had come for the burial, blanched at the sight (to say nothing of the smell). At Aïn Abid and Oued Zenati, the streets were still strewn with bodies on the morning of the twenty-first; the houses were shambles. The Europeans who had been spared huddled together in the town halls, many giving vent to their grief and despair. As M. Soustelle remarks, the victims were people of modest means, "*colons* without fortunes." At the Constantine hospital, M. Soustelle found women and children "groaning in fever and in nightmare, their fingers severed, their throats half-slit."

Constantine itself had a rough time on August 20; eight bombs were thrown in the city as noon approached. One of these exploded in a café, wounding fourteen patrons of the establishment. Another, aimed at a police station, missed its mark, exploded in the street, and wounded two passers-by. But far more significant was the assassination of Allaoua Abbas, nephew and disciple of Ferhat Abbas; more significant too, an unsuccessful attempt made on the life of Chérif Benelhadj-Saïd, U.D.M.A. delegate to the Algerian Assembly for Constantine. The gunmen who killed Abbas, a druggist, at his counter were shot down in their flight by a French patrol; in the pocket of one of them, the police found this "order of execution":

> Army of National Liberation.
> War Jurisdiction.
>
> For collaboration with the enemy and stand against the revolution, the War Jurisdiction sentences the man Abbas, Allaoua, to the death penalty. Executed, August 20, 1955.
>
> The Command.

A handwritten note appended to the order said: "Let other collaborators prepare to pay with their lives for the honor and well-being of others." A second "order of execution," directed at Mostefa Benbahmed, the Socialist deputy, also fell into the hands of the police; luckily for Mr. Benbahmed, the terrorists had not had time to carry it out. Mr. Benelhadj-Saïd, who had opened the door of his home to his assailants, was taken to the hospital with four cruel bullet wounds; he survived. The "executions" had been ordered in compliance with Mohammed Ben Bella's injunction to "liquidate all persons who might be tempted to act as valid interlocutors," in other words, the politicians who looked upon themselves as the possible instruments of a negotiated settlement with France. A warning to Ferhat Abbas—written in blood. In fact, the leader of the U.D.M.A. himself, it later developed, also had been sentenced to death.

It was estimated that the French troops, in standing off the attacks on August 20 and 21 and in pursuing the assailants, had killed upwards of 1,250 Moslems; 1,024 prisoners were taken. Georges Penchenier, a correspondent of *Le Monde,* reported in a dispatch from Philippeville that troops engaged in a mopping-up operation near the city had destroyed a *mechta* (hamlet) three miles away, killing fifty women, children, and old men in cold blood.* An official statement, denying M. Penchenier's version, said the women and children had been killed during a combat between a French force and rebels entrenched in the *mechta.* Though M. Penchenier stuck to his guns, I am inclined to distrust his testimony. He intimated in his first dispatch that he had witnessed the

* See *Le Monde* for August 25, 1955.

action but admitted later that, at the time of his visit to the *mechta*, operations there had ceased; he conceded, too, that the *mechta* had not been destroyed.* In the Oued Zenati and Jemmapes districts, on the other hand, the *mechtas* from which the bulk of the assailants had come and in which the rebels had taken refuge, nine in all, were emptied of their inhabitants and totally destroyed. This measure was, no doubt, justified; others were open to question.

I have particularly in mind an official announcement made on August 22; it said that arms would be distributed to isolated civilians for their own defense. If such civilians remained isolated, each constituted a standing invitation to the rebels to attack and seize his weapon and its ammunition. But if the isolated civilians banded together with their arms, it is hard to see what would have distinguished them from the "self-defense groups" so categorically banned in April. M. Soustelle had declared that under no circumstances would private initiative be tolerated in the fight against terrorism. Was he of a different mind now that the Europeans were burying their dead?

But there was surely reason to fear that weapons that could have served a useful purpose if distributed in good season to properly deputized persons and groups might become dangerous in the hands of men wild with grief and rage. At Aïn Abid, some Europeans, convinced that they had been betrayed by their Moslem neighbors, took the law into their own hands. How many Moslems were executed by these self-appointed agents of retribution I do not know. An indication may, perhaps, be found in the fact that some eighty widows and orphans were admitted to a Moslem charitable institution in Constantine patronized by Mohammed Salah Bendjelloul. Others were cared for by the Association of Ulema.

It is not my purpose to suggest that the arms distributed by the Administration were necessarily put to nefarious use, but only that the right time for such a distribution was before a likely emergency, not after a massacre.

At Philippeville, on August 23, nerves were frayed bare. The crack of rifles was still ringing in people's ears, guns could still be heard rumbling in the *djebels*, and fresh incidents brought new alarms. Two bombs exploded on the outskirts of the city. A European civilian was burned alive at the wheel of his jeep. A rebel flag was hoisted at the summit of a nearby hill. Shots were fired at a French patrol between Philippeville and the fishing village of Stora not two miles away. Never-

* See *Le Monde* for August 30, 1955.

theless, the city was preparing to pay a final tribute to its dead. All shops were closed in sign of mourning; flags were at half-mast; armored cars stood guard at every road; patrols of paratroopers, Republican Security Guards, and gendarmes went their incessant rounds. The mayor, Paul-Dominique Benquet-Crevaux, as a matter of prudence, had ordered that there be no procession and that the funeral ceremony be confined to the cemetery, where sixty victims of the rebel attacks in the Philippeville area were to be buried.

Several thousand Europeans attended the solemn funeral rites, performed in turn by a Roman Catholic priest, a rabbi, and a Protestant minister. A woman fell weeping upon the coffin of her four children. Near her, a ten-year-old girl knelt in tears beside her father's coffin. A young widow joined her voice with that of the Protestant minister in reciting the prayer for the dead. But as the mourners—friends, relatives, and next of kin—were about to leave the cemetery, there arose from the depths of all that grief a voice of bitter accusation if not of vengeance. Pierre Dupuch, Prefect of Constantine (who had been asked not to attend the funeral), was approached in the cemetery by a minor city official, the brother of one of the victims. "Look at what has become of our families," the man cried. "For the past six months we have been demanding arms."

M. Dupuch, without a word, turned and departed, followed by Major General Gaston Lavaud, by the subprefect of Philippeville, and by a thousand hostile shouts. The wreaths sent by M. Soustelle and M. Dupuch were trampled under foot. The mayor and his people broke into the *Marseillaise* as they dispersed.

The evening, Mayor Benquet-Crevaux appeared at the subprefecture with a "proclamation" which said:

> The population of Philippeville mourns its dead. Out of respect for their memory, and in ignorance of the individual responsibilities involved, it tolerated the presence of a representative of the present Government at the funeral. Its intention in doing so was to make clear in the eyes of all its unshakable determination to meet the enemy's defiance with discipline and cohesion.
>
> But so that its silence, big with bitterness, despair, and anger, will not be malignantly interpreted according to the capricious dictates of a policy of abandon which it unanimously rejects, it recalls publicly that the population of the mine of the Fil-Fila hills, comprising workmen, women, and children, the first to be attacked, deprived of arms or protection, went down defenseless before the blows of assassins whose savagery has no equal in the history of the most primitive races. It recalls that numerous and insistent demands for protection or for arms had been made by the

officials of the city by reason of the danger which became each day more threatening, though contrary to the official optimism.

It imperatively requires that those guilty of this unspeakable dereliction, whatever their position, be sought out and severely punished. That the promises of protection officially made by the highest authorities in the country remain without effect is something it cannot tolerate. It requires the urgent establishment of an organization which will make it possible for the civilian population to cooperate legally in the maintenance of order, in pursuance of promises made in the past.*

It demands once again the proclamation of martial law and the initiation of a policy of authority, repeatedly announced but never really pursued. It holds the authorities responsible once and for all for all failures to come, for the disorders, and for the needless loss of life that perseverance in the present policy cannot help but engender. Determined to defend this portion of France which is Algeria, it holds tantamount to the crime of high treason any pol-

---

* M. Soustelle on April 27: "Nobody denies that certain centers must be protected from danger. But to achieve this end, the only lawful solution is to call upon guards who shall be recruited and directed within the scope of the law by the townships and who shall act as rural constables, auxiliary policemen—the name matters little—under the prefectural authority.

"As a matter of fact, the Government has granted me the funds necessary for the establishment of the organization provided for by law under the name of 'restricted security system' but more commonly known as 'civil defense.' What does this law provide? The law makes it possible to assign for the defense of critical points and threatened centers individuals designated by name and officered, belonging to the establishments concerned or, failing that, especially recruited.

"Thus everything will be done to face up to the dangers that could possibly grow out of a situation which, though still disturbed in many places, can be progressively improved by the measures now being taken or contemplated."

M. Soustelle on July 4: "It cannot be denied that the situation in Algeria is improving."

M. Bourgès-Maunoury to the Algerian Assembly on May 28: "It would be unthinkable to reject private initiative tending to protect property and lives, it being expressly provided that such initiative is taken within the compass and under the control of the administrative and military action. Such is the purpose of what is known as the 'restricted security system.' "

M. Bourgès-Maunoury at Bône on May 30: "A large part of the Constantine department has suffered from the crimes of the rebellion. Be assured . . . that the Government is resolved to use every possible means to re-establish calm and public peace everywhere . . ."

M. Bourgès-Maunoury in Paris on June 1: "I return comforted by what I have seen."

> icy that, by weakness, improvidence, or incompetence, could lead it to ruin or to its separation from the home country.

In answer to this sharp demand, M. Soustelle put out the following statement:

> Even the legitimate sorrow of families and friends, even the indignant emotion of the population, cannot justify attacks directed at a government representative who has done and is doing his whole duty. The provocative action of certain emissaries, who removed and trampled upon the floral offerings of the Governor General and of the Prefect, might have been the signal for grave incidents. Thanks to the calm displayed by the majority of those present, these incidents, the consequences of which could have been disastrous, did not occur.

It is true that, on the occasion referred to, serious incidents might have, but did not, occur. It is true that a shocking act had been perpetrated at the cemetery. It is even true that M. Benquet-Crevaux's "proclamation" went considerably beyond the proper bounds of courtesy and deference. But as M. Soustelle, in his statement, side-stepped the issues raised, it may be presumed that he had no very good answer. This is apparent in his book, *Aimée et Souffrante Algérie:* "It would be vain to explain to it [the European population]," he writes, "that the massacres, frightful as they were, had been limited to the victims of the first attack, and that the immediate reaction of the troops had prevented a disaster of appalling dimensions. . . . The search for scapegoats naturally led people to pick on the public authorities. 'They should have . . .' or 'If only they had . . .'—such were the key words that made it possible to pin responsibility for the catastrophe on the Government, the Prefecture, the Army." The best comment on this attitude was an earlier pronouncement by M. Soustelle himself: "The simple duty of any democratic authority is to put an end to murders, to attacks, to acts of pillage and vandalism."

The next problem confronting the authorities was that of a whole area badly disorganized. Though the bulk of the rebel bands had been beaten back into the almost impenetrable mountain regions of Collo and Edough, the countryside was full of vagrant, bewildered, and fear-stricken Moslems. Isolated terrorist raids and troop movements only added to the confusion; many roads remained insecure. The port town of Collo, its land routes in rebel hands, its telephone and telegraph lines down, was in touch with the outer world only by radio and had to be supplied by sea from Philippeville. Few towns, in fact, had been harder hit than Collo on August 20; two factories and several shops had gone up in smoke along with 860 tons of cork (which is a lot, cork being light).

In the cities, the Moslems, fearing reprisals, tried to keep out of sight; for days, the Moslem shopkeepers in Philippeville quaked behind closed shutters. Jittery European civilians, unable to distinguish between good Moslems and bad, opened fire at the drop of a hat. On at least one occasion, a French patrol, mistaken at dusk for a rebel band, had to duck shots fired by such civilians. On September 6, the wife of a gatekeeper at a railway grade crossing was massacred with her two daughters in a rebel raid. Shots fired near the cemetery at Philippeville as the funeral procession was passing, on September 8, led to acts of retaliation in which seven Moslems, including the gravediggers, lost their lives.

Relations between Europeans and Moslems were thus thoroughly poisoned; the economic life of the area was paralyzed. Philippeville suffered an acute shortage of meat, vegetables, and milk. Many merchants were unable to meet their financial obligations. It may, therefore, accurately be said that, although the insurrection had failed, the rebels had won a psychological and strategic victory.

M. Soustelle, acutely conscious of the dangers inherent in this situation, moved quickly to do something about it. On the morning of August 30, 500,000 handbills were dropped from the air over northern Constantinois carrying this message:

> Inhabitants of the *douars:* A horde of assassins deceived you on August 20. They compelled you to follow them in the way of riot. You have fled your homes and abandoned your property. This is a great misfortune for you.
>
> Those are responsible who ordered you to assassinate, to plunder, and to burn and who, very frequently, stayed behind while your own folk went to their death. The guilty will be punished. But all those who took part in no crime can and must return to their *mechtas;* no harm will come to them. Moreover, they may present this handbill to the officers, report their return, and regularize their situation, so that there will be no confusion.

In Philippeville, M. Benquet-Crevaux issued an "appeal" urging the Europeans to resume their normal occupations, to avoid congregating in public places, and to stay off the street in the event of an emergency. The Moslems were urged to do the same; it was specified that passes would be issued to those answered for by their employers.

On September 5, Colonel Georges-Camille Meyer was appointed civil and military commander in the Philippeville and Collo districts under the authority of the Prefect of Constantine and the Subprefect of Philippeville, the latter, newly appointed, being André Nicoulaud, an exceptionally able administrator. The mayors of the two townships were, simultaneously, divested of their police powers. The purpose of these measures was to concentrate law enforcement in the hands of a single man and thus, if possible, avert further rebel depredations.

That this danger was real could hardly be doubted; raids and attacks continued to take their toll in many outlying districts. Even as Army units brought in from other areas undertook a sweep of the Collo hills in search of rebel hide-outs, four civilians were butchered near El Milia, a farm was burned at Condé Smendou, 150 head of cattle were slaughtered at Aïn Abid, and two gendarmes were wounded between Collo and El Ouloudj.

In Kabylia, too, murder, arson, and sabotage had become everyday occurrences. On August 22, Marcel Frapolli, mayor of Fort National, a man of liberal views, beloved of all, was shot in the back on the steps of his home. He died at the age of forty-two, leaving seven children. Moslem merchants in the area had already begun to receive notices ordering them to contribute to the rebellion sums ranging upward from 50,000 francs. Signed "The Intendance," the notices were mimeographed on paper bearing the letterhead, "Army of National Liberation." Such summonses, obviously, could not be ignored.

A sheet containing A.L.N. "Orders and Instructions for June and July" also came to light in August. Among its many prescriptions, those more worthy of note were:

1. "Each leader must keep a register of martyrs and combats."
2. "Each group should have at least one Garand and one sub-machine gun."
3. "Men engaged in supply and liaison must help us without being informed of our organization. They will be dealt with only by the group's paymaster."
4. "Appoint in each region a group of volunteers bound by oath whose task will be to act in the cities against officers and high personalities."
5. "Avoid . . . killing journalists."
6. "As regards those whom you presume to be *goumiers,* kill them once you have proof. Death may also strike the *goumier's* family. Throw the body on the road and pin a note to it. As for war veterans, compel them to share their pensions with you."
7. "Headmen and rural constables must be compelled to resign within a month. If they fail to do so, kill them."
8. "Make contact with greengrocers to see that they poison vegetables supplied to the French Army."
9. "Enrollment is compulsory for persons between the ages of forty-

five and sixty years of age. Employ the civilians for the cutting of telephone lines, for supplies, and for odd jobs."

10. "Agents engaged in intelligence will go into troop cantonments. They shall be between forty-five and sixty years of age, of affable character, capable of worming their way in; they should, if possible, be secondhand dealers, traveling poultry merchants, etc."
11. "Burn farms, farm instruments, cereal crops, and everything owned by the *colons*."
12. "Recite nationalist poems at all times."

27. ASSASSINS AND POLITICIANS

The methods of the F.L.N., especially the methodical recourse to political assassination, are almost as old as Islam itself. As far back as the eighth century, a sect known as the "Stranglers" went in for allegorical interpretation of the Koran and the physical elimination of those who denied it. But it remained for the *Hashshashin*, or "Hashish-eaters," of the twelfth and thirteen centuries to perfect the art and, incidentally, to give the world a new word, "assassin."

The *Hashshashin* traced their origin to a break with the Ismaili sect, a branch of Islam made familiar to all by its forty-eighth Imam, the late Aga Khan. The Ismailis, whose sect is itself an offshoot of the Shiite schism, are at one with the Shiites in considering Ali, son-in-law of the Prophet and fourth Caliph of Islam, to be the rightful successor of Mohammed and in rejecting the legitimacy of the first three Caliphs, Abu Bakr, Omar, and Othman. Shiites and Ismailis have, naturally, even less use for the usurper Muawiya, who overthrew the house of Ali to found the Omayyad dynasty. But whereas the Shiites hold to the twelve Imams of Ali's direct line—the twelfth, the Shiites say, is not dead but will return to redeem the faithful—the Ismailis recognize only six of these Imams, plus a seventh of their own, Ismail. (With the Ismailis, seven is a sacred number.) When, in 760 or thereabouts, Jafar Sadiq, the sixth Imam, passing over his elder son, Ismail, bequeathed the Imamate to his younger son, a fraction of the people refused to accept the arrangement; they proclaimed the legitimacy of Ismail, though he soon died, and went about preaching an allegorical interpretation of the Koran.

One of these Ismailis, Hamdan Qarmath, founded the revolutionary

Carmathian movement in Mesopotamia, while another, Abou Abdallah, won the Berbers of North Africa to his doctrine of an imminent coming of the Mahdi, or Hidden Imam. In time, a certain Obaid-Allah, after many vicissitudes, got himself accepted by the Berbers as the looked-for Mahdi and was proclaimed Emir of the Faithful, descendant of the Prophet through Ali and Fatima. From his capital at Mahdia on the Tunisian coast, Obaid-Allah subdued Abbasside Libya. His grandson, Mansur, took Sicily, and his great-grandson, Moizz, became the first Fatimite Caliph of Egypt in 972.

The eccentric Hakim, whose self-proclaimed deification in 1010 led to the formation of the Druse sect, important even today in Syria and the Lebanon, is perhaps the best known of the Fatimite Caliphs. But one of his successors, Mostansir, also deserves to be remembered, for by appointing his younger son heir presumptive, to the detriment of his elder son, Nizar, he gave rise to the *Hashshashin* sect.* A Persian Ismaili named Hassan Ibn Sabbah took up the cudgels for Nizar, was expelled from Egypt and ultimately established his order in the Persian mountain fortress of Alamut. Soon his ascendancy spread far. His followers, reduced to blind submission, found spiritual release in paradisiac hallucinations induced by the use of hashish and served their master by murdering his enemies.

From 1090 to 1256, eight Grand Masters of of Alamut maintained, first as lieutenants of the Cairo Imam, later as Imams in their own right, an independent principality behind a rampart of terror; they even held strong points in Syria through lieutenants who assumed the title *Sheikh al-Jabal* (c.f., *djebel*) or, as the chroniclers of the Crusades said, Old Man of the Mountain. One of these lieutenants, Rashid-ed-Din Sinan, repudiated his allegiance to the Grand Master of Alamut and went it alone—with hashish and murder; the Crusaders and even Saladin had to reckon with him. The power of Alamut was destroyed in 1256 by the conquering Mongols; that of the Old Man of the Mountain, a little later by the Mameluke sultans of Egypt. But the curious visitor to Syria, if he travels to the mountains between Hama and Latakia, may still see moth-eaten descendants of those redoubtable *Hashshashin* living now in crumbling fortress-towns of a bygone age.

So when, for instance—I cite an example repeated in Algeria many times over—a gang of rebels took the village of Tanefdour near El Milia on the night of September 4, slit the throats of seven dignitaries and cut off the noses of four others, they were faithful to an old tradition. The spirit of Hassan Ibn Sabbah and of Rashid-ed-Din Sinan was not, and is not, dead.

---

* The Indian Ismailis, or Khodjas, also recognize the legitimacy of the Imamate of Nizar.

But if we are to see the most spectacular results of the policy of assassination, if we are fully to apprehend its terrible efficacy, we must examine the case of Ferhat Abbas, moderate leader of the Democratic Union of the Algerian Manifesto (U.D.M.A.). For Mr. Abbas was driven in the space of a few months to espouse without reservation the position of the F.L.N. terrorists who had murdered his nephew.* The first phase of Mr. Abbas's change took the form of a public statement on August 24, 1955, in which by indirection he imputed the death of Allaoua to the French. Here are the essential passages of this remarkable document:

> The U.D.M.A. notes that through the minutely organized attempts on the lives of Allaoua Abbas and Benelhadj-Saïd, a blow was aimed directly at itself and at its secretary-general. It observes that on the occasion of these attempts, both as regards the substance of the facts, in particular their origin, and as regards the identity and status of the perpetrators of this double crime, explanations and theses are being put forward with the object of creating rents and divisions in public opinion and in the Moslem conscience. That thus, and thereby, it is in a position to assert that the masters of the regime—and in the very first place, their press—are not without having a hand in the political confusion, the motives of which are easy to discern. Consequently, it warns public opinion against the exploitation of these attacks both in the psychological domain and in that of politics.
>
> Resolutely determined not to be outmaneuvered, the U.D.M.A. states that under no circumstances can it forget the heavy responsibilities and permanent crimes of the colonial regime. It asserts that, however great the misfortunes that may assail it, the U.D.M.A. will not allow itself to be distracted from the objectives and from the ideal for which it means always to conduct the same fight.

By January, 1956, Mr. Abbas found it expedient to put the U.D.M.A., his snorting charger, out to pasture. In a statement to the Tunisian weekly, *Action,* he denied any thought of being a "valid interlocutor":

> I am in no way qualified to negotiate with France. The men who lead the action are alone entitled to do so. My party and I myself have thrown our entire support to the cause defended by the National Liberation Front. My office, today, is to stand aside for the chiefs of the armed resistance. The methods that I have upheld for fifteen years—cooperation, discussion, persuasion—have shown themselves to be ineffective; this I recognize, but my solution of an autonomous "Algerian Republic" still strikes me as valid.
>
> I shall, however, defend neither this nor any other solution; I shall take no political action unless I am instructed to do so by

* See p. 175.

the National Liberation Front. And for this contingency to arise, the military problem will first have to be solved by negotiation.

The following April found Mr. Abbas in Cairo. "The war is not a fatality," he told a press conference there. "We appeal to the universal conscience, and more particularly to the conscience of liberal Frenchmen. Between the French and Algerian peoples, discussion and negotiation are not only possible but desirable. But there must be no cheating. The French leaders ask with whom they could negotiate. With the men of the National Liberation Front beyond a doubt, we reply, with the men who are struggling for the freedom of their people."

The essential thing to remember amid all this verbiage is that, from mortal peril, Mr. Abbas reached safety in the arms of the F.L.N. He who understands this understands a large part of the Algerian "revolution." But Mr. Abbas was not alone in a funk in late August, 1955. Mr. Benbahmed's anxiety was easy to imagine; it is not given to many of us to gaze upon an order for our own execution. As for Mr. Bendjelloul, the poor man was terror-stricken. "I know that I, too, am condemned to death," he kept saying in a conversation with M. Soustelle. The urgent problem for the politicians of Mr. Bendjelloul's stamp was, if possible, to disarm the assassin's hand by committing themselves a little more to the rebellion without giving up the bed they had feathered for themselves in the French camp and without forfeiting their chances in the event of a compromise settlement. The resourceful M. Bendjelloul took the lead. On August 25, at his instigation, a group of ten Moslem politicians, meeting at Constantine, issued a protest against what they termed "blind repression" and resolved to send another delegation to Paris. This venture was soon to have a luxuriant but ephemeral flowering. But before joining Mr. Bendjelloul in Paris, we must catch up with the doings of the Algerian expatriates.

In Cairo, a number of politicians, including Ahmed Mezerna, Hocine Lahouel, Mohammed Khider, and Ahmed Ahmed-Bioud (alias Bayoud), jockeying for position and hoping perhaps to offset the preponderance of the "military" clique around Mohammed Ben Bella, signed a "Protocol of General Union" on January 11, 1955. It proclaimed Algeria to be "Arab and Moslem," an integral part of the Arab Maghrib, itself a part of the "Arab fatherland." But the "General Union" was quickly sundered by conflicting ambitions and abiding antagonisms among the émigrés. Although Ahmed Mahsas, Ben Bella's turbulent henchman,* described

* In the winter of 1955, Mahsas, then panjandrum of rebel arms smuggling, had words with Ben Bella in a hotel room in Tripoli, Libya. Soon they were hurling Coca-Cola bottles at each other. Although they later made up, Mahsas was consigned to a sort of limbo.

Khider as "rotten" and Aït Ahmed as a "Berbero-materialist," the two managed to remain within the charmed circle of the F.L.N.'s Cairo delegation. Mohammed Boudiaf, who arrived from Europe in May, 1955, became number two man on the "military" side under Ben Bella. At a lower level, the politician Mohammed Yazid managed to keep a grip on Ben Bella's shirttails. Lahouel also straggled along in the background.

The "outcasts"—Sheikh Bachir Brahimi (Ulema), Ahmed-Bioud (U.D.M.A.), Mezerna, Chadly Mekki, and M'Barek Filali (Messalists)—banded together to form the "National Movement for the Liberation of Algeria." The prospects were, however, no brighter for this faction than for Abdel-Krim's "North African Liberation Committee"; neither was in the good graces of the Egyptian Government. In August, Sheikh Bachir Brahimi, under a cloud because of his relations with the outlawed Moslem Brotherhood, managed to stay an expulsion order with a plea of ill-health. In September it was learned that Colonel Nasser had thrown Chadly Mekki and Ahmed Mezerna into prison to get them out of the way of the F.L.N. Ahmed Ahmed-Bioud was to follow Ferhat Abbas into the F.L.N. early in 1956 and there to achieve a position of influence, thanks to his association with Ahmed Kamal, a United States citizen of Turkish descent and a benefactor of the Algerian rebellion.

The Arab League's "Fund to Aid the Liberation Movements" continued to receive contributions for the Algerian rebels; Egypt, notably, came through with £80,000. Abdelkalek Hassouna, secretary-general of the Arab League, was understood to have initiated talks with the F.L.N. looking toward the formation of a provisional Algerian government in exile, but the inner dissensions of the F.L.N. brought the proposal to nought.

28. THE "SIXTY-ONE"

An observer surveying the Algerian scene at the end of August could distinguish little that was not black and ominous. Substantial parts of the Constantine department lay prostrate; the rebellion, or its premonitory symptoms, creeping insidiously through the land, touched more villages, opened more sores, left more scars, claimed more lives. In some areas, evacuated by the French, the rebels held undisputed sway; their contingents drilled, trained, rested at will. In other districts—Tebessa and La Meskiana, for instance—with the schools, forestry stations, and farms burned, with the teachers, foresters, and *colons* gone, a few administrators and gendarmes remained alone to preside over the general ruin in the name of France.

Even on trunk highways, as between Bône and Philippeville, all travel was in convoy. Constantine itself was closely beset; the city was shocked to learn that a farm had been destroyed not seven miles from its gates by a band of 150 rebels, some of them on horseback. French troops, too thinly spread, always on the alert, frequently on the move, were beginning to show signs of fatigue; and even at that, they kept the main roads open only from dawn to 2 P.M. From the middle of the afternoon to the following morning, the rebels ruled supreme.

The rapid march of events had brought French weaknesses into sharp relief. The French were slow; the rebels were swift. The French were irresolute, divided; the rebels, despite dissension in their rear echelons, were "united in action." The French discussed contemplated measures in public and lost the benefit of surprise; the rebels, deliberating in secret, retained the initiative. But of all the sorry spectacles offered by the French, none could equal that of the writers and pamphleteers who, in Paris, labored unceasingly to discredit M. Soustelle's policies, to depict the repression as more heinous than the rebellion, to consign the *colons* to outer darkness, and to arouse sympathy for the rebel cause.

In this effort, the Communists were joined by a variegated lot of leftists, intellectuals, and "progressive" Christians (Roman Catholics for the most part, but with a conspicuous sprinkling of Protestants). I have already mentioned Georges Penchenier of *Le Monde*, whose dispatches from Algeria, presented with a show of impartiality, were slanted to prove the inevitable success of the rebellion; he recommended using Messali Hadj as the pivotal figure in a negotiated settlement. The ball was carried forward by the editors of such weeklies as *L'Express*, *France-Observateur*, and *Témoignage Chrétien*. The slogan of these "paladins of peace and democracy," as M. Soustelle called them, was: "The solution in Algeria can only be political." From this premise they concluded that attempts to restore law and order could only vex the problem and make a settlement more difficult to reach. Robert Barrat, one of the most vocal of the Catholics, warned that Algeria was heading straight for a "revolt of the slaves." To stave this off, he claimed, "shock treatment" was necessary; he explained that nothing short of Algerian home rule would do the trick, that the time had come to treat with the rebels.*

* See *Le Monde* for July 12, 1955.

M. Barrat expressed confidence that Algeria would remain within the French Union but did not say what could be done if the country's new masters demanded full independence, which was, after all, their avowed goal. Nobody, however, was misled by the subtleties of M. Barrat's argumentation; those who agreed and those who did not knew perfectly well that Algerian independence held no terrors for him. I ask the reader to reflect for a moment on M. Soustelle's position; between the rebels in Algeria and the insistent carping of their apologists in France, he had little to be grateful for.

On August 30, the *Journal Officiel* carried a decree making the provisions of the "state of emergency" act applicable to the whole of Algeria. A second decree created nine new *arrondissements* (subprefectures)—Bouïra, Fort National, Aïn Témouchent, Marnia, Relizane, Aïn Beïda, Mila, Bordj Bou Arreridj, and Djidjelli.

On September 1, Mohammed Salah Bendjelloul descended on Paris at the head of a deputation of worried Moslem politicians including Ali Cadi, Allaoua Ben Aly Chérif, Amar Naroun, Mostefa Benbahmed, Mohammed Belhadj Bengana, and Abdelmadjid Ourabah, all deputies for Constantine. The doors of the elegant, eighteenth-century Hôtel Matignon swung open when they appeared, and Mr. Bendjelloul, with the others in tow, found himself in the presence of Premier Edgar Faure, beside whom sat Jacques Soustelle. The "national idea," Mr. Bendjelloul declared, had made such progress in Algeria that nothing now could stop it.

But the delegation had not come merely to promote a propaganda theme borrowed from the F.L.N.; they were also there to show that they were the champions of the downtrodden Algerians. Mr. Bendjelloul, who did all the talking, bitterly denounced the "repression" and insisted that sanctions be taken against certain Europeans, including M. Benquet-Crevaux.

The next day, after the French Government's coordinating committee for North African affairs had approved several aspects of the "Soustelle Plan" and the dispatch of fifteen fresh battalions to Algeria, M. Bendjelloul issued a "communiqué" in which his group again protested with "indignation and deep emotion" against the "recent massacres of Moslems, notably at Philippeville and at Aïn Abid," and demanded an "immediate halt to this odious repression in all its forms, both civil and military, and the arrest of all the European elements guilty of, or inciting to, the assassination of innocent, unarmed inhabitants." It was, the delegation said, abundantly clear that the "repression" could not solve the Algerian problem. "Integration," too, according to the "communiqué," had been tried and found wanting. The delegation called for a "new solution" in harmony with the "present aspirations of the Algerian populations." Mr. Bendjelloul and his satellites could hardly go further than that without declaring openly for the rebels.

Back in Constantine, Mr. Bendjelloul went into a huddle with the U.D.M.A. group; it was announced afterwards that a "congress of second-college deputies and delegates" would be held in Algiers on September 26. M. Soustelle's reforms, scheduled to come up for consideration at a special meeting of the Algerian Assembly at the end of the month, were in advance declared to be "outdated." There was even talk of a new "manifesto" proclaiming the existence of an Algerian nation.

On September 21, M. Soustelle issued a decree summoning the Algerian Assembly into special session on September 27; it was anticipated that the session would last a fortnight. In that time, the delegates would be asked to consider measures for the breakup of the administrative townships into smaller, rural townships, for the freedom of Moslem religious institutions from government control, for the compulsory study of Arabic by all Moslem pupils in the elementary schools, for the abolition of the *khammessat** (to be replaced by sharecropping on a fifty-fifty basis), for the consolidation of dismembered agricultural holdings, for the expropriation of underdeveloped estates, and for aid in the acquisition of farm land by Moslem peasants. On September 25, Premier Edgar Faure, in a radio address, committed the Government without reserve to the policy of integration. He said:

> Among all the systems the mind might devise to regulate the relations between Algeria and Metropolitan France, . . . a choice is not to be made. For more than a century, Algeria has been in the process of integration with France. If this integration has perhaps not always been pursued with sufficient continuity and energy, are we, for that, to condemn the very idea of integration? Certainly not.
>
> Our goal is to achieve in quick stages the complete integration of Algeria, integration that will respect Algeria's originality and personality in such matters as language and religion, but will confer on all its inhabitants, without discrimination, the rights and duties, the opportunities and obligations deriving from French citizenship.
>
> This integration will be rapidly and loyally completed according to methods and stages to be decided on in agreement with all those who can provide useful advice. The day after tomorrow, an initial series of reforms will be put to the Algerian Assembly.

* One-fifth of the crop to the tenant; four-fifths to the landowner.

> The task is to open a road, that of hope; it is to rescue Algeria from skepticism as well as from anguish.
>
> The Government, determined to maintain the sovereignty of France in its African territory, resolved to re-establish order and peace in Algeria, calls upon the human and national solidarity that must unite the whole body of our citizens, European and Moslem alike, so that a true French community may be built in Algeria. The future, in Algeria as everywhere, belongs to those who strive for fraternal solutions.

On September 26, at 10 A.M., about fifty Moslem politicians, responding to Mr. Bendjelloul's call, gathered in Algiers to take a stand in respect to the policy of integration. It may well be imagined by what mixed emotions that meeting was agitated. Mr. Bendjelloul's views were by no means shared by all; many of his colleagues, even among those present at the meeting, were far from ready to disavow the moderate positions that had always been theirs in the past. But M. Bendjelloul won the day by a trick. It was agreed at the outset that those who had subscribed to the meeting, sixty-one in all, would be bound by the majority decision, whatever it might be.

After a tumultuous, eight-hour debate during which Abderrahmane Farès, delegate for Boghari and former speaker of the Algerian Assembly, had crossed swords with Salah Mesbah, delegate for Akbou and arch-anti-integrationist, a motion repudiating integration was put to a vote and carried by twenty-five to seventeen. In other words, if nine of the absentees had unexpectedly trickled in and voted against the motion, Mr. Bendjelloul would have been left holding the bag. This did not happen; consequently, there was much grinding of teeth when the result was known.

Actually, Mr. Bendjelloul had succeeded in getting only twenty-five of a total of ninety Moslem members of the National Assembly, Council of the Republic, Assembly of the French Union, and Algerian Assembly to vote against integration—not 28 per cent. But Mr. Bendjelloul was neither the first nor the last to hit on a system for making minority opinion prevail. His at least had the advantage of causing no blood to flow. The motion read as follows:

> On this twenty-sixth day of September, 1955, by reason of the gravity of the events through which Algeria is living, the undersigned second-college representatives, members of the National Assembly, the Council of the Republic, the Assembly of the French Union, and the Algerian Assembly, met to define their attitude. Their first duty is to denounce and vigorously to condemn the blind repression that, by applying the principle of col-

lective responsibility to defenseless populations, strikes a considerable number of innocent people. They demand an instant halt to this repression and a return to a more wholesome and normal conception of the rules of justice.

Analyzing the deeper causes of the present troubles, they solemnly assert that these causes are essentially political. They are thus led to conclude that the so-called policy of integration, never sincerely pursued despite the reiterated demands of the second-college representatives, is now outdated.

The overwhelming majority of the population now adheres to the Algerian national idea. Faithful interpreters of the popular will, the undersigned representatives hold it to be their duty to direct their action toward the fulfillment of this aspiration.

To this end, they give imperative mandate to all their members in the French Parliament to defend this policy in the councils of Government and of the Parliament, which must be confronted with their responsibility.

They decide to set up a permanent committee to coordinate the action of the representatives at all levels and to follow the development of the political situation.

The names appearing at the bottom of this document were those of ten Moslem deputies out of fifteen, five senators out of seven, four councilors of the French Union out of nine, and forty-two delegates to the Algerian Assembly out of fifty-nine (one second-college delegate having died during the summer recess). The participants were largely from the Constantine and Algiers departments, as will be seen from the following table.

	Oran		*Algiers*		*Constantine*		*Southern Territories*	
	Total	*Signers*	*Total*	*Signers*	*Total*	*Signers*	*Total*	*Signers*
Deputies	3	0	5	3	7	7		
Senators	2	1	2	1	3	3		
Councilors of the French Union	2	0	5	2	2	2		
Delegates to the Algerian Assembly	14	3	17	13	23	22	5	4

It is perhaps not surprising that most of the representatives of the Oran department should have preferred to steer clear of Mr. Bendjelloul.

Of the three departments, Oran is the most deeply penetrated by European settlement; the spirit of cooperation has consistently been better there than elsewhere in Algeria. It was the misfortune of the advocates of integration to be split into two camps. Abderrahmane Farès and his friends had attended the meeting in the hope of winning a majority vote there. Abdelkader Saïah, speaker of the Algerian Assembly, on the other hand, had kept his friends away.

The "coordination committee" was set up with Boudjema Ould Aoudia as secretary-general and Ahmed Francis, U.D.M.A. delegate for Ammi Moussa (Oran department), as deputy secretary-general. The members of the committee were: Mohammed Salah Bendjelloul, Ali Cadi, and Ali Brahimi, deputies; Salah Mesbah, Smaïl Lakhdari, Mohammed Bouchenafa, Abdelmadjid Mecheri, Hachémi Benchennouf, Kaddour Sator, and Aïssa Bensalem, delegates. This committee, on all subsequent occasions, spoke in the name of the "Sixty-One."

I remember Mr. Ould Aoudia well. Delegate for Michelet in Kabylia and a native Roman Catholic lawyer, Mr. Ould Aoudia had in the past been ostentatiously pro-French. "I should like you to come to Kabylia and see how we deal with the rebels," he had boasted to me one day only a few months before. "They won't get far with our villages; the people are armed and will drive them off!" Yet there he was, dancing to Mr. Bendjelloul's tune, as bold as before—in words. The enemy, only, had changed; now it was the French.

It was further resolved at the meeting that the motion of the "Sixty-One" would be read in the Algerian Assembly the following day after the Governor General's speech and that the second-college delegates would then march out of the building.

To avoid a noxious cleavage in the Algerian Assembly, M. Soustelle called the special session off at the last minute. This move had the effect of vexing the first-college delegates, who convened in Algiers on September 27 with all present except René Justrabo, the Communist delegate, to deplore the adjournment. In a motion unanimously adopted, the European delegates expressed their desire to "examine in all objectivity, and in agreement with many members of the second college, the proposed reforms submitted for their consideration." The motion also said:

> Profoundly saddened by the attitude of certain second-college delegates seeking to push Algerian politics in the direction of separatist nationalism, the members of the first college take exception to the methods used, notably threat and constraint, to obtain the signatures of certain of their pro-French colleagues, thus compelled to contradict their most recent statements.

> They reaffirm their profound attachment to the mother country, counter any idea of secession in the most unequivocal manner with an unshakable determination to maintain French sovereignty in Algeria within the context of Franco-Moslem brotherhood, the only warrant for peaceful social progress, and demand of the public powers an attitude of firmness excluding . . . any evasion . . . , the reestablishment of public order, and the inception of a coherent and constructive policy.

On the same day, twenty second-college representatives met at the Palais Carnot in Algiers with Ali Chekkal, delegate for Mascara, in the chair and voted a motion stressing the grave consequences that, in their view, could result from a refusal to consider the proposed reforms. The motion, signed by five deputies, two councilors of the French Union, twelve delegates, and one senator, also said:

> The undersigned second-college representatives, while denouncing all atrocities of whatever sort and whatever may be their origin, press strongly for the quick and loyal adoption of the policy of integration, which seems best to correspond to the aspirations of the Algerian populations.

Abderrahmane Farès, whose name figured so incongruously among the "Sixty-One," went on the air to clarify his position.

> My first thought . . . is for all the innocent victims of the of the painful events through which our country is passing, and the words "terrorism" and "repression" are so odious that our duty is to extirpate them forever from our vocabulary.
>
> As an independent and free representative who has never tried to exploit the dead for political gain, I fought openly at the meeting of Algeria's Moslem representatives for frank, loyal, and total integration into the indivisible Republic in the shortest possible time; I defended this with all my conviction, for it is the ideal of my whole life.
>
> Having been the victim, during this debate, of certain maneuvers which I leave to the appreciation of the consciences of those who perpetrated them, I come here today to tell you all that Farès remains what he has always been, and to appeal earnestly to all the Algerian representatives, and more particularly to the second-college representatives, to understand that in the circumstances we are now experiencing all selfish calculations, even legitimate ones, must give way to the public interest.
>
> My own life is as nothing in comparison to my country's future.
>
> I therefore accept all my responsibilities, and I conjure my colleagues who adopted the same position as I at the last "con-

> gress," and also my young colleagues of the Constantine department who share my convictions and courage, to join us.
>
> I address myself to all the populations of Algeria, to all the second-college representatives wherever they may be, asking them to accept, at this moment, and before the history of our country, their responsibilities.

The case of Mr. Farès must now be mentioned and disposed of. It is not a pretty story, but it is a highly illustrative one. Let us, then, before going further, hear Mr. Farès's amplification as contained in a statement to *Le Monde:*

> I have never varied in my position, and there is to my mind but one solution to the Algerian problem, that of total integration into the French nation. Appearances may have suggested that I had adopted the views of my colleague Bendjelloul and that I had aligned myself according to his motion. . . . This is only a matter of detail. . . . In the positions that I have held at the Constituent Assembly, at the Financial Assembly, at the Algerian Assembly, in the technical posts that have been entrusted to me, those of rapporteur of the budget and president of the finance committee, in the key committees on which I have sat, or again during my recent trip to the United States, I have seen, studied, and compared many things. I have given much thought to the political, economic, and social aspects of Algerian life, and I have only become the more completely possessed with my earlier conviction. The only way to give our populations without delay the wherewithal of happiness lies in integration.
>
> I do not on this point give way to a sentimental weakness or to an illusion. My schoolmasters taught me . . . that the duty of a public man, especially when circumstances are difficult, is to keep a cool head and a sense of realities. Now, an objective and lucid examination of the facts proves that the gigantic means that must be employed if the Algerians are to become citizens in the full sense of the term—I mean by that on the intellectual, physical, and moral planes—cannot be found outside the policy of assimilation of which I speak. . . .
>
> In time of war, our populations proudly accepted their share of the nation's sacrifices and endured the calamity that overcame us. In time of peace, our country, new, underdeveloped, characterized by a runaway birth rate, may perhaps also be said to present the symptoms of a catastrophe, but it must have trust in the solidarity of the nation. . . .
>
> Integration is not to me a mere word, or a cloak for connivances, or even a source of intellectual satisfaction for a man imbued with the culture he has received. It is a legitimate act,

born of a political position thought out in terms of existing realities. How then could I disavow myself?*

How? Mr. Farès was to give us a dramatic demonstration. He was mute for a year; then, in Paris, on September 24, 1956, he spoke—to repudiate everything that he had ever said before. "At the present moment," he declared in an interview spread over three columns in *Le Monde*, "the *moujahidine* represent, whether one likes it or not, the last hope of the Moslem populations."† He spoke of "legalized assassinations," but now implicitly condoned the terrorism. Stating, as others had done before him, that the solution in Algeria would have to be political, not military, Mr. Farès came to the point: "The only valid interlocutor at the present time," he said, "is the F.L.N., which has been able to muster behind it the Algerian people almost to a man." This statement, though quite untrue, is, when closely examined, by way of being a candid personal admission.

The carnage of innocent victims, he went on to explain, and the "financial hemorrhage" that had already been such a drain on the French economy could be brought to an end only through negotiations with the F.L.N. His appeal to the Frenchman's instinctive concern for his pocketbook contrasts sharply with the eloquent words he had used a year before to persuade the French to loosen their purse strings for needy Algeria.

But Mr. Farès was not yet out of the woods. He had only recanted; he still had to expiate a multitude of past sins. In December, 1956, he and several others of the long-since quiescent "Sixty-One" formed a committee in France, ostensibly to provide material and moral support for the Moslem students ordered on strike by the F.L.N. The politicians doing penance with Mr. Farès were Salah Mesbah, former deputy speaker of the Algerian Assembly, Ali Brahimi, former deputy for Algiers, and Aïssa Bensalem, former delegate to the Algerian Assembly for M'Sila (Constantine). Their committee studiously applied itself to the task of being helpful to the F.L.N. in minor ways (with speeches, petitions, and statements to the press); its pretensions were necessarily modest; its rewards, in the event of a rebel victory, would probably be no greater.

In the meantime, the committee was allowed to function freely in France. Why, indeed, should its activities have been curtailed? Its positions were openly defended by any number of French politicians,

* See *Le Monde* for October 1, 1955.

† See *Le Monde* for September 25, 1956.

writers, scientists, ecclesiastics, and partisans of peace. It must not be forgotten, in this connection, that the F.L.N. was indirectly represented in the French National Assembly by 149 Communist and Progressive deputies and could, in addition, count on the sympathy of a handful of Socialists and Radicals. As for Mr. Farès himself, he continued to hold a highly lucrative public post as notary at Koléa, west of Algiers, although he was seldom seen there.

Going back to that critical period in September, 1955, when the Algerian Assembly almost flew apart, we find, among others, three men in clear opposition to Mr. Bendjelloul–Mr. Farès, Ali Chekkal and, more passively, Abdelkader Saïah, delegate for Orléansville and speaker of the Algerian Assembly. Of the three, only Mr. Chekkal remained loyal to himself and to France. Mr. Farès, as we have seen, was later to sacrifice the ideal of his life, but not his life. Mr. Saïah resigned from the Algerian Assembly on March 18, 1956. In his letter to Robert Lacoste, the French Minister Resident, Mr. Saïah said that in view of the failure of the "policy of union" for which he had always stood, he had decided to return to his own people and "to share their life and their risks." Whereupon he retired with his French wife to Versailles.

But M. Chekkal, what of him? In February, 1957, he was appointed a member of the French delegation to the United Nations General Assembly. "Algerian Frenchmen, both Moslem and European," he said in a message before departing, "your interests are intimately linked with those of your French brothers, just as the destiny of French Algeria is intimately linked to that of France, our common fatherland." On May 26, 1957, M. Chekkal was assassinated as he was leaving the presidential box at the Colombes sports stadium in the suburbs of Paris after the *Coupe de France* association football game. The assassin, captured immediately, was identified as Mohammed Ben Saddok, 27 years old, a native of Bône and by trade a plumber's assistant. An F.L.N. spokesman, speaking over Cairo radio on the "Voice of the Arabs" program, said:

> Twice we tried to kill Chekkal, in 1955 and in 1956, but he was well guarded. A member of our secret organization was able to assassinate him on Sunday because the police had relaxed their protection. The Army of National Liberation claims the honor of having organized this assassination, carried out by one of its members. We solemnly express our profound gratitude to the valorous members of the secret organization who have rid Algeria of the greatest traitor our country has ever known and the greatest tool of colonialism. Chekkal was being held in reserve

> to thwart our national demands and to bring Lacoste's reforms into effect. Now that he is dead, all these reforms are doomed.

Ali Chekkal lies in his grave. Abderrahmane Farès and Abdelkader Saïah live in comfort and ease. Of all those who have capitulated to rebel terror, I put Mr. Farès at the bottom of the list. Who can blame the Mzabite grocer for paying his protection money? Excuses can be found for the politician who resigns his office to save his skin. But the public man who deserts the banner he has raised for others to follow purchases safety with ignominy. If there is a speck of decency in Mr. Farès, his punishment is, henceforth, in having to live with himself.

The episode of the "Sixty-One," especially when seen in the light of later events, shows how little the Moslem politicians understood the true nature of the Algerian rebellion. They had not realized that all the chips were down, that this time the F.L.N. was playing for keeps and had no intention of sharing the spoils with anybody else. There was just no middle ground for the politicians to maneuver in; there would be no "round table" for them to sit at. And yet the F.L.N. had been at pains to warn the politicians to beware. On September 22, a message went out to the second-college representatives; it said in substance:

> The standers-by, the stooges of colonialism, now think they can climb aboard with us. Yesterday, they scrambled for the favors and advantages dispensed by the Administration. Today, they issue protests and vote motions. That is less dangerous for them than to take up arms. The idea now in their heads is to divide up the portfolios and key positions in the Algerian Republic. But the people will not forget that these men, instead of helping them, helped themselves. The pitiful lackeys of imperialism already stand convicted; their eleventh-hour speeches cannot ward off the punishment that awaits them.

Jacques Soustelle, no man to take the count from such as M. Bendjelloul, made his intentions clear in a radio address on September 27. He had not, he said, been intimidated by the clamor in the second college; his motive in canceling the special session of the Algerian Assembly had been rather to protect measures vital to the future of the country from the baleful effects of fear and confusion.

> Many representatives of both colleges . . . have, since this morning, imparted to me their alarm at the prospect of the deadlock into which certain intransigent positions could drive Algeria. I persist in hoping that wiser counsel will prevail, that at a moment when discussions to promote progress and the common

> good are to begin, there will be no one to assume the responsibility for rejecting the debate. Since the task was and still is to seal the union of European and Moslem Frenchmen by a realistic and sincere endeavor, I should hate to think that anyone would move to provoke a rupture that could have incalculable consequences.
>
> I must state in unequivocal terms that our objective remains the complete and rapid integration of Algeria; our goal, peace in justice. If unbridled passions prevent us from taking here the necessary decisions, the sovereign Parliament will be called upon to settle the matter in the last resort.

The rebellion itself, as little affected by M. Soustelle's high purpose as by M. Bendjelloul's low scheming, continued in September to thrust upon the authorities a host of problems suffering no debate and no delay; heedless of what was said in Algiers and in Paris, it underlined in blood its claim to absolute priority. Rebel bands in the northern part of the Constantine department had made their junction with those of the south; a continuous, though diffuse, front now extended from the Tunisian frontier to Kabylia. Rebel activity was particularly intense in the Souk Ahras and Ouenza districts, where many farms were burned, roads blocked, telephone and telegraph poles felled, arms stolen, and loyalist Moslems assassinated. Forty-seven farms were destroyed in the Constantine department alone, as against seventeen in August.

Meanwhile, storm clouds were beginning to gather along the Moroccan frontier. Acts of sabotage showed that the virus of the rebellion had come alive in the interior of the Oran department. The lingering aftereffects of the boycott of the Mzabites took a morbid form in Algiers and Blida, where several Mzabite shops were sacked; one Mzabite was killed and another seriously wounded. It was announced that as about 100 rural schools had been forcibly closed or destroyed, at least 3,000 Moslem pupils would be deprived of schooling in the new term.

The Government, absorbed though it was in politics, managed also to increase its military effort; it even sought in new ways to forge an instrument that could enable it to snatch the initiative from the rebels. The call-up of reservists, begun in May with an initial contingent of some 8,000 men, mostly of noncommissioned rank, was now in full swing; 75,000 reservists were already, or would soon be, back in uniform. In addition, about 100,000 national servicemen were being kept under arms beyond the normal time for their release.

Simultaneously, with the reluctant consent of the North Atlantic Treaty Organization, France was withdrawing her best divisions from the "Atlantic shield" in Europe. The Second and Fourth Mechanized

Divisions, both of the NATO type, had already crossed the Mediterranean, the former to occupy positions in Kabylia, the latter to guard the Oujda district on Morocco's eastern frontier. In September, the Twenty-Seventh Alpine Division under the command of Brigadier General Michel Gouraud took over in Kabylia from the Second Division, which moved eastward to the Philippeville-Bône sector. The Seventh Mechanized Division and the Fifth Armored Division were later withdrawn from Germany and sent to Algeria.

In Algeria, small, highly maneuverable units—Mobile Rural Protection Groups (G.M.P.R.), native *harkas* and nomad companies (mounted auxiliaries)—were being recruited and equipped as fast as possible to give the Army the auxiliary support it so badly needed. Nine G.M.P.R. were operating in Kabylia in September. By the end of the month, French effectives in Algeria had reached 120,000 men.

29. DISAFFECTION IN FRANCE

The call-up of the reservists in France led to the mutiny or near mutiny of men opposed to the Algerian fighting. The first of these incidents occurred in Paris' Gare de Lyon on September 11, when 400-odd Air Force reservists scattered instead of boarding the troop train that was to take them to Marseilles for embarkation. Shouts of "We don't want to leave!" reverberated from various parts of the station and even from nearby cafés. The demonstrators, rounded up by the police and put aboard a civilian train—the troop train had left—caused further confusion by pulling the alarm cords each time the train started to move. In the end, they had to be taken back to their barracks at Villacoublay in the southwestern suburbs of Paris.

On September 29, 200 men of the 401st Artillery Regiment, accompanied by two Army chaplains, attended a mass celebrated at the St. Séverin church near the Sorbonne "for peace in Algeria and for the souls of the dead on both sides." A handbill distributed afterwards at the door of the church said:

> We are here regardless of our other opinions, to give solemn witness to our anguish and to our shame at having to serve with

> violence a cause which is not that of the French people as a whole. . . . May those among the French who might accuse us of defeatism or of cowardice go into the barracks and there freely and honestly question the soldiers as to the understanding they may have of their duty to defend France; they will learn that we are neither cowards nor defeatists and that there is among us a great thirst for true justice and for justice for all men, which imposes upon us an imperious duty to know what we are defending and whom we are defending, without contradiction and without remorse.

This document and others like it reflected a strong anticolonial current of opinion in the French church. Obviously, it was not enough to explain to these excited young men that they were being sent to defend the integrity of French territory and to protect the lives of French citizens.

On October 7, an even more extreme demonstration occurred, this time at the Richepanse barracks at Rouen. Refusing to get into the trucks that had been sent to take them to the railway station, about 600 men of the 406th Artillery Regiment, reservists for the most part, flung pieces of furniture in all directions, broke windows and staged a sit-down strike. Orders thundered at them by their officers fell on deaf ears. In the afternoon, the Communist mayor of the suburban village of Petit Quevilly appeared on the scene with a number of his henchmen and, in an emotional pep talk, encouraged the mutineers to keep their spirits up. The Communists sang the *Internationale;* the mutineers sang the *Marseillaise*. Republican Security Guards, moving in to disperse the crowd, were subjected by mutineers and demonstrators alike to a barrage of stones, bricks, and other objects, but managed ultimately to clear the street with the use of tear gas. By midnight, the barracks were invested by what the newspapers described as a "very important force." At 2 A.M., the mutineers were loaded into trucks and sent on their way.

Such incidents were symptoms of a deep division in the French nation. But in fairness it must be recorded that many of the mutinous reservists were later to give, however grudgingly, a good account of themselves in Algeria. Thousands of reservists who, without breaking discipline, had evinced a negative attitude began having second thoughts after landing in Algeria. Algeria, they discovered, was not the God-forsaken place they had imagined it to be, but a precious part of the nation's patrimony and a tribute to French vitality. In the rebellion, they found a challenge that had to be met not only with guns but with the works of heart and mind as well; they realized that if they rose to the occasion, some good could be made to come of the Algerian tragedy.

Their own tragedy was in knowing that their efforts were repudiated in advance by a large body of their countrymen. It was this aspect of the problem that caused the French journalist André Frossard to comment: "What concerns us is not our Algerian policy, if it exists, but French unity itself, which is going to pieces under our eyes. When a country ceases to be fully behind its sons who are fighting and dying in its service, its disintegration is near."

It was Jacques Soustelle who, with the help of his able and devoted staff, devised the instrument of ultimate victory. This instrument was the Specialized Administrative Section (S.A.S.) The S.A.S.'s have already been mentioned as a projected reform; in September, they entered the realm of reality. Explaining the measure at a meeting of the Government's coordinating committee for North African affairs on September 22, M. Soustelle spelled out the problem. The rebels, he said, had shown by the destruction of schools, farms, mines, crops, and cattle, by the assassination of Moslems in contact with the Administration, that their object was to ruin the whole fabric of the country. "A situation of this sort," he said, "cannot be met with military operations alone." His answer was to plot out "pacification zones" within which the S.A.S.'s would spin their web of confidence, protection, and assistance.

A new agency known as the Administrative and Economic Action Services took the job in hand; at its head was Fernand Vrolyk, the man who had directed emergency relief in the Orléansville area after the 1954 earthquake. Twenty-six officers provided by General Lorillot were sent into Kabylia with orders to start the ball rolling. Plans were made to have 250 newly trained Algerian Affairs Officers or officers on detached mission in the field before the end of the year. Each "chief of S.A.S." was given a secretary, an interpreter, a two-way radio set, a motor vehicle, and a guard of about thirty men. This small force was composed of regulars at the outset, but the object was to replace the regulars as quickly as possible with locally recruited auxiliaries. Army physicians, many of them young reservists fresh from their medical studies, were later, by their enthusiasm and sense of mission, to bring into the S.A.S.'s a social component of inestimable value. The rebels, with little to offer but the squeeze, resented these doctors more, perhaps, than anything else and managed to kill several of them. As the first "chiefs of S.A.S." were heading for their isolated posts in the Kabyle mountains, announcement was made in Paris of plans for organizing a territorial force, or home guard, in Algeria. *La Territoriale*, composed of civilians serving in static protection units twenty-four hours a week, has since become a familiar feature of Algerian life.

On September 12, the Government decreed the "dissolution" of the Algerian Communist party (P.C.A.) and its affiliated organizations.* The party publications, including the daily *Alger Républicain*, were placed in public custody and ceased to appear. The "dissolution" decree, it was said, had been motivated by a change in Communist tactics; the party's sympathy for the rebellion had increasingly taken the form of active participation. M. Soustelle reports in his book that the local P.C.A. secretary at Marnia in western Algeria had turned up among the arrested members of an F.L.N. terrorist cell and that the P.C.A. secretary in Bône, urging his followers to support the tobacco boycott, had said: "The Communists must take up arms as soon as possible so that the P.C.A. will not be left in the lurch on victory day, as the Tunisian Communist party was in Tunisia." The P.C.A. had even had a hand, according to M. Soustelle, in organizing the August 20 massacre at the El Halia pyrite mine near Philippeville.

No one, of course, was innocent enough to think that the party would now go out of business. But the loss of *Alger Républicain* was undoubtedly a stinging blow; the paper, fully committed to the rebel cause and widely read among the Moslems, had been the Communists' best card. To salvage something from the wreck, they managed to give independent existence to *Le Travailleur Algérien*, formerly a weekly page in *Alger Républicain*. By September 17, the Communists had recovered sufficiently from their "dissolution" to inform the M.N.A. that the underground party organization was now ready to join in all "anticolonialist" action and that its participation would not be made contingent on a political *quid pro quo* of any kind.

The product of Robert Barrat's "progressive" Catholic brain and the incipient mutiny of a group of Catholic reservists have already been alluded to. In September, M. Barrat, carrying Catholic opposition a step further, published in *France-Observateur* an interview with members of the rebel band led by Amar Ouamrane in Kabylia. A distinction must here be drawn between a legitimate journalistic venture and a political maneuver. It is, I know, easy for a reporter to give expression to his personal views by interviewing some public figure who shares or embodies them. Since the subjective element is bound to color a newspaperman's work, a reasonable margin of tolerance must be allowed in practice. Obviously, however, no such tolerance can be admitted by a responsible editor when the interviewer and the person interviewed are,

* These were: *L'Union des Femmes d'Algérie, Le Secours Populaire Algérien, L'Union de la Jeunesse Démocratique Algérienne, Les Amis de l'Union Soviétique, La Société d'Impression et d'Exploitation d'"Alger-Républicain."*

each for reasons of his own, engaged in special pleading. The Paris publicist had a clear political purpose in going to the mountains of Kabylia; it was to prove that France should capitulate in Algeria because (1) the rebellion was the expression of an irresistible force, and (2) this force was basically good and therefore nothing to be afraid of. A few excerpts from M. Barrat's interview will give the gist of it:

> . . . A group of about fifteen men . . . dressed in khaki uniforms, armed with army rifles and submachine guns. Their chief presents himself: Sergeant Ouamrane, commander of the Kabyle *maquis*. A civilian stands beside him: ". . . I am one of the political commissars of the F.L.N."
>
> They all assert that they are prepared to come to an understanding with "honest Frenchmen" and to respect them . . . "This is not a revolt; it is a war. We will struggle one year, five years, ten years if necessary. If we fall, our places will be taken by those younger than ourselves . . . The combat will cease only when our political objectives are won . . . Today the F.L.N. is the stronger for having drawn into its ranks all the young leaders of the M.T.L.D. . . . The Lahouelists no longer represent anything but themselves. As for Messali, he still has followers in France; in Algeria, his name is still popular, but his authority has practically vanished. The Algerian people are increasingly at one with us . . . We have armed groups and political commissars just about everywhere . . . Our groups, swamped by the number of applicant volunteers, now accept only those who have a certain amount of military training. Even the second-college representatives give us money . . . There is not a single foreigner in our officer corps, but many of our officers are former noncommissioned officers in the French army . . . Time and the repression are working in our favor. We were 3,000 on November 1; now we are 12,000. We shall be 100,000 as soon as we have the requisite number of officers . . . Our men have never committed atrocities . . . We did not wish the death of teacher Monnerot. We have killed collaborators, certainly, but, in the resistance movement, did you not do as much? . . . We demand: (1) The cessation of the repression operations and of all military action . . .; (2) The release of all political prisoners . . .; (3) A declaration by the French Government putting an end to the myth of 'Algeria, three French departments' . . . and recognizing the principle of the Algerian people's right to independence. It will be necessary to organize, a few months after calm has been restored, free elections under the control of a constituent assembly; these elections will bring into existence a government which will negotiate with the French Government the future political status of Algeria and the new ties that will link Algeria to France. We harbor no

grudges against the French . . . It is French doctors who in most cases treat our wounded under the seal of secrecy . . . If, tomorrow, the Europeans of Algeria agree to play the game of democracy and equality loyally here, why should we go elsewhere to look for the technicians, engineers, specialists our country needs? . . . We shall never submit to assimilation or integration . . . We are girding for a long and difficult struggle . . . After the phase of spectacular insurrection (November 1) and of general insurrection in a given region, . . . we shall, as soon as our means are adequate, move on to the third stage—the establishment of a free zone . . ., with a proclamation of independence, a provisional government, and an appeal for outside aid . . ."

In a statement issued to the press on September 26, M. Bourgès-Maunoury took strong exception to M. Barrat's interview.

> The reporter of a weekly . . . went so far as to interview certain rebels and attempted to present them as the authentic mouthpieces of the aspirations of the Algerian populations and as being careful to attack the military only, sparing the European civilians. The Interior Minister wishes to call attention . . . to the exceptional gravity of such suggestions. The rebel chiefs referred to, common-law criminals, have taken part, they and their men, in assassinations which not only do not spare but frequently have as their object European or Moslem civilians, women, children, and old people.*
>
> Since November 1, 1954, miners, postmen, doctors, foresters, trainmen, teachers, farmers, rural constables, administrators have been their vicitims. Attacks have also resulted in the destruction of economic and social installations . . . even schools . . . Elements of the populations that may have joined the rebels on certain occasions have generally done so under duress. Those who sought to resist were attacked . . . It would be dishonoring the Moslem populations to allow the notion that these men could be accepted in France as their representatives. It would also be dishonoring France.

On September 26, M. Barrat was arrested at Dampierre, twenty miles southwest of Paris, and held on charges of consorting with convicted criminals, notably with Ouamrane, several times sentenced to death *in absentia*. The outcry that followed M. Barrat's arrest can hardly be imagined. *France-Observateur* was, naturally, purple with indignation; it vowed it would "remain faithful to our duty of objective information."

* By the end of October, 1955, according to the official figures, the rebels had killed 123 European civilians, including sixteen women, twenty children, and 441 Moslem civilians.

The Socialist party had not yet come to power, and was therefore free to hurl its anathemas as it pleased; its secretariat-general denounced "this new and grave infringement of freedom of expression and of information."

The Catholic Center of French Intellectuals, of which M. Barrat had formerly been secretary-general, protested against the arrest of a man who had "followed his difficult calling as a journalist in a situation that puts to the test consciences at grips with national, democratic, and Christian imperatives." *Témoignage Chrétien* proclaimed its "solidarity" with M. Barrat, listed as one of the publication's contributing editors. Another protest was signed by seventy-two journalists representing twelve newspapers and magazines.* However, nothing happened to M. Barrat beyond the passing annoyance of his arrest (amply compensated for by his increased renown). He was released on September 27 and, although a new charge, that of attempting to demoralize the Army, was brought against him in October as the consequence of an article of his in *Témoignage Chrétien*, he was not otherwise inconvenienced.

30. ALGERIA AND THE CHURCH

We see in the case of many Catholic intellectuals something of the moral fraud that has surrounded the Algerian crisis from the start: a rebellion that falsely presents itself as the expression of a popular aspiration; writers who, making themselves the advocates of this imposture, clothe their actions in the high ethics of a profession which has as its goal the pursuit of truth. But what, one may ask, are their real motives? An adequate answer would require a book in itself. We should have to look into the interesting, complex processes that have drawn the French church, or part of it at least, away from its former allegiance to the French state, that have brought to the fore a host of Catholic writers, thinkers, and ecclesiastics hostile to the national concept as their fathers knew it. I remember being quite startled in 1953, when I was new to North Africa,

---

* *Le Monde, France-Soir, Libération, Franc-Tireur, L'Humanité, Le Populaire, L'Express, Témoignage Chrétien, France-Observateur, Le Jacobin, Le Canard Enchaîné,* and *Le Droit de Vivre.*

to hear a French diplomat in Tunis refer to the church as a "subversive force," intent on proving its "universality" at the expense of the state. But I was soon to learn what he meant.

A strong community of interests, if not of doctrine, binds an expanding church to an expanding state. The state being the vehicle by which new areas may be penetrated, the church is nationalistic. But when the state is weak, when it recedes, when its positions fall, the situation is reversed; the church must then slough off the state if it wants to remain, if it wants to hang on to the conquests it won with the state as its auxiliary. The new situation requires a far-reaching readjustment of values, because the church must, to survive in outlying areas, identify itself, not with the waning power of colonialism, but with the rising power of native nationalisms; it must, if possible, enter into a compact with the new and often non-Christian masters of the former colonies. This policy, revealing as it does an extraordinary degree of moral versatility, may reflect on the church's claim to be the repository of eternal and unchanging truths, but such, frequently, is the price of survival.

Nowhere may this general law be observed and verified with greater clarity than in North Africa. In the nineteenth century, and up until the first World War, the church was resolutely on the side of the conquerors. Its great figures of that period—Charles-Martial Cardinal Lavigerie, Primate of Africa, founder of the Order of the White Fathers, and Father Charles de Foucauld, Trappist missionary of the Sahara—were intense nationalists, despite the church-and-state controversy at home. Indeed, several of Father de Foucauld's letters, recently published, caused no end of embarrassment in church circles now unreceptive to his views. One of his letters, written to the Duke de Fitz-James in 1912, is curiously prophetic:

> My feeling, is that if, little by little, ever so gently, the Moslems of our colonial empire in Africa are not converted, a nationalist movement similar to that of Turkey will emerge. An intellectual elite is being formed in the large cities, educated in the French manner, an elite that will have lost its Islamic faith, but that will retain the outward forms of Islam as a means by which to influence the masses.
>
> On the other hand, the mass of the rural folk and of the nomads will remain ignorant, remote from us, steadfastly Moslem, inclined by their religion, by their *marabouts*, to hatred and contempt of the French, inclined to this also by their contacts with the French (representatives of the public authority, *colons*, merchants), contacts too often of a nature to make us disliked.

> The national or Moorish sentiment will therefore be exalted among the educated elite when the opportunity arises. For instance, when France is beset by internal or external difficulties, the elite will use Islam as a lever to stir up the ignorant masses and will strive for an independent Moslem African empire.
>
> France's northwest African empire—Algeria, Morocco, Tunisia, French West Africa—has 30 million inhabitants; in fifty years, thanks to the prevailing peace, it will have twice this number of people. It will then be in the midst of material progress, rich, spanned by railways and filled with men skilled in the use of our arms; the privileged among them will have been educated in our schools. If we have not been able to make Frenchmen of these peoples, they will drive us out. The only way for them to become French is for them to become Christian.*

In another letter, written to an army captain in September, 1916, Father de Foucauld said:

> I agree with you completely on all points; on the absolute necessity of dealing *severely* with the crimes committed—desertions, refusals to submit to authority, and defections to the enemy; on the necessity of expelling undesirables, spies, and troublemakers; on the necessity of forbidding all contact between our obedient subjects and the enemy, the disloyal, the recalcitrant, etc.; on the necessity of refusing to negotiate with enemy natives, except when they come to us asking pardon and unreservedly submitting to our authority.
>
> Not to act with all severity is to give new courage to criminals and to incite others to follow them; it is to lose the esteem of all, the obedient as well as the disobedient, who in such conduct see only weakness, timidity, fear; it is to discourage the loyal, who see that equal treatment awaits the faithful and the deserters, the obedient and the rebels. Not to drive out the undesirables is to allow the ferments of trouble, weak at first, to develop and work their full effect, which can be most serious, amounting to open rebellion. To treat with enemy or rebel chiefs as equals is to magnify them infinitely and to diminish ourselves proportionately.†

What interests us here is the fact that Father de Foucauld's rules have been repudiated by his successors. A whole body of doctrine and precept has, indeed, grown up around the notion of victory in capitulation; some of the most illustrious minds in French Catholicism, men like François Mauriac and Louis Massignon, the distinguished orientalist,

* See *Le Monde* for May 17, 1956.

† See *Le Monde* for May 23, 1956.

have led the way. The "progressive" Catholic thesis was set forth by Georges Hourdin in a series of articles in *Le Monde* in September, 1956. From the jumble of M. Hourdin's ideas, a few stand out as essential to his line of argument; in summary, these are:

> The rebellion is, in point of morality, no worse than the repression; all atrocities are reprehensible. Springing as it does from the national aspiration of the Algerian people, the rebellion is bound to spread unless its causes are removed. The solution must, therefore, be political, not military. If France persists in trying to put the rebellion down, she will not only fail but forfeit her intellectual and moral prestige, which is her most precious asset. The young Catholics who support the rebellion base their action on "arguments of pure justice."
>
> The concept of Algeria as part of France is an illusion that cannot resist the onslaught of reality; the French had better wake up to this reality before it is too late. Nor is Algeria purely Arab. The rebel leaders recognize this; they are imbued with French culture and pursue an ideal of equality—proof that French culture is "universal." "It cannot be denied . . . that the Arabs and Berbers . . . who lead the political and military movements are influenced much more by the ideology of the rights of man and of the citizen than by religious Islam, from which they are determined to escape at all costs so as to build a modern state, that is, a lay state . . . Nowhere, to my knowledge, has the rebellion assumed the aspect of a holy war . . . This refusal to engage in holy war is imputable, as far as I could gather,* to the deliberate desire of the leaders of the F.L.N. It is due also . . . to the attitude of the Catholic church in Algeria, to the generosity, to the sense of justice, and to the charity displayed there by the lay militants, clergy, and hierarchy . . ."
>
> The solution to the Algerian problem is to be found, not in turning the clock back, for that would be "stupid," but in breaking new ground, in defining the "national personality" of Algeria and the ties that will keep it a part of the French Union. It should be possible to set up a "federation" within Algeria (the entities to be federated are not described) and to establish a "confederal relationship" between Algeria and France.

M. Hourdin, so quick to puncture the "illusions" of others, would seem to cherish a few of his own. His portrait of the rebellion, in particular, is fanciful to say the least; and since his whole case rests upon the premise of rebel enlightenment and tolerance, he leaves himself open to the question: And if you should be wrong, what then? It will be

* On a recent visit to Algeria.

noted, too, that M. Hourdin does not quite dare throw helve after hatchet; he begs the deliquescent state to make one further effort, to accept a last duty as partner in a "confederation." But here again a question arises: And if the new masters of Algeria want no part of your "federation" or of your "confederation," what then?

In attempting to give substance to theories such as those propounded by M. Hourdin, M. Barrat was a precursor; others were to follow. Of these, Mme. Claude Gérard must be mentioned for her variation on the theme: she chose to ride into battle flying the colors of the M.N.A. A heroine of the French resistance movement, Mme. Gérard was credited with having organized one of the first *maquis* in occupied France. She had later been arrested by the Germans, tortured, sentenced to death, and delivered by advancing Allied troops.

After the war, she had been active for a time in Catholic political circles and had subsequently set up an agency called *Inter-Afrique Presse*, specializing in news of African nationalist movements. In the spring of 1956, she took it into her head to visit an M.N.A. *maquis* in Algeria (or possibly only in Algiers, I am not sure). An account of this adventure appeared in the Socialist weekly *Demain* for May 23. Mme. Gérard also gave an interview on the subject to the London *Observer*. She was arrested in Paris on May 29 and charged with plotting against the security of the state.

The air was, of course, immediately filled with protests. A "Committee for the Defense of Claude Gérard" was set in motion by Emile Kahn, president of the League for the Rights of Man, who announced that, while in the Algerian *maquis*, Mme. Gérard had intervened to save the lives of several French soldiers. Jean Pandrigue de Maisonseul, director of city planning for the department of Algiers, said to have acted as internuncio between Mme. Gérard and the Messalists, was arrested in Algiers on May 26, charged with plotting against the state, and released on June 12. Albert Camus, the well-known novelist, wrote to *Le Monde* to express the "indignant stupefaction" he had felt upon hearing of the arrest of his friend, M. de Maisonseul. The case of André Mandouze, the classics professor who published rebel "victory bulletins" in his sheet, *Conscience Moghrébine*, has already been mentioned in these pages; he, too, was a militantly "progressive" Catholic.

In April, 1956, it was announced that three priests of the *Mission de France*, Fathers Augros, Manet, and Kerlan, constituting a "sacerdotal team" assigned to Souk Ahras, had been expelled from eastern Algeria by order of the Prefect of Constantine. These priests, responsible for the cure of souls—Father Augros was in charge of the local parish—had nevertheless directed their attention mainly to the Moslems. They had set up an association for "fraternal mutual aid," the purpose of which was to succor the poor and also to provide opportunities for bringing the different communities into closer contact with one another. The *imam* of the mosque and the rabbi of Souk Ahras were honorary presidents of the association along with Father Augros. It was not denied that the three priests had been in touch with "certain well-known nationalist militants anxious not to lose the possibility of conversing with liberal French elements."* (Here the reader should be advised that by "liberal" is meant someone who sympathizes with the rebel cause.) The rub was that the desired *rapprochement* between the communities miscarried; some European inhabitants of Souk Ahras, indeed, took an extremely poor view of their priests' consorting with the rebels.

However, the Bishop of Constantine, in a message to be read from the pulpit of every church in the diocese, declared that "these priests have been faithful to the spiritual mission entrusted to them." An even more astonishing document was signed by the *Mission de France* under the signature of Achille Cardinal Liénart, Bishop of Lille, and Jean Vinatier, vicar general. It said in part:

> We can assert, as the bishops of Algeria have done, that the sacerdotal team of Souk Ahras pursued above the murderous struggles a work of humanity and justice favorable to a return to peace—protesting without weakness against the crimes, the burnings, the murder of innocent people, on the one hand; protesting with equal force against the collective repressions, the tortures, the destruction of villages, on the other hand; welcoming all Europeans asking for sacerdotal or human assistance; welcoming equally all Arabs confiding in it, and uniting the former and the latter in a common prayer for peace . . .
>
> We insistently demand that these measures be revoked. This would be an act of justice toward the priests of Souk Ahras; it would be an unmistakable sign on the part of the authorities showing that they are sincerely striving to achieve the reconciliation of the European and Moslem communities on Algerian soil; it would be an effective way of mitigating the tragedy that troubles so many consciences.

Apart from equating the rebellion and efforts to quell it—thus conceding a moral victory to the rebels—the cardinal implied, for reasons that may not be entirely disinterested, that the reconciliation in Algeria could be achieved only, or essentially, by those who, like the priests of Souk Ahras, understood the rebel point of view. Nothing, it must be admitted, could be more damaging to the French will to resist. Nor must the reader think the three priests were permanently excluded from their

* See *Le Monde* for April 26, 1956.

charge; the expulsion order was revoked by the Prefect of Constantine on July 27, 1956.

It went rather worse for Father Barthez, also of the *Mission de France*, who had obligingly hidden a rebel mimeograph machine in the parish house at Hussein Dey in the suburbs of Algiers. Haled into court in July, 1957, with eleven other "progressive" Catholics, all accused of activities harmful to the integrity of French territory, Father Barthez told the judges: "I was deeply anxious to bridge the gap between the two communities through common social work." Nevertheless, he was convicted and given a suspended sentence of five months in prison.

Thus, behind a screen of lofty principle and pious endeavor, a segment of the church was preparing for a new day—without France. Saint Augustine, an earlier Algerian bishop, had, in his *City of God*, told the Christians of his age how the church could rise triumphant from the ruins of imperial Rome. A similar ambition stirs many French Christians today, the ruins now being those of France. These Christians lack the genius of St. Augustine; they lack his clarity of purpose, his towering moral authority; yet their discourses remind one irresistibly of the twilight of Rome.

Only one among them, as far as I know, has put the issue squarely and honestly to his coreligionists—and to his countrymen. The superior of a French seminary, quoted by André Frossard in *Le Monde*, made this remark on his return from a visit to Kabylia: "This period, so very tragic, seems to offer the church new possibilities as much for widening the outlook of the faithful as for revealing its mysteries to the Moslems. All future evangelization, perhaps even the very preservation of the church in this land of Islam, is now at stake."* Who can doubt that the priests of the *Mission de France*, and the other "progressive" Catholics, were trying to realize the possibilities to which M. Frossard's unnamed churchman referred, and which result from the misfortunes of France?

An interesting and, I think, valid analogy can be drawn between the attitude of the church toward Algeria and that of the United States. The tendency in the United States, as in the church, is to write French Algeria off as untenable. Both hope, for reasons peculiar to themselves, to retain influence in Algeria after the positions now held by the French state have fallen. The United States, too, must consider its relations with the future masters of the country; it must avoid as much as possible acts and attitudes that might count against it, in other parts of the Arab

* See *Le Monde* for November 28, 1956. More, of course, was at stake than evangelization in Algeria alone. Many Catholic attitudes toward Algeria were, and are, conditioned by the church's hopes and fears in Asia, Madagascar, and Africa south of the Sahara.

world today, in Algeria itself tomorrow. Like the church, the United States fears the anarchy and confusion likely to follow in the wake of a sudden collapse of French positions and of an abrupt withdrawal of French troops. Hence the demand for a negotiated settlement now, on "liberal" terms, yielding to the rebels as much as necessary to obtain in return the promise of future cooperation, particularly in the transitional period between French and Arab rule. The French state will then be expected to see the operation through, absorb the shocks, and pay the bill.

The anti-Americanism so prevalent among the Europeans in Algeria —it became virulent after the failure of the Anglo-French intervention in Egypt in November, 1956—is frequently regarded as irrational and unwarranted. Such is not the case. The anti-American feeling stems from an understanding of American pressures and purposes. The Europeans have only to read the newspapers to realize how little their interests and even their lives are taken into account on the other side of the Atlantic. While the anticolonial demagogy of the American labor unions may, perhaps, be expected, the Europeans cannot help being appalled when as good a friend as Adlai Stevenson expresses the hope that France will become more "realistic" and satisfy the Moslem aspiration for home rule.

But blame should be put where blame is due. In the last analysis, the attitude of the United States, like that of the church, is merely a reflection of French weakness. If French positions, if French authority, were impregnable, it would occur to no one to meddle in Algerian affairs, and the nationalist contenders for power would get about as much of a hearing as those of Puerto Rico.

31. A REBEL VICTORY AT THE UNITED NATIONS

The rebel leaders, even in the moments of their wildest imaginings, probably never anticipated a decision in the field. Much, undoubtedly, could be obtained by attrition, more still by terror. The real hope, however, lay in an assault on the enemy's moral redoubts. For this, the hour was propitious. The fiber of the French nation had never been so slack. Distracted by the clamor of conflicting ideologies, Frenchmen, like the

Romans of Macaulay's ballad, waxed hot in faction but cold in battle. The bitter contempt in which Frenchmen held one another, combined with the sense of guilt that had permeated all classes of French society, opened to the rebels dazzling vistas of opportunity.

Maximum results, it was realized, were to be got by holding up France to the opprobrium of the world, not certainly for her failure to discharge the ordinary duties of a civilized nation, but for her "oppression." Here the rebellion could be used with telling effect—as exhibit A, proving that a subjected and liberty-loving people had risen against its colonial taskmasters. It was rightly surmised in the higher councils of the F.L.N. that the French could not stand indictment at the bar of world opinion, that they would panic at the mere thought of such a thing. And what better place could be found for the public arraignment of France than the vivid and contentious forum of the United Nations? There the rebels could count on the solid backing of the Arab and Asian nations and on that of the Communist bloc. Moreover, the hesitations and embarrassment of many other member nations, the United States included, were bound to offer the Arab delegates and lobbyists scope for their talents. "The Algerian problem is sure to be internationalized," the rebel leaders said, "if not at this session, then at the next." They were not far wrong.

The maneuver began on July 29, 1955, when the delegates of thirteen Asiatic and African nations requested the Secretary-General of the United Nations to place the Algerian question on the agenda of the coming session of the General Assembly. The request was made on the ground that a colonial conquest had prevented the Algerian people from exercising its right to self-determination; the document also stressed the "imperious necessity for negotiations between the French Government and the true representatives of the Algerian people." On September 22, the Assembly's General Committee voted eight to five (with two abstentions) to reject the Asian-African request, but was overruled on September 30 by the Assembly itself, which voted twenty-eight to twenty-seven (with five abstentions) to hear the complaint. The French delegation, headed by Foreign Minister Antoine Pinay, having argued that the Algerian question was a purely internal matter involving part of the territory of the French Republic and therefore wholly outside the competence of the international body,* walked out of the Assembly room in protest.

---

* By virtue of Chapter I, Article 2, Paragraph 7 of the United Nations Charter, which says: "Nothing contained in the present Charter shall authorize the United Nations to intervene in matters which are essentially within the domestic jurisdiction of any state or shall require the Members to submit such matters to settlement under the Charter."

The debate preceding the vote had brought into view some of the basic weaknesses of the United Nations. Once again the concept of an international polity grounded in law, running the gauntlet between passion and demagogy, had emerged much the worse for it. As Pinay had pointed out in his speech, Algeria had been French territory for more than a century and had been recognized as such, implicitly or explicitly, by countless treaties and international instruments, including the United Nations Charter itself. How and by what right, M. Pinay had asked, could such a national and international reality now be called into question? "Measure well the consequences, all the consequences," he had warned: "To what lengths will enterprises of violence and destruction be carried tomorrow if these enterprises receive today the blessing of the United Nations?"

But many delegates saw the matter in an entirely different light. To them, Algeria, far from being a part of France, was a subject nation struggling for its freedom and therefore a natural concern of the United Nations. It was this view, defended notably by Fadil Jamali of Iraq and Krishna Menon of India, that had prevailed.

It appeared at least ironical that small, backward states, some ruled by slave-holding despots, should point an accusing finger at France. Their liberating pretensions, when compared with their achievements, were ludicrous. But more damaging still to the good name of the United Nations: a question of capital importance, fraught with danger for the future, had been decided by a highly dubious majority of one. Who had cast the deciding vote? If the two phantom states, Byelorussia and Ukraine, had been struck from the list, the result would have been reversed. The votes of Costa Rica and Guatemala, both hostile to France, had weighed as heavily in the balance as the favorable votes of the United States and Great Britain.* It is, I think, wise in general to make

* Since writing these lines, I have come upon a comment made at the time by Kesrouan Labaki, an excellent Lebanese journalist, in the Beirut newspaper *Le Soir*. His judgment bears repeating: "This action [of the United Nations] constitutes an unwarrantable interference in the domestic affairs of a country that remains the champion of the rights of man. This intervention was voted by a group of twenty-eight states, most of which do not respect the fundamental freedoms or the rights of man, against France, which has settled the Tunisian affair to the satisfaction of Bourguiba, which is settling the Moroccan affair to the satisfaction of the Istiqlal, and which gives the Algerian French the rights enjoyed by those of Paris, which is the only Western and Christian nation whose Moslem nationals sit in the Parliament and accede to the highest positions in the state. Lebanon sided with twenty-seven countries, at least nineteen of which are subjected to the dictatorship of a minority or never knew what free elections are. Lebanon remains faithful

power roughly commensurate with responsibility. As Sir Winston Churchill recently remarked, "It is anomalous that the vote or prejudice of any small country should affect events involving populations many times exceeding their number, and affect them as momentary self-advantage may dictate."

The French delegation was recalled to Paris immediately after the vote of the General Assembly and took no further part in the session until the Algerian question was removed from the agenda two months later. The rebel leaders and their backers had, however, no reason to be discouraged. The General Assembly had, in effect, endorsed their basic contention, which was that the question in Algeria was one of human rights and self-determination, that it transcended considerations of national sovereignty, and thus came within the purview of the United Nations. This was, indeed, a resounding success; it authorized the most optimistic hopes for victory at a subsequent session—provided, of course, the rebel bands could hold out long enough in the *djebels* of Algeria.

32. DOCUMENTS FOUND IN A CAVE

Late in September, 1955, the French command undertook to reclaim the Nememchas, an area that had been virtually abandoned to the rebels the previous summer. Fifteen battalions, drawn from both sides of the Tunisian frontier and commanded by Brigadier General Michel Lecarpentier de Sainte-Opportune, deputy commander of the French forces in Tunisia, were thrown into the area. Slowly, methodically, they made their way

---

to Saudi Arabia, no doubt, when the Riyadh Government orders the execution of officers and tribal chiefs accused of loving liberty. It is even faithful to Yemen when the Imam has his brothers beheaded. But solidarity must not exceed these limits. We are no longer with Yemen when Yemen undertakes to give France lessons in civilization, when Saudi Arabia seeks to obtain for Algerians, Moroccans, Tunisians, and Mau Mau rights and privileges that none of the sovereign of Riyadh's subjects would dare dream of. In the specific matter that concerns us today, the majority of the Lebanese part company with the Arab countries, condemn the action of the Government, denounce the vote cast by the Lebanese delegation to the United Nations . . ."

across that storm-tossed sea of stone, combing out innumerable valleys, peering into innumerable caves. Now it so happened that Bachir Chihani, alias Si Messaoud, self-styled "Commander in Chief of the Algerian Army of Liberation," and certainly the paramount rebel chief in eastern Algeria, was then holding a council of war in a cave near Djeurf. The rebels scattered like fowl when General de Sainte-Opportune's men closed in. Twelve rebels were killed in their flight, others were caught, but the elusive Chihani got away.*

In Chihani's cave, the French found a briefcase stuffed with documents, among them correspondence (in French) between Chihani and Mohammed Ben Bella. These documents, avidly scrutinized by French intelligence officers, showed that the rebels had begun to implement plans for an "autonomous zone" in the Nememchas, complete with *caïds* and rural constables of their own choice. A letter from Ben Bella, written, according to the sender, "with the agreement of the Big Brother" (meaning Colonel Nasser), contained assurances to the effect that the A.L.N.'s "request," presumably for arms, would be granted; it added, however, that the "principal problem," undoubtedly that of shipping, remained to be solved. Meanwhile, the letter said, the "structure of the revolution"—"Army of Liberation plus political expression in the cities" —was not to be neglected. Ben Bella also reported in the letter that the F.L.N. organization in France had been set up but had still to be consolidated. He reminded the rebels of their duty to "liquidate all personalities that might play the part of valid interlocutors." He asked for the names of three or four qualified Algerians—they should be "honest, politically mature, and fluent in French, English, and Arabic"—who could be called on for "political work."

Another letter, unsigned but undoubtedly written by Ahmed Mahsas, Ben Bella's right-hand man, set the rebels' minds at rest regarding the nefarious activities of the expatriate politicians. Mahsas wrote:

> You may be sure that we have done everything to see that nobody may exploit the revolution for personal or partisan ends. The two clans—the Messalists (Mezerna and Chadly†) and the central committee (Lahouel and Yazid)—are properly muzzled. Nobody recognizes them here.

The letter said that Sheikh Bachir Brahimi and Ahmed Ahmed-Bioud (alias Bayoud) as well as Mezerna and Mekki had repudiated the F.L.N.

* But his end was near. Chihani, who had not hesitated to kill fellow rebels who stood in his way, was murdered by two of his lieutenants before the year was out.

† Chadly Mekki.

Mahsas conceded that Mohammed Khider and Hocine Aït Ahmed, both described as "corrupt like all the other politicians," continued to represent the F.L.N. in Cairo, but added that "they serve merely as a front and have no say in the matter."

Mahsas continued:

> The truth is that we are very badly represented abroad. We have contemplated a change of personnel. We need untainted men. The only person here who might possibly redeem himself is Yazid, and even that is doubtful.
>
> Khider is done for; he has become stodgy and has entered upon the path that leads to decay. He is easily influenced by Aït Hocine and Lahouel. The latter two, however, are not dangerous, since their future is in our hands, and they have no followers to back them up in case of a maneuver of some kind. It is nonetheless true that they fall far short of representing the revolution in a worthy manner.
>
> The danger could come from the Messalists, who are doing everything they can to take over the Army of National Liberation. They have, in this endeavor, neglected neither falsehood, nor slander, nor fraud. They raise funds in the name of the Army. They try to insure that those who denounce them are beaten up (this in France). In the East, their prestige is nil. They do the work of parasites (on the radio) with the help of El Brahimi and Bayoud (U.D.M.A.).
>
> In accordance with the declarations of November, we tried to form a committee of the National Liberation Front. After the usual maneuvers, Brahimi (Ulema), Bayoud (U.D.M.A.), Mezerna and Chadly (Messalists), Lahouel and Yazid (central committee), and Khider and Aït Hocine (representatives of the Algerian delegation; they were close to us then) accepted the principles of the Front, which were:
>
> 1. Recognition of the Army of National Liberation and of its power of decision (internal sovereignty);
> 2. Faith in action as the only way to solve the Algerian problem;
> 3. Faith in North African unity of action.
>
> It was then that we observed all the baseness of those people. Each one tried to use the Front to further his personal interest or that of a party or clan. The spirit of the Front, that is, a repudiation of all bad habits, was absent. The committee split into two groups: 1) Mezerna, Chadly, Brahimi, and Bayoud going their way; 2) Lahouel, Yazid, Khider, Aït Hocine, apparently continuing to accept the Front. We continued to work with the latter group, keeping them under constant and severe control.

Thus it was that the job of clarification took up a lot of our precious time. Especially in France, where amid the attacks of the Messalists and of the Administration it was necessary to make the militants understand that the revolution was above persons and parties. Messali has played the part of a counterrevolutionary. His primary thought has been to keep the followers who adore him. Perish the revolution! He was never willing to accept the principles of the Front and of the Army of National Liberation. Like all the politicians, he took full advantage of the simplicity, ignorance, and faith of the militants. With God's help we have been able to clarify the issue in France; we have a good, growing organization. The Messalists exist also, but it is a matter of time.

In the East, our positions are getting stronger by the day both politically and in point of revolutionary ideology. And thanks to the historic battle which you are fighting and which forces the admiration of the whole world, the enemy is in desperate straits. He has recently admitted that he will never be able to vanquish the glorious Algerian resistance by force of arms. Has he not just announced a change of tactics the aim of which is to isolate the Fighters of the Faith by trying to separate them from the people and, in addition, by making Tunisian-type solutions dance before the eyes of cardboard politicians?

What does the release of the Messalists and the Centralists [Lahouelists] mean? It is clear! The object is to counteract the Revolution advancing toward liberation from the forces of oppression. . . .

The French "democrats" talk a great deal about a Tunisian-type solution in Algeria. Even the question of valid interlocutors is broached. Abbas is considered, and especially Messali, for the "rôle of Bourguiba" (the laying down of arms). . . .

Some people are already making plans. Kiouane, an influential member of the defunct central committee, has written an article for *France-Observateur;* in it he calls for the opening of a conference to include the representatives of all the political tendencies and of France. . . .

Messali, the outworn leader, made a moderate statement published in *La Vérité* (Trotzkyite)* in which, after denouncing the repression less vigorously than a Bendjelloul or any other "administrative," he too calls for the opening of a conversation with France. You can see the maneuver taking shape:

---

* In addition to its monthly organ, *La Voix du Peuple,* printed in Belgium, the M.N.A. had access to *La Vérité,* weekly organ of the French Internationalist Communist party (Trotzkyite). Frequently, the M.N.A. took a whole page in *La Vérité.* It would be interesting to know what the details of the arrangement were.

1. The use of tainted politicians to weaken the revolutionary zeal of the people;
2. The infliction of forceful blows upon the combatants and the people to make them amenable to the solutions of the politicians.

This maneuver has already been denounced long ago; that is, when Messali was moved from Les Sables-d'Olonne, where he could see nobody, to Angoulême, where he is free to receive whom he pleases. Meanwhile, the repression falls ferociously upon the people and upon the combatants.

It is evident that France as well as the trashy politicians will be sadly disappointed. The vigilance of the combatants will, in Algeria, nip Bourguibaism in the bud. The combatants are of higher maturity; they have freed themselves from myths; they rely on themselves. They know that the solution of the problem depends on their force, on their organizational capacity, on their fighting power, on their maturity in all respects. Nine months of their glorious action has thrust the Algerian question upon the world. As the result of nine months of sacrifice, a people chloroformed by the politicians takes hope and courage and rises against the oppressor. The Algerian question has been brought by blood before the United Nations.

Glory to the Army of National Liberation.

It should be recorded as a footnote to this correspondence that at least some of the arms mentioned in Ben Bella's letter apparently got through to the rebels. Here is the evidence: on Christmas eve, Ali Ben Mekki Kerbadou, a minor rebel chief, gave himself up to French troops at Khanga Sidi Nadji on the southern confines of the Aurès and Nememcha ranges. Information provided by Kerbadou led to the discovery of a rebel arms cache; it also enabled the French to smash a rebel band south of Guentis on December 29 (thirty rebels killed). One of the three rebels taken alive that day, a Hocine Benouarja, turned out to be an emissary from Cairo; he said he had been trained as a guerrilla by Egyptian instructors. Benouarja's personal diary yielded a mass of detail on the rebel organization in Cairo and in Tripoli. All this was most interesting, but more was to come. French officers going through documents found in the arms cache came upon a letter written by Chihani on November 1 and addressed to Colonel Nasser. Typed in Arabic and rubber-stamped with the seal of the A.L.N., the letter said:

Praise to God alone.

The Supreme Command of the Algerian Army of National Liberation, under the authority of Sheikh Bachir el Chihani, Commander in Chief of the armed forces, acknowledges delivery of the items listed below:

Four Thompson submachine guns of American manufacture with 800 rounds of ammunition; thirty-three British ten-shot rifles with a supply of 8,600 cartridges; one Bren gun with a supply of 100 cartridges.

Delivery has been effected by the southern Tripolitania route. For this, it warmly thanks the members of the Maghrib committee and its chief, the Commander of the Revolution, Colonel Gamal Abdel Nasser.*

The briefcase that Chihani had left behind in the cave near Djeurf contained, in addition to the correspondence already mentioned, a set of directives penned, so it seems, by the rebel chief himself for the use of his men. This highly cluttered, and in spots unintelligible, document need not be reproduced in full, but a few of its prescriptions will serve as an indication of how Chihani thought the "independence struggle" ought to be conducted:

Any zone remaining inactive is considered to be high treason . . .

Any utility belonging to the enemy must be destroyed . . . The permanence of action on the roads, with the participation of the civilians; destroy the telephone poles and attack those who repair them, and roads. No prisoners except big chiefs; continue the burning of farms and all the houses of the *goumiers,* no pity for the Moroccans.

All *caïds,* presidents, must be killed.

The women, the *colons,* and the French civilians must be killed; if they kill our children and our wives, kill theirs.

Requisition all the goods of the *colons* and of the *goumiers.* All tax collectors must be killed, and he who pays them; boycott of taxes; burn the houses of Moslem sergeants in service. Gather together all the militants to warn them not to smoke, and all those who refuse must be killed; national mourning, no celebrating.

Set up terrorist cells in the cities . . .

Kill the traitors in the cities by suicide commandos; isolate suspects; abduction of suspects; neutralize them, work on them to have them on our side.

He who issues directives himself without orders from the committee must be executed without delay.

---

* This letter was turned over to an examining magistrate in Batna for use in case Chihani should ever be caught and brought to book. But, as Kerbadou was able to testify, Chihani was already dead.

Kill Bourguibaism, our watchword is that of the liberation . . . Our independence will come by force, all those who listen to the political elements must be court-martialed . . .

33. TERROR IN THE WEST

On the night of October 1—Jacques Soustelle had inaugurated a trade fair in Oran that day—the rebels fastened their terror on the mountainous area bordering the Moroccan frontier: a new front had been opened. At Turenne, west of Tlemcen, a *caïd* on his way home for dinner was shot by a terrorist and wounded in the arm. Later that evening, in a nearby *douar*, the president of the local *djemaa*, emerging from his house in response to the call of a friend's voice, was killed in the road by five khaki-clad rebels. Two hours passed. Then at Souila, near the port town of Nemours, twenty rebels in uniform riddled the *caïd's* house with lead. A night watchman was killed, but, luckily for the *caïd*, a detachment of Republican Security Guards arrived in time to put the rebels to flight before further damage was done. At midnight, a group of about thirty rebels armed with automatic weapons swooped down on the frontier village of Benioussine in the Marnia district and abducted three Moslems, who, not long before, had testified in court against a captured terrorist. At Anatra, a neighboring village, a Moslem known for his loyalty to France was assassinated by three masked men, who, departing, left a British-made hand grenade on the ground behind them. The house of a pro-French Moslem in the Sebdou district south of Tlemcen came under rebel fire; again a night watchman was killed. Another Moslem was murdered at 4 A.M. on October 2.

That evil morning brought misfortune to a French light infantry company newly arrived from Germany, then quartered in a farm four miles west of Nedroma. The farm nestled in a deep hollow; from the vantage ground of the hills above, the rebels commanded a plunging view into the French position. With a few bursts of automatic fire, they killed a sergeant and wounded several men before the startled French had got so much as a rifle into play. For three hours, the French blasted away at the rebels with a mortar and other weapons, while the rebels, well ensconced behind their rocks, kept pouring lead into the camp. A Republican Security unit stationed in the area delivered the position, without, however, managing to engage the rebels in combat.

Two foresters also perished that day: one was assassinated under the eyes of his wife and two children; the other was shot down as he was returning on horseback from a tour of inspection. A handbill found on the second forester's body (and elsewhere) said: "The whole department of Oran joins its fighting brothers to illustrate in the most striking way the unity and coordinated action of the rebel forces. French soldiery will soon come to understand that, as was shown in Indochina, it is vain to attempt to maintain domination by force." This message was written in French, Arabic, and—presumably for the benefit of deserters, real or potential, from the Foreign Legion—in German.*

All these terrorist attacks occurred within forty miles of the Moroccan frontier. It was reported that the bands, although composed in the main of peasants recruited or impressed locally, were led by rebels who, having fled to Morocco after the terrorist outbreak in November, 1954, had trained as guerrillas in the Spanish zone, notably at Zaïo, just across the border. Rebel arms and supplies almost certainly came from Spanish Morocco. Mohammed Ben Bella, spurred on no doubt by the successful conclusion of an arms deal in Italy in August, had visited Spanish Morocco in September—in connection, it may be assumed, with preparations for the October "offensive."†

Though the violence was confined to the frontier area, the felling of telephone poles thirty miles east of Tlemcen suggested that the rebellion was already pushing its tentacles well into the Oran hinterland. In an effort to pin the rebels down before they could progress further, Pierre Lambert, corpulent, realistic, hard-hitting Socialist Prefect of Oran, ordered reinforcements sent into the troubled zone. But once again—and, it will be noted, on the morrow of their signal success at the United Nations—the rebels had caught the French unawares, and at small cost to themselves penetrated into the heart of a previously quiet region.

* Sidi Bel Abbès, south of Oran, is the home of the Foreign Legion. The rebels are known to have facilitated desertions, sometimes in return for a fee. That German deserters have served in the rebel ranks cannot be doubted, but I have no idea of their number.

† On October 17, Ben Bella was seen in Madrid, where, according to one report, the Egyptian military attaché gave him £20,000 and a supply of insignia for the rebels.

The saying, "Oranie,* haven of peace," sounded a little hollow after that. And once again, rebel action was following the familiar pattern of assassination and fear, an incomparable formula for asserting power over the minds of the people. Once their lesson had been made manifest in the simple, stark, unforgettable terms of a man lying dead in his blood with a note pinned to his belly, once the primal instinct of self-preservation had been aroused, the psychological battle was won by the rebels. And the French had another occasion to measure the inefficiency of their counterattack—the promise of reforms, of more justice, of greater well-being. The discrepancy between the psychological weapons used by the French and by the rebels was glaring; it was that of a wooden sword against a precision rifle. Clearly, if the French were to succeed, protection and security would have to come first; only then could a way to the heart be found. This is why, as I have said, the S.A.S. was the instrument of ultimate victory; it satisfied social needs, but it also protected.

I was interested two years ago to read in *Time* magazine an article on Southern coercion to prevent the Negro from exercising his constitutional right to vote. These two paragraphs, in particular, struck my attention:

> The specific threat of physical violence looms in relatively few areas (and relatively few white Southerners will stand for it). But where it looms, it is terribly effective. In Liberty County, Fla., last year, all but one of the first ten Negro registrants in the county's history took their names off the voting list after a set of cross-burnings, bomb-throwings, and shots fired into their homes.
>
> In Belzoni, Miss., in 1954, a Negro minister who refused to remove his name from the voting list was shot down—a fact that did not prevent the coroner's inquest from returning a verdict of "accidental death." And in Tensas Parish, La., where not one of 4,500 Negro inhabitants is registered, the only Negro who tried it recently was taken by the registrar to see a law officer, who asked him: "Aren't you happy here? Is something wrong with the way things operate around here? If you aren't happy, perhaps we can arrange for you to leave." The Negro promptly replied that he was happy, that his attempt to register had been a mistake. The Negro stayed on in his community, but his wife lost her job.†

Such stuff, by Algerian standards, is child's play, but it does illustrate a general rule—that if you want to work your will on another, see that he fears for his life, and you seldom fail.

---

* A French geographical term applied to western Algeria as a whole; the counterpart of "Algérois," "Kabylia," and "Constantinois."

† See *Time* for July 29, 1957.

The second-college representatives in the Oran department were, it must be said, far braver in the face of danger than their colleagues in the other two departments. Meeting together in Oran on October 5, they passed a motion in which they denounced the terrorist aggressions committed along the frontier and demanded that the "loyal integration of Algeria into Metropolitan France" be made effective forthwith. They said it was the will of the inhabitants of the troubled area to assist in restoring law and order.

Hundreds of telegrams expressing the same desire poured into M. Soustelle's office and even into the Interior Ministry from *caïds, djemaa* presidents, and other native authorities in western Algeria. It was, therefore, decided that the evident, spontaneous reaction of the inhabitants against the rebel raiders should be exploited to the full. With M. Lambert and Colonel Jean Constans, chief of the Governor General's military staff, directing operations from Oran, fifteen Algerian Affairs Officers, five of them Moslems, went into the frontier zone to supervise the distribution of more than 2,000 rifles to hastily recruited auxiliary defense units (*harkas*) and to coordinate pacification efforts. In all, thirty-seven *harkas* of about fifty men each and seven "protection groups" of comparable strength were organized and armed. At Le Kreider, far to the south, a large *harka* (800 men, some on foot, some mounted) assumed part of the responsibility for guarding Oran's southern approaches. Arms were also allocated for the defense of 326 isolated European farms.

These various measures, though they reflected a laudable desire to associate the Moslems closely with the Europeans in the cause of common safety, bore the fatal mark of makeshift. They came too late; their efficacy was vitiated by haste and overconfidence. In eastern Oranie, as in the northern Constantinois five months before, the French learned that the defenses of an area could not be improvised. Fifty-five more *harkas* were raised in November. But, as the rebels consolidated their hold on the area, the will to resist rotted around them. A few of the *harkas*, on the point of going over to the rebels bag and baggage, had to be hurriedly dissolved. Fifty-eight individual desertions involving the loss of fifty-nine weapons (three of them automatic) were reported in October; sixty-four men deserted with fifty-eight rifles in November; twenty with thirty-four rifles in December. In March, 1956, 130 men of the *harkas* assigned to the Djilalia S.A.S. in the Marnia district deserted, making off with 187 rifles and twenty-two submachine guns.

It must not be thought that all the *harkas* were unreliable; some, indeed, achieved a highly enviable record in combat. What can be inferred is that a house is no better than its foundations; these had not been attended to. The French were in for months of patient effort, of slogging, harassing give-and-take, of slow, uncertain recovery of lost ground before they reached at last that crucial divide, marked by no sign in particular but by a thousand unmistakable indications, beyond which they could truthfully say that time was working in their favor.

Meanwhile, in eastern Algeria and in Kabylia, the situation was worse than ever. The contaminated zone had enveloped Bône; its ramifications stretched east as far as La Calle and west into lesser Kabylia. From its Kabyle citadel, the rebellion was creeping down into the Soummam Valley and on toward Bougie. When the rebels passed, farms, schools, forestry stations, livestock, crops lay wasted behind them; assassinations, abductions, mutilations were the constant emblem of their action. On October 17, a bus on its way from Bône to Herbillon, a fishing village at the foot of the Edough massif, was attacked by a band of about 100 rebels, who butchered the European driver and the seven Europeans among the passengers. The victims included a young couple just starting out on their honeymoon.

In Algiers itself, the atmosphere had undergone a significant change since midsummer. People had previously been able to forget the rebellion in the distant Aurès, even in Kabylia, as one forgets an encysted tumor. The sporadic acts of terrorist agitation could be adjusted to; the human being is an adaptable creature. But the savage attacks of August 20 had put a different face on the matter. The gulf between the European and Moslem communities grew wider and deeper.

Of course, except in the rebel-infested areas, life continued as usual. No one coming to Algiers for the first time and seeing the streets jammed with traffic, the cafés crammed with people, would have suspected anything was amiss. But the visitor who stayed on for a time soon sensed the contained tensions that poisoned the atmosphere. It was not unusual to see a European slip an automatic pistol into his pocket before motoring out into the country (although he would be in trouble if caught with it) or take leave of his friends early so as not to be away from an aged parent after sundown.

In rebel country, on the other hand, conditions were grimly reminiscent of Kenya at the height of the Mau Mau revolt. Civilian travel by road was difficult and in many places impossible. Only heavily armed military convoys ventured through the immense cork forest that lies along the coast between Philippeville and Collo. These convoys were like huge ships sailing upon a silent and ominous sea; they passed with barely a ripple and again the invisible enemy ruled supreme. Collo would have been totally isolated if it had not been for the two veteran *balancelles** that plied between that city and Philippeville. From Philippe-

* The *balancelle* (or *ballanzella* or *paranzella*), pointed at both ends and originally lateen-rigged, is the typical coastal vessel of the western Mediterranean basin.

ville, Stora, or Collo, the apprehensive resident could look up at the lowering hills above and wonder what new threats lay concealed deep in those limitless forests.

The massive gray shape of the cruiser "Montcalm" standing guard over the port city of Philippeville was a reassuring sight to the people there, though it did not incline them to optimism. And nothing could have been more oppressive than the sandbag barricades and machine-gun nests that surrounded every public building throughout the area. But such is the force of habit that as soon as the curfew in Philippeville was set back from 6:30 P.M. to 8 P.M., the townsfolk resumed their traditional evening promenade in Marquet Square. After curfew, however, anyone who failed to respond when challenged by a patrol was shot down.

Some European farmers in the surrounding country had given up and gone elsewhere. Others, particularly those of modest means, clung to their land even though, in many cases, their crops had been burned and their livestock slaughtered. If they could not fortify their farms, they moved their families to the city or to the village and, motoring out each morning, continued to work their land at the daily peril of their lives. It was not a pleasant existence, but for many there was no alternative. A good two-thirds of the Philippeville *arrondissement* had been brought under the control of the rebels; this meant that they were able to dominate a native population of some 70,000 in that area alone.

An estimate of rebel strength in October put the number of "regulars" at about 3,900 divided as follows:

Constantine Department	
North (center, Condé Smendou; chief, Youssef Zighout):	1,400
East (center, Souk Ahras; chief, Amor Djebar):	300
South (Aurès-Nememchas; chief, Bachir Chihani):	1,400
Kabylia	
(Center, Tizi Ouzou; chief, Belkacem Krim):	500
Oran Department (chief, Larbi Ben M'Hidi):	300

34. DEBATE AND INDECISION

Unfortunately, at a time when the situation called more imperiously than ever for unity of purpose and effort, politics took no holiday; in fact, the din of discordant voices only grew louder. The "coordination committee" of the "Sixty-One," meeting on October 5, resolved to maintain its stand against "integration" and to send a new delegation to Paris. This, however, did not save Boudjema Ould Aoudia, the committee's secretary-general, from tortured second thoughts on the matter. In an open letter to the Governor General he explained that, since Algeria could not be other than French, he had personally upheld the principle of integration. According to Mr. Ould Aoudia, the "Sixty-One," without adopting the nationalist idea themselves, had to admit it existed; their job was to express the "aspirations" of their constituents and to call attention to the gravity of the situation. In so doing, he said, the "Sixty-One" had reopened channels of communication with the electorate, a circumstance that would enable them to encourage the people to "enter resolutely into the heart of the French family."

Jacques Chevallier, in an interview carried on the front page of *Le Monde*, chose that critical moment to aim a stinging shaft at M. Soustelle's integration policy. "Practically inapplicable," he said; the *colons* would never stand for it. Just imagine having to pay the same wages as in France! "No," he said solemnly—thereby implicitly conceding to the *colons* a right of veto—"the foreseeable opposition would be insurmountable, interests and feelings being what they are." And what, asked the interviewer, did M. Chevallier think of the federal structure advocated by some Moslem politicians? Answer: inevitable. He said:

> But I hasten to add, . . . that years will be needed to achieve it. For in the present situation, and by reason notably of the international context, it would offer wide scope for threats of secession. But do not go on from there to conclude that the maintenance of the *status quo* is the only solution. If integration pure and simple is impracticable because of the opposition it would encounter, if federalism can be achieved only as a long-term goal,* the possibility of profound reforms remains, reforms having as their real, not as their illusory, object the improvement of the lot of the Moslem mass stricken with unemployment and malnutrition.
>
> But, to save valuable time, it is necessary to proceed by decision and authority, without repeated and prolonged debates in the the assemblies. The example of Algiers shows that where there is action, sedition does not raise its head. We have had almost no attack on the European population, and it is with pride that I ascribe this tranquility of the city to our efforts on behalf of the Moslem population. Widen this concept to other fields than housing, apply it to the whole territory, and you will be close to a solution.†

* The *colons*, apparently, in M. Chevallier's mind, would not be allowed to veto *that* with their opposition.

† See *Le Monde* for October 5, 1955.

We have heard from Jacques Chevallier before; his views will be of little further concern to us once we have brought him around a full 180 degrees. It is interesting to see, though, how this man, a former advocate of the "eye for eye, tooth for tooth" method of dealing with the rebels, reacted when his city, despite all he had done for the Moslems, became the vortex of the rebellion. Here, then, is what he told a correspondent of *France-Soir* in September, 1957—two years later.

> I regret to be unable to share the official optimism, but, judging by what is happening daily in this city of 500,000 inhabitants which I administer, the situation, far from improving, is only getting worse.
>
> Why persist in trying to treat the Algerian affair as if it were a war? In reality, it is a revolution being carried out in political confusion, which to be cured must be treated politically. Now, innumerable statements full of good intentions and, besides, often contradictory, have not resulted in any progress in this respect. Projects are placed side by side but none are discussed—by anybody, much less by an Algerian. Not a single Algerian of the first or second college is consulted as to their contents. As though the fate of ten million individuals in the throes of political fever could be settled without them.

Asked by what means confidence could be restored, M. Chevallier replied:

> It is not by imposing solutions that success will be achieved. It is by restoring the broken contacts, in resuming the colloquy, in discussing solutions together. There is no point in discussions with those who agree with us. Discussion must be with those who disagree. In this respect, the Algerian problem is much more a matter of procedure—that is, to decide how the discussion of it is to be approached and conducted, rather than to prejudice the content of this discussion now. It is from the discussion that the light will come.

From a distant debate in the National Assembly, when the 1947 Algerian statute was under consideration, the voice of Jacques Chevallier comes down to us with its repudiation of Arabic, its denunciation of the Koran.* We remember him next as a "liberal" in the Algerian Assembly,

* M. Chevallier on August 26, 1947: "There are not only Arabs in North Africa. There are 10 million Berbers, of whom 3 million live in Algeria—the Kabyles of greater and lesser Kabylia, the Mzabites, the Tuaregs of the Sahara, and the Matmatas of southern Tunisia and the Tunisian-Algerian confines. . . . These Berbers . . . by their tribal laws, their vernacular tongue, their ancestral customs, live outside Islam as it would be understood if the

proclaiming that it was better to deal with "semirebels than with menials" but acquiescing when his political associates opposed parity of representation in the city councils. As Secretary of State for War in the Government headed by Pierre Mendès-France, he declared that the Aurès was "practically in a state of insurrection," only to announce six days later that all was well. The following year—on May 25, 1955—he delivered himself of the fire-eating statement mentioned earlier: "You do not fight rebels with legal means; you fight them with means identical with theirs." And now we hear him recommend a deal with those same rebels. It is one thing to record the veerings of M. Chevallier's pronouncements, quite another to find the key to his mental processes; however, M. Chevallier is a devout Roman Catholic, and the key may therefore have been a growing concern for future evangelization and even for the survival of the church in Algeria.

Coming as it did on the eve of an important debate on Algeria in the National Assembly, M. Chevallier's dismissal of integration as "practically inapplicable" was certainly no boon to M. Soustelle. His later willingness to meet the rebels halfway—and in the Algerian context halfway is all the way—did much more harm. M. Chevallier may not be regarded as an oracle by many of his countrymen, but, American on his mother's side and fluent in English, he is the darling of visiting foreign correspondents; I know several who swear by him.

It was greatly to be hoped that the Government would seize the opportunity of a new debate on Algeria to make its policy clear, to define its "peace aims" and to give the Algerians a glimpse of a future worth fighting for. In his communications with Paris, M. Soustelle had urged that this chance not be missed; he even issued a public statement calling for a "quick, clear, and definitive decision." And he was right, for as long as the Government's long range intentions were in doubt, or misty at best, political prophets of every stripe could be counted on to confuse

---

Koran were spread everywhere by the use of the Arabic language. . . . We have already made the enormous mistake of Islamizing Kabylia by introducing official Moslem justice there. What, then, are we after in fostering Arabic? The result, in short, is to place the Berbers under Islamic authority through the medium of the Arabic language. . . . It is, finally, to ask them to accept backward ideas. . . . Could it be that those who want a progressive statute would seek to impose the Koran with all its backwardness?. . . . I do not think that a lay state would now wish to turn itself into a missionary . . . to open the door to Moslem proselytism. . . . That would be a way to undermine French influence, diminish French hegemony, and utilize a part of the statute to lessen the influence of our country. . . ."

the issue to the greater comfort of the rebels. For three days and a night, the Assembly debated the Algerian question, but the only reflection in the mirror it held up to the nation was: indecision. Maurice Bourgès-Maunoury was to be congratulated for a masterly presentation of the problem, but unequivocal commitment to a clear goal was not forthcoming. Premier Edgar Faure's utterances were, in this respect, a dismal disappointment.

From M. Bourgès-Maunoury, the Assembly learned that the Government was still determined to give effect to the "solemn undertakings" of the Algerian Statute, itself a "step toward integration." He announced that, since the Algerian Assembly was temporarily paralyzed by dissension, some of the Government's reform measures would be submitted without delay directly to the National Assembly. These would include land reform and the establishment of an agricultural modernization and expansion fund.

Other measures, providing notably for the independence of the mosques, the teaching of Arabic, and the creation of rural townships, would await the next regular session of the Algerian Assembly in November. The minister promised that political reforms amounting to a "new charter" for Algeria would be examined that autumn in consultation with the representatives of both colleges. In the meantime, he said, the Government would concentrate on restoring "total and permanent security" everywhere in Algeria. "This security alone," he added, "will make it possible to bring the two populations back into balance and understanding. To achieve this, the nation will be asked to make all necessary sacrifices, for its future as well as that of Algeria is at stake."

Among the interpellators, Ali Cadi, deputy for Constantine, took the prize for defiance. "Our duty," he said, "is to confront the public powers with their responsibilities and to inform you that no reform decreed from above will enable the Franco-Moslem community to live again. You have no right to integrate against their will populations intent on retaining their personality, their traditions, their religion, and their language. The time has come to give up the policy of fictions." The much-used but little-honored device used by M. Cadi was that of attributing false intentions to an adversary the better to demolish him. It was as though M. Soustelle had never gone to bat for the teaching of Arabic, the independence of the mosques, and the safeguarding of the Moslem heritage in general. M. Cadi had hit well below the belt.

René Moatti, Sétif-born independent deputy for Paris, spoke eloquently in support of M. Soustelle's policies. "As the Algerian Statute is progressively and loyally applied," he said, "the national argument advanced by the authors of the motion [the "Sixty-One"] will lose its force. Perhaps then the Moslem representatives, pulling themselves together, will again become the guides of opinion now deluded." "Never!" shouted M. Cadi from his seat. "I regret," answered M. Moatti, "to see that the hidden sentiments of some men should be thus exposed to public view. Reflect, Mr. Cadi, upon the responsibility you assume in uttering that word when I foresee the happy day of reconciliation."

The reader will forgive me if I pass over the brickbats hurled by Jacques Duclos, leader of the Communist group, and the lesser but still vigorous invective of his colleague, Mme. Alice Sportisse of Oran. To them, M. Soustelle and his associates were automatically fascist beasts. Pierre Cot, a *Progressiste* (crypto-Communist) deputy, argued that the contemplated reforms, though substantial, were not enough; the essential question, he said, was political: "Will we give satisfaction to the Algerian people, who aspire to freedom?" Jacques Chevallier called for an "authentic political life" in Algeria. "If certain sentiments cannot be peacefully expressed," he said, "they will find expression in explosion and rebellion. The existence of a constructive and loyal opposition must be accepted." One wonders whom M. Chevallier had in mind as a possible candidate for this office—M. Bendjelloul, perhaps, or Ben Bella? Edouard Depreux announced that the Socialist group, of which he was the leader, would vote for "peace in Algeria through free negotiations." Again the question comes to mind: with whom and on whose terms? Needless to say, it was not answered.

A "battle of motions"—there were six in all—occupied the long night of October 13 to 14. Paradoxically, Jacques Chaban-Delmas, Social Republican deputy and leader of the parliamentary group to which M. Soustelle belonged, presented a motion hostile to the Government, described as being incapable of carrying out the Algerian policies it advocated. The Socialists, in the person of M. Depreux, put forward a motion calling for free negotiations with a new Algerian Assembly. The Communist motion, presented by M. Duclos, also called for negotiations with the freely elected representatives of the Algerian people; it demanded, in addition, an end to military operations in Algeria. Jacques Chevallier and his wealthy associate in politics, Georges Blachette, entered the lists with a motion demanding the immediate application of the Algerian Statute and the acceptance of a loyal and constructive opposition. Paul Estèbe, a Peasant party deputy, stated flatly in his motion that the Government was without the authority needed to insure the security of life and property in Algeria and the harmonious development of that

French province. The Government's position was expressed in a motion introduced by Roger Gaborit, a Radical deputy. Stripped to its essentials, this document:

1. Reaffirmed the principle of equal rights for all Algerians, Europeans and Moslem;
2. Endorsed the Government's proclaimed policy of fighting terror in Algeria effectively but without collective reprisals;
3. Called for early consideration by Parliament and, if possible, by the Algerian Assembly of reform measures designed to give full immediate effect to the 1947 Statute and to make land available to Moslem peasants;
4. Demanded other measures to improve the lot of the Algerians, notably the upward adjustment of salaries and social benefits to bring them into line with the scales prevailing in France;
5. Barred foreign "intrusion" in Algerian affairs and urged the Government to take "all necessary retaliatory measures" against countries and groups trying to stir up trouble in Algeria;
6. Requested the Government to draw up before the end of the year and in consultation with the Algerian representatives of both colleges a set of proposals for changing Algeria's legislative, administrative, and financial institutions in such a way as to promote greater brotherhood between the Algerian populations and the closer integration of Algeria with France;
7. Welcomed the idea of a loyal and constructive opposition in Algeria.

The Assembly having refused in separate votes to give priority consideration to any of these motions, Premier Faure was compelled to assert his leadership. But instead of the trumpet call that might have sent a salutary tremor through that querulous body, imparting an intimation of its duty and high opportunity, he chose to blow a small toot on a small horn. He was unable even to give strength and substance to the word "integration," to fill it with meaning for those whose lives were to be governed by it. He said:

> In adopting the word "integration," we rejected—and this was in itself a definition—secession and assimilation . . . The application of the Statute must be carried to its conclusion; as for the rest, it will be left up to the National Assembly to determine the tempo of the measures to be taken, to decide what the Algerian

> Assembly should be, to say whether integration should be carried to the point of abolishing or overhauling the Government General, to settle the questions of electoral colleges, of local government, of Algeria's economic and financial autonomy. . . .
>
> All these questions are difficult and will have to be carefully thought out. Today, the Government asks you to decide on four points: first, a general political conception excluding secession and assimilation; secondly, the specific, short-term measures constituting the Soustelle Plan; thirdly, a longer-range economic plan embodying the recommendations of the Maspétiol report and a program of administrative reforms; finally, as regards the political institutions, I ask you to affirm the free and democratic nature of the elections and to go on record as favoring a modification of the Statute in the direction either of more complete integration or of the maintenance of the present system with the desirable differentiations.

When he had thus drawn an opaque veil across the picture, M. Faure stood on M. Gaborit's motion and demanded a vote of confidence. The deputies went home as a new day (October 14) dawned over Paris; it was past five o'clock. It remained for them to decide, by accepting or rejecting the Gaborit motion, whether the Government should live or die. For this, by virtue of a "safety-valve" clause in the French Constitution, they would be allowed at least one full day of silent meditation. Actually, the vote of confidence took place on the morning of October 18; the Government was saved by 305 votes to 274.

A cabinet crisis had been averted; this was something to be thankful for. If the Government had fallen, precious weeks might have elapsed before action could be taken on matters of greatest urgency. But apart from that, what a futile performance! Algeria had been denied a picture of its future. Nobody could fail to see that the Government itself was now virtually adrift. The stoutest hearts were seized with dismay. M. Soustelle, however, with courage that does him credit, lowered his sights and prepared for the November session of the Algerian Assembly.

But he was soon to be buffeted by new difficulties. The Government's decision to dissolve the National Assembly and to hold a general election six months before the appointed time was a calamity as far as Algeria was concerned. This, however, is to anticipate. At first M. Soustelle had reason to think that, with the Algerian debate out of the way, the Government would be able to turn its attention to the problem of security and to his pressing requests for reinforcements.

On October 13, M. Bourgès-Maunoury, appearing before the interior committee of the Council of the Republic, said:

> The maintenance of order and the setting up of a complete and permanent security system would require the dispatch of 60,000 more men. We are asking the Defense Minister for them. But where are they to be found? In Indochina? It would take a long time to repatriate and regroup them. In Morocco? Once the military operations there come to an end and the political situation has clarified, it will be possible to draw upon the large formations arrayed about the *medinas* (native quarters). But these prior conditions do not yet exist.

Nevertheless, M. Bourgès-Maunoury, M. Soustelle, and General Pierre Billotte, the Defense Minister, met with General Lorillot and other responsible civil and military authorities at the Telergma airport near Constantine on October 20 to review the military situation and map strategy. It was there that M. Soustelle got wind of the Government's impending decision to plunge France into the free-for-all of an electoral campaign; if the rebels had appeared on the field with disintegration rockets, he could not have been more appalled. Yet he resolved to keep his hand firmly on the tiller; he could not abandon Algeria at such a moment, even to campaign for re-election as deputy for Lyons. The official party flew from Telergma to Batna and from there to Philippeville for a closer look at conditions in these two vital sectors. Before boarding the plane that was to take him back to Paris, M. Bourgès-Maunoury vowed at Philippeville that those elusive reinforcements would be found and sent to Algeria. However, separated from M. Faure by a widening gulf of disagreement, he was to resign his portfolio before this promise could be fully carried out. General Billotte, having toured Kabylia by helicopter, met the press on the evening of October 21 in one of the spacious, neo-Moorish reception rooms of the Palais d'Eté, the Governor General's official residence in Algiers. The Defense Minister asserted that "Atlantic solidarity" would be a vain word if the Western powers turned their backs on France's problem in North Africa. He held the Algerian rebellion to be an aggression against the Atlantic Community itself and insisted that allied nations taking a contrary view violated the letter and the spirit of the Atlantic Pact.

The final days of the outgoing legislature were devoted, not, as may easily be imagined, to land reform in Algeria—this question was far from the deputies' thoughts—but to passionate and endless discussion of the electoral law and to labyrinthine political maneuvers, all of which, happily for the author and for the reader, lie entirely outside the scope of this book. The National Assembly was dissolved on December 1; the general election was set for January 2—in Algeria, naturally, as well as in Metropolitan France.

On November 29, in the midst of this great dislocation, the Algerian Assembly convened for its ordinary session, with only the U.D.M.A. delegates absent. After an opening address by the speaker, Abdelkader Saïah—he called for concord—M. Soustelle rose to plead at last for his policies in an atmosphere of relative sanity. Algeria, he noted, was not as sick as it was sometimes made out to be; the country's economy, in particular, had proved its resilience; despite insecurity and depredation, production curves showed little if any drop. He described the pacification zones and the S.A.S.'s as the answer to those who would put Algeria on the horns of the "false dilemma—repression or abandonment." He continued:

> If it is objected . . . that no reform should be carried out as long as order has not been entirely restored, I reply that order cannot be lasting unless force is the servant of justice and humanity. If it is declared that the projects are inadequate or imperfect, I reply: it is up to you to propose others or amendments to these. But do not yield to the temptations of nihilism; to do so would be to close the door on hope.
>
> Yes, what I ask of you all today is to open that door. Let it not be said before history that just as it was about to open, we allowed it to swing heavily shut upon the destiny of a people.

The "Sixty-One," by now on the wane—their position was too artificial long to stand the stresses placed upon it—continued to give themselves airs. On December 1, thirty-eight of the "Sixty-One" attended a meeting called for the purpose of rededicating the group to the "Algerian national idea." The meeting was, by all accounts, a stormy affair. After speaking earnestly in defense of integration, Abderrahmane Farès walked out of the room; it was his last manly act. Mohammed Salah Bendjelloul, Ferhat Abbas, Aïssa Bensalem, Mostefa Benbahmed—all old friends—and Allel Bentchicou, councilor of the French Union for Constantine, distinguished themselves that day as the most ardent champions of the "national idea." The "Sixty-One" resolved at this rump session to boycott the debates on the Soustelle Plan. Boudjema Ould Aoudia's "coordinating committee," carrying on from there, undertook to state or restate the views of the "Sixty-One" from time to time as the occasion demanded. It was thus through the voice of Mr. Ould Aoudia that the "Sixty-One" urged the voters to stay away from the polls in the event of an election in Algeria, opposed any campaigning on grounds of "inadequate freedom and security," proclaimed the necessity of negotiations looking toward a new Algerian charter, took up the slogan of "interdependence" then being used as a smokescreen to cover French capitulation in Morocco. Mr. Ould Aoudia and his friends advised the second-college representatives to remain at their "combat posts," whereas Ferhat Abbas was beginning to preach collective resignation; another fragment of the "Sixty-One" was about to fall away.

It is a wonder to me that in the numerous cohort of French intellectuals and "progressives" advocating a deal with the Algerian nationalists, no one stepped forward to make common cause with the "Sixty-One." Yet this was the only native group—especially while it included the U.D.M.A.—even ostensibly in favor of Algerian nationhood as a French benefaction rather than a prize of war. Indeed, apart from Mme. Claude Gérard's quixotic sally, even the M.N.A. was largely ignored. The intellectuals and "progressives," though they recommended a compromise, negotiated settlement, had eyes only for the F.L.N. It seemed not to matter to them that the solution they proposed was repudiated in advance by the F.L.N. as rankest treason. The recurrent theme of "liberal" opinion in France was that peace could not be achieved until the Government was prepared to treat with "*ceux qui se battent*" ("those who fight") or "*ceux qui nous font la guerre*" ("those who make war upon us").

M. Soustelle, himself an intellectual by any standards, was particularly affected by a manifesto adopted on November 5 at a meeting in Paris of the "Intellectuals' Action Committee against the Pursuance of the War in North Africa." The manifesto accused the French Government of fighting an "unjust, shameful, and vain war in Algeria"; it called for: "The cessation of the repression; immediate negotiations with the representatives of the peoples of North Africa, and in particular with those of the Algerian people; the abrogation of the 'state of emergency' in Algeria; the release of the contingent*; no racial discrimination at home or abroad." The "war" in Algeria was, according to the manifesto, "unjust" because it was being waged against men "whose crime is to have chosen to act according to our own principles."

Since when, one may ask, has terror been a French principle? Since when have the French recognized their better selves in those who hack

* The annual contingent of national servicemen, kept in uniform beyond their normal term of service.

their way to power with bullet and knife and drown contradiction in innocent blood? M. Soustelle, in a measured, pained reply, noted that the manifesto rested, not upon a sober analysis of the Algerian crisis, but upon "old, demagogic slogans."

35. AN ELECTION POSTPONED

The electoral campaign was, in a sense, keynoted even before it began by Pierre Mendès-France, who, in a series of speeches, proclaimed that: "It is with those who are fighting us that we must negotiate if we really want to restore peace." Speaking at Caen on October 16, he said:

> Unkept promises are the cause of the present situation in Algeria. We have not respected the 1947 Statute. The elections were rigged. The Algerian representatives derived their power from the Administration.
>
> The Statute, that is, the law, must be applied in all haste and true elections must be held. Undoubtedly we shall see, coming from the ballot boxes, names of men who advance violent demands, but it is with them that we must negotiate if they really represent the Algerian people. The repression will never put an end to the present situation. It is by a political and democratic solution that we must begin if we want to stop the flow of blood.

In the matter of unkept promises, M. Mendès-France was a specialist. The reader will recall his policy statement to the National Assembly on November 12, 1954, when, referring to the rebels, he spoke of the "criminal purpose of a few men," when he declared that the "repression must be without weakness for it is without injustice," when he promised "massive reinforcements," when he warned: "Let no one expect us to have the slightest consideration for sedition or make any concession to it. The defense of the internal peace of the nation and the integrity of the Republic admit of no compromise." But then he had been premier; now he was an opposition leader in pursuit of power. However, since the electoral campaign was to be dominated by a new political alliance, the Republican Front, uniting the Socialists, the Radicals, and lesser fragments of the non-Communist left, and since the Mendès-France recipe for "peace in Algeria" was to provide that coalition with its principal battle cry, the former premier's new thesis warrants our attention.

Peace can, of course, always be had by capitulating to the enemy; it was perfectly attainable in Algeria just as it had been in Indochina. But on what terms? Part of M. Mendès-France's deceit lay in his unproved assumption that acceptable terms could be found through surrender. Each of his listeners was free to form his own idea of acceptable terms. M. Mendès-France was careful not to define them. What remained was a vague vision of "Franco-Moslem brotherhood" and Algerian "emancipation," it being understood that these were potentially real, compatible, and beneficent. Anyone with little knowledge of the problem would gladly accept such a solution. Peace itself is an almost irresistibly attractive prospect. Who does not remember the success of the Republican slogan, "Peace in Korea," in the 1952 American presidential campaign?

Closer examination reveals how misleading the Mendès-France thesis was at every point. The first premise, that of unkept promises as the cause of the Algerian conflict, was, to start with, certainly false, if only because the 1947 Statute, which he described as embodying these promises, was wholly incompatible with the demand for Algerian statehood. But M. Mendès-France recognized the political advantage to be derived from the deep-seated French guilt complex. "Free elections" constituted the core of his peace formula. However, he carefully failed to state for what body or assembly the elections were to be held. If he had done so, his demonstration would have collapsed. It was clear that elections held within the framework of French political institutions—National Assembly or Algerian Assembly—would be spurned by the rebels as a denial of Algerian independence—spurned, boycotted, and disrupted. Yet, under the Algerian Statute, no other elections were possible.

Assuming, however, for the purposes of argument, that elections were held outside the framework of French political institutions, in contravention of the Statute, how could the Europeans be expected to react? Coming, admittedly, as a concession to rebel demands and therefore subject to the pressures of an already half-victorious adversary, such elections would very likely lead to the formation of an Algerian constituent assembly and to the proclamation of Algerian independence. How, then, did M. Mendès-France think "free elections" could solve the problem and promote "Franco-Moslem brotherhood"?

Basically, the Algerian problem involves the relations between two communities rooted in the same soil. It cannot be solved only by changing the nature of the relations between Algeria and Metropolitan France.

Integration, it is true, holds out the promise of economic, social, and political equality for the Moslem community. But proposals for federation or some other form of autonomy leave the basic problem of intercommunity relations unsolved. All this, M. Mendès-France and his political associates chose not only to ignore, but, implicitly or explicitly, to deny. Millions of French voters went to the polls firmly convinced in all good faith that, in casting their votes for Republican Front candidates, they were advancing the cause of peace, justice, and concord in Algeria.

No informed person could fail to apprehend the grave danger to which Algeria would be exposed in the event of a general election there. The prospect was that of jumping into the lion's mouth. Over wide areas, balloting was simply out of the question; elsewhere, it would entail the greatest risk. In the circumstances then existing, few, if any, Moslem candidates would be likely to come forward—in fact, none did—and an election confined to the Europeans would merely drive the two communities further apart. Besides, an undertaking so easy to wreck would, if embarked on, give the rebels an unhoped-for opportunity to turn French authority to derision.

As usual, the F.L.N. made no secret of its intentions; on December 7, it issued a handbill which said:

ELECTIONS FOR THE RENEWAL OF THE FRENCH NATIONAL ASSEMBLY.

Algerian people!

The F.L.N., assuming once again its responsibilities before God, before men, and before history, has decreed:

1. Active abstention to take the form of:
   a) Incessant activity on the part of all patriots (fighters of the A.L.N., militants and sympathizers of the F.L.N.) during the period of the electoral campaign.
   b) Use of force on election day.
2. The execution of all candidates, to whatever party they may belong.
3. The abduction and the slitting of the throats of all electoral agents.
4. The resignation of all representatives in office. These, from deputy to simple *djemaa* member, are required to resign before January 1, 1956.

All representatives without any exception who refuse to resign will be considered traitors to the fatherland and killed without judgment.

> . . . The F.L.N. requests all its militants and sympathizers to procure a weapon and to proceed with direct action. Each patriot will consider it his duty to kill a traitor.

Charming document! Yet to postpone the election in Algeria was also to incur injury. It was an admission of weakness and a differentiation prejudicial to the unity of the Republic—in short, a bitter pill. François Quilici, deputy for Oran; Marcel Paternot, deputy for Algiers; Alain de Sérigny, delegate to the Algerian Assembly for Algiers; and various other first-college representatives insisted that the election be held at all cost. On December 8, however, the Algerian Assembly voted sixty-seven to ten in favor of postponement and the next day refused to vote the election appropriations.

M. Soustelle, meanwhile, in Paris to impress upon the Government the necessity of postponement, was told at first that this was legally impossible. Nevertheless, a way was found. Under the decree of December 12, the election in Algeria was postponed "by reason of the exceptional circumstances that make impossible the conduct of free and sincere electoral operations." The rebels were jubilant, and well they might be, for they had won a base on balls.

The F.L.N. paper, *Résistance Algérienne*, commented gleefully in its third issue on the postponement of the election in Algeria; it described this as an "admission that the French constitution cannot apply to Algeria." The paper also saluted the "cascade of resignations" among the Moslem representatives; it reminded those who had not already done so that they would be expected to resign forthwith. Any compromise with the French was again ruled out. Messali got his usual dose of virulent abuse; he was put down this time as a "traitor to the cause of the Algerian people." The paper upbraided the M.N.A. leader for his relations with the Trotzkyites and accused him of maintaining thugs to beat up honest members of the F.L.N. "Treason comes under the jurisdiction of the High Court," the paper warned, without saying what the "High Court" was.

The dissolution of the National Assembly on December 1 automatically put an end to the "state of emergency." It will be recalled that an amendment linking the "state of emergency" to the life of the legislature had been tacked on to the Government's "state of emergency" bill in committee; the painful consequences of this ill-considered provision were now apparent. All the exceptional measures taken by the authorities to cope with the exceptional situation in Algeria had become illegal overnight—and this at a moment of intense terrorist agitation coupled with political fever. M. Soustelle reports in his book that a swarm of

Communist and "progressive" lawyers from Paris descended on Algiers to demand the immediate release of interned terrorists and suspects* and that some, counting on the success of their political friends at the polls, went so far as to threaten recalcitrant officials with early reprisals. On December 3, the Government, in response to M. Soustelle's urgent representations, put a small plug in the gaping hole of illegality by issuing a decree according to which the Governor-General and the prefects were to report within twenty days on the "measures that the exceptional circumstances will have led them to take to insure the maintenance of order, the safeguard of persons and property, and the maintenance of the integrity of the territory." M. Soustelle makes this comment in his book:

> The prefects and I knew that it would be perfectly possible, especially if the adversaries of French Algeria came to power after the election, to tax us with arbitrary rule, to accuse us of illegal acts and restraint. I decided to assume full responsibility myself. It was under these conditions, in spite of the law and having at our disposal only precarious and dubious legal instruments, that we had to save Algeria from anarchy.

That anarchy was a danger could hardly be doubted. One of the multiple manifestations of this danger was a wave of resignations among Moslem city councilors and *djemaa* members, those belonging to the Lahouelist faction to start with, others later. The M.T.L.D. central committee, as we have seen, disbanded in November at the behest of the F.L.N., its members being free to join the F.L.N. on an individual basis or not, as they pleased. The resignation of the Lahouelist officeholders was part of the agreement. Needless to say, the imperative blanket order to resign on pain of death, issued by the F.L.N. on December 7, gave added impetus to the movement. The Communists, the Messalists, and even the moderates soon began to follow the Lahouelists' lead. On December 23, the U.D.M.A. quit the "Sixty-One" and, in a public statement, summoned its members holding elective office to resign their seats.

Limited at first to the Algiers department, the rash of resignations spread to the Constantine department in December and even affected a few localities in the Oran department. By the end of the year, sixty-nine city councils and forty-eight *djemaas* had lost members in this way; a councilor of the French Union, six delegates to the Algerian Assembly, and thirty-one general councilors also had sent in their resignations.

* There were about 1,500 persons in internment camps in Algeria at the time.

Many a resigning city councilor or *djemaa* member explained tearfully to his subprefect or administrator that he had acted only to protect himself and his family. On January 15, 1956, M. Soustelle called a halt by announcing flatly that no resignations would be accepted and that those already tendered would be considered "null and void."

The F.L.N. had, in this matter, overextended itself. Though its power to kill, destroy, and disrupt was great, the F.L.N. was not omnipotent; it could not be everywhere; obedience to its injunctions varied in relation to the fear it inspired, but since it was frequently unable to carry out its threats, universal submission was beyond its reach. Some *djemaas* were depleted by resignations, but many others continued to function normally. A breakdown in local government was the exception rather than the rule.

36. INCIPIENT ANARCHY

Yet multiple resignations among natives holding elective office were, unhappily, but one aspect of a much wider deterioration. Despite several drubbings at the hands of French troops and savage internecine strife, the rebels continued, as the year ended, to prosper. Their formations, though ragged, were improving in point of command, discipline, and efficacy; liaison between the various "zones of insurrection" was getting better; progression in space was constant.

In the villages, *caïds*, notables, and war veterans—the bedrock of French influence—were being murdered at the rate of three a day. The refusal to pay taxes or to carry (or even to possess) identity cards was, where it occurred, the sure sign of rebel hold on the people. Rumors of possible peace negotiations to follow the election in France had a most demoralizing effect. Since it was not at all clear who might get the upper hand, the Moslems were more inclined than ever to play the waiting game; they could always take sides later when it became easier to discern the designs of providence. The prevailing uncertainty prevented the French from deriving advantage from the growing weariness of villagers preyed upon by rebel bands living on the country.

Conversely, the confusion into which the French had fallen was of immeasurable value to the rebels; it gave them time and a favorable psychological atmosphere in which to operate; it enabled them to sink deeper roots, to put out new ramifications. Of these, the most effective were the rudiments of a parallel civil administration. The rebel chiefs rendered justice, settled disputes.* Even in villages held by the French, F.L.N. political agents were sometimes secretly at work preparing the way for this "administrative" subversion.

In the Canrobert-Aïn M'Lila area, north of the Aurès between Aïn Beïda and Constantine, the F.L.N. was reported to have a "political commissar" and a "tax" collector in each of the tribal districts. The "political commissar" handled propaganda and indoctrination, while his colleague levied "taxes," imposed fines, and received contributions. The "taxes" were collected from the peasants according to a rustic schedule: 5,000 francs for each tractor, 3,000 francs for each French plough, 1,000 francs for each Arab plough (a primitive type), 500 francs for each farm hand. In addition, each landowner was required to turn over eighteen bushels of wheat. Laborers from the area who had migrated to Metropolitan France were given three months to return, failing which their families would be required to pay a 60,000-franc fine for each absent laborer.

The rebel propaganda mills did not concern themselves with villagers only. Handbills by the score were churned out for the purpose of channeling fear to certain specific ends; some were designed to incite the native soldiers to desert, others to impair the morale of French troops, still others to intimidate the *colons*. These efforts were not without effect. Desertions of native soldiers were frequent enough to cast doubt on the reliability of whole units. And no one will ever know how much protection money the rebels collected from *colons* in outlying districts. The ban on smoking and gambling was revived sporadically; the ban on spirits was enforced in several places with the aid of hand grenades thrown into European cafés frequented by Moslems. The F.L.N. tried also to put cinemas out of bounds. On December 12, bombs

* Arbitration lies at the heart of the Arab concept of justice. The Koran, sound principles, and the authority to see that sentences are carried out suffice to make the system congenial. French justice, with its courts, codes, and initiate castes of magistrates and lawyers, with its incomprehensible feature of delayed judgment and punishment, with all its procedural loopholes, is entirely foreign to the Arab tradition. Consequently, the rebels were far more successful in keeping the natives out of the courts than they were in keeping them out of the schools.

exploded in two Algiers cinemas, the Donyazad and the Olympia, both specializing in Egyptian films. In eastern Algeria, all real estate transactions with Europeans were forbidden on pain of death.

The sheet *Résistance Algérienne*, clandestine "official organ" of the F.L.N., began to appear in October. A "special issue" was followed a week later by the first "regular" issue. The latter carried a "Communiqué from the H.Q. of the A.L.N." which said—the figures must have been pulled from a hat—that the French Army had lost thirty-five officers and 3,000 other ranks in combat since the beginning of the rebellion. The F.L.N.'s "political conditions" were set forth. It was the mixture as before: self-determination; negotiations only with the "authentic representatives of the Algerian people"; an end to the repression; the release of persons interned; a sovereign constituent assembly; talks between Algeria and France on an equal footing. The paper warned the faithful to "beware" of the Messalists, those "compromised, deluded, outdated individuals" who, after having undermined the action of the A.L.N., now claimed to represent it. "If they persist in playing into the hands of the police and of the repression forces," the paper said, "the people's justice will fall upon them, implacable."

The spread of the rebellion could never be accurately plotted on a map; the early stages were often too subtle to be noticed, and the rate of development varied from area to area. But some signs were unmistakable. In November, rebels began to be detected for the first time in the mountains of the *Sud-Oranais;* their number could not be ascertained, but three murders were committed in Géryville, and a bus was attacked. Rebel infiltrations were reported also in the Atlas mountains toward Aumale, south and southeast of Algiers, and in the Ouarsenis range southwest of Algiers.

In Kabylia, which I visited at Christmas time, the atmosphere was lugubrious. Rebel-controlled country, I found, began almost at the gates of Tizi Ouzou. Even on roads a few miles from the city, the security forces traveled in convoy only. The city itself, however, seemed relatively safe under the protective wing of General Gouraud's Twenty-Seventh Alpine Division. Belkacem Krim and Amar Ouamrane were not thought to have had more than 800 rifles at their disposal; yet the 12,000 French troops in the area, between static-defense and mobile-offensive duties, were barely holding their own. The rebels, dispersed over a vast mountainous region, were fiendishly hard to catch; but, for them, it was no trick at all to stage a lightning raid and be gone, or to slit a *caïd's* throat under cover of night. They possessed, and profited by, every advantage. French authorities would sometimes find themselves operating in a sort of void. Shunned by silent, terror-stricken inhabitants, they lived in dread of a mass rising. This did not occur, but in those dark days Kabylia was close to the brink of anarchy.

The rebels in Kabylia, it seemed to me, were less inclined to religious fanaticism than their brethren further east. They killed, but usually without going in for the ritualistic mutilation of bodies. However, if the influence of religion was weaker, that of Communism was stronger. Not that the rebel leaders were interested in Marxist abstractions or that they accepted Communist control. What fascinated them, and stimulated them to emulation, was the example of Red China and of the Viet Minh; their heroes were Mao Tse-tung and Ho Chi-minh. In Far Eastern Communism they saw the most potent of all forces against European domination. Its fame was spread by Kabyles who had served with the French Army in Indochina. A few notions regarding its theory and practice were accepted as articles of faith. It is to this influence that we must ascribe the institution of "political commissars," which has been a central element in the rebel organization.

In sharp contrast with Kabylia, the Aurès, which I visited in November, was fully convalescent. Motoring in convoy up into the heart of the reputedly nasty Oued Taga section north of the Batna-Arris road, I was struck, as I had been the previous year, by the singular beauty of that region, an interplay of delicacy and grandeur. All was peace and quiet. Autumn tilling was in full swing, and only bucolic scenes met the eye. Yet these mountains had been the cradle of the rebellion; for months the rebels had roamed at will through the area, taking men and supplies as they went. The awe inspired by these intrepid fighters of Islam had been enormous; at their behest, the men had stopped smoking and the women had removed their ornaments. But soon the fine ardor of nationalism was turned into gall by rebel exactions. Besides, General Parlange and his men had given the lie to the rebel boast that the infidel was on the run. Twenty-two pacification centers were in operation at the time of my visit—seven in the Aurès proper, six in the Khenchela district, six in the Tebessa district, two in the MacMahon district, and one in the Corneille district; others were planned.

Captain Jacques Carreau-Gasherau, whom I met at Bou Hamar, had 130 native volunteers under arms, thirty of them organized as his own auxiliary unit, the others as a guard for the protection of seven surrounding villages. The auxiliaries were beginning to give a good account of themselves; they had already seized a stock of rebel arms, ammunition, and supplies, killed one rebel, and wounded three. One man, who seemed to be particularly pleased with himself, was wearing a war trophy on his feet—a pair of brand-new mountain shoes. Having entrusted his own security and that of his unfinished *bordj* (fort and administrative center) to these native volunteers, Captain Carreau-Gasherau busied himself with works projects and irrigation schemes. He and his colleagues provided, without ostentation and without publicity, a daily, grass-roots example of what M. Soustelle meant when he spoke of making force the servant of justice and humanity.

Although much had been accomplished, it could not be said that the Aurès had been entirely purged of rebels; 1,500 or so were still lurking in its remoter recesses or in the Nememchas. But the rebels had lost the best of their happy hunting grounds and much of their prestige. Their life was no longer the enviable one of victorious heroes. The protected villages had become hornets' nests and, in addition, French troops—paratroopers, Foreign Legionnaires, light infantrymen, men of the mechanized cavalry, and native auxiliaries—were now flung out across the Aurès and the Nememchas. Clearly, for positive results, the rebels would have to try their luck elsewhere.

As a matter of fact, the rebel *Wilaya* 1—Aurès, Nememchas, Tebessa—was soon to lapse into old-fashioned Berber anarchy. The death of Mostefa Ben Boulaïd, following that of Bachir Chihani, opened the door to a long and inconclusive struggle for supremacy, the chief contestants being Omar Ben Boulaïd, Mostefa's vainglorious and incompetent older brother, and Tahar Nouichi, one of Mostefa's earliest companions. Amirouche Aït Hamouda, better known simply as Amirouche, rebel chief in lesser Kabylia, vainly attempted in November, 1956, to persuade the quarreling bands to yield to an unified command. There was even some talk of an "election," though nothing came of it. Ultimately, in the spring of 1957, Omar Ben Boulaïd kicked over the traces and, repudiating his allegiance to the F.L.N. executive, kept the field near Sbeitla in Tunisia with a small band of faithful followers. His moment of defiance was, however, a fleeting one; the Tunisian Government quickly threw him under the wheels of the F.L.N. juggernaut; and when next heard of, Mr. Ben Boulaïd was on his way to Cairo in response to a "summons."

In other parts of eastern Algeria, the rebellion was still gaining ground. The Belezma mountains west of Batna and the Hodna mountains beyond were now fully within its toils; so was the Soummam valley southwest of Bougie; so, in lesser Kabylia, were the wild Guergour district northwest of Sétif and the Biban range northwest of Bordj Bou Arreridj. Rebel strength had gained concomitantly; there were at least 1,600 "regulars" in the northern part of the Constantine department at the end of the year. However, a "pacification zone" had been decreed in the Philippeville-Collo area and was being organized with the help of Brigadier General Gérard de Thomas de Labarthe's Fourteenth Infantry Division.

I visited two of the eighteen new Specialized Administrative Sections (S.A.S.) in their formative stages—at Praxbourg twelve miles southwest of Philippeville and at El Halia in the Filfila hills east of Philippeville (site of the pyrite mine where thirty-seven Europeans had lost their lives in the August massacre). From his improvised billet at Praxbourg, the chief of the S.A.S.—Lieutenant Henri Breysse, twenty-nine years old, formerly of the Thirteenth Half-Brigade of the Foreign Legion—scanned a range of hills inhabited by some 10,000 natives, most of whom, afraid of French troops and rebels alike, had "holed up" in their *gourbis* (huts). His first job was to restore a modicum of confidence among the people and get them back to their normal occupations. He would have to see that each family was present and fully accounted for, revive a languishing *djemaa*, restore the patterns of life. Medical assistance and works projects would follow; native auxiliaries would be levied; a *bordj* would be built. Such was the task that awaited Lieutenant Breysse as he stood for the first time with his *caïd* and surveyed his forbidding "parish."

At El Halia, Captain René Limbach of the Colonial Infantry, seasoned by years of experience in Indochina, French West Africa, and French Somaliland, was moved at the start to have a look round his S.A.S.; he put his hands in his pockets and set out on foot. The jittery citizens of Philippeville, who quaked at the thought of venturing beyond the city limits, would have been staggered if they had seen him; but the best way, I suppose, to banish the fears of others is to have none oneself. At El Halia as at Praxbourg, it came home to me that, once again, the hopes of the many had been entrusted to the few.

An unfortunate incident, indicative of the nervousness and tension then prevailing everywhere in eastern Algeria, occurred on December 4 at Lamy, a village north of Souk Ahras on the road to La Calle. It was market day and Lamy was swarming with native buyers and sellers from the surrounding countryside. At about 10:30 A.M., a fight broke out, accompanied by a rattling barrage of shouts, threats, insults. In the midst of the hubbub, a native auxiliary was shot at and wounded, presumably by a terrorist. The first shot was echoed by others, fired by rebels outside the village. French armored cars manned by gendarmes assigned to the protection of the village returned fire, blasting away at what were assumed to be the rebel positions, but also, apparently, raking the market place. At that moment, a bus filled with frightened natives started up and, ignoring all orders to stop, roared away. Shots were fired from the bus as it passed a military cantonment; again fire was returned. The driver, wounded, lost control of his vehicle, which crashed in a gully. Seventeen Moslems were killed and twelve were wounded that day; many, though not all, were undoubtedly innocent.

On December 12, a convoy of five army vehicles on its way from Guelma to Gounod, twenty-one miles further south, found the road blocked by a bus and a truck. Before a passage could be cleared, the convoy was attacked by a strong rebel band using automatic weapons and hand grenades. Nineteen French soldiers were killed and two were wounded; five were listed as missing. On Christmas Eve, the car of a French forester was machine-gunned on the road between Ampère and Sétif; the forester, his wife, and their twelve-year-old son were killed. In these two actions, the rebels had given the measure of their potential. It was unlikely that they would again be able to drive the people to a rising, but it was evident that they still could and would terrorize the country. There was, perhaps, some comfort in the thought that the Mouloud, the Prophet's birthday and traditionally a time of religious fanaticism—it fell that year on October 29—and the first anniversary of the rebellion had come and gone without the bloody explosion the rebels had promised.

The expatriate leaders, meanwhile, continued to spin their dark intrigues. Mohammed Ben Bella turned up in Tripoli on November 19 to inspect arms depots prepared by the Tunisians. In December he narrowly escaped assassination in a Tripoli hotel at the hands of a Frenchman from Tunis, who was killed by the Libyan police. Mohammed Khider was sighted first in Rome, then in Tripoli. Ahmed Boudaa, whom we remember as treasurer of the old M.T.L.D. central committee, arrived in Cairo on October 31 from Switzerland. A contingent of fifty North Africans was reported to be in training at the Egyptian National Guard camp in Cairo, while thirty-two Algerians were learning the art of guerrilla warfare at the Zanzur camp west of Tripoli.

Early in the following year, attention was focused for a moment on Tlemcen, the most Moslem and the most nationalist of the Algerian cities. On January 16, 1956, a local physician named Benzerjeb, who had been running errands for the F.L.N., was arrested. On the 17th, he was shot and killed "while trying to escape." Dr. Benzerjeb's death caused an explosion of indignation. The nationalists rejected the French explanation; they asserted that the physician had been brought down in cold blood. On the 18th, the agitation flared into violence. A group of demonstrators, returning from the cemetery where they had expected to attend Dr. Benzerjeb's funeral, besieged a villa beside the road. The owner of the villa fired at the crowd, and one of the demonstrators fell, mortally wounded. A nasty spate of rioting ensued. Houses were stoned and damaged; stores were broken into; cars were overturned and burned. Pierre Lambert, Prefect of Oran, clapped a 5 P.M. curfew on Tlemcen and ordered the Republican Security Guards to disperse all gatherings.

The rioting broke out again the next day, however, with the students of the *medersa* (Moslem college) taking the lead. The curfew was advanced to 4 P.M., and armored cars were brought into the city. On January 20, Raymond Blanc, Mayor of Tlemcen, appealed for calm in the name of the city fathers, both European and Moslem. The disorders subsided, but outrage and indignation continued to fester in the city for a long time. In all, eighty arrests had been made for disturbance of the peace. Dr. Benzerjeb was buried on January 19 at dawn with the consent of his family. It was noticed that most of the shops looted by rioters were Jewish-owned.

37. THE MESSALISTS AGAINST THE F.L.N.

The M.N.A., mustering its faithful and straining every nerve to retrieve something of its lost fortunes, began in the autumn of 1955 to take a hand in terrorist agitation and even to maintain a few armed groups in the field, notably in Kabylia, where the F.L.N. had not been able entirely to destroy Messali's "historic" influence. This was the beginning of a bloody contest between the M.N.A. and the F.L.N., the one trying to impinge on the other's jealously guarded monopoly of the Algerian "resistance movement." Perhaps the full story of this contest, reminiscent in some ways of the wartime struggle between General Draja Mikhailovitch and Josip Broz Tito in Yugoslavia, may someday be told by a student curious about the minutiae of history. For present purposes, the highlights will be enough.

The M.N.A. terrorist organization functioned at first under the direction of Mustapha Ben Mohammed, a member of the Algiers city council, arrested on November 10; its strength probably did not exceed

400 members in the Algiers area. The M.N.A.'s doctrinal position, as authoritatively stated in *France-Observateur* for February 23, 1956, differed from that of the F.L.N. only in matters of detail. The M.N.A. made negotiations with France contingent on the prior withdrawal of French troops but was, perhaps, less rigid than the F.L.N. on the requirement for the prior establishment of an Algerian government; in any case, it did not claim to be the sole representative of the Algerian people. "The terms of a cease-fire," the statement said, "would be to negotiate with the Algerian people on the basis of: Algerian nationhood; the release of persons interned; democratic freedoms; a constituent assembly sovereignly elected under popular control; freely defined ties of mutual friendship and assistance with France."

The M.N.A.'s attitude toward the F.L.N., as reflected in the battle of handbills, was ambivalent: overtures and insults came in rapid succession. In December, an M.N.A. handbill called the F.L.N. a "basket of crabs" and accused it of having put the Egyptians up to the arrest of Chadly Mekki and Ahmed Mezerna. The F.L.N., retorting (in a bulletin for internal circulation), charged that the Messalists had "like cowards stabbed the Front in the back." In February, 1956, however, the M.N.A. adopted a conciliatory line. A handbill entitled, "Algerians, the M.N.A. speaks to you," said: "The aim of the M.N.A. is not to direct its efforts . . . against a brother movement . . . The situation makes the achievement of national unity indispensable . . . One objective only: struggle until victory is won . . . To continue the work of disunion would be a crime against the fatherland."

The F.L.N. replied to these advances with a handbill entitled, "When the 'Basket of Crabs' becomes a 'Brother Movement.'" "The F.L.N.," the handbill said, "cannot ally itself with a lot of profiteers and informers . . . Traitors are not to be taken as allies but are to be killed . . . Messali, if he wants to be pardoned, must dissolve the M.N.A. and put himself under the authority of the Front . . ." Despite this rebuff, the M.N.A., still proffering friendship, issued a handbill which said: "We have banished resentment from our hearts . . . Our brothers Mezerna and Chadly in their Cairo prison will understand that our abnegation is motivated by patriotism . . . With all due deference to the pen-pusher who hatched the handbill reviling our movement, the people want unity and they shall have it." But already F.L.N. and M.N.A. bands had clashed near Maillot in Kabylia with loss of life and limb; the blood feud had begun.

In the spring of 1956, M.N.A. bands were reportedly active in the coastal area of lower Kabylia between Tigzirt and Port Gueydon, in the Palestro, Mirabeau, and Maillot districts, and in the Guergour. We hear for the first time of Mohammed Bellounis, identified then as M.N.A. chief in lower Kabylia; he was later to become commander of a vast M.N.A. "province" in the southern part of the Algiers department and in the Sahara. In April, the arrest near Orléansville of a "regional chief" named M'Hamed Benmadjoub brought to fourteen the number of Messalist leaders captured in that area.

On March 13, 1956, a French patrol came upon the bodies of eighteen Messalists, lying in the road with their throats slit, near Seddouk in the Soummam valley northeast of Akbou. Fifteen more bodies were found there on March 20, plus a "notice and warning" which said:

> It is made known to all that these soldiers belonged to the Army of Messali, which has dissociated itself from the National Algerian Union, to which, however, all the other organized parties and groups in Algeria have rallied. These individuals supported the schism contrived by Messali and fought for his cause, refusing to fight in the name of Algeria and in the way of God. Consequently, the Army of National Liberation, which is honored to belong to the National Liberation Front, has sentenced them to death.
>
> This is the fate that henceforth awaits all those who divide the National Union.

A score of Messalists perished in a nocturnal battle with the F.L.N. near Boghni on March 20. The test of strength thus irremediably engaged could end only to the advantage of the F.L.N. This may be why the M.N.A. sought in the months that followed to promote the idea of a united "National Resistance Council"—with no great conviction, however, judging by its continued verbal attacks on the F.L.N. An M.N.A. handbill in May, for instance, denounced the "maneuvers and shady transactions of those who, having taken refuge in Cairo, try to impose their control with lies and demagogy." Another handbill, issued in December under the title, "Down with the Pseudo-Patriots," exalted the memory of the "gallant pioneers" of the M.N.A., "treacherously killed" by the F.L.N. In February, 1957, the M.N.A. was still identifying itself with the A.L.N. A man was found dead near Orléansville; a note pinned to his body said: "Traitor to the fatherland for collaboration with the F.L.N.; assassinated by the A.L.N."

In the autumn of 1956, the M.N.A. bands, driven out of Kabylia and the region of Orléansville (save perhaps for a few remnants), began to make their presence felt far to the south, from Aïn Boucif to Djelfa, from Bou Saâda to Reibel. Bellounis, whose men had previously been operating in the Bouira district, moved down into the Djebel Boutaleb in the Hodna range and on to the region of M'Sila; from there he dominated the northern reaches of the Sahara. Two lesser M.N.A. chiefs, Achoun Ziane and Si Haouès, carved out spheres of their own, the former in the region of Djelfa, the latter in the Biskra-Ouled Djellal area. The Ouled Naïl mountains, home of an Arab tribe famous for the dancing girls it used to send to Bou Saâda to beguile tourists in search of local color, became an M.N.A. stronghold. However, Ziane, self-styled "General of the Sahara," came to grief in the Djebel Bou Kahil between Bou Saâda and Laghouat on November 7. He and two of his lieutenants were among the six rebels killed that day in an encounter with the Foreign Legion. On November 8, Ziane's band was engaged and decimated. Amor Driss, Ziane's second-in-command, took over as M.N.A. chief in the area.

The F.L.N. was bound to look upon the M.N.A. pocket on its southern flank as something that could not long be abided. The Messalists were, in fact, subjected to increasing pressure by Mourad, F.L.N. commander in the *Sud-Oranais*, and by Si Chérif,* chief of the *Wilaya* 6 (*Sud-Algérois* and part of the *Sud-Oranais*). A succession of clashes occurred in the spring of 1957—near Aumale, at Djorf (near M'Sila), at Letourneux (between Boghari and Téniet el Haad), and in the Djebel Nador (southeast of Tiaret). The M.N.A. seems to have got the worst of it in all of them.

In April, the M.N.A. was driven out of the Djebel Amour range west of Djelfa by Mourad. With both the F.L.N. and the French raining blows on them, the Messalists, it was thought, would soon be compelled to accept defeat. That there were defections to the F.L.N. is certain. For instance, Haouès Hamouda Ahmed Ben Abderrazak, known as Si Haouès, pledged allegiance to the F.L.N. early in 1957 and served his new masters well by clearing the Aurès of dissident elements that had been impeding the flow of arms and men from Tunisia. He succeeded Si Chérif as commander of *Wilaya* 6 and was killed in combat on March 28, 1959, with Amirouche, another rebel commander. The two were trying to reach Tunisia by the southern route. A native of M'Chounèche in the Aurès, Si Haouès was thirty-five years old at the time of his death. Amor Driss also went over to the F.L.N. He became Si Haouès's second-in-command and was caught in the action that cost Si Haouès his life.

Early in September, 1957, it was reported that Bellounis had entered into a compact with the French and was operating as their ally. His hatred of the F.L.N. seems to have been inflamed by the Melouza massacre, in which 302 Moslem villagers suspected of pro-M.N.A. sympathies had perished at the hands of an F.L.N. punitive expedition on May 28,

* *Nom de guerre*. Si Chérif later became a colonel in the French Army.

1957.* In November, 1957, Bellounis went over to the French openly at the head of a private army of more than 2,000 men armed and supplied in part by the French. But he continued to fly an Algerian flag—a red crescent and star on a green and white field—and to regard himself as a champion of Algerian independence.

Bellounis broke with the French in the wake of the events that had placed Algeria under army rule in May, 1958. His defection was attributed to his hostility and that of some of his lieutenants toward the policy of integration to which the Army was committed. At first the French attempted to hold Bellounis to his alliance by negotiation. When this failed, they dropped handbills urging his men to desert. In July, 1958, a French force overran his command post in the village of Diar el Chiouk in the Ouled Naïl mountains. Bellounis had fled, but near the village the French discovered three pits in which 400 of Bellounis' men were buried, presumably after execution. On July 14, Bellounis made a stand and was killed in combat. His army was decimated and dispersed by the French.

38. MR. ABBAS'S FLIGHT TO CAIRO

The U.D.M.A., whose delegates were absent, as we have seen, when the Algerian Assembly convened for its ordinary session on November 29, 1955, was consumed by a furious desire to sit at the "round-table conference" on Algeria, then apparently in the offing. To understand the position of the U.D.M.A., we must realize that the political outlook in Algeria at the end of November was dominated by the expectation that M. Soustelle's plans for closer integration would fail and that Algeria

* The massacre, the worst of several of a similar nature, took place at Mechta Kasbah near Melouza at the western end of the Hodna mountains between Bordj Bou Arreridj and Aumale. The victims may also have been on the point of placing themselves under the protection of the French Army. The F.L.N. had issued a handbill in April, 1957, ordering its guerrilla units to "burn all villages that request French protection and kill all their male inhabitants who are more than 20 years old."

would instead move toward greater autonomy. It was anticipated that the government to be formed in January would take positive steps at the outset to define a new relationship between Algeria and France. The Socialists and the Radicals were already talking in terms of federation, and even the outgoing Government had intimated that wide consultation with the representatives of the Algerian people would have to precede the elaboration of further political reforms. Integration had become so problematical that, quite apart from the more compelling considerations of personal safety, few Moslem politicians were still willing to pin their fortunes to it. Comments heard in the corridors of the Algerian Assembly suggested that even the Moslem politicians most favorable to integration saw little use in voting for the Soustelle Plan if profound institutional changes were soon to follow in any case.

Although it represented little more than a handful of ambitious men, the U.D.M.A. saw in the disarray of the French a chance to reap where the rebels had sown. By rivaling the F.L.N. in insolence, the U.D.M.A. hoped to cozen the French into accepting its receivership as a lesser evil. In this way, it was felt, the U.D.M.A. might become a buffer between France and the F.L.N., recommending itself to the one as a guarantee against extremism and to the other as a sharp broker. But it was not enough that the French should be convinced of the inevitability of drastic concessions; they would also have to concede the U.D.M.A.'s claim to be a genuine "third force." A big order, but worth a try, for the alternative was the curtain.

On November 30, the political bureau of the U.D.M.A. issued a ringing blast against the "repression," the Soustelle Plan, and other "false remedies proposed within the framework of existing institutions." The statement also said:

> Despite the bankruptcy of the public powers . . . the U.D.M.A. has again asserted that talks and negotiations are still possible. For this, it is necessary only to face up to the real problem, that of the freedom of man, and to realize that no solution is workable until it is assured of the adhesion of the people concerned. Algeria is not France. Algeria is a colony where exceptional and arbitrary laws have reduced a people to bondage. This cannot longer endure. The salvation of all and the honor of France are at stake. All Algerian and French democrats must therefore unite to undertake decisive action . . .

This and other pronouncements in the same vein elicited no response from the French or from anyone. Then came the F.L.N. summons to resign. For the U.D.M.A., time was running out. Mr. Abbas and his little retinue of disciples could hardly ignore the F.L.N. injunction. There was not one among them ready to stand up in his own person for the "freedom of man," to defy, not the temporizing French, but the F.L.N. killers. Naturally, however, the resignation of the U.D.M.A. representatives was accompanied by another flow of extravagant words, in which (to use a French expression) the fish was drowned.

In January, 1956, Mr. Abbas told the Tunis weekly *L'Action* that he and his party had thrown their entire support to the F.L.N. and would "stand aside for the chiefs of the armed resistance." The interview was carried by the magazine in its January 23 issue. On January 26, Mr. Abbas said he had never made any such statement. To this, *L'Action* replied in its January 30 issue: "Our correspondent asserts that the words as reported were taken down virtually from dictation . . ." Judging by what followed, there can be little doubt that it was Mr. Abbas who lied, not *L'Action*. But the statement was prematurely published.

On January 30, Mr. Abbas and Ahmed Francis conferred in Geneva with Ahmed Ahmed-Bioud, the U.D.M.A. representative in Cairo. It may be assumed that details of the imminent fusion of the U.D.M.A. with the F.L.N. were discussed at this meeting. In any case, Messrs. Abbas and Francis left Algeria for good on April 7. They traveled first to Paris and from there to Geneva, Rome, and on to Cairo with two Ulema, Ahmed Tewfik Madani and Abbas Bencheikh Hocine.

Mr. Abbas held his famous press conference at the Semiramis Hotel in Cairo on April 25. As waiters wove through the room passing orangeade to more than 200 journalists, the "*chefs parachutés*" took their places on the platform under the glare of newsreel floodlights. Mr. Abbas sat in the middle with a microphone in front of him. To his left sat Ahmed Francis and Mohammed Lamine-Debaghine; to his right, Messrs. Tewfik Madani and Bencheikh Hocine. On one side of the room, Mohammed Ben Bella and Mohammed Khider could be seen looking on with the critical eye of probation officers.* Fouad Galal, former Egyptian Minister of National Guidance, also was present. But it was a purely Algerian show.

As has already been noted, Mr. Abbas promised on that occasion that until France agreed to negotiate with the F.L.N. and to accept its terms, there would be "neither peace, respite, nor armistice." He even asserted

* As Ben Bella was certainly aware, Ferhat Abbas and several others had been sentenced to death by the *maquis* inside Algeria and pardoned on condition that they put themselves at the disposal of the F.L.N. committee in Cairo. And Ben Bella must have suspected that the object of the maneuver was to dilute his own authority.

that the French had massacred 100,000 Algerians. Mr. Abbas read from a French text that was distributed afterwards to the press with translations in English and Arabic. The English version contained an added flourish, not found in the other two—a threat to carry the war to Metropolitan France itself if the last French soldier was not promptly withdrawn from Algerian soil. It could not be denied when the performance was over that Mr. Abbas had come through with flying colors. He had yielded to none in nationalist zeal and in political artistry.

The record shows, too—how typical!—that Mr. Abbas had not resigned his seat in the Algerian Assembly in response to his own command. He had, on the contrary, kept his paw in the public till up to the last minute, collecting his delegate's stipend of 250,000 francs ($714) a month and even drawing on his travel allowance for the fiscal year beginning April 1, 1956. In short, he had skipped the country on public funds.

The defection of the U.D.M.A. in December, 1955, left the "Sixty-One" in a painfully exposed position. They could procrastinate, issue statements and manifestos, but they could not indefinitely ignore the F.L.N.'s resignation dictate. Thirty-odd members of the group met on January 4 and, after criticizing the U.D.M.A. representatives for resigning too soon, put out a "communiqué" stating that the Algerian problem was "essentially political and not alimentary, as some would like to believe." Having thus dismissed all reforms designed to improve the well-being of the people, the "Sixty-One," or what was left of them, demanded that the "principle of Algerian nationhood" be recognized by the French Government and ratified by the National Assembly. The group also declared "solemnly":

> That it has no desire to play the part of a valid interlocutor . . ., its object being only, on the one hand, to serve the cause of the people by bringing the Algerian national problem to the attention of the Parliament and Government born of the recent election and, on the other hand, to protect the innocent populations against blind repression;
>
> That if after new representations in Paris and before the end of the first month following the formation of the French Government, this Government shall not have proclaimed its determination to promote a policy in conformity with the legitimate aspirations of the Algerian people, the "Sixty-One" will resign in a body from all their political posts and will incite other Moslem representatives to do likewise.

A fortnight later the Association of Ulema put out a violent manifesto signed by its president, Larbi Tebessi, and by its secretary-general, Ahmed Tewfik Madani. The Ulema protested in this document against the "horrors and infamous atrocities" allegedly committed by the French and they attributed to colonialism the "misfortunes that have devoured this country since 1830." After a word of commiseration for "all the free Algerians upon whom the heavy gates of the prisons have closed" and for the "victims of a blind repression," the Ulema went on in their manifesto to guillotine the reforms:

> Any policy built upon the patching up of the past and carried out by means of "reforms" that are but the avatars of the colonialist order, whatever name may be given them, can be nothing more than an odious and cynical derision of a kind calculated to bring the despair to its most terrible paroxysm . . . It is not possible to solve the Algerian affair in a definitive and peaceful manner otherwise than by recognizing solemnly and without feint: the free existence of the Algerian nation as well as its specific personality, its national government, its sovereign legislative assembly . . .

Mr. Tewfik Madani, his nationalist orthodoxy now firmly established and published abroad, had every reason to look forward to a position of honor and eminence in the F.L.N. He was not disappointed. He travelled to Cairo with Ferhat Abbas in April and became titular head of the F.L.N. in October, following the capture by the French of Mohammed Ben Bella and his four companions.*

A very different fate was to overtake Larbi Tebessi. On the evening of April 4, 1957, a jeep came to a grinding stop in front of the Villa Meriem in the populous (European) Belcourt district of Algiers. Several men, dressed to look like French paratroopers except that they wore motorcycle helmets and dark glasses, appeared at the door of the villa, and, finding Larbi Tebessi there–it was not his home–said:

"We have come to take Abdellatif Soltani† into custody; are you he?"

"Abdellatif Soltani is absent. I am Larbi Tebessi."

"Larbi Tebessi? Very well; follow us."

Mr. Tebessi was neither seen nor heard from again. The French command categorically denied having had anything to do with the disappearance of the elderly and apparently harmless sheikh. The truth

* See p. 58.

† Another *alem.* The dialogue was reported by a witness.

can only be surmised, but some evidence suggests that Larbi Tebessi had identified himself with a Cairo-Tunis faction of the F.L.N. then at odds with the Kabyles of the "internal resistance."

39. THE TESTAMENT OF JACQUES SOUSTELLE

In November, 1955, a half-dozen "liberal" mayors, including Jacques Chevallier, broke away from the powerful mayors' association in protest against the "racist" policies of some of their colleagues and formed an association of their own. Although the hope was that the native presidents of the 134 municipal centers (self-governing villages) in Kabylia could be brought into it, the new association did not afterwards show the slightest sign of life. On December 15, the regular association met in closed session with seventy-six of the Algiers department's 124 mayors present and with Raymond Laquière, Mayor of Saint-Eugène, in the chair. In their motion, the mayors noted with concern that the situation continued to deterioriate, demanded the execution of death sentences, reasserted their opposition to a "federal" solution of the Algerian problem, and threatened to close down the city halls if their demands went unheeded.

The European community was, indeed, oppressed with every sort of evil presentiment. The loss of its deputies when its fate was in the balance was bad enough. But echoes of the electoral campaign, especially talk of federation and of a common electoral roll, to say nothing of the accusations of alleged French torture and brutality, led the Europeans to fear the worst. Their anxiety led to an abortive attempt to amalgamate the principal European pressure groups within a vast *Rassemblement Français Nord-Africain.* On January 13, 1956, however, fifty-two veterans' associations banded together to form a "*Comité d'Entente des Anciens Combattants, Victimes de la Guerre et Cadres de Réserve,*" commonly known as the *Comité d'Entente.* A manifesto adopted by these united veterans demanded that the Government:

1. Solemnly proclaim its irrevocable determination to maintain French sovereignty in Algeria;

2. Re-establish order and security in Algeria by all the means at its disposal so as to insure the protection of the French community, in which European and Moslem Frenchmen are closely united;
3. Order the execution of all sentences imposed by the courts, notably death sentences;
4. Make energetic representations to foreign nations to the end that all encouragement and material aid to the rebels be made to cease.

The Government's committee for the coordination of North African affairs decided on December 21 to send an extraordinary mission to Algeria to "insure closer liaison" between Premier Faure (who also was acting Interior Minister) and M. Soustelle. What useful service such a mission could possibly perform was not adequately explained; nothing, on the face of it, could be more admirably designed to complicate M. Soustelle's already arduous task and to impair his authority. Nevertheless, Lieutenant General Pierre Jacquot, French commander in chief in Indochina, was compelled to travel halfway round the world to join the mission. The other members of the mission were: Jacques Duhamel, director of M. Faure's personal staff; Abel Thomas, assistant director of M. Faure's staff as Interior Minister; and Paul Demange, a former Prefect of Oran. M. Duhamel did not leave Paris; the other three '"missionaries" visited Algiers briefly. Messrs. Thomas and Demange were recalled after forty-eight hours to "report" on an "important conference" held by M. Soustelle on December 26, while General Jacquot stayed on to study the military situation.

The January 2 general election in France gave a clear-cut majority to no party or group of parties. The Communists forged ahead, gaining fifty seats. The Socialists and the Radicals—the core of the Republican Front—lost ground; so did the Popular Republicans and the Moderates. M. Soustelle was re-elected in Lyons, but his party, the ex-Gaullist Popular Republicans, suffered a crushing defeat, losing fifty-one of its seventy-one seats. The ranks of the right were thrown into confusion by the emergence of a powerful new extremist party, that of the anti-tax leader Pierre Poujade (who was not himself a deputy). The fifty-one Poujadist deputies—their number later dwindled as the result of voided elections—called themselves the French Union and Fraternity Group, but nobody could tell how these rank outsiders might behave.

The Republican Front seemed to think it could make up for its weakness at the polls by its arrogance. The Moderates were told where to get off by Gaston Defferre, Socialist deputy and Mayor of Marseilles, who said his party repudiated the idea of a government of national union and would have no part of any government that did not "break brutally with the do-nothingism of the past." With the Republican Front claiming the right to govern by virtue of its preponderance among the non-Communist parties, there could be little doubt that the forthcoming government would bring the Socialists to power with the Radicals as auxiliaries.

It is difficult to convey a notion of what Algeria was like during that appalling month of January, 1956. If campaign promises were to be taken seriously, the prospect of a Socialist government brought the most reckless of adventures within the realm of possibility. Anything might be attempted in pursuit of the supreme goal of peace and repose; a deal with the rebels, home rule, the release of the interned terrorists, a common electoral roll, and heaven knows what other sovereign remedies, were waiting on the apothecary's shelf. And although the new Assembly was apparently as heterogeneous as its predecessor, one fact stood out—counting the Communists, the majority favored some sort of autonomy for Algeria.

This being the case, the French officials and army officers who were trying to restore security in the rebel-infested parts of the country or just to prevent the administration from breaking down began to wonder to what extent their efforts and hardships had meaning. Certainly, if negotiations with the rebels were imminent, a basic "reassessment" was in order. The anxiety of these men was heightened by the fact that they were not alone; beside them, working with them, were numerous Moslems—*caïds*, city councilors, general councilors, *djemaa* presidents and members, rural constables, and lowly *harkis* (volunteer auxiliaries). How would these people fare in the event of a capitulation? How would their fidelity and courage be requited? And how, with the issue in doubt, could they be required to put their lives in further jeopardy?

The dauntless M. Soustelle, concerned to sum up and to draw the conclusions of his experience for the benefit of his successor, drafted a memoir and submitted it to Premier Faure on January 7. The document was a confidential one, for official use only. Since it could not be released to the press, it was "leaked," undoubtedly by those who thought their political interests would be advanced by its publication. As M. Soustelle saw it, the choice facing the new National Assembly was one of exceptional gravity. The French Constitution, that of a highly centralized state, did not provide the institutional flexibility which alone might have enabled the Government to hold a federated Algeria within the framework of the Republic. M. Soustelle rightly feared that, in the absence of any federating machinery, autonomy would put Algeria squarely on the road to secession, Moslem rule, and economic ruin. That is why he continued to make a strong case for integration in the teeth of increasing hostility in Paris.

His memoir was at once a plea, a profession of faith, and a plan for the future. Integration, according to M. Soustelle, would not put a permanent obstacle in the way of federation, whereas premature federation would make integration forever impossible. He advocated a solemn proclamation by which the new Assembly would undertake to make the European and Moslem inhabitants of Algeria fully equal in rights and duties within a given time limit. Such a proclamation, he thought, should be followed by an offer of *aman*, or pardon, to rebels who surrendered and who had committed no common-law crime.

In M. Soustelle's view, nothing was to be begrudged. There was to be no difference whatever between Algeria and Metropolitan France except in the matter of personal status. Regulations governing credit and wages, the cost of power and transport, the system of elections to national bodies—everything was to be exactly the same. And if this meant enormous financial sacrifice, what then? Was Algeria not worth it?

M. Soustelle's plan, or at least what was reported as being his plan, went further. It called for:

1. The abolition of the Government General and of the Algerian Assembly, and the establishment of a special ministry for Algerian affairs in Paris;
2. The division of Algeria into three groups of departments, each group to be headed, as in France, by a "super prefect";
3. The abolition of the administrative townships;
4. Parity of representation for the Europeans in townships where their community was numerically strong;
5. The institution of a common electoral roll for all national elections and the concomitant increase in the number of Moslem deputies.

These proposals, given wide publicity in the press, were the signal for a new outburst of polemics. The "ultras" in Algeria, who saw red whenever the common electoral roll was mentioned, flew right off the handle. Louis Boyer-Banse, head of the *Union Française Nord-Africaine*, ran a vehement attack on M. Soustelle in his paper, *Prestige Français;* his article, entitled "A Criminal Conspiracy to Prepare Our Obliteration," came close to accusing M. Soustelle of treason. General Adolphe Aumeran, deputy for Algiers in the old Assembly, intimated in his paper *L'Africain* that M. Soustelle was in effect handing Algeria over to the Arab League. Even the relatively staid *Echo d'Alger* complained that the common electoral roll proposed by M. Soustelle would drown the Europeans in the Moslem mass.

These reactions could, I think, be attributed in part to a misunderstanding of M. Soustelle's basic purpose, the result of premature publicity without adequate explanation. A common electoral roll in a federal context would indeed crush the Europeans; in the context of integration, however, it could conceivably constitute one of the essential elements cementing Algeria to France. M. Soustelle felt strongly that Algeria could not stand still, that it would have to move in the direction either of closer integration or of greater autonomy, and that autonomy meant ultimate secession. He saw the common electoral roll almost as the seal of integration. How then, in all honesty, could he reject it? He may have been wrong in thinking that the common electoral roll was inseparable from integration, but he could not be accused of trying to destroy the European establishment. On the contrary, his whole effort was to save it, and with it Algeria as a whole.

M. Soustelle, castigated in Algiers, got equally harsh treatment in Paris, but for very different reasons. Those who, long since, had put their money on capitulation were in no mood to concede defeat. M. Soustelle's proposals would have to be laid promptly to rest. The Mendèsist weekly *L'Express,* therefore, now swung its heavy artillery into action against the Governor General. It did not hesitate to describe the Soustelle proposals as a "fraud" that could lead to war; the real alternative, according to *L'Express,* was between "negotiation" and "repression." *Le Monde* joined the chorus, but in a subdued key befitting its dignity. Jacques Fauvet, the paper's editorial writer, commented:

> But if the right holds that these suggestions go too far, the left thinks they come too late. Though they are a logical outgrowth of the 1947 Statute, they come at a moment when events and attitudes are much less amenable to the assimilation of Algeria as part of France. Lost time can never be made up, especially in North Africa. The federalist idea, vague it is true, is progressing; it presupposes a revision of the Constitution. The idea of integration has lost ground, if only in parliamentary circles. The choice, in any case, cannot be put off much longer.

What *L'Express* clamored for in a vulgar, offensive way, what *Le Monde* advocated in muted tones, was capitulation. At the core, their thesis was: Algeria must be left to whatever its fate may be, provided France gets out from under. There was, it seemed to me, a strong strain of Vichy in the settlement-at-all-costs school of thought, a strain made up of mixed emotions, including a desire for restful change, a taste for passive self-mortification, and a belief in purification through renunciation.

Such sentiments were, of course, cynically played upon by politicians vying for power and well content to exercise it in a diminished nation. The same sentiments were encouraged and flattered by Catholics (and Protestants) eager to build a new "City of God" amid the ruins of French settlement in North Africa. But—who knows?—the Parisian intellectual set may yet discover that it is out of step with the bulk of the people of France. Just as, during the war, the voice of General de Gaulle had a resonance against which the Vichy propagandists could not prevail, so perhaps tomorrow the challenge of Algeria will find the nation's multitudes more resolved than its intellectual upper crust. I once had a spirited discussion on this subject with the "super prefect" of an Algerian group of departments. The official asserted in the face of my incredulity that, however beset with problems Algeria might be, there was no "Algerian problem." "France will never abandon Algeria," he said, "and that's that; those who say the contrary are merely deluding themselves and deluding others."

M. Soustelle, quite understandably upset by the "leak" of his memoir, made M. Faure aware of his intense displeasure. This known fact gave rise to rumors to the effect that M. Soustelle had resigned in protest, or was about to do so. Algiers was stunned by these rumors. For a moment it looked as though the evils of a phantom government in Paris would be compounded by those of a headless administration in Algiers. The rumors were quickly denied, however, and on January 12 M. Soustelle went on the air to restate his faith in a closer and more just union with France. After stressing the necessity of a "tenacious and persevering" effort to restore law and order, M. Soustelle said:

> Since Algeria must become an integral part of France, it is imperative that this exigency become more real each day for the good of all. This means that the specific personality of this province of the French Republic be solemnly recognized and guaranteed with all respect for its tradition, for its religion, for its culture. This means, too, that among the French of Algeria, whatever their racial origin, whatever their religion, as also between them and their fellow citizens of Metropolitan France, equality must reign—the equality of rights and duties, of advantages and sacrifices, from Dunkirk to Tamanrasset.
>
> I am profoundly convinced that this is the way of salvation. It is also the spirit of France, generous and humane, that commends us to break with the routines of the past and to reply to

> the defiance of the evil forces that assail us with a long step forward and with a resolute decision in favor of progress and brotherhood.
>
> No!—to the rebellion, to its obscurantism and savagery. No!—to a do-nothingism content with the precarious maintenance of an outdated state of affairs. Let us instead, all those who want peace and progress, pull together to save Algeria by resisting aggression and by promoting the great reform that this country looks forward to. It is essential to create a true community at last, to throw together all that is France and all that is Algeria . . .
>
> Unbridled violence cannot give the rebellion an impossible victory; it can only bring death and ruin to a greater number of Algerians each day. There is no solution outside France and without France. I have no other aim, no other care, than to find that solution and to make it prevail.

The French cabinet decided on January 11 to establish in Kabylia a unified civil and military command on the Aurès model. On January 15, Brigadier General Jean Olié, fifty-two-year-old commandant of the special military school at Coëtquidan in Brittany (the successor to the old Saint-Cyr), was appointed civil and military commander at Tizi Ouzou. To his new post he brought a wealth of experience gained partly in the Foreign Legion—he had commanded its famous *Régiment de marche* in 1944—and partly in Morocco, where he had served for many years as a native affairs officer. Meanwhile the Nineteenth Infantry Division (Brigadier General André Dufourt), newly landed, was taking up positions in the region of Sétif. The number of Algerian Affairs officers in the field had now reached 300.

On January 26, in one of his last pronouncements as Governor General, M. Soustelle assailed the rebels for their systematic destruction of the rural schools, which he described as "symbols of culture, understanding, and peace." Speaking over Algiers radio, he said: "How can they [the rebels] claim to act in the name or in the interest of the Moslem people? The people want to acquire knowledge so as to live better. The rebels would compel them to stagnate in ignorance. The people want peace and concord; the rebels impose upon them a hopeless war, resulting only in the spread of ruin and death."

No one could be more convinced than I that the Algerian rebellion is an attack on the ordinary decencies of life. Yet in the matter of schools, M. Soustelle failed to discern what I believe to be a weakness in French educational policy. Though the villagers wanted the schools and clamored for more, they did not look upon them as being, as it were, of their own substance. They recognized a burned school to be a damaging loss; they did not feel it as a wound in their flesh and as an outrage to their collective integrity. For the schools were French, and the rebels, in attacking them, struck a blow at France.

The schools were remarkably good. They were competently staffed. But from a sociological point of view, something was wrong with them. I am no expert, but it seems to me that the lesson to be learned from the experience of Algeria is that schools should be organically a part, almost a microcosm, of the communities they serve. Schools, even when adapted to native needs (as is the case in Algeria), should not be superimposed on an alien culture. The pupil emerging from such a school is already half-divorced from the ways and outlook of his own people. He is apt to feel himself to be destined for something different and better. Such a lad is ripe for disappointment and disillusion. If bitterness and resentment follow, and they often do, another misfit is thrown upon the world. There are too many disgruntled youths in Algeria's extraordinarily young population.

A revealing incident occurred not far from Algiers in the summer of 1957. A French lieutenant belonging to the infantry regiment responsible for law and order in the district drove in a jeep one day to a little native village off the beaten track. In the back of the jeep he carried the body of a terrorist whose career of murder and arson had been cut short by a burst of French machine gun fire. The officer delivered the body to a village patriarch, the terrorist's father. The old man shuddered to hear in what singular ways his own son had distinguished himself. When the officer had finished speaking, the father spat on his son's body and said: "I have seven sons. Only this one went to school."

I cannot help thinking it would have been better if the French, instead of dotting rural Algeria with their own schools, had fostered the development of native schools, each a tribute to the initiative, resourcefulness, and labor of a village, each the expression of a deep-felt need. Such a system might have come along more slowly. The quality of the schooling would not have been high. But I am sure the French could constantly have exercised an influence for good within a system of native schools, particularly through government-assisted vocational training programs.

It should be recorded in this connection that even now the emphasis is being placed more and more on the teaching of the practical techniques so badly needed by the largely unproductive inhabitants of the underdeveloped country that is Algeria. It would be unfair, too, to criticize the French school system in Algeria for its shortcomings without mentioning its permanent merits. Few outsiders realize what a tremendous effort has been made under appallingly difficult conditions to educate the Moslem children, girls as well as boys. A word of praise must be said for the countless devoted men and women who have spent their working lives in the service of this cause.

Jacques Soustelle reports in his book, *Aimée et Souffrante Algérie,* that he conferred at length with Premier-Designate Guy Mollet in Paris on January 29. The Socialist leader seems to have listened to M. Soustelle's explanations with a mite of skepticism. The left-wing *cénacles* of Paris were hostile to the jolting views defended by M. Soustelle. In fact, word had got around that the Governor General, as he puts it in his book, "lived in the Palais d'Eté like a satrap of the Persian empire, in the midst of a handful of confidants, cut off from any contact with the population." It had even been said that his correspondence was censored by his entourage. Obviously, the whole Algerian problem would have to be learned all over again. Illusions that, in Algeria, had long since collapsed under the impact of reality were, in Paris, desperately clung to by men who refused to let experience disavow their theories. Nevertheless, M. Soustelle handed M. Mollet a memorandum containing his final recommendations.

In his memorandum, M. Soustelle called the new Government's attention to three dangers. The first of these resulted from the relentless campaign of denunciation and misrepresentation to which the Administration and the Army were being subjected by certain French journals of opinion. Something, M. Soustelle said, would have to be done about this, for anxiety, discouragement, and disgust were beginning to gnaw at the vitals of the Army in particular.

The second danger was that of announcing an intention to negotiate with the rebel leaders. Such an announcement, he said, would be enough "to convince the population once and for all that the rebels are winners and to induce it, for fear of reprisals, to take refuge in the camp of the victors."

The third danger lay in a possible attempt to negotiate a settlement with an *ad hoc* Algerian assembly. Rebel terror, he felt, would quickly reduce such a body to subservience, and the delegates, fearing for their lives, would undoubtedly strive to outbid one another for rebel favor. In these circumstances, the assembly could be counted on quickly to proclaim itself sovereign and constituent and Algeria independent.

In his final memorandum, M. Soustelle urged further that the new Government start by proclaiming these three basic principles:

1. Algeria remains and will remain an integral part of the French Republic;

2. The cultural, linguistic, and religious personality of Algeria is solemnly guaranteed;
3. The equality of the French citizens of Algeria is complete as regards rights and duties, without any racial or religious discrimination.

Turning next to more immediate problems, M. Soustelle again dwelt on the imperious necessity of reinforcements. These could be dispensed with, he maintained, only if the Government was willing either to drown the rebellion in a river of blood or else to evacuate the country. Since these alternatives were equally unthinkable, and since security had still to be restored, the Government, in M. Soustelle's view, had no choice but to send more troops to Algeria.

He also spoke of the "untenable situation" created by the abrogation of the "state of emergency." Here, too, he said, remedial action was urgently needed, since the Algerian authorities were operating in a state of semi-illegality. The absence of Algerian deputies at a time when the National Assembly would in all likelihood be called upon to make momentous decisions affecting Algeria's whole future struck M. Soustelle as a serious anomaly; he suggested, therefore, that the terms of the outgoing Algerian deputies be extended. No one could have been more aware than he of the shortcomings of the Algerian Assembly. Yet he did not recommend its dissolution since, under the Algerian Statute, another Assembly would have to be elected within three months. After putting in a word for his cherished reforms, M. Soustelle proposed that, to expedite action on all these pressing matters, the Government secure the adoption by the Parliament of a *loi cadre*, or framework law, which, while defining the goal to be attained, the general policy to be pursued, and the principles to be observed, would give the executive wide powers to see the job through.

Alas, no one is a prophet in his own country. The Socialist Government headed by M. Mollet was to stick like glue for more than a year to an impossible trilogy—cease-fire, free elections, negotiations. It was not until late in the summer of 1957 that a Government headed by Maurice Bourgès-Maunoury returned to the idea of a *loi cadre* for Algeria.

M. Soustelle's term as Governor General, having been extended in July, 1955, for a second six-month period, was normally to end on January 31, 1956. The political conjuncture made a further extension impossible; M. Soustelle was, therefore, at the end of his mission, and the Government was faced with the choice of his successor. Grappling with the Algerian problem—described by M. Mollet himself as one of his "first preoccupations"—the Premier-Designate and his colleagues announced three important decisions: the Governor General would be replaced by a cabinet minister resident in Algiers; the man appointed to hold this new portfolio was General Georges Catroux, Grand Chancellor of the Legion of Honor; the Premier would visit Algeria in person soon after his investiture by the National Assembly.

40. THE FLEETING SHADOW OF GENERAL CATROUX

The appointment of General Catroux was as eloquent as any statement of intentions. It meant that the Socialists, in their quest for a negotiated settlement in Algeria, were ready to consider the most drastic concessions. For despite the laurels that weighed upon his brow, General Catroux had become the ultimate symbol of capitulation. His mission to Antsirabé was still fresh in everyone's memory. Less than five months before he had gone off to that resort town in Madagascar to see the exiled Sultan of Morocco, Mohammed Ben Youssef. There he had been happy to announce the Sultan's acceptance of the liquidation of the French protectorate. The words spoken by General Catroux on that occasion should be engraved on tablets and enshrined in some hall of delusion. He said:

> . . . . First of all, I informed Sidi Mohammed that he would return to France. I laid that down as the starting point of the conversations. It was, from the time I arrived, a settled point . . .
>
> Ben Youssef has agreed to support the policy that aims at creating a free and independent state linked to France by an act of interdependence. French permanence is insured. Our country retains its strategic, diplomatic, political, and cultural interests and sees them guaranteed.
>
> The situation of the French will remain superior to that of other nationalities by virtue of the part they have played in the development of Morocco.
>
> Not once was the "quarrel of the legitimacy" broached. Sidi Mohammed Ben Youssef has, moreover, renewed his undertaking not to indulge in any political action . . .

What happened then? Ten weeks later Sidi Mohammed was back on the throne, and it only remained officially to proclaim Morocco an independent state. This was done on March 2, 1956. As for "interdependence" and all the rest of it, at the time of writing the French have not yet obtained even a treaty of establishment for the protection of their own nationals in Morocco.

In the light of what had already occurred, it was impossible not to understand what the Socialists were up to and what use was to be made of General Catroux. If there were any lingering misapprehensions in this respect, *Le Monde* obligingly undertook to dispel them. It said in an unsigned editorial:

> The innovation of a minister resident, the choice of the occupant of this high office, do not, of course, constitute a solution in themselves. They already point to an intention.
>
> General Catroux will directly commit the authority of the French Government in Algiers; he will participate in governmental deliberations. The appointment of the Grand Chancellor of the Legion of Honor has an even more precise meaning. . . . Since his return from Moscow [where he had been French Ambassador], General Catroux has not ceased to turn the attention of a lucid mind to the development of the Maghrib, where he was the associate and disciple of Lyautey before becoming the companion of General de Gaulle. Beginning in 1952, he presided over a group for the study of oversea affairs . . . This committee advocated for Tunisia solutions similar to those that have finally been adopted by the French Government.* . . . A member of the National Council of the R.P.F. [General de Gaulle's *Rassemblement du Peuple Français*], General Catroux resigned from it in January, 1952, by reason, he wrote, of his "disappointment . . . as regards the solution it proposed for several important problems including those of Tunisia and Morocco." Invited the following year to speak on Lyautey in Casablanca and Marrakech, he was warned by General Guillaume against coming to Morocco, where, the Resident General explained, after General Catroux's approval of M. François Mauriac's position, his talks might provoke infinitely regrettable reactions. The fact remains, nonetheless, that it was General Catroux whom M. Edgar Faure's Government called upon last September to negotiate a solution of conciliation with the Sultan, still in exile at Antsirabé.

* One of the members of General Catroux's study group was Jean Rous, secretary of the Congress of Peoples against Imperialism.

> Wherefore General Catroux's departure for Algiers can only reflect the determination of the new French Government to seek there as well a peaceful solution, necessary not only for Algeria, but also for the equilibrium of the whole of North Africa.*

Was the Moroccan operation to be repeated in Algeria? *Le Monde* hoped it would. So did many others in France. But the Europeans in Algeria balked when asked to trot along after the good general like the oysters after the walrus and the carpenter. At a meeting in Algiers on January 29, 4,000 war veterans passed a resolution in which they "denied" to General Catroux the "honor" of governing them. The appointment of an elderly general, "unfit if not retired"—General Catroux was then just seventy-nine years old—to replace an energetic young governor general struck the *Echo d'Oran* as a "humiliation" for Algeria. Raymond Laquière, Mayor of Saint-Eugène and former speaker of the Algerian Assembly, told *Le Monde* that if General Catroux came to Algiers, no European leader would be on hand to greet him. Actually, a decision to this effect seems to have been taken at a meeting of about forty Algerian deputies and mayors in Paris on January 30. Even Jacques Chevallier was understood to have indicated that he would not be able to welcome General Catroux to Algiers.

In his investiture speech on January 31, Guy Mollet stated his Algerian policy in broad and equivocal terms, conveying the impression that a happy alternative to integration had been found beyond the strict maintenance of French sovereignty (unmentioned), but on the near side of independence. The main objectives of his Algerian policy as outlined on that occasion were:

1. To re-establish peace, putting an end to terrorism and to blind repression;
2. To organize the coexistence of the two Algerian communities;
3. To establish an indissoluble union between Algeria and Metropolitan France;
4. To recognize and respect the "Algerian personality" and, rejecting any unilateral settlement,
5. To hold free elections as soon as possible on the basis of a single electoral roll;
6. To dissolve the Algerian Assembly and hold elections for its renewal;
7. To reform Algeria's municipal and administrative structure;
8. To adapt the Army to its tasks;
9. To promote economic and social advance.

* See *Le Monde* for January 31, 1956.

These objectives became those of the French Government with M. Mollet's investiture by a vote of 420 to 71.

General Catroux, interviewed by *Le Monde*, filled in a few of the gaps left by M. Mollet. The General, too, was backtracking. He said:

> The plan the Government proposes to apply . . . will not be integration, which the Moslems today no longer accept. It will take into account the specific character of the country with its two communities . . . It will respect, as the Premier said in his investiture statement, the "Algerian personality." . . .
>
> But there can be no question of conceding to Algeria a purely Moslem personality. First, this would be to fail to recognize the importance of the Metropolitan contribution to the country's development. In addition, there is no historical basis for the recognition of a national Algerian state . . .
>
> In Algiers, I expect to have talks with those interlocutors whom I consider valid. I naturally exclude the Moslems who have risen against France. It is only on the spot that I shall be able to form a precise idea of the situation. I have already been able to ascertain the ascendancy of the National Liberation Front. I see three reasons for this: intimidation and terrorism, the successes obtained in some regions by the Moslems who are fighting us, the attraction of the appeal to Algerian nationality.
>
> Forces better adapted to their mission, able for instance to oppose guerrilla warfare with guerrilla warfare, would enable us no doubt to win successes that would produce a change in Moslem opinion . . .
>
> At all events, there can be no question of allowing the bonds that link Algeria to France to be impaired. If the Government is resolved to secure for the Moslem community its rights, it does not under any circumstances intend to turn the country into a national state, inevitably marked for independence. Nor can there be any question of reducing the French to minority status. The two communities must accede to equality of rights and duties. It is by putting an end to the injustices that subsist, by improving the human condition of the natives through social and economic measures, that peace and understanding can be restored among inhabitants destined to live together.

At the center of a gathering storm of opposition, General Catroux thus lost his hauteur, ceased to treat his North African compatriots with disdain, parted company with François Mauriac. Yet this was not going to be enough to save him. The circumstances of his sudden fall from ministerial rank will shortly be recounted. But first let us cast a critical glance at his doctrine. Integration was explicitly repudiated. However, Algeria was not, as a result, to be brought one whit closer to nationhood.

The "Algerian personality," though nothing new—M. Soustelle had always sought to preserve it—and the promise of negotiations were now being used as a cover to conceal a shabby offer. The Moslems, denied the hope of nationhood, were also to be denied the benefits of integration. They were to be induced instead to enter a halfway house in which they would be neither completely French nor completely Algerian. And, by the same token, the Metropolitan French might reasonably expect to be spared at least part of the crushing financial burden of Algerian integration to say nothing of its political imponderables. Premier Mollet's investiture statement and General Catroux's elaboration ushered in a painful period of ambiguity.

A delegation of Moslem politicians then in Paris, unaware, apparently, of General Catroux's change of heart—or perhaps only of speech; who could tell?—fairly bubbled with enthusiasm. In a message to the new Minister Resident on February 1, they said:

> They [the Moslem representatives] are convinced that, having contributed so successfully to the right solution of the Moroccan problem, you will not fail to find for the Algerian problem a solution based likewise on the national aspirations of the Algerian Moslem populations.
>
> They hold it to be their duty to warn you against the pretensions of the Federation of Mayors, which is in no way qualified, and has no right, to set itself up as the mouthpiece of the Moslem populations.

The message was signed by two former deputies—Mohammed Salah Bendjelloul, leader of the delegation, and Ali Brahimi; by four senators—Abdennour Tamzali, Chérif Benhabyles, Khelladi Benmiloud, and Abdallah Mahdi; and by four delegates to the Algerian Assembly—Hachémi Benchennouf, Smaïl Lakhdari, Mohammed Madi, and Mohammed Boulsane.

On January 31, M. Soustelle went on the air with a farewell talk to the Algerian people:

> . . . . Europeans and Moslems, . . . you are all equally dear to me as fellow citizens whom I have seen struggling and suffering together. More than ever I remain convinced that there is no salvation outside a fraternal partnership of all Algerians, without discrimination of any sort, with equality of rights and duties in the bosom of the French Republic. There lies dignity; there lies peace . . .
>
> Wherever I may be, wherever I can make my voice heard, it is for Algeria that I shall speak, for its progress, for its pacification, for its happiness . . .

It cannot, I think, be denied that M. Soustelle has since kept his word.

The departure of Algeria's last Governor General—M. Lacoste also carried this title at first but, as a cabinet minister, his position was really rather different—was the occasion for a huge popular demonstration on the waterfront near the quay at which the S.S. "El Djezaïr," bound for Marseilles, was berthed. The war veterans and the students, to be sure, were there, numerous and compact, but it would be a vast mistake to believe, as *Le Monde* insinuated, that the demonstration had been artificially stimulated by the pressure groups. The man in the street, guided by his intuition, is sometimes more discerning than those who claim to be the leaders of opinion. The ordinary people of Algiers knew perfectly well that M. Soustelle was a rock of fidelity, not the conspirator Louis Boyer-Banse had said he was. To that rock they had instinctively moored their hopes. So it was that the workman put down his tools, the merchant closed his shop; and from the populous Bab el Oued and Belcourt districts—melting pots in which Spanish, Maltese, and Italian immigrants quickly become "Algerian French"—even from the aristocratic "heights" of the city, a migration occurred of thousands of people drawn as though irresistibly toward downtown Algiers and the port area.

M. Soustelle, quite unprepared for any such vast flood of humanity, left the Palais d'Eté in the first of a procession of official cars, his intention being to observe established protocol as it applied to departing Governors General. This meant taking leave of the authorities and saluting the massed colors of the veterans' organizations on the esplanade in front of the *Gare Maritime*. As the procession proceeded down the Rue Michelet, the main shopping street, on its way to the port area, as it passed the university, the cafés, the central post office, there were shouts of "Do not leave!" Other Governors General had, no doubt, heard similar shouts on the day of their departure. But never before on such an occasion had the port area been, as then, packed with a solid mass of people.

When M. Soustelle's car, preceded by a troop of Spahis, swung into sight a great clamor arose. A space had, however, been cleared for the ceremony behind a cordon of troops and armored cars. M. Soustelle reached that spot without mishap. The flags held aloft by the veterans cracked in the wind. The band played the *Marseillaise*. Then the police lines broke. As M. Soustelle describes it in his book, everything from the iron gates at the entrance to the port area to the *Gare Maritime* building was engulfed in a raging human sea. Here and there, a general's kepi or an admiral's cap could be seen bobbing on the surface, while the veterans' flags plunged up and down like the masts of a storm-tossed ship. M. Soustelle himself was propelled toward an armored car, upon which he took refuge with several other members of his official party. All efforts to persuade the crowd to make way for the Governor General were vain. By shouting and gesticulating, M. Soustelle managed to obtain a moment's relative silence. "If you want me to continue to defend French Algeria, . . ." he cried. "Yes! Yes!" responded the crowd. ". . . . then let me leave." "No! No!" Laboriously, the armored car inched forward, taking almost an hour to cover 200 yards. M. Soustelle, when he reached the quayside, leaped from the vehicle, made a dash for the "El Djezaïr," clambered up an iron ladder, and was aboard. The crowd sang "*Ce n'est qu'un au revoir*" (French version of "Auld Lang Syne") as the ship pulled out.

But the demonstration was not only one of sympathy for M. Soustelle; it was also one of hostility toward General Catroux and others of the same political stripe. Vivas for the departing Governor were interspersed with such shouts as "Down with Catroux!" and "Death to Mendès!" The correspondent of *Le Monde* naturally made much of this in his dispatch. He went further. Pointing out that, apart from native war veterans, there were few Moslems in the crowd, he conveyed the impression that M. Soustelle had somehow been the Governor General of the Europeans only, if not actually of the "ultras." The events of the day were presented as a sort of plebiscite in which the Europeans had voted for, and the Moslems against, M. Soustelle and his policies. In fact, the absence of the Moslems had little to do with M. Soustelle's policies; it meant essentially that the Moslems had yet to be delivered from their fears. The Arab does not react as a European does. He reacts as a European did when he was no further removed from primitive anarchy and insecurity than is the Arab of our own time. The failure of Europeans to grasp this essential difference has led to endless confusion and misapprehension. In medieval Europe, the ability to protect conferred the right to command. So it is among the Arabs even today. French power in North Africa was never otherwise understood. But by this rule, M. Soustelle had failed in his capacity as chief. The Arabs, therefore, owed him no respect and rendered him no honor. And yet he, as much as any other, was their friend.

On February 3, in the old city of Oran, the P.C.A. incited a mob of striking dock workers and Arab youths to violence, possibly in answer to the European demonstration in Algiers the previous day. The mob, surging into the busy Boulevard Paul Doumer, overturned and set fire to two cars, stoned a bus, battered its way into a jeweler's shop, and wrecked a European café. Charged by a section of Republican Security Guards, the rioters, numbering several hundred, scattered into narrow side streets, came together again behind a public market and resumed their destructive course. That afternoon they were back in the street, smashing and burning cars, pillaging shops. A curfew had to be imposed, and, as darkness fell, the silence of empty streets was broken only by the tread of passing patrols. The police, meanwhile, totted together its figures for the day: one killed and twenty wounded among the rioters; six wounded among the security forces; nine cars burned; fifteen cars and two buses damaged; twenty commercial establishments, including seven Jewish jewelry shops, pillaged or burned; 500 arrests.

It was announced in Paris on February 3, at the end of the new Government's first cabinet meeting, that Premier Mollet would fly to Algiers on February 6 and that General Catroux (whose resignation had been tendered and refused) would be installed as Minister Resident on February 10. The next day, Max Lejeune, Secretary of State for the Armed Forces in charge of Algerian affairs, flew to Algiers by way of Oran, ostensibly to study the military situation in Algeria, but undoubtedly also to take a few soundings prior to the Premier's visit. The precaution was fully warranted, for, despite the words of appeasement uttered by M. Mollet and by General Catroux, the European community was seething with hostility. Already, on February 2, a delegation of first-college politicians headed by Raymond Laquière had spoken its mind in an exchange of views with Premier Mollet. Two days later, the delegation, widened to include most of Algeria's first-college senators and former deputies, sent a memorandum to Premier Mollet. In it the politicians expressed the fear that "dramatic consequences" would follow the arrival of General Catroux in Algiers and "adjured" the Government not to expose Algeria to this "new peril." They also took a strong stand in opposition to the promise of a common electoral roll. They wrote:

> The contemplated unilateral imposition of the single college without prior discussion with the representatives of the two Algerian communities and, in particular, with the European community, which alone would be injured by this new and far-reaching measure, does not seem to be consonant with your desire not to determine Algeria's fate unilaterally.
>
> You cannot fail to realize that the single college would eliminate the French community from Algerian public life. The only conceivable system, therefore, is one that would guarantee to the

community of civil status the equality of representation which you yourself recognize as being indispensable to the interests of the community of Koranic status. This alone implies the maintenance of the double college. . . .

This view was not, and has not yet been, accepted in Paris. The Socialist Government never flinched for an instant in its declared resolve to impose the single college upon Algeria. The succeeding Government headed by Premier Maurice Bourgès-Maunoury stood committed to the same policy. All objections were dismissed with the remark that the common electoral roll was a promise that could not be gone back on. Yet the Mollet Socialists and the Bourgès-Maunoury Radicals unceasingly declared that neither community in Algeria was to be allowed to dominate the other. The idea seemed to be that the superior voting strength of the Moslems could be neutralized by gerrymandering, by the institution of balanced tickets, and by similar devices. In other words, what was given with one hand was to be taken away with the other.

This sort of constant equivocation needlessly vexed the Algerian problem from the first days of the Socialist Government. How much better it would have been to recognize frankly that, since there are two communities in Algeria, one is bound to dominate the other unless parity and equality are the rule in all institutions common to both. When, I wonder, will it be understood that an ethnic majority is vastly different from a political majority, and that it is no more possible to give the Moslem community majority representation in Algeria than it is to give a populous country majority representation in an assembly, or in a partnership, of nations? The pathetic thing about it all is that the Moslem politicians have not for an instant been duped by French semantic trickery. They can be counted on to denounce the fraud of any common electoral roll that does not bring them substantial rewards in terms of power.

The European representatives expressed another evident truth when they pointed out in their memorandum that there could be no free elections in Algeria as long as rebel terror kept the Moslem community in the grip of fear. The memorandum was signed by eleven of the fifteen outgoing first-college deputies. The four who did not sign were Pierre Fayet and Mme. Alice Sportisse, Communists; Maurice Rabier, Socialist; and René Mayer, chairman of the European Coal and Steel Community. Jacques Chevallier, still going in circles, added his name to a list that included such archconservatives as General Adolphe Aumeran and François Quilici. All of Algeria's seven first-college senators and seven of its nine first-college Councilors of the French Union signed, along with seven delegates to the Algerian Assembly and A. Isella, mayor of Hamma-

Plaisance near Constantine and president of the Algerian Federation of Mayors.

The curtain had not yet been rung down on the "Sixty-One." However, the remnants of the group now preferred to expand their chests in Paris rather than in Algiers, where F.L.N. gunmen might be wondering why they were still in office. Who, then, should appear at the Hôtel Matignon on February 4 with a group of second-college politicians in tow but Mohammed Salah Bendjelloul himself. The visitors handed Premier Mollet a message which said:

> We learn from the press that you are about to visit Algeria. We believe that on this occasion you will be minded to make a proclamation to the Algerians. We deem it our duty to advise you that your words will strike no responsive chord among the Moslems unless you solemnly declare the recognition of the Algerian national fact.
>
> Not claiming to be authorized interlocutors, but only ordinary informants, we have to remind you of the so-called "motion of the Sixty-One," which faithfully reflects the unanimous opinion of the Moslem populations, wholeheartedly behind the national idea.
>
> We must also caution you against the pretensions of the first-college representatives, who are in no way qualified, and have no right, to speak in the name of the Algerian Moslems.

The gratuitous implication contained in the last paragraph of this motion raised a question that Mr. Bendjelloul did not answer: Who *was* qualified to speak in the name of the Algerian Moslems? By their own admission, Mr. Bendjelloul and his friends were merely informants and givers of advice. This intermediate function being of little use to anyone, the time was obviously at hand when the last of the "Sixty-One" would have either to declare for the rebels outright and atone as best they could for past sins, or else bow out of the picture.

On February 4, about 10,000 war veterans, responding to the call of the *Comité d'Entente* for a silent demonstration of protest and warning, marched in a driving rain from their headquarters at the *Maison du Combattant* to the Algiers war memorial, where a wreath was laid. There was no disorder; there were no shouts; there was no special police detail. In his dispatch, Gaston-Charles Pignault of *Le Monde* pronounced the demonstration a failure because it had not attracted a crowd comparable with that of February 2. He said it had been "merely an episode, luckily peaceful, in the battle of handbills and communiqués waged since the departure of M. Soustelle."

In a radio fireside chat that same Saturday evening, Premier Mollet said that he would confer in Algiers with all the people of consequence he had not been able to see in Paris, and that he would himself welcome General Catroux to the city and install him as Minister Resident. After expressing indignation at the "base attacks" to which General Catroux had been subjected, the Premier continued in these terms:

> The Government will not choose in advance a stock solution to the Algerian problem. It will not allow itself to be bound by theoretical preconceptions. It has, on the other hand, clearly defined its objectives and the limits beyond which it will not go.
>
> Our aim is first to recognize and respect the Algerian personality and the total political equality of all the inhabitants of Algeria. It is also to reinforce at the same time the indissoluble union between Algeria and Metropolitan France. What would become of France without Algeria and of Algeria without France?
>
> The Government asserts that the future permanent status of Algeria will not, in any case, be imposed unilaterally. It must be the result of free discussion with the qualified representatives of the population.
>
> I know that the immense majority of the Moslems of Algeria aspire only to the maintenance of the ties with France. But, for all that, France must insure total equality of rights for those whose equality of duties has never been contested. For all that, she must make the necessary effort to free from the nightmare of unemployment and hunger these Algerian masses of whom it is not sufficiently realized that one-half is less than twenty years old.
>
> A million and a half Europeans, French for the most part, live in Algeria—farmers, workers, employees, doctors, teachers, merchants. It is by them and through them, by their labor and courage, that France is present in Algeria. They can count on the support of the nation. The nation must also be able to count on their sincere help in the building of the fraternal Franco-Moslem community.

M. Mollet's warm reference to the European inhabitants of Algeria, so unusual in the mouth of a Socialist politician, provided eloquent evidence of the "reassessment" to which the Government had been constrained by the turn of events. But M. Mollet and his colleagues had only themselves to blame for part of their predicament. They should have foreseen that the appointment of General Catroux would strike the Europeans in Algeria as a provocation. The appointment was an unbelievable blunder. Even if the Government had intended to scuttle Algeria, its best course would have been to allay suspicions by entrusting the task to some ambitious former empire-builder still longing for the limelight on the stage of history.

In this respect, a leaf could well have been taken from the book of Mendès-France, who had cunningly shipped Marshal Juin aboard his plane before flying to Tunis on July 31, 1954, to liquidate the French protectorate there. But though Mendès was Minister of State in the Mollet Government, no such precaution was taken. And France was treated to the spectacle of leftist politicians trying to make up for their blunder with professions of undying solicitude for people upon whom they had only recently visited every kind of anticolonial curse.

The words had changed, but General Catroux remained. M. Mollet was not, therefore, at the end of his troubles. In Algiers, the *Comité d'Entente* was preparing a chilly—other groups, a violent—reception for the Socialist Premier. In a statement to the press, the *Comité d'Entente* recommended that there be no demonstration of the usual sort. "It is a closed, silent, unnoticing city that the President of the Council of Ministers must find here," the Committee said. "The *Comité d'Entente des Anciens Combattants* earnestly urges the students to observe the same attitude."

41. THE SIXTH OF FEBRUARY

M. Mollet's plane put down at the Maison Blanche airport near Algiers at 2:45 P.M. Before motoring into the city, the Premier told reporters he had come to inquire into the needs and aspirations of all. He said he would speak frankly to those who called on him and would expect frankness in return. He protested his entire good will and his desire to insure security and even-handed justice everywhere. He spoke of his presence in Algiers as an affirmation of the indissoluble bonds linking Algeria to Metropolitan France. He expressed his profound faith in the Franco-Moslem community.

With that he climbed into his official car and, preceded by motorcyclist outriders, headed for the Algiers war memorial, where he planned to lay a wreath. Despite the recommendations of the *Comité d'Entente*, some 18,000 people, including large and vociferous groups of students, had gathered in the immediate vicinity of the memorial. One group was dispersed as men of the army honor guard took up their positions. But there was no way to calm the excited multitude. The police and large contingents of Republican Security Guards, many of them brought over from Metropolitan France for the occasion, struggled to keep the streets clear and the crowd on the sidewalks. Shouts and imprecations filled the air. Some slogans sent General Catroux to the gallows; others demanded the return of Jacques Soustelle.

When the Premier, followed by dignitaries of the highest rank, advanced to place his wreath at the foot of the monument—an army band had just played the *Marseillaise*—stones, ripe vegetables, and pieces of sod came pelting down around him. His suit was flecked with cabbage leaf and tomato pulp. Generals tried frantically to intercept hurled stones while Security Guards, holding their rifles at both ends, threw themselves against the turbulent demonstrators. The thud and explosion of tear grenades heightened the general din. Nevertheless, Guy Mollet, outwardly calm and collected, deposited his wreath, returned to his car, and vanished in the direction of the Palais d'Eté.

The presence of the Mayor of Algiers among the high officials at the monument had had the effect of oil on fire. "Chevallier to the stake!" shouted the students; "Mollet to Paris!" "Soustelle! Soustelle!" The Premier was already out of sight when the police lines broke in a garden facing the monument. A youthful crowd surged forward and trampled upon the Premier's wreath. The police, blowing whistles, scrambled to prevent this profanation, but in vain. A French flag flying from a nearby flagpole was put at half-mast. The crowd, now massed on the steps leading up from the memorial to an esplanade above, sang the *Marseillaise*. Then came shouts of, "To the Palace! To the Palace!" Until sunset, groups of demonstrators roamed the streets of the city, tying up traffic, provoking the Security Guards to futile pursuit, but not otherwise endangering life and property. A check at the end of the day showed that five wounded demonstrators had been taken to hospital. Casualties among the security forces were put at seventeen wounded, none seriously. It is worth noting that not a single anti-Arab slogan or shout had been heard during the day.

In Paris, where reports of the disturbances were on the front pages of all the evening newspapers, General Catroux resolved, this time in earnest, to resign. There was, indeed, little else he could do. For as long as he figured as a protagonist, the Premier's path was sure to be blocked by a solid wall of distrust. It so happened that General Catroux had an appointment to see President René Coty at 4:30 o'clock that afternoon. At a little before 5 P.M., the President informed Premier Mollet by telephone of the General's decision. The resignation was then officially announced in Paris. At 5:30 P.M., Premier Mollet issued the following statement in Algiers:

> As soon as he learned of today's demonstrations, particularly when he realized that his name could become a cause of discord among his former comrades-in-arms, General Catroux asked me to relieve him of his commitment.
>
> Anxious not to increase the trials by which Algeria is already divided, I have accepted this resignation, but I want to pay tribute to the great soldier for this new proof of his abnegation and patriotism.
>
> I shall myself pursue my conversations here as I said I would when I arrived, and I count on all to facilitate my task.

At 7 P.M., M. Mollet, receiving more than 100 newspaper reporters at the Palais d'Eté, said:

> I had anticipated difficult hours. They have been just that. I am a ward of the nation and a war veteran . . . I regret the misunderstanding of my action that I read this afternoon in the eyes of my wartime comrades.

Some correspondents remarked in their dispatches that M. Mollet must have been dreaming if he thought he had recognized fellow veterans among the youthful demonstrators at the war memorial. However, that there was deep misunderstanding and even hostility nobody could deny.

M. Mollet explained:

> I held it to be unthinkable that my first official contact with Algiers should be the occasion for a clash between men who should, on the contrary, unite to face common difficulties. It is in this spirit that I acceded to General Catroux's request . . .

The rest of M. Mollet's press conference was of little moment. He denied that Albert Gazier, Minister of Social Affairs, had been urgently summoned from Paris. The purpose of M. Gazier's visit, he said, was to study Algerian social problems. It was noted, however, that the Premier was now attended by four members of his cabinet, the other three being Max Lejeune, François Tanguy-Prigent, Minister of Veterans' Affairs, and Marcel Champeix, Secretary of State for the Interior in charge of Algerian affairs.

As night fell over the feverish city, the gates of the palace swung shut, the demonstrating students went home for dinner, and the streets resumed their normal aspect. But the agitation was not at an end. A statement issued to the press that evening revealed that representatives of the *Comité d'Entente*, of the Federation of Mayors, and of various patriotic groups, banding together to form an "Algerian Committee of Public Safety," had drawn up a set of demands which Premier Mollet was being asked to meet forthwith. These were that the French Army be adapted to the conditions of combat forced upon it by "cutthroats and highway bandits armed and directed from abroad," that an end be put to the "intolerable" foreign intervention in Algeria, even if this meant recourse to arms, that the Government unequivocally subscribe to the maintenance of French sovereignty in Algeria, and that it repudiate the policy defined by the Premier in his investiture statement, particularly his promise of a common electoral roll. The committee urged the veterans' organizations and all patriots in Metropolitan France to support the cause of French Algeria and appealed to Algerians of all faiths to continue the struggle until they could be sure of living and dying as Frenchmen.

Le Monde reported on its front page the next day that the *Comité d'Entente*, determined to take full advantage of the situation created by the disturbances in Algiers, had "turned itself into an Algerian Committee of Public Safety." The record, however, shows that the *Comité d'Entente* never signed the committee's "protocol of union." Actually, the moving spirit in the venture was a visiting Paris lawyer named Jean-Baptiste Biaggi, president of the *Anciens Commandos de France*, a veterans' organization without any branch or activities in Algeria. The Poujadists, too, had a hand in it. That the Algerian Committee of Public Safety was a mistake, that it was tainted politically, soon became glaringly apparent. The *Comité d'Entente* was the first to walk out on it; and a few days after its birth, the committee was defunct.

The departmental mayors' association, meeting in plenary session at Saint-Eugène in the suburbs of Algiers on February 7, adopted a resolution calling for the restoration of public peace, the execution of persons sentenced to death,* and the rejection of the common electoral

* No rebel or terrorist had yet been executed. The number of those sentenced to death was not made public. However, in August, 1957, it was stated that of 385 persons sentenced to death in Algeria since November 1, 1954 (persons sentenced *in absentia* presumably excluded), sixty-eight had been executed; in addition 150 death sentences had been commuted to hard labor for life.

roll. The mayors also announced–rashly, for they soon had to back down–that they would take no part in discussions with the central authorities until their demands were met by the Government.

The remnants of the "Sixty-One"–although they had never uttered a word of complaint about the rebels, who by then had butchered 944 Moslem and 162 European civilians–raised their voices in indignant condemnation of the "racist demonstrations instigated by local feudalisms." They welcomed M. Mollet's visit, which they hoped would "ring the knell of colonialism." They repudiated the "use of force" (by the French, of course; not by the rebels) and demanded negotiations with the "qualified representatives of the Algerian people without exception" and the adoption of the common electoral roll. The motion of the "Sixty-One" ended with the announcement that the group, having set itself the task of "enlightening the Government and Metropolitan opinion as to the true aspirations of the Moslem populations," now considered its mission accomplished. The motion was conveyed to M. Mollet by Salah Mesbah, Ali Cadi, Aïssa Bensalem, and Boudjema Ould Aoudia. Exeunt the "Sixty-One." (They were, in fact, still to make a few flitting appearances upon the stage, but as mere shadows, virtually unnoticed.)

At a meeting of the Committee of Public Safety on February 8, M. Biaggi proposed a series of measures by which to bludgeon M. Mollet into compliance with the committee's demands. A mass demonstration in Algiers and another in Paris were among his suggestions. But M. Biaggi, going right off the rails, also suggested that the impenitent members of the "Sixty-One" should be harried out of the country with threats of reprisals.

M. Pignault of *Le Monde*, reporting extreme tension among the Moslems, wrote in a dispatch: "And is it not to be feared that the Moslem population of Algiers, whose restraint until now has been remarkable, will rise up against the threat to the 'Sixty-One'?" As though the threat was to be taken seriously. As though the Moslems cared a rap for the "Sixty-One." M. Pignault was forced to report the following day that M. Tanguy-Prigent had gone unescorted to the war memorial and had placed a wreath there without attracting any particular notice. Obviously, no Moslem "Sixth of February" was to be feared.

The readers of *Le Monde* were also asked to believe that M. Mollet had been made to eat humble pie by a turbulent lot of irresponsible youngsters. The events of February 6 certainly gave this impression. But there was a good deal more to the situation than *Le Monde* was willing to admit. The youthful mob had, no doubt, taken the spotlight. The deeper reality was made up of human anguish; of insecurity, uncertainty, and evil days, not only in Algiers, but in towns and villages across the country. This M. Mollet perceived; *Le Monde* did not, or would not.

The Premier's first reaction threw the Parisian *salons* into spasms of rage. To be so near the goal of capitulation and then to be frustrated was almost more than they could bear. François Mauriac, writing in *L'Express,* set the tone:

> What did he [M. Mollet] go to Algiers for? Was he then uninformed? Were not the replies that he would get in Algiers known to him in advance? You could have remained at the Hôtel Matignon, Mr. Prime Minister; an Aumeran or a Borgeaud would have sufficed for your information right here.
>
> . . . . Toward a man who has, to start with, sacrificed Pierre Mendès-France and General Catroux, I no longer feel a personal bond.
>
> . . . . From M. Edgar Faure . . . we could expect a sudden invention, a flash of crafty intelligence. But this magister, motionless in his chair, facing a howling class, and who yields to spitballs, leaves no recourse to hope.

42. ROBERT LACOSTE GETS THE JOB

It was announced on February 9 that Robert Lacoste, Minister of Economic Affairs, having accepted the Algerian portfolio, would take up his new post the following day. A Socialist politician was thus set to rush in where the general had feared to tread. The two men were, indeed, a study in contrasts. M. Lacoste, then fifty-seven years old, had none of Catroux's urbanity, social graces, and subtle intelligence. The prestige of arms, the luster of ambassadorial rank, and the renown of past proconsular achievements—these belonged to the general, not to the pugnacious deputy for Dordogne. M. Lacoste had been a minor civil servant and a labor leader of sorts in his earlier days. He had distinguished himself in the resistance movement during World War II and had emerged afterwards as a tough, ambitious politician. Built like a wine barrel, M. Lacoste was as blunt in manner as he was inelegant in appearance, but he was a tenacious man. And although he was not above a compromise with political expediency, he seemed always to be guided by a sort of rough-and-ready patriotism.

It is not to be wondered at, therefore, that the Minister Resident should soon have become an object of intense aversion in the *salons* of Paris. I remember reading under the signature of one complaining Paris intellectual that it was no more possible to argue with M. Lacoste than with an earthquake. And I must say this unconscious tribute was deserved. For it is true that M. Lacoste consistently and impatiently refused to listen to all the elaborate reasons why France should abandon Algeria.

Meanwhile, in Algiers, M. Mollet was getting filled in on every conceivable point of view. An endless succession of delegations filed into and out of the Palais d'Eté. Teachers, politicians, trade unionists, war veterans, Moslems, and Europeans—all had their say, and to all M. Mollet lent an attentive ear. His desire to appease and to accommodate was evident, but since he could not make everybody happy without a certain amount of ambiguity, misunderstandings were bound to arise. Smaïl Lakhdari, second-college delegate to the Algerian Assembly for Guelma, said M. Mollet had told him that the common electoral roll would result in man-for-man voting and proportional representation for the two communities. According to a delegation of general councilors from the Oran department, however, M. Mollet had stated that the common electoral roll was not incompatible with parity of representation for the two communities. In other words, the most crucial point of all had yet to be clarified.

On the evening of February 9, after three days of consultations, M. Mollet went on the air to sum up. Addressing himself first to the Europeans, he said:

> You have been depicted as colonialists. I do not share this view. There is, no doubt, among you, a small, selfish minority ready to defend its own interests and political positions to the desperate end. . . . There is also the immense mass of the European population. These farmers, these employees, these tradespeople, these teachers, these doctors, these men who have been established in Algeria for several generations and have their families, their homes, and their dead here—since my arrival, I have heard the voice of all of them and I have been greatly moved by it. In their eyes, Algeria is the grandest country in the world; it is their little homeland, that to which they are most attached. They see France only as it is reflected in Algeria.
>
> These men—you who are listening—believed that France was

going to abandon them. I have understood their despair, the profound despair that holds their whole being in its grip. This is why I say to you in all sincerity that, even though for me the experience was painful, the unfortunate demonstration on Monday had a wholesome aspect. It provided many with an opportunity to express their attachment to France and their fear of being abandoned. If that is what the immense majority of the men and women at the war memorial wanted to make known, I assure them that they have been heard. France will remain present in Algeria. The bonds linking Metropolitan France and Algeria are indissoluble. . . .

To the Moslems he said:

You, too, have your extremists. There is among you a handful of madmen and criminals who get their directives from outside Algeria and serve interests that are anything but Algerian. Others, poverty-stricken and therefore susceptible to their propaganda, have allowed themselves to be led astray . . .

I turn to you, the immense mass of the Moslem people, you who know uncertainty, anxiety, suffering. You hesitate, my Moslem friends, because you have doubts about the intentions of France. You may have feared that France would abandon you. I tell you bluntly: this has been and always will be entirely out of the question. The Government will fight, France will fight to stay in Algeria, and will stay here. There is no future for Algeria without France.

. . . . You are anxious? You fear all the extremists? I declare simply: order and justice will be made rigorously to prevail, rapid and serene, the same for all.

I guarantee the Government's unshakable determination to see that you get justice and full equality before the law . . . You aspire to a regime of freedom. This freedom, only republican France can guarantee it.

We will make the Franco-Moslem community a living reality. It will be an original creation. There is an Algerian personality. Nobody can deny this. It will be brought out within the French community.

France will give Algeria the possibility of atomic energy for its industrialization. France will mobilize her strength to make the miracle of the Sahara come true. The development of the Sahara is the great task of our generation.

You suffer, too; I am profoundly conscious of that. I am aware of your immense distress. I am aware of your poverty. But I also know that you suffer more from injustice than from poverty. You suffer because your human dignity has been offended, because you felt you were being treated as second-class citizens. You are

> free men. Only republican France can guarantee you this freedom . . .
>
> I have here with me the Minister of Social Affairs. I have appointed the Minister of Economic Affairs . . . to take charge in Algeria.* Both will immediately concern themselves with your living conditions. . . . The wealth of the southern territories in coal, iron, oil, and natural gas will be developed . . .
>
> Europeans and Moslems, my stay has given me the intimate conviction that the immense majority among you are profoundly attached to the Franco-Moslem community. Refrain from anything that could compromise the trusting relations between you . . .
>
> The Franco-Moslem community will be founded on an equal division among its members of resources, work, and responsibilities. The Franco-Moslem community will grow out of free discussions. The Government intends to hold fair elections as soon as calm has returned. It will study with the freely elected representatives of the whole Algerian people the structure to be given to the indissoluble Franco-Moslem community. . . .
>
> Europeans and Moslems of Algeria, you may have confidence in the grandeur, in the power of France. You must have confidence in the determination of France to insure equality and justice in peace restored.

This speech was significant in that it set a pattern to which the Socialist Premier was to remain faithful to the end of his incumbency. M. Mollet's education had lasted three days. In that time he had learned much, no doubt—a few truths about the European community had, in particular, entered his head—but the real nature of the Algerian problem still escaped him. The lessons learned by M. Soustelle in the hard school of experience were ignored. The process of adjustment to reality had to start all over again, this time against the pull of Socialist doctrine.

No one could fail to be struck, too, by the fact that the Premier had made no reference to French sovereignty in Algeria. He had, it is true, stated that the bonds linking Algeria to France were "indissoluble," but he had not definded their nature. And although he had promised free elections, he had omitted any mention of the body for which the elections would be held. Was he, in fact, offering the Moslems federation in lieu of independence? Perhaps not, but his words suggested that he was toying with the idea.

There was, of course, no response. The rebels still had the initiative and saw no reason to accept a halfway solution.

---

* M. Lacoste was Minister of Economic Affairs in the Mollet Government before becoming Minister Resident in Algeria.

Besides, the dynamics of their movement committed them to intransigence. Theirs was a revolutionary creed; theirs also a collegial command. This made inevitable a constant struggle for power within the rebel ranks, a struggle already deeply stained in blood. Fidelity to revolutionary principles, even in adversity, alone could protect a rebel leader from elimination on charges of betrayal. It was, therefore, idle to suppose that a rebel leader of any consequence would be willing to talk in terms of federation. On the contrary, M. Mollet's speech, with its inacceptable proposals that also were major concessions, was bound to encourage the rebels to persevere, more convinced than ever of ultimate success.

Of course, M. Mollet had actually appealed to the Moslem community as a whole to repudiate the rebels and, having done so, to collect the rewards awaiting them in the Franch camp. He had assumed that the Moslems were free agents. This mistake, by prolonging the conflict, was to be paid for in human lives.

The Committee of Public Safety, meanwhile, was cooking up a new demonstration designed to drive home its demands. A preparatory meeting on February 9 attracted some 2,000 members of participating groups to the *Maison du Combattant*, where many fighting words were heard. Amédée Froger for the mayors, and Louis Calavassy (of the *Association Rhin et Danube*) and Georges-Edouard Roux (of the *Anciens des Commandos d'Afrique*) for the veterans, summoned the Government to accede instantly to the committee's four principal demands—adaptation of the Army to local conditions, action to put an end to foreign intervention in Algeria, maintenance of French sovereignty, and repudiation of the Premier's investiture statement, particularly as it applied to the Algerian electorial system. Then M. Biaggi, the little Napoleon, rose to speak. He vituperated M. Mollet and all but ordered the French fleet to Alexandria.

As a final piece of business, it was decided that the laying of a wreath at the war memorial the following afternoon would be the occasion for a mass demonstration. The Poujadists undertook to see that the shops were closed. The mayors said no business would be transacted at the town halls. The students promised to help direct the crowd. The committee appealed for "calm and dignity."

But there was a hitch. François Collaveri, Prefect of Algiers, had banned all gatherings of more than three persons in public places. Nevertheless, a fluid crowd converged on the war memorial the next afternoon, eddying through the public gardens, swarming over the steps of the central post office, milling in adjacent streets. Republican

Security Guards, brought up in trucks, cleared the post office steps. The iron gates leading to the war memorial were closed and cordoned off.

At 3:25 P.M., the mayors, arrayed in their tricolor sashes of office, assembled in groups of twos and threes, so as not to violate the prefectural ban on gatherings. The crowd had reached about 10,000 when the police line below the war memorial, subjected to increasing pressure, buckled and broke. Flags were held aloft. From the rear echelons pressing forward came the strains of the *Marseillaise*. M. Froger, having reached the iron gates and hoisted himself above the crowd, pleaded for discipline. The crowd responded by singing the *Marseillaise* and shouting, "Open! Open!"

At that point, the police charged. In an instant, the demonstration was thrown into seething confusion. Fists and sticks flew; whistles sounded. In the midst of the melee, M. Froger was seen trying to parley with the police. A few demonstrators managed to climb over the wrought-iron fence and to reach the cenotaph, where they came to attention with their flag. A moment later they were joined by hundreds more, for the gates had burst open. A mayor started to make a speech, but his words were drowned out. The arrival of police reinforcements, however, soon put a new face on the matter. The crowd was broken up and dispersed, not without a few cracked skulls and a score of arrests. It was noticed that the organized veterans had taken no part in the action.

The next day, M. Biaggi appeared to have been cut down to size. He complained to reporters that M. Collaveri, the Prefect, had sent him packing and that he had not even been able to get a request for an appointment through to M. Mollet. Michel Autier, secretary-general of the *Comité d'Entente*, who also was present at the impromptu press conference in the Aletti Hotel that evening, felt compelled to explain that his organization, dedicated solely to the defense of French Algeria, did not wish to be identified with certain political attitudes and extravagant positions. M. Biaggi glowered.

On February 10, as soon as M. Lacoste had got behind his desk at the *Gouvernement Général*, M. Mollet left Algiers. But before returning to Paris he traveled to Bône with Max Lejeune, Secretary of State for the Armed Forces in charge of Algerian affairs, to examine the military situation at closer range. There, after conferring with Major General Jean Noiret, French commander in eastern Algeria, and other top civil and military officials, the Premier spent the night in an army command truck. The next morning, he flew over rebel-infested areas in a helicopter. He said as he enplaned for Paris that he did not think more reinforcements would be needed and that he was sure the Franco-Moslem community would become a "living, fraternal, and indestructible reality."

Subsequent elaborations did little to clarify the obscure aspects of the Government's Algerian policy. The distinction between French sovereignty and "indissoluble ties," the implications of the common electoral roll—these and other essential points remained swathed in ambiguity. The policy of equivocation kept the European community in a state of uneasiness without for an instant improving the Government's bargaining position vis-à-vis the rebels. The only advantage accruing to the Government from its double talk was a tactical one in the arena of domestic politics; it served as a protective smoke screen.

Addressing the National Assembly on February 16, M. Mollet developed his theory of the primacy of the carrot; he said:

> The action of the rebels . . . derives its strength mainly from its political and psychological appeal. . . . The French response will be inadequate as long as it remains purely military. The military themselves have stated: "The Army can contain terrorism. It cannot, by itself, eliminate terrorism if the terrorists are to continue to have the support of a notable fraction of the population."
>
> The Government will, therefore, take all measures necessary to insure order and respect for the law of the Republic, but it will at the same time give the Moslems reasons for hope and will use political and propaganda weapons as well.
>
> To insure the security . . . of the Europeans and Moslems of Algeria is France's primary duty. It does not, however, provide the solution to the Algerian problem. This solution is of an economic, social, and political order. The Government is resolved to make a considerable effort to develop the Algerian economy and to raise the standard of living of the country's population. The battle will be waged against poverty . . .

These words carry us back to M. Soustelle's early days. The Premier assumed, as M. Soustelle had done, that if the Algerian Moslems failed to eject the rebels from their midst, it was because their aspirations had been denied. The logical answer, therefore, was to promise the Moslems a better life. The resulting "psychological shock," it was felt, would help to cut the ground from under the rebels.

To M. Mollet, security was merely a duty of the state, not a desperate human need. He did not appear to realize that when a man's knuckles are clamped in a vise, what he wants is immediate relief. Fear was the primary enemy, but the Premier leveled his spear at hunger, inequality, and political subjugation. Consequently, his "psychological shock" was a dud; his combat was futile.

The Premier again asserted in his speech that the union of Algeria and France was "indissoluble," but that the "Algerian personality" would be recognized and defended. He continued:

> To the Europeans as to Moslems, . . . the Government solemnly announces that the meaning of the Algerian personality will under no circumstances be defined unilaterally. It will emerge from free discussions with the authentic representatives of the population chosen through loyal and supervised elections. We will not pick our interlocutors; they will be elected by universal suffrage.
>
> One of the Government's primary concerns is to hold free elections at the earliest possible moment. The Government will give priority to the election of the deputies to the National Assembly. It will then hold an election for the Algerian Assembly. . . .

Seldom had M. Mollet strayed so far from reality. He was, by implication, asserting that the rebellion would be contained in short order. For otherwise, how could he reasonably expect to get the Moslem voters to the polls in areas where the rebels were strong? In one important respect, however, the speech brought clarification: the first election, when held, would be for the National Assembly.

Armed with the Government's 1956-57 budgetary estimates, M. Lacoste appeared before the Algerian Assembly on February 21. About half the second-college deputies, including fifteen signers of the original motion of the "Sixty-One," were in their seats. The U.D.M.A. delegates, having ostensibly resigned, were absent. Nor was there any trace of René Justrabo, the sole Communist delegate. The Speaker, Abdelkader Saïah, in his welcoming address, urged the delegates to keep politics out of their deliberations.

M. Lacoste, rising to speak, declared that the "supreme law of the Republic" made it incumbent upon him to "insure with all the French of Algeria the safety of the common homeland," to restore law and order, and to protect the lives of all. He dedicated himself to a policy of human emancipation, justice, and reconciliation, pledging in particular to bring more Moslems into government service, to fight want, to initiate land reform, to promote industrialization, and to implement the Maspétiol recommendations. He announced that the French Treasury would contribute upwards of eighty billion francs ($200 million) to the new Algerian budget—thirty-three billion francs ($94 million) more than the previous year. In conclusion, he said:

> To those who strive desperately to oppose the necessary advances, I say that France fights well only for the cause of progress. As for the blinded fanatics, if their fratricidal folly does not cease, they will learn to their sorrow that France strikes all the harder in that she is conscious of being just.

On February 28, Premier Mollet appealed in a radio address for a cease-fire and promised free elections within three months after the end of hostilities. This was M. Mollet's psychological Big Bertha. The Premier's words were printed on handbills and dropped from the air over the wide areas of Algeria. Therefore they deserve our attention. M. Mollet declared:

> France recognizes and respects the Algerian personality. Algeria is and will remain indissolubly linked to France. The final status of Algeria will under no circumstances be determined unilaterally. It will result from free discussion with the elected representatives of the Algerian population. . . .
>
> In accordance with its promise, the Government will immediately initiate the announced measures for economic and social progress and administrative reform. To this end, a bill conferring upon it the necessary special powers will be submitted to the National Assembly tomorrow.
>
> I now turn to the Moslems, to all the Moslems of Algeria. In the name of the Government, I renew and clarify before them a solemn commitment: the guns must be silenced, and elections will then be organized within the three months that follow the cessation of fighting and of acts of violence. Moslems, . . . today you have a way to make your aspirations known and freely to choose your representatives. . . . Are there any among you who, by their refusal to put an end to the fighting, are prepared to assume before the world and before history the tragic responsibility for making the situation irreversible, for preventing your peaceful emancipation, and for destroying Franco-Moslem brotherhood?
>
> France, loyal and generous, offers you justice and equality. If you refuse these, if you permit the gulf to grow wider, if you do not join with us to prevent the continuation of crimes denounced by all religious and civil laws alike, crimes against women, children, and old people, France will be compelled to mobilize all her strength to insure by all means at her command the security of the population. I cannot believe that this appeal, which I make with all my conviction, will go unheeded. . . .

It was noted that the Premier's remarks were addressed to the Moslems rather than to the rebels, nowhere mentioned. He gave the impression that the whole Moslem population was involved in the rebellion. This was to magnify the strength of the rebellion and to do the Moslem population a grave injustice. If there had been truth in M. Mollet's implication, the French would long since have been driven out of Algeria.

Since M. Mollet was, once more, attacking an imaginary enemy, his appeal did not, and could not, have the slightest positive effect. But many commentators held that he had simply not gone far enough. Among the left-wing Socialists, the Radicals of the Mendès school, and the "liberal" Catholics, M. Mollet's concessions to Arab nationalism were judged inadequate to produce the desired "psychological shock." These groups asserted that the forces of nationalism would have to be propitiated. If this meant the subjection of the European community, what of that? Was not France morally committed to the emancipation of peoples?

The failure of M. Mollet's policy, like that of any national policy, could be ascribed as easily to imaginary as to real causes. I often think of the Spanish Armada in connection with socialist efforts in Algeria. The Great Armada, although it was launched against a heretic nation with the Pope's blessing and the prayers of a whole Catholic people, ended in disaster. Had God, then, deserted Spain? If so, why? No doubt, it was felt, because Spain herself must be full of heresy. This sort of reasoning gave new impetus to the Inquisition and led to the expulsion of the Moriscos.

Similarly, in Algeria, the collapse of Socialist hopes did not invalidate Socialist theory in the eyes of its defenders, but served only to prove that it had been betrayed. Thus we see that the demands of a secular doctrine can be almost as implacable as those of a jealous and wrathful god. A restless minority in the French Socialist party—men like Robert Verdier, Daniel Mayer, André Philip, Jean Rous, Charles-André Julien, and Edouard Depreux—kept M. Mollet under constant fire for not leading the Europeans to the sacrifice. For it is true that, according to orthodox doctrine, national emancipation is a necessary stage on the road to socialism. To deny this proposition is to strike at the underpinnings of the whole structure of socialism.

But socialism is not theory alone. It is also an ideal of human betterment. The Algerian crisis has thrown the doctrinaries into conflict with the idealists. To those who insist that socialist theory must be integrally upheld and that Algeria must, therefore, be given its independence, the idealists reply by asserting that the end result must first be examined. The fact that national independence has, particularly in the Arab world, too often led to political dictatorship, economic stagnation, social regression, and a denial of minority rights is cited by the idealists as an argument against automatic independence for a country in which France holds the interests of millions of human beings in trust.

The case for the idealists has been put by J. Riès, who noted in the *Revue Socialiste* that Arab nationalism sets in motion forces opposed to the socialist ideal. Though far from suggesting that French rule in Algeria was even an approximation of that ideal, M. Riès equated the evils of capitalism with those of a political regime which, by producing lower standards of living, set back civilization itself. His conclusion was that a socialist should strive to see that no people be "disposed of" and thereby deprived of its rights to a fuller, better life.

It is to M. Mollet's credit that he put human considerations ahead of doctrine. Nor was his attitude a passive one. He fought gamely, and on the whole successfully, to win the party to his views.

43. THE REBELLION NEARS ITS APOGEE

While Paris and Algiers were fully immersed in politics, the rebellion, unheeding, pursued its bloody course. On February 17, a French farmer named Fernand Cruet, his wife, and their eighteen-year-old adopted daughter were massacred in their home near Saint Pierre-Saint Paul, only thirty miles from Algiers.

A week later, a bus on its way from Bou Saâda to Algiers was stopped near the Deux Bassins pass, thirty-seven miles south of Algiers, by six rebels disguised as Algerian Riflemen. Others were hiding in thickets beside the road. The passengers, all Moslems, were made to get out of the bus, and one of them, Chief Sergeant Abid Laziri Ben Slimane, was butchered on the spot. The driver, a European, ordered to run the bus into a gully, did so; but just as the heavy vehicle was about to go over the shoulder of the road, he jumped out and got away under heavy submachine-gun fire.

The driver of the next car to come along, Robert Salle of El Biar (a suburb of Algiers), saw the bus in the gully and, thinking there had been an accident, came to a stop. In an instant, the rebels had surrounded the car and compelled its occupants—M. and Mme. Salle, their seven-year-old daughter, Mme. Salle's mother, and a visiting friend from Paris (a M. Charfois)—to stand in the road. First the two men were murdered, then Mme. Salle and her daughter. Mme. Salle's mother, though grievously wounded, survived. The Salle family and their visiting friend had spent the day sight-seeing in Bou Saâda.

The third car to fall into the rebel trap was driven by José Ritter, an Algiers architect. He, too, was murdered then and there. Presently, still another vehicle appeared, a pickup belonging to an electrical firm. George Conte of Blida was at the wheel; four Moslem employees were in the back. M. Conte, who had assumed the rebels to be soldiers, was showing his license when he was pulled from the cab of the pickup, told to walk away, and brought down with a blast of submachine-gun fire in the back. One of the employees blurted out, "But he was our boss." "So, he was your boss!" replied a rebel. The employee was then shot at point-blank range and killed with a bullet in the back of his neck.

M. Ritter's funeral in El Biar on February 26 degenerated into a political demonstration, during which the crowd set upon two British television cameramen who had been mistaken for Americans. The unfortunate cameramen had to be extricated by the police. Later the crowd swarmed through the streets shouting "Mollet to the stake!" "Death to Mendès!" and "Chevallier resign!" Simultaneously, at Blida, a crowd, having attended M. Conte's funeral, marched in the center of town shouting slogans hostile to Premier Mollet and singing the *Marseillaise*.

The fourth section of the second company of the Forty-sixth Battalion of Algerian Rifles, assigned to the protection of the Oran-Oujda railway, had just pitched camp near the Tralimet bridge west of Tlemcen. On February 9, shortly before midnight, a sentinel, hearing a muffled voice say, "They have put up barbed wire," barked, "Who goes there?" No answer. The sentinel fired a shot and got a volley in return. The men of the section, rushing out of their tents, came under the withering automatic fire, not of the rebels, but of one of their number, Chief Corporal Abdelkader Soudani. Of the section's seventeen men, six, including four Europeans, were wounded by the treacherous corporal, who, when his clip was empty, rushed out of the camp with three accomplices and joined the attackers. The French second lieutenant commanding the section found that his radio had been put out of commission and that his submachine gun had been stuffed with dirt. Meanwhile, however, a man had got to a railway gatekeeper's telephone and alerted the colonel commanding at Marnia. The arrival of armored cars put the rebels to flight; they withdrew into Moroccan territory taking with them Corporal Soudani and his booty—three army rifles, a submachine gun, and ammunition.

But the affair at the Tralimet bridge was a mere curtain raiser. In the early hours of February 20, a company of the Fiftieth Battalion of Algerian Rifles (reservists) came under rebel attack at Sebabna, site of an iron mine on the Moroccan frontier near Port Say. Second Lieutenant Fournier of Oran, the acting company commander, had just ordered his men to their guns when the sudden defection of fifty-five Moslem soldiers led by Chief Corporal Abdelkrim, a veteran of the Indochinese fighting, brought disaster. The first soldiers out of the billet were mowed down by their fellows-in-arms. Lieutenant Fournier perished with ten of his men; twenty were wounded.

At Abdelkrim's command, the mutineers cleaned out the company's arms rack before leaving the camp. The rebels, about 200 of them, all in military-type uniform, were waiting outside with donkeys and mules, ready to carry the booty away. The haul was substantial—113 weapons, including four automatic rifles and eight Sten guns. Thirty Moslem riflemen had remained loyal under fire. Sergeant Tahar, seriously wounded in the action, was awarded the *médaille militaire* for bravery.

Psychologically, the French cause had been badly hurt. The fear of betrayal now stalked every native unit, casting its pall over European and Moslem alike.

On February 24, Oran buried its fallen sons—Lieutenant Fournier, Sergeant Picard, Chief Corporal Hernandez, and Corporal Sebban, names that in themselves reflected the ethnic composition of that fascinating city, part French, part Spanish, and part Jewish. A funeral service for the first three was conducted at the Cathedral while, at the Jewish cemetery, Corporal Sebban was buried according to the rites of his faith. When the religious ceremonies were over, a crowd of several thousand fell in behind the banners of the veterans' associations, sang the *Marseillaise* and shouted slogans hostile to the Government. Of the victims of the Sebabna tragedy, most were from the region of Mostaganem. The savage reality of the rebellion had come home to western Algeria as never before.

In eastern Algeria, however, the French could point to at least one success. On the morning of February 14, the leading party of a column composed largely of Foreign Legionnaires ran into rebel fire near Taberdga in the Nememchas. By holding the assailants at bay despite losses, the leading party enabled the bulk of the column to fan out and close in on the rebel band, estimated to number about 200. Forty-two rebels perished; two were caught. The rest managed to break contact under the cover of night. The encounter was, in fact, something of a revelation to the French. The rebels had put up a stiff fight, making good use of difficult terrain. All were in "uniform"; all wore green forage caps adorned with a red crescent. Their arms included Thompson submachine guns and Garand rifles.

The situation in Kabylia at the end of February was hardly less discouraging than in the worst parts of Oranie and of the Constantinois. At Tazmalt, between Maillot and Akbou, for instance, the assassination of the Moslem assistant secretary to the mayor brought to twenty-one the number of terrorist attacks perpetrated in that village since the beginning of the rebellion and eliminated the community's last Moslem still on the public payroll.

The mayor of Haussonvillers, west of Tizi Ouzou, was mortally wounded by a terrorist one day at noon in the center of his village. The administrative township of the Soummam, between Akbou and El Kseur, reported eleven assassinations, twenty-one acts of sabotage, and the destruction of two schools in the first two weeks of February. In sixteen months, that township had lost four *caïds*, five rural constables, one president of a municipal center (Kabyle village), two *djemaa* presidents, one *djemaa* member, and two city councilors, all killed by the rebels.

In February, a total of 176 Moslem civilians, including three *caïds*, were massacred, forty-nine of them in Greater Kabylia.

In February, 1956, the rebellion was near its zenith, not in point of numerical strength but in terms of efficacy. The Algerian Affairs Officers were, in many places, finding it difficult, if not impossible, to throw their operation into gear. The rebels, meanwhile, were more or less successfully consolidating their parallel administration—essentially concerned with "tax" collecting and *shikaiya* (the arbitration of private disputes). Loyal Moslems flocked in increasing numbers to the cities and even to Metropolitan France, while the "political vacuum" was enlarged by a new spate of resignations among the elected Moslem representatives. Desertions from native units of the French Army soared.

In the first two weeks of March, 178 regulars deserted. The number included eighty-five men of the Third Algerian Rifles, who disappeared on March 7 with 160 rifles and side arms, seven automatic rifles, four bazookas, and three mortars. In that case, however, Colonel Bigeard's paratroopers (the Third Colonial Parachute Regiment), in quick retaliation, killed 110 rebels, among them sixty deserters, and recovered most of the lost weapons.

At Nedroma in the Oran department, six native auxiliaries attached to the township were arrested for plotting with the rebels to kill the civil administrator. At Sebdou, south of Tlemcen, the betrayal of a native watchmen enabled the rebels to pillage and burn the offices of the township and to make off with two motor vehicles, twenty-three rifles, and the official files. The S.A.S. (seat of a pacification center) at Sidi Djilali in the Sebdou district was taken and burned under the noses of fifty native auxiliaries.

Improved rebel fighting techniques were reflected in the defense of a well-constructed fort near Thiers in the Palestro district in western Kabylia. To reduce the fort, held by eight rebels, the French had to subject it to the fire of 75-millimeter, no-recoil guns.

According to M. Isella, president of the Algerian Federation of Mayors, 217 farms had been burned in the Constantinois alone by the end of January, 1956, for an estimated loss of $4,500,000. It was reported that 1,555 Europeans other than farmers had given up their livelihoods in the rural parts of the Constantinois, 384 of them seeking refuge in the cities, the rest crossing over to Metropolitan France. The number of fruit trees cut down by the rebels was thought to exceed 45,000 in the Constantinois and 12,000 elsewhere. Sixty-five thousand vine plants had been destroyed in the Algiers department. In some places, the rebels had machine-gunned whole herds of cattle and flocks of sheep.

In the region of Souk Ahras, autumn tilling on farms owned by Europeans had been only 30 per cent of normal. A report issued by the economic section of the Government General said that in Guelma and Souk Ahras the entire patrimony of the European inhabitants was for sale but that there were no takers. Property transactions in the city of Bône were being completed at as little as 50 per cent of the 1954 assessments. With rebel bands roaming almost at will through the cork forests that cover the hills between Philippeville and Collo, the cork harvest was to decline sharply in 1956. Already huge stocks had been burned, forcing the cork stopper plant at Collo to close down. The timber industry, too, had suffered severe losses. The two largest saw mills in the Constantine Department had been burned.

Nevertheless, the Algerian economy as a whole continued to progress. Industrial production in 1956 was slightly below the 1955 level, but was still ahead of 1954. In agriculture, the value of the 1956 cereal crops topped the 1955 figure by 26 per cent. Wine production was up 29 per cent; citrus fruits, up 14 per cent. In other words, for all their wanton destruction, the rebels were finding that Algeria died hard.

Rebel striking power was, however, greater than ever. A French intelligence report in March, 1956, gave the following estimates of rebel strength in men and arms:

Regions	*Regulars* (*Moujahidine*)	*Auxiliaries* (*Mousebbelline*)	*Totals*
Oranie	1,250	3,000	4,250
Greater and Lesser Kabylia and the Mitidja Plain	2,000	6,000	8,000
North Constantinois	1,700	5,000	6,700
East Constantinois	1,300	4,000	5,300
South Constantinois	1,800	3,000	4,800
Totals	8,050	21,000	29,050
Armament:	Machine guns	4	
	Machine rifles	72	
	Machine pistols	530	
	Army rifles	3,200	
	Hunting rifles	18,000	

In the psychological sphere, too, the rebel effort was varied and sustained. A sort of "index" established in March, 1956, made it a sin against the national cause for Moslems to read French periodicals other than *Le Monde*, *France-Observateur*, and the Catholic monthly *Esprit*.

In an early attempt to get the Moslem children out of the public schools, the rebels spread the rumor that the milk distributed to the children was poisoned and that the compulsory vaccinations were lethal.

Many panic-striken Moslem mothers withdrew their children, but after a few days attendance figures were back to normal. The ban on the use of tobacco continued to be enforced wherever possible. In addition, the rebels sought to prohibit the more popular forms of entertainment. There was to be no music, no theatre, no sporting contests. The Arabic theatrical season, scheduled to open at the Algiers Opera House on March 16, had to be canceled for want of spectators. At Canrobert in the Constantine department and in various parts of the Oran department, Moslem women were warned that reprisals would be taken against those who continued to work as servants in European homes. In the Soummam Valley, Moslems employed as farm hands by the *colons* were ordered to stay at home.

Yet, despite their threats and their bloody sanctions, the rebels were unable to deprive the Europeans of the native labor without which European farms and enterprises could not function. The sufferings and sacrifices demanded by the rebels of their coreligionists were too great to be accepted *en bloc* by any but a small minority. In fact, thousands of European farms, lands, and buildings, many of them highly vulnerable, continued to be entrusted to the care of Moslem overseers. If the rebellion had been a truly popular movement, the countryside could have been quickly and easily divested of its European component. And, confined to the coastal cities, French Algeria could not long endure. The European community, attacked by Moslems, was also, to a significant extent, protected by Moslems. The resulting debt of gratitude is one that cannot be forgotten.

Although there is, properly speaking, no Sabbath in Islam—Friday is merely the day of public prayer—the merchants in Sidi Bel Abbès and other towns in the Oran department yielded to a rebel injunction to close their shops on Fridays. Moreover, the wearing of the *chechia* (a brimless cap made of knitted wool dyed red) was prescribed by the rebels to replace the more popular beret. These and other such devices, contrived as a way of accentuating the separate identity of the Moslems, were the work of the psychological services of the rebellion.

Pierre Lambert, the Socialist Prefect of Oran, taking the view that distinctive headgear was no more to be tolerated than the arm bands of certain semi-fascist European organizations, winked at the *chechia* but drew the line when some ardent citizens of Tlemcen donned colored felt fore-and-afters of a type imported from Iraq and made popular by the Sultan of Morocco. He also put his foot down in the matter of Friday closings. Since these were obviously a political demonstration rather than the observance of a religious obligation, he made it clear that any merchant caught with his shop closed on a Friday would be subject to summary rustication. The merchants, many of them happy to have an excuse for defying the rebel injunction, hastened to comply with the Prefect's ruling.

44. NEW POWERS AND REFORMS

The Special Powers Act, adopted on March 12 by a vote of 455 (including the Communists) to 76 in the National Assembly and by 294 to 7 in the Council of the Republic three days later, defined the areas within which the Government could carry its Algerian policies into effect by decree.

The Government was given a free hand, notably in matters pertaining to economic expansion, land reform, agricultural credit, recruiting for public service, wages and working conditions, industrialization, Saharan development, territorial reorganization, and administrative reform. Decrees issued by the Government in pursuance of the Act were to be immediately applicable; if at variance with existing legislation, they would have to be ratified by the Parliament within a year. In addition, the Act authorized the Government to make special appropriations by decree after consulting the finance committees of the two houses of Parliament, such decrees also being subject to parliamentary approval within a year. All laws and decrees in force in Metropolitan France could, under the Act, be made applicable in Algeria, in modified form if necessary, by decision of the cabinet.

As regards public order, the security of persons and property, and the protection of the integrity of the territory, the Government was given almost unlimited latitude to take whatever exceptional measures the circumstances might warrant.

All these special powers were vested in the existing Government only and would lapse with the end of the Government's incumbency, unless its successor requested an extension of the Act within ten days of its initial vote of confidence.

The first decrees issued under the Act had the effect of perpetuating the "state of emergency." Terrorist crimes continued to be within the jurisdiction of the military courts, and night searches were again authorized. Terrorists carrying arms or wearing clothes of military appearance could, if caught in the act of a crime against persons or property, be committed for immediate trial without prior indictment by an examining magistrate. The death sentence was prescribed for soldiers deserting with their arms. The Minister Resident was given authority to regulate the movements of persons and the transport of goods, assign places of residence, create forbidden zones, ban meetings, control the press,* dissolve associations, order searches, collect reparation for willful damage or for aid given to the rebels, suspend or transfer civil servants, deprive elected representatives of their seats, postpone by-elections, and delegate certain civil powers to the military. Travel between Algeria and Metropolitan France was made subject to strict controls.

Several of the reforms drafted under the direction of M. Lacoste were promulgated by decree in the latter part of March, 1956. One of these modified the civil service regulations so as to reserve half of all future openings to Moslem candidates during a period to end on December 31, 1960. It also permitted the recruitment of Moslem candidates on contract outside the process of competitive civil service examinations. It further provided that the age limits applicable to candidates for Government positions would in every case be extended five years for Moslems.

The constitutionality of this measure was, and has since been, seriously questioned, since it violated the principle of the equality of all French citizens before the law. Besides, it was an invitation to the F.L.N. to plant its agents in strategic administrative posts and so to strengthen its "fifth column." That more Moslems should have been brought into the civil service in the past cannot be doubted. But the attempt to improvise a remedy without due regard to the equal rights of citizenship and to the realities of the emergency must be put down as unjust and unwise.

A fund known as the *Caisse d'accession à la propriété rurale* was set up to finance the acquisition, by agreement or expropriation, of arable land for distribution to Moslem small-holders. At long last, it was announced, the much-talked-about land reform was about to get under way. The decree governing the operations of the new fund stipulated that large, company-owned estates formerly ceded by the Government, and parts of smaller, individually-owned holdings irrigated at public

* It is only fair to say that this power was not abused and to commend M. Lacoste's press chief, Michel Gorlin, for his consistently liberal information policies.

expense, were to be divided and that the land thus acquired would be made available to Moslem beneficiaries on easy terms. It was anticipated that 10,000 families would be settled on 150,000 hectares (370,000 acres) in the initial phases of the reform. But the plan proved almost unworkable in practice. It quickly became apparent that any Moslem *fellah* (peasant) settling on divided land was automatically marked out for the attention of the F.L.N. killers.

The first sixteen lots covering an area of 618 acres near Saint-Lucien in the Oran department were to be distributed by Pierre Lambert, the Prefect, on July 23, 1956, but the ceremony was called off because of "insecurity." French troops were in fact operating at the time against rebel bands in the nearby Tessala mountains. A dispatch to *Le Monde* said: "It is also possible that the Administration may have feared that reprisals might be taken against the Moslems to whom the land would have been parceled out."

The fear was amply justified. On May 19, 1957, when 113 lots were about to be distributed near Aïn M'Lila in the Constantine department, two of the prospective recipients were butchered by the rebels. The result was a general defection of all the *fellahin* who were to have got the land. Commenting on the incident, Jacques Soustelle put these words in the mouths of their rebel "protectors": "So, you want to escape poverty and hunger! You want your families to live better! Death to you!" The wretched *fellahin* did the only thing they could do. They returned to their rock-strewn hills and the squalor of their mud huts.

On May 30, several *douars* near Wagram in the Oran department were raided by rebels in search of *fellahin* guilty of accepting divided land. Thirty-five were massacred; several were wounded.

It must be noted, too, that many European landowners looked upon expropriation more as a promise than as a threat. They were eager to let the Government buy land they could not otherwise sell and to invest the proceeds elsewhere. A later decree specified that undeveloped holdings of any size were, if located in irrigated areas, subject to expropriation. As far as I could tell, this decree was wholly inoperative. Any number of irrigated farms, wholly abandoned by their European owners, are still begging for expropriation.

Other reform decrees, however, fared better. Credit terms for Moslem farmers were improved, wages for farm hands were raised, and the *khammessat*—one-fifth, four-fifths sharecropping—was abolished. In the future, all sharecropping was to be on a fifty-fifty basis. This measure did not affect the European landowners, who had always applied the fifty-fifty rule in their sharecropping agreements, but it did change the picture as far as Moslem landowners were concerned. From time immemorial, the sharecropper on Arab land had been forced, under the *khammessat* system, to relinquish four-fifths of his produce to the owner.

On April 11, 1956, the Algerian Assembly was dissolved by decree and its prerogatives were vested temporarily in the Governor General. As new elections were out of the question, Algeria, having already lost its representation in the National Assembly, now became for all practical purposes an administrative territory. The right of citizens to have a voice in the conduct of their own affairs had been summarily suspended by the Socialist Government. However, there was no very audible indignation in France. I count this a sad commentary on the vitality of the democratic reflex of the French nation.

The Algerian Assembly had not been a perfect institution by any means. Its very existence had been hard to reconcile with the political unity of the Republic. But that body had provided a channel through which legitimate opinion could be made to influence public policy. If, in dissolving the Algerian Assembly, the Socialist Government had intended to replace it with a type of representation that did not carry within it the seeds of autonomy, the measure could have been presented as a step in the direction of integration and hence of greater interracial equality. But such was not the case. Indeed, the Socialist party congress held at Lille in June, 1956, came out for wholly autonomous legislative *and executive* institutions in Algeria. Therefore, the dissolution of the Algerian Assembly was all loss and no gain. It was disheartening, too, to see the loyalty and courage of some Moslem delegates requited with the loss of their seats, in other words, with something closely resembling a disavowal.

In June, 1956, eight new Algerian departments were decreed, along with six new *arrondissements*. Algeria was thus to have, in all, twelve departments divided into a total of thirty-seven *arrondissements*. Three "super prefects" officially known as Inspectors General of the Administration on Extraordinary Mission (Igames)—one in Algiers, one in Oran, and one in Constantine—were given jurisdiction over areas corresponding roughly to the three original departments.

These measures, soon carried into effect, were almost universally applauded. They helped fill out a skeletal administration, and, by following the normal French administrative pattern, threw no new obstacles in the way of integration.

Unfortunately, the same cannot be said of the *loi-cadre*, or framework law, adopted in its final form by the French Parliament on January 31, 1958. The *loi-cadre* provided for the establishment of several autonomous territories each with its own government responsible to an elected territorial assembly under the sovereignty of France. The first decrees of application, issued on March 5, 1958, divided Algeria into five self-governing territories—Oran, Chélif, Algiers, Kabylia, and Constantine—and raised the number of departments from twelve to fifteen. The common electoral roll was instituted under a separate law, adopted on January 28, 1958. However, the *loi-cadre* also called for the creation of a consultative council of communities in each territory. The hope was that by giving parity of representation in these councils to citizens of civil and Koranic personal status, the *loi-cadre* would provide the European minority with a measure of protection.

The *loi-cadre* stipulated further that, two years after its election, each territorial assembly could vote to transfer some of its power to federal institutions at the center. If this happened, a federal council, composed of delegates elected in equal number by each of the territorial assemblies, would be expected to carry out the decisions of a federal assembly, itself made up of two sections, the one elected by the territorial assemblies and the other by the councils of communities. In the event of disagreement between the territorial assembly and the council of communities in any of the territories, the Minister for Algeria could either promulgate the decision of the assembly or refer the matter to the arbitration of the French Council of State. The same arbitrational procedure was to be used in case of disagreement between the two sections of the federal assembly.

The authors of the *loi-cadre* apparently felt that by Balkanizing Algeria, the country could be made proof against galloping independence. *Divide et impera.* Another widely held belief was that, even if independence did become inevitable, the *loi-cadre* would lay the groundwork for institutions under which the European community could continue to live without fear for its acquired rights. The weakness of this type of reasoning lay in the assumption that institutions bearing the French trademark—particularly their interracial features—would automatically commend themselves to the future Moslem rulers of Algeria, a highly unlikely prospect.

But, in 1956, official French thinking had not progressed that far. The problems of local government were still receiving primary attention.

One of the June, 1956, decrees abolished the *communes mixtes*, or administrative townships. The territory covered by the seventy-eight *communes mixtes* and also by the tiny municipal centers in Kabylia was to be divided into new, self-governing townships. Proportional representation and the common electoral roll were to be introduced in the new townships as soon as security conditions permitted. As a result of the change, the civil administrators were to become "prefectural delegates" with greatly reduced powers. The *caïds*, it seemed, were fated to disappear altogether. Some observers suspected that the Government might later regret its highhanded treatment of this body of men.

The corps of *caïds* had lost twenty-seven dead, four missing and presumed dead, and nineteen wounded since the beginning of the rebellion. The conduct of the *caïds* in the face of constant peril had often been beyond praise. One of them, Caïd Hamiche, at the head of sixty partisans, had held out for two days near Bougie against 200 attacking rebels before relief could be got to him. Nevertheless, all the *caïds* were to get the axe.

The *caïds*' reaction to the news of their impending dismissal was understandably bitter. One immensely influential *caïd* was heard to remark grimly: "Since France rejects us, she had better not count on us any longer." Another Moslem dignitary made this comment to a French official: "If certain *caïds* are undeserving, they are not the only ones of whom the same may be said. Take individual sanctions by all means, but do not throw opprobrium upon the corps as a whole. The *caïds* now expect to encounter the fate that overtook the pro-French leaders you abandoned in Morocco.* Such measures inevitably redound to the advantage of the rebels."

One of the most unpopular—and therefore courageous—measures taken by the Mollet Government was the massive call-up of young reservists (called *disponibles*, or "availables") for service in Algeria. Under a decree issued on April 13, 1956, Defense Minister Maurice Bourges-Maunoury was able to send about 140,000 fresh troops across the Mediterranean that spring and during the early part of the following summer. The first to go were 65,000 twenty-four-year-olds of the mobilization class of the third quarter of 1952 and 5,000 men of the classes of the fourth quarter of 1952 and of the first quarter of 1953 who had not been taken under the call-up of August, 1955. These were followed by 70,000 men of the class of the second quarter of 1952. Since some 20,000 men were posted to Algeria directly from units and services in Metropolitan France, the total reinforcements available to General Lorillot,

* On November 19, 1955, three days after the Sultan's return from exile, the *khalifa* (lieutenant) of the Pasha of Fez and two lesser notables were massacred by a mob on the grounds of the Imperial Palace in Rabat. Six other Moroccan officials, including three *caïds*, were seriously wounded. In March, 1956, Si Mokhtar, the former Pasha of Meknès, and several *caïds* who, under the French, had exercised authority in the regions of Fez and Meknès, were interned by the new regime.

supreme commander in Algeria, were in the neighborhood of 160,000 men. In addition, approximately 6,000 reserve officers (of a total of 119,400) and several thousand non-commissioned officers of the Army, Navy, and Air Force were recalled to active duty, most of them for service in Algeria.

The young reservists were given accelerated infantry training without regard to their previous military specialties. If this came as a jolt to those who, as national servicemen, had served in the mechanized cavalry and in other specialized branches of the Army, it was perhaps even harder on the Air Force reservists. The latter were for the most part organized into Air Infantry companies whose performance in combat was not always to prove as effective as might have been hoped. (In April, 1956, the Air Force had 55,000 men and 750 aircraft in Algeria.) The pay and allowances received by privates called up for service in Algeria averaged 10,080 francs ($28.80) a month if unmarried; 31,230 francs ($89.20) a month if married, without children. For unmarried sergeants, the pay and allowances averaged 52,620 francs ($150.35) a month; for married sergeants without children, they averaged 68,940 francs ($197) a month.

The Twentieth Infantry Division may be cited as typical of the new divisions formed almost entirely of young reservists. Brigadier General Robert Simon, chosen in May to command the Twentieth Division, then in the process of formation in western France, had to be summoned from Algeria, where he was serving as deputy commander of the Second Mechanized Division in eastern Constantinois. On May 25, General Simon was conducting an operation in the hills north of Tebessa; a radio message, received by the General aboard his helicopter, instructed him to report to Paris as soon as possible. He was in Paris on May 29 and in Rennes the following day. After a quick tour of the camps into which the 8,500 men of his division had poured—they came from Brittany, Normandy, Poitou, and Vendée—he returned to Algiers to be on hand for the arrival of the first units on June 7. These, landing from three troop transports, included two infantry regiments, an artillery group, a light tank regiment, an engineer battalion, and a signal company. A few days later, the Twentieth Division was deployed across Kabylia from Palestro to Les Portes de Fer.

In March, 1956, the French forces in Algeria had numbered about 200,000 regulars. By July, more than 120,000 reservists had already crossed the Mediterranean. The total effectives of the Army, Navy, and Air Force in Algeria were 364,000 at the end of July and 402,000 at the end of August. It was reported at that time that the French forces in Morocco numbered roughly 100,000 while those in Tunisia numbered 43,000. More than half of France's military might was concentrated in the three North African countries.

When the first reservists were called up under the decree of April 13, it was understood—but not officially stated—that their tour of duty would last six months. In September, 1956, the Cabinet decided to demobilize the reservists progressively along with the national servicemen of the class of 1954 who had been kept in uniform beyond the normal tour of eighteen months. Together, the two groups accounted for almost 200,000 men. By the end of November, more than 80,000 reservists had returned to their homes; by the end of December, virtually all were back. Theoretically, their places were taken by national servicemen, but, in fact, the *quadrillage*, or security network, in Algeria slackened perceptibly for want of men. On the other hand, the morale and performance of the national servicemen were on the whole better than those of the reservists had been. Few of the national servicemen were married; all knew military service to be an inescapable duty. Many of the reservists had been too unhappy about being snatched from their jobs and homes to give a really good account of themselves in Algeria.

Max Lejeune, Secretary of State for the Armed Forces in charge of Algerian Affairs, asserted in February, 1957, that the Army had 340,000 men in Algeria and that this number was sufficient "provided they are well employed." Actually, the effectives maintained in Algeria represented a continuing compromise between the needs of the French command and the willingness of the nation to supply them. There were about 1,000 *douars* (native villages) in Algeria, comprising an average of perhaps ten *mechtas* (hamlets) each. For the *quadrillage* to be complete, a section would have had to be quartered in each *mechta.* Ideally, therefore, the *quadrillage* alone should have been able to get 400,000 men. Yet the most perfect *quadrillage,* being static, could be of little offensive value. At least 50,000 mobile troops were needed if the Army was to be successful in its mission of pursuing and destroying the rebel bands. In addition, the protection of roads, railways, bridges, tunnels, dams, water supply systems, power plants, and other public facilities—six or seven thousand vulnerable points in all—could hardly be insured by less than 70,000 men. The total effectives needed by the Army were thus about 520,000 men, not counting the services. The available manpower was, and remains, unequal to the job to be done. The result was, and is, insecurity. The inhabitants of countless hamlets across the country would have been glad to be rid of rebel exactions. To French officers, they repeated endlessly, but often to no avail, the same complaint: "You are here today and gone tomorrow, but we remain. If we cooperate with you today, tomorrow our throats will be slit." And that was the precise truth of the matter.

45. REBEL SANCTUARY IN TUNISIA AND MOROCCO

"It is impossible to avoid the conclusion that France made a major military—and perhaps political—mistake by granting independence to Morocco and Tunisia if she was not going to grant it to Algeria."

HANSON W. BALDWIN

On March 29, Messali Hadj was transferred from Angoulême to Belle-Ile-en-Mer, a charming little island in the Bay of Biscay, where Sarah Bernhardt once had a home.

But two other dates in March, 1956, are more likely to be remembered. On March 2, the independence of Morocco was proclaimed in Paris. That of Tunisia was proclaimed on March 20. These developments were destined to have far-reaching effect on the subsequent course of events in Algeria. For almost immediately, casting aside any semblance of neutrality, the two former protectorates involved themselves in the Algerian rebellion. There can, I think, be little doubt that, but for the aid and protection afforded it by Tunisia and Morocco, the rebellion would have been circumscribed and perhaps crushed before the end of 1957. But, as the United States learned in Korea, it is singularly difficult to destroy an enemy enjoying the sanctuary of an inviolable frontier.

In November, 1957, Christian Pineau, the French Foreign Minister, told the political committee of the United Nations General Assembly that the F.L.N. was so firmly entrenched in the Moroccan province of

Oujda that it levied its own taxes and operated recruiting centers and training camps. He said that from their Moroccan bases the rebels had been able to "carry out incursions into western Algeria with relative impunity." Any number of independent press reports bore him out.

M. Pineau described the situation in Tunisia as "even more serious." He said Algerian rebels had "occupied" part of that country, establishing military headquarters in the heart of the capital city, setting up logistic bases at Souk el Arba, Tadjerouine, and Tozeur, training camps at Teboursouk, Aïn Draham, and Thelepte. "From these centers," M. Pineau continued, "the [rebel] commandos infiltrate Algeria and there regroup to carry out their surprise attacks. No sooner do they feel threatened than they scurry back to the safety of Tunisian soil."

The establishment of rebel strong points on Tunisian and Moroccan soil made it easy for some newspaper correspondents to write sensational reports from "behind the rebel lines." Photographers and television cameramen, too, have given the public what has purported to be an uncensored look at the Algerian underground. It is questionable, however, whether any of these scenes of rebel life were actually photographed or filmed inside the French defenses of Algeria. The evidence suggests that, on the contrary, the work was done either in Tunisia and Morocco, or else within the shadow of a protecting frontier.

The experience of the first two years of Moroccan and Tunisian independence has not been kind to those who held that essential French positions in North Africa could be safeguarded only if the terms of the nationalists were accepted without reservation. We have seen what happened to the notion of "interdependence" as soon as it was subjected to the test of reality. Today that word, which sounded so convincing in the mouth of General Catroux, has become a bitter joke.

Independence would have had manifest merit if it had stabilized France's relations with her former protectorates or if it had promoted the well-being of their inhabitants. Neither has occurred.

The flight of private capital quickly assumed panic proportions. It was estimated that about 50 billion francs ($142,800,000) had left Morocco by the end of 1956; 488 companies had been dissolved. In the first nine months of that year, Moroccan bank deposits dropped 28 per cent. In Tunisia, bank deposits dropped 17 per cent and savings deposits dropped 50 per cent.*

---

* By contrast, Algeria, with bank deposits up 6 per cent and savings deposits up 14 per cent in the same nine-month period, was beginning to look like an island of prosperity in a sea of want. Much of this prosperity was, no doubt, artificially induced. Nevertheless, the Algerian economy showed unmistakable signs of continued vitality.

A document appended to this work will give the reader a glimpse of the conditions prevailing in the *médinas* (native sections) of Casablanca in the spring of 1957. For the first time, in Morocco, we hear of death caused by "physiological want" (starvation).

However, human suffering, unlike outraged ambition, is soft-spoken. The complaints of the sick and hungry, muted by the walls of squalid dwellings, attract little notice. But let an Arab nationalist be thwarted in his quest for power, and his indignant outcries will echo in the corridors of the United Nations and around the world. Impassioned orators will exalt the rights of peoples and the divinity of self-determination.

I do not for an instant deny the mystic pull of Arab nationalism. But I doubt that its protagonists have proved themselves the friends of freedom. As Paul Rivet, the French ethnologist, has put it, "A human being who cannot eat his fill, a human being who cannot read a newspaper, is not free." When nationalism succeeds in a backward country, it seldom relieves either economic or cultural indigence, and the result is dictatorship and minority rule. Yet, with the encouragement of the Western world, nationalism seems to be the predominant ideal in the mid-twentieth century.

The stabilization of French relations with Tunisia and Morocco implies the elimination of the remaining vestiges of French positions of power beyond the Mediterranean. A French naval establishment in Tunisia or a French lead mine in the Atlas mountains of Morocco—each is a present or potential source of grief for Paris.

In the Suez Canal Zone, Britain learned how hard it is to maintain an alien garrison in a newly independent country convulsed with nationalist fervor. In Iran, where Britain had no troops, the nationalist storm engulfed an economic position, the Anglo-Iranian Oil Company's refinery and oil fields. The Dutch have experienced the same sort of thing in Indonesia. There, an explosion of anti-Dutch agitation destroyed what was left of the Netherlands establishment and compelled thousands of Dutch nationals to set out for a distant homeland many of them had never seen. On December 8, 1957, Tillman Durdin wrote in a dispatch from Djakarta to *The New York Times:* "Indonesian actions this week represent a closing chapter for Dutch economic and cultural interests in the island chain that was once the Netherlands' rich East Indies colony." It may be presumed that all will be well between The Hague and Djakarta once the Dutch have pulled out of Netherlands New Guinea.

How much must the French lose in North Africa before Paris may rejoice in the knowledge that its relations with Tunis and Rabat have achieved enduring serenity? Although the last French soldier has left Tunisia, the great Bizerte naval-air base remains as an affront to Tunisian sovereignty. When everything French has been blotted from the soil of Morocco, that country's irredentist claim to "historical frontiers" in French West Africa will still keep the cauldron of trouble boiling. And Algeria itself will have to be abandoned before the promised era of good will will dawn.

As to the French settlers in the two former protectorates, they became the victims of a tragic misapprehension. Encouraged by the Republic to sink roots in alien soil under the perpetual protection of the French flag, they, or their children, lived to see the Tricolor struck and the Crescent raised in its place. Receding French power left them stranded, foreigners in lands they had developed with their hands. They deserve more than the passing tribute of these pages; I wish it were in my power to give it to them.

In the days of Munich, the late Robert Dell, distinguished correspondent of the *Manchester Guardian* at Geneva, wrote a prophetic article entitled "The Disastrous Consequences of the Policy of Capitulation." What Mr. Dell said then is still true. He who capitulates digs his own grave and often drags others into it with him. The Arab lands are weak. Weakness added to weakness produces no strength. The friendship of the new masters of the Arab states, bought by the West at the expense of crucial military and political positions, is made of shifting sands. In the end, the power vacuum will not be filled by rulers wielding arms supplied in pursuance of the Eisenhower Doctrine. The real contest is between American might and the expanding empire of the Soviet Union.

The Chinese, I am told, used to delight in historical pageant dramas lasting several hours. These portrayed in theatrical form the cyclical rise and fall of empires. They would begin with scenes of a dissolute court. The decline of imperial power would encourage the governors of outlying provinces to raise the standard of revolt and to assert their own authority. Their arrogance, hauteur, and pomp would be inversely proportionate to the size of their domains. Incessant strife among these feudal, semi-independent warlords would bring anarchy and desolation to the countryside, subjecting the peasants to grinding poverty. Slowly one of the warlords, emerging as the strongest, would force the others to bend to his rule, would found a dynasty, and build his empire on the ruins of the one that had decayed. Or perhaps the whole land would be overrun by the hordes of a foreign conqueror. In either case, order would be restored; the frontiers would be guarded by a disciplined army; roads, bridges, and palaces would be constructed; tilling would be resumed in the fields, and prosperity would return to the countryside. Then, with time, the new court, giving way to ease and pleasure, would begin to neglect the hard task of government, lose its habits of virility, and sink into sloth. And the cycle would begin all over again to the pure delectation of the spectators.

The kings and dictators who have risen to supremacy in the Arab world as a sequence to the drastic decline of British and French power are now in the phase of hostile maneuverings. One, Gamal Abdel Nasser of Egypt, is in the process of founding a new Arab empire. But, since his United Arab Republic lies in the heart of one of the strategic areas of the world, he cannot disregard the conflicting ambitions of the United States and the Soviet Union. When he chose to ally himself tentatively with the latter, many Americans consoled themselves with the thought that a "positive neutralism" like Nasser's was better than satellite status. But, meanwhile, the tide in the Middle East continued to flow against the West. And ultimately, unless that tide can be made to turn, the Soviets will establish their hegemony in the area. I strongly suspect that the issue will be decided in the end, not by good will, not by appeasement, not by competing offers of economic and military aid, not by propaganda, but by a clear-cut power commitment. Only the inception, highly problematical, of a world order could change this basic rule.

How much better it would have been if the United States had recognized in good time the necessary solidarity of the Western world, of which it is willy-nilly a part! The British betrayed the West—and their French ally—by inciting the Syrians to revolt against the French mandate in 1945. The Americans behaved with equal want of foresight when they nudged the British out of the Suez Canal Zone and when they condemned the Franco-British intervention in Egypt and rescued Nasser in November, 1956. Having forced its allies to relinquish their strategic positions, the United States is left weakened and virtually alone in the arena, face to face with Soviet power and Arab extremism.

This situation calls for political and military statesmanship of the highest order. Yet what do we see? By virtue of the Eisenhower doctrine, United States and Western interests were entrusted to an informal and wobbly alliance based on five Arab kings—Hussein of Jordan, the late Faisal of Iraq, Saud of Arabia, Idriss of Libya, and Mohammed of Morocco—and one dictator—Bourguiba of Tunisia. It is hard to imagine these men actually controlling the destinies of the Arab world in a period of social and political upheaval and of global readjustments of power. They are the lesser chieftains of the traditional Chinese pageant dramas, fated sooner or later to be swept aside. The pity of it is that the Christian Lebanon and Israel, both of them linked to the West by genuine ties of culture and sentiment, each the home of an authentic humanist tradition, must pin their safety to the uncertain course of the United States. They have a right to be concerned.

The fear that the North African nationalist movements might, if abandoned by the United States, turn to Moscow for support has frequently been used in Washington as an excuse for the policy of carrying water on both shoulders. The nationalist leaders themselves have played upon that fear again and again in their attempt to drag the United States into the picture on their side. Habib Bourguiba, for instance, has stated specifically that if the United States fails to sacrifice French interests to his, he will seek the help of the Soviet bloc. To yield to blackmail of this kind is to abdicate real leadership. But it must be understood, too, that Bourguiba's threats rest on the dubious assumption that he is strong enough to make his own decision. If he declares against the West, he will vindicate the position of his most dangerous rival, Salah Ben Youssef, now in Cairo, and will have to bow to those who are not tainted with previous Western leanings.

As regards Algeria, Washington should, I think, ponder this question: Shall we, to appease our Arab friends, support the aims of the Algerian rebellion? Or shall we, rather, help the French build there a land in which two races may, for the first time, work out a common destiny within the framework of a new Eur-African union? If the first course is followed, the United States can hope only to swell the number of poverty-stricken Arab states without internal freedom, strength, or stability. The friendship of an independent Algeria will, in the long run, be of no more value than that, now lost, of Iraq. The Paris-Brazzaville axis will be broken. The Cairo-Casablanca axis will become an attainable object of Soviet policy. If the second course is followed, the dream of racial partnership and of European-African cooperation on a new basis may become a reality.

46. BOYCOTT AND GENERAL STRIKE

In the autumn of 1956, the F.L.N. tried again to impose its will on the Moslem population, this time by ordering a boycott of the schools. The object in keeping the Moslem children at home (or more generally in the street) was to provide spectacular proof of the F.L.N.'s claim to popular support and deny the French an essential avenue of influence.* Imposed by intimidation in the teeth of strong popular resistance—the methods used included threats to parents and pupils and hand grenades thrown into schoolyards (at Algiers, Sétif, Batna, and Biskra)—the boycott order was obeyed only in areas of intense terrorist agitation. Almost total in Algiers at the beginning of the school year, the boycott was 90 per cent effective at Blida, 70 per cent at Oran, 60 per cent at Sétif and in the rural townships of the Algiers *arrondissement,* but negligible or wholly rejected everywhere else. By the middle of the school year, attendance was almost normal again, even in Algiers. The rebels, in attempting to prove their strength, had revealed their weakness.

However, their greatest failure was yet to come. In December, 1956, the F.L.N., after a preliminary series of strikes, decided the moment had come for an all-out test of strength; they resolved to stage a week-long, "general, insurrectional strike" throughout the country. Planned by the F.L.N.'s supreme Coordination and Execution Committee (C.C.E.), the strike was, according to a set of directives found on the body of a rebel chief killed near Djidjelli on January 13, 1957, to attain the following goals:

1. To show in a decisive way the total adhesion of the whole Algerian people to the F.L.N., its sole representative.
2. To give by means of this demonstration an incontestable authority to our delegates at the United Nations . . .
3. To bring more classes of society into the active struggle by converting anticolonialist hatred into concrete and evident action . . . This atmosphere will foster and increase our revolutionary potential.
4. To provide the experience necessary for the general insurrection.

From F.L.N. headquarters in Tunis, the word came: "Our struggle has reached its culminating point and our fate will be decided at the United Nations." A central strike committee was set up; under it, in the *wilayas*, zones, regions, and sectors, the local ramifications of the F.L.N.

* The handbill prescribing the boycott, issued in September, said: "This action will signify that the rupture between the Algerian people and the French authorities has been consummated in all fields including that of culture . . . For a country at war, . . . education is of secondary importance . . . even though our thirst for culture and science is greater than ever. . . ." The previous spring, the F.L.N. had tried with only partial success to make the secondary school and university students leave their classes and join their "brothers" in the ranks of the A.L.N.

undertook to disseminate the propaganda themes, to transmit orders, and see that they were carried out. The new F.L.N. labor organization, the *Union Générale des Travailleurs Algériens* (U.G.T.A.), and its middle-class counterpart, the *Union Générale Commerciale Algérienne* (U.G.C.A.), were assigned the job of bringing industrial and commercial activity to a complete standstill during the strike. Algiers and its suburbs were divided into 100 sectors, each to be controlled by a squad of fifteen stalwarts under the general supervision of Amar Taleb, a former member of the U.D.M.A. executive committee and the moving spirit in the U.G.C.A.

The population was informed that the strike would last eight days, that during the strike all Moslems were to remain indoors, that all shops were to be closed, that infractions would be met by punishments not excluding death, and that the cities were to be "dead," resembling "cemeteries where nothing moves." Moslem families were advised to lay in the necessary supplies; the needy were promised succor from F.L.N. relief funds. News of the impending general insurrection was spread well in advance to heighten the suspense and accentuate the fear psychosis. Tunis and Rabat radios kept up a steady flow of inflammatory broadcasts full of incitement to revolt.

The P.C.A., too weak to contemplate independent action, supported the strike but, in a post-mortem, criticized the F.L.N. for having limited it to eight days instead of making it indefinite and for having kept the people indoors, thereby cutting itself off from the masses. The M.N.A., which had advocated a twenty-four-hour strike, attacked the F.L.N. with red-hot handbills. It deplored what it called "ill-considered mass action that can in the long run only exhaust the people"; it blasted the strike as a "new and terrible trial."

F.L.N. plans called for terrorist action on an unprecedented scale during the strike. An instruction sheet dated December 27, 1956, and seized in the Constantine department said: "The armed groups are to be on the alert throughout the period of the strike. All roads are to be controlled. Prevent all movements of persons and vehicles. In general, paralyze all public life. Acts of sabotage, ambushes, attacks must be stepped up . . ." Young terrorists plotted to hoist the rebel flag on public buildings. Orders from the C.C.E. specified that 500 "seasoned fighters" were to be given shelter on the outskirts of Algiers and that the *fidayoun* (terrorist "martyrs") were to prepare the necessary bombs, grenades, and explosives. The raids, it was stated, would be carried out either by individual terrorists or by "death commandos"—and, according to instructions issued from Tunis on January 14, irrespective of losses.

Moslem householders were told to leave their doors ajar so that their homes could, if necessary, provide the terrorists with places of refuge.

Theoretically, the strike was to coincide with the Algerian debate in the United Nations General Assembly, but since consideration of the Algerian question by that body was repeatedly put off, the strike plans hung fire for days. A false start was made at Bougie on January 6. At last, on January 21, although the Algerian question had not yet come up at the United Nations, the F.L.N. "clandestine" radio station in Morocco, announced that the strike would begin on January 28. A similar announcement was broadcast over Tunis and Damascus radios the following day. An F.L.N. handbill confirmed the date.

No stone had been left unturned to insure the success of the strike; yet, outside the F.L.N., nobody wanted it. The Constantine and Oran tramway employees declared through their spokesmen that they would work if protected. Employers were swamped with requests for sick leave and accumulated off time. The Moslem merchants were, in many cases, openly hostile to the strike and to those who promoted it. A member of the U.G.C.A. was heard to remark: "When will the Government take measures against these young killers who for the past two years have been sponging on us?" On all sides, the predominant hope was that French countermeasures would create an evident state of necessity, provide a shield behind which the strike orders could be ignored without incurring the wrath of the F.L.N. Furthermore, the strike appeared to many to be of dubious value, even from a nationalist point of view; they saw that since it was imposed, it could not, except fraudulently, serve as a demonstration of public sentiment.

The F.L.N. was unlucky in that on January 8, 1957, Brigadier General Jacques Massu, tough commander of the Tenth Parachute Division, had been appointed security chief for greater Algiers. The choice denoted a determination to deal energetically with troublemakers. On January 14, General Massu declared that in the event of a strike all shops would be open; if necessary, he said, they would be forced open, in which case the security of merchandise could not be guaranteed. In a radio message on January 18, he said: "Algiers will be encompassed, compartmented, tightly controlled, that is to say, protected and disinfected." The F.L.N. reacted to General Massu's words with a show of moral indignation. Mohammed Abbas-Turqui, describing himself as president of the U.G.C.A.,*

* Mohammed Abbas-Turqui was a rich Algiers merchant (leathers, hides, shoes) who, after bestowing bountiful benefactions on the F.L.N. at the beginning of the rebellion, joined the F.L.N. committee in Tunis late in 1956.

put out a handbill denouncing General Massu's "invitation to vandalism, murder, and pillage." On January 20, Tunis radio appealed to world opinion for an indictment of such methods.

On January 19, at a meeting of F.L.N. leaders at Staouéli, thirteen miles west of Algiers, it was noted that: "The organization that we had painfully succeeded in building up has been completely destroyed. The reinforcements put at our disposal by the A.L.N. have been forced to take to the hills . . . The situation could be compared to that of a ship in distress." However, the leaders attending the meeting decided to take stopgap measures pending "word from the leaders outside the country."

Despite the dislocation of the terrorist arrangements, the strike was effective in the larger cities on the first day. The postal and telegraph service reported the absence of 71 per cent of its Moslem personnel in the Algiers area, 41 per cent in the Oran area, 28 per cent in the Constantine area. The Algerian railways reported an almost total walkout in the Algiers department, as against 50 per cent in the Oran department and 25 per cent in the Constantine department. The strike began to dwindle on the second day, largely as the result of French countermeasures. In Algiers, a fleet of about 100 army trucks took Moslem workers from their homes to their places of work; most of the trucks plied between the Kasbah and the port area. General Massu's men, among them paratroopers in their distinctive, mottled battle dress, ranged the city, opening closed shops, catching suspected terrorists in a thousand snares.

Between January 20 and February 14, twenty-three gunmen, fifty-one chiefs of terrorist cells, and 174 F.L.N. "tax" collectors were arrested. Handbills dropped over the Kasbah from the air on January 29 informed the inhabitants that the strike would be broken but that shops would be protected against pillagers. (There had been pillaging of Moslem shops.) Other handbills, dropped three days later, said: "The F.L.N., after having been defeated in the countryside, is defeated in the cities." The recrudescence of terrorist attacks promised by the F.L.N. did not occur.

On the other hand, French troops bore down heavily on the rebel bands: 167 rebels were killed on the first day of the strike in engagements on both frontiers; 216 were killed in Kabylia and at Mascara, southeast of Oran, on the last day of the strike. Terrorism, if it did not increase, did not disappear. A man was found hanging by his neck at Boghni in Kabylia and a railway gatekeeper was killed in the Chélif valley southwest of Algiers on January 29; three farm hands were strangled at Maillot in Kabylia on January 31; seven employees of the Algerian power company were abducted at Djidjelli on February 1. An attempt on the life of a non-striking butcher at Médéa, south of Algiers, resulted in the immediate closing of all the Moslem shops in the city.

When the strike was over, it was seen that seventeen people had been killed, twenty-three wounded, and forty-four abducted by terrorists in the course of the week. Four shops had been attacked. These figures were not above previous weekly averages. Employees of essential services who had struck in defiance of individual requisition orders were severely punished. At the Mustapha general hospital in Algiers, 240 such employees were suspended, sixty-four dismissed, and sixty-three arrested. Many shops that failed to open during the strike were compelled by the authorities to remain closed afterwards for varying periods.

The F.L.N.—what else could it do?—proclaimed the strike a success. It is true that an F.L.N. strike order had been issued and, at the outset, widely obeyed. But the strike had quickly ceased to be "general" and had at no point assumed the aspect of an insurrection. All essential services had functioned throughout; the rebel flag had been hoisted nowhere; the cities could not have been likened to "cemeteries" by any stretch of the imagination. And when it was over, when normal conditions returned, the feeling of relief was immense everywhere.

Nor could it be said that the strike had a determining effect on the course of events at the United Nations. At the end of a debate that more than once brought to mind those of the French National Assembly, eighteen African and Asian countries introduced a resolution recognizing Algeria's right to self-determination and calling on France to act accordingly. This resolution was defeated in the Political Committee on August 13 by a vote of thirty-four to thirty-three, with ten abstentions. Two days later, the General Assembly wound up its discussion of Algeria with the unanimous adoption of a resolution expressing "the hope that, in a spirit of co-operation, a peaceful, democratic, and just solution will be found, through appropriate means, in conformity with the principles of the Charter of the United Nations." The resolution made no mention of independence or self-determination; it fell far short of deciding the fate of Algeria. The rebels were no better off than before.

The "general, insurrectional strike" of 1957 may well have been a turning point. It has been said that even if the F.L.N. suffers grievous reverses, terrorist agitation can never be stamped out. I do not agree. In any conflict of this sort, uncertainty as to the final outcome gives the terrorist the margin of complicity he needs for protection. But if it becomes manifest that defeat, not victory, awaits the masters whom the terrorist serves, that protective margin will vanish; the terrorist, isolated, can then be destroyed. In arms, in men, in money, in outside support, the

F.L.N. was, in 1956, strong as never before; but time had perhaps deserted the rebel camp and started working for the French. Of course, what had been won in the field could always be lost round the conference table; this, indeed, was the rebels' great hope.

47. COMMUNISTS AND THE F.L.N.— RIVALS IN TERROR

The Algerian Communist party had, as we have seen, been torn asunder by its total espousal of the rebel cause and by the consequent defection of the bulk of its European members. Eugène Mannoni of *Le Monde* made this pertinent observation in an article on the Algerian Communists:

> Prominent among those who booed M. Mollet when he came to Algeria on February 6, 1956, were organized workers as convulsed as the rightist veterans. The terrorist threat, felt alike by the worker of Philippeville and the landowner of Aïn Abid, begot the same anxiety in all Europeans. The ethnic reflex took precedence over the former class solidarity.*

M. Mannoni also pointed out that the membership of the Algerian Communist party had never exceeded 12,000, and he added: "If three of its five top leaders were Moslem, four-fifths of its members were Europeans. Despite its attempt to become 'Algerian,' it had remained an appendage of the French party." Its cells were concentrated, not in the Kasbah, but in the Spanish-Algerian quarters of Oran and in the populous Bab el Oued and Belcourt sections of Algiers, where, as M. Mannoni put it, workers were the "victims at dawn of terrorists lying in wait for them."

Before the outbreak of the rebellion, the Algerian Communist party had managed to send two first-college deputies to Paris (Mme. Alice Sportisse and Pierre Fayet) and a first-college delegate to Algiers (René Justrabo), but its successes in the second college had been slight. All that was left to the party at the beginning of 1956 was a hard core of confirmed activists struggling to create a guerrilla force capable of hold-

* See *Le Monde* for March 23, 1957.

ing a small area for the Hammer and Sickle. The Communists could not otherwise hope to be cut in some day on the spoils of victory.

The case of Cadet Officer Henri Maillot is illustrative of this design and of the perils attending it. On April 4, 1956, at dawn, an army truck loaded with arms and ammunition left Miliana under escort and headed for Algiers, seventy-four miles to the northeast. It arrived at a little before 9 A.M. As soon as the men of the escort had departed in quest of something to eat, Cadet Officer Maillot, commanding the convoy, climbed into the cab of the truck and ordered the driver, Private Jacques Domergue, to proceed to the Bainem wood just west of Algiers. The vehicle was later recovered. The driver was found bound to a tree. But Maillot had vanished and with him the load of arms and ammunition. Light machine guns, rifles, pistols, and a stock of hand grenades were lost. It was recalled that the clandestine Communist organ, *Liberté*, had ordered party members to "procure in every possible way arms for the forces engaged in the struggle for the liberation of Algeria."

Two days later, a communiqué issued by the Freedom Fighters, the Communist guerrilla organization, announced that Maillot had joined the "resistance forces." The communiqué also contained a list of the stolen weapons. On May 18, Maillot himself sent a mimeographed circular letter to his former comrades of the 504th Transport Battalion, to the police, and to the press. In it, he explained that in joining the ranks of the "fighting Algerians," he had responded to his party's call.

Maillot, it was learned, had been born twenty-eight years earlier in Algiers, the son of a municipal employee who had once been secretary-general of the Communist-dominated Municipal Employees' Union. The younger Maillot had become secretary-general of the *Union de la Jeunesse Démocratique Algérienne*, a Communist-front organization, and had been employed as an accountant by the Communist daily, *Alger Républicain*. He also had represented Algeria at youth congresses in Prague and Warsaw. However, in volunteering for active service in the Army, Maillot, a reservist, had sworn that he had severed all ties with the party. "Conscientious, methodical, devoted, hard-working, perfectly disciplined, robust, well prepared to bear arms"—such were the appraisals of his superiors. But this praise carried little weight with the Algiers military tribunal, before which Maillot was tried *in absentia* on May 22, 1956. The tribunal sentenced him to death.

On June 5, 1956, an armed band was sighted in a previously uncontaminated area near Lamartine east of Orléansville. Pursued by a security unit, the band was attacked outside a native village called Boudouane. Seven rebels fell in the encounter, among them two Europeans. Despite bleached hair and eyebrows, one of the European bodies was quickly identified as that of Henri Maillot. The other European casualty, a certain Maurice Laban, had been a schoolmaster at Biskra in the Constantine department and chief of a Communist cell there. He had been banished from the department in December, 1955. A copy of the Prefect's expulsion order was found on his body.

That the Communists had been trying to establish a guerrilla zone of their own in the Orléansville district was now clear. In this enterprise, they may well have had the support of the local ramifications of Messali Hadj's Algerian National Movement (M.N.A.), still relatively influential in the area but much more in need of allies than the F.L.N. Proof is wanting, but I should not be astonished to learn that the F.L.N. had something to do with the quick destruction of the Communist band at Boudouane.

Only two members of the Communist band got away. They were: Lucien Ahmadou Gherab,* like Maillot a deserter, and Mohammed Boualem, secretary of the Oran Dock Workers' Union and instigator of the political strike in Oran on February 3, 1956.† Both of these men were sheltered for a time by Dr. Michel Martini, principal surgeon at the Orléansville hospital and allegedly a former member of a Communist cell at Saint-Mandé near Paris. Later the two went into hiding in Oran. In August, however, Gherab, leaving Boualem behind, headed south and joined a *maquis* near Tlemcen.

On the night of August 26, 1956, a nomad company (mounted auxiliaries) fell upon a strong rebel band that had abducted four Europeans the previous day. The engagement, which took place north of Tlemcen between Pont de l'Isser and Les Abdellys, cost the rebels fourteen dead. One rebel was caught alive. Information elicited from the prisoner encouraged the security forces to undertake a *ratissage* (combing operation) in the area. A second clash occurred on September 1. This time two rebels were killed and two were caught. One of the prisoners, dressed in khaki and carrying an automatic pistol, turned out to be Gherab. His companion, Miloud Kacemi, wore civilian clothes but sported a Thompson submachine gun. Brought to trial in Oran on Sep-

* Gherab, born in 1926 at Blida, was the son of a Kabyle schoolmaster who had adopted civil personal status. Having abandoned his medical studies in Algiers to throw himself into the Communist movement, the younger Gherab joined the editorial staff of *Alger Républicain*, writing under the name of Ahmed Aghrib. In June, 1955, he was called into active service as a reserve administrative officer in the Medical Corps and assigned to the Ducros Military Hospital at Blida. Second Lieutenant Gherab deserted on April 7, 1956.

† See pp. 274–275.

tember 11, Gherab was sentenced to death, while Kacemi got off with a five-year prison term.

Despite the extremity in which Gherab found himself, or perhaps because of it, his tongue wagged freely, putting the French authorities on to a Communist underground in the Algiers and Oran departments. By September 14, thirty persons, including five Europeans, had been apprehended. Dr. Martini, the Orléansville surgeon, and Boualem, the Oran labor leader, were of the number. The police claimed that the organization had been helping the rebels by obtaining arms and ammunition, providing food, shelter, and ammunition, perpetrating murders and outrages, and making preparations for the sabotage of railway lines.

Meanwhile, the Communists had given up the idea of establishing a guerrilla zone of their own. On July 1, 1956, a communiqué purporting to emanate from the headquarters of the Freedom Fighters announced the dissolution of the Communist units and their "integration" into the F.L.N.'s Army of National Liberation. The document said the Freedom Fighters had been organized to associate Communists and nationalists alike in the "armed struggle." Giving no reasons for the shift in policy, it simply ordered all Freedom Fighters to go over to the Army of National Liberation with their arms and equipment and to accept the control of the F.L.N.*

From that day forward, the aim of the central committee of the Algerian Communist party (headed by Dr. Saddok Hadjerès, a Jewish physician) was to persuade the F.L.N. to agree to the formation of a non-political resistance committee similar to the Resistance Council that had directed the underground movement in France during World War II. Such a committee, as the Communists saw it, would bring together the representatives of all groups wishing to take an active part in the "liberation of Algeria" and would be content to leave basic political decisions in abeyance pending an expression of the popular will, possibly through the medium of a constituent assembly. It would also, of course, give the Communists a voice in the higher councils of the rebellion and an opportunity to maneuver more freely in anticipation of the political struggle to follow.

Communist efforts in this direction were futile, however, for they ran counter to the true nature of the Algerian rebellion. Actually, the

* The Freedom Fighters were commanded by Abdelkader (Lucien) Guerroudj, a former schoolmaster. Prior to its dissolution, the organization had sought to maintain "urban action groups" in Algiers, as well as a red *maquis* in the hills. Guerroudj was arrested in January, 1957.

rebellion differed from the French resistance movement in one essential particular: its promoters sought power for themselves exclusively. Moreover, if the Communists and their sympathizers were numerically strong in France, such was not the case in Algeria. It was not to be expected, therefore, that the F.L.N. would be willing to make concessions to the Communists in return for unneeded cooperation and support.

Larbi Bouhali, secretary of the Algerian Communist party, readily conceded that in failing to throw itself into the "military struggle" at the outbreak of the rebellion, his party had pursued a mistaken course. But he told a journalist in Berlin in January, 1957, that it had since made amends; that under an agreement with the F.L.N., the Communist "armed forces" were joining the ranks of the Army of National Liberation. The party, he added, now hoped to participate in the formulation of F.L.N. policy. He failed to mention, however, that the F.L.N. had long since turned thumbs down on any such idea.

A month earlier, the rebel organ, *El Moudjahid,* had spoken scathingly of the "bureaucratic Communist leadership," which, it said, had lost contact with the people and was unable to "analyze the revolutionary situation correctly." The Algerian Communist party was pronounced defunct as a force to be reckoned with. That was all the thanks the Communists got for "integrating" their bands with the Army of National Liberation and for accepting the control of the F.L.N. The rebel attitude was, in fact, simple enough. The F.L.N. welcomed the Freedom Fighters as *moujahidine* (combatants); but, determined to preserve its monolithic structure, it spurned the overtures of the Communist leaders.

Nevertheless, the Communists continued their dogged efforts to keep a finger in the revolutionary pie. Although they had been unable to maintain independent guerrilla bands or to break into the councils of the rebellion, terrorism still seemed to offer a promising field of endeavor. Here, if enough human lives could be taken, the F.L.N. might be compelled to acknowledge the superiority of Communist techniques and the advantage of some sort of an alliance with the party.

On November 13, 1956, the Algiers police were advised that a suspicious-looking parcel had been deposited in a closet at the Hamma gas works by a latheman named Fernand Yveton. Policemen sent to investigate found a beach bag at the spot indicated. The bag contained a box divided into two compartments. In one of the compartments, a cylindrical bomb was found; in the other, an alarm clock set for 7:30 P.M., two batteries, and wire connections. The word "Betty" appeared on the cylinder. The device was instantly disconnected.

Yveton, who was arrested on the spot, admitted having placed the bag and its contents in the closet. He told the police that "Betty" had been handed to him earlier in the day by an unnamed European woman with blond hair. Another time bomb, he said, was to have been placed at the foot of a gasoline storage tank in suburban Hussein Dey. These tips were false, and the police set out on a wild-goose chase. Actually, Yveton's accomplice was Jacqueline Guerroudj, dark-haired European wife of the commander of the defunct Freedom Fighters. She managed to slip the second bomb into a parked police van, but it failed to explode.

Yveton, it turned out, had been a militant Communist since adolescence. The thirty-year-old latheman, a former secretary of the El Biar section of the Algerian Communist party, had also been a close friend of Henri Maillot and had accompanied Mme. Maillot to her husband's funeral.

Brought to trial on November 25, 1956, under the accelerated procedure authorized in cases of *flagrante delicto*, Yveton denied that he had meant to take human lives. The purpose of "Betty," he said, had been only to attract attention. However, the director of the gas works and two foremen testified that, Yveton's assertions to the contrary, there was always a constant going and coming of personnel between 7 P.M. and 8 P.M. near the closet in which the bomb had been placed. The Algiers military tribunal found Yveton guilty of an "attempt to destroy an inhabited building by explosive substance" and sentenced him to death. He was executed on February 11, 1957.

Yveton, a bungler, had the privilege of giving his life to the cause in which he believed. But some of his colleagues in terror fared better, for they were both more effective and more elusive than he had been. On November 12, 1956, three time bombs, all thought to have been placed by Communists,* exploded, the first in an Algiers streetcar, the second in a notions store in suburban Maison Carrée, and the third in the Hussein Dey railway station. Thirty-six persons were wounded that day, among them eleven women and ten children. Several of the children were maimed for life—a splendid contribution to the freedom struggle. On November 28, another bomb attributed by the police to Red terrorists exploded at a trolley-bus station in the populous Bab el Oued section of Algiers, wounding twelve. The same day, three persons were wounded by a Communist bomb in Hussein Dey.

* In fact, only the mercury fulminate detonators of these bombs came from a Communist laboratory at Birkadem. The explosive itself, a mixture of potassium chlorate, nitronaphthalene, and starch, had been supplied by the F.L.N —a curious instance of cooperation in rivalry.

Yet, despite their efforts, the Communists never managed to spill anything like as much innocent blood as the specialists of the F.L.N. In the single month of September, 1956, the F.L.N. terror organization headed by Saadi Yacef and Ali Ammar, known as "Ali la Pointe," carried out eighty-five separate attacks within the city limits of Algiers, killing twenty-four persons and wounding 116. Fourteen of the dead were Moslem civilians, five were European civilians, and five were soldiers. Among the wounded, twenty-four were Moslem civilians, sixty-four were European civilians, and twenty-eight were soldiers. The cruelest of these feats of terror was the explosion of two time bombs on September 30, one in a cafeteria and the other in a milk bar. One woman was killed; sixty-two persons, about one-half of them women and children, were wounded. By midnight, fifteen amputations had been performed in the hospitals of the city. The little Fernande Pons, eight years old, was among those who lost a leg.

Other notable achievements of Saadi Yacef and his gang were:

> January 27, 1957. The explosion of time bombs placed in two Algiers cafés by young Moslem girls took four lives and sent fifty persons to the hospital.
>
> February 7, 1957. Time bombs exploded in two Algiers stadiums, killing nine persons and wounding forty-five.
>
> June 3, 1957. Time bombs concealed in the bases of lamp posts near bus stops went off during the evening rush hour. The casualties were ten killed and eighty-six injured.
>
> June 9, 1957. A time bomb placed beneath the orchestra dais at the Casino de la Corniche in suburban Saint-Eugène exploded during a dance. Ten persons, including the orchestra leader, were killed; ninety were wounded.

As a result of these outrages, General Massu, who had become security chief for greater Algiers prior to the abortive "insurrectional strike" of January 28 to February 4,* kept the men of his Tenth Parachute Division concentrated in and about the city and began a systematic hunt for the F.L.N. terrorists. This operation came to be known as the "Battle of Algiers."

The methods used by the paratroopers certainly could not be justified on grounds of normal legality. Yet an implacable, half-subterranean war in which innocent lives were used as pawns had fastened itself on the city. The victims of terrorist bombs, knives, and bullets had latterly become more numerous—146 casualties in December, 1956; 194 in Janu-

* See pp. 315–319.

ary, 1957. Armchair moralists verge on inhumanity when, by putting the law above all other considerations, they would in effect deny to ordinary human beings their right to protection, often to life itself.

Paris was swarming with such moralists. One of them, the Roman Catholic author Pierre-Henri Simon, published a small book called *Contre la Torture** in which he selected the most inexcusable acts of police and army brutality to indict an entire policy—a policy that happened to be at variance with the pro-nationalist position taken by M. Simon and other "liberals" within the church. The pamphleteer dared dedicate his "cry for justice and honor" to the French men and women who had resisted Hitler.

That excesses had occurred was certain; but it was equally true that M. Lacoste and his associates had made, and were making, a serious effort to avoid them. And it is not to condone "cruel and unusual punishments" to point out that the crimes General Massu and his men were trying to combat were more vicious than the third degree.†

The paratroopers, then, applied a harsh cure to the morbid state they had found in Algiers. If they were denounced in certain Parisian journals as torturers, they at least won the gratitude of Algiers. M. Simon and his emulators probably had little knowledge of the intense relief that follows deliverance from mortal fear and could not suspect that the Moslems were, if anything, more thankful than the Europeans.

By the end of February, 1957, most of the local F.L.N. leaders in Algiers had fled either to the Kabylia *maquis* or to Tunisia. Larbi Ben M'Hidi, the last member of the F.L.N. executive remaining in the country, had been caught on February 26 by paratroopers under the command

* Paris: Editions du Seuil, 1957.

† In April, 1957, the Mollet Government, under harassing fire from left-wing critics, put up a smoke screen. It announced that it was appointing a Committee to Safeguard Individual Rights and Liberties in Algeria. Composed of twelve distinguished citizens drawn from government service and the professions, this committee held its first meeting on May 10, 1957, at the Hôtel Matignon in the presence of Premier Mollet, Robert Lacoste, and François Mitterrand, the Minister of Justice. Pierre Béteille, a judge of the Court of Cassation, was elected president of the committee. Maurice Garçon, the celebrated trial lawyer, was elected secretary-general. The committee subsequently heard complaints and looked into alleged instances of arbitrary arrest and torture. Unfortunately, the committee's usefulness was vitiated by the fact that it did not include within its frame of reference denials of that primary human right—the right to life and protection. Consequently, it was, in Algeria, largely discredited from the start.

of General Massu's subordinate, Colonel Marcel Bigeard. But Saadi Yacef, who had become rebel chief for Algiers, was still in the city with his adjutant, Ali la Pointe. They lay low until two of General Massu's three regiments were withdrawn in April. The campaign against the paratrooper-torturers, then at its height in Paris, had favored their plans by hastening the respite they so badly needed if they were to go into business again. When the respite came, they immediately applied themselves to the re-establishment of their badly damaged bomb network.

They achieved results surpassing their fondest dreams. Ten lives were snuffed out when the lamp-post bombs exploded on June 3. Ten more persons perished at the Casino de la Corniche on June 9. The total wounded in the two outrages—176—set a new record for a single week. In addition, the June 9 explosion led to a hideous race riot two days later. After the funeral of the victims, about 2,000 Europeans, youths for the most part, sought to avenge the crime of the F.L.N. in innocent Moslem blood. Twelve Moslems were killed by the mob; at least fifteen were wounded. Hooligans set fire to a score of motorcars. Perhaps as many as 100 shops were sacked and burned. Commenting on the riot the next day, *Le Figaro* commented: "That 2,000 demonstrators shouting, 'French Algeria!' should have so powerfully assisted the F.L.N. is something that leaves us speechless." June 9 was indeed a banner day for the rebels.

Obviously, the terror organization had to be broken again. This was done in an ingenious way. A terrorist named Abdelkader Mahmoud having been caught, a French colonel stepped, so to speak, into his boots. Using the prisoner's "drops," Colonel Godard entered into correspondence with Yacef and rose rapidly in the latter's estime. The new Mahmoud's success was apparently phenomenal. When misfortune overtook other key terrorists, Mahmoud always managed to emerge unscathed. His *baraka*, his slipperiness, his ability defied comparison. Ramel, military chief under Yacef, and Chérif Debih, known as Mourad, Yacef's political commissar, lost their lives in August. On September 10, Yacef put Mahmoud in charge of all military action in the Algiers zone. A fortnight later, the French moved in on Yacef himself; they arrested him and a young woman confederate, Zora Driff, in the Kasbah. Ali la Pointe, still at large, then took over as commander of the "autonomous zone of Algiers." On October 7, however, besieged by paratroopers in his Kasbah hide-out, he was blown to bits in the explosion of his own cache of explosives. With that dramatic incident, the long nightmare of urban terror came to an end in Algiers. (Yacef Saadi escaped execution under President de Gaulle's general commutation in January, 1958.)

The Communists had dropped out of the race for supremacy in this field long before and were reduced henceforth to the more ineffectual forms of agitation.

48. TRADE UNIONISM

The Algerian nationalists had long been aware of the use that could be made of a regimented labor movement. In Tunisia, the *Union Générale Tunisienne du Travail* (U.G.T.T.), founded in 1946 by the late Ferhat Hached,* had provided the Neo-Destour party with an incomparable chance to maneuver. By taking his organization out of the Communist-dominated World Federation of Trade Unions and into the American-dominated International Confederation of Trade Unions (I.C.F.T.U.) in 1951, M. Hached had contrived to enlist in behalf of his political cause the unqualified support of the American labor movement. His policy had been followed in 1955, again with satisfactory results, by the newly formed *Union Marocaine du Travail* in Morocco. The Algerian nationalists could hardly fail to be fascinated by the singular achievement of their Tunisian and Moroccan "brothers" and to seek for themselves similar advantages both at home and abroad. Accordingly, plans for an Algerian nationalist labor federation, already generated by the old Movement for the Triumph of Democratic Liberties (M.T.L.D.), were given new and more urgent consideration.

It will be recalled that two M.T.L.D. leaders, Ahmed Mezerna and Abderrahmane Kiouane, had been in touch, before the outbreak of the rebellion, with Irving Brown, European representative of the American Federation of Labor and a substitute member of the executive board of the I.C.F.T.U. These earlier contacts gave Messali Hadj's Algerian National Movement an initial advantage over the rival F.L.N. Much better introduced in world labor circles than the F.L.N. and more conscious, perhaps, of the importance of an effort in the field of labor, the Algerian National Movement (M.N.A.) beat the F.L.N. to the gun in

* Ferhat Hached was murdered, presumably by European extremists, on December 2, 1952.

February, 1956, by setting up the *Union Syndicale des Travailleurs Algériens* (U.S.T.A.) with the blessing of the I.C.F.T.U. Headed by Mohand Ramdani, a Messalist member of the Algiers city council, the new federation began with two unions, one comprising streetcar, and the other power plant, employees. It also launched a drive to organize workers on the docks, in the hospitals, and in the building trades. It applied without delay for membership in the I.C.F.T.U.

The F.L.N., its claim to predominance thus openly challenged, was compelled to counterattack. It did so early in March, 1956, by founding a rival labor federation called the *Union Générale des Travailleurs Algeriens* (U.G.T.A.), already mentioned in these pages in connection with the 1957 "insurrectional strike." The U.G.T.A. issued a manifesto in which it proclaimed its determination to give "to the labor struggle . . . an orientation corresponding to its (labor's) own aspirations, that is, a revolution in the political, economic, and social fields." Abdelkader Amrani, Lahouelist member of the Algiers city council and an employee of the Bastos tobacco company, seems to have been one of the chief architects of the U.G.T.A. The federation focused its first efforts on the hospital, dock, tobacco, and railway workers, winning notable successes.

In Algeria, the contest between the U.G.T.A. and the U.S.T.A. was an unequal one, if only because the threat of F.L.N. reprisals hung over anyone daring to join the Messalist federation. In France, however, where the Messalists were still solidly entrenched, the U.G.T.A. was unable to gain a foothold. To this day, Messali's U.S.T.A. remains a bastion of power wherever Algerian emigrant labor is concentrated.

The creation of the F.L.N.'s federation and its initial successes in Algeria put the I.C.F.T.U. on the spot. For it was clear that the Messalist federation, which the I.C.F.T.U. had held over the baptismal font, was, for reasons closely akin to gangsterism, not going to be "representative." Meanwhile, the U.G.T.A., playing hard to get, let it be known that it would not join the international body unless the U.S.T.A. was barred. In this, it got strong backing from Ahmed Ben Salah, secretary-general of the Tunisian U.G.T.T. and a member of the I.C.F.T.U. executive board. A further complication stemmed from the attitude of the French Socialist *Force Ouvrière* federation, a charter member of the I.C.F.T.U. with ramifications in Algeria. Although *Force Ouvrière* was too weak to exercise a determining influence in the councils of the I.C.F.T.U., it nevertheless opposed the admission of a "national" Algerian federation as an infringement of its own jurisdiction over the whole of French territory, Algeria included.

The Communists, too, were acutely embarrassed, and they had every reason to be. The two new "national" federations were headed by former stalwarts of the Communist-led French General Confederation of Labor (C.G.T.). And since both were eager to secure the benefits of American backing, they could be counted on not only to oppose the Communist *Union Générale des Syndicats Algériens* (U.G.S.A.), but to strip it of the bulk of its members, by intimidation if necessary. The Communists, quite naturally, denounced this "division of the workers" and sought to engage their rivals in "unity" talks. The only response was from the F.L.N., which demanded, as its price for unity, the absorption of the Communist-dominated unions into the U.G.T.A. This price being too high to pay, the Communists were forced to go their starved and solitary way; and their U.G.S.A., now affiliated directly to the World Federation of Trade Unions, dwindled rapidly to almost nothing.

The emergency subcommittee of the I.C.F.T.U. executive board, meeting in April, 1956, to examine the Algerian situation, acceded to a Messalist request to postpone final action, but authorized an on-the-spot inquiry, to be conducted by Omer Becu of Belgium and J. H. Oldenbroek of the Netherlands, respectively president and secretary-general of the I.C.F.T.U., and by Irving Brown. Apart from that, the subcommittee was content to acknowledge Algeria's "deep desire for self-determination."

The Brown mission—as it was inevitably called—did not materialize. On May 8, 1956, it was announced in Algiers that M. Lacoste had barred Mr. Brown from Algeria as an "undesirable" and had ordered the expulsion of Guy Gomis, president of the Algiers Junior Chamber of Commerce, who had apparently aspired to become Mr. Brown's Man Friday. A statement from M. Lacoste's office charged that Mr. Brown, under the cover of trade unionism, was "pursuing a reckless policy with dubious persons in utter contempt for the legitimate interests and incontestable positions of France in Algeria and in North Africa." A few days later, in a telegram to Mr. Oldenbroek, M. Lacoste said he had proof of Mr. Brown's "collusion with dubious individuals for the purpose of giving pecuniary encouragement to the formation of anti-French trade union organizations in Algeria and North Africa." M. Lacoste added that, as a result, he was compelled to oppose Mr. Brown's entry into Algeria "by every legal means" and that his decision was irrevocable.

When M. Lacoste took the further precaution of having the leaders of the two nationalist labor federations rounded up and sent to internment camps, the I.C.F.T.U. people in Brussels were convulsed with indignation. They issued ringing protests and prepared to lodge a complaint with the International Labor Office in Geneva. Irving Brown, in Washington, called M. Lacoste the "dictator of Algeria." In New York, where sympathies for Arab nationalism are tempered with a concern for the future of Israel, Mr. Brown told a meeting of the International Brotherhood of Electrical Workers (at the Waldorf-Astoria Hotel!) that the North African nationalists represented the French tradition of liberal thought. He gave the innocent electrical workers to understand that efforts—his efforts, presumably—to direct North African nationalism into the "channels of democracy" would destroy the totalitarian forces in the Arab world and make for unity between the Arab countries and Israel. Apart from Mr. Brown's curious standards of veracity and judgment, it is interesting to see how he felt he had to present his case to make it palatable in New York. A few days later, George Meany, president of the American Federation of Labor-Congress of Industrial Organizations, was reported to have asked Premier Guy Mollet in a personal letter to disavow M. Lacoste in the name of the Socialist ideal.

It later developed that the ties between the F.L.N. and the U.G.T.A. resembled those of an interlocking directorate. Idir Aïssat was interned in May, 1956, as secretary-general of the U.G.T.A. In February, 1957, he was taken from the Bossuet internment camp and placed under arrest as a member of the F.L.N. executive.

In July, 1956, the I.C.F.T.U. executive board admitted the U.G.T.A. to membership in the international body and barred the Messalist U.S.T.A. on the ground that it was not sufficiently representative. The board announced that it still intended to send a mission of inquiry to Algeria. A resolution also was published. This monument of cynicism paid tribute to the "Algerian trade unionists who have been deprived of their freedom" and to "those who, at the risk of their lives, continue their trade union task indispensable to the establishment of a democratic regime."

What was not said, but what appears to be true, is that the Tunisian U.G.T.T. in the person of its secretary-general, Ahmed Ben Salah, had blackmailed the I.C.F.T.U. by threatening to go over to the Communist-dominated World Federation of Trade Unions if the I.C.F.T.U. failed to admit the F.L.N.'s U.G.T.A. and to exclude the Messalist U.S.T.A. Be that as it may, the I.C.F.T.U. had, in its choice, capitulated to the rankest skulduggery and brought into its fellowship as violent a lot of cutthroats as ever put on the mask of trade unionism. The attentive observer of these maneuvers can only conclude that the I.C.F.T.U. is not above a double standard when it comes to the all-important question of "ethical practices."

Force Ouvrière protested meekly against the shrinkage of its jurisdictional limits. Robert Bothereau, secretary-general of *Force Ouvrière*, explained his organization's position in these terms:

> *Force Ouvrière* believes . . . that the admission of the U.G.T.A. can only increase the tension in a situation already so troubled. But, convinced that whatever the outcome of the Algerian problem may be, a cohabitation will be necessary, *Force Ouvrière* preferred to make a measured protest that would preserve future contacts.*

Force Ouvrière, obviously, was not going to be a problem either to the Socialist Government of France, to which it was tied by doctrinal affinity, or to the I.C.F.T.U., of which it was more or less an offshoot. Once or twice thereafter *Force Ouvrière* seemed to be on the point of stiffening its opposition to the U.G.T.A. In July, 1956, for instance, its executive committee called the I.C.F.T.U.'s decision to admit the U.G.T.A. a "historical error." But nothing ever came of these momentary signs of resolve.

On July 7, 1956, the Tunisian U.G.T.T., the Moroccan U.M.T., and the Algerian U.G.T.A. issued a joint statement expressing their determination jointly to "promote the development of free Algerian trade unionism as embodied in the U.G.T.A. and to give full efficacy to their support of the Algerian national cause."

The Tunisian weekly *Action* commented:

> This statement is of capital importance, for it seals the unity of the North African trade union movement in behalf of the liberation of Algeria and of the social advance of the workers.
>
> The extraordinary power of the unified North African labor movement must not be underestimated. The factors of this power are numerous.
>
> The three North African countries have the unhappy privilege of being afflicted by a degree of unemployment never before equalled in any of the countries of Europe or of the Middle East. . . . This great mass of unemployed, well organized, can weigh, and already does weigh, upon the destinies of the three North African countries. . . .†

One is forced to conclude, in the light of *L'Action's* comment, that freedom from want does not necessarily figure among the blessings of independence. This candid admission is interesting in itself. But *L'Action* went further; it suggested that human misery can and should be exploited by the nationalists in their quest for power. However, the boast of North African unity was not to be taken too seriously; it had yet to be proved by the test of time.

In Algeria, the F.L.N. gave the U.G.T.A. an added boost by recog-

---

* See *Le Monde* for July 7, 1956.

† See *L'Action* for August 6, 1956.

nizing the membership card issued by the federation's affiliated unions as a general safe-conduct. Having established its headquarters in the old M.T.L.D. central offices in the Rue de Chartres, the U.G.T.A. was now ready to back the F.L.N. with strike action at a moment's notice. Opportunities for service to the F.L.N. were soon to present themselves. We have already examined the role played by the U.G.T.A. in the 1957 "insurrectional strike.*

In Brussels, meanwhile, the I.C.F.T.U. had announced its "active support for oppressed Algerian trade unionists." The I.C.F.T.U. *Information Bulletin* for January 15, 1957, said a message calling for the "opening of negotiations between the French Government and the genuine representatives of the Algerian people" was to be sent to the various national delegations to the General Assembly of the United Nations then in progress. In February, 1957, the executive council of the A.F.L.-C.I.O. called on Washington to "mobilize the prestige and influence of the United States" behind the demand for Algerian independence.

Simultaneously, in Prague, the World Federation of Trade Unions proclaimed a "week of action and solidarity in behalf of the Algerian workers and people, for the cessation of hostilities, and the recognition of the independence of the Algerian people." When rival organizations pursue an identical goal, I cannot help feeling that one of them must be playing the part of a dupe.

In the I.C.F.T.U. *Information Bulletin* for April 15, 1957, this item appears:

> On February 16, the I.C.F.T.U. submitted a formal complaint to the I.L.O. against the French Government for the infringement of trade union rights in Algeria and supplied complementary information on March 22. The I.C.F.T.U. General Secretary says that this latest information makes it clear that trade union freedom in Algeria has, in fact, been completely suppressed. "We raise the strongest protest against this flagrant violation of trade union rights by a member government of the International Labor Organization," he writes to the I.L.O. Director General, "and express the hope that the Governing Body will deal with our complaint promptly and vigorously."

Mr. Oldenbroek did not give the source of his "latest information," but it is reasonable to suppose that it had come to him from his affiliated organization in Algeria, in other words, from the labor wing of the F.L.N. A modicum of honesty should, it seems to me, have prompted him to state his source; the issue would then have been much clearer. As to the "complete suppression of trade union freedom," we enter

* See p. 316.

here the realm of demagogy, unworthy of a decent labor organization. The record contains no evidence of French interference with trade unions not involved in the armed rebellion. No complaints were made by *Force Ouvrière*, by the *Confédération Française des Travailleurs Chrétiens* (the Roman Catholic federation), or by any of the independent unions, although all had Moslem members.

Jefferson Caffery once told me when he was United States Ambasador to Cairo that his relations with Colonel Gamal Abdel Nasser's revolutionary junta were "so good as to be almost embarrassing." I doubt if Raymond A. Hare, the present United States Ambassador to Cairo, could say as much. Political conditions in the Arab world are subject to sudden and disconcerting change. This is something our intrepid trade unionists would do well to ponder. They think they have won a victory over Communism when they have brought a nationalist labor federation into the I.C.F.T.U. But is the assumption safe? In my opinion, it is not. Let neutralism, "positive" or otherwise, overtake a few more Arab countries, and—who knows?—the North African labor federation may decide to seek their fortunes outside the American bloc. If that day comes, Messrs. Brown and company may realize the dangers of the game they have so lightly played.

Indeed, an embryonic alternative to the I.C.F.T.U. already exists. In March, 1956, a Congress of Arab Workers at Damascus was attended by labor delegates from Egypt, Syria, Lebanon, Jordan, and Libya. That congress gave birth to an International Confederation of Arab Trade Unions with headquarters in Cairo. In April, 1957, 1957, the *Union Tunisienne du Travail*, a short-lived splinter federation in Tunisia, sent a delegation to Cairo for talks with Arab labor leaders there. Although nothing came of this move, it may still be regarded as a portent. The Cairo group itself has given little sign of life, but it could, of course, be reactivated at President Nasser's pleasure.

49. THE JEWS

On May 12, 1956, at 12:20 P.M., a hand grenade was thrown at a café on the edge of the Shara, the old Jewish quarter of Constantine. Ten patrons of the establishment were wounded, all of them Jews. The culprit, an Arab terrorist, fled, but was shot down by European civilians a few moments later as he tried to take cover in the entrance to a building. Several of his accomplices, overtaken in a nearby café, drew a burst of automatic fire. Nine Moslems who may or may not have been terrorists were wounded. Meanwhile, wild fusillades had broken out inside the Shara. Three Moslems were killed and a fourth was wounded when a barber shop was blasted by vigilantes. But the shooting there seems to have been a two-way affair; an iron storefront across the street was later found to be full of holes. The bodies of three Moslems, presumably hit by stray bullets, were recovered elsewhere in the Shara.

Sirens sounded the general alarm. Groups of Territorials rushed to strategic points, taking up positions mainly along the parapet and road above the deep gorges of the Rhumel that separate the native and European sections of the city. For more than an hour, the rattle of automatic fire echoed in the ravines.

The disorders were the consequence of an attempted terrorist incursion. An all-out rebel attack had apparently been planned. Numbers of unarmed rebels already were converging on the city. Their weapons, it was learned, had been sent in beforehand and placed in the safekeeping of women. But the attack, prematurely begun, miscarried.

The next day, Constantine's Christian community celebrated the feast of St. Joan in an atmosphere of acute tension. At about 6 P.M., the unnatural silence of that Sunday evening was shattered by the report of gunshots in the heart of the Shara. When the police arrived, they discovered the bullet-riddled bodies of six Moslems in the street. Nine Moslems and two Jews were found to have been wounded. It developed that the patrons of an ice cream parlor in the Rue de France, struck with panic at the sight of a suspicious-looking Moslem passerby whose gestures might have been those of a man about to throw a hand grenade, had started shooting more or less indiscriminately. In other parts of the Shara, two Moslems were killed and seven were wounded in circumstances that could not be determined.

On the morning of May 14, Major General Jean Noiret, French commander in eastern Algeria, threw a cordon of troops around the Shara for the double purpose of protecting it against further terrorist infiltrations and of preventing further vigilante action. It was established that most, if not all, of the Europeans who had taken part in the shootings were Jews. That bloody weekend widened the gulf of bitterness between the Jews and the Arabs in Algeria and left the Arabs with a score to be settled.

The Shara, part of the congested old city of Constantine, was naturally sensitive to agitation of all kinds. Memories of the pogrom that had taken about 100 Jewish lives there in 1934 remained painfully alive. Twenty-two years after that earlier explosion of Moslem fanaticism, the Jews of Constantine reacted to rebel terror with a show of violence that revealed the vitality of their European reflex. Yet the Jews are as indigenous to Algeria as the Arabs.

In the past century and a quarter, the cultural advance of the Algerian Jews has been prodigious. Although, as Henri Weiler* observes in an excellent contribution to *Initiation à l'Algérie*,† a few Jews had dominated Algerian commerce prior to the French conquest, the Jewish community as a whole had been despised and mistreated by the Algerian Moslems and by the Turks. From time immemorial, the Algerian Jews had been an Oriental, Arabic-speaking people sunk deep in ignorance and squalor. The arrival of the French enabled them to throw off the shackles of centuries. Today, although many retain a working knowledge of Arabic, their language and culture are French. I do not know of a more striking example of assimilation.

The decree of October 24, 1870, sponsored by the French Jewish politician, Adolphe Crémieux, conferred full French citizenship, including civil personal status, on the Algerian Jews. Without losing their ethnic and religious identity, the Jews struck out enthusiastically on the road to emancipation. City folk for the most part, they flocked to the French schools and to the university. Their commercial and professional aptitudes quickly became a powerful stimulant to the general development of the country. In 1931, the Algerian Jews were estimated to number a little more than 110,000. By 1957, they had increased to about 140,000. Measured in terms of economic strength and productive capacity, they probably outrank the nine million Moslems.

The forward surge of the Jews seems hardly to have been impeded by the strong anti-Semitic feelings that pervade not only the Moslem community, but the non-Jewish majority in the European community as well. The Crémieux decree was actually revoked by the Vichy regime in 1940, and the Algerian Jews, like their Metropolitan coreligionists, lived through a period of official persecution. The revocation of the Crémieux decree was an act of inconceivable folly. How could it not have been understood in Vichy that, since the Jews had become an integral part of the fabric of European life in Algeria, any attempt to hold them to second-class status would betray the whole scheme of French endeavor there? It is difficult to penetrate the workings of the Vichy mind.

Luckily, the Vichy period was brief, and the scars it left have all

---

* Vice-principal of the Franco-Moslem *lycée* at Constantine.

† Paris: *Librairie d'Amérique et d'Orient*, 1957.

but vanished. Most Algerian Jews would now subscribe to the confession of an eminent Algerian Jewish physician, who said recently: "How can I not look upon myself as French? My parents were illiterate and poor, yet I have always found, in school, at the university, and in my career, that no door is closed to ability and willingness to work. Opportunity is, perhaps, the greatest boon that can be conferred by a country upon its sons."

What, one wonders, would Algeria be like if the Moslems, like the Jews, had developed a thirst for learning and progress? The answer cannot readily be given, for no such thing occurred. Too often, the *lycées* and the university have been to the Moslem students less a challenge and an opportunity than a source of frustration and resentment. For Islam is steeped in piety. Its own modes of thought and action are almost as immutable as the revealed word of the Koran. Any venture in the realm of Western culture involves for the Moslem a relinquishing of the divine for the temporal. The unchanging, and therefore reassuring, ways of the race must be left behind by the Moslem *lycée* and university student as he follows the difficult course of Western thought. Anyone who has felt ill at ease in a church of a faith possessing a strange liturgy will have an inkling of the perplexity of the Moslem student in a European school. Frequently, his sense of insecurity and inferiority find compensation in extreme nationalism and other attitudes of rebellion. For while the Jew has proved a true convert to progress, the Moslem is likely to remain an exile.

The Algerian Jew resembles a hermit crab in that, for centuries, he lived in the airless, exiguous shell of the Arab. When the French offered him a mansion, he was struck as by a revelation and turned his back on his former home forever. Only the Moslem remains torn between his own constricting heritage and the uncongenial, but manifestly superior, culture of Europe.

Despite the transformation of their community, however, the Jews are likely to be wiser in the ways of the Moslems than other Europeans. Centuries of living together, of commercial dealings, and endemic persecution have given them an insight few outsiders can match. For observers wishing to deepen their understanding of Moslem affairs, it is usually a good rule to consult the Jews.

One is constantly reading statements in the American press to the effect that the North African Jews have nothing to fear from Arab rule. It is alleged that King Mohammed of Morocco dearly loves his Jewish subjects and that President Bourguiba of Tunisia is proud to have a Jewish leader (André Barouch) as a member of his cabinet (Minister of Housing and City Planning). Such statements do not reflect the predominant feelings of the North African Jews themselves. Of course, in North Africa, as elsewhere, Jews often adjust their opinions and utterances to their personal interests. The discerning observer must allow for this. He will then have to decide whether the deep apprehension of the majority of the Tunisian and Moroccan Jews is warranted or not. But that the apprehension exists he cannot deny.

What the Jewish minorities need essentially, but what they have seldom if ever known under Arab rule, is freedom. The undercurrents of intolerance have always been strong in Islam; and as the Arab "awakening" progresses, they grow no weaker. It would, I think, be rash in the meantime to take royal or presidential professions of friendship at face value or as a long-term guarantee.

A Tunisian Jewish friend of mine, now an immigrant in Israel, merely shrugged one day after hearing Bourguiba praise the Jews. Pressed for a comment, he confined himself to a quotation from the first chapter of Exodus:

> Now there arose up a new king over Egypt, which knew not Joseph.
>
> And he said unto his people, Behold, the people of the children of Israel are more and mightier than we:
>
> Come on, let us deal wisely with them; lest they multiply, and it come to pass, that, when there falleth out any war, they join also unto our enemies, and fight against us, and so get them up out of the land.

The decision to "deal wisely" with the Jews is a recurrent one; it has been made before and will undoubtedly be made again. Thousands of Tunisian and Moroccan Jews, preferring to take their destiny out of the hands of their Moslem rulers, have migrated to Israel, and more would go if they could. But from Algeria, a mere handful have gone.* Unlike their coreligionists in the former protectorates, the Jews of Algeria have tasted the fruits of freedom and equality in the country of their birth.

The abortive rebel attack on the old city of Constantine and the shootings that followed left bad blood in their wake. Before the month of May, 1956, was out, the rebels had shown that they meant to avenge the Moslem dead. At Batna, south of Constantine, several Jews, including the rabbi of the town, had been wounded by terrorists. At Orléans-

---

* It was reported in April, 1957, that a total of 1,685 Jews had left Algeria for Israel since the beginning of the rebellion. Between January 1, 1955, and April 20, 1957, Israel received 42,846 Jews from Morocco and 3,240 Jews from Tunisia.

ville, a synagogue had been burned. A Jewish cemetery near Oran had been desecrated. On June 4, a Jewish shopkeeper in Constantine was assassinated. On June 19, five hand grenades exploded in the center of Colomb Béchar, killing a Moslem and wounding several Europeans. It was reported that the attack had been directed primarily against the town's Jewish inhabitants. Jews were threatened at Biskra, Aflou, and Bou Saâda. A Moslem boycott of Jewish merchants, decreed at Constantine, Batna, and Sétif in July, spread to Algiers and Blida in August.

In September, the M.N.A. (Messali Hadj's Algerian National Movement) issued a handbill taking the Jewish community severely to task for its failure to support the "national struggle." The "neutrality" of the Jews was criticized again by delegates to the September congress of the *Union Générale Commerciale Algérienne.* In September, too, a prominent Jewish cloth merchant was assassinated at Bou Saâda.

The campaign against the Jews had, however, developed haphazardly. It was not until mid-autumn that the F.L.N. moved to inject an element of calculated political direction. The first evidence of this was a message from the F.L.N. to Maurice Eisenbeth, the Grand Rabbi of Algiers, and to other leaders of the Jewish community. Sent in October, the message demanded that the Algerian Jews take a stand for or against the rebellion.

With that, the tone of rebel propaganda changed. Threats and harsh words gave way to overtures and cajolery. "We are all sons of the same soil," the rebel propagandists said in effect. "There is no difference between Moslem and Jew. We must all join hands to liberate our common homeland." Actually, the new "line" appears to have been laid down at a conclave of rebel leaders in the Soummam Valley in August, 1956. A handbill purporting to reflect the doctrinal position of that assembly attributed previous incidents of anti-Semitic violence to French "provocations." The "Algerian revolution," according to the handbill, had shown by its acts that it deserved the confidence of the Jewish community. The Jews, it said, were entitled to a fair share of happiness in the independent Algeria to come. Noting, however, that the Jews had not yet committed themselves to the cause of the F.L.N., it added:

> Despite the silence of the Grand Rabbi of Algiers, so different from the comforting attitude of the Archbishop of Algiers courageously and publicly bucking the tide and condemning colonial injustice,* the great majority of Algerians refuse to re-

* "Equivocal" would perhaps be a better word to describe the pronouncements of Archbishop Léon-Etienne Duval. His 1957 New Year's message was typical. In it, he said: "Sooner or later it will become irresistibly evident that

> gard the Jewish community as having gone over to the enemy camp for good.

The handbill urged Jews to follow the example of those among them who had "given their friendship to the Revolution, already proclaiming with pride their Algerian nationality." The choice of the few, the handbill said, was based on "experience, common sense, and wisdom." The document ended with this curious remark:

> The disappearance of the colonial regime, which has used the Jewish minority as a buffer to absorb the anti-imperialist shocks, will not necessarily result in the pauperization of the Jews. It is an absurd hypothesis to imagine that, without France, Algeria would be nothing. The economic prosperity of the peoples that have become free is evident. Greater national revenue will secure for all Algerians a more abundant life.

In October, 1956, the *Union Générale Commerciale Algérienne*, responsive to the wishes of its parent body, the F.L.N., started wooing the Jewish merchants, letting it be known that those who enrolled as members would be protected against "difficulties" with the rebels.

The Communists, too, eager to break down some of the racial antagonisms that crippled their action, rushed to the support of the new F.L.N. policy. They produced a document in which a "group of Algerian Jews" declared for the rebellion and urged their coreligionists to do likewise. The document said:

> In proclaiming our attachment to the Algerian nation, we give the lie to the colonialists, who, to prolong their domination, seek to convince the French people that the revolt here is nothing but the expression of a medieval fanaticism. In this way, we will shorten the butchery that has steeped Algeria in blood and cost so many innocent people their lives.
>
> However, if the ideas of many of us are unclear as to our national vocation, we all ardently desire a return to peace in Algeria. We know that the only way to achieve this is in negotiations between the French Government and those who are fighting, in particular the F.L.N., which has won the confidence of

---

Algeria can exist only through the peaceful cohabitation of the spiritual communities of which this country is made up. In the end, the arms must be silenced; but, to achieve this, hearts must speak. The initiative for this brotherly dialogue must be taken right here in Algeria." But the F.L.N. was undoubtedly correct in thinking that M. Duval would rather see France expelled from Algeria than the Roman Catholic Church.

the masses. It is for this reason that we hope to hear the Grand Rabbi of Algiers express, as the Grand Mufti has done, a desire for such negotiations.

But even as the F.L.N.'s olive branch was being held out by a variety of hands, two Jews were assassinated at Médéa, and the Jewish cemetery at Saint-Eugène in the suburbs of Algiers was profaned. Rebel advances went hand-in-hand with the implicit threat of reprisals in the event of non-cooperation.

Summoned by the F.L.N. to make their position clear, the leaders of the Jewish community temporized. Nevertheless, at a meeting of Jewish leaders in Algiers on October 27, 1956, it was decided that an understanding with the F.L.N. could not be contemplated.

A month later, the *Comité Juif Algérien d'Etudes Sociales* published in its review, *Information Juive*, a statement to the effect that since the Algerian Jewish community did not constitute a political entity, its various institutions could not express a collective political opinion. The statement continued in these terms:

> As regards the Moslem community, and in spite of the unjust penalty paid by too many of our coreligionists, innocent victims who have fallen these last months, we feel compelled to pay tribute to the rectitude, indeed to the cordiality, that has habitually characterized Jewish-Moslem relations in Algeria, and in particular during the period of Vichy.

In March, 1957, the French section of the World Jewish Congress warned that no non-confessional Jewish group, and no individual Jew, could speak on any subject in the name of the Jewish community as a whole. The section pointed out that, like other ethnic groups, the Jews inevitably held a wide range of opinions.

Since then, although the leaders of the Algerian Jewish community have clung to an attitude of extreme circumspection, its members have remained overwhelmingly hostile to the rebellion. The only notable exceptions have been a few Jewish Communists, pacifists, and left-wing Socialists, who advocate a negotiated settlement with "those who are fighting."

Nor has there been much evidence of a significant change of heart among the rebels. "May God curse them because of their mischief," says the Koran of the Jews (IV, 49). This malediction, intoned in mosques for centuries, provides a good clue to the deeper feelings of the Moslems toward the Jews. Despite their dialectical efforts, the rebel strategists were powerless to adjust the thinking of their followers to the proclaimed need for Jewish-Moslem amity.

On March 27, 1957, Jacob Chekroun, rabbi of Médéa, was assassinated by rebel terrorists on the steps of his synagogue. In April, 1957, the rebels decreed a boycott of Jewish merchants in Tlemcen. As a result, the Jews could not doubt that many in the rebel camp still placed more faith in fear than in persuasion.

50. A LOOK AT THE REBEL CAMP

It will be recalled that the Committee for Unity and Action, formed in the spring of 1954 at the behest of the Algerian expatriates in Cairo, had plotted the armed uprising of November 1, 1954, after its efforts to reconcile the quarreling Messalist and Lahouelist factions within the Movement for the Triumph of Democratic Liberties (M.T.L.D.) had failed. The members of that select committee must, therefore, be regarded as the fathers of the rebellion, the *chefs historiques* as they are called by the F.L.N. propagandists.

The decision to abandon the Messalists and the Lahouelists to their sterile disputes and to strike out on an independent course of violence with Egyptian support seems to have been taken at a meeting in Switzerland early in July, 1954. When that meeting broke up, Mohammed Khider, Hocine Aït Ahmed, and Mohammed Ben Bella went back to Cairo, while the other participants—Larbi Ben M'Hidi, Rabah Bitat, Mourad Didouche, Belkacem Krim, Mostefa Ben Boulaïd, and Mohammed Boudiaf—returned to Algiers, where a "war council" was held. It was on this ocasion that Algeria was divided into six *wilayas* or zones. Of the *wilayas*, five were to be organized as distinct commands at the outset, each falling to one of the chiefs present at the meeting.* The sixth *wilaya*—the Sahara—was left for subsequent attention.

Mourad Didouche, one of the five original commanders, was killed in combat in January, 1955. Mostefa Ben Boulaïd was captured in February, 1955; he escaped from prison in November of that year and was killed in March, 1956, in the explosion of a bomb set by a rival faction. Rabah Bitat was arrested by the French in March, 1955. Mohammed Boudiaf had fled to Cairo before the outbreak of the rebellion. There-

* See pp. 95–96.

fore, the death of Ben Boulaïd left only two *chefs historiques*—Larbi Ben M'Hidi and Belkacem Krim—still in the field.

Meanwhile, however, a new star was rising, that of Ramdane Abane, Krim's chief political lieutenant. An intelligent and well-educated Kabyle from Fort National, a revolutionary by conviction, the thirty-six-year-old Abane had made himself indispensable to his more primitive superior. He organized Krim's political, fiscal, and military apparatus in Kabylia and, when that was done, began in the spring of 1956 to cogitate schemes for concentrating effective control of the rebellion in the hands of a few field commanders and for reducing the Cairo committee to merely representational status. With this in view, he proposed that a supreme rebel congress be held, not in Cairo, not in Switzerland, but in the heart of Algeria itself. For there, the members of the Cairo committee, if they managed to attend, would inevitably appear more or less in the role of outsiders. Such a congress, Abane reasoned, would establish the primacy of the bands and of their leaders over the absentee *sayids.*

Although Mohamed Ben Bella and his associates in Cairo must have been suspicious of Abane's maneuver, they nevertheless agreed to attend the contemplated congress. The time and the place were set by Abane without consultation with Cairo. The distant leaders were merely informed of the decisions that had been made. Then, apparently, with a Machiavellian touch, Abane sent out word to the effect that the French had got wind of the plan and that, consequently, all participants were to stand by for an all-clear signal from him.

In a careful review of this episode of the rebellion, Serge Bromberger notes that Ben Bella and the other members of his committee spent twenty days at San Remo, Italy, poised to make a secret crossing of the Mediterranean at a moment's notice.* But the promised signal did not come. Their patience nearly exhausted, the pilgrims from Cairo resolved to continue their wait at Tripoli in Libya. It was there that the staggering news reached them—the supreme rebel congress had already been held in their absence.

That momentous gathering, held on August 20 in the Soummam Valley, was dominated by two Kabyles—Belkacem Krim and Ramdane Abane—and by two Arabs—Larbi Ben M'Hidi and Youssef Zighout. But the greater influence was exercised by the Kabyles. Ben M'Hidi, titular chief at *Wilaya 5* (Oranie), had just returned from a long sojourn in

* See *Le Figaro* for July 18, 1957.

Cairo and was not fully in the picture. As commander of *Wilaya* 2, Zighout was Krim's next-door neighbor. The credentials of some of the other delegates were rather more dubious. Omar Ben Boulaïd, pretentious brother of the late Mostefa Ben Boulaïd, had been designated as spokesman for the Aurès, then in a state of anarchy. The autonomous zone of Souk Ahras, important as a supply and communications corridor to Tunisia, was not represented at all.

Citing these deficiencies, Ben Bella was later to contest the representative value of the congress and the validity of its decisions. Nevertheless, the congress succeeded in casting the rebellion into a new structural mold.

At the instance of Abane, the congress created a National Council of the Algerian Revolution, whose seventeen titular and seventeen substitute members included the *chefs historiques*, the principal converts to the rebel cause (notably Ferhat Abbas), the F.L.N. leaders in Metropolitan France, and the field commanders in Algeria. Although this council was proclaimed to be the supreme governing body of the rebellion, its members were too scattered ever to convene in plenary session. It is safe to assume that the authors of the council meant it to remain a thing of paper, suitable for window decoration.

The congress also called into being a Committee of Coordination and Execution, described as a subordinate body comprising the chiefs of the six *wilayas*. Theoretically appointed by and responsible to the National Council, the committee could have been mistaken for the executive branch of a representative pseudo-government. In practice, however, since the council was a mere fiction, the committee more closely resembled a Directory. As Abane was well aware, the committee could perpetuate itself only by co-optation.

At least two *wilayas*—number one (the Aurès) and number six (the Sahara)—and possibly a third—number four (Algérois)—were without a titular chief in August, 1956. The anarchy prevailing in the Aurès had destroyed the unified command formerly exercised there by Mostefa Ben Boulaïd and Bachir Chihani. The Sahara was still, for the most part, beyond the rebel sphere of action. And the evidence suggests that Amar Ouamrane had not yet succeeded the late Mourad Didouche as chief of *Wilaya* 4. The rebel executive was, therefore, confined at the outset to Belkacem Krim (appointed supreme rebel commander), Larbi Ben M'Hidi, Youssef Zighout, and Abane. But Zighout fell in combat a month later, and Ben M'Hidi was caught by the French in February, 1957. Krim and Abane would then have been alone on the executive if they had not in the meantime co-opted two new members, Idir Aïssat, secretary-general of the F.L.N. labor federation, and Dalhab Saad, a former secretary to Messali Hadj.*

That Aïssat should have been given a seat on the Directory cannot fail to intrigue the observer. For Aïssat was not a free man. He had been interned by the French at Bossuet, forty miles south of Sidi Bel Abbès, in May, 1956. It is curious, too, that the obscure Saad should have been chosen in preference to, say, Lakhdar Bentobal, Zighout's successor as chief of *Wilaya* 2 (northeastern Constantinois). But one salient fact stood out—the committee was now composed of two Kabyles and two Arab nonentities. For a time, the Kabyle duumvirate of Krim and Abane ruled the rebellion.

The congress in the Soummam Valley defined rebel objectives as follows:

1. Total weakening of the French Army so as to deprive it of any possibility of a victory imposed by force of arms;
2. Large-scale deterioration of the colonialist economy by sabotage so as to make the normal administration of the country impossible;
3. Maximum disturbance of the economic and social situation in France so as to make the continuation of the war impossible;
4. Political isolation of France in Algeria and in the world;
5. Development of the insurrection in such a way as to make it conform to international law (personalization of the army, recognizable political power, respect for the rules of war, normal administration of zones freed by the Army of National Liberation);
6. Constant action to bolster the people against French attempts at extermination.

In addition, the congress made a cease-fire contingent on the following political conditions:

1. The recognition of the indivisible Algerian nation;
2. The recognition of the independence of Algeria and of its sovereignty in all matters, including national defense and diplomacy;
3. The release of all Algerian men and women incarcerated,

* Born in 1919 near Reibel, 230 miles south of Algiers, Saad completed secondary school in Algiers and got a government job in the taxation department. In 1952, he represented the Movement for the Triumph of Democratic Liberties (M.T.L.D.) at the Vienna congress of the Partisans of Peace. Two years later, when the M.T.L.D. split into two factions, Saad abandoned Messali and sided with Hocine Lahouel and the Central Committee. He was arrested in December, 1954, and released a few months later.

interned, or exiled by virtue of their political activity before or after the national insurrection of November 1, 1954;

4. The recognition of the F.L.N. as the sole organization representing the Algerian people and as the sole partner in negotiation. *Per contra,* the F.L.N. is answerable and responsible for the cease-fire in the name of the Algerian people.

A final section committed the F.L.N. to the concept of a North African federation. The declaration was unanimously adopted by the congress.

Mohammed Ben Bella and the members of his group* were in no position openly to disavow the Soummam Valley congress. But they hoped to reassert their claim to undisputed leadership by winning, if they could, a decisive diplomatic victory over the French.

Mohammed V's forthcoming state visit to Tunis, scheduled to begin on October 22, 1956, seemed to offer possibilities in this respect. For the Sultan of Morocco was as anxious as Mr. Bourguiba to promote a negotiated settlement of the Algerian conflict—a settlement based, of course, on prior recognition by France of Algeria's right to independence. The Sultan and the Premier were, indeed, vying for the honor of sponsoring the new Algeria. If, as anticipated, they undertook to draft joint peace proposals in consultation with the Cairo committee, Ben Bella could then reasonably turn to the Algerians and to the Arab states with the question: "What has Abane done to match this?"

The eve of the Sultan's departure for Tunis found Ben Bella, Mohammed Khider, Hocine Aït Ahmed, Mohammed Boudiaf, and Mustafa Lacheraf† in Rabat, where they were warmly received at the Imperial Palace.‡ It was agreed that the five would travel to Tunis as unofficial members of the Sultan's party.

* In February, 1956, the F.L.N. delegation in Cairo had turned itself into a "Committee of Six" comprising a "military commission"' (Ben Bella, Mohammed Boudiaf, and Larbi Ben M'Hidi) and a "political commission" (Mohammed Khider, Mohammed Lamine-Debaghine, and Hocine Aït Ahmed).

† Born at Sidi Aïssa (ninety-seven miles southeast of Algiers) in 1917, Lacheraf had been a schoolteacher and publicist before becoming propaganda chief for the F.L.N. in Metropolitan France. He had joined Ben Bella's group in Madrid.

‡ As a result of the Sultan's action in giving the rebel leaders a reception at the Imperial Palace, the French Government suspended negotiations then in progress between Paris and Rabat. The purpose of the negotiations was to establish conventions for the grant of French technical and financial assistance to Morocco.

The next day—October 22, 1956—the itinerant rebel leaders boarded a DC-3 commercial transport plane chartered from Air Atlas, a French-owned commercial airline in Morocco. Nine journalists, including Thomas Brady of *The New York Times*, also were taken aboard. After putting down briefly at Palma (Majorca), the aircraft headed for Tunis. However, when it reached a point close to the Algerian coast, the pilot was ordered by radio to land at the Maison Blanche airport near Algiers.

The pilot, a Frenchman, acceded to the order but, instead of proceeding directly to the point indicated, circled over the Mediterranean long enough to make his landing at Maison Blanche coincide roughly with the scheduled arrival time at Tunis. The plane's hostess engaged the passengers in conversation so that they would be less likely to notice the deviations from the prescribed course.

The surprise was complete. The passengers were convinced as the plane came in for a landing that they were at the El Aouina airport on the outskirts of Tunis. They realized that something was seriously amiss only when their plane, caught in the glare of searchlights, came to a stop at the center of a circle of armor. The five rebel leaders were instantly taken into custody by the French authorities.

The Sultan, when he heard of the capture of his guests, was in high dudgeon. But it could not be denied that the guests were of a peculiar sort, particularly in the entourage of a sovereign. All five were found to have been traveling under false names with false Moroccan and Egyptian passports. Ben Bella had been carrying, in addition, two weapons—an automatic pistol and a 9-mm. submachine gun—and more than a million francs in cash. A bulging briefcase in his possession yielded an abundance of fascinating material, including an address book containing the keys to two codes, a diary in which the rebel chief had recorded two meetings with Prince Moulay Hassan of Morocco in Seville (on April 8 and 23, 1956), details of arms transactions with prices given in dollars, a plan for an attack on the central police station at Oran, and proposed locations of drop points in Algeria for the parachuting of arms, ammunition, and supplies.

The atmosphere in Tunis on the afternoon of October 22 was, however, one of buoyant optimism. The Sultan and his official party, arriving aboard an Air Atlas Superconstellation, were welcomed at the airport by the Bey of Tunis and Premier Bourguiba in the presence of the diplomatic corps. A guard of honor presented arms while a military band played the Moroccan and Tunisian national anthems. From El Aouina, the Sultan and the Bey rode into town in an open car at the head of a procession of thirty vehicles. Clad in a pastel-blue *djellaba* (robe), the Sultan graciously acknowledged the ovations of enthusiastic crowds lining the streets. Here and there shouts of "Ben Bella!" and of "*Aljezäir yahia!*" ("Long live Algeria!") went up from groups of Algerians who had fallen in behind massed green and white flags of the rebellion.

At one point, a dozen or so Algerians, breaking away from a marching formation and shouting, "Lacoste to the stake!" surged with their flags toward the gates of the French Embassy (formerly the seat of the French Resident General). But the gates swung shut and the Algerians were dispersed by the police.

Later, at the Dar es Saâda palace in suburban La Marsa, where the Sultan and his party were to stay, M'Barek Bekkai, the Moroccan Premier, thanked the Tunisians for the warmth of their welcome. "I hope," he added, "that this visit will mark the beginning of a new era in the relations between our two countries. This will contribute to the liberation of our sister Algeria from colonialism, for Tunisia and Morocco are the wings of the Maghrib, and when the wings are free, the body, too, becomes free."

That evening, Bachir Ben Yahmed, Tunisian Secretary of State for Information, and a group of journalists gathered at El Aouina to await the arrival of the five Algerian rebel leaders. The vigil at the airport ended with gasps of surprise when it was learned that the five had been summarily snatched from the sky. In a midnight statement to the press, Mr. Ben Yahmed said: "The Tunis conference, which was to have been the conference of peace in Algeria, may at the outset and in a dramatic way turn into a war conference."

Mr. Ben Yahmed exaggerated. But the euphoria of the afternoon had certainly given way in the evening to stupefaction and anger. The Sultan remonstrated by telephone with President René Coty of France. Mr. Bourguiba directed Pierre de Leusse, the French Ambassador, to convey a strong protest to Paris. He then convened the Tunisian cabinet and kept it in session until 2:40 A.M. It was announced that Hassan Belkhodja, Tunisian Ambassador to Paris, had been recalled and that all activities scheduled for October 23 in connection with the Sultan's visit had been cancelled.

The next morning, Moroccan Premier Bekkai and his Foreign Minister, Ahmed Balafrej, flew to Paris to have it out with the French Government. Received that evening by Premier Mollet, the Moroccans demanded the immediate release of the five rebel leaders. M. Mollet replied that this could not be done. He argued that, in giving the rebel leaders an official reception at Rabat and in attempting to take them to Tunis as honored guests, the Sultan had acted in a manner regarded in Paris as highly unfriendly to France. Premier Bekkai intimated later that M. Mollet's attitude might lead to a breaking off of diplomatic relations between Paris and Rabat.

In Rabat, Hamad Douiri, Minister of Public Works, called the capture of the five an "act of pure piracy." The Moroccan Deputy Premier, Driss Hammedi, accused the French of having broken their pledged word. He asserted (what seems to have been true) that the Sultan had been trying to promote peace in Algeria "with the consent and encouragement of the French Government."

The Sultan himself said later in an interview that he had been pursuing his "delicate peace mission" with the "semiofficial consent of the French Government." He called the capture of the five the "most stinging blow that has even been struck at my honor not only as a sovereign, but also as a man." The incident served at least to illustrate the acute misunderstandings that were almost bound to flow from the equivocal policy M. Mollet had been pursuing in regard to Algeria.

M. de Leusse, the French Ambassador to Tunis, was so outraged by the capture of the five that, completely forgetting the proprieties of his office, he made bitter representations over the telephone to M. Lacoste in Algiers. As a minister in the Government, M. Lacoste was, of course, in no way answerable to M. de Leusse for his actions. The logic of M. de Leusse's position left him no choice but to resign, which he did forthwith. In Paris, Alain Savary, Socialist Foreign Secretary for Moroccan and Tunisian Affairs, also resigned in protest.

On the afternoon of October 23, Mr. Bourguiba, after handing M. de Leusse a joint Tunisian-Moroccan note of protest, brought his cabinet back into emergency session. He said at a news conference afterwards that the French action—he called it a "trap"—far from quelling the rebellion, would "cause the war to spread east and west from Algeria."

In a sense this had already happened, for on that very day events were taking an ugly turn in both Morocco and Tunisia. Rioting had broken out at Meknès and at Tunis. Casablanca and Rabat seethed with anti-French agitation. The Tunisian labor federation called a general strike. For several days, the French inhabitants of Meknès and French farmers in the surrounding countryside lived through a nightmare of indescribable horror. At least forty-nine men, women, and children were butchered by frenzied Moroccans; many more were wounded. Many homes and shops were destroyed.* About 200 farms were burned. A family of five, including three children, was massacred north of Petitjean.

---

* For the description of one episode of the Meknès riot, see p. 41.

Three French motorists were killed between Taza and Oujda. The world, however, took little notice.

On October 24, the Sultan and his party flew back to Rabat aboard an Italian plane. Four days later, the five captured rebel leaders were transferred to Paris and incarcerated at the Santé prison. Accused of participating in an attempt to demoralize the Army and the nation, they were held for trial before a military tribunal. Nevertheless, on November 19, 1956, acceding to the request of their counsel, the Minister of Justice (François Mitterrand) granted them the status of political prisoners, subject only to certain temporary restrictions described as necessary to the conduct of the judicial inquiry. At the time of writing—more than two years later—the five are still awaiting a problematical trial.

Meanwhile, Pierre Commin, acting secretary-general of the French Socialist party, admitted that he had conferred with three rebel leaders —Mohammed Khider, Abderrahmane Kiouane, and Mohammed Yazid—in Rome in September, 1956. It soon developed that the meeting referred to had been only one of a series of similar "contacts" between French Socialist emissaries and representatives of the F.L.N. On April 12, 1956, according to the Tunis weekly *L'Action,* Joseph Bégarra and Georges Gorse, Socialist members of the Assembly of the French Union, had attended a meeting arranged in Cairo by the Egyptian Government at the request of the French Foreign Minister, Christian Pineau. The F.L.N. representative there seems to have been Yazid. The second meeting took place on June 11 at Belgrade, where M. Commin, accompanied by Pierre Herbant, acting assistant secretary-general of the Socialist party, and Ernest Cazelles, Socialist member of the Assembly of the French Union, reportedly discussed with Yazid the possibility of a cease-fire. The journal *L'Action* asserted that at a third meeting in Rome on September 2, M. Commin had "recognized the natural and legitimate right of Algeria to independence" but had dwelt on the difficulties of making this development acceptable to French public opinion. M. Commin instantly denied having said anything of the sort. The fourth and last meeting brought M. Herbant and Dr. Lamine-Debaghine together in Belgrade later in September. There, if *L'Action* is to be believed, the two emissaries listed the "points of agreement" already arrived at and recognized the need for subsequent encounters.

It matters little what actually was said at these meetings. That they were held at all is sufficiently revealing. For the meetings brought into sharp relief the ambivalent attitude of the French Socialists toward the F.L.N. They were also a measure of Socialist delusions. In defiance of all logic and of the lessons of the recent past, the Socialists were still apparently convinced that the F.L.N. could be persuaded to meet the French Government halfway, that an acceptable compromise settlement could be bought at the price of substantial concessions. Many French Socialists simply could not face up to one of the hard facts of life, which is that in a conflict involving the possession of power a display of weakness is an invitation to defeat. They failed to see that "independence within interdependence" or qualified sovereignty was wholly abhorrent to the forces that had been set in motion with the outbreak of the rebellion. And so, through their misunderstanding of the nature of a conflict in which men were being asked to fight and die, they succeeded only in prolonging the killing. It would have been far better if they had had the clairvoyance and the courage to advocate the real alternative to uncompromising resistance—capitulation. For if peace was the supreme objective, it could always have been had at that price.

The same confusion, the same ambivalence, the same weakness of purpose came out in the episode of the five captured rebel leaders.

But for vacillations in Paris, the dramatic capture itself would probably have impressed the rebels as a sign of resolve and have shaken their morale. The Algerian Moslems were stunned to see pictures showing the indomitable rebel chiefs handcuffed like ordinary criminals on their way to prison. The violent anti-French agitation that followed in the wake of the capture was confined to Tunisia and Morocco. Algeria remained as quiet as a tomb.

Because of the secret encouragement it had given the Sultan of Morocco, Paris recoiled at the idea of bringing the five swiftly to trial and of punishing them for their crimes. And so the Government merely backed and filled, betraying its embarrassment and dissipating every advantage that, in other circumstances, might have accrued to it from the boldness of the capture. Paris was appalled by what Algiers had done but could not undo it.

If the French had meant to force the rebels to a decision in Algeria, the capture of the five would have been a godsend. If, on the contrary, their purpose was to make peace, the capture could still have been turned to good account. They had only to snatch the rebel chiefs from their cells and to lodge them in style at La Celle Saint Cloud, where, the previous November, the Sultan of Morocco had graciously accepted the capitulation of France. The gratitude of the rebel chiefs might then have enabled the French to obtain a semblance of reasonable terms.

Instead, the five were confined to the Santé prison, indicted for a crime punishable by death, given the status of political prisoners, and never brought to trial.

Following the capture of the five rebel leaders, Ben Bella's mantle fell temporarily on Ahmed Tewfik Madani, secretary-general of the Association of Ulema. On October 25, Mr. Tewfik Madani declared over Cairo radio that the Army of National Liberation was "resolved to fight to the end against the French." He said the rebel command had already held a "military conference" somewhere in Algeria and had decided that the capture of the five would have no effect on military operations or on the political objectives of the F.L.N.

The conference referred to may have been a meeting that took place at Belkacem Krim's mountain hide-out in Kabylia. It was an almost purely Kabyle affair, attended by such surviving stalwarts as Ramdane Abane, Amar Ouamrane, Amirouche, and Slimane Dehilès. The problem of *Wilaya* 1 (the Aurès), where the rebel bands had lapsed into anarchy, bulked large at the meeting, eclipsing the misfortunes of the decapitated Cairo committee. The task of restoring discipline in the Aurès devolved upon Amirouche, who promptly set out with plenary powers, only to find on arrival a condition beyond his control. Despite the Aurès, however, the cohesion of the rebellion was impressive enough to count as a tribute to the energy of its Kabyle general staff.

It was announced in April, 1957, that the F.L.N. had moved its external headquarters from Cairo to Tunis. But the Tunis committee, or *Idara*, had begun to assume major importance long before that. By the end of 1956, Tunisia had become a huge drillground, rest camp, and arms depot for the rebels. At least 5,000 armed Algerians were stationed on Tunisian soil; an additional 2,000 were in training there. A total of perhaps 200,000 other Algerians were living in Tunisia. The number included workers in the phosphate mines near Gafsa and all sorts of newer arrivals, among them families fleeing the insecurity of the Algerian frontier zone and men either wanted by the French police or sentenced to death by rebel leaders in the remoter parts of Algeria. Serge Bromberger of *Le Figaro* notes in his book, *Les Rebelles Algériens,** that, with money flowing freely through rebel hands, lucrative activities were available to astute camp followers in Tunisia. Arms, explosives, blankets, food, and medical supplies were bought, sold, and transported by swarms of parasites, while collectors, authorized and unauthorized, levied "taxes" more or less indiscriminately at the point of submachine guns.

* Paris: Plon, 1958.

Influence within the Tunis *Idara* was a fluctuating thing. Ahmed Mahsas, Ben Bella's former henchman, enjoyed a moment of power there, but he incurred Abane's hostility by supporting the "legitimacy" of the *chefs historiques* in opposition to the new executive and by encouraging the "Balkanization" of *Wilayas* 1 and 2. He even had Amar Benouada, titular second-in-command of *Wilaya* 2 under Lakhdar Bentobal, and Brahim Mezhoudi, another of Bentobal's lieutenants, ejected from his headquarters by the Tunisian police. But the Kabyles put an end to such antics by taking over at Tunis themselves.

Belkacem Krim established himself there as representative of the rebel "colonels," leaving Saïd Mohammedi, a forty-seven-year-old Kabyle, in command of *Wilaya* 3 (Kabylia). Amar Ouamrane turned *Wilaya* 4 (Algérois) over to Dehilès and took charge of arms-running from a more commodious and strategically located base of operations at Tunis. The arrest of Larbi Ben M'Hidi on February 25, 1957, left the F.L.N. executive with only one member still active in Algeria—Ramdane Abane, who had become "National Political Commissar." Benyoussef Benkhedda, chief of the autonomous zone of Algiers, stood by him. But both fled to Tunis soon afterwards. Early in 1957, Ouamrane, though not yet a member of the executive, emerged as the most powerful and influential member of the Tunis group.

In an analysis of the relations between the Tunisian Government and the rebel *Idara*, M. Bromberger gives us a conjectural glimpse of what must have passed between Ouamrane and Bourguiba when matters of mutual concern brought them together in the winter of 1957. He writes:

> The head of the Tunisian Government was profoundly and openly worried about the turn of events. Tunisia was submerged by a horde of traffickers over whom it had no control. Along the frontiers, *fellaga* in arms moved about freely, subjecting the peasants to their exactions. Throughout the country, incessant collections of funds depleted the meager resources of the population to the point of compromising the success of the Tunisian Government's bond drive . . . The head of the Government . . . had every reason to fear that the Algerian potential in Tunisia might, despite the anarchy that characterized it, become strong enough to hold the Tunisian Army in check.*

M. Bromberger hazards the guess that it was probably Mr. Bourguiba himself who, in conversation with Ouamrane, proposed the compromise plan that was soon agreed upon. Under this plan, the Tunisian National

* See *Le Figaro* for May 16, 1957.

Guard, an auxiliary force composed largely of former Tunisian *fellaga*—M. Bromberger calls it the Praetorian Guard of the Neo-Destour party—assumed responsibility for the transport of arms and supplies to the frontier. In return, the *Idara* undertook to remove all rebel concentrations to the frontier zone. Specific villages near the frontier were designated as rest areas for the Algerian rebels. It was understood, however, that rebel casualties would continue to be admitted to Tunisian hospitals.

Despite the restrictions imposed on rebel freedom of action in Tunisia, the new arrangements were eminently satisfactory to Ouamrane. They simplified his logistic problems and strengthened his hand in dealing with dissident factions in the rebel camp. For deliveries of arms and supplies were to be made at the frontier to the F.L.N. exclusively. This meant that Ouamrane could stop the flow of arms and supplies to any group showing an inclination to kick against the authority of the F.L.N. executive.

There were, in fact, at least two of these at the time. The first was a band led by Omar Ben Boulaïd, who claimed the right to succeed his late brother, Mostefa, as rebel commander in the Aurès. Unable to vindicate his claim either by force or by persuasion, Omar, breathing defiance, attempted to go it alone with a handful of faithful followers. The Bourguiba-Ouamrane agreement did him in. As has already been noted,* he headed for Cairo in response to a "summons."

The second dissident rebel group was that of Larbi Taleb, self-appointed commander of a *mintaqa* (sector) in the Sahara. Actually, his 400-odd rifles were confined to the region between El Oued and Gafsa, on the edge of the Sahara. From his base at Redeyef, a phosphate-mining center west of Gafsa, he struck northward toward Tunis. He could not, of course, hope to bring the Tunisian Army to its knees. His purpose seems rather to have been to cause so much mischief in the populous mining areas that Mr. Bourguiba would comprehend the advantage of buying him off with access to arms and supplies.

Instead of coming to terms with Taleb, however, Bourguiba sent the Tunisian Army against him. The Tunisian regulars, reinforced by auxiliaries under the command of Lassoued Sassi, a former *fellaga* chief, caught the unfortunate Taleb at Matmata in southern Tunisia on June 18, 1957. It was reported a few days later that 200 men of Taleb's band had also been captured by the Tunisian force. These developments underscored the practical importance of the Bourguiba-Ouamrane agreement to the F.L.N.

Meanwhile, a guerrilla chief who had previously given evidence of a

---

* See p. 246.

rebellious attitude toward the F.L.N. high command was coming to the fore, not as a dissident leader, but as one of Ouamrane's best lieutenants. He was Mahmoud Chérif, a former officer in the French Army. On more than one occasion, Chérif had demonstrated his skill in spotting an opportunity for himself and in turning it to good account. He attracted attention first in the spring of 1956, when efforts were being made to unify three strong but quarrelsome rebel bands along Algeria's eastern frontier.

Sami Farhi and his three brothers, with about 250 Berbers of the T'Kaka tribe under their command, had aroused the enmity of other bands in the area by attempting to control the flow of the contraband arms. The Farhis' main rivals were Mahmoud Guenez, who, at the head of 250 Arabs of the Yahyia tribe, had carved out a zone of influence in the Morsott district north of Tebessa, and Lazhar Cheriet, a former Tunisian *fellaga* chief, whose 700 partisans were Berbers of the Allaouna tribe. Cheriet's domain lay on both sides of the frontier in the region of the Tunisian town of Fériana. During a stormy "unity" meeting held in June, 1956, at Mathildeville near Tunis, one of the Farhis shot and wounded Cheriet. Whereupon Chérif took over Cheriet's command. From that already eminent position, Chérif was later to rise to titular supremacy in *Wilaya* 1 (the Aurès) with the rank of "colonel" and a seat on the F.L.N. executive.

By March, 1957, Tunis was, as we have seen, crawling with rebel "brass." For Amar Ouamrane, Belkacem Krim, Ahmed Mahsas, Mahmoud Chérif, Lazhar Cheriet, and the others, the Tunisian capital undoubtedly had many charms. In addition, various lesser chiefs chose to establish their headquarters on Tunisian soil. Amara Bouglez, known as Amar Laskri, lord of the semiautonomous Souk Ahras corridor, set himself up at Souk el Arba. Abdallah Belouchet, commanding the Sedrata *mintaqa* southwest of Souk Ahras, was to be found at Tadjerouine south of Le Kef. Sami Farhi was safely ensconced at Thala.

These would have been cumbersome guests in any country. In tiny Tunisia, they practically had the Government over a barrel. As a champion of Arab nationalism and a contender for pre-eminence in the North African federation to come, Bourguiba had no choice but to welcome and appease the future probable masters of Algeria. His margin for maneuver was extremely narrow.

But the Tunisian Premier had one hope—that the rebels, taking a page out of his own book, would see the wisdom of coming to terms with the French. It would not have occurred to him to suggest a compromise in ultimate ends. But he understood the value of flexibility as a political expedient. He knew that the French Government, in its desire to throw off the burden of effort in Algeria, would clutch at a straw. If only the rebels could be persuaded to proffer it!

On March 7, 1957, Premier Mollet reiterated his government's unconditional offer of a cease-fire to be followed by free elections. This, Bourguiba felt, was enough to go on. He endeavored to impress his views on the rebel politicians gathered in Tunis for the celebration of the first anniversary of Tunisian independence.

On March 21, he organized at his personal residence a luncheon-conference attended by Premier Bekkai of Morocco, Ferhat Abbas, and Mohammed Lamine-Debaghine.* On that occasion, he reportedly urged the rebel leaders to accept the free elections and the neutral supervision proposed by the French. He was said to have begged them to drop their insistence on a prior recognition by France of Algerian independence if the French agreed in return to accept the verdict of the voters, whatever it might be. But for once Bourguiba's renowned powers of persuasion failed to have their usual magic effect. The rebel politicians, precariously perched at the top of an unstable pyramid, exposed to the mailed fist of the Kabyle revolutionaries, stuck to their guns. There could be no elections, they said, without a prior recognition of Algerian independence and of a provisional government of their own making.

This position was stated the following day by Lamine-Debaghine at a press conference held in the offices of the Federation of Tunisian Civil Servants. Lamine-Debaghine was flanked on the platform by Amar Ouamrane, Ahmed Mahsas, and Ferhat Abbas. Below them sat Amar Benouada and two rebel functionaries (Aït Hassan, a lawyer, and Rachid Abdelaziz, national secretary of the F.L.N. labor federation). Lamine-Debaghine declared:

> Elections are a domestic matter in which Algeria alone is concerned, to the exclusion of France and the United Nations. We demand prior and unconditional recognition of Algerian independence. No cease-fire can be contemplated before the proclamation of our independence.
>
> It cannot be denied that all the Algerians are with us. They have proved this and are proving it every day by their combat against the French troops. In these circumstances, elections are perfectly useless. . . .
>
> There can be only one class of citizens in Algeria—Algerians.

* The previous month, Lamine-Debaghine had succeeded Tewfik Madani as head of the "External Delegation" of the F.L.N. Amar Ouamrane had become chief of the military section. Ouamrane's two assistants were Ben Mostefa and Brahim Mezhoudi.

> Therefore the French must opt. If they remain French, their interests will be respected as will those of all foreigners living in Algeria. . . .

Lamine-Debaghine also thundered his anathema at Messali Hadj's Algerian National Movement (M.N.A.):

> Algeria is the F.L.N.! The F.L.N. can prove that the Algerians are behind it to a man and that it completely controls the Army of National Liberation. Only in France do a few individuals claim allegiance to the M.N.A. This movement has cut itself off from the Algerian community.

While Lamine-Debaghine was speaking, Ouamrane glared at the French correspondents in the room. He fiddled nervously with a pencil and clenched his teeth. After a few vain attempts to interpose his remarks, he leaped to his feet and, pounding on the table, launched into a diatribe against French "atrocities." However, Lamine-Debaghine and Ferhat Abbas managed to calm him; they represented to him in Arabic that they were supposed to be handling political affairs.*

One cannot help wondering what Mohammed Ben Bella in his prison cell thought of all this. For the former generalissimo of the rebel forces did not hold Lamine-Debaghine in high esteem. In a letter sent from the Santé prison and seized by the French, Ben Bella said the *chefs historiques* had lost confidence in Lamine-Debaghine forever. (The letter was addressed to the absent leader's "brothers in Algiers.") Hocine Aït Ahmed, writing to Ramdane Abane, was more explicit. "His bad faith and his intellectual dishonesty," Aït Ahmed said of Lamine-Debaghine, "are not to be doubted. . . . My dear brother, he has disgusted everybody." There seems to be reason to believe that Lamine-Debaghine was, in fact, an inveterate intriguer, sedulous to advance his own interests.

On April 17, 1957, the Tunis newspaper *Al Amal* announced the official transfer of the External Delegation of the F.L.N. from Cairo to Tunis.

One of the constant objectives of the F.L.N. in 1956 and 1957 was the establishment of an Algerian government in exile. Such a scheme could hardly commend itself to Mr. Bourguiba, for if it materialized, positions on both sides of the Mediterranean would be hardened, and the chances of a negotiated settlement would be diminished. Moreover, Mr. Bourguiba had no desire to be bound over to a pseudo-government

* See Max Clos' "*Les Extrémistes algériens ont fait échouer les tentatives de conciliation de Bourguiba*" in *Le Figaro* for March 23, 1957.

that could not possibly be recognized by the United States. It may be surmised that he wanted nothing to jeopardize what his regime needed above all else—the adrenalin of hard dollars.

But to the F.L.N., the idea of a government-in-exile had great appeal. If, as might reasonably be anticipated, such a government was recognized by most or all of the Bandung powers, the F.L.N. would be immeasurably strengthened. Its claim to be regarded as the sole representative of the Algerian people would then have the official backing of populous nations whose influence was felt at Washington and at the United Nations. The difficulty lay primarily in Tunisian and, no doubt, Moroccan reluctance to endorse the scheme; but internal rivalries also were a serious obstacle.

There was talk in January, 1957, of Ahmed Ahmed-Bioud as possible head of an Algerian government in exile. That this former Nazi agent* should have been considered for such a post cannot be understood without reference to his connections. Ahmed-Bioud, more commonly known as Bayoud, was in Cologne at the time with Ahmed Kamal, a United States citizen of Turkish descent. The two had apparently known each other in the past, for Mr. Kamal seems to have been a contributor to Ferhat Abbas's Democratic Union of the Algerian Manifesto (U.D.M.A.) when Ahmed-Bioud was assistant secretary-general of that organization. But in 1957 their association was of another nature. Mr. Kamal had set up a secret society in Tripoli called *Jamaiat el Islam fi Ifriqya al Shamalya* (Islamic Association of North Africa). Purporting to be essentially a cultural group, the society was in fact working for the Algerian rebellion. Propaganda, technical and financial assistance, and arms were the uncultural commodities in which it dealt. What Ahmed Kamal and Ahmed-Bioud were up to in Cologne in 1957 is a matter for conjecture,† but evidently the F.L.N. looked upon the protagonists and their activities with the highest favor. Mr. Ahmed-Bioud undoubtedly had the British-French-Israeli intervention in Egypt in November, 1956—and especially

---

* Born in 1908 at Bou Tlétlis near Oran, Ahmed-Bioud married Margaretha Doppman, a Swiss woman of German descent. He was a schoolteacher before World War II. In 1944, he served the Nazis as head of the North African section of the *Deutsche Arbeits Front* in Berlin, where he was associated with Haj Amin Husseini, Grand Mufti of Jerusalem. After the war, he fled to Cairo. In October, 1952, he was appointed preceptor to the children of Mohammed Naguib, the Egyptian Prime Minister.

† In the summer of 1956, Ahmed-Bioud and Mohammed Boudjemline, another of Ferhat Abbas's disciples, had traveled assiduously between Switzerland, West Germany, and Holland in search of arms for sale. They had been in partnership then with Ahmed Kamal and Idriss Abdelkrim, a son of the exiled Riff leader.

the Egyptian debacle in the Sinai Peninsula—to thank for his sudden rise to prominence. For the events of November had left Gamal Abdel Nasser in no position to continue arms deliveries to the Algerian rebels, and other possible sources were eagerly sought. The revival of the Egyptian dictator's fortunes during 1957 and the consequent resumption of the flow of arms to the rebels once more reduced Mr. Ahmed-Bioud to obscurity, despite his connections.

If, as some said, Ahmed Kamal had access to abundant reservoirs of oil money in the Middle East, his standing with the rebels was easily explained. For the rebellion was an expensive undertaking. Its budget has never, of course, been published in neat columns of revenues and expenditures. But a few clues to its general outline may be garnered pending a more accurate accounting.

The Algerian labor force in France constituted a primary source of revenue. Of some 300,000 Algerian emigrant laborers, an estimated 125,000 were regularly employed in French industry and public works. These wage earners were fair game for F.L.N. and Messalist extortioners, whose methods of coercion were those of the rankest gangsterism. A total of 618 attacks involving Algerians was reported in 1956. The number included forty-six crimes listed as "political murders." In 1957, the Algerian crime rate in France climbed sharply. In the first two months of that year, 436 Algerians were stabbed, clubbed, or shot; forty-three of these were killed. Since the F.L.N. and Messalist "collectors" were constantly at each other's throats, it is impossible to know how many of the victims were simply recalcitrant contributors. The overwhelming majority of the wage earners undoubtedly contributed to both factions without demur. The standard monthly contribution for laborers was 2,000 francs ($5.70).

Algerian merchants and coffeehouse-keepers were compelled to pay much more than this. Although the exact amount cannot easily be ascertained, an incident in Morocco may be cited as an indication. On April 17, 1957, Saad Rahal, thirty-four years old, an Algerian pharmacist in Meknès, perished with his mother when a parcel sent to him through the mails exploded in his home. It was discovered that, two months running, M. Rahal had refused to pay his contribution to the F.L.N. For Algerian pharmacists in Morocco, the contribution was set at 100,000 francs ($285) a month. A comparable scale may well have prevailed in France, with the added problem of rival collecting agencies.

A French estimate put the total monthly contribution of the emigrant Algerians in France to the F.L.N. alone at 500 million francs ($1,428,000). A sum at least as great was thought to be levied each month in Algeria itself. According to one report, for instance, the rural township of Tebessa (100,000 inhabitants) was pouring 30 million francs ($85,700) a month into the rebel coffers, despite the fact that the Moslem farmers in the area were 330 million francs ($940,000) in debt to the local Provident Society. In other words, the F.L.N.'s revenue from individual contributions must have been in the neighborhood of one billion francs ($2,857,000) a month.

How was the money spent? The maintenance of one guerrilla fighter in the field probably cost close to 30,000 francs ($85) a month. With rebel strength at approximately 20,000 regulars early in 1957, the fighting force as a whole cost perhaps 600 million francs ($1,714,000) a month. The balance—400 million francs ($1,143,000)—presumably went for services, propaganda, overhead, and pocket-lining. The French believed, no doubt rightly, that the substantial contributions made by the Arab states and funds collected from other outside sources were used primarily for the purchase and shipment of arms and ammunition. Rebel armament was estimated in April, 1957, to include ten mortars, seventy-three machine guns, 224 machine rifles, 1,100 submachine guns, and upwards of 10,000 army rifles.* New weapons were thought to be reaching the rebels at the rate of about 1,000 a month. Among the new weapons seized by the French were British 303 army rifles, Lewis guns from Egypt, and Beretta pistols imported directly from Italy.

The externals of military organization and even of political power had been an important consideration with the rebels from the start. Uniforms, badges, and shoulder patches gave the individual *moujahid* (combatant) a sense of being an authentic soldier. The sanctity of rank dwelt in the minds of officers and men alike. Civil authority, too, though unstable, acquired a measure of prestige wherever the rebels could impose it on the population. Communiqués, typewritten travel orders, rubber stamps, and a vocabulary of heterogeneous European origin clothed the rebellion in the trappings of bureaucratic legality. Maps with military and civil divisions and subdivisions plotted in graced the walls of humble mountain *gourbis* (huts) occupied by rebel leaders. *Wilayas* were divided into *mintaqa* (zones), *mintaqa* into *nawahi* (areas), and *nawahi* into *fouroua.*

In many places, of course, the administrative arrangements of the F.L.N. were purely theoretical. In others, however, they actually functioned. There, the key figure was usually the *raïs,* or political commissar. Acting as civil affairs officers for the commander of the *mintaqa,* the

---

* It is interesting to compare these figures with the estimates of the previous year. See p. 299.

raïs had charge of propaganda, finances, intelligence, and, occasionally, relations with European settlers. Lesser officials, controlled by the *raïs*, policed the *douars* (native villages), collected "taxes," settled disputes, and victualed such bands as might be quartered in the sector. In some villages, little, elected "liberation committees" came into existence as a sort of democratic adjunct to the F.L.N., but their pretensions seem always to have been extremely modest. The whole system was, of course, dependent on the fortune of rebel arms; in adversity, it vanished; but it could as easily sprout again.

The anomaly of a rebel executive committee composed of four living men only,* one of them in prison, had sooner or later to be corrected. This was particularly true in that a measure of power had latterly passed into the hands of two non-members—Amar Ouamrane and Mohammed Lamine-Debaghine. The matter was attended to with a minimum of fuss at a meeting of F.L.N. leaders in Cairo on August 25, 1957. The simplest of expedients was used. The *ad hoc* gathering assumed the attributes of sovereignty by calling itself the National Council of the Algerian Revolution. It then proceeded to revamp the executive committee.

On September 5, 1957, Ferhat Abbas announced the new executive committee in a press release distributed at Geneva. As for the National Council, it was said only that the number of members had been increased from thirty-four—seventeen regular and seventeen substitute—to fifty-four, all regular; no names were given. The new Committee of Coordination and Execution was composed of nine members, three of them drawn from the old executive committee and the Tunis *Idara,* three from the External Delegation, and three from the powerful group of field commanders. In addition, five imprisoned *chefs historiques*—Mohammed Ben Bella, Mohammed Khider, Hocine Aït Ahmed, Mohammed Boudiaf, and Rabah Bitat—were listed as honorary members. The nine who now sat on the committee were:

From the External Delegation:

Ferhat Abbas, 58 years old.

Dr. Mohammed Lamine-Debaghine, 40 years old.

Abdelhamid Mehri, 31. Once a member of the Lahouelist faction in the old Movement for the Triumph of Democratic Liberties, Mehri seems to have turned up in Cairo toward the end of 1955. Mohammed Khider put him to

---

* Belkacem Krim, Dalhab Saad, Ramdane Abane, and Idir Aïssat. The latter was a prisoner of the French. Dalhab Saad was so obscure and inconspicuous that the French thought his seat on the executive was occupied by Benyoussef Benkhedda, chief of the autonomous zone of Algiers.

work organizing "Algerian Bureaus" in Damascus, Beirut, and Amman.

From the old executive and Tunis *Idara*:

Amar Ouamrane, 38, former sergeant in the French Army.

Belkacem Krim, 35, former corporal.

Ramdane Abane, 37, former secretary of the administrative township of Châteaudun-du-Rhumel in the Constantine department.

From the corps of field commanders:

Abdelhafid Boussouf, 31, commander of *Wilaya* 5 (Oranie), former member of the Revolutionary Committee for Unity and Action (C.R.U.A.).

Mahmoud Chérif, 40, commander of *Wilaya* 1 (the Aurès), former lieutenant in the French Army.

Lakhdar Bentobal, 34, commander of *Wilaya* 2 (North Constantinois).

The Kabyle hegemony was at an end, on paper at least; but Krim, Ouamrane, and Abane* retained control of military affairs and arms procurement. They could afford to concede the claims of the External Delegation and of the field commanders to seats on the somewhat shadowy Committee of Coordination and Execution.

51. THE REVOLUTION OF MAY 13, 1958

The French bombing of the Tunisian frontier village of Sakiet Sidi Youssef on February 8, 1958, did not have the consequences predicted by most observers. For instead of internationalizing the Algerian conflict and of precipitating a negotiated settlement there, the bombing marked

* Ramdane Abane died in Tunisia in the spring of 1958. The circumstances of his death were veiled in mystery. *El Moudjahid*, the F.L.N. organ printed at Tunis, reported in its issue for May 28, 1958, that Abane had been mortally wounded "on the field of honor" early in April while on an inspection tour of the guerrilla army. The French, however, believed that Abane was in the "protective" custody of his fellow insurgents in Tunisia at the time of his death.

the beginning of the end of the Fourth French Republic and, by the same token, gave French Algeria a chance of survival.

Sakiet, it will be recalled, was not only a frontier village; it was also an Algerian rebel position. From machine-gun nests inside the village, the rebels had been firing—not without some success, apparently—at French aircraft on patrol over the frontier area across the border. The previous month, fifteen French soldiers had been killed and five captured in an ambush laid by rebels based on Sakiet. The bombing raid was ordered by the French command to silence rebel guns at Sakiet and to put an end to rebel incursions from that village.

The brutality of the attack, however, shocked the world. Sakiet was subjected to daylight bombing and strafing by three waves of planes, including United States-made B-26 bombers and Corsair fighters. According to official Tunisian figures, sixty-eight persons were killed in the raid, among them eleven women and twenty children; 100 persons were wounded. Although the identity of the male victims was not disclosed by the Tunisian Government, Premier Félix Gaillard told the French National Assembly on February 12 that the "majority of the victims were soldiers of the F.L.N." This assertion cannot be checked since, to my knowledge, no newspaper correspondent on the spot made any effort to ascertain the identity of the male victims. Perhaps M. Gaillard was right.

For Tunisian Sakiet—as distinct from the parts of the village occupied by the Algerians—the raid was a catastrophe. Apart from the death that had been rained down upon it, the material damage was considerable. Visiting correspondents reported that private dwellings, a school, stores, and "public buildings" had been hit. What the "public buildings"—including a Tunisian National Guard post—had been used for was not stated.

Defending the action in the French National Assembly, Premier Gaillard placed responsibility for the civilian casualties on the Tunisian Government for its willingness to harbor and aid the rebels who had kept France at war in Algeria for more than three years. M. Gaillard could, it seems to me, have put the matter in more explicit terms. For the Tunisian Government had been warned that the right of pursuit would be exercised against Algerian rebels attacking the French from positions on Tunisian soil. It therefore had a clear duty to its own people to see that the Algerian rebels did not set up machine-gun nests in inhabited villages; that they did not, in effect, hide behind the bodies of Tunisian women and children. The French, on the other hand, if they had permitted the rebels to kill with impunity from such a sanctuary, could never have hoped to insure security along the frontier. The loss of innocent lives at Sakiet was an appalling tragedy. But the man primarily responsible for it was Habib Bourguiba.

The Tunisian Government retaliated the next day by informing Paris that French troops stationed in Tunisia by virtue of a mutual defense convention would not be allowed to circulate outside their camps. President Bourguiba ordered a blockade of the Bizerte navy yard and naval air base and swore the Tunisians were ready to "lay down their lives" if France refused to evacuate her garrison.

On February 13, Tunisia submitted a formal request for a meeting of the Security Council to consider a French "act of aggression" against her. Mongi Slim, the Tunisian ambassador to the United States, informed Soviet delegate Arkady A. Sobolev, then chairman of the council, that Tunisia would regard herself as in a state of "legitimate self-defense" in the event of a violation of the newly imposed restrictions on the movements of French ground, naval, and air units within Tunisian territory. The device had been cleverly contrived! Any French unit commander in Tunisia unwilling to accept the humiliating barrier thrown about him would have to shoot his way out, setting fire to the international powder keg prepared by Bourguiba. Though sorely provoked, the French Army wisely chose to drink the cup of humiliation.

Meanwhile, France filed a countercomplaint in the Security Council, charging that Tunisia permitted Algerian rebels to operate from Tunisian soil against the territorial integrity of France and against the security of persons and property. Paris could undoubtedly have stolen the initiative from Tunisia by lodging a prior complaint coupled with a demand for neutral observation of the Tunisian-Algerian frontier. As a result of its commitments to the Algerian rebels, Tunisia would almost certainly have refused to receive neutral observers, thereby weakening its position. But, as usual, French diplomacy failed to meet the challenge.

The Tunisian complaint to the United Nations and the fettering of the French Army were only part of an operation designed to bring the United States, and possibly even the United Nations, into the picture in such a way as to hasten a negotiated settlement of the Algerian conflict. Mr. Dulles had, in fact, already opened a vista that seemed to lead in that direction. On February 11, he had said at a news conference: "It is very difficult to isolate the problem of Algeria from the problem of Tunisia and, perhaps, Morocco . . . I don't think we would be excluded by any purely arbitrary legal views from taking any course of action which we thought would really improve the situation." This was Mr. Bourguiba's contention as well; and, in addition, Sakiet provided a splendid opportunity to prod the United States into action.

Washington was painfully anxious to avoid a Security Council debate involving a delicate issue between Tunisia and France, for that would only put the "honest broker" in an uncomfortable corner. There was also the fear that such a debate would enable the Soviet Union to make a propaganda killing at the expense of the West. Mr. Bourguiba was, of course, fully alive to these apprehensions. Therefore, on the very day of the Tunisian complaint, he suggested a way out. He said in Tunis that, if France accepted United States mediation, Tunisia also would accept it and would withdraw her complaint to the Security Council.

On February 15, a Government spokesman in Paris said after a cabinet meeting that France would accept the "good offices" of the United States, but would not submit her dispute with Tunisia to American arbitration. The next day, Mr. Bourguiba made the alternative to a mediation effort even more disagreeable to the United States and France; he instructed Mr. Slim in New York to bring the Algerian question before the Security Council as an extension of the Tunisian complaint on the bombing of Sakiet. On February 17, France and Tunisia accepted a joint offer by the United States and Britain to use their good offices toward a settlement of the dispute. The Security Council then postponed the scheduled debate on the Franco-Tunisian issue to allow time for conciliation by the United States and Britain. Mr. Bourguiba made no secret of what he expected to come of this. He said on February 18 that the settlement of the Algerian conflict would have to result from pressure by the United States and other Western powers on France.

The man chosen to be the American mediator was Robert D. Murphy, Deputy Under-Secretary of State. This appointment provided still another clue to American intentions. We have already encountered Mr. Murphy in these pages. It was he who, as President Roosevelt's personal envoy, had told the Algerian nationalists in 1942 that the end of colonialism figured among the American war aims.* There was no reason to believe that his views had changed substantially in the interval. Mr. Murphy's British partner in mediation was Harold Beeley of the Foreign Office.

At the first meeting between Mr. Murphy and Mr. Bourguiba in Tunis on February 25, the Tunisian President reportedly gave great emphasis to his central contention—that the Algerian conflict necessarily came within the purview of the mediation effort. It cannot be doubted that Mr. Murphy concurred fully with Mr. Bourguiba on this point; but, of course, he could not say so openly without ruffling the French and compromising his mission.

In the three weeks that followed, the Murphy-Beeley mediation team shuttled between Tunis and Paris, trying to hammer out a set of pro-

---

* See p. 20.

posals acceptable to the French and Tunisians as a basis for discussion. The task was complicated by the French insistence on Tunisian "non-belligerence" in Algeria and by Tunisia's refusal to consider joint or neutral surveillance of her frontier with Algeria to prevent the passage of rebel reinforcement and supplies.

Mr. Bourguiba was, in the meantime, blowing hot and cold. At one moment he was summoning the West to choose clearly between the Tunisian and French positions (or, as one American correspondent put it, "making a last-ditch stand to prove that cooperation with the free world pays"); at the next moment, he was extending an olive branch to the West and to France. In a speech before the Tunisian Constituent Assembly on March 20, he proclaimed his readiness to cooperate with France and thanked Britain and the United States for their role in keeping the case from degenerating into violence.

The *New York Times* correspondent in Tunis attributed Mr. Bourguiba's "startling change in tone" in part to "assurances given him privately by the United States and Britain that the allies of France would make forceful efforts to bring about a negotiated end to the three-year-old nationalist insurrection in neighboring Algeria." Here we reach the heart of the matter!

On March 17, Messrs. Murphy and Beeley returned to Paris from Tunis with their completed set of proposals. These included: withdrawal of most of the 22,000 French military personnel in Tunisia; neutral surveillance of former French military airports to prevent their use by or for the Algerian rebels; recognition by France of Tunisian sovereignty over Bizerte and the negotiation of a new basis for continued French occupancy; re-examination of the cases of French residents expelled from their homes in Tunisia during the acute phase of the crisis; and reinstatement of ousted French consular officials. On April 10, Christian Pineau, the French Foreign Minister, told the Foreign Affairs Committee of the National Assembly that Messrs. Murphy and Beeley had been unable to resolve the deadlock over control of the Algerian-Tunisian frontier. Nevertheless, the cabinet, at the end of a twelve-hour meeting, decided on April 12 to accept the Murphy-Beeley proposals as a basis for discussion and to open direct negotiations with Tunisia on all disputed points except that of the frontier itself (the one that had touched off the crisis and mattered most).

C. L. Sulzberger, foreign affairs columnist of *The New York Times*, stated an evident truth when he wrote that the ultimate goal of the mediation effort was "to produce a situation in which a settlement of the Algerian civil war could be attempted." A realization of what was afoot and of the probable consequences for France and Algeria if the maneuver should succeed brought the Gaillard cabinet to the ground in the early hours of April 16. The 321-255 vote against M. Gaillard in the National Assembly constituted a rejection of the proposals made by the Anglo-American good-offices mission.

It is extraordinary to observe, however, that this slight *contretemps* seemed not to dismay Mr. Murphy in the least. On April 17, Robert Doty, chief of the *New York Times* Paris bureau, reported on "unimpeachable" authority—the source can hardly have been other than Mr. Murphy himself—that the United States was "increasingly convinced of the need for a non-military settlement of the Algerian rebellion." Mr. Doty added, significantly, that the United States did not exclude the "possibility of negotiations with the National Liberation Front." He also described Washington as being convinced that M. Gaillard's successor "would probably be led by events to resume the good-offices effort on terms much the same as those on which M. Gaillard fell."

Although the State Department issued a denial the following day, it was impossible to believe that Mr. Doty and the other correspondents who had filed similar reports had dreamed the whole thing up. Certainly, in Metropolitan France and in Algeria, the American position was widely assumed to be exactly as stated on April 17. France, in the words of Robert Lacoste, had been heading straight for a "diplomatic Dien Bien Phu."

In Paris, the political consultations, party caucuses, and other rituals connected with the process of finding a new government lasted nearly a month. During that period, two events of a less futile nature occurred in North Africa. The first of these was a Pan-North-African conference held in Tangier and attended by leaders of the two ruling nationalist parties—the Istiqlal and the Neo-Destour—and of the F.L.N. (The F.L.N. delegation was headed by Ferhat Abbas.) In a final communiqué on April 30, the conference recommended the formation of a revolutionary Algerian government in exile "after consultation with the governments of Tunisia and Morocco."* The conference also committed the "Moroccan and Tunisian peoples and governments" to the "total support" of the "Algerian people . . . in the war for independence."

The second notable event of that interregnum period was the execu-

* The formation of a "Provisional Government of the Algerian Republic" was announced in Cairo on September 19, 1958. It included all the living members of the Committee of Coordination and Execution (the F.L.N. executive) as set up in Cairo in August, 1957 (see pp. 362–363), with the sole and unexplained exception of Amar Ouamrane.

tion, undoubtedly in Tunisia, of three French soldiers who had been prisoners of the Algerian rebels for more than eighteen months. An announcement made by the F.L.N. *bureau de presse* in Tunis on May 9 said the three had been accused of torture, rape, and murder, sentenced to death by a special tribunal of the Army of National Liberation sitting in "national territory," and executed for their crimes.

Despite this reference to a judicial procedure, the reaction in Algeria and Metropolitan France was one of horror. In the absence of any neutral corroboration, the presumption was that there had been no semblance of a fair trial. The evidence suggested, on the contrary, that the three unfortunate soldiers had been chosen at random and killed as a reprisal for the execution of convicted Algerian terrorists in French prisons. The previous issue of the rebel organ, *El Moudjahid*, had put the French on notice in these terms: "The blade of the guillotine must stop. Let French opinion be warned. Beginning tomorrow, each Algerian patriot to mount the scaffold signifies one French prisoner before the firing squad." On April 24, the day before the alleged sentencing of the three French soldiers, Abderrahmane Taleb, a chemistry student at the University of Algiers and a former purveyor of bombs to the F.L.N., and two other convicted terrorists had been guillotined in Algiers.

The hardening of the rebel position as reflected in the Tangier conference and in the execution of the three French soldiers came at a time when the Paris regime gave the impression of being irremediably lost in mediocrity and instability. When, on April 22, Georges Bidault abandoned his attempt to form a government, it became clear that those who had defeated M. Gaillard by rejecting his proposal for renewed talks with Tunisia could not rally a majority of their own behind a policy tougher than the one previously pursued. On May 2, the Socialist party decided not to participate in a new government, presumably in the hope that if matters got worse, Guy Mollet would be called upon to save the situation. In the interim, however, the party's decision meant that Robert Lacoste's incumbency as Minister for Algeria was at an end.* M. Lacoste had been a stout fighter for the defense of French Algeria, but he had been forced to wage most of his battles in Paris—against the friends of the rebels and others in his own party, on neighboring benches in the National Assembly, and in the press. The loss of this plucky man was deeply felt in Algeria.

René Pleven, a former Premier with a weak attitude toward Algeria, was about to form a new government on May 8 when he was ditched

* M. Lacoste had been Minister Resident in Algeria under Premier Guy Mollet. He had become Minister for Algeria when the Bourgès-Maunoury Government was formed in June, 1957.

by the Radicals in a dispute over the person of the Defense Minister designate, André Morice, a dissident Radical. Several key portfolios in M. Pleven's ephemeral cabinet were held by advocates of a "liberal" or, as it was sometimes called, an "evolutive" policy in Algeria. These were: Maurice Faure, a Radical (Foreign Affairs); Edgar Faure, a Radical (Finance); and Pierre Pflimlin, chairman of the Roman Catholic Popular Republican party (Oversea France). But Pierre Mendès-France and his Radical associates could not stomach M. Morice, who was closely identified with the group favoring a policy of resistance in Algeria. As Defense Minister under Premier Maurice Bourgès-Maunoury from June to September, 1957, he had initiated the right of pursuit as a weapon against rebel incursions from Tunisia. The electrified barbed-wire entanglements strung along the Algerian side of the frontier were known as the "Morice Line." For these reasons, the Radicals felt that M. Morice's presence in the Government as Defense Minister was incompatible with the "liberal" policies they were hoping to pursue.

On May 13, Pierre Pflimlin went before the National Assembly to seek investiture as Premier. In political coloration, his cabinet could not be distinguished from its stillborn predecessor—except that M. Morice had been eliminated. M. Pleven got Foreign Affairs; Edgar Faure retained Finance; Maurice Faure was given Interior; and Pierre de Chevigné, a Popular Republican (Catholic), went in as Defense Minister. M. Pflimlin's formal appeal to the National Assembly for support included a pledge of further military action against the Algerian rebels as a prelude to cease-fire negotiations, possibly with the help of Tunisian and Moroccan intermediaries. It was anticipated that, with the Communists voting against him, M. Pflimlin stood little chance of winning a majority.

The politicians in the Palais Bourbon were apparently unaware of the mounting perils. They acted as if the "system" could go through an indefinite number of receiverships without dangerous public protest. They were impervious to the growing disgust, nausea, and despair on both sides of the Mediterranean and to the revolutionary currents then gathering force in Algeria. They ignored the exacerbated patriotism of the standing army, sent again and again to defend the interests of France on bloodstained fields only to see victory forfeited by the Government of the moment. And yet the portents of an impending storm had been numerous and unmistakable.

M. Soustelle and his associates, although they had been unable to muster a majority behind M. Bidault, were determined to bar the way to M. Pleven. In this, they had strong backing in Algiers. To prove it, the *Union pour le Salut et le Renouveau de l'Algérie Française*, a group headed by M. Soustelle, invited the population of Algiers to take part in a peaceful demonstration on April 26. M. Lacoste, who at first had taken a favorable view of the contemplated demonstration, changed his mind at the last minute and forbade it; no mention of it was allowed to appear in the press. But handbills went out, and the demonstration was held in spite of M. Lacoste. "The gathering and the march," according to Alain de Sérigny, publisher of the *Echo d'Alger*,* "took place in the greatest calm. This was what the Paris newspapers called the 'oath of the twenty-sixth of April,'† which was nothing more than a warning designed to show the public powers that neither Algeria nor the Algerians could be delivered up to others. A resolution was handed to the Igame,‡ Prefect of Algiers, M. Serge Baret, by the patriotic associations represented by a Vigilance Committee. There was no mention whatever of General de Gaulle. But it should be noted that M. Léon Delbecque, head of M. Chaban-Delmas's psychological action service § and a member of the U.S.R.A.F.,¶ had come to Algiers on a personal visit and had had much to do with the organization of the April 26 demonstration."

When, despite this warning shot across its bows, the "system" in Paris continued to go its insouciant way, many people in Algeria began to wonder to what hope they could still cling. In this climate of despair, the wildest enterprises stood some chance of success. A prerevolutionary situation was developing.

On May 8, 1958, the thirteenth anniversary of V-E Day, the Army honored M. Lacoste, the departing Minister for Algeria, with an imposing march-past, a medal, and a citation. For twenty-seven months, the citation said, M. Lacoste had set a high example of patriotism, courage, and abnegation. When General Raoul Salan, supreme commander in Algeria, made the presentation of the medal—the Cross of Military Valor with palm—shouts of "Stay with us!" went up from the crowd. In an order of the day to the troops, M. Lacoste expressed his confidence in ultimate

---

* In his book, *La Révolution du 13 Mai* (Paris: Plon, 1958).

† The oath, taken by about 8,000 demonstrators, was: "Against whatever odds, on our tombs and on our cradles, taking our dead on the field of honor as our witnesses, we swear to live and die as Frenchmen in the land of Algeria, forever French."

‡ An acronym formed from the full title, *Inspecteur général de l'administration en mission extraordinaire*; in other words, a "super prefect," responsible for a group of departments.

§ Chaban-Delmas, Gaullist deputy for, and mayor of, Bordeaux, was Defense Minister in the Gaillard Government.

¶ *Union pour le Salut et le Renouveau de l'Algérie Française.*

victory. "It [victory] will be certain," he said, "the day those who lead France understand that there is no longer any room for pessimism and manifest a steadfast and fully demonstrated determination, in spite of the want of understanding shown by certain of our allies."

These words seemed, in Algiers, to echo the popular demand for a government of national union; in Paris, they sounded like a repudiation of the Socialist party's decision not to join the Moderates, Radicals, and Independents in any new government. M. Lacoste was not more explicit, but it may safely be assumed that he was in something less than wholehearted agreement with either his party's leadership or the efforts then being made to resurrect the ideal of government by the Left alone, of a new Popular Front.

On the night of May 9, a telegram was carried by a general officer to the Elysée Palace in Paris. It had been sent earlier in the day by General Salan to General Paul Ely, Chief of Staff of the Armed Forces; but it was meant for President Coty. This is what it said:

> The present crisis shows that the political parties are profoundly divided on the Algerian question. Press reports suggest that the abandonment of Algeria may be contemplated by means of a diplomatic process that could begin with negotiations toward a cease-fire. I take the liberty of reminding you of my conversation with M. Pleven, in the course of which I stated categorically that the sole clauses of a cease-fire could not be other than these: "France, confirming her appeal for a cease-fire, invites the rebels in Algeria to turn over their arms and guarantees, with a large amnesty, their return to the bosom of a reinvigorated Franco-Moslem community."
>
> The Army in Algeria is oppressed by the sense of its responsibility: toward the men who are fighting and who risk a useless sacrifice if the national representation is not determined to maintain French Algeria, as stipulated in the preamble of the *Loi Cadre;* toward the French population of the interior, which feels abandoned; and toward the Moslem French, who, in greater numbers each day, have again placed their reliance in France, confident that our reiterated promises never to abandon them will be kept.
>
> The French Army in its entirety would feel the abandonment of this national patrimony to be an outrage. Its reaction of despair could not be foretold. I ask you kindly to call our anguish to the attention of the President of the Republic; it can be dispelled only by a government resolutely determined to maintain our flag in Algeria.*

* The text of General Salan's telegram is taken from Alain de Sérigny's book, *La Révolution du 13 Mai.*

A copy of this telegram was handed to M. Lacoste in the presence of Generals Allard and Jouhaud.* The next day, without waiting for a new government to be formed, M. Lacoste left Algiers for Périgueux, his political bailiwick, via Paris. He knew a demonstration was planned for May 13 to honor the memory of the three French soldiers executed by the F.L.N.; apparently, although he was said to favor the demonstration, he did not want to be a party to it. In any case, the effect of his departure was to create a power vacuum in Algiers. Into this vacuum, the Army was soon to step. If it had not done so, there is no telling what might have happened.

The events that followed can best be described under separate date lines.

May 13

In response to a decision of the Vigilance Committee, places of business and workshops in Algiers closed their doors on the afternoon of May 13. Activity subsided almost everywhere, and streets normally clogged with trucks and buses on a Tuesday afternoon were free of traffic. The gates of the university had been closed by order of the rector. Only primary schools remained in session.

Although the official ceremony in memory of the three executed soldiers was not scheduled to begin at the War Memorial until 5 P.M., the first formation of demonstrators appeared in the heart of downtown Algiers at a little past 2:30 P.M. Several hundred strong, it marched past the central post office, the War Memorial and the university, and up the Rue Michelet—the Fifth Avenue of Algiers—singing the *Marseillaise* and shouting "*Algérie française!*" There was a hesitation when the crowd reached the vicinity of the United States information center. Then a rock was hurled through the plate-glass window. This seems to have been the signal for a general attack. In a matter of minutes, before the security forces could intervene, the place was sacked and the street was littered with books and magazines.

Later, demonstrators belonging to another formation attempted to pillage the offices of the *Journal d'Alger*, a daily newspaper published by Georges Blachette, close political friend of Jacques Chevallier. This time, however, a unit of the Third Colonial Parachute Regiment moved in and cleared the building.

* As commander of the Algiers Army Corps, Major General Paul Allard was one of General Salan's senior aides. Major General Edmond Jouhaud was commander of the French Air Force in Algeria. Like Rear Admiral Bertrand Géli, the Navy commander in Algeria, General Jouhaud came under General Salan's authority.

Delegations from the suburbs and from the surrounding towns were, meanwhile, converging on the center of Algiers behind their banners and flags. Marching secondary school students and teachers held aloft a banner marked with the words, "French Algeria against all comers." The motto, "Act and prevail," was inscribed on another banner; a third said, "No Government of surrender." Handbills were scattered from passing motorcars. Horns sounded *Algérie française* in code—three shorts and two longs. The shouted slogans were mostly: "The Army to power!" "Soustelle with us!" and "Bourguiba to the stake!" Strains of the *Marseillaise* echoed from near and far.

Little by little, the steps leading up from the Plateau des Glières, opposite the central post office, to the "G.G." (*Gouvernement Général*) above—the War Memorial stands on a slight elevation at the foot of the steps—came alive with people. When government employees peering from windows of the G.G.* were hissed and booed, a detachment of Republican Security Guards in full riot kit took up positions at the top of the steps. At that point, the arrival of a delegation of Moslem war veterans created an opportune diversion; its flag-bearers were wildly acclaimed.

By 4:30 P.M., there were perhaps 100,000 people in and around the Plateau des Glières. Symptoms of nervousness and impatience could be detected as groups of demonstrators surged forward and back. A loud-speaker rigged to the building housing the offices of the Army magazine, *Le Bled*, blared out patriotic slogans, while the crowd responded with shouts of "*Algérie française!*" The names of Pflimlin, Mendès-France, Chevallier, and other public figures were booed. Stentorian voices from the crowd rose above the clamor to announce that: "All decisions not emanating from a government of public safety will be considered null and void." Or that: "The people will not obey a government that does not cement the French Union." Huge applause.

The War Memorial was now completely encompassed. Nevertheless, the veterans advanced toward it in column formation while students and others spontaneously linked hands to open a passage through the crowd. Two cars equipped with loud-speakers preceded the flag-bearers. From one of them, an amplified voice declared: "The European and Moslem veterans, shoulder to shoulder here as they were at the front, come to pay honor to the three assassinated soldiers—Sergeant Richomme and Privates Decourteix and Feuillebois."

A tremendous ovation greeted the war veterans. Kisses were thrown.

* If many civil servants remained at work despite the decision of the Vigilance Committee, it was because they had been notified that sanctions would be taken against absentees.

Words of thanks were addressed in particular to the Moslem veterans for their presence. The *Marseillaise* was sung. "These flags," said the loud-speaker, "have been brought back from wars where we fought for freedom . . . We must know whether we have the right to call ourselves Frenchmen." Wreaths having been placed at the foot of the monument, the flags were lowered, and a minute of silence was observed. An *Echo d'Alger* reporter noted simply in his account of the ceremony: "It was impressive, this immense crowd that all at once became silent."

But the tumult resumed instantly afterwards, so that an air force band and an honor guard encountered the greatest difficulty in taking up positions below the monument prior to the arrival of the "authorities." At 5:55 P.M., fumes of tear gas wafted down from the G.G. caused added confusion. Although, from below, it was hard to tell what had happened, there had apparently been a scuffle involving some turbulent youths and Republican Security Guards on the esplanade in front of the G.G.

Immediately, however, from another direction, the sound of police sirens announced the approach of the "authorities"; they arrived moments later. General Raoul Salan, the supreme commander, was there, accompanied by Air Force General Edmond Jouhaud and Admiral Philippe Auboyneau, French naval commander in the Mediterranean. Next came Generals Paul Allard and Jacques Massu. The civil authority was present in the person of Serge Baret, "super prefect" of Algiers. Escorted by military police, the group advanced to the foot of the monument and deposited there a wreath of roses. Bugles sounded taps and the band played the *Marseillaise*, but both were almost lost in the shouts and acclamations of the crowd.

The official group left the monument to cries of "Massu to power!" Overhead, helicopters buzzed by at low altitude. Instead of departing by car as they had come, the "authorities" headed for army headquarters on foot. Some observers thought Massu, in mottled battle dress, his sleeves rolled up, seemed a little embarrassed to be almost the sole object of the crowd's enthusiasm. General Salan, his superior, led the way, but the cries were, "Massu!" "Massu!"

The ceremony was over. The crowd was beginning to disperse. It was then that voices shouted, "All to the G.G.!" A loud-speaker took up the refrain, adding: "The C.R.S.* provoked us without any violence on our part. All to the G.G. We will join the others again up there." By 6:15 P.M., compact groups of youths had set out to take the G.G. by storm.

The man who, by all accounts, was the first to shout, "All to the G.G.

* *Compagnies Républicaines de Sécurité.* The initials are often used to designate the members of this state police formation. In this book, I have generally referred to them as Republican Security Guards.

against the rotten regime!" and who certainly did more than anyone else to stimulate the attack on the government building was Pierre Lagaillarde, president of the *Association Générale des Etudiants d'Algérie*. Although no longer a student—he was, in fact, a lawyer at Blida—Lagaillarde had unflaggingly used his influence within the student movement to combat any threat to French Algeria. He was much in evidence on the afternoon of May 13. Dressed for the occasion in the uniform he had once worn as a parachute lieutenant in the Army, he operated from a sort of command car that enabled him to move swiftly from one place to another on the fringes of the demonstration. At no point were Lagaillarde and his youthful companions tempted merely to mingle with the crowd and to shout *Algérie française* until they were hoarse without doing anything about it.

At 6:15 P.M., then, the scene abruptly shifted. The center of the demonstration was no longer in the Plateau des Glières or in the vicinity of the War Memorial, but on the splendid esplanade above, or the Forum, as it is usually called,* with a plunging view of downtown Algiers, the port, and the sea. The functional, modern building rising on the northeast side of the Forum was the seat of the Government General. A bust of Marianne, symbol of the Republic, in the spacious lobby was a reminder that the structure belonged to the masters of the regime and was the bastion of their power in Algeria.

After a first encounter with the Republican Security Guards during the official ceremony at the War Memorial, the youthful insurgents had, apparently, backed away from the acrid fumes of tear gas. But the arrival of reinforcements, summoned by Lagaillarde, gave them new courage, and the attack was resumed. Subjected to a barrage of stones, the guards fell back to the doors of the G.G.; heavy iron gates swung closed behind them. More tear grenades burst in the Forum. Although relatively few in number, the guards could, no doubt, have repulsed the insurgents at the price of a few cracked heads; their performance suggests that they did not have their heart in their work.

In any case, commandeering a heavy truck for the purpose, the insurgents rammed the gates and, almost before they knew it, had the building at their mercy. There followed an hour or more of perfect anarchy, marked by scenes of wanton destruction. While a vanguard of youths swept through the corridors and offices of the G.G., plundering files, flinging dossiers out of windows by the armful, ripping out telephone wires, and breaking things under the noses of startled functionaries, the destructive rage of other insurgents vented itself upon cars

* Its official name is Place Georges Clemenceau.

parked in the Forum, presumably those of fainthearted government employees who had stuck to their office chairs instead of joining the demonstration. Windshields were smashed; tires were punctured; car bodies were dented. The insurgents made havoc, too, of the library on the ground floor of the G.G. The statue of Marianne was unbolted and removed from its pedestal. A fire broke out but was quickly extinguished. Suddenly, Lagaillarde appeared on a third-floor cornice, standing with his feet apart and his arms in the air. At this signal, more attackers surged forward. Papers, letters, and administrative forms of various colors continued to flutter down from the upper stories of the building.

Was a revolution in progress? Or were these merely students on the rampage? The question must have occurred to the many *Algérois* who, instead of going home after the ceremony at the War Memorial, filtered through cordons of paratrooopers and climbed the steps to see what was going on at the G.G. above. With their arrival, the crowd on the Forum grew denser. Insurgents waving flags from cornices and from the roof of the building shouted encouragement to those below. More and more people poured into the Forum until, by 7 P.M., the crowd there had reached some 30,000. Once again, the shouted slogans were heard: "*Algérie française!*" "The Army to power!" and "Soustelle with us!"

From the first-floor balcony of the G.G., Colonel Paul Ducournau, chief of M. Lacoste's military staff, pleaded for calm. He might as well have been addressing the ocean in a storm; his lips moved, but his words were completely lost. Unable to speak, he held up a blackboard. On it he had chalked this message: "I have just telephoned to Paris. We have demanded a government of public safety." He turned the blackboard around. The words on the back were: "The Army is the guarantee of French Algeria." The crowd applauded, but the demonstration continued. At 7:30 P.M., General Massu swung into the Forum aboard a jeep stuffed with paratroopers. The crowd reacted with a thunderous ovation.

Not expecting a second demonstration, still less an attack on the G.G., General Massu had, at the close of the ceremony, returned to the headquarters of the Tenth Parachute Division at Hydra on the outskirts of the city. Hearing that the G.G. had been taken by bands of youths, he rushed to the scene, fully determined to put an end to the disorders. Once inside the building, he sought out the ringleaders and expostulated vehemently with them. He upbraided Lagaillarde with particular severity, calling his reserve officer's uniform a "disguise."

But General Massu was quick to realize that matters could not so easily be sorted out. The invasion of the G.G. had, no doubt, been the work of a youthful horde; yet this act, despite the accompanying destruction, had been charged with the anguish and also with the hope of countless Algerians. Moreover, the youths inside obviously had the passionate sympathy of the crowd outside; and the feelings that had erupted with such violence after the memorial ceremony were also to a large extent shared by the Army. It is reasonable to suppose that, amid the hubbub and confusion, General Massu sensed that the day could not end simply with the expulsion of the insurgents from the G.G. Something positive had to emerge.

A few moments after General Massu's arrival, General Salan and his staff also appeared. They had come through an underground passageway linking the headquarters of the Tenth Military Region (Algeria) on the Place d'Isly to the G.G. Three separate groups were now present in the building. The first of these was made up of top officials of M. Lacoste's proconsulate, including Pierre Chaussade, who, as secretary-general, had been M. Lacoste's immediate deputy. In this group, all but Colonel Ducournau had played a passive role. General Salan and his officers constituted the second group. They had already covertly repudiated the regime in Paris, but they remained the defenders of the Republic and the natural enemies of anarchy. The third group, an extremely curious one, had been born of the day's events; it was composed of the insurgent leaders, of men who, by their audacity and eloquence, had acquired an ascendancy over the crowd. M. Lagaillarde was, of course, one of them. Another was a man whose speeches from the balcony had been particularly forceful. Asked whom he represented, he replied, "The crowd." He was later identified as André Baudier, a clerk in the city housing authority. Others were: Rodolphe Parachini, an employee of the Shell Company; Paul Moreau, a film distributor; Armand Perrou, a salesman; Gabriel Montigny, an employee of a cash register company; and Joseph Jolivet, a foreman. These were the revolutionaries. They belonged to no political party. They had not previously known each other. From total obscurity, they had been catapulted to a position from which they could shake the Republic to its foundations.

Tense moments were experienced on both sides when the army group and the insurgent group met face to face. The next day, at a press conference, General Massu gave this account of the proceedings:

> Scarcely had I entered [the building] when I was harpooned by a bunch of young fellows in M. Maisonneuve's* office. I tried

* Pierre Maisonneuve, on leave as president of *Electricité d'Algérie,* was director of M. Lacoste's civil and military cabinets.

> to convince them that their demonstration was, to say the least, misplaced. But there was no loud-speaker by which to make myself heard by the demonstrators scattered through the building.
>
> It was then that General Salan arrived. He did not approve of the demonstration either. He tried to speak. The crowd did not want to listen to him; besides, the lack of a loud-speaker hampered him as well.
>
> It was then that the young fellows and young men who were there . . . explained to me that only a committee of public safety could channel the emotions of the crowd. "We are setting up this committee," said one. "Come into it with us. Your repute will enable you, and you alone, to calm them."
>
> General Salan said, "After all, that is the best solution." I agreed then to participate in the committee, judging that this was, no doubt, the only way of controlling its action. I must say, in addition, that all those chaps seemed to be motivated by undeniably patriotic sentiments.
>
> Thus it was . . . that the committee was formed. I then brought in: my chief of staff, [Lieutenant] Colonel Ducasse; [Lieutenant] Colonel Trinquier,* who I knew was held in high esteem by the people of Algiers; and Colonel Thomazo,† who, because of his post at the Army Corps, would enable me to keep in constant touch with the superior command, and also with veterans groups, for he was very close to them . . .‡

Beginning at a little past 8 P.M., Colonel Trinquier's paratroopers, having thrown a cordon around the G.G., set about clearing the building. This was done quietly but firmly. No untoward incidents occurred. At 8:40 P.M., a huge French flag was draped from the first-floor balcony, and General Salan appeared. He was greeted with boos and catcalls, for he was thought to be a pillar of the regime. He withdrew. Then this announcement was read by one of the insurgent leaders: "The Army is with us. We have formed a Committee of Public Safety. Salan is with us." After a moment's silence—while this extraordinary piece of news was being assimilated—the crowd roared its approval. It also shouted for

---

* Colonel Trinquier had succeeded Colonel Marcel Bigeard as commander of the Third Colonial Parachute Regiment.

† Colonel Jean Thomazo was assistant to General Allard, commander of the Algiers Army Corps.

‡ This version of General Massu's remarks is taken from Raymond Dronne's book, *La Révolution d'Alger* (Paris: Editions France Empire, 1958). According to the *Echo d'Alger*, General Massu said: "I looked at General Salan. . . . He said nothing. I had barely thirty or forty seconds in which to reflect. I decided to accept in order to control the action of this committee. . . ."

General Massu, who, stepping to the front of the balcony, said: "The Army is at one with you. You will serve the cause of French Algeria by remaining calm and disciplined. We have agreed to await with vigilance the news which you hope to hear from Paris."

At the suggestion of a civilian member of the committee, many of the demonstrators sat down in the Forum. They realized that they might have a long wait ahead of them and also, no doubt, that their continued presence there would strengthen the hand of their representatives inside the building. Meanwhile, loud-speaker cars, assisted by other vehicles tooting the three short and two long signals of *Algérie française*, took the news of the formation of the committee to the rest of the city. The midnight curfew automatically lapsed. All Algiers was in a state of effervescence. In a thousand cafés, glasses were lifted to "victory."

One of General Massu's first acts as president of the Committee of Public Safety was to send a telegram to President Coty. It said:

> WE INFORM YOU CREATION CIVIL AND MILITARY COMMITTEE PUBLIC SAFETY IN ALGIERS PRESIDED OVER BY MYSELF GENERAL MASSU BY REASON GRAVITY SITUATION AND ABSOLUTE NECESSITY MAINTENANCE ORDER AND THIS TO PREVENT EFFUSION BLOOD. WE REQUIRE FORMATION IN PARIS OF A GOVERNMENT OF PUBLIC SAFETY ALONE CAPABLE OF PRESERVING ALGERIA INTEGRAL PART METROPOLITAN FRANCE.

Later in the evening, the committee was enlarged to include four Moslems–Saci Mahdi, a retired major; Saïd Mohand Madani, an employee of a chemical company and an active trade unionist; Mohammed Berkani, an accountant; Taieb Chikh, a landowner–and representatives of the Vigilance Committee and of the *Union pour le Salut et le Renouveau de l'Algérie Française*–Auguste Arnould, airline pilot; Dr. Bernard Lefèvre, physician; Robert Martel, farmer; and Jacques Merlo, engineer. Léon Delbecque, a convinced Gaullist, was made vice-president of the committee on the strength of his claim to be M. Soustelle's representative. Subsequent accretions during the night brought in eighteen others who had distinguished themselves in the defense of French Algeria, among them Alain de Sérigny, publisher of the *Echo d'Alger*, and Lucien Neuwirth.* The full committee was, therefore, made up of thirty-eight members.

M. Delbecque stated–erroneously–that M. Soustelle himself was

* M. Neuwirth had been an assistant to M. Delbecque in Algiers. A native of Saint-Etienne, he later became spokesman for the committee. He was thirty-four years old on May 18, 1958.

about to arrive from Paris. This news, relayed to the crowd, filled the Forum with joy. When a plane flew overhead at about 11:30 P.M., many jumped to the conclusion that M. Soustelle was in it and prepared to give him a triumphal welcome. Unfortunately, M. Soustelle, under police surveillance in Paris, had not yet eluded the vigilance of those assigned to "protect" him.

At 9:30 P.M., a telegram marked "urgent" and "very secret" was handed to General Salan. Signed by the outgoing Premier, Félix Gaillard, the telegram said: "General Salan, C.S.I.A.,* is authorized to take all measures for the maintenance of order, the protection of property and persons until further notice."† This was, perhaps, M. Gaillard's last act of authority.

At the Palais Bourbon, M. Pflimlin's chances of investiture were improving by the minute. News of the insurrection in Algiers had been flashed to Paris. Conscious of the threat to its very existence, the National Assembly was beginning to rally around the Premier designate. Pierre Montel (Independent), Léopold Senghor (African Convention), and Pierre André (Independent) addressed the evening session, but their speeches, prepared in advance, had lost all relevance and only exasperated the deputies present. It was past 10 P.M. when M. Pflimlin asked for a short recess. A Communist deputy, Waldeck Rochet, leaping to his feet, urged all "republican" deputies to close ranks against the "factionists" and to defend "republican legality" to the end. "It is true," M. Pflimlin answered angrily, "that grave events are taking place in Algiers. But the Communist party is in no position to save the Republic. I have requested a recess so that those who are responsible for the maintenance of republican order may cope with the situation. This very night the Assembly will be called upon to assume its responsibilities at a moment when I am myself prepared to assume mine." The recess was granted at 10:40 P.M.

At about the same time, the studios of Algiers radio were taken over in the name of the Committee of Public Safety. The task had been entrusted to two members of the committee, who, when they arrived with an order signed by General Massu, were stopped at the door by a police detail. But the difficulty was easily overcome. Paratroopers escorting the committee members merely thrust the policemen aside. The director of the station having acceded gracefully to a request that he remain in his office, Armand Perrou went on the air with a message

---

* *Commandant supérieur interarmées en Algérie,* General Salan's official title.

† Quoted from Alain de Sérigny's *La Révolution du 13 Mai.*

announcing the formation of the committee. "The battle has been won," he concluded.

At midnight, a message from General Massu was read to the thousands still camped in the Forum. It said in substance:

> Your movement has met with the warm response of the whole of Algeria and is leading to the formation of Committees of Public Safety in the principal cities—Oran, Constantine, Bône, etc.
>
> We appeal to General de Gaulle, who alone is capable of heading a Government of Public Safety, above all parties, to insure the permanence of French Algeria, an integral part of France.

The hand of Léon Delbecque was evident in this brief statement. Until midnight, the insurrection had had two goals—the overthrow of the "system" and the establishment of a government of national union for the safeguarding of French Algeria. A name, a symbol, a precise objective—these were now added. To M. Delbecque's political mind, it had long been evident that General de Gaulle was the only figure in France about whose person the forces of regeneration could crystallize. This view was held also by M. Soustelle and many others.* To be sure, the general's own position on Algeria, as far as it was known, seemed to be highly ambiguous. This could not be helped; it was De Gaulle or nothing. Besides, it could always be argued that General de Gaulle would, if he came to power, respond so intuitively to the deeper aspirations of the nation that the preservation of Algeria would impress itself upon him as a paramount duty.

Alain de Sérigny, who was present at the G.G. that evening, reports in his book, *La Révolution du 13 Mai*, that between 10 P.M. and 11 P.M. General Salan sent a telegram to M. Pflimlin begging him to step down and pleading for the formation of a government of public safety headed by a person of "high national authority." Similar telegrams went to the speakers of the two houses of Parliament and to Pierre Montel, chairman of the national defense committee of the National Assembly. General Salan also conferred by telephone with M. Lacoste and General Ely.

In Paris, however, events were taking a course very different from the one hoped for in Algiers. When the Assembly resumed its session at 1:15 A.M., M. Pflimlin asked the seven deputies still waiting their turn

---

* On May 11, *Dimanche Matin,* Sunday edition of the *Echo d'Alger,* had carried an editorial by M. de Sérigny entitled, "*Parlez, parlez vite, mon Général.*" In it, M. de Sérigny had urged General de Gaulle to break his silence and, in so doing, to restore hope to ten million Algerians.

to speak to forgo their privilege so that the investiture vote could be taken at once. This being agreed to, M. Pflimlin restated his Algerian policy and ended with these words: "We are perhaps on the verge of a civil war, and it is the Communists who would be the beneficiaries. I ask you to rise to the responsibilities that face you on this historic hour and to make your decisions."

It was announced at 2:45 A.M. that M. Pflimlin had been invested by the Assembly by a vote of 274 to 129, with 137 abstentions. An analysis of the vote showed that Mendès-France, Mitterrand, and the other Radical advocates of a "liberal" policy in Algeria had given their votes to M. Pflimlin *en bloc*. Four of six pro-Communist Progressives also had voted for M. Pflimlin. The Communists themselves had abstained. If the Communists and Progressives had voted against M. Pflimlin, as they certainly would have done in other circumstances, M. Pflimlin would have emerged with a majority of six—hardly the wide basis of confidence that alone enables a government to govern. And although it is true, as *Le Monde* pointed out, that M. Pflimlin was not a prisoner of the Communists, he was very close to being one, and he was certainly very beholden to M. Mendès-France and to the Radical group. With the Communists, the Radicals, and many Socialists poised to pounce on him if he failed to pursue an "evolutive" policy in Algeria, M. Pflimlin could expect nothing but hostility in Algiers. In the rest of France, his authority was below average for the Fourth Republic. Yet he was to cling to what power he had with remarkable obstinacy.

The news of M. Pflimlin's investiture, received at the G.G. at 3 A.M., was immediately relayed to the Forum. M. Delbecque then read this message from General Salan: "It being my mission to protect you, I am taking the destinies of Algeria temporarily into my hands. I ask you to have confidence in the Army and in its commanders and to show by your calm your determination." At 4 A.M., the Committee of Public Safety issued its "Communiqué No. 1." The document, which had General Salan's approval, was read from the balcony by General Massu. It said:

> We inform the population of Algiers that Pflimlin's government of surrender has just been invested . . . as a result of the complicity of the Communists.
>
> We express our gratitude to those of the population who, as a result of the announcement made earlier, have stayed up to greet M. Jacques Soustelle. M. Jacques Soustelle has twice been prevented from coming to join us . . .
>
> The Committee earnestly begs General de Gaulle to break his silence by speaking to the country with a view to the formation

of a government of public safety, which alone can save Algeria from abandonment and, by the same token, from the "diplomatic Dien Bien Phu" spoken of on several occasions by M. Robert Lacoste.

In any case, the Committee of Public Safety, which represents you, continues to insure the liaison between the population and the Army, which is assuming power until final victory is won.

Pending the arrival of Jacques Soustelle, the officers of the Committee are: General Massu; M. Delbecque, serving as M. Soustelle's deputy; M. Madani; and M. Lagaillarde.

We decree as of this moment the mobilization of all French energies in the service of the country and ask you to be ready to respond to the first call put out by the Committee of Public Safety.

We are proud to prove to the world that the population of Algiers can provide a perfect demonstration of the total fraternity of the French populations, European and Moslem, united under the French flag.

The news from Paris had been a cruel disappointment to the Forum, but many anxieties were dissipated by General Massu's communiqué. This, combined with a need for sleep and the promptings of the loudspeaker, induced most of the crowd to disperse; only a few indomitable groups remained until dawn. The members of the Committee of Public Safety spent the rest of the night in M. Maisonneuve's office. As to the dignitaries of the Lacoste regime, they had long since departed, using the underground passageway to General Salan's headquarters.

The Mediterranean sun, rising that morning in a crystalline sky, seemed to emphasize by contrast the murky impasse into which the events of the previous night had driven France and Algeria. Paris had not understood, had failed to respond, had decreed a test of strength with Algiers. A holding operation would now have to be undertaken. What were its chances of success? This question must have preoccupied the protagonists of the revolution, the Army, and also the masters of the regime in Paris. The latter had won the first round. Technically speaking, they now occupied the seats of power by the will of the people. It was obviously going to be hard to dislodge them.

But the dismay felt in Algiers was partially relieved by two messages that had reached the G.G. in the final hours of the night. The first committed the Sahara to the revolution. Signed by the officers commanding the posts of Fort Flatters, Edjelé, Tamanrasset, In Salah, and Fort Polignac, it said:

> Tired of the successive surrenders of those who govern us, we, officers, noncommissioned officers, enlisted men, associations, and civilians of the Sahara, rally to the Committee of Public Safety.

The second communication was a telephone call from the Hôtel Matignon in Paris; M. Pflimlin had orally confirmed the special powers granted to General Salan by M. Gaillard a few hours earlier. (According to some reports, it was General Salan who had booked the call; the effect, in any case was the same.) In refusing to burn its bridges, the Government put prudence ahead of valor; it also showed a realistic appreciation of its inability to crush the revolution in Algiers by direct assault. The paradoxical result was that General Salan now ruled Algeria in agreement with both the legitimate Government in Paris and the insurrectional committee in Algiers. But the Government was playing a double game. Its intent, soon demonstrated by acts, was to hamstring General Salan by putting Oran and Constantine directly under the authority of Paris and then to starve Algiers into submission.

On May 15, an official of the Algiers Prefecture, returning from a trip to Paris, handed General Salan the Government's order confining the exercise of his special powers to the central departments alone. Maurice Faure, who held the Interior portfolio briefly before being shunted over to the newly created Ministry of European Institutions, was heard to say: "How can you believe this to be a revolt having the slightest hope of success? We will cut off all supplies to Algeria. They will be without fuel, food, medicine. They will be compelled to capitulate." Pierre de Chevigné, Minister of Defense, promised to bring the "generals guilty of insurrection in the face of the enemy" to their senses in forty-eight hours.

May 14

It must be recorded that the "guilty" generals acted a little on the day after the insurrection as though they would have liked nothing better than to extricate themselves from their new revolutionary entanglements; in a word, to be off the hook. M. Pflimlin was now Premier; M. Soustelle had not arrived, and General de Gaulle remained silent in the seclusion of his home at Colombey-les-Deux-Eglises. The immediate object on May 14 could only be to gain time and, if possible, to see that the civilians refrained from rocking the boat. The great hope was that M. Pflimlin would, in a moment of patriotic abnegation, heal the breach by resigning. It was essential, therefore, to temporize; to do nothing that might put M. Pflimlin's back up or stiffen his will to stay in power.

General Salan issued a communiqué on May 14 stating that he had temporarily assumed civil and military power for the purpose of maintaining law and order, protecting life and property, and directing military operations. The communiqué said the function of the Committee of Public Safety, "set up under the pressure of events to express the determination of the Franco-Moslem population to remain French," was to insure the liaison between the population and the army command and to serve as a channel through which the command could transmit its orders. The communiqué also stressed the necessity of getting the administrative machinery functioning normally again. It urged the people to place their trust in the Army and to resume their usual tasks.

Two press conferences were held that evening, one by General Massu at General Salan's headquarters, the other by M. Delbecque at the G.G. They provided striking evidence that the military and civilian leaders of the Committee of Public Safety had not yet synchronized their operations.

After recounting the events of the previous day and night, General Massu stated that the Committee of Public Safety had been formed with a double objective—to restore law and order and to bring a government of public safety into existence in Paris, if possible with General de Gaulle as Premier. He was pleased to observe that order had been restored without damage to life or limb, but conceded that the investiture of M. Pflimlin had been a disappointment. He explained that his actions had also been motivated by a desire to make the civilian members of the committee realize that, since the war against the nationalist rebels continued, nothing should be done to impede the military operations or to disrupt the unity of the Army. "It was urgent, therefore," he continued, "to put an end to the insurrectional atmosphere so as not to run the risk of a break with Metropolitan France, which would have had enormous disadvantages for us." He insisted that the committee was clearly subordinate to General Salan and that the military hierarchy was unimpaired. "That, by the way," he added, "is why this press conference is being held at the Tenth Military Region rather than at the Government General."

General Massu also stressed the temporary nature of the Committee of Public Safety, stating that it would dissolve itself as soon as a new Minister for Algeria could take over. "Including a minister appointed by M. Pflimlin?" asked a reporter. The General repeated, "As soon as a new minister can take over."

Other questions and answers were equally revealing, for instance:

"General, do you not fear widespread troubles in the event a government of pubilc safety is not formed in France?"

"I have no idea. As you know, I am like someone who has thrown himself into the water. Believe me, there is nothing of the factious general in me, and I only wish I had never been given this sort of a job."

At another point he said, "I am in this thing merely by chance and do not play politics." And again: "Where are we going? I haven't a notion." He insisted—and no one there could doubt his sincerity—that he had acted on the spur of the moment, essentially to prevent any spilling of blood.

General Massu's words, as well as the reality of the situation, were in curious contrast with the headlines then appearing in the American press.* This was not, in the first instance, an army coup. The junta and the pronunciamento, such as they were, had been more or less rammed down the Army's throat, and the Army would have considered itself well rid of both. But the revolution had been started; there was no turning back now, despite the violence done to the Army's tradition and natural inclinations.

General Salan and General Massu were cast in very different molds; but, bound by a common allegiance to the Army, they inevitably stood together. General Massu, though not the blockhead he was made out to be by many commentators, was essentially a man of action. His dash and vigor, combined with a measure of personal magnetism, made him a natural leader of men. These qualities were foreign to General Salan, whose approach to military problems rested rather on careful study and attention to detail. Courteous and soft-spoken, General Salan had generally been regarded as a model of circumspection. In Indochina, where he had served as supreme French commander from April, 1952, to May, 1953, he had been criticized for overcautious leadership in operations against the Communist forces. He was attracted by Buddhism and had a predilection for the easygoing Kingdom of Laos.

Every inch a republican general, noted for his undeviating deference to constituted authority, General Salan had been chosen by Premier Guy Mollet's Socialist Government to succeed Lieutenant General Henri Lorillot as supreme commender in Algeria in November, 1956. That this man should now endorse a rebellion against the Government was almost past belief. But actually General Salan had never walked in the labyrinth

* Apart from a couple of correspondents regularly stationed in North Africa, the only American or British newsman on hand for the revolution of May 13 was John Wallis of the London *Daily Telegraph*, who had flown to Algiers on a hunch that something might happen.

of French politics or indulged in speculation about France's mission in Algeria. His notion of patriotism was simple and straightforward. To him, Algeria was a part of France that it was his duty to protect. And although he was very loath to throw down the gauntlet to the new government in Paris, his first loyalties were to what he believed to be the higher interests of the nation.

While General Massu, at Tenth Region headquarters, was trying to apply the brakes, M. Delbecque, at the G.G., was stepping on the accelerator. He announced that the Committee of Public Safety had extended its authority to the whole of Algeria. He said in substance:

> What has happened in Algeria was not contrived in advance, but was instead the result of a concurrence of circumstances. First there were M. Pflimlin's repeated statements on the subject of cease-fire negotiations with the F.L.N. We could never allow the rebel bands to remain in Algeria with their arms. In addition, when three French soldiers were basely assassinated by the F.L.N., there was no official reaction. This aroused the indignation of the people of Algiers.
>
> The Committee of Public Safety will remain in existence until the present Government yields to a government of public safety headed by General de Gaulle. The Committee of Public Safety functions under the authority of General Salan.

In answer to a question, M. Delbecque added significantly, "The Committee of Public Safety does not recognize the Government of M. Pflimlin."

Meanwhile, the revolutionary fervor had spread to Oran. In the afternoon of May 14, a huge crowd of civilians and Territorials ranged behind their flags and banners heard the mayor, Henri Fouques-Duparc,* read a proclamation from the balcony of the city hall and announce the formation of a Committee of Public Safety. Afterwards, the crowd, more than 50,000 strong, marched to the War Memorial, where M. Fouques-Duparc placed a flag. Later, while a "commando" of Territorials seized the central telephone exchange,† columns of demonstrators, shouting the familiar slogans of the revolution and singing the *Marseillaise*, surged toward the Prefecture. The Republican Security guards on duty there

* Actually, the elected city council had been dissolved in Oran as in many other Algerian cities and replaced by a "special delegation" appointed by the Administration. M. Fouques-Duparc, the former mayor, was president of that delegation. He was also a former Gaullist deputy.

† Normally under army control, the Territorials seem to have taken the law into their own hands in Oran on May 14.

were quickly overwhelmed; the iron gates in front of the building gave way. Shouts of "Lambert to the stake!" and "Resign!" followed M. Fouques-Duparc as he entered the Prefecture at the head of a deputation.

The Prefect-Igame, Pierre Lambert, a Socialist of M. Lacoste's stamp, was at his post. He had pledged his loyalty to the Pflimlin Government earlier in the day. This cost him in an instant the popularity he had won over the months and years by his courage, tenacity, and vigor. Now, with a howling multitude at his door and no one to protect him, he was compelled to yield to the will of the street. He therefore relinquished his authority to Major General Jean Rethoré, commanding the Oran Army Corps. While this was being done, however, the crowd had invaded the Prefecture, spreading destruction in its path. M. Lambert, jostled as he tried to make an exit and even slightly injured on the steps outside, was extricated by the Army and whisked away in a staff car.

In Constantine, where the previous day a turbulent demonstration had prevented Jean Chatel, Igame and Prefect of Constantine, from reaching the War Memorial, a Committee of Public Safety was set up on May 14 amid considerable confusion. M. Chatel and Major General Jean Gilles, commanding the Constantine Army Corps, issued a statement asserting their determination to defend French Algeria and appealing for calm. Other Committees of Public Safety were formed in cities and towns all over the country. In most cases, their first move was to send telegrams to General Massu declaring their solidarity with the central Committee of Public Safety and to President Coty demanding the establishment of a government of public safety.

In Paris, the Socialists rushed to the aid of the Government in peril. Their parliamentary group voted 61 to 6 to allow its members to enter the cabinet. Although no requests were made for specific portfolios, the Socialists indicated that they were prepared to accept the heaviest ministerial responsibilities.

May 15

The salient event of the following day was the statement of availability put out by General de Gaulle. Lieutenant Colonel de Bonneval, the General's aide-de-camp, carried the statement from Colombey-les-Deux-Eglises to Paris, reaching the General's offices in the Rue Solférino at 5 P.M. There the document was mimeographed and distributed to 150 eager reporters. It said:

> The degradation of the state leads infallibly to the estrangement of the associated peoples, the distress of the Army in action, national dislocation, the loss of independence. For twelve years,

France, beset by problems too harsh for the regime of the parties, has been caught in a disastrous process.

Not so long ago, the country from its depths put its trust in me to guide all of it to its salvation. Today, in the face of the trials that again are mounting toward it, it should know that I am ready to assume the powers of the Republic.

The effect of this pronouncement was to change the whole picture to the decisive advantage of Algiers. Its resonance in those very depths of the nation to which General de Gaulle had referred was enough to break the brittle foundations of the "system" and to leave it tottering. For the Algiers revolution, it was more than the fulfillment of a prayer; it was the promise of victory. The previous day, the Committee of Public Safety—as exemplified by General Massu, at least—had resembled the cursed Jackdaw of Rheims:

His feathers all seemed to be turned the wrong way;
His pinions drooped—he could hardly stand . . .

But by the evening of May 15, the revolution had assumed the aspect of the jackdaw after plenary absolution:

He grew sleek and fat;
In addition to that,
A fresh crop of feathers came thick as a mat . . .

Since morning, the Forum had again become the focal point of the revolution. General Salan—the object now of lusty applause—had spoken from the balcony at 10:30 A.M. He had said:

All the Moslems are behind us. The day before yesterday, at Biskra, 7,000 Moslems went with their wreaths to the War Memorial to honor the memory of our three soldiers executed in Tunisian territory. My friends, the action that has been undertaken here has brought the Moslems of this country back to us. Now, for us, all of us here, the only possible outcome is victory with the Army that you have unceasingly supported, that you like, and that likes you.

The General had ended his speech with the words, "My friends, I cry, 'Long live France! Long live French Algeria!' " He had been about to leave the balcony when, prompted apparently by M. Delbecque, he had returned to add, "Long live De Gaulle!"

All afternoon, loud-speakers had kept the crowd in a patriotic frame of mind by playing martial music. At 6 P.M., Auguste Arnould, a member of the Committee of Public Safety, walked out on the balcony, took the microphone and said, "M. Delbecque has an important communication to convey to you." In a voice described by the *Echo d'Alger* as "heavy with emotion," M. Delbecque read General de Gaulle's statement. The crowd gave thunderous expression to its joy; ten thousand voices broke into the *Marseillaise*. There were shouts of "*Vive de Gaulle!*" and "*Vive l'Algérie française!*" Major Mahdi, a Moslem member of the committee, asked for a minute of silence "in memory of our sons and brothers who have fallen for the grandeur of France and for French Algeria." The news of General de Gaulle's statement swept Algiers, buoying up its hopes. "After months of anguish," the *Echo* commented, "Algeria again takes heart."

Meanwhile, in Paris, Guy Mollet, slated to become Vice-Premier, conferred feverishly with M. Pflimlin on ways and means of saving "republican legality." The most important of the measures contemplated in this connection was a bill to exhume the old "state of emergency" law of April 3, 1955,* and to apply it to Metropolitan France for a period of three months. This law, it will be recalled, had been drafted nearly five months after the outbreak of the nationalist rebellion in Algeria; its purpose had been to make more effective the drive against an armed uprising that had not been contained within the framework of ordinary "republican legality." The same law was now to be pushed through Parliament with lightning speed and used this time, not against nationalist guerrillas, but against citizens whose opposition to the Government resulted in part from the failure of the regime ever to achieve the original objectives of the law. This was in itself an admission of impotence. Moreover, the prospects could not be said to be good for a government with liberal pretensions—and Socialist participation—that deprived citizens of their republican freedoms in order to save republican legality.

Nevertheless, the "system" managed to put its remaining authority to rather damaging use. Interior Minister Maurice Faure's blockade of Algeria having gone into effect, twelve passenger and cargo vessels lay idle in the port of Marseilles. Since air traffic between Algeria and Metropolitan France also was halted, the French mails ceased to function across the Mediterranean. These restrictions exasperated the Algerians without weakening the revolution.

May 16

In scores of Algerian towns and villages, Moslems had taken part in the establishment of local Committees of Public Safety and given unmis-

* The main provisions of the original bill are summarized on pp. 142–143. The amendments are noted on pp. 143–144.

takable proof of their adherence to the revolution. But the Forum had remained very largely in the hands of the Europeans. This anomaly was at least partially corrected on May 16, the day of the great outpouring of Moslems from the ancient Kasbah and from the other Moslem sections of greater Algiers. They came in two columns, perhaps 30,000 in all—men, women, and children of every condition of life, especially the lowest. They, too, carried flags and banners; they, too, shouted the slogans of the revolution—"De Gaulle to power!" "The Army to power!" "Soustelle with us!" "Long live Massu!" "Long live Salan!" and "*Algérie française!*". But some of their slogans had special meaning, for instance: "The Kasbah answers, Present!" and "We remain French!". Behind a prominent banner inscribed with the words, "Algiers Kasbah–Committee of Public Safety," marched a contingent of Moslem girl scouts in blue skirts, white blouses, and red neckcloths, each carrying a tricolor bouquet. And still they came: veterans, stevedores, merchants, artisans, schoolteachers, *yaouleds* (street urchins), all marching to the cadence of *Algérie française.*

After a brief halt near the War Memorial, where the *Marseillaise* was sung, the two columns proceeded to the Forum. There the Moslems mingled, as they arrived, with thousands of Europeans who had already heard General Massu define the functions of the Committees of Public Safety. The enthusiasm of that moment was, perhaps, as great as any that had yet been felt in the Forum. Everyone had heard that a Moslem demonstration was to take place that day; no one had expected it to be anything like this.

Deafening applause greeted the announcement that Saïd Mohand Madani, member of the Committee of Public Safety, was about to speak. Advancing to the microphone on the balcony of the G.G., the fifty-three-year-old employee of a chemical company, trade unionist, and father of seven, read this appeal in French:

> The Committee of Public Safety . . . has recorded with pride the moving response of the Moslem populations in gathering around the local committees that have been formed spontaneously over the whole of Algerian territory.
>
> These men who open to their compatriots the road to integration have a right, from this moment on, to the gratitude of the country. We ask them to persevere in the local committees and in the action that has been undertaken by gathering around them the hesitant populations that, only yesterday, were perplexed by the irresolution of France.
>
> They should know that France will never abandon them. We shall, all of us together, throw the enemy that serves a foreign

master out of our territory. We shall build an Algeria from which fear shall be banished, a brotherly and human Algeria in which the words of equality, fraternity, and justice shall recover their full meaning.

All of us who have taken up the fight to assert the permanence of France in Algeria bind ourselves to it here by solemn oath.

In Arabic, M. Madani said:

The Moslems, linked to their Christian brothers of Algeria, are ready to struggle with them until final victory.

For 127 years France has been in Algeria. When she came here, she found two million Moslems. It is thanks to her, to her civilization, to her methods, thanks to all her achievements, that the Moslems today number nearly ten million.

The United States, on the other hand, rapidly brought about the disappearance of the thousands of men of red race that inhabited the conquered territories, whereas here France has made us men worthy of the name.

The F.L.N. must disappear. Algeria is French and must remain French.

Generals Jouhaud and Massu also spoke briefly. Then a member of the Kasbah Committee of Public Safety,* introduced by M. Delbecque, read a message that said:

The Committee of Public Safety of the Algiers Kasbah, representing 75,000 inhabitants of many origins, offers General Salan and the central Committee of Public Safety the assurance of its confidence and of its determination to fight with all its strength for the salvation of all.

The next speaker was Auguste Arnould, airline pilot and member of the Committee of Public Safety, who had an inspiration that was perfectly to symbolize the meaning of the occasion. "A moment ago," he said, "M. Madani made an oath to pursue the fight until victory is won. I also make that oath, for a single heart beats within us." After a pause, M. Arnould added: "And now we are going to show the world the strength of our union. To do this, we are going to take one another by the hand and form a great chain of friendship." A few silent seconds passed; then, in an instant, thousands upon thousands of hands grasped each other and were lifted up, locked together, toward the sky. At the same time, the multitude broke into the *Marseillaise*.

* The Kasbah committee was composed of twenty-five Moslems, four Jews, and two Christians, plus four army officers and two noncommissioned officers.

Some reports in the American press suggested that the demonstration on May 16 had been stage-managed; that the Moslems had, in fact, been rounded up by the authorities and herded into the Forum. One dispatch said merely that the members of the Kasbah Committee of Public Safety had marched to the Forum "accompanied by several hundred Moslems." This kind of reporting made it difficult for Americans to understand the significance of what had happened.

The authorities, and in particular the officers of the *Sections Administratives Urbaines* (S.A.U.)—the city equivalents of the S.A.S.—had, of course, assisted in the formation of the Kasbah Committee of Public Safety. But the demonstration could never have developed as it did without the spontaneous participation of thousands of Moslems. A French captain assigned to the Upper Kasbah wrote in a private letter to a former school classmate: "The day my comrades and I went up to the Forum, 15,000 Moslems followed us. Who would have thought this possible even a year ago? The charge of constraint has been made. But there were barely fifteen of us in all, and none of us even carried side arms. It was a truly spontaneous movement . . . Whatever may be said, this was a splendid recompense for us. The rest will follow automatically."

Le Monde was, of course, hostile to the revolution. Nevertheless, its special correspondent in Algiers, Eugène Mannoni, saw more on May 16 than did many of his Anglo-Saxon colleagues. He noticed, for instance, that, among the advancing Moslem delegations, several were neither preceded nor escorted by S.A.U. officers. These demonstrators, according to M. Mannoni, shouted "*Algérie française!*" and "*De Gaulle au pouvoir!*" with genuine gusto and, as they passed, saluted the Europeans who acclaimed them. M. Mannoni reported that the Moslems from Castiglione, a town on the coast twenty-eight miles west of Algiers, had come into the city with only their mayor and their flute and tambourine players to guide them. The Mzabites, a religious minority group made up largely of grocers and petty shopkeepers, were particularly enthusiastic. As M. Mannoni put it, "Their faces, at once fat and subtle, reflected their feelings without reserve."

Since M. Mannoni belittled as much as he could the claims made in Algiers for the events of May 16, his observations are of special interest. He wrote:

> What conclusions are to be drawn from the demonstrations? If some Moslems came because they feared that reprisals might await them in case they refused and who behaved like simple extras, others—how can it be denied when it was seen?—demon-

strated that they still desired to become full-fledged Frenchmen despite the many disappointments and revolts.

That a "psychological shock" had been felt, and deeply felt, by the Moslem community was so evident that few even tried to deny it. At most, the reactions of the Moslems were attributed to fanciful causes, notably to the promise of equality implicit in the drive for "integration" or to the personal magic of General de Gaulle. Actually, integration, soon to become one of the rallying cries of the revolution, had as yet hardly been mentioned. And if General de Gaulle's name was revered among the Algerian Moslems, it was not because he had put a few thousand Moslem veterans and civil servants on the first-college voting roll but because he had won renown as the victorious commander. The psychological shock that brought the Moslems into the Forum and into the local Committees of Public Safety was produced by the fact that the Army had taken power and given its pledge that Algeria would never be forsaken. Security and the right to live—these were the aspirations that found in the revolution of May 13 the promise of fulfillment.*

The Moslems are no fools. They know, or instinctively sense, that except for those at the top of the economic scale, equality is something no French government can give them this year or next. For equality to come within the grasp of any but the favored few, there would first have to be an economic and social revolution in Algeria; the whole country—not just portions of it—would have to be converted from an archaic to a productive economy. This goal is not impossible of attainment; indeed, it will have to be relentlessly pursued if Algeria's skyrocketing population is to be saved from hunger. But it was not, I am sure, with this thought uppermost in their minds that the Moslems flocked to the standards of the revolution of May 13. Their motivations were far simpler and more elemental. They were tired of being caught between the hammer and anvil of endless rebellion and repression. A Frenchman, like the citizen of any civilized nation, has a right to protection against terror. This right had been denied to the inhabitants of Algeria, particularly the Moslems, for too long. The Army, which had already decontaminated Algiers, now stood pledged to make the right to protection prevail everywhere. It is not to be wondered at, therefore, that the Moslems should have responded with enthusiasm.

---

* The desire for social emancipation was there, too, however. It revealed itself in the action of the Moslem women who, on May 17, snatched off their veils and burned them in the Forum. Unfortunately, this courageous example was neither widely followed nor universally applauded among the Algerian Moslems.

As a result of the massive adherence of the Moslems, the revolution continued to gain in assurance. Its position with regard to Paris stiffened as its momentum increased. This was reflected in an appeal sent to President Coty by General Massu on behalf of the central Committee of Public Safety. The appeal said:

> The patriotic upsurge that has taken hold of the whole of French Algeria is rallying the Moslem people around their Committees of Public Safety, which they are asking to join in droves.
>
> France, in your person, runs the risk of losing her best chances if you do not respond to the popular fervor of Europeans and Moslems, united under the same ideal, by accepting the arbitration of the Liberator of the country so that a government of public safety headed by General de Gaulle can then be formed.
>
> Any other solution will breed sorrow, misery, and despair.
>
> The patriotic upsurge in Algeria is not a factious movement. The whole of Algeria is animated by a desire to submit itself to a strong republican central authority, capable of creating the French Union. It is thus the best rampart against all factions of whatever sort.
>
> You should know that our resolve is unshakable and that all the vital forces of Algeria will remain united until final victory.

The Moslem response had another, more subtle effect on the course of events in Algeria. Stemming as it did from the assumption of power by the Army, it increased the preponderance of the military within the councils of the revolution from top to bottom. Even though the European members of the local Committees of Public Safety could by no stretch of the imagination have been thought to be contemplating a return to the privileges of former times, the presence of army officers on these committees was undoubtedly regarded by some Moslems as a guarantee of fairness and regularity. The confidence of the Moslems made the position of these officers one of special trust. At the top, General Salan, General Massu, and the others drew from their successes the conclusion that they could, and should, run the show with little or no civilian counsel or interference.

Another growing conviction at Tenth Region headquarters was that M. Pflimlin could not last much longer. His authority had already deteriorated noticeably. The generals were, therefore, more anxious than ever to avoid any action likely to result either in a desperate attempt by M. Pflimlin to hang on against all odds or in a revulsion of republican sentiment in Metropolitan France, always sensitive to men on horseback. Certain defensive energies not yet available to the Government were best left dormant. In their effort to steer the revolution away from the paths of extremism, the generals inevitably kept an apprehensive eye on the activities and pronouncements of their civilian auxiliaries. This led to some bridling among the civilians. But the spirit of compromise was there, and it is to the credit of the leaders on both sides that the inevitable frictions and misunderstandings were not allowed to deflect the revolution from its objectives or to impair its essential cohesion.

The first man to experience the Army's distaste for extremists was our old friend, Jean-Baptiste Biaggi,* who, since February, 1956, had blossomed forth in Paris as head of something called the *Parti Patriote Révolutionnaire*. Burning with zeal for the Algerian cause, M. Biaggi arrived at Maison Blanche airport aboard a plane from Madrid on May 16. But the joys and satisfactions to which he had, no doubt, been looking forward were denied him. In execution of an order signed by General Salan, M. Biaggi was shipped to Adrar, a desolate spot in the Sahara 375 miles south of Colomb Béchar. But the extraordinary M. Biaggi was to manage the unusual exploit of escaping from Adrar and of making his way first to Algiers and then to Europe without getting caught.

Subsequent arrivals were to include: Jean Le Pen and Jean Demarquet, rightist deputies, on May 20; Jean-Louis Vigier, Independent deputy for Paris, on May 24; and Robert Pesquet, Gaullist deputy, on May 25. All of them were to be compelled to retrace their steps. In the end, General Salan agreed, somewhat reluctantly it seems, to the presence in Algiers of only three deputies—Jacques Soustelle, Raymond Dronne, and Pascal Arrighi.

The functions of the Committees of Public Safety, as defined by General Massu in a speech that preceded the giant demonstration in the Forum on May 16, threw an interesting light on the manner in which the Army proposed to guide the revolution. He said:

> The Committees of Public Safety established in all the townships of Algeria must obligatorily represent the two communities of Algeria—Europeans and Moslems. The number of members will vary according to the size of the population.
>
> It is essential that the Army be made a part of these committees by the appointment to them of one or more career officers. Only in this way will the union of the Army and of the nation . . . be exemplified.
>
> I remind you that the role of the Committees of Public Safety is to insure the liaison between the population, from which they

---

* See p. 282.

sprang, and the military authority, in which all the powers are vested. In no case will they substitute themselves for the regular administrative agencies, with which they must cooperate fully. City governments, special delegations, subprefectures, and prefectures will continue as in the past to conduct public affairs in accordance with the laws of the Republic.

The Committees of Public Safety are not revolutionary committees, for we are not factionists; and their essential mission is to tighten the bonds uniting the two communities, to keep the population informed on the trend of events, and to maintain it in a state of vigilance.

I wish also to make it clear that the Territorial units must assist the military authority fully and without reservation. Under no circumstances are they to forget their duty as soldiers in the service.

Thus . . . the Committees of Public Safety, which I ask you to fill out so as to make them as representative as possible, will be the image of this country, united shoulder to shoulder in cohesion and order under the unimpaired authority of its military leaders.

In this way, our action will influence the decisions we expect from Metropolitan France and will make our countrymen . . . and the world . . . know the calm, resolute, and wise countenance of the whole of Algeria. And, above all, do not forget that we must pursue the military operations. This duty rests upon the Army, but it is imperative that our soldiers feel themselves to be the combatants of the entire nation, united and coherent, and that the enemy have no illusion about our inner strength and our determination.

You may be sure that Metropolitan France, despite the attempts being made there to stifle opinion, will shortly understand the action undertaken by Algiers for the nation's common salvation. Send us your motions and resolutions. We shall see that they are made known. They will influence that misled opinion to break down the sordid wall of party interests and to insist on the formation of a government of public safety, through which we shall see our victory bear fruit and our beloved France shine in the world.

In Paris, however, the Government was marshaling what strength it had to avert the outcome for which General Massu had so fervently pleaded and to save France for the "system." It was engaged on May 16 in the process of ramming its "state of emergency" bill through Parliament with application of Article Eleven of the enabling act (authorizing night and day searches and government control of press, radio, cinema, and the theater).

In an eloquent speech during the debate, former Premier Georges

Bidault charged that the Government had demanded special repressive powers for the defense, not of the nation, but of the regime. He described as "intolerable" the imputation that General de Gaulle, who had restored the Republic after its darkest eclipse, was now preparing to harm it. "What is contested," he continued, "is not the legality of the Government but the means at its disposal, the policy it is pursuing, and its support. Realism compels you to take into account developments that go beyond your ability, if not your will, to terminate them peacefully." In conclusion, he urged M. Pflimlin—who was, of course, chairman of his own Popular Republican party—to yield to a government of national union. To this, M. Pflimlin replied in effect that, as head of the legal government of France, it was his duty to hold the fort against every onslaught.

The "state of emergency" bill was adopted by the National Assembly at an evening session by a vote of 462 (Communists included) to 112. The Council of the Republic passed it by a vote of 211 to 94.

In another move to bolster his defenses, M. Pflimlin brought four Socialists into his cabinet. Guy Mollet became Vice-Premier. Jules Moch, noted in the past for his tough anti-Communist attitude, took over from Maurice Faure as Interior Minister, while Albert Gazier went in as Minister of Information with responsibility for censoring the press. Max Lejeune was made Minister of State. The portfolio of European Institutions was invented to console Maurice Faure and the Radical party for the loss of the Interior Ministry.

May 17

It must have seemed to some of those in the Forum during the great Moslem demonstration of May 16 that the revolution had reached the hour of its apotheosis. But the following day was to be marked by moments of equal, if not greater, intensity. This time, however, Tenth Region headquarters had neither planned nor anticipated them. They were the result of the unexpected arrival of Jacques Soustelle.

On the evening of May 13, the general and colonels gathered at the G.G. would, in their perplexity, have welcomed M. Soustelle with outstretched arms and a sigh of relief. But by the seventeenth, matters stood in a very different light. To the Army, which, in the meantime, had assumed the role of destiny in Algeria with notable success, M. Soustelle was now *ipso facto* an actor without a part. It was felt, too, that his presence upon the stage at that particularly delicate juncture might frustrate the attempts then being made to bring about M. Pflimlin's resignation by a subtle combination of defiance and restraint.

When, therefore, M. Soustelle and his four traveling companions* stepped from the chartered plane that had brought them from Geneva, they were quickly escorted to a room at the Maison Blanche military air base. A few moments later, they found themselves face to face with a galaxy of generals and colonels intent on securing their immediate departure. General Salan himself was there. It is safe to assume that M. Soustelle, quite unprepared for such a reception, took vigorous exception to it. Alain de Sérigny, who entered the room soon after M. Soustelle's arrival, reports in his book, *La Révolution du 13 Mai,* that he heard M. Soustelle and the generals in "animated conversation." M. de Sérigny takes credit for dissipating the misunderstanding. He writes:

> Jacques Soustelle, advised by me of the plans that had been laid, recognized at once that his sudden appearance in Algiers would, at that juncture, be interpreted by M. Pflimlin as a sort of challenge, and that it would be better to give the Premier a chance to choose freely between resignation and an aggravation of the conflict.
>
> "General," he said to the supreme commander, "I came here to put myself at the service of French Algeria and of the country. Everything must be subordinated to that goal. I do not want to do anything that might interfere with the steps you plan to take."
>
> The tension vanished. Faces beamed. Hands were stretched forward. It would not be said that Algiers, in a moment of impatience, had deprived M. Pflimlin of the opportunity of letting wisdom guide his choice.

The upshot of the encounter at Maison Blanche was that M. Soustelle would be kept under wraps at M. de Sérigny's home until General Salan had made further representations to M. Pflimlin. By 2:30 P.M., M. Soustelle was in M. de Sérigny's car speeding toward Algiers by a circuitous route. But word of his arrival leaked before he reached his destination, and cheering throngs began to gather in the streets of the city. Despite this slight miscarriage of the compromise agreed to, General Salan pleaded again with M. Pflimlin by telephone. In vain; the Premier was adamant. At 3:45 P.M., General Salan acquainted M. Soustelle with the negative result of his call to Paris. In M. de Sérigny's words, this meant

* They were: General Guillain de Bénouville, a wartime resistance leader; Geoffroy de la Tour du Pin, a career diplomat; Charles Béraudier, deputy mayor of Lyons; and René Dumont, an official of the *Union pour le Salut et le Renouveau de l'Algérie Française.* M. Soustelle had given his police bodyguards the slip the previous afternoon and had crossed the Swiss frontier in General de Bénouville's car at 5 o'clock in the morning. Their chartered plane landed at Maison Blanche at about 1 P.M.

that M. Soustelle's "hour had come." From the windows of M. de Sérigny's villa, overlooking the city and the bay, M. Soustelle could hear in the distance the shouts of the crowd—"Soustelle! Soustelle!" and "*Algérie française!*"—and the singing of anthems.

Something of the atmosphere of that afternoon is reflected in these lines of a personal letter written by a Frenchwoman who took no part in any of the mass demonstrations:

> Saturday afternoon as Aunt M . . . and I were knitting in the living room and listening to the horns of motorcars that kept sounding the three short and two long blasts of *Algérie française,* suddenly we heard through our closed panes a voice cry, "Soustelle has arrived!" I opened the window. M. M . . . on the balcony of his apartment at number fifty-one across the street, shouted to me, "Soustelle has arrived!" He was radiant. He was hanging out a flag from his balcony. From balconies on all sides, other flags appeared. With the help of Lolita and Antoinette we sewed together a blue bath towel, a piece of an old sheet and the front of a red apron to make a magnificent flag for our balcony. What fever! What emotion! Cars passed in the street; voices from them shouted, "All to the Forum!" And we could see the most varied, the hugest crowd imaginable, issue forth from every door and make its way toward the Forum . . .

The Forum and all its approaches were soon packed solid. Flags and banners fluttered here and there above a sea of heads. To beguile a long wait under a scorching sun, the crowd sang the *Chant des Africains* and the *Chant du Départ* each ten times over. At 4:05 P.M., detachments of paratroopers and Territorials cleared a passage for the official cars. At 4:10, General Salan, General Allard, and Serge Baret, the Prefect-Igame of Algiers,* rolled up to the G.G. amid the cheers of the crowd. They were followed five minutes later by M. Soustelle and his party, and by several prominent members of the Committee of Public Safety. The crowd, almost beside itself with enthusiasm, shouted "Sous-TELLE! Sous-TELLE!" Thousands raised their hands to wave a welcome to the returning champion of French Algeria.

Greeted on the steps of the G.G. by General Salan, M. Soustelle entered the building to reappear moments later on the balcony. Lucien Neuwirth had the greatest difficulty in obtaining a measure of silence. As soon as his voice could be heard, he introduced M. Soustelle with

* Of Algeria's three Igames, only M. Baret joined the revolutionary movement. He did so without hesitation (on the night of May 13) and without reservation. He was later appointed Secretary-General in succession to M. Chaussade. In this capacity, he was General Salan's chief civilian assistant.

these words: "When Jacques Soustelle departed, you said, 'It is only an *au revoir*.'* Here he is back with you again!"

After paying a vibrant tribute to the Army and its chiefs, M. Soustelle recalled that before leaving Algiers on February 2, 1956, he had pledged all his energies to the salvation of Algeria.† He said that for two years and four months he had unceasingly striven to keep that promise. He continued:

> Only three days ago I was at my post in the National Assembly so as to pursue my efforts there, but I was subjected to constant surveillance. [Boos.] With my freedom threatened at every moment, I could no longer fulfill my duty. I therefore decided to return to Algiers. [Applause.]
>
> In your midst, at the Army's side, I have chosen at once freedom and the fatherland. [Applause.] I have put myself at the disposal of French Algeria, which has just given a magnificent example of European and Moslem brotherhood. I have no other ambition than to help repair the national unity on both sides of the Mediterranean . . . [Applause.]

The demonstration lasted well into the evening. Delegations of Europeans and Moslems pouring in from the Mitidja plain—from Fort de l'Eau, Rovigo, Le Corso, Aïn Taya, and many other villages—were greeted by General Massu in a speech from the balcony. Ahmed Touami, vice-president of the Committee of Public Safety of Maison Carrée, vowed that the whole population would stand together in defense of French Algeria. At 5:30 P.M., M. Soustelle returned briefly to the balcony in response to the clamor of the crowd before leaving the G.G. to attend a military conference at Tenth Region headquarters.

In the evening, the crowd was startled by a fire near the entrance to the G.G. When it was learned that a group of Moslem women had burned their veils, a wave of enthusiasm swept the Forum. M. Soustelle, appearing on the balcony for the third time, praised the Moslem women for their "marvelous and comforting" act, symbolic of their "will for emancipation." He formed a V-sign with his arms in the air as the crowd sang the *Marseillaise*.

M. Soustelle's arrival was the occasion for other demonstrations throughout Algeria. At Tiaret, Moslems and Europeans embraced one another in the public square. Moslem leaders addressed crowds at Sidi Bel Abbès, Affreville, and Constantine. The whole country was, in fact, buoyed up by the conviction that, with M. Soustelle in Algiers, all would be well.

---

* See. p. 274.
† See p. 272.

As seen from Paris, however, the Algerian picture was more shadow than light. In a television address to the nation, M. Pflimlin attributed the "disturbances" that had broken out in Algeria to the "anxieties of our compatriots of Algeria, deceived by tendentious reports." He said the reactions of the Algerians were justified in so far as they stemmed from a passionate desire to remain French. "But," he added, "we must be much more severe with those who, systematically, misled them and sought to turn the demonstrations into an insurrection."

May 18

Addressing innumerable delegations of Moslem women massed in the Forum on the afternoon of the eighteenth, M. Soustelle expressed the hope that future historians would note the date and the nature of the event—a gathering of women, the first of its kind in Algeria, attesting to the fact that the old bars had been thrown down and that the country was now inhabited simply by ten million French men and women. Chérif Sid-Cara, former Radical deputy for Oran, succeeded M. Soustelle on the balcony. He testified to the solidarity of the "province of Oran" with the other parts of Algeria in their common determination to remain part of the French fatherland. M. Sid-Cara was followed by a young woman from the Mahieddine Moslem quarter of Algiers who urged her sisters to cast off their traditional garments, to repudiate the reclusion to which they had been used, and to strike out boldly on the path of emancipation. A few women removed their veils, but most seemed to feel that the time was not yet ripe for such a radical step. Still, it must be counted for something that they were there at all.

In the days that followed, M. Soustelle was given a triumphal welcome almost from one end of the country to the other. At Boufarik, Tizi Ouzou, Oran, Constantine, Biskra, and Bône he addressed crowds remarkable for their size, color, and enthusiasm. At Algiers, delegations of all sorts and people from all walks of life crowded into the Forum every evening to demonstrate their solidarity with the revolution and to hear its leaders exalt its purposes and achievements. These evenings of renewal and exultation are remembered in Algiers as the "*grandes heures du Forum.*" Concomitantly, the organs of the revolution—notably the Army command as an agency of civil government and the Committees of Public Safety—began to function more smoothly and efficiently. For the benefit of the French and foreign journalists who had swarmed into Algiers, daily press conferences were held. At these, Colonel Charles Lacheroy spoke for General Salan, while Lucien Neuwirth spoke for the Committee of Public Safety. The new arrangements made for better coordination; the revolution ceased to speak with discordant voices.

May 19

The nineteenth was the day of General de Gaulle's press conference at the Palais d'Orsay Hotel in Paris before 1,000 journalists and guests, fourteen microphones, and fourteen television and newsreel cameras. The general's words riveted the attention of France, if not of the world. Those that had, perhaps, the greatest impact were:

> What is happening at this moment in Algeria with regard to Metropolitan France and in Metropolitan France with regard to Algeria could lead to an extremely serious national crisis. But it could also be the beginning of a kind of resurrection. This is why the moment seemed to me to have come when it would be possible for me once again to be directly useful to France . . .
>
> When someone assumes the powers of the Republic, it can only be because the Republic will itself have delegated them . . .
>
> In Algeria there is a population that for years has had to face war, murders, attacks. This population has found that the system established in Paris is unable to solve its problems. Worse still! It has seen this system turn recently to the good offices of foreigners. It has heard a man, who, moreover, is my friend and who happened to be Minister for Algeria at the time, declare publicly, "We are heading toward a diplomatic Dien Bien Phu." It has seen crisis follow crisis in Paris, impotence added to impotence, the same representatives of the same parties substituting themselves for each other *ad infinitum* in the same ministerial positions without ever coming up with anything clear, precise, and effective. How could this population not be expected to revolt in the end? How could it not seek recourse for its misfortunes elsewhere than in parliamentary combinations? This is inevitably what has occurred . . .
>
> In these circumstances, the Army, observing the immense popular emotion, concluded that its duty was to prevent a reign of disorder. This is what it has done and done well. Besides, the Army is itself profoundly affected by the tragedy resulting from the bankruptcy of the public powers and inflicted on the country the Army serves with great merit and sacrifice . . .
>
> I therefore fully understand the attitude and the action of the military command in Algeria and I hope, in the national interest, that the Army will remain coherent and united, an example at a time when examples are so few . . .

General de Gaulle had hardly taken leave of the press when his words were echoed by a Moslem in the Forum at Algiers. Azem Ouali, president of the association of the mayors of Kabylia, said: "The weakness of the regime keeps pushing us toward the abyss. The Europeans and Moslems of Algeria have felt this and have broken down the wall of fear . . ."

General Salan, judging the moment to be propitious, extended to the rebels a new offer of *aman* (pardon). A handbill issued by Tenth Region headquarters called on the rebels to surrender their weapons and to take their places in the "new French Algeria." The response has not, to my knowledge, been reported, but there was apparently a slight increase in the number of rebels surrendering to the Army.

May 20

The central Committee of Public Safety, meeting at the G.G. on the twentieth with General Massu in the chair, solemnly declared for the integration of Algeria with Metropolitan France. Its "Motion No. 1" proclaimed all the citizens of the French province of Algeria to be Frenchmen in every respect.

That evening, in the Forum, M. Soustelle developed the theme of integration with his usual skill and vigor. He said:

> Always my mind comes back to this idea, so simple that many have not understood it, particularly on the other side of the sea. It is that if Algeria is to be and remain French, it follows that all Algerians, without exception, must be Frenchmen like the others, nothing but Frenchmen, with the same rights and the same duties.
>
> "French Algeria"—these words are not only, as some propagandists of defeatism and of treason have gone about saying and have pretended to believe, the slogan of a minority; they are a cry from the heart of ten million Frenchmen who, whatever their ancestry, religion, given name, and manner of dress, want to be forever Frenchmen.
>
> One day—already three years ago—I had occasion to declare at Oran, "We no longer want to hear of anything other than Frenchmen from Dunkirk to Tamanrasset." It is thus with great joy that today, at General Salan's side, with the French Army, I say, "This is no longer an idle phrase, no longer just a hope; it is a reality."

Unfortunately, if M. Soustelle was not entirely wrong, he was only partly right. The Moslem community had shown clearly that it did aspire to many of the benefits of citizenship. But it must not be thought that it had lost a deep sense of its separate identity. It still clung to its own archaic codes of law, to its special manner of dress, and to the communal structure of its society. The Moslems continued to be set apart from other Frenchmen by the privilege of a way of life in harmony with the venerable truths of their own revealed religion; and also, for most of them, by the grinding poverty of their estate.

If there is really to be but one sort of Frenchmen from Dunkirk to Tamanrasset, the Moslems will have to sacrifice a substantial part of their legacy in the process. But they stand to gain much, in this life if not in the next. For one thing, they cannot, as Frenchmen, be allowed to starve. With or without her Algerian province, France is rich enough—and is conscious of the duty—to provide for all her sons. As much could probably not be said for an independent Algeria.

The deterioration of governmental authority had already been illustrated when, following General Paul Ely's resignation as chief of staff of the Armed Forces on May 16,* the regime was unable to find a successor of equal rank and had to give the job to Lieutenant General Henri Lorillot, compliant former supreme commander in Algeria. The next damaging blow to the Government's authority came from the Navy.

That the Navy, and especially Vice-Admiral Philippe Auboyneau, commander in the Mediterranean, were in communion of ideas with the Army in Algeria was common knowledge. But Rear Admiral Bertrand Géli, commander of the French Navy in Algeria, made the fact plain and public on May 20. In an order of the day issued from his headquarters at Oran, Admiral Géli said in part: "In the grave circumstances of the moment, when the fate of Algeria and of France is at stake, our duty is to remain perfectly united behind our chief, General Salan, until our hopes are realized and our efforts justly rewarded." A few hours later, the Navy's Mediterranean headquarters at Algiers released the text of a telegram in which Admiral Auboyneau had commended Admiral Géli for his order of the day. As a result, the world knew where the Navy stood. It was evident that in the event of a prolonged test of strength between Paris and Algiers, the Government could not for an instant count on the Navy to enforce a blockade of Algeria.

Actually, the Government had already thrown in the sponge in this respect. The freighter "Isée" from Marseilles docked at Algiers on May 20; the freighter "Miliana" and the packet "Lyautey" entered the port the following day, and maritime activity quickly returned to normal.

* In an order of the day banned by the Government, General Ely said he had submitted his resignation so as not to be in a position of having to answer for measures that would go against what he believed to be essential.

Commercial telegrams and telegraphic money orders were resumed on May 22. All this struck Pierre Mendès-France as an abject capitulation to the factious generals. He was quoted as having said in the corridors of the National Assembly: "Algeria must be starved. For the past ten days I've been telling M. Pflimlin to hold up the ships."

May 21

On the evening of the twenty-first, General Salan made what was probably his shortest and certainly his most effective speech from the balcony overlooking the Forum. The crowd had been chanting the slogan, "*L'Armée au pouvoir!*" at the top of its lungs. "Thank you," the General said, "for these complimentary words—'The Army to power.' But you must know that we are now all united and that thus we shall march together up the Champs-Elysées, and we shall be covered with flowers!"

May 22

The Committee of Public Safety issued a statement on the twenty-second, calling on all members of the French Parliament to stay in Paris and to regard themselves as "mobilized on the spot" to pursue the good fight. The choice, the statement said, lay between a government of public safety headed by General de Gaulle, or that of cooperation with the "Communist plot." It appealed to the members of both houses to choose the "path of honor and resurrection," warning that in any case they would be judged according to their acts.

Coming as it did immediately after the summary expulsion from Algeria of Jean Le Pen and Jean Demarquet, both ex-Poujadists, the committee's statement was an effective deterrent to other prospective visitors from the National Assembly. It reflected General Salan's determination to prevent the formation of anything resembling a rump parliament on his doorstep. But there were other prospective travelers in Paris. One was André Mutter, M. Pflimlin's Minister for Algeria, then waiting to take up his post. Another was General Lorillot, the new chief of staff of the Armed Forces, whose imminent departure for Algiers had been announced by the Government. General Salan persuaded both to remain in Paris.

May 23

In the night of May 22 to 23, three special planes took off from points in the Sahara—one from Ouargla, one from Ghardaïa, and one from El

Abiod Sidi Cheikh (east of Aïn Sefra). The passengers aboard these planes were the European and Moslem delegates chosen to represent the Sahara on the expanded Committee of Public Safety to be set up that day. Early in the morning, the delegates representing Oranie and the Constantinois reached Algiers aboard other planes. As they arrived they were taken to the Palais d'Eté, where they were greeted by the members of the original Committee of Public Safety (now to be known as the Committee of the Thirteenth of May). At 10:30 A.M., General Salan called to order the first plenary session of the Committee of Public Safety of Algeria and the Sahara. Jacques Soustelle and Chérif Sid-Cara sat at General Salan's right; General Massu and Léon Delbecque, at his left.

The new committee's initial order of business was to vote the "statutory decision" by which General Salan had brought it into existence. This done, General Salan and M. Soustelle withdrew, and General Salan and M. Sid-Cara took over as co-presidents. General Jouhaud, M. Delbecque, and Azem Ouali were elected vice-presidents. The new committee undoubtedly derived additional authority and effectiveness from its wider geographical basis. Its functions and purposes were the same as those of the original committee (which, of course, remained as its nucleus). General Salan's "statutory decision" specifically committed the committee to work for the establishment of a "government of public safely headed by General de Gaulle."

May 24

Paris was shocked—and Algiers, delighted—to learn on the twenty-fourth that the revolution of May 13 had spread to Corsica. The dissidence in Algeria, though not condoned, could at least be understood and explained. In Corsica, there were no extenuating circumstances. Besides, it was easy to think of Algeria as a separate country that might one day go its own way. But Corsica was part of the homeland. "No popular emotion," M. Pflimlin was to declare in a radio broadcast, "can justify the acts committed [there] by a handful of factionists."

What the Alsatian in M. Pflimlin failed to comprehend was that Algeria and Corsica are two kindred segments of the Mediterranean world. The ties of race and sentiment that bind them together are so close that Corsica inevitably throbbed to all the emotions aroused in Algeria by the events of May 13. In some ways these were, perhaps, heightened by the island's Napoleonic tradition. Messages had been exchanged, some in the form of cryptic bulletins broadcast over Algiers radio. Pascal Arrighi, Radical deputy for Corsica, had reached Algiers from Spain aboard a small plane on May 19, to find plans for the Corsican operation already well advanced.

At Ajaccio, on the night of May 23, a group of Gaullists met at a café just opposite the Prefecture for the purpose of setting up a Committee of Public Safety and of preparing an irresistible demonstration for the following afternoon. The meeting had been organized by Antoine Serafini, a former Gaullist deputy and a former mayor of Ajaccio, and by Henri Maillot, a cousin of General de Gaulle and a local Gaullist leader. The next day, before dawn, a military plane left Algiers with M. Arrighi and three other Corsicans aboard. The "mission" from Algiers, accompanied by an officer with an order signed by General Salan, landed at Calvi, twenty-three miles north of Ajaccio. Joining forces with a unit of paratroopers stationed there, the mission set out for Ajaccio in Army trucks in the afternoon of the twenty-fourth.

In Ajaccio, meanwhile, M. Serafini and M. Maillot did the decent thing by explaining their plans to the Prefect, Marcel Savreux, and by asking him to lead the demonstration. Instead, M. Savreux advised Jules Moch, the Interior Minister, of what was afoot, with the result that a company of Republican Security Guards was instantly dispatched from Nice in two planes to maintain "republican" order in Ajaccio. With the Republican Security Guards on their way to Ajaccio by air and the paratroopers rumbling in their trucks down the road from Calvi, much might now depend on which of the two forces would be the first to reach Ajaccio.

The paratroopers, winning the race by minutes, were ready, when the Republican Security Guards arrived, to give them a welcome tailored to their needs. But since, as it turned out, the intentions of the Republican Security Guards were by no means hostile—fifty of the 150 men were Corsicans—there was no problem. They were merely instructed to take up guard duty in the city.

By late afternoon, when the paratroopers and the mission from Algiers swung into De Gaulle Square, the Gaullist demonstration was in full swing. At 6:30 P.M., the Prefecture was submerged by a crowd of several thousand. M. Savreux, still faithful to the regime, took refuge with his wife in their private apartment while the new masters of the Nancini Palace harangued the crowd from its windows. M. Maillot stimulated the crowd to new heights of enthusiasm by shouting the names of Salan, Massu, and De Gaulle. M. Serafini, reconciled now with his enemy, M. Arrighi, spoke to demand General de Gaulle's return to power at the head of a government of public safety. The formation of a Committee of Public Safety with Maillot and Serafini as co-chairmen was announced. The *Marsellaise* and the *Ajaccienne* were sung up and down the Cours Napoléon, which echoed also with shouts of "*Vive De Gaulle!*"

Other Committees of Public Safety were set up at Calvi, Corte, and Bastia. At Bastia, however, where the Subprefecture was invested by Gaullist demonstrators, the Socialist assistant mayor, a Sébastien de Casalta, operating from the City Hall, tried to organize a countermovement. He set up a Committee of Vigilance, announced a popular demonstration for the following morning, and informed the Interior Ministry in Paris that Bastia and part of Corsica were determined to resist the "factionists." The Communists, rushing to M. de Casalta's assistance, put out a handbill that said: "The Government of the Republic, by the voice of its chief, orders all Corsicans to defend republican legality." The Socialist-Communist "resistance" fizzled the next morning, however, when only about a hundred demonstrators turned out to defend republican legality. No one paid much attention to them. A detachment of paratroopers had occupied the airport; Algerian riflemen had taken up positions in and around the city; the Committee of Public Safety was functioning. There was no danger that Bastia would be lost to the revolution. On May 26, M. de Casalta surrendered the City Hall to Colonel Thomazo of the Algiers Committee of Public Safety, who had just been appointed civil and military governor of Corsica by General Salan.*

The abortive Socialist-Communist attempt to make a stand at Bastia, although of no importance in itself, was to have decisive consequences in Paris. The Government, convinced on the strength of M. de Casalta's assertions that Bastia and a substantial part of the island were solid for the regime, resolved to send naval support. The failure, if not the refusal, of the Navy to cooperate in this undertaking was a shattering rebuke to the Government's pretensions to effective power. From this blow, it was not to recover.

May 27

Events were now moving swiftly to the inevitable conclusion. On the twenty-seventh, General de Gaulle announced that he had begun the "regular process" of forming a republican government. Algiers was greatly elated by the news. But M. Pflimlin, yielding to Socialist pressures, still hung on. In the National Assembly, his constitutional reform bill was carried by a vote of 408 (Communists included) to 165. This victory was, however, offset by the withdrawal of three of M. Pflimlin's

---

* Nevertheless, M. de Casalta was immediately rewarded with the Legion of Honor for his "heroic resistance." On the other hand, the National Assembly voted to deprive M. Arrighi of his seat.

four Independent ministers (the remaining Independent being André Mutter, Minister for Algeria!). A series of Communist-led strikes failed to develop into a full-blown movement of solidarity with the beleaguered Government. Yet it was becoming increasingly evident that unless M. Pflimlin was prepared to pave the way for a Communist-dominated popular front, the game was up. At dawn on the twenty-eighth, it was announced that the Pflimlin Government had resigned.

May 28

The twenty-eighth also was the day of the great march of the "anti-fascists" from the Place de la Nation, through populous quarters where the Jacobin heart of Paris once beat so loudly, to the Place de la République. But the 50,000 marchers taking part in that imposing demonstration were no revolutionary cohort; this was no lashing out of popular fury against the Bastilles of tyranny and pride. It was more in the nature of a funeral procession. The Communists, of course, had called out their militants in large numbers. But here also were the beneficiaries and supporters of the dying regime; here were its mourners. Although all demonstrations were banned under the Pflimlin Government's "state of emergency" law, the Socialist chief censor, Albert Gazier, figured among the leaders of the demonstration along with Jacques Duclos, François Mitterrand, Pierre Mendès-France, Edouard Daladier, Christian Pineau, André Philip, and many other politicians. Among the shouted slogans of the occasion were: "Long live the Republic!" "Long live the Popular Front!" and "Fascism shall not pass!"

May 29

The next day, President Coty, asserting a degree of leadership rarely associated with his office, took resolute action to end the crisis on General de Gaulle's stringent yet possible terms. The President and the sixty-seven-year-old wartime leader conferred at the Elysée Palace in the early morning. An announcement from the palace afterwards said that General de Gaulle, asked by President Coty to form a new government, had accepted. But the General also made his conditions clear. Essentially, these were that the Government be given plenary powers for a fixed period, with a special mandate to prepare and submit to the country by referendum constitutional changes providing for the separation of powers—in other words, a strong executive—and for new relationships between France and her oversea territories. General de Gaulle insisted also that these powers be granted with the "great and broad confidence of the nation."

President Coty was fully aware that such a program, involving as it did the virtual abdication of the regime, was bound to meet with fierce hostility on the left and center benches of the National Assembly. But since the alternative was almost certain civil war, he took the exceptional and dramatic step of warning the National Assembly and the Council of the Republic in separate messages that he would resign if the General was rejected.

In the Forum at Algiers, excitement was, quite naturally, running high on the twenty-ninth. "We are in sight of our goal," M. Soustelle declared. At Oran, the naval cadets of the training ship "Jeanne d'Arc," then making her last call at the end of a round-the-world cruise, were received by the local Committee of Public Safety. Admiral Auboyneau told the young cadets that they were fortunate in being able to witness the "Algerian miracle," which he described as a prelude to the "French miracle." "The ground, sea, and air forces," he said, "must put a single soul at the service of the country. A better future is in the making; it will banish the memory of the surrenders and indignities of the past. On the threshold of your careers in the Navy, it will have been given to you to see the break of a glorious day."

On the morning of the twenty-ninth, a vast concourse of Moslems from the Titteri, a mountainous region lying to the south of Algiers and encompassing Médéa to the west and Aumale to the east, had converged on the Forum to see and hear the leaders of the revolution. The principal speaker was Colonel Si Chérif, a former rebel chief who, in August, 1957, had gone over to the French with 400 guerrillas. Now the commander of a battalion of Moslem troops, Si Chérif appeared on the balcony alongside General Salan, General Massu, and M. Soustelle. Addressing his countrymen in Arabic, he spoke of the pride he felt at being one of the many Algerians who had returned to the bosom of the common fatherland. He urged the rebels who had not done so to accept the French offer of *aman* (pardon):

> Do not listen to foreign parasites who want to profit from the wealth of our country. I know their means of persuasion and their tricks, for I have led the life that you are leading. What are you doing now in your mountains? All our brothers have returned; there are ten million of us. Do you think you are serving a good cause in pillaging and ruining our country like locusts? If, through blindness or pride, you do not listen to my wise words, I shall be the first to fight you . . .

May 30–June 1

General de Gaulle had motored back to Colombey-les-Deux-Eglises after his conference with President Coty on the twenty-ninth. Returning to Paris on the thirtieth, he plunged into the political consultations that must always precede the formation of a new republican government. On June 1, in the National Assembly, he demanded and obtained—by a vote of 329 to 224*—his investiture as Premier on the basis of a program outlined in a seven-minute address. He had made it clear that he intended to govern by decree for six months without parliamentary interference and to prepare far-reaching constitutional changes for approval or rejection, not by Parliament, but by the people.

In Algiers, the General's program was well received. By contrast, his cabinet was construed almost as a betrayal of the very ideal for which he stood. Obviously, the General had gone to extreme lengths to conciliate the parties of the Fourth Republic and especially the party leaders. For here at his side, in what was supposed to have been a government of regeneration, were some of the most tarnished princes of the old "system." Guy Mollet and Pierre Pflimlin had been appointed to the cabinet as Ministers of State along with Félix Houphouet-Boigny, Negro deputy for the Ivory Coast and a perennial minister, and Louis Jacquinot, a former Minister for Oversea France. Antoine Pinay, who, as Foreign Minister in the Edgar Faure Government, had helped liquidate the French protectorate in Morocco in cooperation with General Catroux, was Minister of Finance. And the Socialist Max Lejeune, although temporarily without a portfolio, seemed to be slated to become Minister for Algeria.†

Several key ministries had gone to "technicians," men who had never entered the arena of party politics. The Foreign Minister, for instance, was Maurice Couve de Murville, a former ambassador to Washington. The most extraordinary of the new cabinet ministers was André Malraux, the distinguished novelist, who was to hold the Information portfolio for several weeks before turning his attention to other matters. The only minister identified in any way with the aims of the revolution that had brought General de Gaulle to power was Michel Debré, Social Republi-

* Including 141 Communists, forty-nine Socialists, and eighteen Radicals. Forty-two Socialists and twenty-four Radicals voted for General de Gaulle's investiture.

† He was, in fact, to become Minister for the Sahara. General de Gaulle was to announce in Algiers his decision to keep the Algerian portfolio himself and to delegate his powers to General Salan.

can senator, ardent Gaullist, and author of a devastating indictment of the previous regime.* He was Minister of Justice.

In Algiers, Léon Delbecque and several of his colleagues on the Committee of Public Safety were frank to say that this was not at all the government they had hoped for. The Army, too, was bitter. As to the Moslems, it need hardly be noted that, in the light of past performance, they had little confidence in the ability or in the determination of the politicians of the Fourth Republic to restore security in Algeria. General de Gaulle had assumed, perhaps, in making his deals with the party leaders, that his personal prestige was enough to dispel all doubts and reservations in Algeria. If so, he was mistaken. The misgivings that were born on June 1 were to be dispelled, and then only partially, only when General de Gaulle had appointed M. Soustelle to his cabinet as Minister of Information early in July. On the other hand, General de Gaulle had, at the price of damaging compromise, come to power in an entirely legal manner, without the aid of grenadiers or bayonets. His government was immaculately conceived; only the midwifery had, possibly, been a little dubious.

June 2-3

On the second, less than twenty-four hours after his investiture, General de Gaulle marched to the rostrum of the General Assembly to deliver an ultimatum. It was that, if that reluctant body failed to pass his emergency program, he would resign forthwith. Actually, two-thirds of his program—authority to rule by decree for six months and the renewal of special powers in Algeria†—had already been passed. It was the final measure—a preliminary constitutional amendment paving the way for subsequent sweeping constitutional changes—that made the deputies balk. They objected to this measure mainly because, by depriving them of a voice in the formulation of the changes, it could well be their own death warrant. However, since the alternative to General de Gaulle was almost certain civil war, the Assembly capitulated. Shortly after midnight, the measure was carried by a vote of 350 to 161. (The Council of the Republic was to ratify it by a vote of 256 to 30.)

Two events of lesser importance but not without significance also occurred on June 3. The first was the reappointment of General Paul Ely as chief of staff of the Armed Forces. The second was the resignation of Jacques Chevallier as mayor of Algiers. On May 31, M. Chevallier

* *Ces Princes qui nous gouvernent* (Paris: Plon, 1957).

† The same powers that had already been exercised by four previous governments. See p. 301.

had proclaimed his faith in General de Gaulle; but in spite of this he must have felt out of place in the new order of things. He submitted his resignation to General Salan; it was accepted.

June 4

After a preliminary conference with General Salan in Paris on the third, General de Gaulle flew to Algiers on the fourth in a Caravelle jet airliner. From the Maison Blanche airport to the Palais d'Eté, at the War Memorial, on board the cruiser "De Grasse" in the harbor—wherever he went that day, it was in an atmosphere of triumph. The setting could hardly have been more splendid, the day more luminous. *Alger-la-Blanche* had become *Alger-la-Tricolore.* Flags and bunting fluttered from every façade. Huge Lorraine crosses superimposed on the letter "V," prominently displayed, recalled the glorious days of the liberation of France. On the sidewalks, the *yaouleds* did a lively business in little Lorraine crosses and in tricolor cockades. At 7 P.M., General de Gaulle, accompanied by his official party, entered the Forum. From every corner of that vast plaza, from all its approaches, now crammed with people, peals of applause and shouts of "De Gaulle! De Gaulle!" greeted the General as he reviewed the honor guard drawn up in front of the G.G. Met on the steps of the building by General Allard, M. Delbecque, and the members of the Committee of Public Safety, General de Gaulle disappeared from sight. A few moments later, General Salan, stepping out on the balcony, addressed the crowd briefly. "Our great cry of joy and hope has been heard!" he declared. M. Soustelle, who spoke next, received such a mighty personal ovation that he had to plead repeatedly for silence. "Now at last," he said, "the moment has come for which we have waited so long. General de Gaulle is among us!"

At 7:10 P.M., dressed in the uniform of a brigadier general but bareheaded, the Premier appeared on the balcony.* Another great burst of enthusiasm and applause went up from the crowd. Waving arms reached into the air from the gates of the G.G. to distant roofs and balconies. Flags and banners were held aloft. For three full minutes, the General was unable to speak. The joy was spontaneous and unfeigned, for the General's presence on the balcony where his name had been so fervently invoked was in itself the fulfillment of uncounted hopes. But an under-

* The two ministers who had accompanied the General from Paris, Max Lejeune and Louis Jacquinot, might have followed him onto the balcony with regrettable consequences if they had not been kept prisoners in an office of the G.G. by vigilant members of the Committee of Public Safety. Their incarceration lasted about fifteen minutes.

current of anxious expectation could also be detected in the crowd. What was De Gaulle going to say? Would his words banish the suggestion of ambiguity attached to his ministerial bargaining in Paris? Would they gratify every tingling anticipation?

To a large extent they did. The happy inspiration of his first sentence brought the General into close communion with that frantically cheering multitude. Calling for silence by raising his arms to form a V-sign, he declared, "I have understood you!" As soon as he could make himself heard again, he continued in these terms:

> I know what has occurred here. I see what you have sought to accomplish. I see that the road you have opened in Algeria is that of renewal and fraternity.
>
> I say renewal in every respect. But, very rightly, you wanted it to begin at the beginning; that is, with our institutions; and that is why I am here.
>
> I say fraternity, for you will provide the magnificent example of men who, from one end to the other, share in the same ardor and live hand in hand.
>
> Well then, of this I have taken cognizance in the name of France! And I declare that from this day forward, France considers that in the whole of Algeria there is only one category of inhabitants, that there are only Frenchmen in the full sense, with the same rights and the same duties.
>
> This means that opportunities must be opened that, for many, have until now been closed. This means that a livelihood must be given to those who have not had it. This means that the dignity of those who have been deprived of it must now be recognized. This means that a country must be given to those who may have thought they had no country.
>
> The Army, the French Army, coherent, ardent, disciplined, under the orders of its commanders; the Army, tested by so many trying circumstances, and which none the less has accomplished here a magnificent work of understanding and pacification; the French Army has been on this soil the leaven, the witness, and it is the sponsor of the movement that has developed here.
>
> It was able to dike the current so as to channel the energy. I depend on it for the present and for the future.
>
> French in the full sense, enrolled in the same single electoral college—we shall make this manifest in no more than three months' time, on the solemn day when all Frenchmen, including the ten million Frenchmen of Algeria, will be called to decide their own destiny.
>
> As to the ten million Frenchmen here, their votes shall carry the same weight as those of the others. They will be called to the

polls to elect—I repeat, in a single electoral college—their representatives for the public powers as will all other Frenchmen. With these representatives, we shall see how to accomplish the rest.

May all those of your cities, your plains, your *djebels* participate in this immense demonstration in great numbers! May that participation include even those who, through despair, have felt called upon to engage in a combat which I myself recognize to be courageous—for courage is not lacking in this land of Algeria—to be courageous, but to be none the less cruel and fratricidal.

I, De Gaulle, open to them the doors of reconciliation.

Never more than here, nor more than this evening, have I felt how beautiful, how great, how generous is France!

Long live the Republic. Long live France!

It was noticed that General de Gaulle neglected to say, "Long live French Algeria!" It was noticed, too, that, while dwelling on the goal of internal integration within Algeria, the integration of Algeria into Metropolitan France was included as an objective only by implication. And who could be quite sure what he meant when he said that France and the elected representatives of the Algerian people would see "how to accomplish the rest"?

The striking feature of the General's emotional improvisation was, paradoxically, the total absence of innovation. Though very different in style, it was, in content, an almost exact replica of the formula devised by Guy Mollet in February, 1956, to provide a decisive "psychological shock"—equality, a single electoral roll, free elections, no unilateral settlement, but instead discussions with the elected representatives of the Algerian people. Like M. Mollet, General de Gaulle studiously avoided any explicit commitment on the question of French sovereignty in Algeria. Was Algeria part of France? Was it an associated territory? Presumably, these could be points of discussion at some future conference table.

M. Mollet had undoubtedly thought in 1956 that equalitarian proposals made by a Socialist leader would have dramatic effect on a population aspiring to full equality. We have already examined the folly of such a belief. In making the same proposals, General de Gaulle appears to have been convinced that since "I, De Gaulle, open the doors of reconciliation," the weapons would really drop this time from the hands of the rebels in a great *élan* of gratitude, or that the Moslem population would spontaneously eject them from its midst. Both men failed utterly to understand the nature of the Algerian rebellion and to take into account the ravages of fear. The psychological shock had occurred prior to General de Gaulle's return to power. His words, repeated with minor variations at Constantine, Bône, Oran, and Mostaganem, served only to deaden it.

The rebel reaction was, inevitably, hostile and caustic. An F.L.N. spokesman in Tunis called the General's proposals "ludicrous." He said the General had merely put himself in the "Western colonialist camp" with Salan and Massu.

El Moudjahid, in its issue of June 13, 1958, singled out General de Gaulle's tribute to the French Army for its bitterest remarks. The rebel organ said:

> These words will remain engraved in letters of fire on the heart of each Algerian man and woman. Never before has French cynicism been displayed with such impudence. . . . The unspeakable crimes of the colonialists have been raised to the rank of exceptional virtues; the torturers of the Algerian people have been travestied as heroes and magicians. . . .
>
> One must have a servile soul . . . to see "words of truth, nobility, and hope" where there is in fact only imposture, cynicism, and contempt for the Algerian nation and the Maghrib as a whole. De Gaulle's single sentence gratifying the F.L.N. with a tribute to its courage is a reflection of contempt in all its quintessence . . .

In all that has been written about the plots alleged to have led up to the events of May 13, it is not always easy to distinguish between fact and supposition. But there can be no doubt that at least two separate groups had been trying, each in its own way, to hasten the advent of a new day.

The first of these was composed of proponents of a Gaullist revolution—men like Michel Debré, who was probably the moving spirit; Léon Delbecque, the indefatigable go-between and coordinator; and, of course, M. Delbecque's superior, Jacques Chaban-Delmas, Defense Minister under Premier Gaillard. Jean-Baptiste Biaggi was, curiously enough, a prominent member of this group. Jacques Soustelle, on the other hand, does not seem to have been among the Gaullist plotters. General de Gaulle himself, needless to say, had nothing to do with the schemes then being concocted in his name and for his benefit.

The second group, sometimes referred to as the "Group of Seven," were right-wing Algerian activists intent on bringing the Army to power by any means, including riot and civil commotion. These men—Pierre Lagaillarde, Robert Martel, Dr. Bernard Lefèvre, and their associates—could hardly have been called Gaullists; an Army pronunciamento was all they required.

We have seen how M. Lagaillarde's activists turned the demonstration of May 13 into a successful revolutionary assault on the seat of power in Algiers. We have also seen how the Gaullists, chiefly in the person of M. Delbecque, usurped a revolution not of their making and channeled it toward their own more clearly-defined ends. The two groups, though quite distinct, had sometimes pulled together, as on the occasion of the "oath of the twenty-sixth of April." More often, they had pursued separate paths. Ultimately, they were bound to meet in a contest of sorts, for they counted on the same force, the Army, to make their respective ambitions prevail.

It may not have been entirely by chance that, in the end, the Army chose to place its trust in De Gaulle rather than in one of its own leaders. The brothers, Serge and Merry Bromberger, authors of a recent book on the plotting that preceded and followed May 13,* ascribe an important role in bringing this about to Brigadier General André Petit, who, besides being a convinced Gaullist, was for a time General Ely's emissary in Algiers.

The fear that Paris was about to sell Algeria out had become almost an obsession in Army circles, particularly since Robert Lacoste had spoken of a possible "diplomatic Dien Bien Phu." General Ely's primary concern, both before and after his resignation as commander-in-chief of the Armed Forces on May 16, was for the maintenance of the unity of the Army in the face of a widening breach between Paris and Algiers. He was ready, if necessary, to favor Algiers at the expense of Paris; but in that eventuality, he much preferred De Gaulle to adventure. General Petit argued for De Gaulle in Algiers and, apparently, he won the quick acquiescence of General Massu. General Salan, however, chose De Gaulle only under the pressure of events and after some anguished writhing.

M. Delbecque, it seems, had been planning coordinated agitation to occur simultaneously in Algiers and Paris on May 14. He had traveled to Algiers to take charge there, leaving M. Biaggi in charge of arrangements in Paris. He had, no doubt, been relying heavily for success on the Vigilance Committee that had brought out 8,000 demonstrators on April 26. Serge and Merry Bromberger assert that M. Delbecque was having a telephone conversation with M. Debré when M. Lagaillarde and his student "commandos" took the G.G. Arriving belatedly on the scene, M. Delbecque was reportedly greeted by M. Lagaillarde with the remark, "I admit I am a little ahead of your scenario!"

The threat of a military *Putsch*, to be spearheaded by paratroopers

---

* *Les 13 Complots du 13 Mai* (Paris: Arthème Fayard, 1959).

already stationed in Metropolitan France or flown there from Algeria, loomed very large in the days following May 13. Plans for the coup, dubbed "Operation Resurrection," were, in fact, drawn up in great detail. Various region commanders in Metropolitan France were privy to the preparations. One of them, Lieutenant General Roger Miquel, commanding at Toulouse, was named Metropolitan commander of "Operation Resurrection," ostensibly by General Salan. Actually, General Miquel's mission seems to have originated with General Massu and the Committee of Public Safety; how much General Salan knew about it is not entirely certain. In any case, on May 23, General Miquel received a thirty-two-page plan of operation containing the rotation schedule for the transport planes that were to bring the paratroopers in from Algiers. Air Force General Maurice Challe, chief assistant to General Ely, ordered the necessary aircraft to Algiers before being banished to Brest by the Defense Minister for trying to influence the civil authority.* Meanwhile, Algiers radio had begun broadcasting such ominous messages as "Ernestine is in the kettle" and "The chicken is going to lay its egg." The plans for "Operation Resurrection," as described by the Bromberger brothers in their book, called for diversionary movements by French troops at widely separated points and for the simultaneous occupation of key government buildings in Paris by the paratroopers. Zero hour was set for the night of May 27-28.

On learning that a coup was imminent, General de Gaulle moved quickly to forestall it by removing its justification. He announced on the morning of May 27 that he had begun the "regular process" of forming a republican government and warned the armed forces in Algeria to remain "exemplary under the orders of their chiefs." As a result, the contemplated action was called off for that night; a new zero hour was set—May 30 at 1 A.M.

How much of the planning for "Operation Resurrection" was seriously intended? And how much was bluff, designed merely to rattle the Government, to precipitate M. Pflimlin's resignation, and so to open the way to De Gaulle's return to power? The whole truth is still hard to get at, but certainly the plans had to be genuine to be effective even as bluff. To that extent, it can be said without hesitation that the danger of a military coup truly existed in May, 1958. Some aspects of the preliminary operation were, however, intended solely for their psychological effect. The cryptic messages broadcast over Algiers radio had no other purpose than to heighten the sense of danger in Paris. In addition, accord-

* He had, in an unauthorized interview, attempted to impress the dangers of the situation on Guy Mollet, Minister of State.

ing to the Bromberger brothers, Major General Guy Grout de Beaufort, one of General Ely's closest associates, did yeoman's service in Paris by making certain that the most startling information reached the ears of the highest authorities. He did not have to exaggerate; the truth was sufficient. And the General was in a position to know the facts; he had been designated Paris commander for "Operation Resurrection."

But what of De Gaulle? Was he a party to the Army's campaign of psychological warfare against the legally constituted government? This seems hardly likely. Perhaps he, too, was taken in by the campaign—before becoming its beneficiary. Certainly, he contributed in large measure to its success by his pronouncements and activities. In the end, as Serge and Merry Bromberger point out, the action of the Army had the truly astounding result of enabling De Gaulle to receive power directly from the hands of the elected representatives of the sovereign people.

52. REFERENDUM AND ELECTION

> *"Ce qui est certain, c'est que si jamais la France quittait l'Algérie, ce serait faute d'avoir réellement voulu y rester."*
>
> JACQUES SOUSTELLE

In September, 1958, the Algerian electorate, registered on a single roll and expanded to include the Moslem women, was called to the polls to vote for or against the constitution proposed by the Government of the Republic. The same yes-or-no question was put to the registered voters of Metropolitan France and of the entire French community from Polynesia to the North Atlantic archipelago of Saint-Pierre and Miquelon. But in Algeria, the referendum had special meaning. There the voting was for or against France and, by the same token, for or against the four-year-old nationalist rebellion.

The issue was made clear to every voter. Slogans proclaiming the alternative in the simplest terms—France or the rebels—were painted on countless walls across the country and broadcast from sound trucks in hundreds of busy market places. The army, campaigning for a large "yes" vote, saw to that. The rebels, therefore, faced a straightforward challenge to their claim to represent the Algerian people. They could establish the strength of their following in one of two ways—either by keeping a majority of the Moslem voters away from the polls or by running up a high "no" vote. An impressive number of blank ballots would also have been significant. Their failure was to be complete.

When plans for the referendum were announced in June, 1958,

Premier de Gaulle appealed to those who had taken up arms against France to accept a peaceful contest at the polls. The rebels responded to this invitation with violence and intimidation. They resolved to disrupt the referendum at all costs. The men who directed the rebellion from Cairo and Tunis sent out word to the effect that participation in the balloting would be tantamount to treason and that offenders would receive a traitor's death. They threw their bands into action to prevent, first, the registration of Moslem voters and, later, the voting itself.

Rebel terror, the threat of rebel reprisals, and the insecurity prevailing in many parts of the country placed a heavy burden on the Army, responsible for the protection of the population. But the security forces, assisted by Moslem auxiliaries and self-protection groups, managed to keep sabotage and violence to a minimum in the weeks that preceded the referendum. The country's defenses also were strengthened along the frontiers to prevent rebel infiltrations and the buildup of rebel striking power.

Lashed into emergency action by the crisis confronting them, the rebel leaders hastened to set up at last a "government in exile." They hoped, no doubt, in so doing, to secure wide formal recognition among the nations of Africa and Asia and thus to galvanize the flagging energies of their bands in the field. The formation of a "Provisional Government of the Algerian Republic" was announced simultaneously in Cairo, Tunis, and Rabat on September 19. A spokesman said this "government" considered itself "in a state of war with France under international law." The "government" was immediately recognized by the United Arab Republic, Morocco, Tunisia, Libya, and Iraq. Essentially the old executive committee in a new guise, the Algerian "cabinet" was made up as follows:

Premier: Ferhat Abbas.
Vice-Premier and Minister of the Armed Forces: Belkacem Krim.
Vice-Premier: Mohammed Ben Bella (imprisoned in Paris).
Ministers of State: Hocine Aït Ahmed, Mohammed Boudiaf, Mohammed Khider, and Rabah Bitat (all imprisoned in Paris).
Foreign Affairs: Dr. Mohammed Lamine-Debaghine.
Armament and Supply: Mahmoud Chérif.
Interior: Lakhdar Bentobal.
Communications: Abdelhafid Boussouf.
North African Affairs: Abdelhamid Mehri.
Finance and Economic Affairs: Ahmed Francis.
Information: Mohammed Yazid.
Social Affairs: Benyoussef Benkhedda.
Cultural Affairs: Ahmed Tewfik Madani.

Secretaries of State: Lamine Khan (eastern Algeria), Omar Oussedik (central Algeria), and Mustapha Stambouli (western Algeria).

The F.L.N. also announced an imminent "general offensive" to coincide with the balloting. Nothing of that nature materialized. There was a rash of F.L.N. terrorism and sabotage in Metropolitan France, but in Algeria the rebels were powerless to bring back the fear psychosis that their bloody exploits had created prior to the 1956 legislative election.*

If the rebels failed in this respect, however, it was not for want of trying. On August 16, a rebel band swooped down on a group of Moslem peasants picking almonds near Honaïne east of Nemours and soon afterwards massacred them all. It was noticed that of the twenty-five innocent Moslems who perished that day, eight were women (all potential voters) and two were children. Of the four Moslems butchered by the rebels at Ouled Malek on August 18, three were women between the ages of twenty-nine and thirty-five years.

The fear of betrayal seems to have gripped Amirouche, who had become supreme rebel chief in Kabylia, for he carried out a pitiless purge among his own followers a few days before the referendum. The French Army found four hundred bodies—estimated to represent about one-fourth of Amirouche's total effectives—rotting in a charnel pit at Akfadou, a former forestry station that had been used by Amirouche as a command post.†

In defiance of the rebel boycott and the various forms of physical and moral intimidation that went with it, four-fifths of the Moslems of voting age registered as voters. Of the registered voters, four-fifths took part in the referendum, voting "yes" in more than nine cases out

* The 1956 election was "postponed" in Algeria "by reason of the exceptional circumstances that make impossible the conduct of free and sincere electoral operations." See Chapter 35.

† Amirouche was killed on March 28, 1959, together with Si Haouès, commander of *Wilaya* 6, while trying to escape to Tunis by the southern route, that is, south of the Morice Line. Born in Kabylia in 1926, Amirouche was a jeweller in Relizane when he joined the O.S. (nationalist underground) in 1950. He took part in the conference in the Soummam Valley in August, 1956, and later became the chief lieutenant of Saïd Mohammedi, commander of *Wilaya* 3. He succeeded Mohammedi as commander of *Wilaya* 3 in the summer of 1957 and soon emerged as the very symbol of the rebellion. At the time of his death, he was the only well-known rebel leader left in Algeria itself. The action in which he was killed cost the rebels seventy-one dead and sixteen captured.

of ten. In fact, when the results were in, it was seen that an absolute majority of the Moslem population of voting age had voted "yes."

Since the army could not be everywhere at once, the voting was staggered over a period of three days—September 26, 27, and 28. At several points, the contemplated date for the balloting was changed at the last moment so as to throw the rebels off balance. It is almost certain that some aggressive rebel designs were thwarted in this manner. On the whole, the measures taken to protect the polling places and insure the safe transport of the ballot boxes to the counting centers were effective. In many of the remoter parts of Algeria, itinerant voting stations moved from village to village under armed guard to enable the inhabitants to cast their votes.

Measures of civil supervision were another important feature of the referendum. As in Metropolitan France, all parties and groups desiring to take part in the campaign were free to do so. Control commissions, whose members were drawn mainly from the judiciary, functioned throughout under the direction of Ambassador Henri Hoppenot, a career diplomat. While the voting was in progress, the civil commissioners and their 8,000 delegates had the power to intervene at any moment in behalf of a voter deprived of the free exercise of his rights. At the close of voting, the ballot boxes were sealed in the presence of a commissioner or delegate and taken to a counting center under armed guard, with a civilian representative of the control commission in constant attendance.

In spite of the various precautions taken, the referendum did require of many Moslem participants a measure of courage. The rebels were held in check, but they had not vanished. In the evening of September 27, for instance, a bomb exploded in the heart of Perrégaux, a town east of Oran. Rebel terrorists carried out a number of raids in the difficult sectors of Tiaret, Tlemcen, and the Dahra. At Souk Ahras, near the Tunisian frontier, an itinerant voting station struck a mine. Three members of a local government council at Aïn Beïda, southeast of Constantine, were abducted and murdered. The inhabitants of a village near La Calle, on the Tunisian frontier, refused to vote at all on the ground that the danger was too great. However, another village in the same area voted 1,584 to 4 in favor of the constitution, even though ten of its inhabitants had been abducted and were being held as hostages by the rebels. In the mountains of Kabylia, where Amirouche's bands were entrenched, the turnout was rather less than elsewhere in Algeria. Nevertheless, it exceeded 60 per cent everywhere. At Tassaft, Amirouche's birthplace, it reached 85 per cent.

In the absence of candidates and seats to be filled, no difficulties arose from the fact that Europeans and Moslems were voting for the first time on a common electoral roll. The spirit of May 13 was still running high, and the referendum was seen by the many as a way to further the hopes aroused by the revolution of Algiers. Observers were also struck by the notable enthusiasm of the Moslem women, many of whom evidently regarded the right to vote as an initial long stride in the direction of social emancipation. After centuries of seclusion and semi-bondage, they stood happily on the threshold of a new age.

The progressive attitude of some of the country's religious leaders undoubtedly had much to do with the large turnout of women voters. At El Oued, for instance, where a local Moslem dignitary had urged the women to awake from their torpor, 17,000 women registered, and almost all of them cast their votes on September 26 in an atmosphere of unrestrained gaiety. Even in the distant M'Zab, inhabited by members of the puritanical Abadite sect, a religious leader, Sheikh Bayoud, preached the word of progress, and the women flocked to the polls.

The over-all results for Algeria and the Sahara were:

Registered voters:	4,694,270
Participants:	3,751,522
(Participation: 79.9 per cent)	
Valid votes cast:	3,711,796
Yes:	3,589,876
(Percentage of electorate: 76.4; of vote: 96.7)	
No:	121,920
(Percentage of electorate: 2.6; of vote: 3.3)	

The high "yes" vote exceeded the most optimistic expectations. Of course, it was not to be supposed that many Moslems would defy the rebel boycott, accept the risk of rebel reprisals, and in some cases travel long distances merely to vote "no" or to cast a blank ballot once inside the booth. But there was more to it than that. The French Army stood pledged to the defense of French Algeria. Its leaders had given their solemn word of honor as soldiers, not as politicians. In accordance with the ancient proprieties of their tradition, the Moslems had requited protection with fidelity. The circumstances had provided a clear path to be followed and clear reasons for following it. The response was instinctive and virtually unanimous.

In a major speech at Constantine on October 3, Premier de Gaulle announced the inception of a great, new five-year development plan for Algeria, to be accomplanied by a tremendous increase in the number of Algerian Moslems in public employ on both sides of the Mediterranean. He also asserted that the results of the referendum committed

France and Algeria to each other for all time, but he failed to state in what manner. That he was still dreaming the wishful dream of a united Maghrib linked to France by close ties of culture, commerce, and sentiment suggested itself as a strong possibility when, on October 23, during a press conference in Paris, he called on the rebels to conclude with him a "peace of the brave." In his elaboration, he explained that his proposal was for a cease-fire to be negotiated in Paris without consideration of Algeria's political future. This, he said, would have to be worked out later with the elected representatives of the Algerian people.

The Premier's reference to a "peace of the brave" was a slap at everyone who had voted "yes" or who had advocated a "yes" vote in the referendum in Algeria. If the rebels were "the brave" with whom peace was to be made, it would have been better to vote "no" and thereby to hasten the inevitable negotiations. One shudders, too, at the thought of the crimes implicitly elevated by De Gaulle to acts of bravery.

If the F.L.N. had taken up the Premier's offer, it is probable that both sides could have agreed on the names of mutually acceptable candidates who, once elected in the normal way, would have been in a position to act as intermediaries between the F.L.N. and the French Government. The process leading to Algerian independence would then have been fully and irreversibly brought into play.

This did not occur. The F.L.N. spurned the Premier's offer and, in a communiqué issued in Cairo, insisted instead on full military and political negotiations to be held in neutral territory. "To the efforts of the Provisional Government of the Algerian Republic to find a peaceful solution through negotiation," the communiqué said, "he [De Gaulle] responds with a request for unconditional surrender."

The F.L.N.'s blunt refusal to meet with De Gaulle in Paris apparently came as a shock to the Premier and to his associates. For a secret understanding had, it was thought, already been reached. De Gaulle had appropriately chosen a turncoat—Abderrahmane Farès, former speaker of the Algerian Assembly—to act as go-between with the F.L.N. in an attempt to lay the groundwork for the coming cease-fire negotiation. After several encounters with Ferhat Abbas and other rebel leaders in Switzerland, Farès had returned to Paris on October 20 or thereabouts with the word that the F.L.N. was prepared to drop its stipulation regarding neutral territory and to tone down its demand for prior political guarantees.

What prompted the F.L.N. so cruelly to disappoint the hopes aroused in Paris by Farès' report? The answer can only be surmised. Gamal Abdel Nasser, the Egyptian dictator, may have been against the contemplated cease-fire talks as likely to bring the F.L.N. more fully within the Tunisian orbit. The field commanders may have been fearful for their authority in the event of a cease-fire without prior recognition by France of Algeria's right to independence; for this was, after all, their primary war aim. And they no doubt resented De Gaulle's suggestion that their parliamentaries should come forward carrying white flags. In Algerian eyes, there is little difference between a flag of truce and a flag of surrender. Or the Cairo committee may simply have decided that the element of risk was too great. Its members could not afford to be cast in the role of dupes.

The F.L.N.'s rejection of De Gaulle's "peace of the brave" proposal naturally caused great dismay among the "liberals" in Paris. "A fault," said Maurice Duverger in *Le Monde*. And he added: "What does the F.L.N. expect to gain by refusing to meet General de Gaulle? It must know that no French government could go further than the present Premier in his offers of negotiation." No government? What makes you so sure, M. Duverger?

It is certainly paradoxical, in any case, that the chain of events stemming from the danger of a "diplomatic Dien Bien Phu" apprehended by Robert Lacoste—and also by De Gaulle—should have brought French Algeria to the brink of disaster in the space of a few short months. The country was given another chance, thanks to the F.L.N.; it remained to be seen what would be done with it.

The logic of the Algerian situation has—to the dismay of the theorists—a perverse way of imposing its own law. Each time an irrational hope has been converted into policy there, the revenge of reality has been swift and stringent, and it will no doubt ever be so. Guy Mollet and his Socialist dream were early vicitims. General de Gaulle himself has been disappointed more than once.

There are, on the face of it, three possibilities for France in Algeria. She can offer integration; that is, the best she has. Or independence; that is, abandonment. Or something in between. But is not integration, in fact, the only alternative to independence? All attempts to push Algeria into an intermediate position, far from hastening a settlement, have merely prolonged the country's agony. For Algeria is refractory to what is euphemistically called a "large measure of autonomy"—in other words, to a semi-national existence. The general election held in Algeria on November 28, 29, and 30, 1958, provided a new striking illustration of this.

In his speech to the Forum in Algiers on June 4, 1958, Premier de Gaulle had announced an early election and had promised to do what remained to be done in Algeria in consultation with the elected representatives of the Algerian people. He seems to have been confident that the election would produce a crop of moderate nationalist deputies with whom he could work out a compromise solution. Instead, the election produced seventy-one Algerian deputies (twenty-three Europeans and forty-eight Moslems) overwhelmingly committed to integration.

To the mass of the Moslems, the election was needless and incomprehensible. They had already voted for De Gaulle once—in September—and had believed, as they cast their "yes" votes, that the Algerian problem was about to be settled. No such thing occurred. Instead, they were called to the polls again, this time in the midst of appalling confusion. The Government's intentions were obscure. The number of candidates (197) was bewildering. Conducted in these circumstances, and against a background of attempted negotiations with the F.L.N., the election had the effect of throwing the country back upon its former doubts. The events of May 13, confirmed by the referendum, had seemed to herald an early end to the nightmare of insecurity. But who, as the election approached, could confidently predict the outcome of the conflict between France and the F.L.N.? The great psychological shock of May 13 had been allowed to die out, while the rebellion continued its bloody course.

Much publicity surrounded the attempts of Alain Savary, the Socialist politician, and Jacques Fonlupt-Esperaber, the Catholic politician, to form "liberal" tickets in Algeria.* It was widely reported that the two "liberals" had gone to Algeria with the blessing of the Premier's office. However, unable to persuade moderate Moslem nationalists to enter the lists, they returned to Paris. To cover their retreat, they charged that, with the Army in control in Algeria, the election there could not be free.

In a dispatch to his newspaper in New York, an American correspondent said: "French *officials* found it impossible to persuade *representative* Moslems to become candidates for the French National Assembly."† This and other similar reports conveyed the impression that the integrationist candidates, of whom there was no dearth, were somehow non-representative. It would be hard to find a clearer instance of news reporting slanted to fit a bias.

The failure of moderate nationalists to rally to the "liberal" banner in defiance of the F.L.N. injunction prescribing death as the penalty for

* Under the provision of the electoral decree requiring that balanced tickets, shared by one or two Europeans and from one to four Moslems, be formed in each constituency, according to the relative strength of the two communities. Split-ticket voting was barred. The device was designed to take some of the sting out of the common electoral roll.

† Italics added.

participation in the "colonialist" election does not necessarily prove that —in the words of the correspondent quoted above—"the rebel movement had virtually complete control over the elite among the Algerian Moslems." But it does prove that the centrifugal pressure of events had driven the moderates from an untenable middle position. The chief weakness of the middle position was that it had no popular support. None but fools could expect many aspiring Moslem politicians in 1958 to risk their lives in defense of it.

The writer of an unsigned letter published by *Le Monde* in its issue for November 20, 1958, was close to the mark when he said:

> What the Algerians want is, first of all, peace; then dignity; third, education; finally, assured employment.
>
> The great majority are ready to applaud any policy which provides these basic benefits, whether it be called "integration" or "independence." As for autonomy, this word, except among a few intellectuals who think of independence when they utter it, evokes no response.
>
> France and the F.L.N. must fight it out on this basis. I believe the odds to be greatly in favor of France. The day the four basic conditions are met—peace being perfectly obtainable through an extension of the security network to the exclusion of any discussion—the problem will be solved. Both France and Algeria will be regulated by the same laws conferring the same rights upon their inhabitants, and it will matter little whether or not this is called integration.

But perhaps it matters a great deal. Max Lerner has remarked, in speaking about revolutions, that where there is an idea, the arms and men grow, but where there is no idea or a hollow one, the arms and men fall away. It cannot be denied that there is an idea—national independence— behind the Algerian rebellion. But if resistance to that rebellion is to be fully successful, it must be based on an equally compelling idea. Autonomy or home rule simply will not do. The referendum proved that many Algerians, Moslems as well as Europeans, responded strongly to the idea of integration.

Chérif Sid-Cara described the content of this word perfectly when he said in a speech to the French National Assembly: "My dear Metropolitan colleagues, you have in common a feeling that you do not have to express at every moment; it is that of possessing a common fatherland. We desire to share this feeling with you. We would like to have the impression, without having to proclaim it incessantly, of possessing the same fatherland that you possess." Premier de Gaulle himself had declared in his speech to the Forum on June 4, 1958, that a "country must be given to those who may have thought they had no country." It was, therefore, immensely discouraging to Algerians who had come forward eagerly with their "yes" votes in September to realize that integration—both the word and the idea—had been dropped.

Nevertheless, despite the Government's efforts to promote a measure of diversity among the candidates, despite the bickering that had brought the Committees of Public Safety on evil days, integration triumphed easily at the polls in November. In many constituencies, even the semblance of an opposition failed to develop. The contests were between persons and spheres of influence rather than ideas. Fierce campaigns were waged all over Algeria by candidates standing on virtually identical platforms.

Such was the case in Algiers itself, where Pierre Lagaillarde's *Algérie française* ticket defeated three rival tickets, at least two of which were about as integrationist as his own. One of the defeated tickets was headed by Auguste Arnould, airline pilot and prominent member of the original Committee of Public Safety. Another was headed by the veteran politician Raymond Laquière, former speaker of the Algerian Assembly.

During the electoral campaign, M. Lagaillarde had promised the voters that he would resign as deputy on July 1, 1959, if Algeria's integration with France had not become a fact by that date. His running mates were: René Vinciguerra, a Gaullist who had stood at Léon Delbecque's side on May 13; Ahmed Djebbour, who had unsuccessfully contested a by-election in Paris and who had been grievously wounded by an F.L.N. gunman; and Kaouah Mourad, an employee of the Algerian gas and power monopoly.

In the suburbs of Algiers, which formed a single constituency, an integrationist ticket headed by Philippe Marçais, dean of the Faculty of Letters of the University of Algiers, defeated three rival but equally integrationist tickets. M. Marçais' running mates were: Marc Lauriol, professor at the Algiers School of Commerce; Mlle. Nefissa Sid-Cara, sister of the Oran politician; and Robert Abdesselam, lawyer and former tennis champion. Mlle. Sid-Cara was to become a Secretary of State in the cabinet formed by Michel Debré on January 8, 1959. Her brother, Chérif Sid-Cara, won handily in Oran's rural constituency. One of his running mates was Pierre Laffont, distinguished publisher of the *Echo d'Oran.*

In the city of Oran, General Roger Miquel, formerly Army regional commander at Toulouse, challenged the entrenched power of Henri Fouques-Duparc, the former mayor, deputy, and cabinet minister (Secretary of State for Civil Aviation under Premier Pierre Mendès-

France for a brief period in 1955). The campaign was vigorously fought, but the General went down to defeat on election day. A Socialist ticket headed by Maurice Rabier, former deputy for Oran, and a right-wing ticket headed by François Quilici, another former deputy for Oran, were overwhelmed at the polls.

A stouthearted advocate of integration was elected at Médéa in the person of Pierre Vignau, formerly a delegate to the Algerian Assembly. Similarly, at Batna, Ali Mallem, backed by the movement of May 13, routed Alfred Malpel, a former mayor of Batna whose hostility to the local Committee of Public Safety had suggested "liberal" leanings. A well-known lawyer, M. Mallem had once been close to Ferhat Abbas and had even defended Mostefa Ben Boulaïd, the first rebel commander in eastern Algeria. More recently, however, he had become one of the leading Moslem proponents of integration and, politically, an associate of Jacques Soustelle. At Bône, Pierre Portolano, an ardent integrationist, defeated a Socialist candidate, Raoul Borra, a former mayor of the city. Azem Ouali, president of the mayors' association of Kabylia and a prominent figure in the movement of May 13, was elected at Tizi Ouzou.

Tickets that might have been described as "dissident" in that they did not swell the chorus for integration were successful in only three of Algeria's eighteen northern and two Saharan constituencies. At Philippeville, Leopold Morel, lawyer, *colon*, politician, and publisher of the *Dépêche de Constantine*, defeated Mme. Suzanne Lefort, wife of the colonel commanding the Second Foreign Parachute Regiment (Foreign Legion). One of M. Morel's running mates was Mohammed Boulsane, former delegate to the Algerian Assembly and member of the "Sixty-One." A Socialist ticket headed by Dr. William Widenlocher won at Sétif. At Tlemcen, Yvon Grasset, Mayor of Eugène Etienne (formerly Hennaya, a town six miles north of Tlemcen), defeated an integrationist and a Socialist. He had based his campaign on the economic objectives outlined by De Gaulle in his Constantine speech and had stressed the need for "brotherhood" and "dignity."

The number of abstentions was, not unexpectedly, far greater in November than it had been the previous September. The overall participation was 65 per cent of the electorate, as compared with 80 per cent for the referendum. At Bougie and Sétif, only 52 per cent of the registered voters went to the polls. The figure was 60 per cent at Algiers. At Oran and Mostaganem, on the other hand, the participation reached 75 per cent.

A glance at the results in the Orléansville constituency provides interesting evidence of some conscious discrimination on the part of the voters. Only one ticket had been formed there; it was headed by Bachaga

Saïd Boualem, member of an influential family, major in the army reserve, and commander of a *harka* (native auxiliary unit). The *bachaga* was a strong candidate and would undoubtedly have won a seat in the National Assembly in the face of the stiffest competition. But about 15,000 voted against him by casting blank ballots. The results in that constituency were:

Registered voters	271,642
For the single ticket	175,928
Blank ballots	15,040

What prompted so many voters to cast blank ballots when they could just as well have stayed at home? The answer may never be known with any degree of accuracy. But the fact that a protest vote did develop in a single-slate constituency is worth recording as an indication of the manner in which nationalist sentiment might have made itself felt all over the country if there had been enough of it.

In most places, the Moslem electorate was plainly confused by the competition between candidates professing the same opinions. It is reported that, at Médéa, a Moslem woman announced that she was for "France, Algeria, and the Arabs." Assured by election officials that the candidates on both tickets in the constituency shared her views, she entered the booth with a blank expression and voted—heaven knows for whom!

In Metropolitan France, the general election was held on November 23, with runoff balloting a week later. There, the candidates stood alone and not, as in Algeria, with running mates on the same ticket. The debacle of the traditional Left and the emergence of Jacques Soustelle's Union for the New Republic as the dominant party, with 189 of the 465 Metropolitan seats in the new Assembly, gave rise to intense satisfaction in Algeria. Pierre Mendès-France, the very symbol of surrender, bit the dust on November 23 (one of his opponents having won an absolute majority). The runoff balloting toppled a host of other "liberal" candidates, including such princes of the Fourth Republic as François Mitterrand, Edgar Faure, Gaston Defferre, Christian Pineau, and Albert Gazier. If many in Algeria deplored the defeat of Robert Lacoste and André Morice, they were heartened to learn of the success of Colonel Jean Thomazo (at Bayonne), Léon Delbecque (at Lille), and Lucien Neuwirth (at Saint Etienne). It was noted, too, no doubt with mixed emotions, that the energetic Jean-Baptiste Biaggi had won a seat as deputy for the fourteenth constituency of Paris. He had got almost twice as many votes as the incumbent, a Communist. M. Biaggi had dissolved his own *Parti Patriote Populaire* to run for election under the colors of the Union for the New Republic. On the whole, the election was judged to have gone well for French Algeria.

On December 8, 1958, sixty of the seventy-one Algerian deputies, meeting in Paris, resolved to:

1. Oppose any attempt to turn the Algerian departments into a separate political entity.
2. Oppose any move to put Algeria under an authority other than the French Parliament and Government.
3. Demand the administrative fusion of Algeria and Metropolitan France, the abolition of all customs barriers between Algeria and Metropolitan France, the abolition of Algerian bank notes and of the separate Algerian budget, the fusion of the Metropolitan and Algerian light and power monopolies and of the two railway administrations.
4. Insure the advancement of the Moslems within the framework of French citizenship.

Three days later, sixty-three Algerian deputies formed a parliamentary group of their own dedicated to the "ever greater fusion" of Algeria with Metropolitan France. The group called itself an "administrative formation." Three other Algerian deputies joined it later, bringing the total number of members to sixty-six. Among the Algerian deputies who did not join the group were Henri Fouques-Duparc and François Lopez, deputies for Oran, who joined the parlimentary group of the Union for the New Republic (U.N.R.). Ali Mallem, deputy for Batna, also joined the U.N.R. group. Dr. Widenlocher, deputy for Sétif, joined the Socialist group.

Having promised to work out Algeria's future in consultation with the elected representatives of the Algerian people, De Gaulle was embarrassed to be confronted with an almost solid phalanx of integrationist deputies from across the Mediterranean. But instead of accepting the verdict of the electorate he had himself called to the polls, he declared in an address on December 7, 1958, that the time was not yet ripe for a political settlement in Algeria. "Our problem," he said, "is above all a human problem—to give each Algerian his liberty, his well-being, and his dignity." The address marked the end of a five-day visit to Algeria. (In giving the human problem priority over the political problem, De Gaulle adopted a line of reasoning frequently used in the past by Algerian "ultras" intent on preserving the political *status quo*. The Premier's purpose was, of course, different. But it is curious to note, in this connection, that the "liberals," who had previously insisted that the Algerian problem, being essentially political, demanded a political solution, let De Gaulle's statement go unchallenged. The "ultras," however, contested it.)

The Premier apparently went further. According to *Le Monde*,* he actually advised various Algerians through René Brouillet, his Secretary-General for Algerian Affairs, that the election did not necessarily constitute the only way of accomplishing what remained to be done in Algeria. *Le Monde* attributed the Premier's attitude to a desire not to "mortgage" Algeria's future. As though the possible options were legion!

Meanwhile, despite the burdensome presence of more than sixty integrationist deputies from Algeria, De Gaulle continued to undo the revolution of May 13 by degrees. A decisive step in this direction was taken on December 12, 1958, when General Salan was relieved as Delegate-General in Algeria and given the newly-created post of Inspector-General of Defense. His successor in Algeria was a civilian, Paul Delouvrier. Air Force General Maurice Challe was appointed commander-in-chief under M. Delouvrier.

The return to civilian control before the achievement of integration was of tremendous symbolic importance. It meant that the Army, which had pledged itself to the defense of French Algeria, was now in a sense being forced to stand down. De Gaulle made this clear in a letter to General Salan. "Our essential concern," he wrote, "is going to shift toward economic and administrative development. In view of this, I hold it preferable to entrust the task to a civilian specialist, the military command resuming its former character. . . ."

M. Delouvrier, a 44-year-old *inspecteur des finances* with wide experience in the field of economics, was a specialist *par excellence*. That he was willing to accept the Algerian post in a time of crisis with no other pretensions than those of a technician made some people question his grasp of the situation. For, as events were soon to show, the "essential concern" was not going to shift to economic development. Other considerations are of far greater moment both to those who kill and to those who may die.

Seven months after coming to power, De Gaulle had yet to face up to the ultimate alternative in Algeria—integration or independence. On the contrary, the notion that France could still reasonably pin her hopes on moderate Algerian nationalism continued to hold De Gaulle and many of his supporters in tragic and infinitely costly illusion. This illusion was

* See *Le Monde* for December 28, 1958.

reflected in De Gaulle's inaugural address as President of the Republic on January 8, 1959. Speaking of the newly-instituted French Community, he said:

> It is a question of giving life to this magnificent institution, which, by virtue of a contract entered into in complete independence, unites, on the one hand, Metropolitan France, together with the Oversea Departments and Territories, and, on the other, the Republics born in the lands of Africa, where liberty, equality, and fraternity have flourished under the tricolor flag. In the union thus formed, a special place is destined for the Algeria of tomorrow, an Algeria that will be pacified and transformed, developing her personality herself and closely associated with France.

The inauguration was, as required by tradition, accompanied by measures of clemency and of pardon. The President commuted to hard labor for life all death sentences—180 of them—for which recourse to appellate jurisdiction had been exhausted. He reduced by one-tenth the prison sentences of all Algerian rebels and terrorists convicted by Algerian courts. Roger Frey, Minister of Information, announced that, concomitantly, the Government had decided to:

1. Release 7,000 persons interned in Algeria by administrative order.
2. Terminate the house arrest of Messali Hadj and allow him the freedom of Metropolitan France.
3. Transfer Mohammed Ben Bella, Mohammed Boudiaf, Hocine Aït Ahmed, Mohammed Khider, and Mustapha Lacheraf to a fort.

As a result of the Government's decisions, the five rebel leaders were taken from the Santé prison in Paris and accommodated on the Ile d'Aix in the Bay of Biscay.* Messali Hadj and his retinue established themselves in a comfortable hotel at Chantilly.

When Michel Debré, the new Premier, went before the National Assembly on January 15 to explain his Government's program, he asserted that Algeria would evolve in its own way but that French sovereignty there would remain unimpaired. (The Government's program was approved on January 16 by a vote of 453 to 56, with 29 abstentions.)

And so the new regime, under Debré, continued to give the dizzying impression of going two ways at once. In holding a parliamentary elec-

---

* The fortifications there were built by Vauban in the seventeenth century as part of the Rochefort defenses. Napoleon sojourned on the island from July 12 to July 15, 1815, before leaving French soil forever aboard the British frigate *Bellerophon.*

tion in Algeria as well as in Metropolitan France, De Gaulle had moved toward integration. In attempting to negotiate a cease-fire with the rebel high command, he had moved toward independence. Similarly, the measures of pardon and of clemency that had marked De Gaulle's inauguration as President made sense politically only as a prelude to new overtures to the rebels. Instead, Premier Debré veered off in the opposite direction by affirming French sovereignty in Algeria and by barring (as De Gaulle had already done) political negotiations with the rebels.

In Tunis, Mohammed Yazid, "Minister of Information" in the "Provisional Government of the Algerian Republic," dismissed the measures of clemency as a "maneuver" without political significance and as a "pitiable attempt to delude world public opinion."

In Algeria, the measures of clemency were seen by many as a wholly incomprehensible bonus to the enemies of France. *Algérie Française*, an organization newly formed for the defense of French Algeria, put out a statement to the effect that, following the official ban on the word "integration," the measures of clemency had helped create an atmosphere of "anxiety and terror."

A news dispatch on January 26, 1959, said that terrorist attacks in Algeria had "returned" to a frequency of fifty a week and had increased in effectiveness. This item stood as a stark comment on De Gaulle's policy of pushing Algeria back to the *status quo ante.*

Deliberate ambiguity in the matter of ultimate aims obscured the nature of the Algerian conflict, bred enervating speculation, and cast doubts on the ability of France to restore peace in Algeria except through capitulation. And so the war dragged on, costing $2,000,000 or more a day in hard cash and inestimable treasure in human lives.

It is ironical that French repugnance against integration should stem in part from the fear that such a course would put an unbearable strain on the French pocketbook. In December, 1958, a study group headed by Christian Pineau, the former Socialist Foreign Minister, cited the supposed economic and financial burdens of integration as a compelling reason for preferring a "more prudent" middle policy based on a recognition of the "Algerian personality."

"Let's work out a cut-rate solution for Algeria," M. Pineau's group said in effect. The instinctive reaction of many hard-pressed and heavily-taxed Frenchmen will, of course, always be to welcome advice of this kind. But Socialists, in responding to so materialistic an impulse, seem curiously out of character. The worst of it is that M. Pineau's recommendations stemmed from a false premise. The premise was that the idea of "personality" could somehow be substituted for the idea of sovereignty

to the satisfaction of a significant number of Algerian nationalists and that a lasting association between Algeria and Metropolitan France could therefore be founded upon it. Four years of war in Algeria were there to prove the folly of such a belief. The sanctity of the Algerian personality had been proclaimed again and again (and never with greater solemnity than by M. Pineau's fellow Socialist, Guy Mollet). Yet the fighting had only gained in virulence. In fact, the "more prudent" middle policy advocated by M. Pineau and his associates was the most ruinous of all. By exposing the weakness of French resolve and confidence, by exacerbating nationalist sentiment in the rebel camp, by depriving the loyal Moslems of a goal worth fighting for, the middle policy could only result in protracted war and, if persisted in, ultimate defeat.

If, as seems likely, the hour of the last chance has struck for France in Algeria, a resolute attempt had better be made to see the realities of the Algerian situation as they are, not as they may appear to be in the light of a particular political doctrine. A service to truth is, at this moment, more than ever a service to Algeria.

The strength of the national ideal within a limited circle of educated and semieducated Algerians—the only possible beneficiaries of independence—cannot be denied. It is idle to believe that the rebellion will be disarmed by the common electoral roll or by the promise of other good things to come. If the French Army is not master of the disputed field, Algeria will be lost. France cannot elude the duty of protecting her citizens, even the humblest of them, and expect respect for her flag.

No greater mistake could be made than to interpret the fraternal demonstrations of May, 1958, and the referendum that followed in September, as meaning that the Moslem community is ready to give up its separate identity and structure. That moment has not yet come. On the other hand, an injustice is done when it is asserted that the Moslems are indifferent to the notion of integration. *Autonomy without independence is a trick to deprive the Moslems of a country they can call their own.* If the French are unwilling to receive the Moslems into their community on some equitable basis, a sense of rejection will develop that can only strengthen the forces of independence. There must be nothing in the nature of a vote of no confidence in the ability of the Moslems to become fully qualified Frenchmen.

Meanwhile, it is nonsense to make the common electoral roll synonymous with equality. There can be no equality in Algeria until two conditions are satisfied *in advance*. The first is the total conversion of the native economy so that the Moslems will no longer be living, most of them, in an archaic world, and only a few in the modern world. In

present circumstances, any election is bound to be more or less a travesty. It is as if the Navaho reservation in Arizona were expected to pass on the complex issues confronting the American electorate. That the Navahos cannot do so because they are backward and illiterate is a reflection, not on them, but on ourselves.

The second prior condition is the acceptance by all Algerians of a common system of ordinary civil law, in harmony with the modern, not the archaic, world. Modern society is a society of law, binding equally on all men, regardless of their religion, or lack of it. So it must be in Algeria.

In my opinion, only the first of these conditions presents a real problem. For if it were dealt with effectively, the second would undoubtedly sort itself out as a natural result. When all Algerians acknowledge the same justice in matters of personal status, as they already do in the fields of criminal and commercial law, it will mean that the communal structure of Moslem society has been abandoned; it will mean that the Moslems have been integrated into a society based on assumptions shared by all its members and geared to the necessities of the contemporary world. There will then no longer be the slightest excuse for a double-college system of voting. The common electoral roll should be the mark of fusion, not a mask for cleavages.

The conversion of Algeria's archaic economy and the necessarily concomitant conversion of the country's archaic society are the great challenge facing France. The problems involved are formidable; the cost is enormous. There is a demographic curse on Algeria—exploding birth rate, static resources—and only France can remove it in the foreseeable future. The alternative is bottomless poverty. If Algeria is not given a truly productive economy—itself the best antidote to excessive natality—the population spiral must ultimately meet the counterforce of starvation.

One of the lessons of the revolution of May 13 and of the referendum is that the overwhelming majority of the Algerian Moslems still want to live in a French context. The French cannot fail to respond. And for all their trials, I count them lucky. Few nations today can offer their citizens such vast opportunities for service at once to other human beings and to a transcendent ideal. What Algeria requires is an emergency rescue operation on a scale not yet attempted by a Western country. This is the very sort of task to which China has set herself in her own immense territories. It would be comforting to think that the job could be done without the iron discipline of Communism and the loss of freedom. For sooner or later it may have to be done under whatever auspices will make it possible.

In the immediate future, the essential imperative in Algeria is security. This is a biological need and a primordial right. And nothing constructive can be accomplished in a climate of fear, amid the clash of arms.

53. SOME REFLECTIONS ON ARAB NATIONALISM

Arab nationalism has been vexed from its inception by confusions resulting from the conflict between Moslem tradition and the modern world. For centuries, Moslem society was static. This will be apparent to anyone visiting the old city of Fez in Morocco or the Zitouna Islamic university in Tunis. Even the practical arts were reduced to the endless repetition of patterns handed down from generation to generation. The *fellah*, for instance, is still faithful to ancestral methods of agriculture that make him less productive than almost any other tiller of the soil.

When the modern world broke over the still waters of Islam—in Morocco, this happened within living memory—the Arabs were ill prepared to receive it. Their reactions have ranged from almost total rejection, as in Yemen, to a large measure of acceptance, as in Egypt. But everywhere Arab leaders are faced with a tough choice. If they decide to hold fast to their tradition, they must attempt to seal themselves off against a rapidly contracting world. But if they decide to accept some of the changes that are thrust upon them, they must reconcile themselves to forms that are purely imitative and have no roots in their own past. The so-called Arab awakening has always struck me as essentially a collision.

The old Moslem society is full of dignity, simplicity, and serene docility in the face of providence. Desert Arabs, in particular, brave, honest, and untarnished, continue to receive the traveler with the fine courtesies of another age. T. E. Lawrence and others have known and praised these virtues.

Progress is wholly foreign to the Moslem tradition, just as it was to antiquity. The traditional Arab is not what might be termed a historical man. History is unimportant to him because he never believed he could shape events and, through them, his own destiny within the confines of time and space. The Arab's hope, based on divine warranty, reaches out to eternity. Rejecting self-realization, the Arab lives in daily communion with the revealed word of God, takes refuge in the fellowship of the faithful, and often endures with unbelievable patience tyranny, injustice, back-breaking toil, disease, and affliction. Immutable custom has served the Arab as a primary security factor, protecting him against dangers seen or unseen, real or imagined. His total fusion with the group prefigures a common salvation. Since the individual in this scheme of things is of little account, the traditional Arab has never learned to think socially. His idea of government is rudimentary. His notion of social responsibility has rarely evolved beyond the obligation of almsgiving and other forms of direct succor.

Is it any wonder, then, that the modern world should have torn many Arabs from their moorings? For the West, dynamic, rational, and individualistic, is at sharp variance with Moslem tradition in every particular of thought, action, and mode of life. Nothing could be more interesting to observe than the phenomena of change and interchange produced by the impact of the West upon the Moslem East. A moving object may be deflected and warped when it strikes and dislodges a stationary object. In like manner, Western influences injected into the Moslem world toppled the existing edifice only to be themselves distorted. And just as some microbes are harmless in one climate and virulent in another, so Western ideas that have been forces for good in their home ground may become destructive of good in the East. Certainly their effects are never the same. It is enough to consider what has happened to such concepts as democracy, popular sovereignty, and parliamentary rule.

Inevitably, for better or for worse, these alien influences are engulfing much of the Moslem East, making the Arabs strangers in a world not their own and creating psychological tensions that were not there before. People who had been fully competent within the older context are now groping for a place in the newer one. And as in adolescence, the desire for emancipation brooks no delay. Aggressive attitudes compensate for want of assurance. Thus we find educated Arabs resorting to exaggeration, overemphasis, verbal violence in the expression of precarious opinions. I am reminded in this connection of a speech at the United Nations by Farid Zeineddine of Syria, who asserted that Algeria in 1830 had been as culturally advanced as France. He went on to accuse the French of "genocide" and had to be called to order when he stated flatly that the French in Algeria were "conducting themselves like Nazis."

It will be objected, and rightly, that demagogy and extravagant language are at home in all countries. But it seems to me that these habits are, in the Arab world to a greater extent than elsewhere, accepted as normal. Indeed, I often wonder how many Arabs have been truly assimilated into the twentieth century. I remember discussing this question in Benghazi some years ago with a distinguished British Arabist. Having assumed for the purpose of argument that universal curiosity combined with a willingness to compare results was the mark of the modern mind at its best, we cast about for the name of a single contemporary Arab who, by this criterion, could be called representative of our time. The Englishman—how normal!—suggested Nuri es-Saïd of Iraq. I was not able to contest this choice. Perhaps a better one could not be made. But I do know that Nuri es-Saïd was an object of repugnance to most Arab nationalists.

It is curious to note, too, that political satisfactions do little to alleviate the stresses placed upon the Arab psyche by the invasion of the West. Egypt, for instance, has realized in abundant measure the fondest dreams of Saad Pasha Zaghlul and his nationalist followers. The country is free and independent; its power is expanding; its capital is the seat of the greatest universities in Islam. Yet the Egyptian intellectual is as tormented as his Algerian cousin. Both are in a hurry to prove their worth, always in Western terms. Both press on, intense, touchy, insatiable, at odds with the world, toward ever elusive horizons.

A "liberal" in Algeria is a European who professes admiration for the Moslem nationalists, or at least for the force they represent. An "ultra" is frequently described as a reactionary steeped in paternalism, a back number akin to an advocate of white supremacy in our own South. An invincible nostalgia for the good old days when an Arab knew his place is supposed to prevent the "ultras" from recognizing the nationalists as the men of tomorrow. But something more than this is behind the preference of many Europeans for Moslems who, in "liberal" eyes, are a lot of outdated feudal lords, *caïds*, and tribal chiefs. Quite apart from the relative merits of the new order and of the old, Europeans are apt to feel they can meet an authentic Moslem, one who is a true product of his own culture, on equal terms. Such a man is not embarrassed to be himself or to be seen for what he is. Since he is under no compulsion to imitate strange people and strange ways, he is troubled by no awkward comparisons.

Equality between European and Moslem is difficult when the latter is, in fact, an ersatz European. The only way to friendly intercourse with the Europeanized Moslem lies in sincere acceptance of his claims and values. Hypocrisy will not do; it creates a strain and will be sensed by the Moslem. Some Europeans cannot make the necessary adjustment without experiencing an intolerable degree of self-abdication. For others, it is quite possible. I have always been interested to observe the attitudes of Europeans called to live among the Moslems, and I have come to believe that the European who is attracted to the Europeanized Arab intellectual is usually one who shares his conflicts and limitations.

It is true, of course, that the new Arabs, not the old, are now governing the politics of the Middle East and of part of North Africa. Such is the strange legacy of Europe to the Arab peoples it so recently held in tutelage. I am aware, too, that the educated elite among the Algerian Moslems, impressed by the conquests of Arab nationalism elsewhere—especially Nasserism—longs to be caught up in the mainstream of Arab life. The emotional charge stemming from this emotional commitment is not to be underestimated; it helped beget the rebellion and helps keep it alive.

But the vision of a few Algerian Moslems goes beyond nationalism. They may be conservatives like Mohammed Aït-Ali, president of the Algiers regional assembly, or modernists like Chérif Sid-Cara, a former French cabinet minister. They may be Arabs or Berbers. What they have in common is a conviction that, without France, the clock would be turned back in Algeria. They look to the association with France for orderly evolution, material progress, and individual opportunity. Above all, they hold in high value a human ideal that they believe can still enlist the devotion of Frenchmen on both sides of the Mediterranean, European and Moslem alike. A failure to make that ideal prevail against wind and tide would constitute the most abject of capitulations, and the world itself would be the loser.

APPENDIX I
WHEN CHILDREN DIE OF HUNGER*

By *Hafid Jellabi*

Among the leprous shanties in which a luckless people are huddled, there stands an occasional new building where statistics accumulate on bare wooden tables—the Hygiene Bureau. Bent over a table, a man writes on a death certificate, opposite the word "cause," "physiological misery." Not far from the hovels, at the end of bumpy dirt alleys, is the cemetery. For lack of bread, a little more earth is removed, and that is all. At Sidi Othman, as elsewhere, people die of hunger, casually. . . .

Strange world of want, built on the joy of others, swarming with little bony faces, with women whose hungry children clutch at flaccid breasts, with an indiscriminate collection of old men leaning motionless against the tin of the shanties and muttering I know not what sufferer's prayer. Along the ground creep unspeakable odors mixed with the polluted waters of the gutters. A child nibbles a piece of stale bread, hard as a rock; envious, a group of little girls stare at him with the shiny eyes of desire. . . .

Early in the morning, men emerge from wretched dwellings to make their way toward the modern city, where untroubled consciences, still asleep, will soon be sitting down to breakfast. . . . They come from all about, from the Carrières Centrales, from Ben M'Sik, from the Djerb D'Jid, from Sidi Othman, and from all those foetuses of future shantytowns where Moroccan misery wallows. On empty stomachs, they wan-

* This article appeared in the Moroccan French-language weekly *Démocratie* for March 11, 1957. The issue was seized by the Moroccan authorities. *Démocratie* was the organ of the Democratic Independence party (P.D.I.), a group opposed to the dominant Istiqlal party.

der through the city of others, awaiting for hours the inevitable refusal. The leitmotiv recurs with the cadence of a stabbing metronome: "No work. We are no longer hiring." Today, a factory closes its doors, and tomorrow a few more will join the wretched wandering . . .

In the evening, when files of workers leave the factories, the "luckless" head back toward the tin cities where the poor, questioning look of wife and children awaits them. Today, as yesterday, it will be necessary to make do with a glass of half-sweetened tea, which will also serve to soften a bit of stale bread bought at a discount from an understanding baker. Tomorrow, the teapot or the tray will have to be sold, for household utensils are disposed of one by one.

Tomorrow, perhaps, it will be possible to work a little in the garden of a European or to wash a car, and even then, there will be fifty applying for the job; for among the "luckless" a bank-of-the-perhaps exists, where one in a thousand wins in the distribution of life-giving hope.

One trade flourishes in the shantytowns, that of the ragpicker. In refuse bins, bits of cloth are found, and these can be sold to the "luckless." Not for much, to be sure—five francs, ten francs, which enable the seller to wear trousers that are a little more presentable, a shirt that closes a little better. These ragpickers of misfortune also buy the torn shirt that can be converted into a couple of pounds of bread soaked in rancid oil or a little coal for the preparation of the tea that is taken in winter just before a man goes to sleep on the ground, wrapped up in sacking and paper.

It is hard to get to sleep with children who cry, a wife who groans in hunger, quietly, so as to disturb no one. The shantytown dwellings open upon a little courtyard shared by three or four families, twenty or thirty people who quarrel, who bawl with hunger. Sometimes a person disappears, to turn up on a card at the Hygiene Bureau. During the past three months, at Sidi Othman alone, more than 330 children under five and more than fifty old people have died; forty children have been stillborn. Next come the women, with twenty for February; and, last, the men—twelve. The other shantytowns are in the same boat. The process is always the same: first, unemployment, then undernourishment, and finally death. This seems hardly to concern the responsible authorities, since the medical social centers have had their budgets cut by 80 per cent in recent months.

Here is strange therapy! Is the aim to cure evil with evil by using the rising death rate as a means for doing away with the shantytowns? A remnant of the Protectorate, the shantytowns—which, after all, did not exist before the arrival of the French—today constitute a wound that must be cauterized without delay. One year after independence, men, children, and women are dying of starvation in face of the strange passivity of the authorities. . . .

Inside the tin shacks of the shantytowns, when there is no work and nothing to eat, there is time for thought, and with all deference to the Government, it must be said that this is indulged in. . . . Here are some reflections gathered at random in alleys where men without work dream of a loaf of bread:

"The Government has promised work for all, and there is more unemployment than before, and, what's more, all these receptions for ministers and foreigners cost money. Why not give us this money? Soup kitchens could be set up. The Welfare Bureau promised to do this, but nothing has happened."

"I have been to the employment agency to ask for work, and I was thrown out. His Majesty will not see your letter. The ministers will tear it up, they who ride in motor cars."

The nights and the days bring talk of politics in the shantytowns, and the hope placed in His Majesty is still as strong as it was in the dark days of exile. "But his ministers hide from him the poverty of his people." How true is the phrase which the Glaoui meant as an expression of contempt, but which is probably His Majesty Mohammed V's greatest title to fame: "He is the Sultan of the Carrières Centrales." In all the shantytowns, people made sacrifices to be able to hang on their blackened walls of tin and planks the portrait of the Sultan of Morocco, of their Morocco.

He is there, representing the hope that, in spite of all, helps relieve the meanness of certain existences. At the heart of that existence, there are also superb young women, Moroccan and French, who attempt the impossible, listening, helping out to the best of the inadequate means put at their disposal. These young women are social workers. I know some who, when night comes, throw themselves in tears upon their beds, because, all the same, one may be permitted to cry with rage at the sight of so much want for which one can do so little.

"Mademoiselle l'Espoir" is a social worker. Like the others, she goes from hovel to hovel trying to remedy little matters always involving the money needed to live.

It is not always easy to lavish encouragement on those who no longer believe in anything much. Not easy, either, to explain the reason for certain delays in the payment of pensions and relief. The habitués of hunger are sometimes bad-tempered. And yet, says "Mademoiselle l'Espoir": "I assure you that, on the whole, they are very decent people. Their needs are not great—a little work, security for the morrow, so that they may live with smiles as wide as this."

All day long, she comes in contact with the beggars' meetings of the *bidonvilles* . . . Everywhere she hears the same prayers, the same requests, the same recriminations: unemployment, hunger, illness. It's an apostolate, the work of the anonymous friends of the poor. All of them have told me the same stories with almost imperceptible variations. Their problems are made up of the problems of others, of the hunger of others. In a dry voice, touched, however, with tenderness for her fellow beings, one of them described to me the life that is hers, a life that seizes poverty in full embrace every day:

"The physical appearance of the children is frightful. Deaths are a daily occurrence, and I am not speaking of tuberculosis cases, which in the promiscuity of the shantytowns are more and more frequent. Infectious diseases spread with terrible speed. But the question is not only one of curing the ill; it is also one of prevention. All these tin shacks are an appalling breeding ground for germs. If they were wiped out, the anticipated number of tuberculosis cases would be reduced by three-quarters."

And the long litany of complaints and of what should be done continues. Debilitated women do their utmost, to the detriment of their health, to nurse their babies to the age of two. Among those who are compelled to wean their babies sooner, 99 per cent do not have enough money to buy milk.

"It is horrible," another social worker told me. "I must show women how to swaddle their babies, how to prepare a bottle, teach them the precautions of ordinary hygiene. I seem to be mocking these people who live in congested shacks and who can afford neither diapers nor milk. Sometimes we give them a little money from our pockets."

In the dispensaries, the practice now is to give milk only to babies already receiving it. With rare exceptions, the newborn are not admitted to the distributions. Complaints to the Ministry of Public Health remain a dead letter. At a welfare bureau, a widow, accompanied by a social worker, comes with her two children to ask for relief. The answer she gets is astonishing for its cynicism: "She is not entitled to relief; she begs for a living."

Thus beggary is recognized in the New Morocco as a calling like that of dock worker or metal-fitter. This woman at least had the courage to beg, but how many able-bodied men . . . would dare demean themselves to that extent? Sometimes the social workers are reduced to advising, in a small trembling voice, certain women to try their luck in the street.

Day laborers are 80 per cent unemployed; qualified workers in certain specialized fields, fancy pastry bakers for instance, are out of work; half the small craftsmen are high and dry, and the rest idle along. Prostitution and juvenile delinquency are the subject of spiraling statistics. The day comes when a girl leaves her family and goes out to put her youth up for sale so as to be able to eat her fill. The day comes when a boy, tempted by the bicycle that will, perhaps, enable him to find work, mounts it and steals it as though he were in an Italian neo-realistic film, only, this time, it is not cinema. . . .

From the countryside—for there, too, hunger is felt—comes a steady flow of the cities' future pariahs. A few shacks are added to others; an alley grows longer. For a time, those who arrive will be the object of general envy, since some still have a little money preciously saved up to try their fortune in the city. Two months, three months later, they have become just like the anonymous others lost in the swarming masses of the fragile city of dangling roofs.

Works projects must be got under way as a matter of extreme urgency; it is imperative to abolish this unspeakable evil, which is the residue of the colonialist era, but which some of those in power today contrive to make worse.

Babies must not suck the dry breasts of crying mothers. It is cheaper to build decent homes than sanatoria. We must reject the false pride that induces some to hide Morocco's sores. There is no such thing as a disgraceful illness; the crime is to cover it up. It is a national duty to abolish the shantytowns. . . .

There would be more valid reality in the smile of a child who, at last, eats his fill than in the smug satisfaction of certain ministers who think that statements of intention have a miraculous curative power. It is all very well to go after prostitutes and delinquent youth, but it would be better to eliminate the causes of their ills.

APPENDIX II
THE FIRST FRENCH SETTLERS IN ALGERIA*

By *Albert Mousset*

One hundred and eight years ago, on October 8, 1848, the first convoy of settlers heading for Algeria left the Quai de Bercy. There were 843 of them. General Lamoricière delivered a patriotic address, and the *curé* of Bercy blessed their flag. Irony of toponymy: these Parisians were being sent 800 leagues from the capital to a village in the region of Oran that was called . . . Saint-Cloud.†

A decree issued the previous September 19 had set aside 50 million francs for the establishment of agricultural communities. The settlement of 12,000 families was contemplated; holdings of from nine to ten-and-a-half acres, seed, livestock, and implements were to be distributed to them; for three years they were to be fed by the state. The candidates for this exodus were required to produce a certificate of good character and a certificate of physical fitness.

Many workers were unemployed at the time, with the result that numerous applications were submitted, especially in Paris.

A scholar whose works are authoritative, M. Henri Lemoine, was curious enough some twenty years ago to examine the archives to see what they revealed about the candidates' professions. Very few of them, to tell the truth, had the necessary qualifications for their new calling. The lists drawn up in the eighth and ninth *arrondissements* (then the first and the second) contained, to be sure, the names of a hundred or so farmers or gardeners and a certain number of government workers. But unexpected professions were also listed—jewelers, bookbinders, engravers,

* The following article appeared in *Le Monde* for May 22, 1956.

† The name of a suburb of Paris.

artists, actors, three concierges, two former notaries, a jurist, a professor of penmanship, and an instructor in the use of the hunting horn!

Between October 8 and December 10, there were sixteen departures, each accompanied by the same ceremonial. And applications for 1849 were already pouring in.

Exhumed by M. Lemoine, the letters addressed by the settlers to the mayor of their *arrondissement* reflected more disappointment than enthusiasm. "Our position," one of them wrote, "is wretched. We have been lodged ten to twelve together in uncovered shacks, and the rain comes down in torrents. Treated like slaves; I do not inflate the matter, but write literally!"

All of them complained about the abolition of the little allowance of ten centimes a day, which had enabled them to buy some extra food for their children. Two sous—quite a sum in those days!

Those wishing to earn two francs a day had to work ten hours for the Corps of Engineers. The daily ration provided by the Government was the same as for the soldiers—750 grams [about one pound and ten ounces] of bread, 250 grams [a little less than nine ounces] of meat, twelve grams [not quite half an ounce] of coffee and sugar, and a quarter of a liter [about half a pint] of wine.

Complaints were not well received. "You ask politely and you get a brutal answer, and if you persist, you are thrown out. We are called a band of ruffians and other things too foul to be repeated."

There were optimists though, as witness the man who had a well of saline water but who hoped it would become sweet with time. Nonetheless, he wished he still had his "two sous of pocket money and the candle, which were a great comfort."

The Frenchman is faithfully reflected in this modest complaint: "We could wish that the accountant in charge of the distribution of liquids was not so afraid that we would get headaches, in other words, that he would not put so much water in our wine."

The settlers wanted arms and national guard uniforms to be issued to them: "We would be happy to find ourselves in our new country as we were in Paris."

In brief, their requests were aimed at three reforms:

1. To be rid of the military administration, "which treats us like convicts";
2. To receive again the ten-centime allowance;
3. To possess healthful, well-built homes.

A brochure by General Le Pays de Bourjolly contained a critical analysis of this settlement operation. He objected to the location of the

villages. He held that the Arabs should not have been expropriated, even though compensation was paid, that they would never understand why the land in which their ancestors were buried had to be taken from them. He complained that the settlers had been indiscriminately selected, that there were sluggards and rakes in the lot.

Finally, he estimated that the operation had cost 7,000 francs per family and concluded that the agricultural communities, extremely expensive to start with, would never be economical.

In many respects, experience was to bear him out.

In any case, the first letters from Algeria created an atmosphere of discouragement. Of 347 applicants who had signed up in the first *arrondissement* for the Spring 1849, departure, 300 dropped out.

A commission was appointed to conduct an official inquiry. It left Paris on June 27, 1849, visited the villages one after another, recorded the grievances of the settlers and the explanations of the directors. In November, it submitted its report to the War Ministry. The report stressed the shortcomings inherent in an improvised operation. It pointed out that the absence of a compulsory minimum yield after three years had encouraged some settlers to do nothing and to live at the expense of the state. There were among them too many jewelers, cabinetmakers, and bookbinders, whereas only experienced farmers should have been recruited. Mortality (especially infantile) was much too high; the medical corps should be required to make a new effort in the direction of more wholesome housing.

The most serious question was that of replacing the military authority by a civil administration. But in a new country, subject to the possibility of uprisings and in no position to administer itself, such action seemed premature.

The report was debated in the Chamber of Representatives in June and July, 1850. This debate resulted in the Law of July 20, which set aside an appropriation of 5 million francs for the improvement of the villages established in 1848 and 1849. But the recruiting requirements were completely revamped: only veterans who had served in Africa and French and Algerian farmers would henceforth be eligible to make good the losses incurred by the first communities and to populate the newer ones. Military directors were to be maintained until 1851, but they were to be assisted by consultative committees composed of village notables. It was definitely decided to establish no further communities.

By that year, there were a total of 10,376 settlers living in 3,745 houses and forty-two villages. Of 56,632 acres distributed, 25,923 were under cultivation. A total of 311,350 fruit trees had been planted.

In short, these city folk, Parisians for the most part, who in 1848 had

tried their luck, had shown themselves to be excellent farmers despite their setbacks at the beginning.

It is only fair to call to mind their tribulations and their efforts at a time when the social problem in Algeria is posed in a new light and when the old methods of colonization are relegated to the state of memory.

Author's note: Actually, the great waves of European immigration occurred at a later date. In 1872, the European community was made up of 130,000 Frenchmen, 71,000 Spaniards, 18,000 Italians, 12,000 Maltese, and some 14,000 of other nationalities. The Franco-Prussian War resulted in an influx of settlers from the lost provinces of Alsace and Lorraine. In addition, the phylloxera blight that devastated the French vineyards in the latter part of the nineteenth century gave tremendous impetus to Algerian viticulture. The European population reached 633,850 in 1901, and 800,000 in 1922; the present figure is in the neighborhood of 1,200,000 (including about 140,000 Jews, most of whom are, of course, indigenous).

APPENDIX III

STATISTICS OF LOSSES, NOVEMBER, 1954 – APRIL, 1957

MONTHS	KILLED				WOUNDED				CAPTURED, ABDUCTED, or MISSING			
	Security Forces	Civilians		Rebels	Security Forces	Civilians		Rebels	Security Forces	Civilians		Rebels
		Europeans	Moslems			Europeans	Moslems			Europeans	Moslems[1]	
Nov., 1954.– Oct., 1955	345	123	441	2,265	649	88	301	241	41	6	204	Un-known
Nov., 1955	43	11	156	254	153	16	56	46	70	1	67	113
Dec.	87	14	164	280	188	36	105	42	53	0	45	148
Jan., 1956	86	14	183	503	272	27	113	36	53	1	85	322
Feb.	106	12	176	385	196	2	91	40	7	1	71	142
March	133	15	304	1,256	341	46	129	84	24	0	85	349
April	165	27	370	1,730	321	52	132	67	22	5	103	543
May	184	54	346	1,995	374	51	169	88	85	4	110	371
June	190	43	328	1,807	493	147	175	80	84	3	189	761
July	195	37	488	1,448	468	93	166	110	10	9	91	243
Aug.	220	31	344	1,722	480	35	206	100	103	8	100	763
Sept.	192	47	325	1,473	498	154	259	67	85	10	61	229
Oct.	240	50	317	1,450	501	172	280	121	75	8	73	156
Nov.	215	75	206	1,440	510	206	269	103	146	16	65	303
Dec.	200	91	213	1,609	490	259	255	113	11	25	88	699
Jan., 1957	178	75	285	1,997	452	249	269	143	16	13	170	790
Feb.	200	67	294	2,995	484	143	202	104	23	12	114	1,198
March	147	46	315	2,693	402	100	158	100	18	7	107	1,692
April	312	59	321	2,738	735	133	195	168	22	10	122	1,873
TOTAL	3,438	891	5,576	30,040	8,007	2,009	3,530	1,853	948	139	1,950	10,695

STATISTICS OF WEAPONS LOSSES, NOVEMBER, 1955 – APRIL, 1957

MONTHS	ARMS OF WAR LOST	
	French	Rebels
Nov., 1955	131	168
Dec.	180	224
Jan., 1956	101	451
Feb.	302	191
March	Unknown	Unknown
April	547[2]	566
May	306	612
June	308	681
July	130	730
Aug.	162	774
Sept.	158	237
Oct.	499	291
Nov.	211	586
Dec.	137	757
Jan., 1957	256	442
Feb.	85	593
March	120	556
April	213	544
TOTAL	3,846	8,403

[1] The majority of the Moslem civilians listed as captured, abducted, or missing were presumed dead.

[2] Including 270 weapons delivered to the rebels by a deserter, the Communist Henri Maillot, on April 4, 1956. See Chapter 47.

SELECTED BIBLIOGRAPHY

It would be impossible to list all the sources from which the factual content of this book was drawn. My personal files of some 16,000 newspaper clippings and hundreds of other papers and documents collected over a period of more than four years were of inestimable value. My reporter's notebooks, too—twenty-two of them, all stuffed with information—were of great help. Published reports of all sorts, but particularly the Government General's annual *Exposé de la Situation Générale de l'Algérie*, were consulted and often proved useful. In addition, I was fortunate enough to have access to official material not previously tapped for any public use. I also poked my nose into dozens of books. Some of these are referred to in the text or in footnotes. Some I quickly laid aside as being of no interest. The titles given in the list below were those which for one reason or another were not discarded:

Algérie-Tunisie in the series of the *Guides Bleus*. Paris: Librairie Hachette, 1950. Indispensable.

ARON, Raymond. *L'Algérie et la République*. Paris: Plon, 1958. A sequel to M. Aron's *La Tragédie Algérienne*, published by Plon in 1957. This is the complete Aron, more brain than heart. It uses figures and statistics to prove that France cannot afford not to dump Algeria.

ARRIGHI, Pascal. *La Corse: Atout Décisif*. Paris: Plon, 1958. A lively book about the role of Corsica in the events of May, 1958.

BIDAULT, Georges. *L'Algérie, l'Oiseau aux Ailes Coupées*. Paris: La Table Ronde, 1958. M. Bidault, a stout defender of French Algeria, at his best.

BOUSQUET, Georges-Henri. *L'Islam Maghrebin*. Fourth edition. Algiers: La Maison des Livres, 1954. A standard work by a professor at the Faculty of Law of the University of Algiers.

BOYER de LATOUR, Pierre. *Vérités sur l'Afrique du Nord*. Paris: Plon, 1956. Bitter truths by a former French Resident General in Tunisia and in Morocco.

BROMBERGER, Merry and Serge. *Les 13 Complots du 13 Mai.* Paris: Arthème Fayard, 1959. The fascinating results of a six months' inquiry by two top-flight journalists.

BROMBERGER, Serge. *Les Rebelles Algériens.* Paris: Plon, 1958. The most careful and detailed description of the rebel camp available.

DRONNE, Raymond. *La Révolution d'Alger.* Paris: Editions France Empire, 1958. An account, in part eyewitness, by a Social Republican (Gaullist) deputy.

GAUTIER, E. F. *Le Passé de l'Afrique du Nord: les Siècles Obscurs.* Paris: Payot, 1952. An original and provocative work. The late Professor Gautier taught geography at the University of Algiers.

Initiation à l'Algérie. Paris: Librairie d'Amérique et d'Orient, 1957. Eighteen specialists contributed chapters to this very informative volume.

JEANSON, Colette and Francis. *L'Algérie hors la Loi.* Paris: Editions du Seuil, 1955. A pro-rebel tract written by a French couple and published in France.

JUIN, Alphonse. *Le Maghreb en Feu.* Paris: Plon, 1957. The thoughts of a son of Bône who became Resident General in Morocco, Marshal of France, and a member of the French Academy.

JULIEN, Charles-André. *L'Afrique du Nord en Marche.* Paris: Julliard, 1952. The rise of North African nationalism as seen through the sympathetic eyes of a French Socialist.

LARNAUDE, Marcel. *Algérie.* Paris: Editions Berger-Levrault, 1950. A descriptive volume containing much basic information.

MASSE, Henri. *L'Islam.* Sixth revised edition. Paris: Librairie Armand Colin, 1952. The best one-volume treatise on Islam that I have encountered. The author, a noted French orientalist, is administrator of the National School of Oriental Languages in Paris.

PAJAUD, Henri. *La Révolution d'Alger.* Paris: Les Quatre Fils Aymon, 1958. The events of May, 1958, described by an Algiers journalist.

SCHAEFER, René. *Révolution en Algérie.* Paris: Editions France Empire, 1956. A discussion of the economic, social, and cultural aspects of the Algerian problem.

SERIGNY, Alain de. *La Révolution du 13 Mai.* Paris: Plon, 1958. The revolution described by one of its leading protagonists.

SERVIER, Jean. *Dans l'Aurès sur les Pas des Rebelles.* Paris. Editions France Empire, 1955. Despite its title, this interesting book is primarily concerned with Algerian ethnology.

SIMON, Pierre-Henri. *Contre la Torture,* Paris: Editions du Seuil, 1957. A political pamphlet written by a "liberal" Catholic polemicist attacking the action of the French authorities in Algeria.

SOUSTELLE, Jacques. *Aimée et Souffrante Algérie*. Paris: Plon, 1956. M. Soustelle's very illuminating account of his year as Governor General of Algeria.

TILLION, Germaine. *L'Algérie en 1957*. Paris: Les Editions de Minuit, 1957. (Published in English translation under the title, *Algeria, the Realities*. New York: Knopf, 1958.) A compendium of broad generalizations, some of which are extremely penetrating. Mlle. Tillion, an ethnologist, deals primarily with the problem of survival in Algeria.

VALLET. Eugène. *Un Drame Algérien*. Paris: Les Grandes Editions Françaises, 1948. A book about the May, 1945, uprising.

N.B. The Koranic quotations are from the E. H. Palmer translation, published by the Oxford University Press in the series, "The World's Classics."

INDEX